UNITED STATES V. NIXON

UNITED STATES V. NIXON

The President before the
Supreme Court

Introductory Essay by
Alan Westin

Edited by Leon Friedman

New York
CHELSEA HOUSE PUBLISHERS

Project Coordinator: Nat LaMar

Paperback edition 1980

Library of Congress Cataloging in Publication Data

Friedman, Leon, comp.
    U. S. versus Nixon

    1. Executive privilege (Government information)—
United States—Cases. 2. Nixon, Richard Milhous,
1913-   3. Watergate Affair, 1972-   I. Title.
KF4570.A7F74   342'.73'062   74-16403
ISBN 0-87754-144-2

JAMES ST. CLAIR: "The President is not above the law. Nor does he contend that he is. What he does contend is that as the President the law can be applied to him in only one way, and that is by impeachment."

LEON JAWORSKI: "Now, the President may be right in how he reads the Constitution. But he may also be wrong. If he is wrong, who is to tell him so? This nation's constitutional form of government is in serious jeopardy if the President, any President, is to say that the Constitution means what he says it does, and that there is no one, not even the Supreme Court, to tell him otherwise."

from the oral argument in the
Supreme Court, July 8, 1974

CONTENTS

Preface — Leon Friedman   ix

The Case for America — Alan F. Westin   xi

Judge Sirica's First Opinion on Presidential Tapes   1

Court of Appeals Decision in Nixon v. Sirica   21

Judge Sirica's Opinion in United States v. Nixon   162

The Petitions to the Supreme Court   169

Special Prosecutor's Main Brief in United States v. Nixon   209

Special Prosecutor's Supplemental Brief in
United States v. Nixon   307

The President's Main Brief in United States v. Nixon   319

Special Prosecutor's Reply Brief in United States v. Nixon   427

The President's Reply Brief in United States v. Nixon   469

The ACLU Amicus Brief in United States v. Nixon   501

The Oral Argument in United States v. Nixon   521

The Supreme Court Decision in United States v. Nixon   597

PREFACE

The documents in this collection tell the story of one of the most important legal and constitutional events in our history: the Supreme Court decision in *United States* v. *Richard M. Nixon.* The title of the case itself illustrates the drama. It is usually the President who represents the people and embodies the power of the nation. But in this case the equation was reversed: it was the nation and the people against the President. And the great authority of the Presidency ultimately bowed to the courts and to the people represented by that uniquely pragmatic institution of our times, the Watergate Special Prosecution Force.

The case against the President—and its process—is important on many levels. Politically it was the immediate cause of the first resignation of a President of the United States. The Supreme Court decision, announced on July 24, 1974, played a significant role in the vote of the House Judiciary Committee to report to Congress three articles of impeachment within a week. It made a vote for impeachment respectable for members of the Committee and of Congress generally. More important, the first tapes to be produced under the Supreme Court's order revealed that the President had indeed known about and approved a cover-up plan to protect his aides from criminal liability, thereby obstructing justice in the Watergate prosecution. Three incriminating tapes were made public on August 5, 1974. By August 9, 1974 the nation had a new President, sworn in by the Chief Justice whose opinion had helped bring about the change.

But the Supreme Court decision had far-lasting importance beyond its immediate political consequences. It established certain basic propositions about our constitutional form of government and settled certain "issues of final power in the American system," as Anthony Lewis of *The New York Times* has called them. Among the issues confronted and decided were: Does the principle of separation of powers grant the President an absolute privilege to protect his confidential communications? How far does the doctrine of executive privilege extend? Can a special prosecutor subpoena the President under whom he serves? Is it more important that a criminal trial proceed with all the evidence available than that the President protect his personal documents and materials? And, above all, what acts of the President are not reviewable by the courts? Is he supreme in his interpretation of his own constitutional powers and prerogatives?

The materials in this collection contain Judge Sirica's first decision on the Presidential tapes as well as the Court of Appeals decision in *Nixon* v. *Sirica*, which served as the curtain-opener for the later Supreme Court decision in *United States* v. *Nixon*. Also included are all the briefs filed by the parties in the case, containing some of the most sophisticated and incisive constitutional arguments in Supreme Court history. I have also included the petitions for review in the Supreme Court and other preliminary documents relating to the scope of the Supreme Court's review in the case. One of the crucial portions of this book is the complete transcript of the oral argument before the Supreme Court, and behind its publication here lies another story.

Some years ago, Professor Yale Kamisar of the University of Michigan Law School urged Chelsea House Publishers to undertake a program of publishing Supreme Court oral arguments. We began with the oral arguments in *Brown* v. *Board of Education*, which were published under the title *Argument*. When we investigated further, we discovered that only a few of the oral arguments had been transcribed by a commercial court reporter, though the Supreme Court itself—irony of ironies—had preserved the audio tapes of all the oral arguments before it dating back to the early 1950's. Professor Kamisar asked Chief Justice Earl Warren to make them available to the public for research purposes, but the Court declined to do so (by an unofficial vote, we were told, of 7 to 2). A year later we again wrote to the Court suggesting that the tapes be transmitted to the National Archives. Shortly thereafter the Court announced that it would deposit at the Archives at the end of each term tapes of all the oral arguments held in the previous year, at last making these vital research tools generally available to interested lawyers, scholars and students.

The transcript itself does not identify which Justice said what in the course of the argument; each question is simply headed "Question." To determine the identity of each questioner, I examined published accounts of the argument and spoke to a number of persons who were present on this historic occasion. I am especially indebted to Philip A. Lacovara, who argued part of the case for the Special Prosecutor, and patiently answered my many inquiries. It was not possible to determine the questioning Justice in every instance, but I hope that there is sufficient identification to give a more personal flavor to the questioning and to indicate the style of individual Justices as they test the historic constitutional problems—and the lawyers—before them.

Leon Friedman
August 1974

THE CASE FOR AMERICA

On Wednesday, July 24, 1974, shortly after 11 A.M., Chief Justice Warren Burger began reading the opinion of the United States Supreme Court in *United States* v. *Nixon*.[1] The courtroom was jammed with lawyers, Washington notables, and members of the public, some of whom had stood in line since early the previous afternoon in anticipation that this would be the day the Justices ruled in the Nixon tapes case. Outside, the Supreme Court's flag flew at half-mast, in honor of former Chief Justice Earl Warren, who had recently died. Across the street from the Court's building, two men wearing rubber masks of Richard Nixon and Henry Kissinger paraded back and forth carrying a banner with a quote on it from one of the already released presidential tapes:

"I don't give a shit what happens. I want you all to stonewall it. Let them plead the Fifth Amendment, cover up or anything else that will save the plan. That's the whole point."

Richard M. Nixon, March 22, 1973.

As the Chief Justice read his opinion in a calm, almost icy tone, the tension in the courtroom shifted into an excited awareness that this was an historic event. By an 8-0 ruling, the Supreme Court had decided that President Nixon must produce for District Judge John Sirica the tapes of 64 White House conversations sought by the Special Watergate Prosecutor for use in the pending obstruction of justice trial of seven former White House aides. The two-year saga of the Watergate break-in and cover-up was reaching its climax. Two weeks later, on August 8th, Richard M. Nixon would announce that he was resigning his presidential office. A reconstruction of that decision by a team of *New York Times* reporters would conclude that "the collapse of Mr. Nixon's fight to stay in office was a consequence of the ruling of the Nixon court."[2]

[1] This account of the Court's decision day is drawn from the *Washington Post* and *New York Times* of July 25, 1974, and from *Time* and *Newsweek* stories of August 5, 1974.

[2] "Nixon Slide From Power: Backers Gave Final Push," *New York Times*, August 12, 1974. See also the account of Saul Friedman, "Walkout Threat by Haig and St. Clair Put Nixon on Narrow Road to Resignation," *Boston Globe*, August 11, 1974, and William Safire, "Last Days in the Bunker," *New York Times Magazine*, August 18, 1974.

From start to finish, the case of *United States* v. *Nixon* was as distinctively American as apple pie a la mode. In no other country in the world would it have been both legally and politically possible for a court of law to force a chief executive to yield up the recordings of his confidential conversations with personal aides.

Indeed, in many nations, the Watergate affair would not have been a matter for the courts to consider at all. In some of these, the crisis would have led to the rumbling of tanks around the capitol following a presidential declaration of martial law. In parliamentary democracies, it would have meant a vote of no-confidence in the national legislature, the resignation of the president, and new national elections. But in the American governmental system, with our fixed term of office for the president and the cumbersome process of impeachment as our sole means of presidential removal, the Watergate crisis had to play out its slow constitutional course. And as it did, once President Nixon refused to deliver subpoenaed White House tapes to the Special Prosecutor, it became inevitable that the legality of his action would be brought to the Supreme Court for review.

As this essay is written, in mid-August 1974, the Supreme Court ruling in the Nixon case is only a month old. But it will be surprising if, a year or even a decade from now, analysts of our constitutional politics do not agree about five major aspects of the case:

1. Given conditions in the nation in July of 1974, the ruling was highly predictable.

2. It was one of the Supreme Court's "better" exercises of judicial statecraft.

3. The decision proved to be highly effective, in its immediate Watergate impact.

4. It was not at all typical of previous Court-versus-President conflicts in our history.

5. Its definition of executive privilege promises to be a source of fertile legal and political disputes in the future.

Let us examine each of these judgments, and then venture an over-all estimate of the place that *United States v. Nixon* will occupy in our constitutional scheme.

1. THE PREDICITABILITY OF THE DECISION

Ever since the famous case of *Marbury* v. *Madison*, 170 years ago the Supreme Court has followed a set of basic, unwritten rules when reviewing politically charged and controversial presidential actions

    a. When the political situation is too dangerous for the Supreme Court (e.g., if a ruling against the President is likely to be disobeyed by him or to produce serious reprisals against the

Court's powers or prestige), the Court should find a way to duck the issue or to deflect it, leaving its immediate resolution to the larger political process.

b. But if the political situation is favorable (that is, if a ruling against the President will enjoy broad public and Congressional support and virtually compel presidential compliance), then the Court is free (if the case warrants it) to do the two things most beloved by American judges — uphold the "rule of law" against claims of prerogative or privilege by the executive, and expand still further the discretionary power of the judiciary in the American constitutional system.

Seen in this tradition, *United States* v. *Nixon* was one of the most predictable rulings in the history of American constitutional law. The political situation was not only hospitable to a ruling against the President but almost irresistably pressing for it. Public opinion was solidly against the President's course of conduct in the Watergate affair and the cover-up. A solid, bi-partisan majority in Congress opposed presidential claims to withhold critical information. And the way in which Nixon had conducted his defense (including the firing of Special Prosecutor Archibald Cox and the forcing of Attorney General Elliot Richardson's resignation) collided with deep-seated American norms about the rule of law, thus creating special pressures on the courts to reassert the primacy of this value in the use of presidential authority.

In this sense, the *Nixon* case closely resembled the Supreme Court's situation in 1952, in passing on President Truman's seizure of the steel mills, under a claim of inherent executive power, to avert a dangerous strike during the last stages of the Korean War.[3] When that case came to the Justices, public opinion was hostile to the Truman administration (only 23% of the public expressed support for Truman); there was broad Congressional opposition to the economic burdens of the Korean War at that point and to the seizure of the steel industry without Congressional sanction. Furthermore, the way in which the President's lawyers had argued his case in the early stages of the litigation collided with public beliefs in "limited government" principles.

(At one key point in 1952, Assistant Attorney General Holmes Baldridge told Judge Pine in the federal district court hearing that the Constitution "did not limit the powers of the Executive" under Article II, even though the powers of the Congress and the judiciary *were* limited by the Constitution. This set off a violent reaction in Congress and in public opinion that was never effectively repaired by

[3] A full account of the *Steel Seizure* case can be found in Alan F. Westin, *The Anatomy of a Constitutional Law Case* (New York: Macmillan, 1958).

the President and his lawyers, despite their public repudiation of the Baldridge assertion.)

Thus the Supreme Court, in a 6-3 decision, declared Truman's seizure of the steel mills to be unconstitutional.[4] "With all its defects, delays, and inconveniences," Justice Robert Jackson wrote in his eloquent concurring opinion, "men have discovered no technique for long preserving free government except that the Executive be under the law, and that the law be made by parliamentary deliberations."

In other words, the Supreme Court generally tends to be a prudent body; it has had to be for the unique power of judicial review to have survived so long in a majority-rule republic. But when one of the fundamental tenets of the American constitutional system is widely regarded by the public as under assault by one of the elected branches of national government, the Justices can and do unite in defense of such basic values. In the *Nixon* case, it was the supremacy of the law, as interpreted by the courts and not the President, that was seen as being at stake.

2. THE SKILLFUL EXERCISE OF JUDICIAL STATECRAFT

The *Nixon* case, because it involved a major interpretation of presidential power and would necessarily affect the progress of the pending impeachment investigation, called for the Court to be unanimous, clear, and "non-controversial." The fact that the Court, highly divided on most sensitive issues of current constitutional law, was able to achieve those goals made the *Nixon* decition one of the Supreme Court's "better" efforts at judicial statecraft.

During the 1973-74 term, a *New York Times* analysis of 144 decisions handed down between October and the *Nixon* ruling showed the court to be split 5-4 or 6-3 in a large number of major constitutional cases.[5] In the majority were the four Nixon appointees — Chief Justice Burger and Justices Blackmun, Powell, and Rehnquist — "solidified into a bloc that is increasing in both unity and capacity to produce a working majority for their views of the law and the constitution." They were joined most frequently by Justice Byron White, a Democrat and a Kennedy appointee to the Court (85% of the time), and almost as often (82%) by Justice Potter Stewart, a Republican appointed by President Eisenhower. This left the Court's three liberals — Democrats William O. Douglas, appointed by Franklin Roosevelt; William J. Brennan Jr., appointed by Dwight

---

[4] *Youngstown Sheet and Tube Co. et al.* v. *Sawyer,* 343 U.S. 579 (1952).

[5] Warren Weaver Jr., "Four Nixon Justices on High Court Vote in Bloc That Could Become Majority," *New York Times,* July 26, 1974.

Eisenhower; and Thurgood Marshall, appointed by Lyndon Johnson — as the consistent dissenters, voting together as a block in 74% of the 144 decisions analyzed. As if to underscore how deeply the Court was divided in 1974, the Court delivered its last opinion of the term the day after the *Nixon* ruling; in a straight ideological as well as party-line division, the Court held, 5-4, that Detroit's plan for busing school children to effect better racial integration was invalid, since the majority said that such a scheme can be imposed on suburban communities in a metropolitan area only when the suburbs can be shown to have participated in unlawful educational segregation.[6]

Given these divisions, the challenge to Chief Justice Burger and his colleagues was to find a way to unite behind one unanimous opinion in the *Nixon* case, thus putting the greatest weight of judicial authority behind the Court's ruling, earning the greatest support from the public, and applying the greatest pressure on the President to comply with such a "definitive ruling." There were eight Justices to be persuaded to such a course, Justice William Rehnquist having withdrawn from participation because of his earlier Justice Department relationship with several of the defendants in the case.

What goes on in the conference room of the Supreme Court is kept entirely confidential, with no record published and no law clerks or other Court personnel even allowed to be present. But a combination of journalistic accounts based on "Court sources" and an unusual official explanation of how Chief Justice Burger worked on the Court's opinion gives us what seems to be a reliable account of what went on among the Justices.[7] According to these reconstructions, when the Court gathered for its conference on July 9th, the day after oral argument had been presented, the Chief Justice urged his colleagues to try to reach a unanimous judgment and to join in a single opinion, a goal to which they assented. After a review of where each Justice stood, it became clear that the President had no support among the eight Justices for his position as to executive privilege. However, Chief Justice Burger and Justice Blackmun — the so-called Minnesota twins — were troubled about the issue of justiciability, that is, whether the Special Prosecutor had the standing to bring this suit to enforce a subpoena against his formal superior, the President of the United States. Justice Stewart stressed the clear autonomy that the Special Prosecutor had been given when this office was created by the President and confirmed by the Senate, and the

[6] Reported in *New York Times,* July 26, 1974.

[7] See "Burger's 41-day Ordeal Told," *New York Times,* August 6, 1974; "A Very Definitive Decision," *Newsweek,* August 5, 1974; "A Unanimous No to Nixon," *Time,* August 5, 1974.

discussions brought Burger and Blackmun around to that view. Four of the Court's liberals — Douglas, Brennan, Marshall, and Stewart — favored drafting a broad opinion limiting the concept of executive privilege, while White and Powell favored the writing of a narrow opinion that would leave the Court flexibility on this issue. After about six hours of discussion, the Justices agreed on the main lines of a decision, and Chief Justice Burger assigned to himself the drafting of this opinion. The other Justices contributed memoranda for his use, and one account states that it was Justice Stewart who contributed the draft of the opinion's treatment of the justiciability issue.

This account of what went on within the Court may or may not be entirely accurate; in the main, it has the ring of credibility. But what is entirely certain is that the 31-page unanimous opinion delivered in the *Nixon* case reads like a perfect committee product. It proceeds with measured tread along its course, avoiding lofty rhetoric or slashing prose. Most of all, it sounds like the cool lecture on constitutional fundamentals that a rather pedantic school master might deliver to a pupil who has handed in a very poor paper on the constitutional fundamentals of the American system, and deserved a lesson in basics. Again, there is a striking parallel to the *Steel Seizure* case, where a similar opinion in tone and treatment was written by Justice Hugo Black for the six-Justice majority in that case. But here, of course, the similarity ends. In the *Steel Seizure* case, each of the Justices in the majority (besides Black) also wrote a concurring opinion. This gave us the brilliant constitutional exegesis of Robert Jackson on our checks and balances system; Felix Frankfurter's painstaking analysis of congressional policies toward executive seizure of private property; and William O. Douglas' effort to soften the blow to President Truman by saying that the attempted expansion of executive power was being done by a "kindly president . . . " But these opinions also diluted and fragmented the holding of the *Steel Seizure* case, so much so that legal commentators despaired of saying just what view of inherent presidential powers the six majority Justices had really agreed upon beyond the fact that President Truman had not acted legally here. It was, Professor Edward Corwin has said, "a judicial brick without straw."

The *Nixon* opinion avoided that pitfall carefully. There were no concurring opinions to raise points of differing emphasis or suggest divided views. There was only the majesty that a unanimous opinion of liberals and conservatives, Democrats and Republicans, can convey to the public, of the rule-of-law defended against attack. Time, and later tests cases in non-Watergate settings, may reveal that there is considerable uncertainty lurking in the Court's certitudes in the

Nixon case, as we will explore shortly. But for an embattled Richard M. Nixon, there was not the slightest shred of comfort in the Court's ruling: the taped conversations were to be delivered, now, to Judge John Sirica. They would be screened to suppress any conversations whose disclosure might jeopardize "military, diplomatic, or sensitive national security secrets." But as to discussions of what the President knew about Watergate and did to cover up its investigation and prosecution, the cat was officially ordered to be let out of the bag.

3. THE POLITICAL EFFECTIVENESS OF THE DECISION

Before the tapes case was argued in the Supreme Court, and even after the President's counsel had appeared before the Justices, no spokesman for the President, or the President himself, would say that he would obey the Court's decision if it proved to be adverse. Even when pressed during the oral argument, the President's attorney James St. Clair stated that "the President . . . has his obligations under the Constitution," implying that he might conclude that his "responsibilities" as head of a coordinate branch of national government required him to refuse to deliver the tapes.

We know from a variety of "inside" accounts, many of these from sources within the Nixon White House and among his supporters in Congress, that the President argued with his counsel for several hours on July 24th that he had a constitutional duty to reject the Supreme Court's ruling and that he could refuse to comply.[8] His lawyer told the President that if he did so, he would certainly be impeached (the House Judiciary Committee had not yet voted on bringing Articles of Impeachment) and just as certainly convicted in the Senate. In addition, St. Clair informed Mr. Nixon that legal ethics would not permit him to stay on as the President's lawyer if he defied the Court's order. Only after this pressure did the President agree to have a statement issued that he would obey the ruling. This came eight hours after the Court had handed down its unanimous decision.

At first, commentators assumed that Nixon would attempt to win further delays in furnishing the tapes to Judge Sirica, perhaps by saying time was needed to prepare copies or transcripts, etc. But Special Prosecutor Jaworski asked Judge Sirica to order a speedy, batch-by-batch timetable, and the judge not only agreed but directed St. Clair personally to listen to the tapes and be responsible for compliance with the schedule.

Among the tapes to be turned over to Judge Sirica on August 2nd were three conversations held on June 23, 1972, just six days after the Watergate burglary. What Mr. Nixon knew was that these three conversations were political and legal dynamite — they would supply

[8] See the accounts noted in note 2, *supra.*

precisely the "smoking gun" that Mr. Nixon's supporters on the House Judiciary Committee had argued had been missing from the case made against the President: clear and convincing proof that the President knew of the Watergate affair and had used his authority in an attempt to cover up the episode. Now, Mr. Nixon realized, his two-year fight to keep the secret in the bottle was about to be lost. On the June 23rd tapes was the clear and convincing evidence that the President had ordered the CIA to be brought into the case in an effort to derail the FBI's investigation. What was even more heinous was that these conversations showed that the President had lied to the American public in several of his statements as to what he knew; had failed to tell his own counsel what the extent of his knowledge and involvement had been; and had failed to provide this material to the House Judiciary Committee.

After the President listened to these tapes while at Camp David during the August 3-4 weekend, and when these were, at last, heard by St. Clair, General Alexander Haig, and a few other key staff members, the last act of the drama began to unfold. Under intense pressure from his aides and several of his most fervent defenders in Congress who were informed of what was on the tapes, the President was persuaded to release transcripts of the June 23rd conversations on the afternoon of August 5th. Three days later, after these disclosures had drained away virtually all of his support in Congress and the nation, the President announced that he was resigning.

It would be claiming too much for the Supreme Court's ruling to say that, had it not occurred, the President would still be in office today, or would have served out his term until 1976. The House Judiciary Committee had compiled a powerful record and had voted out strong Articles of Impeachment. Observers agreed that, even before the August 5th revelations, the House was certain to vote impeachment and the Senate was more than likely to convict. But it was the tape disclosures ordered by the Supreme Court's decision that pushed the President's situation into the critical stage, dissipated his last-ditch support, and forced his resignation. It is hard to think how an outcome could have vindicated any more fully the underlying (and carefully unenunciated) assumption of the Justices that the President's claim of executive privilege in this instance was essentially spurious.

4. THE ATYPICAL CHARACTER OF THIS DECISION IN TERMS OF COURT-PRESIDENTIAL CONFRONTATIONS

United States v. *Nixon* does not fit at all the general character of major executive-judicial encounters in our constitutional history. Professor Glendon Schubert reports that about 800 cases in the federal and state courts dealt with questions of presidential power

etween 1790 and 1956.[9] Of these, 38 rulings held presidential
rders to be invalid, with only 14 of these rulings coming from the
ᶠnited States Supreme Court. Almost half of the total 38 dealt with
ᵉe exercise of presidential powers during national emergencies, such
s Madison's embargo proclamation in 1809, Lincoln's suspension of
abeas corpus during the Civil War, and Franklin Roosevelt's actions
uring World War II. And only two Supreme Court decisions
etween 1790 and 1956 invalidated a major program or policy of the
xecutive — the *Steel Seizure* in 1952 and a 1956 decision (*Cole* v.
ᶠoung) limiting executive loyalty-security programs because of due
ᶜocess failings.

Between 1957 and 1974, and especially during the last two years
f the Nixon presidency, the federal courts did decide some
ᵐportant cases that curtailed presidential claims of authority.
xamples of these are the Supreme Court's decision in 1958, limiting
ᵉe President's power to remove members of independent commis-
ᵒns[10] and the 1972 decision denying that the President's national
ᵉcurity powers provided the basis for the Attorney General to
ᵐploy electronic surveillance against domestic organizations with-
ut the judicial warrant required by the 1968 Omnibus Crime
ᶜontrol and Safe Streets Act.[11] There has also been a series of lower
ᵉderal court rulings in 1973-74 striking down the President's
ᵐpoundment of funds appropriated by Congress,[12] and several
ther exercises of power by President Nixon.[13]

Viewed as a whole, however, the major relationships between the
ᵘpreme Court and the Chief Executive has been for the Court either
ᵒ uphold presidential authority, though at times with some limiting
ᵒnstruct, or to decline to pass on uses of presidential power because
f special circumstances, such as Congressional ratification of the
resident's action or the problem becoming moot owing to the
assage of time.

Yet there is a sense in which the Nixon decision is quite untypical
ᶠ famous collisions between "Court" and "President" in our
ᶦstory. In most of these, such as the conflicts between Thomas

[9] Glendon A. Schubert, Jr., *The Presidency in the Courts* (Minneapolis: University of
ᶦnnesota Press, 1957), Part IV and Appendices A, B, and C.

[10] *Wiener* v. *United States,* 357 U.S. 349 (1958).

[11] *United States* v. *United States District Court,* 407 U.S. 297 (1972).

[12] See *National Council of Community Mental Health Centers* v. *Weinberger,* 361
Supp. 897 (1973) and *People ex. rel Bakalis* v. *Weinberger,* 368 F. Supp. 721 (1973).

[13] In July of 1974, the United States Customs Court ruled that President Nixon had
ᵗed illegally in 1971 when he imposed a 10% surcharge on all dutiable imports, *New York
ᶦmes,* July 9, 1974. And on August 14, 1974, the United States Court of Appeals for the
ᶦstrict of Columbia held that President Nixon had acted illegally when he claimed to have
ᵗoed a bill by withholding his signature when Congress went into a five-day Christmas
ᶜess, *New York Times,* August 15, 1974.

Jefferson and the Court, Andrew Jackson and the Court, or Frank
D. Roosevelt and the Court, it was federal or state legislati
supported by the President and a majority in Congress that ca
under the judicial guillotine.

In these kinds of battles, with basic social programs being stru
down by the judiciary, Presidents have rallied their supporters
overcome judicial vetoes. Constitutional amendments have be
passed, new Justicies have been appointed to vacancies, a
legislation has sometimes been revised to take the objections of t
Court into account. Franklin D. Roosevelt even threatened to pa
the Supreme Court by enlarging its size, in an effort to influence t
swing Justices to modify their positions on New Deal legislation
1937.

United States v. *Nixon* was not that kind of case at all. He
Congress was actively hostile to the President's claims of authority
withhold information, leaving him without the Congressional suppc
necessary to the classic court-versus-elected branches conflict.

Whatever the type of court-Presidential conflict involved, thoug
every President of the United States, now including Richard
Nixon, has obeyed a "definitive" decision of the Supreme Cou
directing him to do or not to do something. The oft-quoted episo
in which President Andrew Jackson is supposed to have said, "Jol
Marshall has made his decision; now let him enforce it," was not
situation in which the President was directed to do anything. T
Court's ruling was directed to a Georgia state court, and Preside
Jackson did nothing to interfere with that situation.

5. THE COURT'S RULING ON EXECUTIVE PRIVILEGE WIL
ENGENDER LIVELY DISPUTES IN THE FUTURE

Great Supreme Court cases, especially those dealing with separ
tion-of-powers review over presidential and legislative authority a
sometimes like delayed-fuse aerial bombs. They have an initi
impact when they first hurtle to earth, but their greater effect com
later, when their full explosive force is released.

That is quite likely to be the legacy of *United States* v. *Nixon.* T
decision's immediate effect was to order 64 taped conversations
be delivered. And the immediate rule of law in the public focus
that the President cannot withhold information from a crimin
proceeding in which such information is directly relevant, on t
grounds of a *general* claim that this would impair the confidentiali
of executive communications and not be in the public interest.

But the decision declared a larger premise that will be far mo
significant in the long run. It rejects the argument of son
populist-minded commentators that there is no constitutional ba
at all for executive privilege. The Justices were unanimous

declaring that in many key areas — the court stipulated "military, diplomatic or sensitive national security secrets" — the President has a constitutional basis for asserting privileges and can have this enforced by the courts.

In my view, this judgment about the Executive's need for and right to confidential communications is entirely right in principle. What it will mean in practice, however, is that from now on, the federal courts have been given the role of arbitrating both the general definitions and the document-by-document review of those presidential communications that may become central to criminal proceedings.

In the long run, therefore, the ruling is a loss for executive power in our constitutional system and a major gain for judicial authority, one that will surely stimulate platoons of litigation in the future. And it was the sheer demonstration of illegitimacy by President Nixon — the invocation of a long-maintained tradition of executive secrecy to protect illegal and immoral conduct in the White House — that compelled the Supreme Court to act.

Future generations of Americans, for better or for worse, will have Richard Nixon to thank for what will probably become one of the most important expansions of judicial authority in the history of the Republic.

Alan F. Westin

Cape Cod
August 18, 1974

I
JUDGE SIRICA'S FIRST
OPINION ON PRESIDENTIAL
TAPES

While testifying before the Senate Watergate Committee on July 6, 1973, Alexander Butterfield first revealed the existence of a recording system in the White House and the availability of hundreds of Presidential tapes covering conversations between President Nixon and his chief aides. Within a week, both the Ervin Committee and Special Prosecutor Archibald Cox subpoenaed a group of tapes which they claimed were relevant to their inquiries. The Ervin Committee's claim was eventually rejected by the courts, but Cox's subpoena was upheld by Judge John Sirica. His initial opinion held merely that (1) the President was subject to a judicial order to produce the tapes, (2) claims of executive privilege were reviewable by the courts, and could not be made solely by the President, and (3) the tapes would be examined by the judge in secret (in camera) to determine whether they were relevant to the criminal investigations under the jurisdiction of the Special Prosecutor's office. Judge Sirica's opinion follows:

In re Grand Jury SUBPOENA Duces Tecum Issued TO Richard M. NIXON, or any Subordinate Officer, Official, or Employee with Custody or Control of Certain Documents or Objects.

Misc. No. 47-73
United States District Court,
District of Columbia.

Aug. 29, 1973

360 F. Supp. 1

Archibald Cox, Watergate Special Prosecutor Force, Philip A. Lacovara, Peter M. Kreindler, Washington, D.C., James F. Neal, Nashville, Tenn., for movant.

Leonard Garment, New York City, J. Fred Buzhardt, McCormick, S.C., Charles Alan Wright, Austin, Tex., Douglas M. Parker, Robert T. Andrews, Thomas P. Marinis, Jr., Washington, D.C., for respondent.

ORDER

SIRICA, Chief Judge.

This matter having come before the Court on motion of the Watergate Special Prosecutor made on behalf of the June 1972 grand jury of this district for an order to show cause, and the Court being advised in the premises, it is by the Court this 29th day of August, 1973, for the reasons stated in the attached opinion,

Ordered that respondent, President Richard M. Nixon, or any subordinate officer, official or employee with custody or control of the documents or objects listed in the grand jury subpoena *duces tecum* of July 23, 1973, served on respondent in this district, is hereby commanded to produce forthwith for the Court's examination *in camera*, the subpoenaed documents or objects which have not heretofore been produced to the grand jury; and it is

Further ordered that the ruling herein be stayed for a period of five days in which time respondent may perfect an appeal from the ruling; and it is

Further ordered that should respondent appeal from the ruling herein, the above stay will be extended indefinitely pending the completion of such appeal or appeals.

OPINION

On July 23, 1973, Watergate Special Prosecutor Archibald Cox acting on behalf of the June 1972 grand jury empanelled by this court, caused to be issued a subpoena duces tecum to the President of the United States, Richard M. Nixon.[1] The subpoena required the President, or any appropriate subordinate official, to produce for the grand jury certain tape recordings and documents enumerated in an attached schedule. The President complied with the subpoena insofar as it related to memoranda of Gordon Strachan and W. Richard Howard, but otherwise declined to follow the subpoena's directives. In a letter to the Court dated July 25, 1973, the President advised that the tape recordings sought would not be provided, and by way of explanation wrote:

> . . . I follow the example of a long line of my predecessors as President of the United States who have constantly adhered to the position that the President is not subject to compulsory process from the courts.

Thereafter, the grand jury instructed Special Prosecutor Cox to apply for an order requiring production of the recordings. On July 26, the Special Prosecutor petitioned this Court[2] for a show cause order directed to the President. At the time of this application a quorum of the grand jury was polled in open court, and each juror expressed his or her desire that the Court order compliance. Subsequently, the Court ordered that the President or any appropriate subordinate official show cause "why the documents and objects described in [the subpoena] should not be produced as evidence before the grand jury."

In response to the show cause order, the President, by his attorneys, filed a special appearance contesting the Court's jurisdiction to order the President's compliance with the grand jury subpoena.[3] The Court allowed for the filing of a response

---

[1.] The Special Prosecutor has been designated as the attorney for the Government to conduct proceedings before the grand jury investigating the unauthorized entry into the Democratic National Committee Headquarters and related offenses. Order of the Attorney General No. 517-73, 38 Fed. Reg. 14688 (June 4, 1973). A grand jury subpoena *duces tecum* was issued by the clerk under seal of the court. F.R. Crim.P. 17(a), (c). The Special Prosecutor appears before the Court on behalf of and under the specific authorization of the grand jury, seeking compliance with the subpoena (Transcript of Hearing of July 26, 1973, on Petition for Order to Show Cause 8-12). In this capacity he appears as an officer of the Court and counsel for the grand jury, in addition to being the attorney for the United States.

[2] Local Rule 3−6 provides:
In addition to the trial of such cases as he may undertake and other duties provided by these rules, the Chief Judge shall:
(3) empanel the grand jury and hear and determine all matters relating to proceedings before the grand jury.

[3] No objections to the technical adequacy of the subpoena or service of process have been raised.

by the Special Prosecutor and reply by the President, and the matter came on for hearing on August 22nd.

The parties to the controversy have briefed and argued several issues including the Court's jurisdiction in the matter of compulsory process, the existence and scope of "executive privilege" generally, applicability of "executive privilege" to the tape recordings subpoenaed, and waiver of privilege. The Court has found it necessary to adjudicate but two questions for the present: (1) whether the Court has jurisdiction to decide the issue of privilege, and (2) whether the Court has authority to enforce the subpoena *duces tecum* by way of an order requiring production for inspection *in camera.* A third question, whether the materials are in fact privileged as against the grand jury, either in whole or in part, is left for subsequent adjudication. For the reasons outlined below, the Court concludes that both of the questions considered must be answered in the affirmative.

I

A search of the Constitution and the history of its creation reveals a general disfavor of government privileges, or at least uncontrolled privileges. Early in the Convention of 1787, the delegates cautioned each other concerning the dangers of lodging immoderate power in the executive department.[4] This attitude persisted throughout the Convention, and executive powers became a major topic in the subsequent ratification debates.[5] The Framers regarded the legislative department superior in power and importance to the other two and felt the necessity of investing it with some privileges and immunities, but even here an attitude of restraint, as expressed by James Madison, prevailed:

> Mr. Pinckney moved a clause declaring "that each House should be the judge of the privilege of its members."

*   *   *   *   *   *

> Mr. Madison distinguished between the power of Judging of privileges previously & duly established, and the effect of the motion which would give a discretion to each House as to the extent of its own privileges. He suggested that it would be better to make provision for ascertaining by *law*, the privileges of each House, than to allow each House to decide for itself.

[4] See *e. g.,* 1 Farrand, The Records of the Federal Convention of 1787, 64—69 (1967).

[5.] The Federalist Nos. 67—77. J. E. Cooke, ed., The Federalist, 452-521 (1961).

He suggested also the necessity of considering what privileges ought to be allowed to the Executive.[6] (Emphasis in original). The upshot of Madison's final suggestion regarding a definition of executive privileges was that none were deemed necessary, or at least that the Constitution need not record any. As Charles Pinckney, the South Carolina delegate later explained in a Senate speech.

I assert, that it was the design of the Constitution, and that not only its spirit, but letter, warrant me in the assertion, that it never was intended to give Congress, or either branch any but specified, and those very limited, privileges indeed. They well knew how oppressively the power of undefined privileges had been exercised in Great Britain, and were determined no such authority should ever be exercised here. They knew that in free countries very few privileges were necessary to the undisturbed exercise of legislative duties, and those few only they determined that Congress should possess; they never meant that the body who ought to be the purest, and the least in want of shelter from the operation of laws equally affecting all their fellow citizens, should be able to avoid them; they therefore not only intended, but did confine their privileges within the narrow limits mentioned in the Constitution.

. . . Let us inquire, why the Constitution should have been so attentive to each branch of Congress, so jealous of their privileges, and have shewn [sic] so little to the President of the United States in this respect . . . . No Privilege of this kind was intended for your Executive, nor any except that which I have mentioned for your Legislature. The Convention which formed the Constitution well knew that this was an important point, and no subject had been more abused than privilege. They therefore determined to set the example, in merely limiting privilege to what was necessary and no more.[7] (Ellipsis in original)

Pinckney's words just quoted, "They therefore determined to set the example, in merely limiting privilege to what was necessary and no more," constitute an apt description of the Convention's purpose and outlook. Are there, then, any rights or privileges consistent with, though not mentioned in, the Constitution which are necessary to the Executive? One answer may be found in the Supreme Court decision, *United States* v.

[6.] 2 Farrand, The Records of the Federal Convention of 1787, 502, 503 (1967).

[7.] 3 Farrand, The Records of the Federal Convention of 1787, 384, 385 (1967). See also, 2 Elliot's Debates, 480 (1836).

Reynolds, 345 U.S. 1, 73 S.Ct. 528, 97 L.Ed. 727 (1953). The Court recognized an executive privilege, evidentiary in nature, for military secrets. *Reynolds* held that when a court finds the privilege is properly invoked under the appropriate circumstances, it will, in a civil case at least, suppress the evidence. Thus, it must be recognized that there can be executive privileges that will bar the production of evidence. The Court is willing here to recognize and give effect to an evidentiary privilege based on the need to protect Presidential privacy.[8]

The Court, however, cannot agree with Respondent that it is the Executive that finally determines whether its privilege is properly invoked. The availability of evidence including the validity and scope of privileges, is a judicial decision.

Judicial control over the evidence in a case cannot be abdicated to the caprice of executive officers.[9]

It is emphatically the province and duty of the judicial department to say what the law is. Those who apply the rule, to particular cases must of necessity expand and interpret that rule. If two laws conflict with each other, the courts must decide on the operation of each.[10]

In all the numerous litigations where claims of executive privilege have been interposed, the courts have not hesitated to pass judgment.[11] Executive fiat is not the mode of resolution.[12] As

[8.] The Court agrees with Respondent that Presidential privacy, in and of itself, has no merit. Its importance and need of protection arise from "the paramount need for frank expression and discussion among the President and those consulted by him in the making of Presidential decisions." Brief in Opposition at 3. This comports with the court's statement in Kaiser Aluminum & Chemical Corp. v. United States, 157 F.Supp. 939, 944, 141 Ct.Cl. 38 (1958) that the executive privilege is granted "for the benefit of the public, not of executives who may happen to then hold office."

[9.] United States v. Reynolds, 345 U.S. 1, 10, 11, 73 S.Ct. 528, 533, 97 L.Ed. 727 (1953). For the courts to abdicate this role to Presidents or anyone else, to make each officer the judge of his own privilege, would dishonor the genius of our constitutional system and breed unbearable abuse. Respondent maintains that an adequate remedy for abuse is provided in the impeachment power. Impeachment may be the final remedy, but it is not so designed that it can function as a deterrent in any but the most excessive cases. The argument overlooks the many possible situations in which only a few may suffer the consequences of abuse; situations where impeachment is not a reasonable solution. The Court intends no suggestion that Respondent could not be trusted as his own judge in matters of privilege, but it would hesitate to set a precedent, in contravention of basic constitutional principles, that might permit or encourage some future high executive officer to become a despot.

[10.] Marbury v. Madison, 1 Cranch 137, 177, 2 L.Ed. 60 (1803).

[11.] See *e.g.,* the cases and authorities cited at 8 Wright & Miller, Federal Practice and Procedure, 167-173 (1970).
These statements are not represented as necessarily accurate where an executive privilege is asserted in opposition to Congressional demands for information.

[12.] While it is true that Attorneys General have never hesitated to claim an uncon-

has been stated most recently in this Circuit.

[N]o executive official or agency can be given absolute authority to determine what documents in his possession may be considered by the court in its task. Otherwise, the head of an executive department would have the power on his own say so to cover up all evidence of fraud and corruption when a federal court or grand jury was investigating malfeasance in office, and this is not the law.[13]

The measures a court should adopt in ruling on claims of executive privilege are discussed under Part III herein.

II

If after judicial examination *in camera*, any portion of the tapes is ruled not subject to privilege, that portion will be forwarded to the grand jury at the appropriate time. To call for the tapes *in camera* is thus tantamount to fully enforcing the subpoena as to any unprivileged matter. Therefore, before the Court can call for production *in camera* it must have concluded that it has authority to order a President to obey the command of a grand jury subpoena as it relates to unprivileged evidence in his possession. The Court has concluded that it possesses such authority.

Analysis of the question must begin on the well established premises that the grand jury has a right to every man's evidence and that for purposes of gathering evidence, process may issue to anyone.

The court can perceive no legal objection to issuing a subpoena *duces tecum* to any person whatever, provided the case be such as to justify the process.[14]

The important factors are the relevance and materiality of the evidence.

The propriety of introducing any paper into a case, as testimony, must depend on the character of the paper, not on

trolled executive discretion in this area, such opinions usually come in response to Congressional demands for information, and therefore have little relevance to the present issue. Insofar as they may have any bearing here, however, assertions that the courts have stamped their approval on this doctrine of absolutism should not be left unchallenged. Such claims rest on unsteady foundations. See *e. g.*, Bishop, The Executive's Right of Privacy; An Unresolved Constitutional Question, 66 Yale L.J., 477, 478, n. 5 (1957).

13. Committee for Nuclear Responsibility, Inc. v. Seaborg, 149 U.S.App.D.C. 385, 463 F.2d 788 (1971).

14. United States v. Burr, 25 Fed.Cas. pp. 30, 35 (Case No. 14,692d) (1807).

the character of the person who holds it.[15]

The burden here then, is on the President to define exactly what it is about his office[16] that court process commanding the production of evidence cannot reach there. To be accurate, court process in the form of a subpoena *duces tecum* has already issued to the President and he acknowledges that pursuant to *Burr*, courts possess authority to direct such subpoenas to him. A distinction is drawn, however, between authority to issue a subpoena and authority to command obedience to it. It is this second compulsory process that the President contends may not reach him.[17] The burden yet remains with the President, however, to explain why this must be so. What distinctive quality of the Presidency permits its incumbent to withhold evidence? To argue that the need for Presidential privacy justifies it, is not persuasive. On the occasions when such need justifies suppression, the courts will sustain a privilege. The fact that this is a judicial decision has already been discussed at length, but the opinion of Chief Justice Marshall on the topic deserves notice here. When deciding that a subpoena should issue to the President, the Chief Justice made it clear that if certain portions should be excised, it being appropriate to sustain a privilege, the Court would make such a decision upon return of the subpoena.

There is certainly nothing before the court which shows that the letter in question contains any matter the disclosure of which would endanger the public safety. If it does contain such matter, the fact may appear before the disclosure is made. If it does contain any matter which it would be imprudent to disclose, which it is not the wish of the executive to disclose, such matter *if it be not immediately and essentially applicable to the point, will, of course, be suppressed.* It is not easy to conceive that so much of the

---

[15] *Id.* at 34.

[16] No claim is made for the President, nor can it be, that apart from his office, he is immune from the obligations of subpoenas and court orders.

[17] In oral argument, the Court put a hypothetical situation to the President's counsel regarding the production of unprivileged evidence. Counsel responded as follows:

MR. WRIGHT: On the set of facts that Your Honor puts, the President would have no privilege, since you have hypothesized the President obtained the evidence wholly independent of any official duties. I must say that in my submission a court would lack power, neverthless, to compel the President to produce the evidence so long as he remains President. I cannot concede that a court has power to issue compulsory process to an incumbent President of the United States. (Misc. 47-73, Transcript of Proceedings, August 22, 1973, at 16, 17.)

It is certainly arguable that a subpoena is compulsory process as well as any subsequent order mandating production either *in camera* or to a grand jury. Be that as it may, the

letter as relates to the conduct of the accused can be a subject of delicacy with the president. *Everything of this kind, however, will have its due consideration on the return of the subpoena.*[18]

And Again:

The propriety of requiring the answer to this letter is more questionable. It is alleged that it most probably communicates orders showing the situation of this country with Spain, which will be important on the misdemeanor. *If it contain matter not essential to the defence, and the disclosure be unpleasant to the executive, it certainly ought not to be disclosed. This is a point which will appear on the return.*[19]

To argue that it is the constitutional separation of powers that bars compulsory court process from the White House, is also unpersuasive. Such a contention overlooks history. Although courts generally, and this Court in particular,[20] have avoided any interference with the discretionary acts of coordinate branches, they have not hesitated to rule on non-discretionary acts when necessary.[21] Respondent points out that these and

---

Court recognizes a distinction between issuing a subpoena to the President and commanding that he honor it.

[18.] United States v. Burr, *supra,* n. 14, at 37. President Jefferson, upon forwarding the subpoenaed letter to Mr. Hay, counsel for the United States, authorized Hay to excise those portions of the letter "not material for the purposes of justice." Mr. Hay was willing to refer the "accuracy" of his opinion on that matter "to the judgment of the court, by submitting the original letter to its inspection." United States v. Burr, 25 Fed.Cas. pp. 187, 190 (Case No. 14,694) (1807).

[19.] *Id.*

[20.] See In Re Application of the senate Select Committee (DCDC 1973), Misc. No. 70-73 (June 12, 1973).

[21.] See *e. g.,* United States v. United States Dist. Ct., 407 U.S. 297, 92 S.Ct. 2125, 32 L.Ed.2d 752 (1972); Powell v. McCormack, 395 U.S. 486, 89 S.Ct. 1944, 23 L.Ed.2d 491 (1969); Youngstown Sheet & Tube Co. v. Sawyer, 343 U.S. 579, 72 S.Ct. 863, 96 L.Ed. 1153 (1952); D.C. Federation of Civic Assn's. v. Volpe, 316 F.Supp. 754, 760, n. 12 (DCDC 1970).

Discretionary duties and acts are not at issue here. The grand jury does not ask that the Court command or forbid the performance of any discretionary functions. The President is not asked to account in any way for the conduct of his office. The questions here concern the obligation of the President to provide evidence, something more akin to a ministerial duty if indeed it concerns official duties at all.

Nor is this a case, as Respondent suggests, where the Court in deciding the applicability of privilege, substitutes its judgment for that of the President on a matter committed to Presidential discretion, the public interest. Where a court, for example determines whether probable cause existed for an arrest, it does not substitute its judgment for that of the arresting officer. A judge simply decides whether the condition is met, whether there were reasonable grounds. He does not decide whether he would have arrived at the same conclusion as the officer did on the need to arrest. Here, the Court must determine whether the conditions for privilege exist. Should it so find, it does not then judge the wisdom of withholding evidence in the public interest.

other precedents refer to officials other than the President, and that this distinction renders the precedents inapplicable. Such an argument tends to set the White House apart as a fourth branch of government. It is true that *Mississippi* v. *Johnson,* 4 Wall. 475, 18 L. Ed. 437 (1866) left open the question whether the President can be required by court process to perform a purely ministerial act, but to persist in the opinion, after 1952, that he cannot would seem to exalt the form of the *Youngstown Sheet & Tube Co.* case over its substance.[22] Though the Court's order there went to the Secretary of Commerce, it was the direct order of President Truman that was reversed.

The Special Prosecutor has correctly noted that the Framers' intention to lodge the powers of government in separate bodies also included a plan for interaction between departments. A "watertight" division of different functions was never their design. The legislative branch may organize the judiciary[23] and dictate the procedures by which it transacts business.[24] The judiciary may pass upon the constitutionality of legislative enactments[25] and in some instances define the bounds of Congressional investigations.[26] The executive may veto legislative enactments,[27] and the legislature may override the veto.[28] The executive appoints judges and justices[29] and may bind judicial decisions by lawful executive orders.[30] The judiciary may pass on the constitutionality of executive acts.[31]

An attempt to dictate to or require an account of the President in the discretionary matters committed to him under Article II would truly be an instance of one branch pitting itself against another. Such is not the case here.

22. Youngstown Sheet & Tube Co. v. Sawyer, 343 U.S. 579, 72 S.Ct. 863, 96 L.Ed. 1153 (1952).

23. United States Constitution, Article III, Section 1.

24. See *e. g.,* 28 U.S.C. §§ 2, 44(c), 144, 1731-1745, 2403; 18 U.S.C. §§ 2519, 3331(a), 6003(a).

25. Marbury v. Madison, 1 Cranch 137, 2 L.Ed. 60 (1803).

26. See *e. g.,* Barenblatt v. United States, 360 U.S. 109, 79 S.Ct. 1081, 3 L.Ed.2d 1115 (1959); United States v. Rumely 345 U.S. 41, 73 S.Ct. 543, 97 L.Ed. 770 (1953); Sinclair v. United States, 279 U.S. 263, 49 S.Ct. 268, 73 L.Ed. 692 (1929).

27. United States Constitution, Article I, Section 7.

28. *Id.*

29. United States Constitution, Article II, Section 2.

30. See *e. g.,* Environmental Protection Agency v. Mink, 410 U.S. 73, 93 S.Ct. 827, 35 L.Ed.2d 119 (1973).

31. See *e. g.,* United States v. United States Dist. Ct., 407 U.S. 297, 92 S.Ct. 2125, 32 L.Ed.2d 752 (1972).

While the Constitution diffuses power the better to secure liberty, it also contemplates that practice will integrate the dispersed powers into a workable government. It enjoins upon its branches separateness but interdependence, autonomy but reciprocity.[32]

That the Court has not the physical power to enforce its order to the President is immaterial to a resolution of the issues. Regardless of its physical power to enforce them, the Court has a duty to issue appropriate orders.[33] The Court cannot say that the Executive's persistence in withholding the tape recordings would "tarnish its reputation," but must admit that it would tarnish the Court's reputation to fail to do what it could in pursuit of justice.[34] In any case, the courts have always enjoyed the good faith of the Executive Branch, even in such direct circumstances as those presented by *Youngstown Sheet & Tube Co.* v. *Sawyer* 343 U.S. 579, 72 S.Ct. 863, 96 L.Ed. 1153 (1952), and there is no reason to suppose that the courts in this instance cannot again rely on that same good faith. Indeed, the President himself has publicly so stated.

It is important also to note here the role of the grand jury. Chief Justice Marshall, in considering whether a subpoena might issue to the President of the United States observed:

In the provisions of the constitution, and of the statute, which give to the accused a right to the compulsory process of the court, there is no exception whatever.[35]

Aaron Burr, it will be remembered, stood before the court accused though not yet indicted. The Chief Justice's statement regarding the accused is equally true with regard to a grand jury: "there is no exception whatever" in its right to the compulsory process of the courts. The Court, while in a position to lend its process in assistance to the grand jury, is thereby in a position to assist justice.

The grand jury is well known to Anglo-American criminal justice as the people's guardian of fairness. Ever since the Earl of Shaftesbury relied upon its integrity, the grand jury has been promoted as a shield for the innocent and a sword against the

32. Youngstown Sheet & Tube Co. v. Sawyer, *supra*, n. 22.

33. See Baker v. Carr, 369 U.S. 186, 82 S.Ct. 691, 7 L.Ed.2d 663 (1962).

34. See United States v. Burr, *supra*, n.14, at 37. In the words of the Chief Justice:
It cannot be denied that to issue a subpoena to a person filling the exalted position of the chief magistrate is a duty which would be dispensed with more cheerfully than it would be performed; but, if it be a duty, the court can have no choice in the case. United States v. Burr, 25 Fed.Cas. pp. 30, 34 (Case No. 14,692d) (1807).

35. United States v. Burr, *supra*, no. 14, at 34.

guilty.[36] Among the Bill of Rights enacted by the First Congress was the Fifth Amendment which reads in part: "No person shall be held to answer for a capital, or otherwise infamous crime, unless on a presentment or indictment of a Grand Jury." The grand jury derives its authority directly from the people,[37] and when that group, independent in its sphere, acts according to its mandate, the court cannot justifiably withhold its assistance, nor can anyone, regardless of his station, withhold from it evidence not privileged.[38] Marshall concluded that, contrary to the English practice regarding the King, the laws of evidence do not excuse anyone because of the office he holds.[39]

. . . The single reservation alluded to is the case of the king. Although he may, perhaps, give testimony, it is said to be incompatible with his dignity to appear under the process of the court. Of the many points of difference which exist between the first magistrate in England and the first magistrate of the United States, in respect to the personal dignity conferred on them by the constitutions of their respective nations, the court will only select and mention two. It is a principle of the English constitution that the king can do no wrong, that no blame can be imputed to him, that he cannot be named in debate. By the constitution of the United States, the president, as well as any other officer of the government, may be impeached, and may be removed from office on high

[36.] For a full exposition of the purpose and role of grand juries see Branzburg v. Hayes, 408 U.S. 665, 92 S.Ct. 2646, 33 L.Ed.2d 626 (1972).

[37.] Hale v. Henkel, 201 U.S. 43, 61, 26 S.Ct. 370, 50 L.Ed. 652 (1906); In Re April 1956 Term Grand Jury, 239 F.2d 263, 269 (7th Cir. 1956).

[38.] Sullivan v. United States, 348 U.S. 170, 75 S.Ct. 182, 99 L.Ed. 210 (1954); United States v. United States Dist. Ct., 238 F.2d 713 (4th Cir. 1956), cert. denied, 352 U.S. 981, 77 S.Ct. 382, 1 L.Ed.2d 365 (1957); In Re Miller, 17 Fed.Cas. p. 295 (Case No. 9,552) (1878); In Re Times Mirror Company, 354 F.Supp. 208 (DCDC 1972).

[39.] The practical obstacles to compliance alluded to by Chief Justice Marshall in the Burr case are not a factor here. At page 34 the Chief Justice wrote:

If, upon any principle, the president could be construed to stand exempt from the general provisions of the constitution, it would be, because his duties as chief magistrate demand his whole time for national objects. United States v. Burr. 25 Fed.Cas. pp. 30, 34 (Case No. 14,692d) (1807).

The President here need not respond in person to the subpoena inasmuch as it is directed to "Richard M. Nixon, or Any Subordinate Officer, Official, or Employee with Custody or Control of Certain Documents or Objects." The Court is advised that the tape recordings have previously been entrusted to the custody of others and no reason appears why they could not again be held in the possession of a subordinate official for purposes of answering the Court's order.

crimes and misdemeanors. By the constitution of Great Britain, the crown is hereditary, and the monarch can never be a subject. By that of the United States, the president is elected from the mass of the people, and, on the expiration of the time for which he is elected, returns to the mass of the people again. How essentially this difference of circumstances must vary the policy of the laws of the two countries, in reference to the personal dignity of the executive chief, will be perceived by every person.[40]

In all candor, the Court fails to perceive any reason for suspending the power of courts to get evidence and rule on questions of privilege in criminal matters simply because it is the President of the United States who holds the evidence. The *Burr* decision left for another occasion a ruling on whether compulsory process might issue to the President in situations such as this. In the words of counsel, "this is a new question," with little in the way of precedent to guide the Court. But Chief Justice Marshall clearly distinguished the amenability of the King to appear and give testimony under court process and that of this nation's chief magistrate.[41] The conclusion reached here cannot be inconsistent with the view of that great Chief Justice nor with the spirit of the Constitution.

III

In deciding whether these tape recordings or portions thereof are properly the objects of a privilege, the Court must accommodate two competing policies. On the one hand, as has been noted earlier, is the need to disfavor privileges and narrow their application as far as possible. On the other hand, lies a need to favor the privacy of Presidential deliberations; to indulge a presumption in favor of the President. To the Court, respect for the President, the Presidency, and the duties of the office, gives the advantage to this second policy. This respect, however, does not decide the controversy. Such a resolution on the Court's part, as Chief Justice Marshall observed, "would deserve some other appellation than the term respect."[42] Nevertheless, it does not hurt for the courts to remind themselves often that the authority vested in them to delimit the scope and application of privileges, particularly the privileges and immunities of governmnent, is a trust. And as with every trust, an abuse can

---

[40.] United States v. Burr, *supra*, n. 14 at 34.

[41.] *Id.*

[42.] *Id.*

reap the most dire consequences. This Court, then, enters upon its present task with care and with a determination to exercise the restraint that characterizes the conduct of courts.

The teaching of *Reynolds* is that a court should attempt to satisfy itself whether or not a privilege is properly invoked without unnecessarily probing into the material claimed to be privileged.[43] A decision on how far to go will be dictated in part by need for the evidence.

> In each case, the showing of necessity which is made will determine how far the Court should probe in satisfying itself that the occasion for invoking the privilege is appropriate. Where there is a strong showing of necessity, the claim of privilege should not be lightly accepted, but even the most compelling necessity cannot overcome the claim of privilege if the court is ultimately satisfied that military secrets are at stake. A fortiori, where necessity is dubious, a formal claim of privilege, made under the circumstances of this case, will have to prevail.[44]

The grand jury's showing of need here is well documented and imposing. The Special Prosecutor has specifically identified by date, time and place each of the eight meetings and the one telephone call involved. Due to the unusual circumstances of having access to sworn public testimony of participants to these conversations, the Special Prosecutor has been able to provide the Court with the conflicting accounts of what transpired. He thus identifies the topics discussed in each instance, the areas of critical conflict in the testimony, and the resolution it is anticipated the tape recordings may render possible.[45] The relative importance of the issues in doubt is revealed. One example, quoted from the Special Prosecutor will suffice:

---

[43]. United States v. Reynolds, 345 U.S. 1, 10, 73 S.Ct. 528, 97 L.Ed. 727 (1953).

[44]. *Id.* at 11, 73 S.Ct. at 533.

Occasionally when the executive privilege question comes before a court, need for the evidence cannot be termed great because it is possible to indirectly satisfy the need without breaching the privilege claimed. This is accomplished in criminal cases, for example, by requiring the government to choose between foregoing its prosecution or coming forward with the information claimed to be privileged. Whichever choice the government makes does justice to the defendant. In addition the situation creates an incentive for the government to critically evaluate its claim of privilege. Compare Vaughn v. Rosen, 484 F.2d 820 at 825, 826 (D.C.Cir. 1973). This case, however, is more akin to those arising under the Freedom of Information Act, 5 U.S.C. § 552. There, as here, the party petitioning access to information gains absolutely nothing from dismissal of the action. The questions of need must be directly confronted.

[45]. See Brief in Support at 10, 11.

Meeting of September 15, 1972. On September 15, 1972, the grand jury returned an indictment charging seven individuals with conspiracy and other offenses relating to the break-in. Respondent met the same day with Dean and Haldeman in his Oval Office from 5:37 to 6:17 p. m. Both Dean and Haldeman have given lengthy but contradictory accounts of what was said (S.Tr. 2229-33, 6090-93).

According to Dean, the purpose of the meeting was to brief respondent on the status of the investigation and related matters. Dean said that respondent then congratulated him on the "good job" he had done and was pleased that the case had "stopped with Liddy." Dean said that he then told respondent that all he had been able to do was "contain" the case and "assist in keeping it out of the White House." (S.Tr. 2230.) If this testimony is corroborated, it will tend to establish that a conspiracy to obstruct justice reached the highest level of government.

Haldeman, after reviewing a tape recording of the meeting, has agreed that there was discussion of the Watergate indictments, of the civil cases arising out of the break-in, of the possibility of a continuing grand jury investigation, of internal politics at the Committee for the Re-Election of the President, and of other matters. He denies, however, that respondent congratulated Dean on Dean's efforts to thwart the investigation. (S.Tr. 6090-93, 6456).

If Haldeman's innocuous version of the meeting can be sustained, it is because the meeting only involved an innocent discussion of political interests. The question of Dean's perjury would then arise. Resolution of this conflict between two of the three persons present and an accurate knowledge of plans or admissions made on this occasion would be of obvious aid to the grand jury's investigation. [46]

The point is raised that, as in *Reynolds,* the sworn statements of witnesses should suffice and remove the need for access to documents deemed privileged. Though this might often be the case, here, unfortunately, the witnesses differ, sometimes completely, on the precise matters likely to be of greatest moment to the grand jury. Ironically, need for the taped evidence derives in part from the fact that witnesses *have* testified regarding the subject matter, creating important issues of fact for the grand jury to resolve. It will be noted as well in contradistinction to *Reynolds,* that this is a criminal

[46.] See Brief in Support at 6, 7.

investigation. Rather than money damages at stake, we deal here in matters of reputation and liberty. Based on this indusputably forceful showing of necessity by the grand jury, the claim of privilege cannot be accepted lightly.

In his Brief in Support, the Special Prosecutor outlines the grand jury's view regarding the validity of the Respondent's claim of privilege. Its opinion is that the right of confidentiality is improperly asserted here. Principally, the Special Prosecutor cites a substantial possibility, based on the sworn testimony of participants, that the privilege is improperly invoked as a cloak for serious criminal wrongdoing.

According to the testimony of John W. Dean, many of the conversations in which he participated were part and parcel of a criminal conspiracy to obstruct justice by preventing the truth from coming out about the additional participants in the original conspiracy to break into and wiretap the offices of the Democratic National Committee. He has testified that in the presence of H. R. Haldeman he told respondent on September 15, 1972, that "all [Dean] had been able to do was to contain the case and assist in keeping it out of the White House." Dean also told respondent that he "could make no assurances that the day would not come when this matter would start to unravel." Respondent allegedly congratulated him on the "good job" he was doing on that task. (S.Tr. 2229-30). Dean also has testified that on March 13, 1973, respondent told him that respondent had approved executive clemency for Hunt and that there would be no problem in raising $1 million to buy the Watergate defendants' silence (S.Tr. 2324). In addition, there is uncontradicted testimony that respondent was briefed on Watergate on June 20, 1972, three days after the arrests, by Haldeman, Ehrlichman and Mitchell, his closest political advisors (S.Tr. 5924, 3407-08). If these three told respondent all they allegedly knew, respondent would have been aware of details of the nascent cover-up.

It is true, of course that other testimony indicates that the conversations did not include direct evidence of criminal misconduct. While this is not the time or place to judge credibility, Dean's testimony cannot be dismissed out of hand. In fact, Haldeman has confirmed many of the details of the meetings at which both he and Dean were present. The opposite conclusions he draws are based upon a different interpretation and different recollection of some of the details.[47]

47. See Brief in Support at 48, 49.

If the interest served by a privilege is abused or subverted, the claim of privilege fails. Such a case is well described in *Clark* v. *United States*, 289 U.S. 1, 53 S.Ct. 465, 77 L.Ed. 993 (1933), a decision involving the privilege of secrecy enjoyed by jurors.

The privilege takes as its postulate a genuine relation, honestly created and honestly maintained. If that condition is not satisfied, if the relation is merely a sham and a pretense, the juror may not invoke a relation dishonestly assumed as a cover and cloak for the concealment of the truth.

* * * * * *

With the aid of this analogy [to the attorney-client privilege] we recur to the social policies competing for supremacy. A privilege surviving until the relation is abused and vanishing when abuse is shown to the satisfaction of the judge has been found to be a workable technique for the protection of the confidences of client and attorney. Is there sufficient reason to believe that it will be found to be inadequate for the protection of a juror? No doubt the need is weighty that conduct in the jury room shall be untrammeled by the fear of embarrassing publicity. The need is no less weighty that it shall be pure and undefiled. A juror of integrity and reasonable firmness will not fear to speak his mind if the confidences of debate are barred to the ears of mere impertinence or malice. He will not expect to be shielded against the disclosure of his conduct in the event that there is evidence reflecting upon his honor.[48]

These principles are, of course, fully applicable throughout government.[49] A court would expect that if the privacy of its deliberations, for example, were ever used to foster criminal conduct or to develop evidence of criminal wrongdoing, any privilege might be barred and privacy breached. So it is that evidentiary privileges asserted against the grand jury may be ruled inapplicable if the interest served by the privilege is subverted.

Nevertheless, without discrediting the strength of the grand jury's position, the Court cannot, as matters now stand, rule that the present claim of privilege is invalid. The President contends that the recorded conversations occurred pursuant to an exercise

[48.] Clark v. United States, 289 U.S. 1, 14, 16, 53 S.Ct. 465, 469, 470, 77 L.Ed. 993 (1933).

[49.] See *e. g.,* Gravel v. United States, 408 U.S. 606, 92 S.Ct. 2614, 33 L.Ed.2d 583 (1972); United States v. Brewster, 408 U.S. 501, 92 S.Ct. 2531, 33 L.Ed.2d 507 (1972); Spalding v. Vilas, 161 U.S. 483, 498, 16 S.Ct. 631, 40 L.Ed. 780 (1896); Bivens v. Six Unknown Narcotics Agents, 456 F.2d 1339 (2nd Cir. 1972).

of his duty to "take care that the laws be faithfully executed."[50] Although the Court is not bound by that conclusion, it is extremely reluctant to finally stand against a declaration of the President of the United States on any but the strongest possible evidence. Need for the evidence requires that a claim not be accepted lightly, but the vitality of Presidential deliberations in like manner requires that the claim not be rejected lightly. The Court is simply unable to decide the question of privilege without inspecting the tapes.

It is true that if material produced is properly the subject of privilege, even an inspection *in camera* may constitute a compromise of privilege. Nevertheless, it would be an extremely limited infraction and in this case an unavoidable one. If privileged and unprivileged evidence are intermingled, privileged portions may be excised so that only unprivileged matter goes before the grand jury (which also meets in secret proceedings). If privileged and unprivileged evidence are so inextricably connected that separation becomes impossible, the whole must be privileged and no disclosure made to the grand jury.

It should be observed as well that given the circumstances in this case, there is every reason to suppose an *in camera* examination will materially aid the Court in its decision. The fact that extensive accounts of the recorded conversations given under oath by participants are available, will enable the Court to make an intelligent and informed analysis of the evidence.

The Court is unable to design a more cautious approach consistent with both a demonstrated critical need for the evidence and the serious questions raised concerning the applicability of the privilege asserted. The Court has attempted to walk the middle ground between a failure to decide the question of privilege and one extreme, and a wholesale delivery of tapes to the grand jury at the other. The one would be a breach of duty; the other an inexcusable course of conduct. The approach comports with precedent in this district,[51] and honors the injunction of *Reynolds* and *Burr* to pursue fairness and protect essential privacy.[52]

50. United States Constitution, Article II, Section 3.

51. Nader v. Butz, C.A.No.148-72 (DCDC August 20, 1973).

52. The President urges that a production order from the Court would open the floodgates to innumerable subpoenas. The above procedure is designed to prevent such a result. It should be noted as well that this is apparently the first time since the *Burr* decision in 1807 that a subpoena of this sort has been directed to the President. If we may rely on history, there is little indication that the President will be subjected to the "parade of horrors" he describes.

Chief Justice Marshall was sensitive to the need to protect the President against

To paraphrase Chief Justice Marshall,[53] if it be apparent that the tapes are irrelevant to the investigation, or that for state reasons they cannot be introduced into the case, the subpoena *duces tecum* would be useless. But if this be not apparent, if they *may* be important in the investigation, *may* be safely heard by the grand jury, if only in part, would it not be a blot on the page which records the judicial proceedings of this country, if, in a case of such serious import as this, the Court did not at least call for an inspection of evidence in chambers?

abuse that would employ judicial process to gain its end:

The guard, furnished to this high officer, to protect him from being harassed by vexatious and unnecessary subpoenas, is to be looked for in the conduct of a court after those subpoenas have issued; not in any circumstance which is to precede their being issued. United States v. Burr, *supra*, no. 14 at 34.

Later in the pretrial proceedings, the Chief Justice had occasion to elaborate on the judicial procedures that might be useful as presidential "guards". The passage is too lengthy for an exposition here, but interested persons are referred to United States v. Burr, 25 Fed.Cas. pp. 187, 191, 192 (Case No. 14,694) (1807). The Court has here attempted to implement the Chief Justice's guidelines.

[53.] United States v. Burr, *supra*, n. 14 at 35.

II
COURT OF APPEALS
DECISION IN
NIXON v. SIRICA

Judge Sirica's decision was appealed to the Court of Appeals in the District of Columbia through the unusual procedural device of a writ of mandamus. Seven judges of the Court of Appeals heard the case (two others disqualified themselves). Argument in the case took place on September 11, 1973. Ten days later the court suggested that the parties get together and try to settle the issue themselves without any court order. When counsel for both sides (Archibald Cox, the Special Prosecutor, and Charles Alan Wright, the President's lawyer) indicated that they could not come to an agreement, the Court announced its decision on October 12, 1973 upholding Judge Sirica's order by a 5 to 2 vote. The Court gave the President five days to seek review of its order in the Supreme Court. That period lapsed on Friday, October 19, 1973 without any appeal by the President. Thus the order became final.

The President indicated that he would comply with the order by submitting partial transcripts of the subpoenaed tapes which would be verified by a third party—Senator John Stennis. When Archibald Cox asserted he would not accept the President's plan, he was fired and Attorney General Elliot Richardson and his deputy William Ruckelshaus, resigned in the famous "Saturday Night Massacre" of October 20, 1973. The uproar that followed the resignations compelled the President to agree to comply fully with the Court of Appeals decision.

Richard M. NIXON, President of the United States,
Petitioner

V.

The Honorable John J. SIRICA, United States District Judge,
Respondent

and

Archibald Cox, Special Prosecutor,
Watergate Special Prosecution Force,
Party in Interest.

UNITED STATES of America,
Petitioner

V.

The Honorable John J. SIRICA, Chief Judge,
United States District Court for the District of Columbia,
Respondent

and

Richard M. Nixon, President of the United States,
Party in Interest.

In re GRAND JURY PROCEEDINGS.
Nos. 73-1962, 73-1967 and 73-1989.

United States Court of Appeals,
District of Columbia Circuit.

Argued Sept. 11, 1973.

Decided Oct. 12, 1973.

As amended Oct. 12 and Oct. 25, 1973.
487 F. 2d 700

Charles Alan Wright, Washington, D.C., with whom Douglas M.
Parker, and Robert T. Andrews, Washington, D.C., were on the
brief, for petitioner in No. 73-1962.

Archibald Cox, Washington, D.C., with whom Philip A. Lacovara and Peter M. Kreindler, Washington, D.C., were on the brief, for petitioner in Nos. 73-1967 and 73-1989.

Anthony C. Morella, Rockville, Md., and George D. Horning, Jr., Washington, D.C., for respondent.

Sherman Cohn, Eugene Gressman, Jerome A. Barron, Samuel Dash, Chief Counsel, Rufus Edminsten, Deputy Counsel, James Hamilton, Asst. Chief Counsel, and Ronald D. Rotunda, Asst. Counsel, were on the brief as amicus curiae.

Before BAZELON, Chief Judge, and WRIGHT, McGOWAN, LEVENTHAL, ROBINSON, MacKINNON and WILKEY, Circuit Judges, sitting en banc.

PER CURIAM:

This controversy concerns an order of the District Court for the District of Columbia entered on August 29, 1973, by Chief Judge John J. Sirica as a means of enforcing a grand jury subpoena *duces tecum* issued to and served on President Richard M. Nixon. The order commands the President, or any subordinate official, to produce certain items identified in the subpoena so that the Court can determine, by *in camera* inspection, whether the items are exempted from disclosure by evidentiary privilege.[1]

Both the President and Special Prosecutor Archibald Cox, acting on behalf of the grand jury empanelled by the District Court in June, 1972,[2] challenge the legality of this order. All

[1.] The District Court's order is reproduced here in its entirety:

This matter having come before the Court on motion of the Watergate Special Prosecutor made on behalf of the June 1972 grand jury of this district for an order to show cause, and the Court being advised in the premises, it is by the Court this 29th day of August, 1973, for the reasons stated in the attached opinion,

Ordered that respondent, President Richard M. Nixon, or any subordinate officer, official or employee with custody or control of the documents or objects listed in the grand jury subpoena *duces tecum* of July 23, 1973, served on respondent in this district, is hereby commanded to produce forthwith for the Court's examination *in camera*, the subpoenaed documents or objects which have not heretofore been produced to the grand jury; and it is

Further Ordered that the ruling herein be stayed for a period of five days in which time respondent may perfect an appeal from the ruling; and it is

Further Ordered that should respondent appeal from the ruling herein, the above stay will be extended indefinitely pending the completion of such appeal or appeals.

[2.] By Order of the Attorney General No. 517-73, 38 Fed.Reg. 14, 688 (June 4, 1973), the Special Prosecutor is designated as the attorney for the United States to conduct proceedings before the grand jury investigating the unauthorized entry into the Democratic National Committee Headquarters and related offenses. He is specifically authorized "to contest the assertion of 'executive privilege.'" See *also* Hearings before the Senate Comm. on the Judiciary, 93d Cong., 1st Sess. 159, 180-81 (1973). The Special Prosecutor, as Attorney for the United States, appears in this Court and the court below as counsel to the grand jury and an officer of the court.

members of this Court agree that the District Court had, and this Court has, jurisdiction to consider the President's claim of privilege.[3] The majority of the Court approves the District Court's order, as clarified and modified in part, and otherwise denies the relief requested.

I.

We deem it essential to emphasize the narrow contours of the problem that compels the Court to address the issues raised by this case. The central question before us is, in essence, whether the President may, in his sole discretion, withhold from a grand jury evidence in his possession that is relevant to the grand jury's investigations. It is our duty to respond to this question, but we limit our decision strictly to that required by the precise and entirely unique circumstances of the case.

On July 23 of this year, Special Prosecutor Cox caused to be issued a subpoena *duces tecum* directed to the President.[4] The subpoena called upon the President to produce before the grand jury certain documents and objects in his possession—specifically, tape recordings of certain identified meetings and telephone conversations that had taken place between the President and his advisers in the period from June 20, 1972 to April 15, 1973.[5] In a letter dated July 25, 1973, addressed to the Chief Judge of the District Court, the President declined to produce the subpoenaed recordings. The President informed the Court that he had concluded "that it would be inconsistent with the public interest and with the Constitutional position of the Presidency to make available recordings of meetings and telephone conversations in

[3.] This, of course, does not signify agreement on the scope of the President's privilege, the proper content of any judgment by the Court, or the District Court's constitutional authority to issue an order to the President. Circuit Judges MacKinnon and Wilkey concur in part II of the Court's opinion and otherwise dissent for the reasons stated in their separate opinions.

[4.] The subpoena, issued by the clerk under seal of the District Court pursuant to F.R. Crim.P. 17(a) and (c), was addressed to the President or "any subordinate officer, official or employee with custody or control" of the documents and objects specified in the attached schedule.

[5.] For the Special Prosecutor's explanation of the relevance of those discussions, see Appendix II, *infra*. The subpoena also required production of two memoranda that had been written by and sent to certain of the President's advisers. The President has complied with the subpoena in so far as it concerned these items.

which [he] was a participant. . . ."[6]

On July 26, at the instruction of the grand jury, the Special Prosecutor applied to the District Court for an order requiring production of the evidence. Having determined by poll in open court the grand jury's desire for the evidence, the District Judge ordered the President, or any appropriate subordinate official, to show cause "why the documents and objects described in [the subpoena] should not be produced. . . ." On August 7, in answer to the order, the President filed a Special Appearance and Brief in Opposition, stating that the letter of July 25 constituted a "valid and formal claim of executive privilege" and that, therefore, the District Court "lack[ed] jurisdiction to enter an enforceable order compelling compliance with the subpoena. . . ."[7]

The District Court then allowed the Special Prosecutor to submit a memorandum in response to that of the President and in support of the Court's order. This memorandum contains a particularized showing of the grand jury's need for each of the several subpoenaed tapes[8]—a need that the District Court subsequently and, we think, correctly termed "well-documented and imposing."[9]

The strength and particularity of this showing were made possible by a unique intermeshing of events unlikely soon, if ever, to recur. The President had previously declared his intention to decline to assert any privilege with respect to testimony by his present and former aides, whether before the grand jury or the Select Committee of the Senate on Presidential Campaign Activities, concerning what has come to be known as the "Watergate" affair.[10] As a result, detailed testimony by these aides before the Senate Committee enabled the Special Prosecutor to show a significant likelihood that there existed conspiracies among persons other than those already convicted of the Watergate break-in and wiretapping, not only to commit those offenses, but to conceal the identities of the persons involved. Moreover, the Special Prosecutor was able to show from the public testimony that important evidence relevant to

---

[6.] Appendix to the Supplemental Brief for the United States (Special Prosecutor), at 30-31.

[7.] Special Appearance at ¶¶ 3 and 6, In re Grand Jury Subpoena Duces Tecum to Nixon, 360 F.Supp. 1 (D.C.D.C.1973).

[8.] Memorandum in Support at 3-11, *id.*

[9.] In re Subpoena to Nixon *supra* note 7, 360 F.Supp. at 11.

[10.] *See* text at note 81, *infra.*

the existence and scope of the purported conspiracy was contained in statements made by the President's advisers during certain conversations that took place in his office. Most importantly, perhaps, significant inconsistencies in the sworn testimony of these advisers relating to the content of the conversations raised a distinct possibility that perjury had been committed before the Committee and, perhaps, before the grand jury itself.

Thus, the Special Prosecutor was able to show that the tape recordings of the disputed conversations—conversations specifically identified as to time, place, and content—were each directly relevant to the grand jury's task. Indeed, the Memorandum demonstrates, particularly with respect to the possible perjury offenses, that the subpoenaed recordings contain evidence critical to the grand jury's decisions as to whether and whom to indict.

On August 29th, the Chief Judge of the District Court entered the order at issue in this case. In the accompanying opinion, 360 F. Supp. 1, he rejected the President's challenge to the Court's jurisdiction and to its authority to enter orders necessary to the enforcement of the subpoena. The President, petitioner in No. 73-1962, asks this Court for a writ of mandamus commanding the District Court to vacate its August 29th order. In No. 73-1967, the United States, through the Special Prosecutor and on behalf of the grand jury, petitions for a writ commanding the District Court to order full and immediate disclosure of the tapes to the grand jury and, in the alternative, for instructions to govern any *in camera* inspection that takes place. The United States has, in addition, filed an appeal from the order below.[11]

Because of the public interest in their prompt resolution, we consolidated the cases and ordered briefing on an expedited schedule. For the reasons stated herein, we decline to command the District Court to vacate its order, and dismiss both the petition and appeal of the United States. We direct, however, that the District Court modify its order in certain respects, and that it conduct further proceedings in this case in a manner consistent with the criteria and procedures defined in this opinion.

In their petitions for relief, both the President and the Special Prosecutor invoke this court's statutory authority to issue "all

---

[11.] No. 73-1989.

writs necessary or appropriate in aid of" its jurisdiction.[12] As the Supreme Court has noted, the peremptory writ of mandamus, one of the group authorized by the All Writs Act, "has traditionally been used in the federal courts only 'to confine an inferior court to a lawful exercise of its prescribed jurisdiction or to compel it to exercise its authority when it is its duty to do so.' "[13] And although jurisdiction, for purposes of the writ, need not be defined in its narrow, technical sense, "it is clear that only exceptional circumstances amounting to a judicial 'usurpation of power' will justify the invocation of this extraordinary remedy."[14] Beyond these considerations, the writ may not be used as a substitute for an appeal, nor to subvert the general congressional policy against appeals from interlocutory orders,[15] a policy that is particularly strong in criminal cases.[16]

With these general parameters in mind, we turn first to the President's petition, which seeks to accommodate a well settled limitation on direct appeals challenging subpoenas. As recently restated by the Supreme Court, ordinarily "one to whom a subpoena is directed may not appeal the denial of a motion to quash that subpoena but must either obey its commands or refuse to do so and contest the validity of the subpoena if he is subsequently cited for contempt on account of his failure to obey."[17] Contrary to the argument of the respondent Chief Judge, we see no basis for broadly differentiating an order to produce evidence for an *in camera* inspection to determine whether its is privileged from disclosure to a grand jury.

From the viewpoint of mandamus, however, the central question that the President raises—whether the District Court

[12]. "The Supreme Court and all courts established by Act of Congress may issue all writs necessary or appropriate in aid of their respective jurisdictions and agreeable to the usages and principles of law." 28 U.S.C. § 1651(a) (1970).

[13]. Will v. United States, 389 U.S. 90, 95, 88 S.Ct. 269, 273, 19 L.Ed.2d 305 (1967), *quoting* Roche v. Evaporated Milk Ass'n. 319 U.S. 21, 26, 63 S.Ct. 938, 87 L.Ed. 1185 (1943). For a full discussion of the general rules governing our authority to issue the writ, *see* Donnelly v. Parker, — U.S. App. D.C. —, —, —, 486 F.2d 402, 405, 407-410 (1973).

[14]. Will v. United States, *supra* note 13, 389 U.S. at 95, 88 S.Ct. at 273, *quoting* De Beers Consol. Mines v. United States, 325 U.S. 212, 217, 65 S.Ct. 1130, 89 L.Ed. 1566 (1945).

[15]. Parr v. United States, 351 U.S. 513, 520-521, 76 S.Ct. 912, 100 L.Ed. 1377 (1956).

[16]. Will v. United States, *supra* note 13, 389 U.S. at 96-98, 88 S.Ct. 269.

[17]. United States v. Ryan, 402 U.S. 530, 532, 91 S.Ct. 1580, 1581, 29 L.Ed.2d 85 (1971). *See also* Cobbledick v. United States, 309 U.S. 323, 60 S.Ct. 540, 84 L.Ed. 783 (1940). *But see* Carr v. Monroe Mfg. Co., 431 F.2d 384 (5th cir. 1970).

exceeded its authority in ordering an *in camera* inspection of the tapes—is essentially jurisdictional.[18] It is, too, a jurisdictional problem of "first impression" involving a "basic, undecided question."[19] And if indeed the only avenue of direct appellate review open to the President requires that he first disobey the court's order, appeal seems to be "a clearly inadequate remedy."[20] These circumstances, we think, warrant the exercise, at the instance of the President, of our review power under the All Writs Act,[21] particularly in light of the great public interest in prompt resolution of the issues that his petition presents.[22]

We find the Special Prosecutor's petition much more problematic.[23] The Supreme Court "has never approved the use of the writ to review"—at the instance of the Government—"an interlocutory procedural order in a criminal case which did not have the effect of a dismissal."[24] And while the Court has not decided "under what circumstances, if any, such a use of mandamus would be appropriate,"[25] we have grave doubt that it would be appropriate in this case. It is by no means clear that a writ directing the District Court to dispense with an *in camera* inspection and order immediate production to the grand jury could fairly be characterized as aiding this Court's jurisdiction,

---

[18.] *Compare* Schlagenhauf v. Holder, 379 U.S. 104, 110-111, 85 S.Ct. 234, 13 L.Ed.2d 152 (1964).

[19.] *Id.*

[20.] Bankers Life & Cas. Co. v. Holland, 346 U.S. 379, 385, 74 S.Ct. 145, 98 L.Ed. 106 (1953), *quoting* Ex parte Fahey, 332 U.S. 258, 260, 67 S.Ct. 1558, 91 L.Ed. 2041 (1947).

[21.] In so concluding, we do not discard the direct appeal as an alternative basis for review in the particular situation before us. The final-order doctrine, as a normal pre-requisite to a federal appeal, is not a barrier where it operates to leave the suitor "powerless to avert the mischief of the order." Perlman v. United States, 247 U.S. 7, 13, 38 S.Ct. 417, 419, 62 L.Ed. 950 (1918). In the case of the President, contempt of a judicial order—even for the purpose of enabling a constitutional test of the order—would be a course unseemly at best. To safeguard against any possible miscarriage of justice, we make known our view that our jurisdiction exists by way of appeal if for any reason the President's application is not properly before us on the jurisdictional predicate he invokes.

[22.] *See* United States v. United States District Court, 444 F.2d 651, 655-656 (6th Cir. 1971), aff'd, 407 U.S. 297, 301, n. 3, 92 S.Ct. 2125, 32 L.Ed.2d 752 (1972).

[23.] We think it clear, in any event, that the District Court's August 29th order is unappealable at the instance of the Special Prosecutor, either under 28 U.S.C. § 1291 or § 1292 (1970). In addition, since the order in no way finally decides that any of the subpoenaed material must be denied the grand jury, it cannot be deemed an order "suppressing or excluding evidence," or otherwise within the contemplation of the Criminal Appeals Act, 18 U.S.C. § 3731 (1970). *But see* note 100, *infra*.

[24.] Will v. United States, *supra* note 13, 389 U.S. at 98, 88 S.Ct. at 275.

[25.] *Id.*

however non-technically jurisdiction might be defined.

Moreover, any resolution of the President's petition necessitates consideration of the validity of the projected *in camera* inspection—the object of the Special Prosecutor's sole objection—and of the need for instructions governing any such inspection—the subject of his sole request in the alternative. In Schlangenhauf v. Holder,[26] the Supreme Court sustained the inherent power of the courts of appeals in special circumstances to review by mandamus a "basic, undecided question,"[27] and "to settle new and important problems."[28] Although one of the problems raised in that case would not normally have justified an exercise of mandamus authority, the Court recognized the propriety of avoiding piecemeal litigation by resolving all issues arising out of the same set of operative facts.[29] Surely the extraordinary importance of the issues that the Special Prosecutor tenders demands no less.

Mandamus is generally withheld when relief is available in another manner.[30] Our review of the President's contentions will necessarily subsume the Special Prosecutor's present concerns. Since we do not consider the question of jurisdiction of his petition essential to a full disposition of this consolidated proceeding, we exercise our discretion[31] to dismiss the petition without deciding it.

III.

We turn, then, to the merits of the President's petition. Counsel for the President contend on two grounds that Judge Sirica lacked jurisdiction to order submission of the tapes for inspection. Counsel argue, first, that, so long as he remains in office, the President is absolutely immune from the compulsory process of a court; and, second, that Executive privilege is absolute with respect to Presidential communications, so that disclosure is at the sole discretion of the President. This

---

26. *Supra* note 18.

27. *Supra* note 18, 379 U.S. at 110, 85 S.Ct. 234.

28. *Id.* at 111, 85 S.Ct. at 239.

29. *Id.*

30. *See* Ex parte Republic of Peru, 318 U.S. 578, 584, 63 S.Ct. 793, 87 L.Ed. 1014 (1943).

31. *See, e. g.,* Ex parte Skinner & Eddy Corp. 265 U.S. 86, 95-96, 44 S.Ct. 446, 68 L.Ed. 912 (1924).

immunity and this absolute privilege are said to arise from the doctrine of separation of powers and by implication from the Constitution itself. It is conceded that neither the immunity nor the privilege is express in the Constitution.

A.

It is clear that the want of physical power to enforce its judgments does not prevent a court from deciding an otherwise justiciable case.[32] Nevertheless, if it is true that the President is legally immune from court process, this case is at an end. The judiciary will not, indeed cannot, indulge in rendering an opinion to which the President has no legal duty to conform. We must, therefore, determine whether the President is *legally* bound to comply with an order enforcing a subpoena.[33]

We note first that courts have assumed that they have the power to enter mandatory orders to Executive officials to compel production of evidence.[34] While a claim of an absolute Executive immunity may not have been raised directly before these courts, there is no indication that they entertained any doubts of their power. Only last term in Environmental Protection Agency v. Mink,[35] the Supreme Court "may order" *in camera* inspections of certain materials to determine whether they must be disclosed to the public pursuant to the Freedom of Information Act. [36]

The Court's assumption of legal power to compel production of evidence within the possession of the Executive surely stands on firm footing. Youngstown Sheet & Tube Co. v. Sawyer,[37] in

---

[32.] Glidden v. Zdanok, 370 U.S. 530, 568-571, 82 S.Ct. 1459, 8 L.Ed.2d 671 (1962); Baker v. Carr, 369 U.S. 186, 208-237, 82 S.Ct. 691, 7 L.Ed.2d 663 (1962). *See also* South Dakota v. North Carolina, 192 U.S. 286, 318-321, 24 S.Ct. 269, 48 L.Ed. 448 (1904); La Abra Silver Mining Co. v. United States, 175 U.S. 423, 461-462, 20 S.Ct. 168, 44 L.Ed. 223 (1898).

[33.] If the judiciary's want of *de facto* power to enforce its judgment has any relevance, is that the third branch of government, posing little physical threat to coordinate branches, need not hesitate to reject sweeping claims to *legal* immunity by those coordinate branches. *See* United States v. Lee, 106 U.S. (16 Otto) 196, 223, 1 S.Ct. 240, 27 L.Ed. 171 (1882).

[34.] *See, e. g.,* United States ex rel. Touhy v. Ragen, 340 U.S. 462, 465-466, 472, 71 S.Ct. 416, 95 L.Ed. 417 (1951) (Frankfurter, J., concurring); Westinghouse Electric Corp. v. city of Burlington, Vermont, 122 U.S.App. D.C. 65, 351 F.2d 762 (1965); Boeing Airplane Co. v. Coggeshall, 108 U.S.App.D.C. 106, 280 F.2d 654 (1960).

[35.] 410 U.S. 73, 93, 93 S.Ct. 827, 35 L.Ed.2d 119 (1973).

[36.] *See* text at notes 92-97 *infra*.

[37.] 343 U.S. 579, 72 S.Ct. 863, 96 L.Ed. 1153 (1952).

which an injunction running against the Secretary of Commerce was affirmed, is only the most celebrated instance of the issuance of compulsory process against Executive officials. *See, e. g.,* United States v. United States District Court, 407 U.S. 297, 92 S.Ct. 2125, 32 L.Ed.2d 752 (1972) (affirming an order requiring the Government to make full disclosure of illegally wiretapped conversations); Kendall v. United States ex rel. Stokes, 37 U.S. (12 Pet.) 524, 9 L.Ed. 1181 (1828) (issuing a mandamus to Postmaster General, commanding him fully to comply with an act of Congress); State Highway Commission v. Volpe, 479 F2d 1099 (8th Cir. 1973) (enjoining the Secretary of Transportation).

It is true that, because the President has taken personal custody of the tapes and is thus himself a party to the present action, these cases can be formally distinguished. As Judge Sirica noted, however, to rule that this case turns on such a distinction would be to exalt the form of *Youngstown Sheet & Tube* over its substance, Justice Black, writing for the *Youngstown* majority, made it clear that the Court understood its affirmance effectively to restrain the President. There is not the slightest hint in any of the *Youngstown* opinions that the case would have been viewed differently if President Truman rather than Secretary Sawyer had been the named party.[38] If *Youngstown* still stands, it must stand for the case where the President has himself taken possession and control of the property unconstitutionally seized, and the injunction would be framed accordingly. The practice of judicial review would be rendered capricious—and very likely impotent—if jurisdiction vanished whenever the President personally denoted an Executive action or omission as his own. This is not to say that the President should lightly be named as a party defendant. As a matter of comity, courts should normally direct legal process to a lower Executive official even though the effect of the process is to restrain or compel the President. Here, unfortunately, the court's order must run directly to the President, because he has taken the unusual step of assumg personal custody of the Government property sought by the subpoena.

The President also attempts to distinguish United States v. Burr,[39] in which Chief Justice Marshall squarely ruled that a

[38]. In Land v. Dollar, 89 U.S.App.D.C. 38, 190 F.2d 623 (1951), vacated as moot 344 U.S. 806, 73 S.Ct. 7, 97 L.Ed. 628 (1952), as well, it was clear that the court realized that its order countered the executive will of the President. The *Land* court acknowledged that the President had directed the cabinet officials to disregard the initial judicial decision. *Id.* at 54, 190 F.2d at 639.

[39]. 25 Fed.Cas. p. 30 (Case No. 14,692d) (1807).

subpoena may be directed to the President. It is true that *Burr* recognized a distinction between the issuance of a subpoena and the ordering of compliance with that subpoena, but the distinction did not concern judicial power or jurisdiction. A subpoena *duces tecum* is an order to produce documents or to show cause why they need not be produced. An order to comply does not make the subpoena more compulsory; it simply maintains its original force. The Chief Justice's words merit close attention. His statement:

> Whatever difference may exist with respect to the power to compel the same obedience to the process, as if it had been directed to a private citizen, there exists no difference with respect to the right to obtain it[,]

is immediately followed by the statement:

> The guard, furnished to this high officer, to protect him from being harassed by *vexatious and unnecessary* subpoenas, is to be looked for in the conduct of a court after those subpoenas have been issued; not in any circumstance which is to precede their being issued.[40]

The clear implication is that the President's special interests may warrant a careful judicial screening of subpoenas after the President interposes an objection, but that some subpoenas will nevertheless be properly sustained by judicial orders of compliance. This implication is borne out by a later opinion by the great Chief Justice in the same case. When President Jefferson did not fully respond to the subpoena issued to him, Colonel Burr inquired why the President should not comply. The Chief Justice's answer should put to rest any argument that he felt the President absolutely immune from orders of compliance:

> The president, although subject to the general rules which apply to others, may have sufficient motives for declining to produce a particular paper, and those motives *may be* such as to restrain the court from enforcing its production * * *. I can readily conceive that the president might receive a letter which it would be improper to exhibit in public. * * * The occasion for *demanding* it ought, in such a case, to be very strong, and to be fully shown to the court before its production could be *insisted* on. * * * Such a letter, though it be a private one, seems to partake of the character of an official paper, and to

---

[40.] *Id.* at 34. (Emphasis supplied.)

be such as ought not on *light ground* to be forced into public view.[41]

A compliance order was, for Marshall, distinct from an order to show cause simply because compliance was not to be ordered before weighing the President's particular reasons for wishing the subpoenaed documents to remain secret. The court was to show respect for the President in weighing those reasons, but the ultimate decision remained with the court.[42]

Thus, to find the President immune from judicial process, we must read out of *Burr* and *Youngstown* the underlying principles that the eminent jurists in each case thought they were establishing. The Constitution makes no mention of special presidential immunities. Indeed, the Executive Branch generally is afforded none. This silence cannot be ascribed to oversight. James Madison raised the question of Executive privileges during the Constitutional Convention,[43] and Senators and Representatives enjoy an express, if limited, immunity from arrest, and an express privilege from inquiry concerning "Speech and Debate" on the floors of Congress.[44] Lacking textual support, counsel for the President nonetheless would have us infer immunity from the President's political mandate, or from his vulnerability to impeachment, or from his broad discretionary powers. These are invitations to refashion the Constitution, and we reject them.

---

[41] United States v. Burr, 25 Fed.Cas. pp. 187, 190, 191-192 (Case No. 14,694) (1807). (Emphasis supplied.)

[42] In 1818, several years after the *Burr* case, a subpoena was also issued to President James Monroe. It summoned the President to appear as a defense witness in the court martial of Dr. William Burton, naming a specific date and time. A copy of the summons is in Attorney General's Papers; Letters received from State Department, Record Group 60, National Archives Building. Attorney General Wirt advised Monroe, through Secretary of State John Quincy Adams, that a subpoena could "properly be awarded to the President of the United States," but suggested that the President indicate on the return that his official duties precluded a personal appearance at the court martial. William Wirt to John Quincy Adams, Jan. 13, 1818, Records of the Office of the Judge Advocate General (Navy), Record Group 125, (Records of General Courts Martial and Courts of Inquiry, Microcopy M-272, case 282), National Archieves Building. In conformance with this advice, Monroe wrote on the back of the summons that he would "be ready and willing to communicate, in the form of a deposition any information I may possess, relating to the subject matter in question." President James Monroe to George M. Dallas, Jan. 21, 1818, *id.* Subsequently, President Monroe did in fact submit answers to the interrogatories forwarded to him by the court. President James Monroe to George M. Dallas, Feb. 14, 1818, *id.*

[43] II Farrand, The Records of the Federal Convention of 1787, 502-503 (1967).

[44] U.S.Const., art. I, § 6, ¶ 1.

Though the President is elected by nationwide ballot, and is often said to represent all the people,[45] he does not embody the nation's sovereignity.[46] He is not above the law's commands: "With all its defects, delays and inconveniences, men have discovered no technique for long preserving free government e x c e p t t h a t t h e E x e c u t i v e b e u n d e r t h e law . . . ."[47] Sovereignty remains at all times with the people, and they do not forfeit through elections the right to have the law construed against and applied to every citizen.

Nor does the Impeachment Clause imply immunity from routine court process.[48] While the President argues that the Clause means that impeachability precludes criminal prosecution of an incumbent, we see no need to explore this question except to note its irrelevance to the case before us. The order entered below, and approved here in modified form, is not a form of criminal process. Nor does it compete with the impeachment device by working a constructive removal of the President from office. The subpoena names in the alternate "any subordinate officer," and the tasks of compliance may obviously be delegated in whole or in part so as not to interfere with the President's official responsibilities.[49] By contemplating the possibility of post-impeachment trials for violations of law committed in office, the Impeachment Clause itself reveals that incumbency does not relieve the President of the routine legal obligations that confine all citizens. That the Impeachment Clause may qualify the court's power to sanction non-compliance with judicial orders is immaterial. Whatever the qualifications, they were equally present in *Youngstown:* Commerce Secretary Sawyer, the defendant there, was an impeachable "civil officer,"[50] but

---

[45.] Myers v. United States, 272 U.S. 52, 123, 47 S.Ct. 21, 71 L.Ed. 160 (1926).

[46.] *See, e. g.,* United States v. Burr, *supra* note 39, 25 Fed.Cas. at 34.

[47.] Youngstown Sheet & Tube Co. V. Sawyer, *supra* note 37, 343 U.S. at 655, 72 S.Ct. at 880 (1952) (Jackson, J., concurring).

[48.] U.S.Const., art. I, § 3, ¶ 7:
Judgement in Cases of Impeachment shall not extend further than to removal from Office, and disqualification to hold and enjoy any Office of Honor, Trust or Profit under the United States: but the Party convicted shall nevertheless be liable and subject to Indictment, Trial, Judgment and Punishment, according to Law.

[49.] On this point, too, Chief Justice Marshall was instructive:
If, upon any principle, the president could be construed to stand exempt from the general provisions of the constitution, it would be, because his duties as chief magistrate demand his whole time for national objects. But it is apparent that this demand is not unremitting.
United States v. Burr, *supra* note 39, 25 Fed. Cas. at 34.

[50.] Because impeachment is available against all "civil Officers of the United

the injunction against him was nonetheless affirmed. The legality of judicial orders should not be confused with the legal consequences of their breach; for the courts in this country always assume that their orders will be obeyed, especially when addressed to responsible government officials. Indeed, the President has, in this case, expressly abjured the course of setting himself above the law.

Finally, the President reminds us that the landmark decisions recognizing judicial power to mandamus Executive compliance with "ministerial" duties also acknowledged that the Executive Branch enjoys an unreviewable discretion in many areas of "political" or "executive" administration.[51] While true, this is irrevelant to the issue of presidential immunity from judicial process. The discretionary-ministerial distinction concerns the nature of the act or omission under review, not the official title of the defendant.[52] No case holds that an act is discretionary merely because the President is the actor.[53] If the Constitution or the laws of evidence confer upon the President the absolute discretion to withhold material subpoenaed by a grand jury, then

States," not merely against the President, U.S.Const. art. II, § 4, it is difficult to understand how any immunities peculiar to the President can emanate by implication from the fact of impeachability.

[51.] *See, e.g.,* Marbury v. Madison, 5 U.S. (1 Cranch) 137, 165, 2 L.Ed. 60 (1803); Kendall v. United States ex rel. Stokes, 37 U.S. (12 Pet.) 524, 710, 9 L.Ed. 1181 (1838).

[52.] [T]he question, whether the legality of an act of the head of a department be examinable in a court of justice or not, must always depend on the nature of that act. Marbury v. Madison, *supra* note 51, 5 U.S. (1 Cranch) at 165.

The mandamus does not seek to direct or control the postmaster general in the discharge of any official duty, partaking in any respect of any executive character; but to enforce the performance of a mere ministerial act, which neither he *nor the President* had any authority to deny or control.

Kendall v. United States ex. rel. Stokes, *supra* note 51, 37 U.S. (12 Pet.) at 610. (Emphasis supplied.)

[53.] In this regard, the President's reliance on Mississippi v. Johnson, 71 U.S. (4 Wall.) 475, 18 L.Ed. 437 (1866), is misplaced. In that case, the State of Mississippi sought to enjoin President Johnson from enforcing the Reconstruction Acts. Though Attorney General Stanbery argued that the President was immune from judicial process, the Court declined to found its decision on this ground, choosing instead to deny the bill of injunction as an attempt to coerce a discretionary, as opposed to ministerial, act of the Executive. The Attorney General rehearsed many of the arguments made by the President in this case, claiming that the President's dignity as Chief of State placed him above the reach of routine judicial process and that the President was subject only to that law which might be fashioned in a court of impeachment. *Id.* at 484. We deem it significant that the Supreme Court declined to ratify these views. *Compare* Georgia v. Stanton, 73 U.S. (6 Wall.) 50, 18 L.Ed. 721 (1867), where the Court declined jurisdiction of a similar bill of injunction even though sub-presidential Executive Branch officials were named as defendants.

of course we would vacate, rather than approve with modification, the order entered below. However, this would be because the order touched upon matters within the President's sole discretion, not because the President is immune from process generally. We thus turn to an examination of the President's claim of an absolute discretion to withhold evidence from a grand jury.

B.

There is, as the Supreme Court has said, a "longstanding principle" that the grand jury "has a right to every man's evidence" except that "protected by a constitutional, common law, or statutory privilege."[54] The President concedes the validity of this principle. He concedes that he, like every other citizen, is under a legal duty to produce relevant, non-privileged evidence when called upon to do so.[55] The President contends, however, that whenever, in response to a grand jury subpoena, he interposes a formal claim of privilege, that claim without more disables the courts from inquiring by any means into whether the privilege is applicable to the subpoenaed evidence. The President agrees that, in theory, the privilege attached to his office has limits; for example, he explicitly states that it "cannot be claimed to shield executive officers from prosecution for crime."[56] Nonetheless, he argues that it is his responsibility, and

[54] Branzburg v. Hayes, 408 U.S. 665, 688, 92 S.Ct. 2646, 2660, 33 L.Ed.2d 626 (1972). We reject the contention, pressed by counsel for the President, that the Executive's prosecutorial discretion implies an unreviewable power to withhold evidence relevant to a grand jury's criminal investigation. The federal grand jury is a constitutional fixture in its own right, legally independent of the Executive. See United States v. Johnson, 319 U.S. 503, 510, 63 S.Ct. 1233, 87, L.Ed. 1546 (1943). A grand jury may, with the aid of judicial process, Brown v. United States, 359 U.S. 41, 49-50, 79 S.Ct. 539, 3 L.Ed.2d 609 (1959), call witnesses and demand evidence without the Executive's impetus. Hale v. Henkel, 201 U.S. 43, 60-65, 26 S.Ct. 370, 50 L.Ed. 652 (1906). If the grand jury were a legal appendage of the Executive, it could hardly serve its historic functions as a shield for the innocent and a sword against corruption in high places. In his eloquent affirmation of unfettered prosecutorial discretion in United States v. Cox, 342 F.2d 167, 189 (5th Cir.), cert. denied, 381 U.S. 935, 85 S.Ct. 1767, 14 L.Ed.2d 700 (1965), Judge Wisdom recognized the grand jury's independent and "plenary power to inquire, to summon and interrogate witnesses, and to present either findings and a report or an accusation in open court by presentment." As a *practical,* as opposed to legal matter, the Executive may, of course, cripple a grand jury investigation by denying staff assistance to the jury. And the Executive may refuse to sign an indictment, thus precluding prosecution and, presumably, effecting a permanent sealing of the grand jury minutes. United States v. Cox, *supra.* These choices remain open to the President. But it is he who must exercise them. The court will not assume that burden by eviscerating the grand jury's independent legal authority.

[55] Brief of Petitioner Nixon at 84: Reply Brief of Petitioner, Nixon at 30 n.6.

[56] Brief of Petitioner Nixon at 69, citing Gravel v. United States, 408 U.S. 606, 627, 92 S.Ct. 2614, 33 L.Ed.2d 583 (1972).

his alone, to determine whether particular information falls beyond the scope of the privilege. In effect, then, the President claims that, at least with respect to conversations with his advisers, the privilege is absolute, since he, rather than the courts, has final authority to decide whether it applies in the circumstances.

We of course acknowledge the longstanding judicial recognition of Executive privilege. Courts have appreciated that the public interest in maintaining the secrecy of military and diplomatic plans may override private interests in litigation.[57] They have further responded to Executive pleas to protect from the light of litigation "intra-governmental documents reflecting * * * deliberations comprising part of a process by which governmental decisions and policies are formulated."[58] In so doing, the Judiciary has been sensitive to the considerations upon which the President seems to rest his claim of absolute privilege: the candor of Executive aides and functionaries would be impaired if they were persistently worried that their advice and deliberations were later to be made public.[59] However, counsel for the President can point to no case in which a court has accepted the Executive's mere assertion of privilege as sufficient to overcome the need of the party subpoenaing the documents. To the contrary, the courts have repeatedly asserted that the applicability of the privilege is in the end for them and not the Executive to decide.[60] They have, moreover, frequently ordered *in camera* inspection of documents for which a privilege was asserted in order to determine the

---

[57.] Totten v. United States, 92 U.S. 105, 23 L.Ed. 605 (1875); United States v. Reynolds, 345 U.S. 1, 73 S.Ct. 528, 97 L.Ed. 727 (1953); United States v. Burr, *supra* note 39.

[58.] Carl Zeiss Stiftung v. V.E.B. Carl Zeiss, Jena, 40 F.R.D. 318, 324 (D.C.D.C,1966), aff'd on opinion below, 128 U.S.App.D.C. 10, 384 F.2d 979, cert. denied, 389 U.S. 952, 88 S.Ct. 334, 19 L.Ed.2d 361 (1967).

[59.] *See, e. g., id.* 40 F.R.D. at 329-335; Kaiser Aluminum & Chemical Corp. v. United States, 157 F.Supp. 939, 141 Ct.Cl. 38 (1958).

[60.] *See e. g.,* United States v. Reynolds, *supra* note 57; Olson Rug Co. v. NLRB, 291 F.2d 655 (7th Cir. 1961); Timken Roller Bearing Co. v. United States, 38 F.R.D. 57 (N.D.Ohio 1964); United States v. Procter & Gamble Co. 25 F.R.D. 485 (D.N.J.1960); Kaiser Aluminum & Chemical Corp. v. United States, *supra* note 59; *see also* the cases cited at 8 C. Wright & A. Miller, Federal Practice & Procedure 167-173 (1970). Despite our peculiar constitutional tradition of judicial review, American law is not in fact unusual in subjecting claims of Executive privilege to court scrutiny. Indeed, no common law country follows the rule, urged by the President in this case, that mere executive assertions of privilege are conclusive on the courts. In Conway v. Rimmer, [1968] 1 A11 E.R. 874, the House of Lords explicitly reversed its long held view, as expressed in Duncan v. Cammell Laird & Co., [1842] 1 A11 E.R. 587, that executive privilege is absolute. *Conway* held that proper adjudication of a privilege

privilege's applicability.[61]

It is true, as counsel for the President stress, that Presidents and Attorneys General have often said that the President's final and absolute assertion of Executive privilege is conclusive on the courts.[62] The Supreme Court in United States v. Reynolds, however, went a long way toward putting this view to rest. The *Reynolds* Court, considering a claim based on military secrets, strongly asserted: "The Court itself must determine whether the circumstances are appropriate for the claim of privilege;"[63] "judicial control over the evidence in a case cannot be abdicated to the caprice of executive officers."[64] It is true that, somewhat inconsistently with this sweeping language, the Court formally reserved decision on the Government's claim that the Executive has an absolute discretion constitutionally founded in separation of powers to withhold documents.[65] However, last term in Committee for Nuclear Responsibility, Inc. v. Seaborg,[66] we confronted directly a claim of absolute privilege and rejected it: "Any claim to executive absolutism cannot override the duty of the Court to assure that an official has not exceeded his charter or flouted the legislative will."[67]

We adhere to the *Seaborg* decision. To do otherwise would be effectively to ignore the clear words of Marbury v. Madison,[68] that "[i]t is emphatically the province and duty of the judicial department to say what the law is."[69]

claim may require *in camera* inspection of documents over which the privilege is asserted. [1968] 1 All E.R. at 888 (opinion of Lord Reid), and 896 (opinion of Lord Morris of Borth-y-Gest). Similar recognition of judicial power to scrutinize claims of privilege may be found in almost every common law jurisdiction. *See, e.g.,* Robinson v. South Australia (No. 2),[1931] All E.R. 333 (P.C.); Gagnon v. Quebec Securities Comm'n, [1965] 50 D.L. R.2d 329 (1964); Bruce v. Waldron, [1963] Vict.L.R. 3; Corbett v. Social Security Comm'n, [1962] N.Z.L.R. 878; Amar Chand Butail v. Union of India, [1965] 1 India S. Ct. 243.

61. In Environmental Protection Agency v. Mink, *supra* note 35, the Supreme Court relied on cases in which claims of Executive privilege were reviewed by the court, often *in camera,* in interpreting how the judiciary should apply the intragovernmental communication exemption to the public disclosure mandate of the Freedom of Information Act. *Id.* at 88 & cases cited at notes 14 & 15.

62. *See, e. g.,* 40 Op.Atty.Gen. 45, 49 (1941) (Attorney General Jackson); 100 Cong.Rec. 6621 (1954) (President Eisenhower).

63. *Supra* note 57, 345 U.S. at 8, 73 S.Ct. at 532.

64. *Id.* at 9-10, 73 S.Ct. at 533.

65. *Id.* at 6 & note 9, 73 S.Ct. 528.

66. 149 U.S.App.D.C. 385, 463 F.2d 788 (1971).

67. *Id.* at 390, 463 F.2d at 793.

68. *Supra* note 51, 5 U.S. (1 Cranch) at 157.

69. The purpose of the explicit constitutional privilege against self-incrimination,

Seaborg is not only consistent with, but dictated by, separation of powers doctrine. Whenever a privilege is asserted, even one expressed in the Constitution, such as the Speech and Debate privilege, it is the courts that determine the validity of the assertion and the scope of the privilege.[70] That the privilege is being asserted by the President against a grand jury subpoena does not make the task of resolving the conflicting claims any less judicial in nature. Throughout our history, there have frequently been conflicts between independent organs of the federal government, as well as between the state and federal governments. When such conflicts arise in justiciable cases, our constitutional system provides a means for resolving them—one Supreme Court. To leave the proper scope and application of Executive privilege to the President's sole discretion would represent a mixing, rather than a separation, of Executive and Judicial functions. A breach in the separation of powers must be explicitly authorized by the Constitution,[71] or be shown

like that of Executive privilege, is defeated by too much judicial inquiry into the legitimacy of its use, *see* United States v. Reynolds, *supra* note 57, 345 U.S. at 3-9, 73 S.Ct. 528, but the courts have never held the mere invocation of the privilege to be sufficient to free the invoker from questioning. The judge must first determine whether the privilege is properly invoked. *See, e. g.,* Hoffman v. United States, 341 U.S. 479, 486-487, 71 S.Ct. 814, 95 L.Ed. 1118 (1951).

[70.] The Supreme Court has repeatedly made clear that it is for the courts to determine the reach of the Speech and Debate Clause, U.S.Const. Art. I, § 6, ¶ 1. *See, e.g.,* Gravel v. United States, *supra* note 56; United States v. Brewster, 408 U.S. 501, 92 S.Ct. 2531, 33 L.Ed.2d 507 (1972); United States v. Johnson, *supra* note 54. Indeed, very close judicial review is needed to determine whether the activities concerning which questioning or prosecution is sought are:
integral part[s] of the deliberative and communicative processes by which Members participate in committee and House proceedings with respect to the consideration and passage or rejection of proposed legislation or with respect to other matter which the Constitution places within the jurisdiction of either House.
Gravel v. United States, *supra* note 56, 408 U.S. at 625, 92 S.Ct. at 2627. If separation of powers doctrine countenances such a close review of assertions of an express constitutional privilege, the doctrine must also comprehend judicial scrutiny of assertions of Executive privilege, which is *at most* implicit in the Constitution. *Gravel* deals on its facts only with an assertion of privilege by an individual legislator. As collective bodies, the Houses of Congress have frequently made unilateral declarations of an absolute privilege to withhold documents in their custody from court process. *See, e. g.,* Senate Resolution, Oct. 4, 1972, 92nd Cong., 2d Sess. These claims have never been pressed to a judicial resolution, and we have no occasion here to decide them. It is sufficient to note that they rest on a footing different from the President's claim of absolute privilege in this case. The President's claim has been previously litigated, and repudiated, in United States v. Burr, *supra* note 39. Further, Congress' claims draw upon two express constitutional privileges unavailable to the President, the aforementioned Speech and Debate Clause, and the Secrecy Clause in Art. I, § 5, ¶ 3. Even so, we note that *Gravel* states that the scope of the Speech and Debate privilege cannot be unilaterally "established by the Legislative Branch." Gravel v. United States, *supra,* 408 U.S. at 624 n. 15, 92 S.Ct. 2614.

[71.] *See* Myers v. United States, 272 U.S. 52, 116, 47 S.Ct. 21, 71 L.Ed. 160 (1926).

necessary to the harmonious operation of "workable government."[72] Neither condition is met here. The Constitution mentions no Executive privileges, much less any absolute Executive privileges. Nor is an absolute privilege required for workable government. We acknowledge that wholesale public access to Executive deliberations and documents would cripple the Executive as a co-equal branch. But this is an argument for recognizing Executive privilege and for according it great weight, not for making the Executive the judge of its own privilege.

If the claim of absolute privilege was recognized, its mere invocation by the President or his surrogates could deny access to all documents in all Executive departments to all citizens and their representatives, including Congress, the courts as well as grand juries, state governments, state officials and all state subdivisions. The Freedom of Information Act could become nothing more than a legislative statement of unenforceable rights. Support for this kind of mischief simply cannot be spun from incantation of the doctrine of separation of powers.[73]

Any contention of the President that records of his personal conversations are not covered by the *Seaborg* holding must be rejected. As our prior discussion of United States v. Burr makes clear, Chief Justice Marshall's position supports this proposition. At issue in *Burr* was a subpoena to President Jefferson to produce private letters sent to him—communications whose status must be considered equal to that of private oral conversations. We follow the Chief Justice and hold today that, although the views of the Chief Executive on whether his Executive privilege should obtain are properly given the greatest weight and deference, they cannot be conclusive.

The President's privilege cannot, therefore, be deemed absolute. We think the *Burr* case makes clear that application of Executive privilege depends on a weighing of the public interest protected by the privilege against the public interests that would be served by disclosure in a particular case.[74] We direct our

---

[72.] *See* Youngstown Sheet & Tube Co. v. Sawyer, *supra* note 37, 343 U.S. at 635, 72 S.Ct. 863 (Jackson, J., concurring).

[73.] The doctrine of separation of powers was adopted by the Convention of 1787, not to promote efficiency but to preclude the exercise of arbitrary power. The purpose was not to avoid friction, but, by means of the inevitable friction incident to the distribution of the governmental powers among three departments, to save the people from autocracy.

Myers v. United States, *supra* note 71, 272 U.S. at 293, 47 S.Ct. at 85. (Brandeis, J., dissenting).

[74.] Chief Justice Marshall wrote two opinions concerning the production of the letters. In the first of these opinions, the Chief Justice ruled that a subpoena to

attention, however, solely to the circumstances here. With the possible exception of material on one tape, the President does not assert that the subpoenaed items involve military or state secrets;[75] nor is the asserted privilege directed to the particular kinds of information that the tapes contain. Instead, the President asserts that the tapes should be deemed privileged because of the great public interest in maintaining the confidentiality of conversations that take place in the President's performance of his official duties. This privilege, intended to protect the effectiveness of the executive decision-making process, is analogous to that between a congressman and his aides under the Speech and Debate Clause; to that among judges, and between judges and their law clerks;[76] and similar to that contained in the Fifth Exemption to the Freedom of Information Act.[77]

produce the letters could be issued to the President and that the Chief Justice himself would consider and weigh any specific objections interposed by the President that the letters contained matter "which ought not to be disclosed." United States v. Burr, *supra* note 39, 25 Fed. Cas. at 37; *see* page 710 *supra.* Statements of the Chief Justice in the first *Burr* opinion suggest that he contemplated that he would actually inspect the letters *in camera.*

If it contain matter not essential to the defense, and the disclosure be unpleasant to the executive, it certainly ought not to be disclosed. This is a point which will appear *on the return.* * * * If they contain matter interesting to the nation, the concealment of which is required by the public safety, that matter will appear *upon the return.*

United States v. Burr, *supra* note 39, at 37. The United States Attorney Hay seems to have read the Chief Justice's first opinion to contemplate inspection by the court. As Judge Wilkey notes in his dissent, after Burr had renewed his request for the letters, Hay offered to submit them to the court for copying of "those parts which had relation to the cause." Hay further expressed his willingness to transmit the letters to Burr's counsel so that they could form their own opinions on what portions should be kept confidential from Burr and the public. Hay anticipated that differences between the opinions of Burr's counsel and himself would be arbitrated by the court. United States v. Burr, *supra* note 41, 25 Fed.Cas. at 190. The prosecution in the *Burr* case thus seems to have read Chief Justice Marshall's first opinion to support a procedure analogous to *in camera* inspection by Judge Sirica and Special Prosecutor Cox.

It was only after Burr's counsel rejected Hay's position and demanded direct submission of the entire letters to Burr himself that Marshall found it necessary to issue his second opinion. In this opinion the Chief Justice addressed the remaining question of whether the President should be ordered to release the letters directly to Burr or whether the court should first inspect the documents to screen out privileged portions. Marshall made clear that before frustrating Burr's efforts to obtain the letters, the court would have to balance the opposing interests:

The president may himself state the particular reasons which may have induced him to withhold a paper, and the court would unquestionably allow their full force to those reasons. At the same time, the court could not refuse to pay proper attention to the affidavit of the accused.

Id. at 192

[75] *See* United States v. Reynolds, *supra* note 57.

[76] Soucie v. David, 145 U.S.App.D.C. 144, 158, 448 F.2d 1067, 1081 (1971) (Wilkey, J., concurring).

[77] 5 U.S.C. § 552(b) (5) (1970); *see* Environmental Protection Agency v. Mink,

We recognize this great public interest, and agree with the District Court that such conversations are presumptively privileged.[78] But we think that this presumption of privilege premised on the public interest in confidentiality must fail in the face of the uniquely powerful showing made by the Special Prosecutor in this case. The function of the grand jury, mandated by the Fifth Amendment for the institution of federal criminal prosecutions for capital or other serious crimes, is not only to indict persons when there is probable cause to believe they have committed crime, but also to protect persons from prosecution when probable cause does not exist.[79] As we have noted, the Special Prosecutor has made a strong showing that the subpoenaed tapes contain evidence peculiarly necessary to the carrying out of this vital function—evidence for which no effective substitute is available. The grand jury here is not engaged in a general fishing expedition, nor does it seek in any way to investigate the wisdom of the President's discharge of his discretionary duties. On the contrary, the grand jury seeks evidence that may well be conclusive to its decision in on-going investigations that are entirely within the proper scope of its authority. In these circumstances, what we said in Committee for Nuclear Responsibility v. Seaborg becomes, we think, particularly appropriate:

> But no executive official or agency can be given absolute authority to determine what documents in his possession may be considered by the court in its task. Otherwise the head of an executive department would have the power on his own say so to cover up all evidence of fraud and corruption when a federal court or grand jury was investigating malfeasance in office, and this is not the law.[80]

Our conclusion that the general confidentiality privilege must recede before the grand jury's showing of need, is established by the unique circumstances that made this showing possible. In his public statement of May 22, 1973, the President said: "Executive privilege will not be invoked as to any testimony concerning possible criminal conduct or discussions of possible criminal conduct, in the matters presently under investigation, including

supra note 35.

[78]. *See* Carl Zeiss Stiftung v. V.E.B. Carl Zeiss, Jena, *supra* note 58, 40 F.R.D. at 324-325.

[79]. *E. g.,* Branzburg v. Hayes, *supra* note 54, 408 U.S. at 687-688, 92 S.Ct. 2646.

[80]. *Supra* note 66, 149 U.S. App. D.C. at 391, 463 F.2d at 794. (per curiam); *see* Gravel v. United States, *supra* note 56, 408 U.S. at 627, 92 S.Ct. 2614.

the 'Watergate' affair and the alleged cover-up."[81] We think that this statement and its consequences may properly be considered as at least one factor in striking the balance in this case. Indeed, it affects the weight we give to factors on both sides of the scale. On the one hand, the President's action presumably reflects a judgment by him that the interest in the confidentiality of White House discussions in general is outweighed by such matters as the public interest, stressed by the Special Prosecutor, in the integrity of the level of the Executive Branch closest to the President, and the public interest in the integrity of the electoral process—an interest stressed in such cases as Civil Service Commission v. National Association of Letter Carriers[82] and United States v. United Automobile Workers.[83] Although this judgment in no way controls our decision, we think it supports our estimation of the great public interest that attaches to the effective functioningof the present grand jury. As *Burr* makes clear, the courts approach their function by considering the President's reasons and determinations concerning confidentiality.

At the same time, the public testimony given consequent to the President's decision substantially diminishes the interest in maintaining the confidentiality of conversations pertinent to Watergate. The simple fact is that the conversations are no longer confidential. Where it is proper to testify about oral conversations, taped recordings of those conversations are admissible as probative and corroborative of the truth concerning the testimony.[84] There is no "constitutional right to rely on possible flaws in the [witness's] memory. * * * [N]o other argument can justify excluding an accurate version of a conversation that the [witness] could testify to from memory."[85] In short, we see no justification, on confidentiality grounds, for depriving the grand jury of the best evidence of the conversations available.[86]

[81.] Statement by the President, May 22, 1973, *quoted* in Appendix to the Brief for the United States (Special Prosecutor), at 14, 24.

[82.] 413 U.S. 548, 93 S.Ct. 2880, 37 L.Ed.2d 796 (1973).

[83.] 352 U.S. 567, 575, 77 S.Ct. 529, 1 L.Ed.2d 563 (1957).

[84.] Lopez v. United States, 373 U.S. 427, 437-440, 83 S.Ct. 1381, 10 L.Ed.2d 462 (1963); Osborn v. United States, 385 U.S. 323, 326-331, 87 S.Ct. 429, 17 L.Ed.2d 394 (1966).

[85.] Lopez v. United States, *supra* note 84, 373 U.S. at 439, 83 S.Ct. at 1388.

[86.] Where, as here, a conversation attended by the President, Mr. Dean and Mr. Haldeman has been the subject of divergent accounts by Mr. Dean and by Mr. Haldeman, without any restriction by the President on their testifying on the ground

The District Court stated that, in determining the applicability of privilege, it was not controlled by the President's assurance that the conversations in question occurred pursuant to an exercise of his consitutional duty to "take care that the laws be faithfully executed," The District Court further stated that while the President's claim would not be rejected on any but the strongest possible evidence, the Court was unable to decide the question of privilege without inspecting the tapes.[87] This passage of the District Court's opinion is not entirely clear. If, however, the District Judge meant that rejection of the claim of privilege requires a finding that the President was not engaged in the performance of his constitutional duty, we cannot agree. We emphasize that the grand jury's showing of need in no sense relied on any evidence that the President was involved in, or even aware of, any alleged criminal activity. We freely assume, for purposes of this opinion, that the President was engaged in performance of his constitutional duty. Nonetheless, we hold that the District Court may order disclosure of all portions of the tapes relevant to matters within the proper scope of the grand jury's investigations, unless the Court judges that the public interest served by nondisclosure of *particular* statements or information outweighs the need for that information demonstrated by the grand jury.

V.

The question remains whether, in the circumstances of this case, the District Court was correct in ordering the tapes produced for *in camera* inspection, so that it could determine whether and to what extent the privilege was properly claimed. Since the question of privilege must be resolved by the Court, there must be devised some procedure or series of procedures that will, at once, allow resolution of the questions and, at the same time, not harm the interests that the privilege is intended to protect.

Two days after oral argument, this Court issued a Memorandum calling on the parties and counsel to hold conversations toward the objective of avoiding a needless constitutional adjudication. Counsel reported that their sincere efforts had not been fruitful.[88] It is our hope that our action in

of confidentiality, there is no objection to presentation by the tape recorder of that part of the conversation that relates to Watergate, any more than to testimony on this point by another witness who had perfect auditory memory.

[87.] In re Subpoena to Nixon, *supra* note 7, 360 F.Supp. at 21-22.

[88.] The Memorandum and replies of counsel are set forth in Appendix I, *infra*.

providing what has become an unavoidable constitutional ruling, and in approving, as modified, the order of the District Court, will be followed by maximum cooperation among the parties. Perhaps the President will find it possible to reach some agreement with the Special Prosecutor as to what portions of the subpoenaed evidence are necessary to the grand jury's task.

Should our hope prove unavailing, we think that *in camera* inspection is a necessary and appropriate method of protecting the grand jury's interest in securing relevant evidence. The exception that we have delineated to the President's confidentiality privilege depends entirely on the grand jury's showing that the evidence is directly relevant to its decisions. The residual problem of this case derives from the possibility that there are elements of the subpoenaed recordings that do not lie within the range of the exception that we have defined.

This may be due, in part, to the fact that parts of the tape recordings do not relate to Watergate matters at all. What is apparently more stressed by the President's counsel is that there are items in the tape recordings that should be held confidential yet are inextricably interspersed with the portions that relate to Watergate. They say, concerning the President's decision to permit testimony about possible criminal conduct or discussions thereof that:

testimony can be confined to the relevant portions of the conversations and can be limited to matters that do not endanger national security. Recordings cannot be so confined and limited, and thus the President has concluded that to produce the recordings would do serious damage to Presidential privacy and to the ability of that office to function.[89]

The argument is not confined to matters of national security, for the underlying importance of preserving candor of discussion and Presidential privacy pertains to all conversations that involve discussion or making of policy, ordinary domestic policies as well as matters of national security, and even to personal discussion with friends and advisers on seemingly trivial matters.[90] Concerning the inextricability problem, the President's counsel say:

Recordings are the raw material of life. By their very nature they contain spontaneous, informal, tentative and frequently

[89.] Brief of Petitioner Nixon at 69.

[90.] *Id.* at 41-43.

pungent comments on a variety of subjects inextricably intertwined into one conversation. * * * The nature of informal, private conversations is such that it is not practical to separate what is arguably relevant from what is clearly irrelevant.[91]

The "inextricable intermingling" issue may be potentially significant. The District Court correctly discerned that *in camera* inspection is permissible, even though it involved what the President's counsel agree is a "limited infraction" of confidentiality, in order to determine whether there is inextricable intermingling. In EPA. v. Mink, the Supreme Court declared that *in camera* inspection was an appropriate means of determining whether and to what extent documents sought in litigation were disclosable as factual information even though the Government argued that the documents "submitted directly to the President by top-level Government officials" were, by their very nature, a blending of factual presentation and policy recommendations that are necessarily "inextricably intertwined with policymaking processes."[92] The Supreme Court stated that it had no reason to believe that the District Judge directed to make *in camera* inspection "would go beyond the limits of the remand and in any way compromise the confidentiality of deliberative information." The Court acknowledged that "the encouragement of open expression of opinion as to governmental policy is somewhat impaired by a requirement to submit the evidence even [*in camera*]." Yet the Court stated: "Plainly, in some situations, *in camera* inspection will be necessary and appropriate."[93] It further noted: "A representative document of those sought may be selected for *in camera* inspection." And it suggested that the agency may disclose portions of the contested documents and attempt to show, by circumstances, "that the excised portions constitute the barebones of protected matter."[94]

In this case, the line of permissible disclosure is different from that in *Mink*, since even policy and decisional discussions are disclosable if they relate to Watergate and the alleged coverup. But *Mink* confirms that courts appropriately examine a disputed item *in camera*, even though this necessarily involves a limited intrusion upon what ultimately may be held confidential, where

[91.] *Id.* at 61.

[92.] *Supra* note 35, 410 U.S. at 92, 93 S.Ct. at 838.

[93.] *Id.* at 93, 93 S.Ct. at 839.

[94.] *Id.*

it appears with reasonable clarity that some access is appropriate, and *in camera* inspection is needed to determine what should and what should not be revealed.[95]

Mink noted that the case might proceed by the Government's disclosing portions of the contested documents,[96] and also noted an instance in which the "United States offered to file 'an abstract of factual information' contained in the contested documents (FBI reports)."[97] We think that the District Judge and counsel can illuminate the key issue of what is "inextricable" by cultivating the partial excision and "factual abstract" approaches noted in *Mink*.

The District Court contemplated that "privileged portions may be excised so that only unprivileged matter goes before the grand jury." Even in a case of such intermingling as, for example, comment on Watergate matters that is "pungent," once counsel, or the District Judge, has listened to the tape recording of a conversation, he has an ability to present only its relevant portions, much like a bystander who heard the conversation and is called to testify. He may give the grand jury portions relevant to Watergate, by using excerpts in part and summaries in part, in such a way as not to divulge aspects that reflect the pungency of candor or are otherwise entitled to confidential treatment. It is not so long ago that appellate courts routinely decided cases without an exact transcript, but on an order of the trial judge settling what was given as evidence.

VI.

We contemplate a procedure in the District Court, following the issuance of our mandate, that follows the path delineated in *Reynolds, Mink*, and by this Court in Vaughn v. Rosen.[98] With the rejection of his all-embracing claim of prerogative, the President will have an opportunity to present more particular claims of privilege, if accompanied by an analysis in manageable segments.

Without compromising the confidentiality of the information, the analysis should contain descriptions specific enough to identify the basis of the particular claim or claims.

[95.] Carl Zeiss Stiftung v. V.E.B. Carl Zeiss, Jena, *supra* note 58, 40, F.R.D. at 331.

[96.] *Supra* note 35, 410 U.S. at 93, 93 S.Ct. 827.

[97.] *Id.* at 88, 93 S.Ct. at 836, *citing* United States v. Cotton Valley Comm., 9 F.R.D. 719, 720 (W.D.La.1949), aff'd by equally divided court, 339 U.S. 940, 70 S.Ct. 793, 94 L.Ed. 1356 (1950).

[98.] —— U.S. App.D.C. ——, 484, F.2d 820 (1973).

1. In so far as the President makes a claim that certain material may not be disclosed because the subject matter relates to national defense or foreign relations, he may decline to transmit that portion of the material and ask the District Court to reconsider whether *in camera* inspection of the material is necessary. The Special Prosecutor is entitled to inspect the claim and showing and may be heard thereon, in chambers. If the judge sustains the privilege, the text of the government's statement will be preserved in the Court's record under seal.

2. The President will present to the District Court all other items covered by the order, with specification of which segments he believes may be disclosed and which not. This can be accomplished by itemizing and indexing the material, and correlating indexed items with particular claims of privilege.[99] On request of either counsel, the District Court shall hold a hearing in chambers on the claims. Thereafter the Court shall itself inspect the disputed items.

Given the nature of the inquiry that this inspection involves, the District Court may give the Special Prosecutor access to the material for the limited purpose of aiding the Court in determining the relevance of the material to the grand jury's investigations. Counsels' arguments directed to the specifics of the portions of material in dispute may help the District Court immeasurably in making its difficult and necessarily detailed decisions. Moreover, the preliminary indexing will have eliminated any danger of disclosing peculiarly sensitive national security matters. And, here, any concern over confidentiality is minimized by the Attorney General's designation of a distinguished and reflective counsel as Special Prosecutor. If, however, the Court decides to allow access to the Special Prosecutor, it should, upon request, stay its action in order to allow sufficient time for application for a stay to this Court.

Following the *in camera* hearing and inspection, the District Court may determine as to any items (a) to allow the particular claim of privilege in full; (b) to order disclosure to the grand jury of all or a segment of the item or items; or, when segmentation is impossible, (c) to fashion a complete statement for the grand jury of those portions of an item that bear on possible criminality. The District Court shall provide a reasonable stay to allow the President an opportunity to appeal.[100] In case of an

---

99. *See id.* at —— ,484 F.2d at 828.

100. Since the subpoenaed recordings will already have been submitted to the District Court, the opportunity to test the Court's ruling in contempt proceedings

appeal to this Court of an order either allowing or refusing disclosure, this Court will provide for sealed records and confidentiality in presentation.

VII.

We end, as we began, by emphasizing the extraordinary nature of this case. We have attempted to decide no more than the problem before us—a problem that takes its unique shape from the grand jury's compelling showing of need.[101] The procedures we have provided require thorough deliberation by the District Court before even this need may be satisfied. Opportunity for appeal, on a sealed record, is assured.

We cannot, therefore, agree with the assertion of the President that the District Court's order threatens "the continued existence of the Presidency as a functioning institution,"[102] As we view the case, the order represents an unusual and limited requirement that the President produce material evidence. We think this required by law, and by the rule that even the Chief Executive is subject to the mandate of the law when he has no valid claim of privilege.

The petition and appeal of the United States are dismissed. The President's petition is denied, except in so far as we direct the District Court to modify its order and to conduct further proceedings in a manner not inconsistent with this opinion.

The issuance of our mandate is stayed for five days to permit the seeking of Supreme Court review of the issues with which we have dealt in making our decision.

So ordered.

would be foreclosed. And any ruling adverse to the Special Prosecutor would clearly be a pretrial "decision or order . . . suppressing or excluding evidence . . . in a criminal proceeding . . .." Thus the District Court's rulings on particularized claims would be appealable by the President as final judgments under 28 U.S.C. § 1291 (1970), and by the Special Prosecutor under 18 U.S.C. § 3731 (1970). See United States v. Ryan, 402 U.S. 530, 533, 91 S.Ct. 1580, 29 L.Ed.2d 85 (1971); Perlman v. United States, 247 U.S. 7, 12-13, 38 S.Ct. 417, 62 L.Ed. 950 (1918); United States v. Calandra, 455 F.2d 750, 751-753 (6th Cir. 1972).

[101.] Judge Wilkey, in dissent, adheres to the abstract in his discussion of who has the right to decide; he makes no reference to the facts before us framing that issue. John Marshall addressed it in the context of President Jefferson's decision to reveal the contents of a private letter to the extent of characterizing it, in a message to congress, as containing overwhelming evidence of Burr's treason. So here, we must deal with that issue not in a void but against the background of a decision by the President, made and announced before the existence of the tapes was publicly known, to permit participants in private conversations with him to testify publicly as to what was said about Watergate and its aftermath. That decision—and the resulting testimony containing conflicts as to both fact and inference—has made it possible for the Special Prosecutor to make a powerful showing of the relevance and importance of the tapes to the grand jury's discharge of its responsibilities. What the courts are now called upon primarily to decide, as distinct from what the President has already decided with respect to the relative importance of preserving the confidentiality of these particular conversations, is how to reconcile the need of the United States, by its grand jury, with the legitimate interest of the President in not disclosing those portions of the tapes that may deal with unrelated matters.

102. Brief of Petitioner Nixon at 94.

MEMORANDUM AND REPLIES

UNITED STATES COURT OF APPEALS
FOR THE DISTRICT OF COLUMBIA CIRCUIT

September Term, 1973

[Filed Sep. 13, 1973, United States Court of Appeals for the
District of Columbia Circuit, Hugh E. Kline, Clerk]

No. 73-1962

RICHARD M. NIXON, President of the United States,
Petitioner

v.

The Honorable JOHN J. SIRICA,
United States District Judge, Respondent

and

ARCHIBALD COX, Special Prosecutor, Watergate Special
Prosecution Force, Party in Interest

No. 73-1967

UNITED STATES OF AMERICA, Petitioner

v.

The Honorable JOHN J. SIRICA, Chief Judge, United States
District Court for the District of Columbia, Respondent

and

RICHARD M. NIXON, President of the United States,
Party in Interest

Before BAZELON, Chief Judge, and WRIGHT, McGOWAN,
LEVENTHAL, ROBINSON, MacKINNON, and WILKEY, Circuit
Judges.

MEMORANDUM

PER CURIAM.

From the able exposition by counsel in the unusually full oral argument allowed by the Court in this case, it appeared to the Court that the issues dividing the parties might be susceptible of resolution by procedures other than those set forth in either District Judge Sirica's opinion or the briefs of the parties. The Court has been, and is, conscious of the public importance of this matter and the public interest in the earliest possible resolution of it.

The doctrine under which courts seek resolution of a controversy without a constitutional ruling is particularly applicable here. The possibility of a resolution of this controversy without the need for a constitutional ruling is enhanced by the stature and character of the two counsel charged with representation of each side in this cause, and by the circumstance that each was selected for his position, directly or indirectly, by the Chief Executive himself.

Whereas Judge Sirica contemplated an *in camera* examination of the subpoenaed tapes, which would have necessitated the presence of the Judiciary, we contemplate an examination of the tapes by the Chief Executive or his delegate, assisted by both his own counsel, Professor Wright, and the Special Prosecutor, Professor Cox.

We say this without intimating a decision on any question of jurisdiction or privilege advanced by any party. Apart from noting that the likelihood of successful settlement along the lines indicated contemplates a voluntary submission of such portions of the tapes to the two counsel as satisfies them, we do not presume to prescribe the details of how the Chief Executive will work with the two counsel.

This procedure may permit the different approaches of the parties to converge. The President has maintained that he alone should decide what is necessarily privileged and should not be furnished the grand jury. The Special Prosecutor has maintained that he should have the opportunity of examining the material and asserting its relevance and importance to the grand jury investigation. If the President and the Special Prosecutor agree as to the material needed for the grand jury's functioning, the national interest will be served. At the same time, neither the President nor the Special Prosecutor would in any way have surrendered or subverted the principles for which they have contended.

If, after the most diligent efforts of all three concerned, there appear to be matters the President deems privileged and the

Special Prosecutor believes necessary and not privileged, then this Court will discharge its duty of determining the controversy with the knowledge that it has not hesitated to explore the possibility of avoiding constitutional adjudication. Even if this were to occur, the issues remaining for resolution might be substantially narrowed and clarified.

We have issued this Memorandum without interrupting the schedule for post-argument memoranda by the parties. The overriding public interest in this case demands our best and most expeditious efforts in the meantime. The Court asks that it be advised, by both counsel, no later than September 20, 1973, whether the approach indicated in this memorandum has been fruitful.

The Clerk is directed to transmit this Memorandum to all parties to the instant proceedings and to file it in the record.

THE WHITE HOUSE
WASHINGTON

20 September 1973

[Filed Sep. 20, 1973, United States Court of Appeals
for the District of Columbia Circuit
Hugh E. Kline, Clerk]

Mr. Hugh E. Kline
Clerk
United States Court of Appeals
Washington, D.C. 20001

In re Grand Jury Subpoena, Nos. 73-1962, 73-1967

Dear Mr. Kline:

This is to advise you that counsel in the above-entitled matter have had lengthy meetings, pursuant to the suggestion in the Court's memorandum of September 13th. Mr. Cox and Mr. Buzhardt met on September 17th and 18th and today Mr. Cox and Mr. Lacovara of his office met with Mr. Buzhardt, Mr. Garment, and myself. I regret to advise the Court that these sincere efforts were not fruitful.

All participants in these conversations have agreed that we shall say nothing about them except to make this report to the Court.

I understand that Mr. Cox will similarly advise you of these meetings and of their unsuccessful outcome.

Respectfully,

/s/   Charles Alan Wright
CHARLES ALAN WRIGHT
An Attorney for the President
cc: Honorable Archibald Cox

WATERGATE SPECIAL PROSECUTION FORCE

United States Department of Justice
1425 K Street, N.W.
Washington, D.C. 20005

September 20, 1973

[Filed Sep. 20, 1973, United States Court of Appeals
for the District of Columbia Circuit
Hugh E. Kline, Clerk]

Hon. Hugh E. Kline
Clerk, United States Court of
    Appeals for the District of
    Columbia Circuit
Washington, D.C.

Re: *Nixon* v. *Sirica* et al. (Nos. 73-1962, 73-1967)

Dear Mr. Kline:

This is to advise you that counsel in the above entitled matter have had lengthy meetings pursuant to the suggestion in the Court's memorandum of September 13. Mr. Buzhardt and I met on September 17 and 18 and today Mr. Lacovara of my office and I met with Messrs. Wright, Buzhardt, and Garment. I regret to advise the Court that these sincere efforts were not fruitful.

All participants in these conversations have agreed that we shall say nothing about them except to make this report to the Court.

I understand that Mr. Wright will similarly advise you of these meetings and of their unsuccessful outcome.

Sincerely,

/s/   Archibald Cox
ARCHIBALD COX
Special Prosecutor

cc: Hon. John J. Sirica
Charles Alan Wright, Esq.

In a "Memorandum in Support of an Order to Produce Documents or Objects in Response to the Subpoena" (pp. 5-10), filed with the court below on August 13, 1973, the Special Prosecutor provided the following description of the nine communications, tapes of which are sought by the grand jury. (The transcript references throughout are to the transcript of the hearings of the Senate Select Committee on Presidential Campaign Activities.)

1. *Meeting of June 20, 1972.* Respondent met with John D. Ehrlichman and H.R. Haldeman in his Old Executive Office Building (OEOB) office on June 20, 1972, from 10:30 a.m. until approximately 12:45 p.m. There is every reason to infer that the meeting included discussion of the "Watergate" incident. The break-in had occurred on June 17—just three days earlier. Dean did not return to Washington until June 18 (S. Tr. 2166). Mitchell, Haldeman and LaRue had also been out of town and did not return until late on June 19 (S. Tr. 3305, 3307, 6195). Early on the morning of June 20, Haldeman, Ehrlichman, Mitchell, Dean and Attorney General Kleindienst met in the White House. This was their first opportunity for full discussion of how to handle the Watergate incident, and Ehrlichman has testified that Watergate was indeed the primary subject of the meeting (S. Tr. 5923-5924). From there, Ehrlichman and then Haldeman went to see the President. The inference that they reported on Watergate and may well have received instructions, is almost irresistible. The inference is confirmed by Ehrlichman's public testimony that the discussion with respondent included both Watergate and government wiretapping (S. Tr. 5924-25). The contemporary evidence of that meeting should show the extent of the knowledge of the illegal activity by the participants or any effort to conceal the truth from the respondent.

2. *Telephone call of June 20, 1972.* Respondent and John Mitchell, the director of respondent's campaign for re-election, spoke by telephone from 6:08 to 6:12 p.m. on June 20, 1972.

Mitchell has testified that the sole subject was the Watergate break-in and investigation (S. Tr. 3407-08). This apparently was the first direct contact after the break-in between respondent and Mitchell, so that what Mitchell reported may be highly material. Indeed, although Mitchell already may have been briefed at this time by Robert C. Mardian and LaRue about Liddy's involvement in the break-in (S. Tr. 3629-32, 4590, 4595), Mitchell maintains that he told the President that only the five arrested at Watergate—not including Liddy—were involved. (S. Tr. 3407-08, 3632). Evidence of this conversation with a man who had no public office at the time and was concerned solely with respondent's political interests will either tend to confirm Mitchell's version or show a more candid report to respondent.

3. *Meeting of June 30, 1972.* Respondent met with Mitchell and Haldeman for an hour and 15 minutes in his EOB office, apparently the first meeting between respondent and Mitchell since June 17, 1972. The topic of conversation, according to Mitchell, was his impending resignation as Chairman of the Committee for the Re-Election of the President (S. Tr. 3442-43), which in fact was announced the next day. This is a meeting most of which almost surely did not involve any official duties of the President. It also strains credulity to suppose that Watergate and how Watergate affected Mitchell and the campaign were not topics of conversation. The records of the meeting are clearly the most direct evidence of the knowledge and intentions of the participants as of a date shortly after the grand jury began its investigation.

4. *Meeting of September 15, 1972.* On September 15, 1972, the grand jury returned an indictment charging seven individuals with conspiracy and other offenses relating to the break-in. Respondent met the same day with Dean and Haldeman in his Oval Office from 5:27 to 6:17 p.m. Both Dean and Haldeman have given lengthy but contradictory accounts of what was said (S. Tr. 2229-33, 6090-93).

According to Dean, the purpose of the meeting was to brief respondent on the status of the investigation and related matters. Dean said that respondent then congratulated him on the "good job" he had done and was pleased that the case had "stopped with Liddy." Dean said that he then told respondent that all he had been able to do was "contain" the case and "assist in keeping it out of the White House." (S. Tr. 2230.) If this testimony is corroborated, it will tend to establish that a conspiracy to obstruct justice reached the highest level of government.

Haldeman, after reviewing a tape recording of the meeting, has agreed that there was discussion of the Watergate indictments, of the civil cases arising out of the break-in, of the possibility of a continuing grand jury investigation, of internal policies at the Committee for the Re-Election of the President, and of other matters. He denies, however, that respondent congratulated Dean on Dean's efforts to thwart the investigation. (S. Tr. 6090-93, 6456.)

If Haldeman's innocuous version of the meeting can be sustained, it is because the meeting only involved an innocent discussion of political interests. The question of Dean's perjury would then arise. Resolution of this conflict between two of the three persons present and an accurate knowledge of plans or admissions made on this occasion would be of obvious aid to the grand jury's investigation.

5. *Meeting of March 13, 1973.* Respondent again met with Dean and Haldeman on March 13, 1973, from 12:42 to 2:00 p.m. Dean testified at length about the meeting. (S. Tr. 2323-2325.) Haldeman gave evidence that he has no independent recollection of what was said. (S. Tr. 6100).*

The White House briefing for the Senate Committee suggests that the meeting related primarily to Watergate and that respondent asked Dean for a report on the involvement of Haldeman and others.** Dean, on the other hand, testified that respondent told Dean that respondent had approved executive clemency for defendant Hunt and that there would be no problem about raising $1 million to buy all defendants' silence. (S. Tr. 2324). Unquestionably, confirmation of Dean's testimony would aid the grand jury in determining the existence, membership, and scope of a cover-up conspiracy. Conclusive disproof, on the other hand, would raise a question of perjury by Dean before the Senate Committee, a matter directly within the grand jury's jurisdiction.

6, 7. *Meetings of March 21, 1973.* On March 21, 1973, respondent met with Dean and Haldeman from 10:12 to 11:55 a.m. and with Dean, Haldeman, Ehrlichman and Ronald Ziegler from 5:20 to 6:01 p.m. (Not all parties were present all of the time.)

Both Dean and Haldeman (who reviewed the recording of the morning meeting) have testified extensively about that meeting

* It is interesting that Haldeman, who had reviewed recordings of other meetings, did not review the recording of this meeting in view of the serious nature of the allegations by Dean.

** *The New York Times,* June 21, 1973, p. 28 (notes of Minority Counsel of Senate Select Committee or oral briefing by Counsel to the President).

(S. Tr. 2329-34, 6112-15, 6273-95, 6394-6400), and it is also discussed in the White House briefing for the Senate Committee. All accounts confirm that the sole subject was the Watergate break-in and wiretapping and the subsequent cover-up. All agree that Dean talked about a "cancer" affecting the Presidency and revealed a theory of the cover-up and the possible liability of White House and Committee officials, including Magruder, Mitchell, Strachan, Colson, Ehrlichman, Haldeman, and himself. (S. Tr. 2330-31, 6112-15, 6286-94, 6640-41.) All agree that there was discussion of Hunt's threat to expose his "seamy" work for the White House unless he received a considerable sum of money. Haldeman testified that it was at this meeting that respondent indicated that $1 million easily could be raised; according to Haldeman, however, respondent went on to say that it would not be right to pay the money. This discrepancy, which can be resolved by a contemporary recording, is manifestly significant.

Haldeman, Ehrlichman and Dean each have testified about the afternoon meeting as well, and the White House briefing gives a separate account. Again, the sole topic of conversation was Watergate. The participants discussed the possibility of present and former White House officials, as well as employees of the Committee, testifying before the grand jury. (S. Tr. 2334-35, 5650, 5710, 6118.) Dean has testified that it was clear to him after this meeting that the cover-up would continue (S. Tr. 2335). Evidence of this meeting is pertinent to determining the existence of a cover-up, its thrust, and its membership.

8. *Meeting of March 22, 1973.* Respondent met with Dean, Ehrlichman, Haldeman and Mitchell from 2:00 p.m. to 3:43 p.m. on March 22, 1973. (Mitchell, of course, was a private citizen at this time.) Dean, Mitchell, Ehrlichman, and Haldeman each have testified that the meeting centered in general on Watergate and in particular on the problems that would be presented by the upcoming Senate Select Committee hearings (s. Tr. 2337-40, 3413-15, 5720, 5128, 6119-22). This meeting was apparently concerned, at least in major part, with political assessments and operations, not exclusively with establishing "government" policy, and is likely to reveal the knowledge and motives of the participants.

9. *Meeting of April 15, 1973.* Respondent met with Dean from 9:17 to 10:12 p.m. on April 15, 1973. Dean has testified in detail about the substance of this hour-long conversation, allegedly telling respondent of his meetings with the United States Attorney's Office. Dean also testified that respondent said

that he had been "joking" when respondent approved raising $1 million for the Watergate defendants and acknowledged that he had been "foolish" to discuss executive clemency with Charles Colson. (S. Tr. 2371-75.) If true and accurate, this testimony would indicate an important dimension to the cover-up conspiracy. If false and misleading, a perjurious injustice has been done for which the grand jury can return an indictment.

MacKINNON, Circuit Judge, concurring in part and dissenting in part:

I concur in the decision on the jurisdiction of this court as expressed in Part II of the Per Curiam opinion, but I respectfully dissent from its conclusion on the principal issue. I also concur in the result reached by Judge Wilkey's dissent and concur generally in his reasoning. However, I rely on some points not discussed by Judge Wilkey and as to points that are common to our two dissenting opinions there are at times differences in emphasis.

I. INTRODUCTION

This case presents for consideration an important consitutional question which has not confronted the courts in the 186 years since the Constitution was written. While the issues involved have arisen many times in the relations between the Congress and the President, there are no controlling judicial precedents. The immediate issue involves the requested disclosure of confidential discussions between the President and his close advisers, but the ultimate issue is the effect that our decision will have upon the constitutional independence of the Presidency for all time.

Justice Frankfurter prefaced his concurring opinion in Youngstown Sheet & Tube Co.[1] with the following admonition, which is peculiarly appropriate the the present case:

Rigorous adherence to the narrow scope of the judicial function is especially demanded in controversies that arouse appeals to the Constitution. The attitude with which this Court must approach its duty when confronted with such issues is precisely the opposite of that normally manifested by the general public. So-called constitutional questions seem to exercise a mesmeric influence over the popular mind. This eagerness to settle—preferably forever— a specific problem on the basis of the broadest possible constitutional pronouncements may not unfairly be called one of our minor national traits. An English observer of our scene has acutely

---

[1.] Youngstown Sheet & Tube Co. v. Sawyer, 343 U.S. 579, 72 S.Ct. 863, 96 L.Ed. 1153 (1952).

described it: "At the first sound of a new argument over the United States Constitution and its interpretation the hearts of Americans leap with a fearful joy. The blood stirs powerfully in their veins and a new lustre brightens their eyes. Like King Harry's men before Harfleur, they stand like greyhounds in the slips, straining upon the start." The Economist, May 10, 1952, p. 370.

*　*　*　*　*　*

[W]ith the utmost unwillingness, with every desire to avoid judicial inquiry into the powers and duties of the other two branches of the government, I cannot escape consideration of the legality of [the President's order.] [2]

Like Justice Frankfurter in *Youngstown*, it is my view that a constitutional decision in this case is unavoidable.

It is my opinion that the preservation of the confidentiality of the Presidential decision-making process is of overwhelming importance to the effective functioning of our three branches of government. Therefore, I would recognize an absolute privilege for confidential Presidential communications. The privilege is grounded upon an historically consistent interpretation of the constitutional structure of our government, and derives support from common law principles of evidentiary privileges. Since the privilege is designed to enhance a President's ability to perform the duties of his office, it only protects presidential communications related to the performance of Article II duties. It is unnecessary to define the parameters of the privilege beyond the precise facts of this case, but at the least the privilege must protect the recordings subpoenaed here. To compel disclosure of these tape recordings, which contain communications between a President and his most intimate advisers, would endanger seriously the continued efficacy of the presidential decision-making process.

II. THE HISTORICAL PERSPECTIVE

The established usage and custom between the executive, legislative and judicial branches warrant the most respectful consideration, especially in view of its consistency over such an extended period of time. Usage and custom are a source of law in all governments [3] and have particular force where, as is the case here, the applicable written law is ambiguous or unclear. "Even

[2] *Id.* at 594-596, 72 S.Ct. at 889-890 (Frankfurter, J., concurring).

[3] United States v. Arredondo, 31 U.S. (6 Pet.) 691, 714, 8 L.Ed. 540 (1832).

constitutional power, when the text is doubtful, may be established by usage."[4] Early in our nation's history, the Supreme Court relied upon usage and custom to establish firmly its own constitutional authority to review decisions of the highest appellate courts of a state.[5] More recently, the Supreme Court explained the importance of custom and usage as follows:

It may be argued that while these facts and rulings prove a usage they do not establish its validity. But government is a practical affair intended for practical men. Both officers, lawmakers and citizens naturally adjust themselves to any long-continued action of the Executive Department—on the presumption that unauthorized acts would not have been allowed to be so often repeated as to crystallize into a regular practice. That presumption is not reasoning in a circle but the basis of a wise and quieting rule that in determining the meaning of a statute or the existence of a power, weight shall be given to the usage itself—even when the validity of the practice is the subject of investigation.[6]

[4] Inland Waterways v. Young, 309 U.S. 517, 525, 60 S.Ct. 646, 651, 84 L.Ed. 901 (1940).

[5] Cohens v. Virginia, 19 U.S. (6 Wheat.) 264, 418-419, 5 L.Ed. 257 (1821); Martin v. Hunter's Lessee, 14 U.S. (1 Wheat.) 304, 350, 4 L.Ed. 97 (1816). Martin v. Hunter's Lessee, *supra,* established the power of the Supreme Court to review state court decisions in civil cases. Later, in the decision upholding the Court's power to review state criminal decisions, Chief Justice Marshall pointedly remarked:
This concurrence of statesmen, of legislators and judges, in the same construction of the Constitution, may justly inspire some confidence in that construction.
Cohens v. Virginia, *supra* 19, U.S. (6 Wheat.) at 419.
Other important constitutional decisions evidence Supreme Court reliance upon custom and usage. Cooley v. Board of Wardens, 53 U.S. (12 How.) 299, 13 L.Ed. 996 (1851), involved the constitutionality of a state law which required vessles to take a pilot in certain waters. In finding that the law did not violate the Constitution, the Court relied upon the existence of such state laws since the adoption of the Constitution and the fact that "similar laws have existed and been practiced in the states since the adoption of the federal Constitution," and that Congress in its legislative acts had recognized the existence of such laws. This contemporaneous construction was held to be entitled to great weight. *Id.* at 315.
In Stuart v. Laird, 5 U.S. (1 Cranch) 299, 2 L.Ed. 115 (1803), the Court relied upon contemporaneous construction of the Constitution, followed by practice and acquiescence, in affirming Congress' power to authorize Supreme Court Justices to sit as circuit judges without receiving additional commissions. This usage was held to be of the "most forcible nature" and "too strong and obstinate to be shaken or controlled." *Id.* at 309.

[6] United States v. Midwest Oil Co., 236 U.S. 459, 472-473, 35 S.Ct. 309, 313, 59 L.Ed. 673 (1915).

A. *Presidential Refusals to*
Comply with Congressional
Subpoenas

Throughout our nation's history, the greatest number of the important instances where information has been requested or demanded of the executive department by Congress have involved the President himself. The precedents created by these confrontations are vital here, because Congress and the courts have similar subpoena powers.[7] These precedents gain additional vitality from the fact that they involved highly critical issues, issues that caused Congress to demand, and the President to resist, disclosure based on the strongest national interest grounds. As Professor Corwin wrote with respect to these instances:

> The point at issue, however, has generally been not justice to the official involved but the right of the Executive Department to keep its own secrets.

Corwin, The President—Office and Powers 1787-1957, 111 (1957). Mindful of the tremendous forces that shaped these precedents, we turn to a few of the most important.

In 1948, following an abortive attempt by a Republican-controlled Congress to obtain certain information and papers from the executive department, a bill was prepared which, if enacted, would have required every President to produce confidential information even though he considered that compliance would be contrary to the public interest. President Truman thought that such a law would be unconstitutional and in preparation for the 1948 presidential election campaign he had a lengthy memorandum prepared[8] (hereinafter referred to as the "Truman Memorandum"). The Truman Memorandum recites all the principal instances, beginning in 1796, where Presidents have refused to furnish information or papers to Congress. A resume of the refusals by seventeen of our Presidents and their heads of departments, as set out in the Truman Memorandum, is printed in the margin.[9] We can profit from these examples of

---

[8] *New York Times,* Sept. 3, 1948, at 5. The Truman Memorandum consists of 102 pages and the original now rests in the Harry S. Truman Library at Independence, Missouri.

Résumé and Conclusions

[9] A bird's-eye view of the refusals by seventeen of our Presidents, and their heads of departments, to comply with congressional requests for information and papers from the Executive, beginning with 1796 to the present time, follows *

President	Date	Type of Information Refused
George Washington	1796	Instruction to U.S. Minister

presidential refusals and the precedents they created.

The March 1792 resolution of the House of Representatives empowering the committee investigating the military expedition

President	Date	Type of Information Refused
		concerning Jay Treaty.
Thomas Jefferson	1807	Confidential information and letters relating to Burr's conspiracy.
James Monroe	1825	Documents relating to conduct of naval officers.
Andrew Jackson	1833	Copy of paper read by President to heads of departments relating to removal of bank deposits.
	1835	Copies of charges against removed public official. List of all appointments made without Senate's consent, since 1829, and those receiving salaries, without holding office.
John Tyler	1842	Names of Members of 26th and 27th Congresses who applied for office.
	1843	Report to War Department dealing with alleged frauds practiced on Indians, and Col. Hitchcock's views of personal characters of Indian delegates.
James K. Polk	1846	Evidence of payments made through Senate Department, on President's certificates, by prior administration.
Millard Fillmore	1852	Official information concerning proposition made by King of Sandwich Islands to transfer islands to U.S.
James Buchanan	1860	Message of Protest to House against Resolution to investigate attempts by Executive to influence legislation.
Abraham Lincoln	1861	Dispatches of Major Anderson to the War Department concerning defense of Fort Sumter.
Ulysses S. Grant	1876	Information concerning executive acts performed away from Capitol.

Rutherford B. Hayes	1877	Secretary of Treasury refused to answer questions and to produce papers concerning reasons for nomination of Theodore Roosevelt as Collector of Port of New York.
Grover Cleveland	1886	Documents relating to suspension and removal of Federal officials.
Theodore Roosevelt	1909	Attorney General's reasons for failure to prosecute U.S. Steel Corporation. Documents of Bureau of Corporations, Department of Commerce.
Calvin Coolidge	1924	List of companies in which Secretary of Treasury Mellon was interested.
Herbert Hoover	1930	Telegrams and letters leading up to London Naval Treaty.
	1932	Testimony and documents concerning investigation made by Treasury Department.
Franklin D. Roosevelt	1941	Federal Bureau of Investigation reports.
	1943	Director, Bureau of the Budget, refused to testify and to produce files.
	1943	Chairman, Federal Communications Commission, and Board of War Communications refused records.
	1943	General Counsel, Federal Communications Commission, refused to produce records.
	1943	Secretaries of War and Navy refused to furnish documents, and permission for Army and Naval officers to testify.
	1944	J. Edgar Hoover refused to give testimony and to produce President's directive.
Harry S. Truman	1945	Issued directions to heads of executive departments to permit officers and employees to give information to Pearl Harbor Committee.
	1945	President's directive did not include any files or written material.
	1947	Civil Service Commission records concerning applications for positions.

Truman Memorandum at 44a, b,c, (1948).

under Major General St. Clair to call for "such persons, papers, and records, as may be necessary to assist their inquiries"[10] was the first such request ever made by Congress. It met with the rebuke by President Washington, after consulting his cabinet, that the "House was an inquest" and "might call for papers generally," but that the Executive should "exercise a discretion . . . to communicate such papers as the public good will would permit."[11] Washington also refused the request of the House for confidential papers which related to the negotiation of the Jay Treaty with Great Britain, notwithstanding a threat by the House that it would not appropriate the required funds unless its request for information and papers was satisfied.[12] The extortive demand by Congress was not successful.

President Jefferson asserted a similar position in refusing to expose the names of those involved in the alleged Burr conspiracy, except that of the principal actor.[13] This apparently is the first instance where a President refused to divulge confidential information involving an alleged substantial criminal offense. President Jackson followed suit in 1835 when he refused to comply with a Senate resolution requesting information in aid of its investigation of frauds in the sale of public lands.[14] In refusing to produce papers to the House, which was investigating the integrity and efficiency of the executive departments in 1837, President Jackson stated in part:

> I shall repel all such attempts as an invasion of the principles of justice, as well as of the Constitution, and I shall esteem it my sacred duty to the people of the United States to resist

---

* In the birds-eye picture, reference is made to the refusals of Presidents Monroe, Fillmore, Lincoln, and Hayes [.] Monroe's refusal may be found in a message dated January 10, 1825, 2 Richardson, Messages and Papers of President's, p. 278' [sic] Fillmore's in 5 Richardson, p. 159; Lincoln's in 6 Richardson, p. 12, and the refusal in Hayes' adminstration is dealt with in 17 Cong.Rec. 2332 and 2618.

10. 3 Annals of Congress 493 (1972).

11. 1 Writings of Thomas Jefferson 303-04 (1905).

12. Brinkley, President and Congress 441 (1947), in Truman Memorandum at 6.

13. 1 Richardson, "Messages and Papers of the Presidents" 412 (1807); in Truman Memorandum at 8.

14. Truman Memorandum at 9.

them as I would the establishment of a Spanish Inquisition.[15]

President Tyler's refusal in 1842 to furnish to the House certain requested information established the principle that papers and documents relating to applications for office are of a confidential nature. President Tyler vigorously asserted that the House of Representatives could not exercise a right to call upon the Executive for information, even though it related to a subject under deliberation by the House if, by so doing, it attempted to interfere with the discretion of the Executive.[16] He further stated:

> It is certainly no new doctrine in the halls of judicature or of legislation that certain communications and papers are privileged, and that the general authority to compel testimony must give way in certain cases to the paramount rights of individuals or of the Government. Thus, no man can be compelled to accuse himself, to answer any question that tends to render him infamous, or to produce his own private papers on any occasion. The communication of a client to his counsel and the admissions made at the confessional in the course of religious discipline are privileged communications. In the courts of that country from which we derive our great principles of individual liberty and the rules of evidence, it is well settled, and the doctrine has been fully recognized in this country, that a minister of the Crown or the head of a department can not be compelled to produce any papers, or to disclose any transactions relating to the executive functions of the Government which he declares are confidential, or such as the public interest requires should not be divulged; and the persons who have been the channels of communication to officers of the State are in like manner protected from the disclosure of their names. Other instances of privileged communications might be enumerated, if it were deemed necessary. These principles are as applicable to evidence sought by a legislature as to that required by a court.[17]

Presidents Polk and Buchanan subscribed to similar positions in opposition to congressional demands for information. Polk

---

[15.] C. Warren, Presidential Declaration of Independence, 10 B.U.L.Rev. 11, 12 (1930); 13 Cong.Deb. Part 2, App. at 202 (1837).

[16.] 3 Hind's Precedents 181 (1907).

[17.] *Id.* at 182.

refused to turn over information that his predecessor as President had considered to be confidential and ought not to be made public.[18] Buchanan refused to comply with a request for information as to whether "money, patronage or other improper means" had been used to influence Congress.[19] Again, this information related to a possible crime.

The request made of President Grant, which he refused, is too political and trivial to discuss,[20] but not so in Grover Cleveland's administration. There, the "Relations between the Senate and the Executive Departments" amounted to a major confrontation and the issues were debated in the Senate for almost two weeks. They dealt with the removal of substantial numbers of office holders by the incoming President; Congress requested the papers and reasons related to the dismissals. Such requests were refused for the usual reasons and one result was the passage of a separate resolution condemning the Attorney General's refusal.[21] President Cleveland pointed out that the Senate was assuming "the right . . . to sit in judgment upon the exercise of my exclusive discretion and Executive function, for which I am solely responsible to the people from whom I have so lately received the sacred trust of office."[22]

On January 4, 1909, the Senate passed a resolution directing the Attorney General to inform the Senate whether legal proceedings had been instituted by him against the United States Steel Corporation because of a certain merger, and if not, they required him to state the reasons. President Theodore Roosevelt took up the cudgel and delivered a special message to the Senate, stating that there were insufficient grounds for legal proceedings against the company. He additionally instructed the Attorney General not to state reasons for his nonaction.[23] Thereafter, when the Senate attempted to get certain papers on this subject from the Commissioner of Corporations, the papers were turned over to the President upon the advice of the Attorney General, and the Senate then introduced a strong resolution:

Resolved by the Senate, That any and every public

18. IV Richardson, *supra* note 13, at 433.

19. *Id.,* Vol. V, at 618-19.

20. *Id.,* Vol. VII, at 362.

21. *See* Senate Miscellaneous Documents, Vol. 7, 52nd Cong., 2d Sess. 232-72; Truman Memorandum at 21.

22. Grover Cleveland, Presidential Problems 63-64 (1904).

23. 43 Cong.Rec. 527-28 (1909).

document, paper, or record, or copy thereof, on the files of any department of the Government relating to any subject whatever over which Congress has any grant of power, jurisdiction, or control, under the Constitution, and any information relative thereto within the possession of the officers of the department, is subject to the call or inspection of the Senate for its use in the exercise of its constitutional powers and jurisdiction.

43 Cong. Rec. 839 (1909). This resolution is remindful of the bill introduced to compel President Truman to turn over papers and of some of the statements being currently made in connection with this general controversy. The resolution was debated extensively but never came to a final vote.

In 1924, during the administration of President Coolidge, information relating to his Secretary of the Treasury was sought in a Senate resolution strongly supported by Senator Couzens. President Coolidge termed it an "unwarranted intrusion" and asserted it was the duty of the Executive to resist it. Other Senators then stated that they never sought "confidential records" and therafter the committed operated with voluntary witnesses and through departmental courtesy.[24]

Next came President Hoover's refusal in 1930 to furnish the Senate Foreign Relations Committee with confidential telegrams, letters and other papers leading up to the London Conference and the London Treaty.[25]

And President Franklin D. Roosevelt received the same treatment at the hands of Congress in 1941 some months prior to Pearl Harbor, when the House requested the FBI to furnish detailed reports and correspondence in connection with investigations arising out of strikes, subversive activities in connection with labor disputes and labor disturbances in industrial establishments with Naval contracts. Attorney General Jackson replied:

It is the position of this Department, restated now with the approval of and at the direction of the President, that all investigative reports are confidential documents of the executive department of the Government, to aid in the duty laid upon the President by the Constitution to "take care that the laws be faithfully executed," and that congressional or public access to them would not be in the public interest.[26]

[24.] 65 Cong.Rec. 6087, 6108 (1924).

[25.] 72 Cong.Rec. 12029 (1930).

[26.] 40 Ops.Atty.Gen. 46 (1941).

The Attorney General further pointed out *inter alia* that:

> . . . disclosure would seriously prejudice the future usefulness of the Federal Bureau of Investigation, for keeping faith with confidential informants was an indispensable condition of future efficiency . . .[27]

Later during the same administration, FBI Director Hoover refused to disclose to a House committe the directive he had received from President Roosevelt in 1944 directing him not to testify as to any correspondence relating to internal security.[28] There were other similar requests during the Roosevelt administration, some of which related to national security, while others were resisted merely because they were "confidential."[29]

President Truman refused to surrender to Congress information and papers relating to loyalty investigations of Government employees, personnel files and FBI files.[30] Subsequently, on the advice of Attorney General Brownell, President Eisenhower made his famous decision refusing to turn over certain information requested in the McCarthy-Stevens investigation.[31]

In each of these instances the Congress sought information from the President or the executive branch in order to enable it to legislate upon subjects within its constitutional power, and in each instance cited the request was refused by the President, who determined that to furnish the information would be an unconstitutional intrusion into the functioning of the executive branch and contrary to the public interest. The numerous confrontations between Congress and prior Presidents over the confidentiality of presidential information firmly establish a custom and usage that a President need not produce information which he considers would be contrary to the public interest.

---

27. Truman Memorandum at 33.

28. Letter of January 22, 1944, Francis Biddle, Attorney General.

29. Truman Memorandum at 39-40.

30 *New York Times*, May 18, 1954, at 24 (Attorney General Brownell's Memorandum).

31 *New York Times*, May 18, 1954, at 1, 24. An extensive memorandum by Attorney General Herbert Brownell recites numerous instances where outstanding Presidents had refused congressional demands for confidential information and papers. These included Presidents Washington, Jefferson, Jackson, Tyler, Buchanan, Grant, Cleveland, Theorodre Roosevelt, Coolidge, Hoover, Franklin D. Roosevelt and Truman, *New York Times*, May 18, 1954, at 24.

B. *The Similarity Between Congressional and Judicial Subpoenas*

The Special Prosecutor contends that custom and usage between the executive and legislative branches are not controlling because the subpoena in this case was not issued by Congress, but by a federal court pursuant to a grand jury investigation. However, a congressional subpoena issued for the purpose of obtaining facts upon which to legislate carries at least as much weight as a judicial subpoena issued for the purpose of obtaining evidence of criminal offenses. The only differences between these two types of subpoenas occur in the subject matter to which the subpoena power may be directed. Congressional subpoenas seek information in aid of the power to legislate for the entire nation while judicial subpoenas seek information in aid of the power to adjudicate controversies between individual litigants in a single civil or criminal case. A grand jury subpoena seeks facts to determine whether there is probable cause that a criminal law has been violated by a few people in a particular instance. A congressional subpoena seeks facts which become the basis for legislation that directly affects over 200 million people. Thus, both congressional and judicial subpoenas serve vital interests, and one interest is no more vital than the other.

Furthermore, both congressional and judicial subpoenas are compulsory documents enforceable with criminal sanctions. Congress always has possessed the inherent power to punish witnesses who refuse to disclose information. And since the enactment in 1857 of a statute making it a misdemeanor to refuse to answer or to produce papers before Congress,[32] the

---

[32.] The Act of Jan 24, 1857 provided:

CHAP. XIX.—*An Act more effectually to enforce the Attendance of Witnesses on the Summons of either House of Congress, and to compel them to discover Testimony.*

Be it enacted by the Senate and House of Representatives of the United States of America in Congress assembled, That any person summoned as a witness by the authority of either House of Congress to give testimony or to produce papers upon any matter before either House, or any committee of either House of Congress, who shall wilfully make default, or who, appearing, shall refuse to answer any question pertinent to the matter of inquiry in consideration before the House or committee by which he shall be examined, shall in addition to the pains and penalties now existing, be liable to indictment as and for a misdemeanor, in any court of the United States having jurisdiction thereof, and on conviction, shall pay a fine not exceeding one thousand dollars and not less than one hundred dollars, and suffer imprisonment in the common jail not less than one month nore more than twelve months.

* * * * * *

SEC. 3, *And be it further enacted,* That when a witness shall fail to testify, as provided in the previous sections of this act, and the facts shall be reported to the

power of the courts has been an additional sanction available to enforce a congressional request or subpoena.[33] In Kilbourn v. Thompson,[34] the Court remarked that Congress has "the right to compel the attendance of witnesses and their answers to proper questions, in the same manner and by the use of the same means, that courts of justice can in like cases."[35] Congress and the courts stand equal in their power to issue subpoenas and equal in their power to enforce them with criminal sanctions.

For these reasons, a judicial subpoena cannot be exalted over a congressional subpoena, and the historic precedents involving congressional requests to the executive department are persuasive authority in the present dispute over a judicial subpoena to a President. However, it is unnecessary to rely entirely on instances of presidential assertions of privilege. The other branches of government have been no less disposed to recognize an absolute privilege on their own behalf.

C. *Congressional Privilege*

Congress has asserted a privilege with respect to subpoenas addressed to members of Congress for documents in its possession and for the testimony of its employees. The practice which has been consistently followed is that no documents can be taken from the possession of either House except by the express consent of such House.

In 1876 a Representative from Indiana was subpoenaed to appear before the grand jury of the District of Columbia.

House, it shall be the duty of the Speaker of the House or the President of the Senate to certify the fact under the seal of the House or Senate to the district attorney for the District of Columbia, whose duty it shall be to bring the matter before the grand jury for their action.

Approved, January 24, 1857.

11 Stat. 155.

[33.] *See* Jurney v. McCracken, 294 U.S. 125, 151, 55 S.Ct. 375, 79 L.Ed. 802 (1935). 2 U.S.C. § 192 (1970) provides the present authority:

§ 192. Refusal of witness to testify or produce papers. Every person who having been summoned as a witness by the authority of either House of Congress to give testimony or to produce papers upon any matter under inquiry before either House, or any joint committee established by a joint or concurrent resolution of the two Houses of Congress, or any committee of either House of Congress, willfully makes default, or who, having appeared, refuses to answer any question pertinent to the question under inquiry, shall be deemed guilty of a misdemeanor, punishable by a fine of not more than $1,000 nor less than $100 and imprisonment in a common jail for not less than one month nor more than twelve months. (R.S. § 102, June 22, 1938; ch. 594, 52 Stat. 942.)

[34.] 103 U.S. 168, 26 L.Ed. 377 (1880).

[35.] *Id.* at 190.

Congress asserted the "well settled" privilege which protects a member who is subpoenaed to testify before a grand jury or in court:

> Inasmuch as it seemed to be well settled that the privilege of the Member was the privilege of the House and that privilege could not be waived except with the consent of the House, they had thought it their duty to submit the matter to the House.[36]

Whereupon a resolution was offered and the member was "authorized to appear and testify under the said summons."[37]

Upon service of a subpoena duces tecum by a court-martial, Congress asserted with respect to the documents:

> They belong to the House, and are under its absolute and unqualified control. It can at any time take them from the custody of the Clerk, refuse to allow them to be inspected by anyone, order them to be destroyed, or dismiss the Clerk for permitting any of them to be removed from the files without its express consent.[38]

Whereupon the resolution asserted the House privilege and consented to the parties to a general court-martial making copies of documents in the possession of the House.[39]

Usually, when personal attendance or documents are requested of members of Congress, Congress permits compliance with such request, but not always. In 1876 the House refused to permit its committee investigating William W. Belknap, late Secretary of War, who had been impeached by the House, to produce before the Supreme Court of the District of Columbia in response to process certain documents relating to the acceptance of bribes.[40] In 1926, Mr. Fiorello LaGuardia of New York rose to a question of personal privilege in the House of Representatives, reported he had been subpoenaed before a federal grand jury in Indianapolis, that he could "not obey that subpoena without the permission of the House" and that if any member of the House introduced a resolution granting him "permission to go [he would] not resist it. No resolution was offered and no further

36. 3 Hinds' Precedents § 2663, at 1112.(1907).

37. *Id.*

38. *Id.* § 2663, at 1113.

39. *Id.* at 112-14.

40. 14 Cong.Rec. 1525 (1876).

record appears."[41]

Essentially the same practice exists in Congress at this time. On October 13, 1970, in a case which subsequently came before this court entitled United States Servicemen's Fund (USSF) v. Eastland,[42] the Senate subpoenaed certain documents in aid of its power of investigation for legislative purposes. The subject (the USSF) of the documents intervened and in aid of a deposition had a subpoena issued to the Chief Counsel of the Internal Security Subcommittee of the Committee on the Judiciary calling for his personal "testimony regarding activities of the Subcommittee, and calling also for production of certain records and other papers in the Subcommittee."[43] The Senate thereupon passed the usual resolution with respect to its documents and the requested appearance of the Chief Counsel. It provided, *inter alia:*

Resolved, That the Chief Counsel, Jullen [*sic*] G. Sourwine, of the Senate Internal Security Subcommittee of the Committee on the Judiciary, is authorized to comply with an appropriate notice of deposition in the case aforesaid, but *shall not testify respecting matters of which he obtained knowledge by virtue of his position or activities as Chief Counsel of the Subcommittee, which are not matters of public record* and shall not without further action by the Senate surrender any papers or documents on file in his office or under his control or in his possession as Chief Counsel of the Senate Internal Security Subcommittee of the Committee on the Judiciary.[44]

Later, when the Chief Counsel appeared for the deposition, he refused to give evidence in violation of the "Senate's mandate"[45] as to matters "which were not at a public hearing."[46]

The common thread throughout these proceedings is that the House or the Senate itself judges and controls the extent to which its members and documents should be produced in courts and before grand juries in response to subpoenas. Congress since 1787 has claimed that it has the absolute privilege to decide itself

---

41. 6 Cannon's Precedents § 586, at 825 (1936).

42. ——U.S.App.D.C. ——,F.2d —— (1973).

43 116 Cong.Rec. 36481 (1970) (emphasis added).

44. Transcript of testimony of Julien G. Sourwine, Nov. 18, 1970, at 16, United States Servicemen's Fund v. Eastland, Civil Action No. 1474-70 (D.D.C., Oct. 21, 1971).

45. *Id.*

46. *Id.*

whether its members or employees should respond to subpoenas and to determine the extent of their response. As far as I have been able to discover, that practice has never been successfully challenged.

D. *Judicial Privilege*

The judicial branch of our government claims a similar privilege, grounded on an assertion of independence from the other branches. Express authorities sustaining this position are minimal, undoubtedly because its existence and validity has been so universally recognized. Its source is rooted in history and gains added force from the constitutional separation of powers of the three departments of government. Chief Justice Burger has asserted that this privilege is grounded in the courts, "inherent power" to protect the confidentiality of their internal proceedings:

With respect to the question of inherent power of the Executive to classify papers, records, and documents as secret, or otherwise unavailable for public exposure, and to secure aid of the courts for enforcement, there may be an analogy with respect to this Court. No statute gives this Court express power to establish and enforce the utmost security measures for the secrecy of our deliberations and records. Yet I have little doubt as to the inherent power of the Court to protect the confidentiality of its internal operations by whatever judicial measures may be required.[47]

In his concurring opinion in Soucie v. David, involving the exemptions from disclosure of certain information in the executive department under the Freedom of Information Act,[48] Judge Wilkey based the privilege upon the common law and the Constitution:

To put this question in perspective, it must be understood that the privilege against disclosure of the decision-making process is a tripartite privilege, because precisely the same privilege in conducting certain aspects of public business exists for the legislative and judicial branches as well as for the executive. It arises from two sources, one common law and the other

---

[47.] New York Times v. United States, 403 U.S. 713, 752 n. 3, 91 S.Ct. 2140, 2160, 29 L.Ed.2d 822 (1971) (Burger, C. J., dissenting).

[48.] 5 U.S.C. § 552(b), (c) (1970).

constitutional.[49]

Counsel for the President in their brief cite additional support for the judicial claim of confidentiality:

It has always been recognized that judges must be able to confer with their colleagues, and with their law clerks, in circumstances of absolute confidentiality. Justice Brennan has written that Supreme Court conferences are held in "absolute secrecy" for "obvious reasons." Brennan, Working at Justice, in An Autobiography of the Supreme Court 300 (Westin ed. 1963). Justice Frankfurter has said that the "secrecy that envelops the Court's work" is "essential to the effective functioning of the Court." Frankfurter, Mr. Justice Roberts, 105 U.Pa.L.Rev. 311, 313 (1955).

* * * * * *

The Judiciary works in conditions of confidentiality and it claims a privilege against giving testimony about the official conduct of judges. Statement of the Judges, 14 F.R.D. 335 (N.D.Cal.1953). See also the letter of Justice Tom C. Clark, refusing to respond to a subpoena to appear before the House Un-American Activities Committee, on the ground that the "complete independence of the judiciary is necessary to the proper administration of justice." N.Y. Times, Nov. 14, 1953, p. 9.[50]

The *Statement of the Judges*,[51] to which counsel for petitioner refers, asserted that the separation of powers prohibits any branch of government from unlawfully interfering with the others, to the extent that Congress had no authority to summon a United States District Judge to appear before a House subcommittee investigating the Department of Justice. The *Statement* went on to say:

[W]e know of no instance, in our history where a committee such as yours, has summoned a member of the Federal

---

[49.] Soucie v. David, 145 U.S.App.D.C. 144, 157, 448 F.2d 1067, 1080 (1971) (Wilkey, J., concurring). Writing for the court in *Soucie*, Chief Judge Bazelon recognized that disclosure of information under the Freedom of Information Act was not to harm specific governmental interests:
The touchstone of any proceedings under the Act must be the clear legislative intent to assure public access to all governmental records whose disclosure would not significantly harm specific governmental interests.
Soucie v. David, *supra* at 157, 448 F.2d at 1080.

[50.] Brief for Petitioner at 32-33.

[51.] 14 F.R.D. 335 (1953).

judiciary.[52]

Thus, the judicial branch asserts the same immunity from being compelled to respond to congressional subpoenas that past Presidents have asserted.

Further assertions of judicial independence surfaced in the aftermath of Justice Fortas' resignation.[53] At that time a special story by Max Frankel reported the reaction among some of the other Justices of the Supreme Court to their suggestion that they should compose a code of conduct to assure their objectivity and probity:

[I]f drawn, they are not likely to diminish the *absolute independence traditionally asserted by the high court for itself and by each of its nine members as individuals.*

In fact, the Justices are said to be determined to resist any effort by Congress or other outside authority to impose ethical standards or enforcement methods upon them. Above all, they remain committed to the principle that *each Justice must be free to work beyond the control or censure even of his colleagues, and they were careful to protect that principle* while concerning themselves with the Fortas case over the last two weeks.

* * * * * *

[T]he Justices are believed to have turned their thoughts to the ways in which they could create a body of standards without compromising the great tradition of professional independents.

* * * * * *

It will be a long exercise, in any case, the Justices expect, and the "standards" that emerge may be no more than each Justice's interpretation of the informal discussions that began around the Court with the Fortas revelations.

* * * * * *

Some members of Congress now believe that they have a duty to impose some standards on the entire Federal judiciary,

[52.] *Id.* at 336.

[53.] It is an intersting footnote to history that the Justice Department, headed by then Attorney General John N. Mithcell, furnished the investigatory material in its possession to Chief Justice Earl Warren but resisted congressional demands for full disclosure of its information in the Fortas controversy. N.Y. Times, May 18, 1969, at 1, col. 2.

including the Supreme Court, and after the Fortas affair some Justices appear to understand this impulse.

But since they refuse to yield to the control of their own Chief Justice or their colleagues, the Justices will plainly resent and resist Congressional supervision if they possibly can.

*   *   *   *   *   *

It is the conclusion of most Justices, therefore, that they must observe the very highest standards but that *they must be their own final judges.* Whether they can combine these two doctrines into a reassuring public body of Supreme Court ethics will not be evident for some time.[54]

The above excerpts express the judiciary's conception of its own privileges as it so far has been made public.

A recent example of the exercise of the judiciary's privilege to protect the confidentiality of its internal decision-making process occurred in this court in February of this year. It arose in the very important case involving the validity of the right of way and permits granted by the Department of the Interior for the construction of the 789-mile Alaska Pipeline. The estimated cost of this pipeline was upwards of $3½ billion. Following the argument of the case on appeal and while the case was under advisement by the judges of this court, a United States Senator wired the Chief Judge of this court as follows:

I have been told one or more judges have disqualified themselves in the trans-Alaska pipeline case currently under advisement. Kindly advise me of their identities and reasons if this is the case. I would appreciate a reply in writing as soon as possible. Thank you very much.

In the reply for the court by Chief Judge Bazelon, this court exercised its privilege to protect the confidentiality of its deliberations, stating:

In re your telegram of February 5, 1973 inquiring as to whether 1 or more judges have disqualified themselves in the trans Atlantic [sic] pipeline cases currently under advisement and in which you request their identities and reasons if this is the case. The opinion, when issued, will reveal the names of the judges who have participated therein. With great respect, we believe that further reply to your inquiry would not be appropriate with cordial wishes.

54. *New York Times,* May 18, 1969, at 1, col. 3 (emphasis added).

It thus appears that the judiciary, as well as the Congress and past Presidents, believes that a protected independence is vital to the proper performance of its specified constitutional duties. It is my conclusion that the deliberative functions of the President's office should be afforded the same essential protection that has been recognized for, and asserted and enjoyed by, the legislative and judicial branches of our government since 1787.

III. THE PRESIDENTIAL COM-MUNICATIONS PRIVILEGE

The Per Curiam opinion recognizes the "great public interest" in maintaining the confidentiality of the presidential decision-making process, but concludes that the national interest in presidential confidentiality may be subordinated in particular situations to a strong countervailing need for disclosure.[55] Thus, the majority recognizes only a qualified privilege for presidential communications.

The focus of my disagreement with this conclusion is that in my opinion an absolute privilege exists for presidential communications. At least where a President discusses matters of official concern with his most intimate advisers, strict confidentiality is so essential to the deliberative process that it should not be jeopardized by any possibility of disclosure.

A. *The Importance of Confidentiality*

By recognizing an absolute privilege, my opinion places the presidential communications privilege on an equal footing with that recognized for military or state secrets in United States v. Reynolds.[56] Military or state secrets are never subject to disclosure regardless of the weight of countervailing interests.[57] Once the court is satisfied that military or state secrets are at stake, its inquiry is at an end. The court cannot balance the importance of secrecy in a particular case against the necessity demonstrated by the party seeking disclosure.[58]

The rationale underlying the absolute privilege for military or state secrets is the policy judgment that the nation's interest in keeping this information secret always outweighs any particularized need for disclosure. A similar policy judgment

[55.] Per Curiam opinion at 717.

[56.] 345 U.S. 1, 73 S.Ct. 528, 97 L.Ed. 727 (1953).

[57.] *Id.* at 11, 73 S.Ct. at 533.

[58.] *Id.*

supports an absolute privilege for communications between a President and his advisers on matters of official concern.

The interest supporting an absolute privilege for presidential communications is the confidentiality essential to insure thorough and unfettered discussion between a President and his advisers. This widely recognized necessity for confidentiality in any decision-making process[59] is especially important in the office of the Presidency. Confidentiality is indispensable to encourage frankness and to allow a President's advisers to advance possibly unpopular arguments without fear of public criticism. Working at the highest level of government, a President and his advisers must be free to explore all aspects of an issue so that final decisions are based upon completely thorough analysis. Their discussions must be informal, candid and blunt. If there is a danger that the words spoken at these discussions will be disclosed to the public, the participants inevitably will speak more guardedly, they will hesitate to suggest possibly unpopular opinions, and the discussions will lose their spontaneity. This loss of spontaneity and freedom would severely restrict a President's ability to conduct thorough and frank discussions on issues of national and world-wide importance.

An essential attribute of the presidential communications privilege is that the President must have absolute discretion in its exercise. To the majority's fear that it would be dangerous to vest absolute discretion in the President because of possible abuse in the future,[60] we need only refer to Justice Story's telling refutation of that argument in Martin v. Hunter's Lessee:

It is always a doubtful course to argue against the use or existence of a power, from the possibility of its abuse. It is still more difficult, by such an argument, to ingraft upon a general power a restriction which is not to be found in the terms in which it is given. From the very nature of things, the absolute right of decision, in the last resort, must rest

---

59. *See, e. g.*, EPA v. Mink, 410 U.S. 73, 87, 93 S.Ct. 827, 35 L.Ed.2d 119 (1973); New York Times Co. v. United States, 403 U.S. 713, 752 n. 3, 91 S.Ct. 2140, 29 L.Ed.2d 822 (1971) (Burger, C. J., dissenting); Carl Zeiss Stiftung v. V.E.B. Carl Zeiss, Jena 40 F.R.D. 318, 324-326 (D.D.C.1966), aff'd on the opinion below, 128 U.S.App.D.C. 10, 384 F.2d 979, cert. denied, 389 U.S. 952, 88 S.Ct. 334, 19 L.Ed.2d 361 (1967); 5 U.S.C. § 552(b) (5) (1970) (Freedom of Information Act); Bishop, The Executive's Right of Privacy: An Unresolved Constitutional Question, 66 Yale L.J. 477, 487 (1957).

60. Per Curiam opinion at 717, *quoting* Committee for Nuclear Responsibility, Inc. v. Seaborg, 149 U.S.App.D.C. 385, 391, 463 F. 2d 788, 794 (1971).

somewhere—wherever it may be vested it is susceptible of abuse.[61]

To allow the courts to breach presidential confidentiality whenever one of 400 federal trial judges considers that the circumstances of the moment demonstrate a compelling need for disclosure would frustrate the privilege's underlying policy of encouraging frank and candid presidential deliberations. If it is possible to convince a court to compel the disclosure of presidential conversations, then a President cannot guarantee confidentiality to his advisers and they must operate always under the hazard that their conversations might be publicly exposed at the behest of some trial court in the future.

By enacting the Presidential Libraries Act of 1955,[62] Congress recognized the importance of maintaining presidential confidentiality. The Act bestows an absolute privilege upon

[61.] 14 U.S. (1 Wheat.) 304, 344-345, 4 L.Ed. 97 (1816). *See also* Bishop, *supra* note 59, at 488.

The plain and short answer to this is that neither can there be a menace to constitutional government by an executive which has to go to Congress for every cent it spends, which has not power by itself to raise and maintain armed forces and which cannot jail its citizens except under a law passed by Congress and after proceedings presided over by an independent judiciary. These are the factors that make the essential difference between an American President and Big Brother . . . . .
Id.

EPA v. Mink, 410 U.S. 73, 93, S.Ct. 827, 35 L.Ed.2d 119 (1973), involved nine documents whose production was sought under the Freedom of Information Act of 1966. 5 U.S.C. § 552 (1970). Six of those documents were held absolutely privileged and were exempt even from *in camera* inspection under Exemption 1 of the Act simply upon their classification by Executive order as military or state secrets.

Thus the vesting of absolute discretion in the President is nothing new. The Congress had sufficient faith in the Presidency to do so under Exemption 1:

[The legislative history] makes wholly untenable any claim that the Act intended to subject the soundness of executive security classifications to judicial review at the insistence of any objecting citizen. It also negates the proposition that Exemption 1 authorizes or permits *in camera* inspection of a contested document bearing a single classification so that the court may separate the secret from the supposedly non-secret and order disclosure of the latter.

410 U.S. at 84, 93 S.Ct. at 834. Indeed, that faith was redeemed when the President instituted new procedures more consistent with the policy underlying the FOIA to insure that only specific documents or protions thereof were classified Secret or Top Secret. *Id.* at 102-103, 93 S.Ct. at 843-844 (Brennan, J., dissenting).

The three documents not within Exemption 1 apparently were not even direct communications to the President, as in the case here, but were actually transmitted to a Mr. Irwin, Chairman of the "Under Secretaries Committee." *Id.* at 76 n.3, 93 S.Ct. at 831 n.3. *Mink* also held that the deliberative portions of the documents, as distinguished from the purely factual portions, were privileged and that if the privileged were inextricably intermixed with the unprivileged materials, then neither was to be produced. *Id.* at 91-94, 93 S.Ct. at 838-839.

[62.] Pub.L. No. 373, 69 Stat. 695 (Aug. 12, 1955) (now 44 U.S.C. § § 2101, 2107, 2108).

papers and sound recordings[63] deposited with the Government-administered presidential libraries by providing that presidential papers and recordings may be accepted "subject to restrictions agreeable to the administrator [of General Services] as to their use."[64] The presidential papers of Presidents Eisenhower, Kennedy and Johnson are subject to the restriction that "materials containing statements made by or to" the President are to be kept in confidence and held under seal and not revealed to anyone except the donors or archival personnel until "the passage of time or the circumstances no longer require such materials being kept under restriction." Restrictions imposed by letters from President Eisenhower and from President Johnson additionally prohibit disclosure to "public officials" on the ground that "the President of the United States is the recipient of many confidences from others, and . . . the inviolability of such confidence is essential to the office of the presidency . . . ."[65] Thus Congress by statute has recognized the confidential nature of presidential papers and recordings, and has subjected them to restrictions against disclosure. It would be incongruous to accord a greater confidence to the materials of a deceased President than to the materials of a living, incumbent President.

The Special Prosecutor contends that in view of the unique circumstances in the present case, disclosure would not infringe seriously upon the confidentiality of the presidential deliberative process. However, the ultimate decision in this case will have repercussions far beyond the narrow factual confines of the present events. The decision here will be the first definitive judicial statement on the issue of presidential privilege. To recognize only a qualified privilege is to invite every litigant, both civil and criminal, to demonstrate his or her own particularized need for evidence contained in presidential deliberations. Already several claims of this nature are pending.[66] The lessons of legal history teach that it will be impossible to contain this breach of

---

[63.] 44 U.S.C. § 2101 (1970).

[64.] *Id.* § 2107(1).

[65.] Letter from President Eisenhower to Administrator of General Services, April 13, 1960; Agreement of February 25, 1965 between Mrs. Jacqueline B. Kennedy and the United States; Letter from President Johnson to the Administrator of General Services, August 13, 1965.

[66.] *See eg.,* Nader V. Butz, 60 F.R.D. 381 (D.D.C.1973), appeal docketed, No. 73-1935, D.C.Cir., Aug. 15, 1973.

presidential confidentiality if numerous federal judges may rummage through presidential papers to determine whether a President's or a litigant's contentions should prevail in a particular case. Furthermore, the decision in this case inevitably will be precedent for assaults on the presently asserted absolute privileges of Congress and the Judiciary.[67]

B. *The Executive Privilege Cases*

The majority relies on a line of cases which recognize a qualified "executive privilege" where a civil litigant seeks disclosure of relevant government documents.[68] In formulating this qualified privilege, the courts concluded that the interest in confidentiality to insure a free deliberative process is weaker than that recognized as necessary to protect military or state secrets.[69] Consequently, the courts have recognized only a qualified, not an absolute, privilege where the government has resisted disclosure solely on the ground of protecting the confidentiality of the deliberative process.

However, none of the "executive privilege" cases involved personal communications between a President and his closest advisers. There is a great distinction between the office of the President and the myriad other agencies and departments that comprise the executive branch.[70] Virtually every decision emanating from a President's office has a direct and immediate

[67.] *See* pp. 738-742 *supra.*

Concurring in *Youngstown Sheet & Tube Co.*, Justice Frankfurther opined:

It ought to be, but apparently is not, a matter of common understanding that clashes between different branches of the government should be avoided if a legal ground of less explosive potentitalities is properly available. Constitutional adjudications are apt by exposing differences to exacerbate them.

Youngstown Sheet & Tube Co. v. Sawyer, 343 U.S. 579, 595, 72 S.Ct. 863, 96 L.Ed. 1153 (1952) (Frankfurter, J., concurring). This was the result in the recent Pentagon Papers case. New York Times v. United States, 403 U.S. 713, 91 S.Ct. 2140, 29 L. Ed.2d 822 (1971). There both sides lost. The newspaper lost in its attempt to have a wider privilege upheld for the press, and the Government lost in its attempt to block the publication of most of the papers. If the President's claim here is denied, the Congress and the Judiciary may find that such precendent will be used as the authority for each of them at the behest of the other to lose substantial protions of their presently asserted independence.

[68.] *E. g.*, Committee for Nuclear Responsibility, Inc. v. Seaborg, 149 U.S.App.D.C. 385, 463 F.2d 788 (1971); Kaiser Aluminum & Chemical Corp. v. United States, 157 F. Supp. 939, 141 Ct.Cl. 38 (1958); *see* 8 Wright & Miller, Federal Practice and Procedure § 2019, at 167-75 (1970).

[69.] *E. g.*, Kaiser Aluminum & Chemical Corp. v. United States, 157 F.Supp. 939, 947, 141 Ct.Cl. 38 (1958); *see* Proposed Fed. Rules of Evidence, Rule 509, Comment (a) (2) (Feb. 1973).

[70.] *See generally* Kendall v. United States, 37 U.S. (12 Pet.) 524, 610, 9 L.Ed. 1181 (1838).

effect on the entire, or a substantial part of, the nation. Lesser executive departments and agencies do not hold such awesome responsibility and power. Each has responsibility for and operates upon only a small segment of the nation. As important as the lesser executive departments and agencies are, their decisions do not have the sweeping and immediate impact which characterizes the decisions and policies of a President.

The national interest in maintaining presidential confidentiality to insure that a President's deliberative process remains completely unfettered is at least as strong as the national interest in protecting military or state secrets. As explained earlier, secrecy is not the ultimate goal of the presidential communications privilege. The ultimate goal is to guarantee that Presidents will remain comprehensively informed throughout their decision-making processes. The importance of the military or state secrets privilege is most apparent when, for example, it prevents disclosure of emergency defense or invasion plans, foreign espionage programs or summit meeting strategy. But if a President is unable to conduct thorough and unfettered deliberations with his advisers, these plans, programs and strategies may never be formulated. Furthermore, whereas the confidentiality of military or state secrets is important primarily with respect to this country's international relations, the presidential privilege promotes informed decisions in both the international and domestic spheres. In view of the immediate national and world-wide impact which accompanies presidential decisions, the need to protect the presidential deliberative process is at least as great as the need to protect military and state secrets. If military and state secrets are absolutely privileged based on the need for confidentiality, then conferences between a President and his close advisers should enjoy a similar absolute privilege based on the need for confidentiality.

C. *Presidential Privilege Against a Grand Jury*

The foregoing discussion demonstrates that the courts should afford presidential communications the same absolute privilege

---

Distinguishing the Presidency from lesser executive agencies does not establish a "Fourth Branch" of government. This distinction merely recognizes the practical realities of the government's operation. Our "living Constitution" and the general separation of powers concept it embodies do not mandate a decision which blindly applies the same privilege to the entire executive branch. It is unnecessary at this time to decide whether the absolute privilege should extend beyond the President to protect cabinet officers and other high executive officials.

which protects military and state secrets. However, the *Reynolds* decision, as well as the "executive privilege" cases, arose from civil litigation and did not discuss the assertion of privilege against a grand jury subpoena. The final issue which must be resolved before recognizing an absolute presidential communications privilege in this case is whether the policy supporting the privilege prevails over the competing interests which arise from a court order to produce information for a grand jury investigation.

Common law evidentiary privileges based on encouraging frank and candid communication apply equally in criminal and civil cases. For example, the husband-wife and attorney-client privileges may be invoked by a witness for either the prosecution or defense in a criminal trial, regardless of the claimed necessity for disclosing the evidence.

Nevertheless, an interest which supports the existence of a privilege in a civil context might be outweighed by stronger countervailing interests which arise in the administration of criminal justice. In Gravel v. United States[71] the court of appeals had fashioned a nonconstitutional testimonial privilege which protected a Congressman's aide from questioning by a grand jury regarding allegedly criminal activity committed in the course of his duties.[72] The court analogized the privilege to that which protects executive officials from civil liability. Since government officers are immune from civil liability, the court of appeals reasoned, a similar doctrine should immunize government officers from criminal prosecution. Carrying this reasoning one step further, the court concluded that a grand jury could not question government officers about crimes for which they could not be prosecuted. The Supreme Court disagreed, explaining:

> But we cannot carry a judicially fashioned privilege so far as to immunize criminal conduct proscribed by an Act of Congress or to frustrate the grand jury's inquiry into whether publication of these classified documents violated a federal criminal statute. The so-called executive privilege has never been applied to shield executive officers from prosecution for crime.[73]

[71.] 408 U.S. 606, 92 S.Ct. 2614, 33 L.Ed.2d 583 (1972).

[72.] *Id.* at 627, 92 S.Ct. at 2628, *see* United States v. Doe, 455 F.2d 753, 760-761 (1st Cir. 1972), vacated & remanded sub nom. Gravel v. United States, 408 U.S. 606, 92 S. Ct. 2614, 33 L.Ed.2d 583 (1972).

[73.] 408 U.S. at 627, 92 S.Ct. at 2628.

It is important to recognize that the "executive privilege" referred to in *Gravel* is the doctrine also known as official immunity.[74] It is not the evidentiary "executive privilege" upon which the majority in this case relies.[75] The express purpose of the official immunity doctrine is to shield executive officers from civil suits so they will not be deterred in the performance of their duties.[76] The quoted language from the *Gravel* decision recognizes that the underlying purpose of official immunity, while supporting immunity from civil liability, does not support total immunity from criminal prosecution.

The only relevance of the *Gravel* dictum to the present case is to suggest that the interest in protecting the confidentiality of the deliberative process may not support absolute immunity from criminal prosecution for executive officers. But the presidential communications privilege, as here outlined, does not immunize executive officers from criminal prosecution. This evidentiary privilege, which protects the presidential deliberative process by preventing disclosure of the exact details of that process, is not premised on any notions of immunity from civil or criminal liability. It is unnecessary in this case to decide the issue touched upon by *Gravel*, which is whether the interest in confidentiality that supports the evidentiary privilege would also preclude the indictment of participants in the deliberative process.

The possibility that an occasional criminal prosecution may be hampered by the privilege does not justify abandoning the compelling long-range necessity for presidential confidentiality. The inability of a prosecutor or grand jury to obtain specific privileged information will seldom prevent a successful criminal prosecution. Understandably, a prosecutor desires to obtain all evidence relevant to a case. But particular evidence frequently is unavailable because of commonly recognized privileges, such as the husband-wife, attorney-client or self-incrimination privileges.

---

[74] *See* Barr v. Matteo, 360 U.S. 564, 79 S.Ct. 1335, 3 L.Ed.2d 1434 (1959); Gregoire v. Biddle, 177 F.2d 579 (2d Cir. 1949).

[75] *See* notes 68-69 *supra* and accompanying text.

[76] The official immunity doctrine . . . confers immunity on government officials of suitable rank for the reason that "officials of government should be free to exercise their duties unembarrassed by the fear of damage suits in respect of acts done in the course of those duties—suits which would consume time and energies which would otherwise be devoted to governmental service and the threat of which might appreciably inhibit the fearless, vigorous, and effective administration of policies of government."

Doe v. McMillan, 412 U.S. 306, 318, 93 S.Ct. 2018, 2028, 36 L.Ed.2d 912 (1973), *quoting* Barr v. Matteo, 360 U.S. 564, 571, 79 S.Ct. 1335, 3 L.Ed.2d 1434 (1959).

In such instances, non-privileged information remains available and convictions routinely are obtained despite various claims of privilege by witnesses.

The 1807 decision in United States v. Burr,[77] upon which the majority relies,[78] does not preclude recognition of an absolute privilege in the present case. In that case, the accused sought to obtain allegedly exculpatory evidence contained in a letter which had been written to President Jefferson by General Wilkinson, an essential witness against the accused.[79] Chief Justice Marshall, sitting alone as the trial judge in the case, issued a subpoena to the President for production of the letter, but the President, through his attorney, refused to disclose certain passages. The Chief Justice appreciated the weight which attaches to a presidential assertion of privilege:

> The president, although subject to the general rules which apply to others, may have sufficient motives for declining to produce a particular paper, and those motives may be such as to restrain the court from enforcing its production.

* * * * * *

> Had the President, when he transmitted it, subjected it to certain restrictions, and stated that in his judgment the public interest required certain parts of it to be kept secret, and had accordingly made a reservation of them, all proper respect would have been paid to it . . . .[80]

---

[77] 25 Fed.Cas. p. 30 (No. 14,692d) (Marshall, Circuit Justice, 1807); *id.* at 187 (No. 14,694)

[78] The Per Curiam opinion states, "We think the *Burr* case makes clear that application of Executive privilege depends on a weighing of the public interest protected by the privilege against the public interests that would be served by disclosure in a particular case." Per Curiam opinion at 716.

[79] 25 Fed.Cas. at 36 (No. 14,692d).

[80] 25 Fed.Cas. at 191, 192 (No. 14,694).

Other important decisions also recognize the strength of assertions of privilege by Presidents and cabinet officers. In United States v. Cooper, a prosecution charging the publication of a libel against the President, Justice Chase, a colleague of Chief Justice Marshall, "refused to permit a subpoena to issue directed to the president of the United States." 25 Fed.Cas. 631, 633 (No. 14,865) (Chase, Circuit Justice, 1800).

Later, during the trial in Marbury v. Madison, when a question arose as to whether the Attorney General, who had been acting as Secretary of State during the period relevant to the trial should answer as to facts which came to his knowledge through his official capacity, Chief Justice Marshall stated:

There was nothing confidential required to be disclosed. If there had been he was not obliged to answer it; and if he thought that any thing was communicated to him in confidence he was not bound to disclose it.

5 U.S. (1 Cranch) 137, 144, 2 L.Ed. 60 (1803).

However, since the President had relied upon his attorney's discretion and had not communicated directly with the court,[81] the Chief Justice allowed the attorney time to consult with the President. Several days later, the Chief Justice accepted "a certificate from the President, annexed to a copy of General Wilkinson's letter, excepting such parts as he deemed he ought not to permit to be made public."[82] From all that appears these excisions were not contested.[83]

The *Burr* case involved a subpoena by a defendant in a criminal trial, and the defendant's demand for the letter was an exercise of his sixth amendment right "to have compulsory process for obtaining witnesses in his favor."[84] Although Chief Justice Marshall was never called upon to enforce the subpoena against the President,[85] and therefore never was required to

---

[81.] It does not even appear to the court that the president does object to the production of any part of this letter. The objection, and the reasons in support of the objection, proceed from the attorney himself, and are not understood to emanate from the president.

25 Fed.Cas. at 192 (No. 14,694).

[82.] *Id.* at 193.

[83.] The incident had other overtones of interest to historians, some of whom appear to have different versions. *See* 3 Beveridge, The Life of John Marshall 518-22 (1919); Rossiter, The American Presidency 70 (1956); Berger, Executive Privilege v. Congressional Inquiry, 12 U.C.L.A.L.Rev. 1043, 1107 (1965).

The case presently under discussion was the misdemeanor trial of Aaron Burr. There are conflicting claims as to whether President Jefferson ever co mplied with a subpoena in the earlier treason case against Burr. Professor Corwin states that "Jefferson when President [refused] to respond to Chief Justice Marshall's subpoena in Aaron Burr's trial for treason." Corwin, The President-Office and Powers, 1787-1957, at 113 (1957).

[84.] U.S.Const. amend. VI.

The eight amendment [*sic*] to the constitution gives to the accused, "in all criminal prosecutions, a right to a speedy and public trial, and to compulsory process for obtaining witnesses in his favor."

25 Fed.Cas. at 33 (No. 14,692d). This right includes the right to compel production of papers in a witness' possession. *Id.* at 34.

[85.] Chief Justice Marshall distinguished the power to issue a subpoena from the power to compel obedience to it:

If, then, as is admitted by the counsel for the United States, a subpoena may issue to the president, the accused is entitled to it of course; and whatever difference may exist with respect to the power to compel the same obedience to the process, as if it had been directed to a private citizen, there exists no difference wit respect to the right to obtain it. The guard, furnished to this high officer, to protect him from being harassed by vexatious and unnecessary subpoenas, is to be looked for in the conduct of a court after those subpoenas have issued; not in any circumstance which is to precede their being issued.

25 Fed.Cas. at 34 (No. 14,692d). This passage reflects Marshall's understanding that the mere issuance of a subpoena to a person does not necessarily mean that the issuance is proper or that the individual to whom it is directed is required to comply in

resolve the ultimate conflict between the President's privilege and the sixth amendment right to compulsory process, he took the opportunity in dicta to discuss whether a President's claim of privilege should be upheld in the face of a criminal defendant's demand for possible exculpatory evidence. Recognizing that he could not "precisely lay down any general rule for such a case,"[86] the Chief Justice suggested that "perhaps" a presidential claim of privilege could be overridden in a criminal trial where the defendant demonstrates a particularly compelling need for the evidence.[87] Quite clearly, this suggestion was not a final disposition of the issue, nor even a holding of the case.

The case before this court involves a grand jury proceeding, not a criminal trial of an accused. A grand jury, of course, is an accuser, not an accused, and has no sixth amendment right to compulsory process for obtaining witnesses. Thus, the express guarantee of the sixth amendment which was present in *Burr* is not applicable to the present case. Moreover, although the grand jury's authority to subpoena witnesses is essential to its task, grand juries always have operated under the constraints of evidentiary privileges.[88] Any conflict between the presidential communications privilege and the sixth amendment rights of a criminal defendant is better the Sixth Amendment when a court has before it an indicted defendant who is able to demonstrate

---

all circumstances. Hoever, the "guard" to which Marshall refers in the quoted passage is never definitively explained in the opinion.

[86]. 25 Fed.Cas. at 192 (No. 14,694).

[87]. Perhaps the court ought to consider the reasons which would induce the president to refuse such a letter as conclusive on it, unless such letter could be shown be absolutely necessary in the defense. The president may himself state the particular reasons which may have induced him to withhold a paper, and the court would unquestionably allow their full force to those reasons. At the same time, the court could not refuse to pay proper attention to the affidavit of the accused. But on objections being made by the president to the production of a paper, the court would not proceed further in the case without such an affidavit as would clearly show the paper to be essential to the justice of the case. On the present occasion the court would willingly hear further testimony on the materiality of the paper required, but that is not offered.
Id.

[88]. Branzburg v. Hayes, 408 U.S. 665, 688, 92 S.Ct. 2646, 33 L.Ed.2d 626 (1972).
It can be argued that the fifth amendment guarantee of indictment by a grand jury presents considerations of fairness that are comparable to the sixth amendment right involved in the *Burr* case. The function of a grand jury is not only to indict the guilty, but also to shield innocent persons from prosecution, *id.* at 686-687, 92 S.Ct. at 2659, and the inability of a grand jury to obtain privileged information might result in the indictment of innocent persons. But in my opinion the inherent strength of the grand jury process affords sufficient protection against indictment of innocent persons where the grand jury believes that exculpatory evidence has been wrongfully withheld.

the materiality of the evidence to his particular defense.[89]

D. *Constitutional Dimensions of the Privilege*

The foregoing discussion has demonstrated the soundness of an absolute, evidentiary privilege for conversations and deliberations of a President with his close advisers. But the privilege also has constitutional dimensions which derive both from the separation of powers doctrine and from the logical principle that inherent in any constitutional right are the means requisite to its effective discharge.

The effective discharge of the presidential duty faithfully to execute the laws requires a privilege that preserves the integrity of the deliberative processes of the executive office. It would be meaningless to commit to the President a constitutional duty and then fail to protect and preserve that which is essential to its effective discharge. Thus the term "effective" is the sine qua non that imbues the presidential decisional process with a constitutional shield. The genius of our Constitution lies, perhaps as much as anywhere, in the generality of its principles which makes it susceptible to adaptation to the changing times and the needs of the country. But this much is explicit: "[The President] shall take Care that the Laws be faithfully executed . . . ." U.S. Const. art. II, § 3. Is it plausible that the Framers should have charged the President with so basic a responsibility, one upon which every ordered society is premised, and yet left him without the ability effectively to satisfy that high charge? Emphatically, the answer must be, "No." The duty and the means of its discharge coalesce and each, the one explicit and the other implicit, finds its source in the Constitution.

The constitutional nature of the presidential communications privilege is reenforced by the doctrine of separation of powers. It is clear, of course, that our Constitutional System of checks and

---

89. Under certain circumstances, the Government's unwillingness to disclose relevant evidence may result in dismissal of the indictment. *See, e. g.,* Alderman v. United States, 394 U.S. 165, 184, 89 S.Ct. 961, 22 L.Ed.2d 176 (1969) (illegal electronic surveillance); Brady v. Maryland, 373 U.S. 83, 87, 83 S.Ct. 1194, 10 L.Ed.2d 215 (1963) (favorable and material evidence); Roviaro v. United States, 353 U.S. 53, 61, 77 S.Ct. 623, 1 L.Ed.2d 639 (1957) (identify of material witness); 18 U.S.C. § 3500 (1970) (Jencks Act). Although the Chief Executive ordinarily retains ultimate control over criminal prosecutions by the United States, a Special Prosecutor has been appointed to conduct the prosecutions related to this case. This unique division of authority within the executive branch may distinguish the cases cited above. *See generally* United States v. Eley, 335 F.Supp. 353, 358 (N.D.Ga. 1972). Since the issue is not squarely presented in the present case, I express no view on its proper resolution.

balances makes each branch dependent upon the other branches in some instances. The trial court and the majority of this court rely in part on this interdependency to decide that the courts have both the power to compel a President to comply with the subpoena and the right to obtain recordings of conversations that were part of the presidential decision-making process. The flaw in their analysis becomes apparent upon closer examination of the nature of both separation of powers and checks and balances. James Wilson[90] in his "Lectures on the Law" accurately stated both concepts:

[E]ach of the great powers of government should be independent as well as distinct. When we say this, it is necessary—since the subject is of primary consequence in the science of government—that our meaning be fully understood, and accurately defined. For this position, like every other, has its limitations; and it is important to ascertain them.

The independence of each power consists in this, that *its proceedings, and the motives, views, and principles, which produce those proceedings, should be free from the remotest influence, direct or indirect, of either of the other two powers.* But further than this, the independency of each power ought not to extend. Its proceedings should be formed without restraint, but when they are once formed, they should be subject to control.

We are now led to discover, that between these three great powers of government, there ought to be a mutual dependency, as well as a mutual independency. We have described their independency: let us now describe their

[90.] James Wilson was an advocate of a strong executive. Early in the Constitutional Convention on June 1, 1787, "Mr. Wilson moved that the Executive consist of a single person. . . . Mr. Wilson preferred a single magistrate, as giving, most energy, dispatch and responsibility to the office." 1 Farrand, Records of the Federal Convention 67 (1966). He was a member of the Continental Congress, a signer of the Declaration of Independence, and an associate justice of the United States Supreme Court, appointed by Washington in 1789.

As a constructive statesman Wilson had no superior in the Federal Convention of 1787. He favored the independence of the executive, legislative and judicial departments, the supremacy of the Federal Government over the State Governments, and the election of senators as well as representatives by the people, and was opposed to the election of the President or the judges by Congress. His political philosophy was based upon implicit confidence in the people, and he strove for such provisions as he thought would best guarantee a government by the people. Together with Gouverneur Morris he wrote the final draft of the Constitution and afterwards pronounced it "the best form of government which has ever been offered to the world." In the Pennsylvania ratification convention (November 21 to December 15, 1787) he was the constitution's principal defender.

23. Encyclopedia Britannica 632 (1954).

dependency. It consists in this, that *the proceedings of each, when they come forth into action and are ready to affect the whole,* are liable to be examined and controlled by one or both of the others. (Emphasis added).

2 Wilson, Works 409-10(1804).

Thus the system of checks and balances begins to operate only at the point "when [the proceedings of any branch] come forth into action and are ready to affect the whole." It is only necessary to cite several examples. The Executive may veto acts of Congress and Congress may override such a veto.[91] The Executive nominates, and the Senate confirms, ambassadors, justices of the Supreme Court and all other officers of the United States.[92] The courts may declare acts of Congress unconstitutional,[93] or constitutional and the Executive faithfully executes the laws in conformance with such decisions. That these principles establish the mutual dependency of the three branches is obvious, but it is equally obvious that each of the above instances involves a restraint by one branch on a final action of a coordinate branch.[94]

The doctrine of separation of powers, by contrast, requires that each branch's "proceedings, and the motives, views, and principles, which produce those proceedings, should be free from the remotest influence, direct or indirect, of either of the other two powers." *Id.* This doctrine, then, prohibits intrusion in any form by one branch into the decisional processes of an equal and coordinate branch. And it is clear, of course, that "[t]he grand jury is an arm of the court and its *in camera* proceedings constitute 'a judicial inquiry.' "[95] Thus, recordings of presidential

91. U.S.Const. art, I, § 7.

92. *Id.,* art. II, § 2.

93. Marbury v. Madison, 5 U.S. (1 Cranch) 137, 2 L.Ed. 60 (1803).

94. Indeed, Youngstown Sheet & Tube Co. v. Sawyer, 343 U.S. 579, 72 S.Ct. 863, 96 L.Ed. 1153 (1952), stands for nothing more than this. There, the seizure of the steel mills constituted the "final action" which the Supreme Court held unconstitutional and ordered undone. The Court, however, did not inquire into the decisional process or the wisdom of the decision in terms of military necessity—it simply held that the act of seizure was unconstitutional. We fully agree that this was a legitimate check on an unconstitutional final action.

95. Levine v. United States, 362 U.S. 610, 617, 80 S.Ct. 1038, 1043, 4 L.Ed.2d 989 (1960).
A grand jury is clothed with great independence in many areas, but it remains an appendage of the court, powerless to perform its investigative function without the court's aid, because powerless itself to compel the testimony of witnesses. It is the court's process which summons the witness to attend and give testimony, and it is the court which must compel a witness to testify if, after appearing, he refuses to do so.
Brown v. United States, 359 U.S. 41, 49, 79 S.Ct.539, 546, 3 L.Ed.2d 609 (1959).

deliberations cannot be the subject of a judicial subpoena if it would even remotely influence the conduct of such deliberations or their final outcome. Enforcement of the subpoena demonstrably would have just such an effect in this case. The conversations that are the subject of the subpoena presumptively occurred as part of the ongoing decisional process involved in the President's constitutional duty faithfully to execute the laws.[96] The end product of this process would be the decision whether crimes had been committed and whether to prosecute such crimes, and whether to discharge or retain certain government employees. These decisions would be the "final action" comparable to the seizure of the steel mills in *Youngstown Sheet & Tube Co.*[97] The conversations themselves, however, were an integral part of the deliberative process and thus not subject to judicial intrusion by means of enforcement of the subpoena. Moreover, it appears insignificant that such a judicial intrusion into that process is for the purpose of laying open those presidential conferences before the grand jury. To hold otherwise would, to paraphrase the district court, exalt the form of the intrusion over its substance,[98] since the pervasively adverse effect on the candor of the deliberations and the soundness of the decisions reached there flows from the breach of confidentiality itself, whatever the purpose of the intrusion.

But the greatest vice of the decision sought by the Special Prosecutor is that it would establish a precedent that would subject every presidential conference to the hazard of eventually being publicly exposed at the behest of some trial judge trying a civil or criminal case. It is this precedential effect which transforms this case from one solely related to the recordings sought here, to one which decides whether this President, and all future Presidents, shall continue to enjoy the independency of executive action contemplated by the Constitution and fully exercised by all their predecessors.

96. *See* note 109 *infra. See generally* notes 109-112 *infra* and accompanying text.

97. *See* note 94, *supra.* The fact that the final decision to prosecute or not to prosecute is not ministerial, but purely discretionary and thus not subject to judicial review is, at the least, irrelevant, and at the most, a factor that further strengthens the separation of powers argument in this particular case.

98. In re Grand Jury Subpoena Duces Tecum issued to Richard Nixon, etc., 360 F.Supp. 1, at 11 (D.C.D.C., 1973).

IV. THE PRIVILEGE IN THIS CASE

A. *The Privilege Was Properly Invoked*

For the foregoing reasons, my opinion recognizes an absolute privilege for presidential communications. To be privileged, the communications must occur under an aura of confidentiality, and, because the privilege is designed to protect a President's ability to perform his duties, the communications must relate to the performance of Article II duties.

The presidential communications privilege was properly invoked by the President under the circumstances of this case. In Reynolds v. United States[99] the Supreme Court discussed the procedures and formalities necessary for a proper invocation of the absolute privilege for military or state secrets.[100] Since the presidential communications privilege resembles the military or state secrets privilege, the *Reynolds* procedures are instructive in the present case.[101]

Initially, there must be "a formal claim of privilege lodged by the head of the department which has control over the matter, after actual personal consideration by that officer."[102] Although an earlier statement by the President indicated that he did not intend to invoke executive privilege with regard to the investigation,[103] the President's letter in response to the subpoena from the District Court expressed a clear intent to claim his constitutional privilege to withhold recordings of conversations with his advisers.[104]

[99.] 345 U.S. 1, 73 S.Ct. 528, 97 L.Ed. 727 (1953).

[100.] *Id.* at 7-11, 73 S.Ct. at 531-534.

[101.] The courts frequently have applied the *Reynolds* procedures to the Government's claims of privilege. *E. g.,* Carter v. Carlson, 56 F.R.D. 9, 10 (D.D.C.1972); Carl Zeiss Stiftung v. V.E.B. Carl Zeiss, Jena, 40 F. R.D. 318, 326-327 n.33 (D.D.C.1966), aff'd on the opinion below, 128 U.S.App.D.C. 10, 384 F.2d 979, cert. denied, 389 U.S. 952, 88 S.Ct. 334, 19 L.Ed.2d 361 (1967).

[102.] 345 U.S. at 7-8, 73 S.Ct. at 532.

[103.] On May 22, 1973, the President stated: Considering the number of persons involved in this case whose testimony might be subject to a claim of Executive privilege, I recognize that a clear definition of that claim has become central to the effort to arrive at the truth. Accordingly, Executive privilege will not be invoked as to any testimony concerning possible criminal conduct or discussions of possible criminal conduct, in the matters presently under investigation including the Watergate affair and the alleged cover-up.

After the President has claimed the privilege, the court must satisfy itself that "the circumstances are appropriate for the claim of privilege."[105] In determining whether the privilege is appropriate in a particular case, the only inquiry is whether there is a "reasonable danger" that disclosure of the evidence would expose matters which the privilege is designed to protect.[106] Since the presidential communications privilege is an absolute rather than a qualified privilege, there is no occasion to balance the particularized need for the evidence against the

[104.] Letter from President Nixon to Chief Judge Sirica, July 25, 1973:

THE WHITE HOUSE

WASHINGTON
July 25, 1973

Dear Judge Sirica:

White House Counsel have receive on my behalf a subpoena duces tecum issue of the United States District Court for the District of Columbia on July 23rd at the request of Archibald Cox. The subpoena calls for me to produce for a Grand Jury certain tape recordings as well as certain specified documents. With the utmost respect for the court of which you are Chief Judge, and for the branch of government of which it is a part, I must decline to obey the command of that subpoena. In doing so I follow the example of a long line of my predecessors as President of the United States who have consistently adhered to the position that the President is not subject to compulsory process from the courts.

The independence of the three branches of our government is at the very heart of our Constitutional system. It would be wholly inadmissible for the President to seek to compel some particular action by the courts. It is equally inadmissible for the courts to seek to compel some particular action from the President.

That the President is not subject to compulsory process from the other branches of government does not mean, of course, that all information in the custody of the President must forever remain unavailable to the courts. Like all of my predecessors, I have always made relevant material available to the courts except in those rare instances when to do so would be inconsistent with the public interest. The principle that guides my actions in this regard was well stated by Attorney General Speed in 1865:

Upon principles of public policy there are some kinds of evidence which the law excludes or dispenses with.   *   *   *   The official transactions between the heads of departments of the Government and their subordinate officers are, in general, treated as "privileged communications." The President of the United States, the heads of the great departments of the Government, and the Governors of the several States, it has been decided, are not bound to produce papers or disclose information communicated to them where, in their own judgement, the disclosures would, on public consideration, be inexpedient.

These are familiar rules laid down by every author on the law of evidence. A similar principle has been stated by many other Attorneys General, it has been recognized by the courts, and it has been acted upon by many Presidents.

In the light of that principle, I am voluntarily transmitting for the use of the Grand Jury the memorandum from W. Richard Howard to Bruce Kehrli in which they are interested as well as the described memoranda from Gordon Strachan to H.R. Haldeman. I have concluded, however, that it would be inconsistent with the public interest and with the Constitutional position of the Presidency to make available recordings of meetings and telephone conversations in which I was a participant and I must respectfully decline to do so.

Sincerely,
/s/   Richard Nixon

[105.] 345 U.S. at 8, 73 S.Ct. at 532.
[106.] *Id.* at 10, 73 S.Ct. at 533.

governmental interest in confidentiality. The balance between these competing interests was examined and resolved when the absolute presidential communications privilege was formulated.[107] Having concluded that the privilege is available, the only inquiry is whether the President's invocation of the privilege promotes the policy which the privilege was designed to protect. Regarding the absolute privilege for military or state secrets, the Reynolds Court stated:

> Where there is a strong showing of necessity, the claim of privilege should not be lightly accepted, but *even the most compelling necessity* cannot overcome the claim of privilege if the Court is ultimately satisfied that military secrets are at stake.[108]

The presidential communications privilege protects the confidentiality of communications between the President and his close advisers which are related to his Article II duties. Since the subpoena covers recordings of confidential communications between the President and his closest advisers, the privilege is appropriate in this case if the recorded conversations related to the President's Article II duties. My starting point is the presumption, in the absence of clear evidence to the contrary, that as a government official the President was discharging his constitutional duties.[109] The nature of the Presidency often makes it difficult to distinguish private from official concerns of the President. Because of his position in the nation, actions which might be commonplace if performed by a private individual assume national importance when performed by the President. As Chief Justice Marshall stated in the *Burr* decision: "Letters to the president in his private character, are often written to him in consequence of his public character, and may relate to public concerns."[110]

From the circumstances already in the public record, it is reasonable to conclude that the conversations at issue related to the President's Article II duty to "take Care that the Laws be

---

107. *See* notes 71-89 *supra* and accompanying text.

108. 345 U.S. at 11, 73 S.Ct. at 533 (emphasis added).

109. United States v. Chemical Foundation, Inc., 272 U.S. 1, 14-15, 47 S.Ct. 1, 71 L.Ed. 131 (1926); *see* United States v. Crusell, 81 U.S. (14 Wall.) 1, 4, 20 L.Ed. 821 (1872); *cf.* NLRB v. Shawnee Industries, Inc., 333 F.2d 221, 225 (10th Cir. 1964); United States v. Washington, 233 F.2d 811, 816 (9th Cir. 1956).

110. United States v. Burr, 25 Fed.Cas. 187, 192 (No. 14,694) (Marshall, Circuit Justice, 1807).

faithfully executed."[111] The break-in at the Democratic Party headquarters soon became a pervasive topic of conversation throughout the country. There occurred constant and widespread speculation concerning the possible involvement of high public officials, and some suspected that the Justice Department was not investigating the matter thoroughly. There is evidence that the President, like other citizens, was concerned that the laws were not being fully enforced. Especially in view of allegations linking the burglary to the White House staff, it was appropriate for the President, as the nation's chief law enforcement officer, to discuss these matters with his advisers.[112] Thus, it is reasonable to conclude that the discussions covered by the subpoena related to the President's Article II duty to execute the laws. The possibility that the President also may have been concerned about the political effect of the offenses on the Republican Party is not inconsistent with the performance of his Article II duties.

Since the subpoenaed tapes are recordings of the President's confidential conversations and there is a reasonable probability that the discussions related to the President's Article II duties, there exists at least a "reasonable danger" that disclosing the tapes would jeopardize the very interest which the presidential communications privilege is designed to protect. Just as the *Reynolds* Court found only a "reasonable danger" that disclosure would jeopardize protected interests,[113] it is not necessary in this case to conclude with the absolute certainty that disclosure would violate presidential confidentiality in matters of official concern. *Reynolds* only requires a "reasonable danger," and that standard is satisfied here.

Since there exists a reasonable danger that disclosing the recordings would infringe upon protected presidential confidentiality, an examination of the tapes by a judge even in chambers would be improper. Once a President asserts his privilege, a court's only function is to determine whether the circumstances are appropriate for the claim of privilege.[114] Yet the court must take this determination without forcing disclosure

[111.] U.S.Const. art. II, § 3.

[112.] The fact that some participants in the conversations were not Government officials does not divest the conversations of their official character. A President must be free to receive advice from both within and without the Government. Soucie v. David, 145 U.S.App.D.C. 144, 155 n. 44, 448 F.2d 1067, 1078 n. 44 (1971).

[113.] 345 U.S. at 10-11, 73 S.Ct. at 533.

[114.] *Id.* at 8, 73 S.Ct. at 532.

of the very communication which the privilege protects.[115]   Thus an *in camera* inspection is proper only if the court cannot otherwise satisfy itself that the privilege should be sustained. In the present case, I am satisfied that appropriate circumstances do exist and, therefore, would hold that even *in camera* inspection is improper.

B. *Privilege Not Destroyed by Possibility of Criminal Conspiracy by Advisers*

The Special Prosecutor also argues that the privilege disappears upon a *prima facie* showing that the conversations occurred as part of a criminal conspiracy by certain of the President's advisers.[116]   He strenuously argues that abuse of the privileged relationship vitiates any otherwise valid privilege possessed by the President. The argument is fatally defective, however, since the President alone holds the privilege which is designed to ensure the integrity of his decisional processes. The possibility that those close to him may have perverted the relationship cannot destroy the privilege held in the public interest exclusively by the President.

The Special Prosecutor relies heavily upon Clark v. United States, 289 U.S. 1, 53 S.Ct. 465, 77 L.Ed. 993 (1933), to sustain his position, but that case is not to the contrary. *Clark* involved a prospective juror who on *voir dire* concealed facts and falsely swore in order to be accepted as a juror. Whatever privilege she might have possessed as a juror could "not apply where the relation giving birth to it was fraudulently begun or fraudulently continued." *Id.* at 14, 53 S.Ct. at 469. It is questionable, of course, whether the privilege of a jury is at all comparable to the presidential communications privilege. In any event, the privilege discussed in *Clark* is designed to protect the deliberations of the entire jury and thus belongs to the jury as an entity. A single juror cannot waive the privilege for all other jurors and make public against their wishes the discussions that occurred in the secrecy of the jury room. A corollary of this principle is that, although a nonculpable juror properly may invoke the privilege, a juror who has abused the privileged relationship cannot assert the privilege to shield himself from criminal sanction if the remaining jurors wish to testify. There is not the slightest indication in *Clark* that the nonculpable jurors attempted to interpose their privilege to keep the jury deliberations secret. Thus *Clark* only

---

115. *Id.*

116. Supplemental Brief of the United States at 19–30.

decided that a juror who abuses the relationship which creates the privilege loses any privilege he otherwise might have possessed; such a juror may not validly interpose a privilege retained by nonculpable jurors who are willing to testify.

Indeed, the analogy of the attorney-client privilege referred to in *Clark*[117] supports the view that an innocent holder of a privilege does not lose it because of misconduct by another. The client, not the attorney, is the holder of that privilege and thus, as *Clark* states, "the loss of the privilege [does not] depend upon the showing of a conspiracy, upon proof that client and attorney are involved in equal guilt. The attorney may be innocent, and still the guilty client must let the truth come out." *Id.* at 15, 53 S.Ct. at 469. By contrast, where the client is innocent, his privilege does not fail because of any misconduct by his attorney. The client cannot control the use to which his attorney puts information confided to him during the course of their relationship, but relies simply upon the attorney's sense of professional integrity. It would be manifestly unjust to penalize the ordinary client by exposing to public scrutiny the intimate details of his personal and financial life upon a *prima facie* showing that his attorney had utilized such information in an illegal enterprise. Similarly, possible abuse of the privileged relationship by advisers to the President cannot vitiate the privilege held by him alone to protect the integrity of the presidential deliberative process.

C. *The Impeachment Clause and the Possibility of Presidential Misconduct*

Thus the Special Prosecutor's case finally rests upon a showing of probable cause to believe that the President himself was guilty of misconduct. However, the Special Prosecutor has never strongly urged the point, preferring to rest his case upon the showing of criminal involvement by those close to the President. Although I would be reluctant to consider a contention never directly pressed, my greater reluctance is premised more fundamentally upon the ground that such a determination at this stage of the proceedings is constitutionally inhibited. I state here not a firm conclusion, but one of sufficient merit to circumscribe judicial inquiry. The constitutional inhibition essentially derives from implications inherent in the Impeachment Clause:

Judgment in Cases of Impeachment shall not extend further than to removal from Office, and disqualification to hold and

117. 289 U.S. at 15, 53 S.Ct. 465.

enjoy any Office of Honor. Trust or Profit under the United States: but the Party convicted shall nevertheless be liable and subject to Indictment, Trial, Judgment and Punishment, according to Law.

U.S. Const. art. 1, § 3 ¶ 7. And, of course, a President may be removed from office only upon impeachment. *Id.*, art. II, § 4.

My starting point is the proposition that a President is subject to the criminal laws, but only after he has been impeached by the House and convicted by the Senate and thus removed from office. The contemporaneous views of the Framers clearly support the view that all aspects of criminal prosecution of a President must follow impeachment. For example, Gouverneur Morris stated during the debates on impeachment that:

A conclusive reason for making the Senate instead of the Supreme Court the Judge of impeachments, was that the latter was to try the President *after* the trial of the impeachment.

2 Farrand, Records of the Federal Convention 500 (rev. ed. 1966) (emphasis added). And Alexander Hamilton in the Federalist Papers twice reiterated the proposition that removal from office must precede any form of criminal process against an incumbent President:

The punishment which may be the consequence of conviction upon impeachment, is not to terminate the chastisement of the offender. *After* having been sentenced to a perpetual ostracism from the esteem and confidence, and honors and emoluments of his country, he will still be liable to prosecution and punishment in the ordinary course of law.

The Federalist No. 65, at 426 (Modern Library ed. 1937).

The President of the United States would be liable to be impeached, tried, and, upon conviction of treason, bribery, or other high crimes or misdemeanors, removed from office; and would *afterwards* be liable to prosecution and punishment in the ordinary course of law.

The Federalist No. 69, at 446 (Modern Library ed. 1937).

A modern commentator similarly argues that the Impeachment Clause:

sharply separates removal from office from subsequent punishment after indictment . . . . Removal would enable the government to replace an unfit officer with a proper person, leaving "punishment" to a later and separate proceeding, if indeed the impeachable offense were thus punishable.

Berger, Impeachment: The Constitutional Problems 79 (1973). *See generally* authorities collected in Brief for Petitioner at 17-26.

Sound policy reasons preclude criminal prosecution until after a President has been impeached and convicted. To indict and prosecute a President or to arrest him before trial, would be constructively and effectively to remove him from office, an action prohibited by the Impeachment Clause. A President must remain free to travel, to meet, confer and act on a continual basis and be unimpeded in the discharge of his constitutional duties. The real intent of the Impeachment Clause, then, is to guarantee that the President always will be available to fulfill his constitutional duties.

Finally, having established that criminal prosecution of an incumbent President must follow impeachment, I come to the reasons this court cannot consider questions of presidential guilt, at least at this stage of the proceedings. Counsel for the President seem to place their argument upon the irrelevance of presidential guilt to the grand jury because of its inability to indict the President:[118]

> . . . there seems to be a suggestion at pages 19-22 of the Opinion [below] that an otherwise valid claim of privilege by the President would be overriden if the evidence sought would show that the President himself had been guilty of a crime. But if there were such evidence of crime against an incumbent President—and there is none in this case—it could not be relevant to the work of a grand jury or of the District Court because of the inability to indict a President prior to impeachment.

This is an insufficient reason, however, since evidence of presidential involvement in a criminal conspiracy might be relevant to establish the case against his advisers.[119] I prefer to rely upon a discrete, but closely related proposition. That is, that

---

[118.] Brief of Petitioner at 20-21.

[119.] For example, if only one adviser had conspired with the President to obstruct justice, it would be necessary to show presidential involvement to prosecute that adviser, since conspiracy requires at least two conspirators. Rogers v. United States, 340 U.S. 367, 375, 71 S.Ct. 438, 95 L.Ed. 344 (1951); United States v. Thomas, 468 F.2d 422, 424 (10th Cir. 1972); *see* 18 U.S.C. § 371 (1970).

The fact that an incumbent President may not be prosecuted because of the Impeachment Clause, however, might not preclude criminal prosecution of any co-conspirators. *Cf.* Rogers v. United States, *supra*; Feldstein v. United States, 429 F.2d 1092 (9th Cir.), cert. denied, 400 U.S. 920, 91 S.Ct. 174, 27 L.Ed.2d 159 (1970); Cross v. United States, 392 F.2d 360 (8th Cir. 1968).

a judicial determination of a *prima facie* case against the President and a grand jury determination of whether or not to indict are sufficiently comparable in the impeachment context so that if one is constitutionally prohibited, the other must be also, for each is a finding that is probable that the President has committed a crime. There is a distinction, of course, in that an indictment initiates actual criminal prosecution, but this is not a dispositive distinction; a judicial determination that it is more probable than not that the President himself is guilty of criminal activity would just as effectively disable a President in the discharge of his constitutional duties. The courts cannot properly, in effect, *ex cathedra* stamp their own imprimatur of guilt upon an incumbent President, if to do so would vitiate the sound judgment of the Framers that a President must possess the continuous and undiminished capacity to fulfill his constitutional obligations. In my opinion such a judicial determination of the probability of presidential guilt would have just such an effect. For these reasons, a court should not directly confront an only obliquely urged assertion of a *prima facie* case against an incumbent President.

D. Prior Testimony by Presidential Advisers Does Not Require Disclosure of the Tape Recordings

The Special Prosecutor contends that whatever privilege the President may have possessed has been waived by the President's statement of May 22, 1973 allowing testimony by his counsel and aides.[120] He argues that a distinction between tape recordings and testimony would be "an intolerable distinction [because] [c]onfidentiality no longer exists in any real sense."[121]

As a starting point, the privilege has not been waived at least as to any matters not already testified to by his advisers. The confidentiality surrounding as yet undisclosed conversations has not been impaired. As to those portions of the tape recordings that have been the subject of testimony before the Senate Investigating Committee, the resolution of the waiver issue is more complex, but the answer appears equally clear.

---

120. [E]xecutive privilege will not be invoked as to any *testimony* concerning possible criminal conduct or discussions of possible criminal conduct, in matters presently under investigation, including the Watergate affair and the alleged cover-up.
Brief of United States, app. at 24 (emphasis added).

121. Supplemental Brief of United States at 33.

There has been no waiver. This conclusion rests upon three factors: the strict standards applied to privileges of this nature to determine waiver; the distinction between oral testimony and tape recordings; and, most important, considerations of public policy that argue persuasively for a privilege that permits the Chief Executive to disclose information on topics of national concern without decimating entirely his right and duty to withhold that which properly ought to be withheld in the public interest.

The determination of whether the President has waived his privilege does not depend upon whether it is purely one of constitutional dimensions, only an evidentiary privilege or one that partakes of attributes of both. For, whatever its source, the privilege is sufficiently essential to the effective functioning of the Presidency to require that the standards employed to determine its waiver be as rigorous as those applied to protect constitutional rights generally.

This simply recognizes that the present and future ability of Presidents effectively to discharge their consitutional duties is as fundamental to our democratic form of government as are the rights guaranteed by the Constitution to each individual. It is well established in the law that the presumption is against waiver of fundamental or constitutional rights. Indeed, "courts indulge every reasonable presumption against waiver" of such rights. Johnson v. Zerbst, 304 U.S. 458, 464, 58 S.Ct. 1019, 1023, 82 L.Ed. 1461 (1938); Aetna Ins. Co. v. Kennedy 301 U.S. 389,57 S.Ct. 809, 81 L.Ed. 1177 (1937); Hodges v. Easton, 106 U.S. 408, 1 S.Ct. 307, 27 L.Ed. 169 (1882). Thus a heavy burden must be met by the Special Prosecutor to establish waiver in this case.

In *Reynolds* the Supreme Court indicated that at least some of the significance attached to the fifth amendment privilege against self-incrimation applied as well to the military or state secrets privilege. The adoption in *Reynolds* of similarly stringent procedures to establish a valid invocation of the privilege implicitly recognized that the two privileges are of equal significance in our governmental system.[122] While counsel for the President are not entirely correct in their assertion that *Reynolds* is dispositive of the waiver issue here,[123] that case

---

[122.] *See* notes 99-115 *supra* and accompanying text.

[123.] Counsel for the President argue:

Indeed, the short answer to any claim of waiver with regard to the materials now sought may be found in United States v. Reynolds, 345 U.S. 1, 73 S.Ct. 528 97 L.Ed. 727 (1953). In that case the United States refused to produce an Air Force investigation report of an airplane crash as well as written statements by the survivors

nonetheless suggests a helpful framework for analysis. Suppose in that case the Government was willing to permit testimony not only as to non-classified matters, but also as to general descriptions of classified matters. Such an offer could not be construed as a waiver of the Government's privilege to refuse to produce the specifications and blueprints of the secret military technology there in question.[124]

Similarly, in this case there exists a valid and tenable distinction between testimony and tape recordings. Confidentiality is composed of many elements and the difference in degree between allowing generalized, selective testimony and the recordings themselves is sufficiently great to constitute a difference in kind. Counsel for the President have well stated that distinction:

> Recordings are the raw material of life. By their very nature they contain spontaneous, informal, tentative, and frequently pungent comments on a variety of subjects inextricably intertwined into one conversation.[125]

The distinction between testimony and tape recordings is not drawn for the purpose of preserving the right, in itself, of public officials to speak pungently and bluntly. Rather, what is sought to be preserved are the qualities of directness and candor that flow from discussions where it is unnecessary for the participants to dissemble, to seek the felicitous phrase or to be concerned

---

of the crash. It offered to allow the survivors to give depositions and to testify as to all matters except those of a "classified nature." The Supreme Court sustained the claim of privilege with regard to the documents sought. The offer to allow the witnesses to testify, far from being a waiver of privilege as to the documents, was expressly relied on by the Supreme Court as a reason for upholding the claim of privilege. 345 U.S. at 11, 73 S.Ct. 528.

Brief in Opposition in the District Court at 20.

The military secrets privilege asserted in *Reynolds* applied only to classified, non-privileged matter and thus the offer could not effect a waiver as to classified, privileged matter. The more interesting point, however, is that *Reynolds* held the entire document privileged, apparently recognizing the distinction between selective testimony and production of the document itself, and refused even to permit *in camera* inspection.

124. Indeed, Machin v. Zuckert, 114 U.S.App.D.C. 335, 316 F.2d 336, cert. denied 375 U.S. 896, 84 S.Ct. 172, 11 L.Ed.2d 124 (1963), extends beyond the limits of the suggested hypothetical. There, a private litigant, against a claim of executive privilege, sought an investigative report of an aircraft accident. He already had been permitted to see it briefly, although he could not copy it or make notes from it. In addition, the Secretary of the Air Force offered to provide a list of the names of witnesses and sent a "releasable summary" of the report to the litigant. *Id.* at 336, 337, 316 F.2d 336. There was never any speculation in the *Machin* decision that waiver of privilege resulted from such actions.

125. Brief of Petitioner at 61.

about interpretations that may be skewed if heard by an unfriendly audience. Failure to recognize the distinction between testimony and recordings here would impede, rather than promote, open and frank discussions. Thus a waiver as to testimony cannot be construed as a waiver of the right to withhold the tape recordings.[126]

The proper resolution of the waiver issue depends more fundamentally, however, upon a reasoned compromise between two clear and well-established principles that sustain the efficacy of democratic government in modern times. That is, the general right and need of the public to be well informed, and the imperative need of government to maintain secrecy and confidentiality in certain situations.[127] Although seemingly antagonistic, both principles emerge from, and are but the recognized end result of, that determination ever present in the law: "Where lies the public interest?" The continued vitality of these two principles perforce demands that any rule on waiver of presidential privilege be formulated to, at once, preserve the privilege to the greatest extent consistent with the public interest and promote as full disclosure by high public officers as possible. In this case that goal would best be achieved by holding that the privilege has not been waived. The policy favoring openness in government dictates that a President should be able to disclose certain selected information relevant to topics of national concern and to permit testimony by subordinate executive

126. The Per Curiam opinion at 718 quotes Lopez v. United States, 373 U.S. 427, 439, 83 S.Ct. 1381, 10 L.Ed.2d 462 (1963), for the proposition that "[t] here is no 'constitutional right to rely on possible flaws in the [witness's] memory. * * * [N] o other argument can justify excluding an accurate version of a conversation that the [witness] could testify to from memory.' " While this language nicely phrases their point, *Lopez* in unpersuasive in the context of this case. *Lopez* involved an Internal Revenue Agent who on the invitation of the defendant discussed defendant's tax return with him, during the course of which an attempt was made to bribe the agent. The agent then testified to this bribe at trial and the recordings of their conversations were introduced as corroborative evidence. The Court held that since the conduct of the conversations were introduced as corroborative evidence. The Court held that since the conduct of the conversations themselves did not violate the fourth amendment, neither did the "surreptitious seizure" of the conversations by recording them. Thus *Lopez* simply involved a question of the admissibility of certain cooroborative evidence against a fourth amendment objection. Whether certain evidence is admissible and whether such evidence is in the first instance privileged and thus not subject to compulsory process are two different questions. A criminal confession is admissible but it may not be compelled absent waiver. Thus the question in the last analysis depends upon whether the President has waived his privilege and I conclude that he has not, principally on the policy grounds discussed at pp. 760-761 of this opinion.

127. Of course, military and state secrets are only the most celebrated of these instances.

officers on such topics, without being compelled to make a complete disclosure of that which is essential properly to maintain the confidentiality and integrity of advice and information furnished to the Presidency.[128]

The majority prefers not to confront this problem directly, but merges what is essentially a question of waiver into its initial balancing process to determine that the need to preserve confidentiality in this case is lessened. Having done this, the majority then strikes the balance against presidential privilege. But this does not resolve the dilemma posed. Whether future Presidents perceive the question of partial disclosure to enter at the balancing stage or as a waiver determination, they will be reluctant partially to disclose information if such disclosure would, under either mode of analysis, increase the probability of compelled full disclosure. The strong public interest in preserving this latitude for future Presidents requires a finding that on the facts presented in this case executive privilege has not been waived.

V. CONCLUSION

For the reasons above stated it is my conclusion that the presidential communications privilege may be exercised to decline to produce the recordings, and that this privilege has not been waived. I would thus enter judgment accordingly in all cases.

If this rule were recognized, the President would then be free voluntarily to type up a transcript of the recordings that are the subject of this litigation and present it to the grand jury with the material deleted that he considers confidential. He could explain the deleted matter.[129] As to the deleted material the President's action would be submitted to the test of public opinion and

---

[128.] On this point, Professor Alexander Bickel is persuasive:

Again, the issue is not whether the President has waived his privilege to keep the tapes secret. To the extent that it exists and with respect to matter that it covers, I do not see how the privilege can be waived. Naturally, if a document or a tape is no longer confidential because it has been made public, it would be nonsense to claim that it is privileged, and nobody would trouble to subpoena it either, since it would be available.

But nature and reason of the privilege are rather to repose in the President and in him alone the subjective judgment whether to maintain privacy or release information—and which, and how much, and when, and to whom. Far from being waived, the privilege, it seems to me, is as much exercised when information is released as when it is withheld.

Bickel, *Wretched Tapes (cont.,* N.Y. Times, August 15, 1973, at 33).

[129.] This would accord with President Jefferson's action in the *Burr* case, *supra* note 82 and accompanying text, and with the following colloquy between Judge Wilkey and Professor Wright (Counsel for the President) at oral argument before this court:

eventually, when the tapes are released for posterity, to the test of history.[130]

WILKEY, Circuit Judge, dissenting. **

The critical issue on which I part company with my five colleagues is, in the shortest terms, *Who Decides?*

There is no issue as to the existence of Executive Branch privilege, and questions as to its scope and applicability to a given set of facts will be relatively easy to determine once the principal question is settled. The basic issue is *who decides* the scope and

JUDGE WILKEY: * * *

You recall, of course, that President Jefferson took the document, the Wilkinson letter, called for by the subpoena. He then deleted from the document those matters which he felt that needed to be confidential, shall we say secrets of State, and then with the deleted version sent an affidavit to the Prosecutor for lodging in the court as to what in summary, without revealing any secrets, the President had deleted and why. And then the exerpted [sic] letter was given with the affidavit to the court in answer to the subpoena.

President Jefferson never furnished the full letter.

MR. WRIGHT: That's right.

JUDGE WILKEY: Now, why should not the President here exercise his privilege in regard to the tapes, deleting State secrets in the same way, but forwarding everything else, in the same way as President Jefferson?

          *   *   *   *

[L]et's add to that not only State secrets, but other matters of confidentiality, which neither of the parties concerned nor the public have any right to know, that would be dangerous to know at this time, in the President's own judgment.

And then why should he not send the rest of it for such use as the Prosecutor in [sic] the defense and the trial judge may deem relevant?

MR. WRIGHT: That would seem to me not an untenable possibility.

Transcript of Proceedings, Sept. 11, 1973 at 102-03.

130. The foregoing opinion was amended after it issued to add the following:

On October 12, 1973, the day this opinion issued, the New York Times published a letter of the Honorable Burton K. Wheeler, former distinguished United States Senator from Montana and nominee in 1924 for Vice President on the Progressive Party ticket with Senator LaFollette. Senator Wheeler had been requsted by a number of Democratic and Republican Senators to lead the opposition to the bill to pack the Supreme Court. (S.1392, 75th Cong.) In his letter to the New York Times he wrote that he considered it necessary to deny charges that the Supreme Court was delinquent in its consideration of cases and discussed with Justice Brandeis the possibility that he and Chief Justice Hughes testify before the Senate Committee on the Judiciary. Justice Brandeis "responded that under no circumstances would he testify or recommend that the Chief Justice testify" because "it just would not be the right thing to do. It might establish an unfortunate precedent." Chief Justice Hughes considered that the Court-packing plan "would destory the Court as an institution" but even in the face of this dire threat, he refused to testify but did write a letter denying the charge of Court delinquency. Senator Wheeler's letter further stated: "[I] f [the Supreme Court] holds that Congress, in other than an impeachment proceeding can obtain the records of Presidential conferences, [it] will set a precedent for Congress to obtain records or other evidence of Court deliberations ... Pursuit of the tapes may result in a precedent-setting decision by the Supreme Court which will ill serve the future of democracy and our form of government."

For a more complete report of the defeat of President Roosevelt's plan to pack the Supreme Court, see the chapter entitled "Saving the Supreme Court' in *Yankee from the West*, Burton K. Wheeler with Paul F. Healy, pp. 319-340 (Doubleday & Co. 1962).

Per Curiam

applicability of the Executive Branch privilege, the Judicial Branch or Executive Branch?

Throughout the *Per Curiam* this issue appears obfuscated; there is an effort to slide away from the square confrontation produced by the Judicial Branch ordering the Executive Branch to turn over records of private conversations in the Chief Executive's own office. The reluctance of my colleagues is understandable; no court has ever done this before. Even the great Chief Justice Marshall shied away from making a final order to the Chief Executive to produce the full text of correspondence, a final order which, if it had ever been issued, President Jefferson was fully prepared to ignore.[1]

---

* For the convenience of the reader, an outline of this dissenting opinion is herewith appended.

I.   *The Dual Origin of the Privilege Asserted*
   A.   *The Common Sense-Common Law, Statutory Origin of Privilege*
      1.   Historically
      2.   Litigation in Which the Government is a Party
      3.   Individual Inquiry of a Governmental Official or Agency
      4.   The First Amendment
      5.   The Chief Executive
   B.   *Separation of Powers—The Tripartite Privilege*
      1.   Judicial versus Executive
      2.   Legislative versus Executive
      3.   Judicial versus Legislative
      4.   Who Decides?
II. *Development of the Tripartite Privilege with Reference to Executive Documents*
   A.   *The Legislative Decision of 1789*
   B.   *Congressional Demands for Executive Papers*
   C.   *Judicial Demands for Executive Papers—The Trials of Aaron Burr*
III. *Relationship of the Grand Jury to the Judiciary and to the Executive*
   A.   *Background*
   B.   *Relationship of the Grand Jury to the Judiciary*
IV. *Amenability of the President to Judicial Process—An Illusory Issue in the Instant Case*
V.   *Application of the Constitutional Tripartite Privilege*
   A.   *Procedures and Practicalities—Statues and the Constitution*
      1.   The Authorities
      2.   Pragmatic Considerations
   B.   *A Healthy Tension*

** Judge MacKinnon has stated his general concurrence in the result reached in this dissent and that differences in the two dissenting opinions are mainly matters of emphasis. That is my position also in regard to Judge MacKinnon's dissent. Given the compressed time frame in which we must write, it has seemed better to write separate opinons rather than to seek specific concurrent language on the important and delicate matters at issue here.

[1.] See Part II.C. *infra,* for the full discussion of the trial of Aaron Burr in 1807. President Jefferson was prepared to instruct the U.S. marshal, an employee then and now of the Executive Branch, not to serve any such order on the President. 9 P. Ford, The Writings of Thomas Jefferson 62 (1898) [hereinafter Writings of Jefferson] . *See* note 118 *infra.*

The *Per Curiam* here never confronts the fundamental Constitutional question of separation of powers, but instead prefers to treat the case as if all were involved was a weighing and balancing of conflicting public interests. There *are* conflicting public interests involved, they must be carefully weighed, balanced, and appraised; the President says he has done just that. Therefore, the most fundamental, necessarily decisive issue is, Who Does the weighing and balancing of conflicting public interests? The District Judge or the President? The answer to this question necessarily involves the Constitutional question of separation of powers. But the whole line of reasoning, the whole line of authorities, relied on by the *Per Curiam* does not deal with the separation of powers issue at all.

I respectfully submit that the errors in the *Per Curiam's* analysis stem from a frequent source of confusion, the failure to recognize and separate the two origins of the Executive Branch privilege: on one hand, the common sense-common law privilege of confidentiality necessary in government administration, which has been partly codified in statutes such as the Freedom of Information Act; on the other hand, the origin of the privilege in the Constitutional principle of separation of powers. The answer to the overriding issue, Who Decides, and answers to all the subsidiary questions hinge upon the correct analysis of the nature and source of the privilege. Historical practice, by the Judiciary, the Congress, and the Executive, reflects implicitly the dual origin of the privilege of confidentiality asserted at one time or another by each Branch.

To understand the legal principles on which the *Per Curiam* relies, and why they cannot be decisive of this case, I proposed first to discuss the nature of the common sense-common law origin of governmental privilege. To understand the legal principles on which this case, in my opinion, necessarily turns, the remainder of the opinion is devoted to the Constitutional principle of separation of power as applied to the case at bar.

A. *The Common Sense-Common Law, Statutory Origin of Privilege*

1. *Historically*

The oldest source of Executive Branch privilege, the common sense-common law privilege of confidentiality, existed long before the Constitution of 1789, and might be deemed an inherent power of any government. As President Thomas Jefferson wrote to George Hay, United States Attorney for Virginia, on 17 June 1807:

> With respect to papers, there is certainly a public and a private side to our offices. To the former belong grants of land, patents for inventions, certain commissions, proclamations, and other papers patent in their nature. To the other belong mere executive proceedings. *All nations have found it necessary, that for the advantageous conduct of their affairs, some of these proceedings, at least, should remain known to their executive functionary only.* He, of course, from the nature of the case, must be the sole judge of which of them the public interests will permit publication.[2]

Historically, apart from and prior to the Constitution, the privilege against disclosure to the public, the press, or to other co-equal branches of the Government arises from the undisputed principle that not all public business can be transacted completely in the open, that public officials are entitled to the private advice of their subordinates and to confer among themselves freely and frankly, without fear of disclosure, otherwise the advice received and the exchange of views may not be as frank and honest as the public good requires.

> No doubt all of us at times have wished that we might have been able to sit in and listen to the deliberation of judges in conference, to an executive session of a Congressional committee or to a Cabinet meeting in order to find out the basis for a particular action or decision. However, Government could not function if it was permissible to go behind judicial, legislative or executive action and to demand a full accounting from all subordinates who may have been called upon to make a recommendation in the matter. Such a process would be self-defeating. It is the President, not the White House staff, the heads of departments and agencies, not their subordinates, the judges, not their law clerks, and members of Congress, not their executive assistants, who are accountable to the people for official public actions within their jurisdiction. Thus, whether the advice they receive and act on is good or bad there can be no shifting of ultimate responsibility.[3]

[2.] *Id.* at 57 (emphasis supplied). It is significant that President Jefferson had twice earlier in writing Hay, on 2 June and 12 June, cited the Constitutional separation of powers as the ground for his privilege. *Id.* at 53, 55.

[3.] Rogers, The Right to Know Government Business From the Viewpoint of the Government Official, 40 Marq.L.Rev. 83, 89 (1956). *See generally* Bishop, The

The Framers of the Constitution itself understood this principle very well. One of the first acts of the Constitutional Convention, 29 May 1787, was to resolve "that nothing spoken in the House be printed, or otherwise published, or communicated without leave."[4] In that historic summer in Philadelphia the Framers produced "the most wonderful work ever struck off at a given time by the brain and purpose of man."[5] But at the conclusion of their historic labors they thought it wise to preserve the confidentiality of exactly how they had done it. On 17 September 1787, as one of their final acts, they directed that all their records on the Convention be turned over to George Washington, not only their presiding officer but one whose complete discretion and probity had long been established.[6] As late as 1831, forty-four years after the Convention, Madison thought it was not yet appropriate for his *Notes* to be published.[7] He thought "no Constitution would ever have been adopted by the Convention if the debates had been public."[8]

2. *Litigation in Which the Government is a Party*

Passing from the Constitutional Convention of 1787 to the most recent Supreme Court case on this point in 1973, Environmental Protection Agency v. Mink,[9] the Court quoted with approval the earlier statement of Mr. Justice Reed, "There is a public policy involved in this claim of privilege for this advisory opinion—the policy of open, frank discussion between subordinate and chief concerning administrative

Executive's Right of Privacy: An Unresolved Constitutional Question, 66 Yale L.J. 477 (1957); Kramer and Marcuse, Executive Privilege—A Study of the Period 1953-1960, 29 Geo.Wash.L.Rev. 623 (1961); Hardin, Executive Privilege in the Federal Courts, 71 Yale L.J. 879 (1962).

[4.] 1 Farrand, Records of the Federal Convention of 1787, at 15 (rev.ed.1966) [hereinafter Farrand].

[5.] Gladstone, Kin Beyond the Sea (in the North American Review, September 1878).

[6.] 2 Farrand 648.

[7.] 3 Farrand 497. Although by resolution of Congress in 1818 (3 Stat. 475) the Journal of the Convention, the bare record of motions and votes, but not the speeches of the delegates, was made public, it was not until 1840, fours years after Madison's death, that his *Notes* of the Convention were made public. 1 Farrand XV.

[8.] 3 Farrand 479.

[9.] 410 U.S. 73, 93 S.Ct. 827, 35 L.Ed.2d 119.

action. . . ."[10] Mr. Justice Reed also pointed out that discussions of this kind are regarded as privileged and are "granted by *custom or statute* for the benefit of the public, not of executives who may happen to then hold office."[11] Observe that Mr. Justice Reed referred to the privilege as being "granted by custom or statute," and not derived from a Constitutional source. This is accurate when we are dealing with this age-old, common sense-common law privilege, which has been codified in statutes from time to time, the latest being the Freedom of Information Act.[12]

Judge Robinson of this court, when sitting as a District Judge, discussed the source of the Executive Branch privilege in these terms, "This privilege, as do all evidentiary privileges, effects an adjustment between important but competing interests . . . in striking the balance in favor of nondisclosure of intragovernmental advisory and deliverative communications. . . ."[13]

United States v. Reynolds[14] illustrates the application of this common sense, common law privilege to a situation in which the sought evidence contained military secrets. It was stated, and has been often quoted, that "[j]udicial control over the evidence in a case cannot be abdicated to the caprice of executive officers."[15] This language may lead to confusion if it is not recognized that in *Reynolds* the Supreme Court dealt only with this long established (custom or statute, according to Mr. Justice Reed) privilege of confidentiality in government in the format of a Tort Claim Act suit against the Government. It specifically did not decide any Constitutional claim of Executive discretion based on separation of powers.[16] Though the Court contrived a "balancing" or "necessity" formula, the Court held that "even the most compelling necessity cannot overcome the claim of privilege if the court is ultimately satisfied that military secrets

---

10. *Id.* at 87, 93 S.Ct. at 836. Mr. Justice Reed was sitting by designation in the Court of Claims in Kaiser Aluminum and Chemical Corp. v. United States, 157 F.Supp. 939, 946, 141 Ct.Cl. 38 (1958).

11. 157 F.Supp. at 944 (emphasis added).

12. 5 U.S.C. § 552 (1970).

13. Carl Zeiss Stiftung v. V. E. B. Carl Zeiss, Jena, 40 F.R.D. 318, 324-325 (D.C.D.C.1966), aff'd on the opinion below, 128 U.S.App.D.C.10, 384 F.2d 979, cert. denied, 389 U.S. 952, 88 S.Ct.334, 19 L.Ed.2d 361 (1967).

14. 345 U.S. 1, 73 S.Ct. 528, 97 L.Ed. 727 (1953).

15. *Id.* at 9-10, 73 S.Ct. at 533.

16. *Id.* at 9, 73 S.Ct. 528.

are at stake."[17] It further held that military secrets *were* at stake, and even *in camera* inspection would not be permitted.

Reynolds, like innumerable other cases in which a court has pronounced that it is up to the Judiciary to decide the existence and applicability of a privilege, represents civil litigation, in which either the United States or some Government agency *as a party* is opposed to some private individual or corporation. Cases under the Jencks Act[18] are examples illustrating the same situation in the criminal field. In *none* of these cases has the Government ever been *required to disclose* the matter which it desired to retain confidential. Whether the action is civil or criminal, the Government always has had the option of disclosure or dismissing the action and retaining the confidentiality of the material.

More relevant to the immediate point under discussion, in these cases the courts did engage in a *balancing* of conflicting public interests, *i. e.*, the public interest in seeing justice done between litigants in the court, and the public interest in seeing Governmental matters of the highest importance kept confidential. Observe that in this typical litigation situation, in which the court balanced conflicting public interests, the ancient common sense-common law Government administrative privilege of confidentiality is all that is ever involved. There is no question of the principle of separation of powers derived from our Constitution, as the Supreme Court specifically said in *Reynolds*.

3. *Individual Inquiry of a Governmental Official or Agency*

Another example of the same ancient governmental privilege of confidentiality is involved when a private individual or corporation requests information from a Government official or agency, and such is denied. For many years the Government bureaucracy engaged in a self-protective exercise of claiming "Executive privilege," sometimes based on ordinary "housekeeping" statues,[19] sometimes invoking the Constitutional

[17.] *Id.* at 11, 73 S.Ct. at 533. See Hardin, *supra* note 3, at 892-895, for a well-reasoned critique of the rationale of *Reynolds*.

[18] The Jencks Act is codified at 18 U.S.C. § 3500(d) (1970).

[19] Among those commonly referred to as "housekeeping statutes" are Rev. Stat. 161 (1878), now codified at 5 U.S.C. § 301 (1970), revised in 1958, and the Administrative Procedure Act, 60 Stat. 237 (1946) (now codified in scattered sections of 5 U.S.C.), which was revised by the addition of the Freedom of Information Act, 5 U.S.C. § 552 (1970). Revisions of both statutes were made to prevent citation as authority for withholding information from Congress and the public.

principle of separation of powers, although what that could have to do with rejection of a request when ordinary members of the public, not another branch of the Government, were seeking information, was never made clear. In order to assure the American public the necessary access to Governmental information, and to prohibit the abuse of so-called "Executive privilege," the Congress finally passed the Freedom of Information Act.[20]

In so doing, the *Congress itself did the balancing in advance* between the competing public interests represented by the right of the people to know how their Government conducts its business, and the recognized necessity of keeping certain types of information strictly confidential. The Freedom of Information Act contains seven categories of documents or information which are exempt from disclosure. In other words, the Congress has judged that, if the material sought falls within one of these seven exemptions, the public interest in maintaining confidentiality outweighs the public interest in the right to know Governmental affairs. The first exemption deals with secrets of state or national security, the others represent categories perhaps of lesser importance, but all are kept confidential, once it is determined the material sought falls within one of the seven exempt categories.

If the member of the public does not accept the denial by the Governmental agency, he can go to court to seek the information. If litigation results, in the typical Freedom of Information Act case, the court properly does not balance the public interest represented on both sides; the court merely determines into which category, exempt or non-exempt from disclosure, the material sought belongs. Once, this is determined, then the Congress has already given the answer in the Freedom of Information Act itself. If the court determines the material falls outside one of the claimed exempt categories, then the private individual is granted access. There is no constitutionally derived privilege involved at all; the rights are purely statutory, a codification of many categories of information previously swept within the vague penumbra of "Executive privilege," and many known to the common law and to the jurisprudence of other nations in which separation of powers is unknown.[21]

---

[20] 5 U.S.C. § 552 (1970).

[21] Vaughn v. Rosen, – U.S. App. D.C. –, 484 F.2d 820 (1973); Cuneo v. Schlesinger, – U.S. App. D.C. –, 484 F.2d 1086 (1973); Soucie v. David, 145 U.S. App. D.C. 144, 448 F.2d 1067 (1971).

4. *The First Amendment*

I am aware of, and impressed by, the strong argument which can be made that the Executive (as well as the Congressional and Judicial) right to privacy is likewise found in the First Amendment, but I resist going into it at length here. Certainly the Chief Executive's right to be fully, frankly, and confidentially informed is equal to that of any other citizen in the land; his need is undeniably greater. To breach his privacy would unquestionably have a "chilling effect" on those who otherwise would counsel and confide in the President with complete candor and honesty.[22]

Legal support for the relevance of the First Amendment here is found in such decisions as Eastern Railroad Presidents Conference v. Noerr Motor Freight, Inc.,[23] and NAACP v. Alabama:[24] In *Noerr* the Supreme Court relied at least in part on the First Amendment to legitimatize joint efforts by businessmen to influence legislative or executive action, even if designed to injure their competitors.

Rather than consider the First Amendment as a *separate* ground for sustaining the Executive's right to privacy, I find it easier to say that the First Amendment in 1789 provided a Constitutional underpinning for the long recognized customary Governmental privilege of privacy. Such a First Amendment right in the Executive would apply, as does the ancient common sense-common law privilege now partly codified in statute, in the Executive's relations with the public and the press, as well as other branches of the Government.

5. *The Chief Executive*

In theory, if only the ancient customary Governmental confidentiality privilege is involved, whether the Chief Executive should disclose the information should be decided no differently from the case of any other Government official. Even though the

---

[22] "There are serious weaknesses in the assumption, popular among liberals who happen at the moment not to be thinking about Senator McCarthy, that public policy ought to draw a sharp distinction between 'military and diplomatic secrets' on the one hand and all other types of official information on the other, giving Congress free access to the latter. In the first place, the line is by no means easy to draw, even when the best of faith is used . . . . More fundamentally, however, the executive's interest in the privacy of certain other types of information is not less than its interest in preserving its military and diplomatic secrets. One obvious example is the data, derogatory or otherwise, in the security files of individuals. Another, perhaps still more important, is the record of deliberations incidental to the making of policy decisions." Bishop, *supra* note 3, at 488.

[23] 365 U.S. 127, 81 S.Ct. 523, 5 L.Ed.2d 464 (1961).

[24] 357 U.S. 449, 78 S.Ct. 1163, 2 L.Ed.2d 1488 (1958).

President represents the repository of information of the highest confidentiality, it would be permissible for the courts to talk in terms of balancing the public interest of those seeking disclosure versus the public interest of the President in retaining confidentiality, while recognizing that any President's assertion of the confidential nature of documents or communications must be accorded the greatest deference by the courts.

As a practical matter, as history shows, the theory breaks down. Not only is the grist of the Presidential mill of a higher quality than that processed by the average bureaucrat, but the institutions or individuals daring to confront the Chief Executive directly have been of a character and power to invoke immediately the other source of the Chief Executive's privilege, the Constitutional doctrine of separation of powers. In the only instances in history of which I am aware, in which demand for documents was made directly upon the President, the demand came from one of the other two co-equal Branches, the Congress or the Judiciary. Beginning with Washington's administration, the Congress has made repeated demands on the Chief Executive for documents, demands which have never been adjudicated by any court employing a balancing test of the public interest involved. The trial of Aaron Burr is the only instance[25] in which demand by subpoena on the President himself was ordered by a court, and this by the Chief Justice himself at the behest of a former Vice President of the United States, then on trial for his life on a charge of treason. In other words, the men and issues were large.

We have read and heard eloquent language on the unique nature of the American presidency from both counsel, who agree as to overriding importance of "preserving the integrity of the Executive Office of the President."[26] We are cautioned that "[n]o substitute offers itself for the American presidency, either domestically or in the world. It will be easier to tear down than to build back."[27] This argument in itself may be good and sufficient reason to sustain the President's assertion of privilege in the circumstances of this case, yet this appears to necessitate a Constitutional value judgment not specifically made in the Constitution itself. Further, analytically it may be that such

[25] We were informed by counsel at oral argument that in the court-martial of Dr. William Burton a subpoena was issued to President Monroe for the President's testimony. It was complied with by a deposition. No documents were involved. *See Per Curiam, supra* at 710 n. 42.

[26] Special Prosecutor's Supplemental Brief at 22.

[27] President's Reply Brief at 37, *quoting from* Professor Charles Black's letter to the *Washington Post,* 12 September 1973.

argument on the unique nature and supreme importance of the presidency in our system is but the long established Governmental privilege of confidentiality raised to the Nth power.

In summary of the common sense-common law privilege of Governmental confidentiality, codified in statute as in the Freedom of Information Act, the *courts do decide* whether the privilege exists and the *courts do decide* as to its scope and applicability to a given state of facts. In so doing, the *courts do balance* one public interest versus another. If custom, common law, and statute were the only sources of the Chief Executive's privilege, he, too, might find his view of the public interest overriden by the "balancing" of competing public interest done by a court. But the President has another source of power.

B. *Separation of Powers—the Tripartite Privilege*

1. *Judicial versus Executive*

We now turn to the second source of the Executive Branch privilege, the principle of separation of powers in our Constitution. Congressional legislation, *e. g.*, the Freedom of Information Act, merely redefined the common sense-common law privilege of confidentiality in the conduct of Government business. It is not unreasonable that the Congress should define how much of Governmental business can safely be made public. But none of this legislation, not even the Freedom of Information Act, touches the Constitutional basis of Executive Branch privilege derived from the principle of separation of powers—nor could it.

My colleagues in the *Per Curiam* reject separation of powers, and concentrate entirely on the common sense-common law, statutorily defined source of the privilege, which is part of the story; but this part, as is made clear in the *Per Curiam* opinion and in the Briefs of the Special Prosecutor, is subject to balancing, weighing, showing of need, and in general a comparative evaluation of conflicting "public interests" *by the courts.*

Not so the Executive Branch privilege which arises from the principle of the separation of powers among the Legislative, Executive, and Judicial Branches of our Government. We must recognize that this Constitutional privilege, if derived from the separation of powers, as it is, is *tripartite.* Chief Justice Taft was keenly aware of this when he wrote: "Montesquieu's view that the maintenance of independence as between the legislative, the executive and the judicial branches, was a security for the people had [the Framers'] full approval . . . . From this division on principle, the reasonable construction of the Constitution must be that the branches should be kept separate in all cases in which they were not expressly blended, and the Constitution should be expounded to blend them no more than it affirmatively requires. Madison, 1 Annals of Congress, 497. This rule of construction has been confirmed by this Court . . . . "28

Observe that it is the Judicial Branch, according to District Judge Sirica's opinion, to whom the tapes are to be handed over for examination *in camera.* Likewise, it is the grand jury to whom the Special Prosecutor wishes to present the tapes with or without the intervention of the District Judge. The grand jury, as is shown by an analysis developed later, is nothing but an appendage of the Judicial Branch, and has always been recognized as such. The Supreme Court unanimously expressed the principle applicable to this situation:

> The fundamental necessity of maintaining each of the three general departments of government entirely free from the control or coercive influence, direct or indirect, of either of the others, has often been stressed and is hardly open to serious question. So much is implied in the very fact of the separation of powers of these departments by the Constitution; and in the rule which recognizes their essential coequality. The sound application of a principle that makes one master in his own house precludes him from imposing his control in the house of another who is master there.[29]

If the Chief Executive can be "coerced" by the Judicial Branch into furnishing records hitherto throughout our history resting within the exclusive control of the Executive, then the Chief Executive is no longer "master in his own house."

This is not a matter of "coercing" the Executive to "obey the law"; there has never before in 184 years been any such law that the Executive could be compelled by the Judiciary to surrender Executive records of the Judiciary.This is an assertion of privilege by the Executive, not a refusal to obey a court's interpretation of the law. This the Executive has *always* done, even when the Executive's interpretation of the law was different from the

[28] Myers v. United States, 272 U.S. 52, 116, 47 S.Ct.21, 25, 71 L.Ed. 160 (1926).

[29] Humphrey's Executor v. United States, 295 U.S. 602, 629-630, 55 S.Ct. 869, 874, 79 L.Ed. 1611 (1935).

Court's, *e. g.*, Youngstown Sheet & Tube Co. v. Sawyer.[30] But also, the Executive has *always* been the one who decided whether the Executive Branch privilege of confidentiality of its records should be asserted, and to what extent, when confronted with demand of another Branch for such records.

In the case at bar we have an assertion of privilege by the Executive Branch in response to a demand by the Judicial Branch for the records of the Executive Branch. This is the first time that this precise situation has occurred since the famous trials of Aaron Burr,[31] but whereas this confrontation between the Judicial Branch and the Executive Branch is almost unique, the tripartite privilege has been asserted innumerable times in various alignments of conflict among the three Branches.

2. *Legislative versus Executive*

The most highly publicized conflicts have been, of course, the demands by Congress on the Executive for Executive papers and information. The first two examples occurred in Washington's administration, the call for the papers relative to General St. Clair's military expedition and later the Jay Treaty.[32] The historical evidence shows that Washington rejected the demands of Congress squarely on the ground of separation of powers. Numerous other examples occurred. Never in 184 years, until Senator Ervin's committee filed the pending action in Judge Sirica's court for these same Watergate tapes, has the Congress desired to take the Constitutional separation of powers issue to a court for adjudication. The reasons are obvious: (1) if the Constitutional principle of separation of powers was valid and effective as a barrier, Congress would lose; (2) acutely aware of its own assertions of privilege, even if Congress won and established that the separation of powers was no barrier to a demand of one Branch for the papers of another, on a reciprocal basis Congress would have to abandon its equally time-honored practice of refusing the demands of the Judicial Branch for its papers; and (3) submitting a dispute between two co-equal Branches to the third Branch would recognize that the Judiciary is "more equal" than the other two.

---

[30] 343 U.S. 579, 72 S.Ct. 863, 96 L.Ed. 1153 (1952).

[31] *See* note 25 *supra.* "There seems to be no case which presents the question of whether a court would attempt to compel actual production of information in the possession of the executive." Bishop, *supra* note 3, at 482 n. 19.

[32] Discussed in detail in next accompanying notes 75-77 *infra.*

To see the relevance of the Congressional demands on the Executive to the Judicial subpoena on the Executive in the case at bar, it is helpful to note that a Legislative and Judicial subpoena have precisely the same coercive effect on the recipient, and both Congress and the courts have independent power to punish for contempt. Under 2 U.S.C. § 190b(a) standing committees of Congress and their subcommittees are authorized "to require by subpoena or otherwise the attendance of such witnesses and the production of such correspondence, books, papers, and documents . . . as they deem advisable."[33]

Wilful noncompliance with a Congressional subpoena constitutes contempt of Congress, a misdemeanor.[34] In such instances, the Speaker of the House or President of the Senate certifies a statement of the facts to the appropriate United States Attorney, whose duty is to bring the matter before a grand jury.[35] However, these provisions do not impair Congress' power to punish for contempt by its own action.[36] In Jurney v. MacCracken the Supreme Court noted "[t]he power to punish a private citizen for a past and completed act [of contempt] was exerted by Congress as early as 1795 [footnote omitted]; and since then it has been exercised on several occasions."[37] Here the Court was concerned "with vindication of the established and essential privilege of requiring the production of evidence. For this purpose, the power to punish for a past contempt is an appropriate means."[38]

[33] The effect of a Congressional subpoena is described in Watkins v. United States, 354 U.S. 178, 77 S.Ct. 1173, 1 L.Ed.2d 1273 (1957):
It is unquestionably the duty of all citizens to cooperate with the Congress in its efforts to obtain the facts needed for intelligent legislative action. It is their unremitting obligation to respond to subpoenas, to respect the dignity of the Congress and its committees and to testify fully with respect to matters within the province of proper investigation. This, of course, assumes that the constitutional rights of witnesses will be respected by the Congress as they are in a court of justice. 354 U.S. at 187-188, 77 S.Ct. at 1179.
The primary limitation on the Congressional subpoena power is that its exercise must relate to a valid legislative function. Usually, Congressional committees issue subpoenas pursuant to some investigation. The limits on Congress' investigative powers were described by this court in Shelton v. United States, 131 U.S.App.D.C. 315, 319-320, 404 F.2d 1292, 1296-1297 (1968).

[34] 2 U.S.C. § 192 (1970).

[35] 2 U.S.C. § 194 (1970).

[36] Jurney v. MacCracken, 294 U.S. 125, 151, 55 S.Ct. 375, 79 L.Ed. 802 (1935).

[37] Id. at 148, 55 S.Ct. at 378. For a discussion of Congress' contempt power, see id. at 147-150, 55 S.Ct. 375. See also Emspak v. United States, 91 U.S.App.D.C. 378, 381, 203 F.2d 54, 57 (1953).

[38] Jurney v. MacCracken, 294 U.S. at 149-150, 55 S.Ct. at 379.

Years ago a distinguished scholar attempted to visualize how an authoritative determination of the Executive's assertedly *Constitutional* right to privacy might be brought about. After pointing out that while "the President and the heads of executive departments have repeatedly, and sometimes brusquely, rejected such congressional demands," and Congress had never sought the aid of the Attorney General or the courts, nor exercised its "power to punish contempts without invoking the aid of the executive and the judiciary," Professor Joseph Bishop concluded:

> Such an episode . . . would furnish the courts an admirable occasion to decide the precise question of the constitutional authority of the executive to withhold the desired data. But it is not likely to arise . . . .
>
> It is, however, conceivable that the Supreme Court may yet be called upon to face *the closely related and logically indistinguishable question of the executive's power to reject a judicial subpoena.* If, in litigation to which the government is not a party, a court becomes convinced that a document in the possession of the government is relevant, and if it somehow manages to satisfy itself that that information is unprivileged, . . . the courts may yet have to decide the ultimate reach of the executive's discretion to grant or withhold information.[39]

Professor Bishop's hypothetical of 1957 is not precisely with us, but almost. Instead of "litigation to which the government is not a party," we have "litigation in which the government is on both sides" (the President and the Special Prosecutor), which gives us the same Constitutional confrontation and question foreseen by Professor Bishop, *i. e.*, "the executive's power to reject a judicial subpoena."

The critical points to be understood from the hypothetical situation, which Professor Bishop foresaw would pose the ultimate Constitutional issue, are these:

(1) The Congressional demand for Executive papers (tapes) is "logically indistinguishable" from the demand on the Executive by Judicial subpoena, *i. e.*, both test the Constitutional separation of powers basis of Executive privilege; and

(2) Both the Congressional and the Judicial demands on the Executive are to be distinguished from the false confrontation found in innumerable examples of litigation (*e. g.*, *Reynolds*) in which the Government (Executive) is a party, because the

---

[39] Bishop, *supra* note 3, at 484-85 (emphasis supplied).

Executive always has an out (abandon the litigation), and thus is never confronted with a true unavoidable demand for the papers or information.

3. *Judicial versus Legislative*

Turning to the other type of repeated conflict, the Legislative Branch has never acceded to a demand of the Judicial Branch for papers in any case without an assertion and preservation of Congressional privilege. The latest example of Congressional refusal to furnish to a court papers relevant to a criminal prosecution was in United States v. Brewster.[40] There the Senate, in accord with ancient and invariable precedent, on 4 October 1972 resolved:

> Whereas in the case of the United States of America against Daniel B. Brewster, et al. (criminal action numbered 1872-69), pending in the United States District Court for the District of Columbia, a subpena ad testificandum and duces tecum was issued by such court addressed to David Minton, staff director and counsel of the Committee . . . .
>
> *Resolved*, That by the privileges of the Senate of the United States *no evidence in the possession and under the control of the Senate* of the United States *can*, by the mandate of process of ordinary courts of justice, *be taken* from such possession or control *but by its permission;* be it further
>
> * * * * * * *
>
> *Resolved*, That David Minton . . . *be authorized to appear* at the time and place and before the court named in such subpena, *but shall not take with him any papers*, documents, or evidence on file in his office, under his control, or in his possession as staff director and counsel . . .[41]

The comparison with the case at bar is striking. Here we have a Judicial subpoena duces tecum directed to the Executive for documents and tapes. The President has said his individual aides who were present at the times the tapes were recorded may testify as to all matters relevant to any criminality which is the subject of the Watergate grand jury inquiry, but may not furnish the tapes.[42] In *Brewster* we had a Judicial subpoena duces tecum directed to the Senate for documents. The Senate permitted the individual aide to testify personally (as did the President) but

---

[40] 408 U.S. 501, 92 S.Ct. 2531, 33 L.Ed.2d 507 (1972).

[41] 118 Cong.Rec. S.16,766, 92nd Cong., 2d Sess. (emphasis supplied).

[42] The President has also permitted two subpoenaed documents to be furnished.

forbade him to produce any of the documents (as did the President with regard to the tapes). The responses of the President and the Senate to the Judicial subpoenas are precisely equal, and equally justified (or unjustified) on the same Constitutional ground of separation of powers.

One further point of comparison: with reference to the Judicial subpoena issued for the Senate papers in the criminal prosecution of Senator Brewster, *Who Decided* how much, if any, of the subpoenaed papers would be produced? The United States court? Not in *Brewster*, and not in any case for 184 years. The Senate, a Branch of the Government co-equal under our Constitution, decided what would be furnished the court and what retained as confidential, precisely as has the Chief Executive in the case at bar.

To cite but two of the best known recent examples, similar assertions of Legislative privilege took place with reference to criminal prosecution in United States v. Calley[43] and United States v. Hoffa.[44] Other similar precedents in both Houses are ancient, numerous, and established beyond question in the Legislative Branch.[45]

---

[43] CM 426402, 1 Military L. Rep. 2077 (ACMR, 16 Feb. 1973); 116 Cong.Rec. 37,652 (17 Nov. 1970).

[44] 205 F.Supp. 710 (S.D.Fla.), cert. denied sub nom. Hoffa v. Lieb, 371 U.S. 892, 83 S. Ct. 188, 9 L.Ed.2d 125 (1962); 108 Cong. Rec. 3626, 3627 (1962).

[45] *See* 3 Hinds' Precedents of the House of Representatives § 2661, 7 March 1876; § 2662, 21 March 1876; § 2663, 22 April 1879; § 2664, 9 February 1886 (1907); Soucie v. David, 145 U.S.App.D.C. 144, 159 n. 4, 448 F.2d 1067, 1082 n. 4 (1971) (Wilkey, J., concurring).

My colleagues rely upon Gravel v. United States, 408 U.S. 606, 92 S.Ct. 2614, 33 L.Ed.2d 583 (1972), for the assertion that "[w]henever a privilege is asserted, even one expressed in the Constitution, such as the Speech and Debate privilege, it is the courts that determine the validity of the assertion and the scope of the privilege." (Per Curiam, *supra* at 714.) *Gravel* was a far different question. First, there was never any issue as to Who Decides the scope of the privilege; Senator Gravel himself invoked the jurisdiction of the courts.

Second, the issue to be determined was "whether the activities concerning which questioning or prosecution is sought are: 'integral part[s] of the deliberative and communicative processes by which Members participate in committee, and House proceedings . . . ' " *(Per Curiam, supra* at 715 n. 70), *i.e.*, the nature of the actions involved. This is reminiscent of the factual categorizing to be done in Environmental Protection Agency v. Mink, 410 U.S. 73, 93 S.Ct. 827, 35 L.Ed.2d 119 (1973), Vaughn v. Rosen, – U.S.App.D.C. –, 484 F.2d 820 (1973), Cuneo v. Schlesinger, – U.S.App.D.C. –, 484 F.2d 1086 (1973), all discussed in text accompanying notes 167-175 *infra*. Once the nature of the action or category of information is determined, the applicable rule of law is clear. The vital question here is Who Decides this.

Thirdly, even if *Gravel* had involved questions of a demand for documents similar to the case at bar, and the Senator himself had not invoked the aid of the courts, yet the basic distinction of *Gravel* from the case at bar may be that, even though Senator Gravel was protected by the specific Constitutional privilege of the Speech and Debate

The principle of separation of powers, with a resulting judicial privilege, works reciprocally when the demand is made by the Congress instead of to the Congress. In 1953 Mr. Justice Tom Clark refused to respond to a subpoena to appear before the House Un-American Activities Committee, on the ground that the "complete independence of the Judiciary is necessary to the proper administration of justice."[46]

Senator Stennis once summed up the Congressional privilege and its origin very well:

> We now come face to face and are in direct conflict with the established doctrine of separation of powers . . . . I know of no case where the court has ever made the Senate or the House surrender records from its files, or where the Executive has made the Legislative Branch surrender records from its files—and I do not think either one of them could. So the rule works three ways. Each is *supreme* within its field, and each is *responsible* within its field.[47]

4. Who Decides?

I thus reach the conclusion, differing from the majority of my colleagues, that the privilege asserted by the President here derives *both* from the Constitutional principle of separation of powers and from the common sense-common law, statutory privilege of confidentiality of Governmental decision-making, whatever the Branch. The latter may be subject to weighing and balancing of conflicting public interests, as many of the cases have done, but never in a case involving the President as a party. But where the privilege of the Chief Executive is derived from the *Constitutional principle* of separation of powers, it is no more subject to weighing and balancing than any other Constitutional privilege can be weighed and balanced by extraneous third parties.

Every President, beginning with Washington and Jefferson, has asserted that the privilege and the scope and applicability are for him alone to decide. This is precisely what Congress does when it either grants or withholds documents in response to the request of a court for evidence in a criminal case. This is what no doubt

Clause applicable only to the Congress, yet Gravel is only a *single* member, *not the whole independent Branch of Government,* as is the President. If we were dealing with a grand jury demand for the records of the *Senate* as a *whole* resisted by the Senate as a whole, far different considerations would come into play.

[46] New York Times, 14 November 1953, p. 9.

[47] Committee on Armed Services, U.S. Senate Military Cold War Escalation and Speech Review Policies, 87th Cong., 2d Sess. 512 (1962) (emphasis supplied).

124

this court would do if confronted with a demand by a Congressional committee for any of our internal documents. We would weigh and decide and assert the privilege as *we* saw it, not as a Congressional committee would see it. *We* would do so on the Constitutional ground of separation of powers. And this is what the President has done here.

We all know that when a Constitutional privilege under the Fifth Amendment is asserted by the humblest individual, the court does not weigh and balance the public interest in having the individual's testimony. All the court can do is make a preliminary inquiry as to prima facie justification for the assertion of the privilege. It is up to the individual to decide whether he will assert the privilege. Other privileges, such as husband-wife, lawyer-client, priest-penitent, when recognized by the law, come into being on a showing that the relationship exists. There is no weighing of the public interest in having the testimony compared to the public interest in the particular individual maintaining his privileged communication or document. Nor does the court invite the holder of the privilege to disclose the privileged information *in camera* so that the court may weigh the "conflicting public interests" involved in disclosure or confidentiality. Even to hint at such a procedure in regard to these privileges is to demonstrate the inherent incongruity of positing the existence of the privilege and yet asserting that someone other than the holder of the privilege will decide by a balancing of interests test whether it can be exercised.

Nor is logical analysis advanced by a parade of examples in which the public interest in disclosure is heavily exaggerated. Of course one can imagine innumerable instances in which a court, Congress, or the Executive, *ought* to disclose the documents in the public interest, and probably *would*. The more exaggerated the example, the more certain it is that a court would decide to disclose to the Attorney General or a Congressional committee, or the Executive would decide to disclose to a court or Congressional committee, internal documents which otherwise would be kept confidential. But the more certain it is that the holder of the documents—the holder of the privilege—will decide to disclose does not alter the fact that *it is the holder of the Constitutional privilege Who Decides.*

In conclusion, I find the suggested procedure by the *Per Curiam (supra* at 720-721) a very logical exercise in determining what evidence should be made available. But going back to the fundamental question of *Who Decides*, this procedure is one which might be gone through by the President, but not by the

Judicial Branch. If the Constitutional privilege has been asserted, then no court has the right to determine what the President will or will not produce.

The *Per Curiam* completely ignores the Constitutional principle of separation of powers as the source of the President's privilege asserted here. The *Per Curiam* treats the privilege as being *solely* derived from the age-old common sense-common law recognition that Government business cannot be conducted without *some degree* of confidentiality, and therefore the Judiciary should "weigh" and "balance" the degree of confidentiality permitted in light of "conflicting public interests" in that confidentiality compared to disclosure, just as if the Executive were engaged in litigation with another party and could be compelled to disclose on pain of losing the litigation if the court's view of the public interest were not accepted by the Executive. But this is no such case, and everything else in the *Per Curiam* opinion logically hinges on the validity of this analysis. But neither we nor any other court can so easily discard the Constitution, including the principle of separation of powers, and including the tripartite privilege universally derived from that principle of separation of powers.

II. DEVELOPMENT OF THE TRIPARTITE PRIVILEGE WITH REFERENCE TO EXECUTIVE DOCUMENTS

A. *The Legislative Decision of 1789*

In 1789 the First Congress faced the issue of the proper relationship between the Executive and the Legislature. Specifically, the Congress considered the questions of who should have custody of Executive papers and who should have power of removal of Executive officers subordinate to the President. The First Congress' deliberation on these matters is especially significant because many members of the Congress had also actively participated in the drafting of the Constitution.[48]

The background for the Legislative decision of 1789 lay in the earlier decision of the Continental Congress to establish a Department of Foreign Affairs. The Continental Congress passed a resolution providing that the Foreign Affairs department would be headed by an officer appointed by the Congress, who would hold office "during the pleasure of Congress."[49] The resolution

---

[48] *See generally* Myers v. United States, 272 U.S. 52, 111-136, 47 S.Ct. 21, 71 L.Ed. 160 (1926); Wolkinson, Demands of Congressional Committees for Executive Papers (Part III), 10 Fed.Bar.J. 319, 328-30 (1949).

[49] The resolution of the Continental Congress is printed at 1 Stat. 28-29 (1789).

further required that the officer take custody of the books, records, and papers relating to his department, *and that any member of Congress should have access to any of these papers.*[50] Thus, the Department of Foreign Affairs as envisioned by the Continental Congress was under the control of the Congress.[51]

After the enactment of the Constitution, the First Congress considered the proper position of the Department of Foreign Affairs and its Secretary. The Act finally passed by the Congress changed the status of the Secretary and his department significantly. The Act specifically made the department an Executive department, and the Secretary subject to the direction of the President.[52] The Secretary was to take charge and custody of all papers relating to the department, except that "whenever the [Secretary] shall be removed from office by the President of the United States, or in any other case of vacancy,"[53] the Chief Clerk, appointed by the Secretary, was to take custody. *Nothing* was said in the Act *concerning either the Congress' right to access to the papers, nor the Congress' right to determine removal* of the Secretary.

---

[50] The resolution provided that the books, records, and other papers of the United States, that relate to this department, be committed to his custody, to which, and all other papers of his office, any member of Congress shall have access: Provided, That no copy shall be taken of matters of a secret nature, without the special leave of Congress. *Id.* at 28.

[51] Other provisions of the resolution which indicate the relationship between the Congress and the Department include sections requiring the Secretary to "report on all cases expressly referred to him for that purpose by Congress, and on all others touching his department, in which he may conceive it necessary," requiring him to "answer to such inquiries respecting his department as may be put from the chair by order of Congress," etc. *Ibid.*

[52] Section 1 of the Act provides:
That there shall be an Executive department, to be denominated the Department of Foreign Affairs, and that there shall be a principal officer, to be called the Secretary for the Department of Foreign Affairs, who shall perform and execute such duties as shall from time to time be enjoined on or intrusted to him by the President of the United States, agreeable to the Constitution . . . respecting foreign affairs . . . ; and furthermore, that the said principal officer shall conduct the business of the said department in such manner as the President of the United States shall from time to time order or instruct.
Act of 27 July 1789, ch. 4, § 1, 1 Stat. 28.

[53] The full text of Section 2 is:
That there shall be in the said department, an inferior officer, to be appointed by the said principal officer, and to be employed therein as he shall deem proper, and to be called the chief Clerk in the Department of Foreign Affairs, and who, whenever the said principal officer shall be removed from office by the President of the United States, or in any other case of vacancy, shall during such vacancy have the charge and custody of all records, books and papers appertaining to the said department.
Act of 27 July 1789, ch. 4, § 2, 1 Stat. 28.

The omission of the provision granting the Continental Congress access to the papers of the department is a glaring omission with no illumination provided by the debate in the First Congress. The reports of the debates do not indicate that the question was even discussed.[54] This omission is explained only by the fact that the Department was to be an arm of the Executive, unlike the predecessor department which was an arm of the Continental Congress, an explanation which is not only inherently persuasive, but demonstrated by the rationale in the debate and action on the allied removal provision. The omission could not have been other than a conscious one, as many members of the First Congress had participated in the Continental Congress.[55]

On the other hand, however, there was strenuous controversy and debate in the First Congress over the question of removal of the Secretary. The first draft of the bill before the House, as proposed by James Madison, had provided specifically that the Secretary was to "be appointed by the President, by and with the advice and consent of the Senate; and to be removable from office by the President."[56] During more than a month's discussion,[57] the House considered various aspects of removal of the Secretary, including the question of how the removal power fit within the Constitutional division into three governmental branches.

Some members of the House feared that the original wording in the Madison bill suggested that the legislature was granting to the President the power of removal, and that this power might be taken from the President by a later Congress.[58] These men felt that the Constitution had already provided the President the power to remove his subordinates, and no statute was necessary. Consequently Mr. Benson of the House suggested an amendment to the bill to delete the clause "to be removable by the President" and to put that phrase in a position in the bill where it would not appear as a legislative grant but merely a statement of

[54] Wolkinson, *supra* note 48, at 329-30.

[55] *See* Wolkinson, *supra* note 48, at 330.

[56] 1 Annals of Congress 385 (1789).

[57] The discussion ran from 19 May 1789 to 24 June 1789. *See* 1 Annals 385-614.

[58] The Congress after the Civil War attempted to do just that with the Tenure of Office Act, Act of 2 March 1867, 14 Stat. 430, ch. 154, which was eventually held invalid "in so far as it attempted to prevent the President from removing executive officers who had been appointed by him by and with the advice and consent of the Senate." Myers v. United States, 272 U.S. 52, 176, 47 S.Ct. 21, 45, 71 L.Ed. 160 (1926).

legislative construction of the Constitution.[59]

After lengthy debate, Mr. Benson moved to insert the clause concerning removal in the description of the duties of the clerk, where it now appears. Madison, who had been persuaded by the wisdom of Benson's suggestions, seconded the motion, and it carried by a vote of 30 to 18.[60] Subsequently the House voted on the second part of Benson's motion, to delete the clause concerning removal which appeared in the first section of the bill. This, too, was supported by Madison, who felt that Congress did not have power to grant the removal power to the President.[61] The amendment passed, 31 to 19.[62] The full bill later passed in the House and was sent to the Senate.

Chief Justice Taft believed that James Madison's "arguments in support of the President's constitutional power of removal independently of Congressional provision, and without the consent of the Senate, were masterly, and he carried the House."[63] Among those voting with Madison in support of the final bill were Carroll, Clymer, Fitzsimons, and Gilman; of the opposite view were Gerry and Sherman; all had been in the Constitutional Convention two years before.[64]

Since the bill enacted at the same session establishing the Department of the Treasury contained somewhat different language, it is illuminating to see how that came about. The original bill contained a clause making it the duty of the Secretary "to digest and report plans for the improvement and management of the revenue . . . . "[65] This had been drafted by Hamilton, the Secretary-designate in the Washington administration, as a device to establish his liaison and influence with the Congressional branch. Hamilton's motives did not go long undetected. Significantly, the revulsion of and opposition in the House was based on the Constitutional principle of separation of powers. A motion was made to strike the offending words, on the ground "that to permit the secretary to go further than to prepare estimates would be a dangerous innovation on

---

[59] 1 Annals 525-527.

[60] *See* 1 Annals 601-603.

[61] *Id.* at 604.

[62] *Id.* at 608.

[63] Myers v. United States, 272 U.S. 52, 115, 47 S.Ct. 21, 25, 71 L.Ed. 160 (1926)).

[64] 1 Annals 614. *See* Myers v. United States, 272 U.S. 52, 114, 47 S.Ct. 21, 71 L. Ed. 160 (1926).

[65] 5 J. Marshall, The Life of George Washington 200 (1807).

the constitutional privilege of that house."[66] It was noted that "the authority contained in the bill to prepare and report plans would create an interference of the executive with the legislative powers, and would abridge the particular privilege of that house to originate all bills for raising a revenue."[67] Madison observed that "the words of the bill were precisely those used by the former [continental] congress on two occasions."[68]

This was not to be acceptable here, for the First Congress realized it was structuring a government in accordance with a new Constitutional principle, the separation of powers, and the members were resolved to be faithful to that hitherto untried principle. Finally, in this debate on the Treasury, an amendment was adopted. The word "prepare" was substituted for "report" in order that "[t]he secretary would then only report his plans if requested by the house."[69] Thus was the Constitutional principle of separation of powers scrupulously adhered to by the First Congress.

It is significant that the bill establishing the War Department[70] was on the Foreign Affairs Department model, not that of the Treasury. The same held true of other subsequently established departments. The Treasury statute remained unique in its specific reference to the Secretary's duty "to make report . . . as he may be required"; this is in part explainable perhaps by the House's Constitutional duty to originate revenue bills (although the statute refers to "either branch"), but certainly because the draft statute originated with Hamilton, who put in the clause for his own purposes, only to see it modified (but not eliminated) in a manner to reflect the House's preoccupation with the principle of separation of powers.

The Legislative decision of 1789, in establishing the Departments of Foreign Affairs (State), Treasury, and War, made by the First Congress, guided by the men who had drafted the Constitution only two years before, vividly demonstrates their understanding of separation of powers as established by the Constitution.[71]

---

[66] Ibid.

[67] Id. at 201.

[68] Id. at 204.

[69] Id. at 205.

[70] 1 Stat. 49 (1789). Brief debate occurred at 1 Annals 615.

[71] As William P. Rogers wrote when he was Attorney General, the Legislative decision of 1789 established the principle that the reasonable construction of the Constitution must be that the three branches of the Federal Government should be kept separate in all cases in which they were not expressly blended, and that no

B. *Congressional Demands for Executive Papers*

Throughout this nation's 184-year Constitutional history, Congress and the Executive have succeeded in avoiding any near-fatal confrontation over attempts by Congress to procure documents in the Executive's possession. In recognition of the delicate balance created by the doctrine of separation of powers, the two Branches have generally succeeded in fashioning a *modus vivendi* through mutual deference and cooperation. Thus, when a Congressional committee calls on an Executive official to produce documents or other needed material, "the call is usually qualified by the softening phrase 'if the public interest permits.' "[72] Similarly, as one commentator observed:

> It is obvious that in a large majority of cases it is greatly to the advantage of the executive to cooperate with Congress, and in a large majority of cases it does so. Congressional control over appropriations and legislation is an excellent guarantee that the executive will not lightly reject a congressional request for information, for it is well aware that such a rejection increases the chance of getting either no legislation or undesired legislation.[73]

In certain instances, however, the Chief Executive has asserted a privilege to withhold information from Congress, and such assertions have often been grounded on a Constitutional separation of powers rationale. When made, the Executive assertion of privilege has always prevailed.[74]

Historically, the first time Congress attempted to probe into documents under the Executive's custody was in March 1792, when the House of Representatives passed a resolution providing:

---

legislation should be enacted by the Congress which would tend to obscure the dividing lines between the three great branches or cast doubt upon the prerogatives properly belinging by the Constitution to any one.

[72] E. Corwin, The President: Office and Powers, 1787-1957, at 113 (4th rev. ed. 1957). For examples of Congressional recognition of Executive privilege see Kramer & Marcuse, *supra* note 3, at 900-02.

[73] Bishop, *supra* note 3, at 486.

[74] It has prevailed without any attempt by Congress to secure adjudication of its claim versus the Executive. Nothing so illustrates the extent to which heat may have replaced light in the appraisal of this entire Watergate affair than the fact that the United States Senate has reversed the strategy of 184 years, and put the question of its right to obtain papers from the Executive into the hands of the Judiciary to determine.

Resolved, That a committee be appointed to inquire into the causes of the failure of the late expedition under Major General St. Clair; and that the said committee be empowered to call for such persons, papers and records, as may be necessary to assist their inquiries.[75]

When the committee asked President Washington for the papers relevant to General St. Clair's campaign, the President called a meeting of his Cabinet. Washington reasoned that since the committee's request was the first of its kind, his response would set a precedent and therefore should be well considered. Secretary of State Jefferson, Treasury Secretary Hamilton, Secretary of War Knox, and Attorney General Randolph attended the meeting. The unanimous conclusion reached by Washington and his Cabinet was, as described by Jefferson:

First, that the House was an inquest, and therefore might institute inquiries. Second, that it might call for papers generally. Third, that the Executive ought to communicate such papers as the public good would permit, and ought to refuse those, the disclosure of which would injure the public: consequently were to *exercise a discretion*. Fourth, that neither the committee nor House had a right to call on the Head of a Department, who and whose papers were under the President alone, but that the committee should instruct their chairman to move the House to address the President.[76]

The Washington administration thus expressed the view that it is in the *President's* discretion to determine whether disclosure of Executive documents would be consistent with the public interest.

In 1796 the House made its second attempt to procure documents from the Washington administration when it passed a resolution asking the President to give the House a copy of papers and correspondence pertaining to the negotiation of the Jay Treaty with Great Britain. The House contended that it

Reciprocally, of course, this means that the Executive at some future date would be able to put the same "logically indistinguishable" issue for the Judiciary to determine in regard to access to Congressional papers. No longer would the Senate be able to withstand the demands of a prosecutor, operating through the process of a court just as in the case at bar, for the records of Senate committees, which were denied by resolution of the Senate in the case of United States v. Brewster and many others. *See* notes 40-45 *supra* and accompanying text.

[75] Subcomm. on Constitutional Rights of the Senate Comm. on the Judiciary, 85th Cong., 2d Sess., The Power of the President to Withhold Information from the Congress, Memorandums of the Attorney General 4 (Comm. Print 1958) [hereinafter Power of the President], *quoting from* 3 Annals of Congress 493.

[76] 1 Writings of Jefferson, *supra* note 1, at 189-90 (emphasis supplied).

could not appropriate funds to implement the treaty until it was allowed access to the papers that it sought. On 30 March 1796 President Washington responded in part as follows:

As therefore it is perfectly clear to my understanding that the assent of the house of representatives is not necessary to the validity of a treaty; . . . and as it is essential to the due administration of the government that the boundaries fixed by the constitution between the different departments should be preserved; a just regard to the constitution, and to the duty of my office, under all the circumstances of this case, forbid a compliance with your request.[77]

Clearly, the President was asserting a Constitutional basis for withholding evidence from Congress.

President Jackson forcefully claimed Executive privilege in 1835 when the Senate requested that he hand over copies of the allegations that resulted in the discharge of Gideon Fitz from the office of Surveyor-General. The President refused to furnish the information requested on the ground that it related to subjects exclusively committed to the Executive Branch. The President's message to the Senate referred to similar requests in the past, all of which he regarded as unconstitutional:

Their continued repetition imposes on me, as the representative and trustee of the American people, the painful but imperious duty of resisting to the utmost any further encroachment on the rights of the Executive.[78]

During the administration of President Tyler, the House directed the Secretary of War to disclose to the House reports made to the Department of War by Lieutenant Colonel Hitchcock regarding the affairs of the Cherokee Indians and alleged frauds that he had been commissioned to investigate. In a message dated 31 January 1843 President Tyler refused to turn over much of the requested information, with the following observations which bear a particular relevance to the case at bar:

The injunction of the Constitution that the President "shall take care that the laws be faithfully executed," necessarily. confers an authority, commensurate with the obligation imposed, to inquire into the manner in which all public agents perform the duties assigned to them by law. To be effective, these inquiries must often be confidential. They may result in

---

[77] 5 J. Marshall, *supra* note 65, at 658.

[78] Power of the President, *supra* note 75, at 7, *quoting from* 1 Richardson's Messages and Papers of the President 133.

the collection of truth or of falsehood; or they may be incomplete, and may require further prosecution. To maintain that the President can exercise no discretion after the time in which the matters thus collected shall be promulgated, or in respect to the character of the information obtained, would deprive him at once of the means of performing one of the most salutary duties of his office. An inquiry might be arrested at its first stage, and the officers whose conduct demanded investigation may be enabled to elude or defeat it. To require from the Executive the transfer of this discretion to a coordinate branch of the Government is equivalent to the denial of its possession by him and *would render him dependent upon that branch in the performance of a duty purely executive.*[79]

The President further stated that "[t]he practice of the Government since its foundation has sanctioned the principle that there must necessarily be a discretionary authority in reference to the nature of the information called for by either House of Congress,"[80] and showed through historical precedent that that authority had always been exercised by the President. So again separation of powers was invoked as a barrier to disclosure of documents in the custody of the Executive.

President Cleveland delivered a famous message to the Senate on 1 March 1886 in which he responded to frequent Senate demands for papers from heads of Executive departments which had been created by Congress. He stated:

The requests and demands which by the score have for nearly three months been presented to the different departments of the Government, whatever may be their form, have but one complexion. They assume the right of the Senate to sit in judgment upon the exercise of my exclusive discretion and Executive function, for which I am solely responsible to the people from whom I have so lately received the sacred trust of office. My oath to support and defend the Constitution, my duty to the people who have chosen me to execute the powers of their great office and not relinquish them, and my duty to the chief magistracy which I must preserve unimpaired in all its dignity and vigor, compel me to refuse compliance with these demands.[81]

[79] 3 Hinds' Precedents of the House of Representatives 181 (1907) (emphasis supplied).

[80] *Id.* at 182.

[81] Power of the President, *supra* note 75, at 15-16.

In 1909 the Senate attempted to obtain from Theodore Roosevelt's Attorney General papers relating to the administration's decision not to proceed against United States Steel Corporation for its absorption of Tennessee Valley Coal & Iron Company. In a message to Congress on 6 January 1909, President Roosevelt described his response to the Senate's demands and cited his reasons therefor:

I have thus given to the Senate all the information in the posession of the executive department *which appears to me to be material or relevant,* on the subject of the resolution. I feel bound, however, to add that I have instructed the Attorney General not to respond to that portion of the resolution which calls for a statement of his reasons for nonaction. I have done so because I do not conceive it to be within the authority of the Senate to give directions of this character to the head of an executive department, or to demand from him reasons for his action. Heads of the executive departments are subject to the Constitution, and to the laws passed by the Congress in pursuance of the Constitution, and to the directions of the President of the United States, but to no other direction whatever.[82]

On 20 January 1944, FBI Director J. Edgar Hoover appeared in answer to a subpoena before the House Select Committee to Investigate the Federal Communications Commission. Mr. Hoover was asked to produce a copy of the directive to him from the President ordering him not to testify before the committee with respect to certain matters. Hoover refused, for reasons stated in a letter from the Attorney General to the chairman of the committee:

It is my view that as a matter of law and of *long-established constitutional practice,* communications between the President and the Attorney General are confidential and privileged and not subject to inquiry by a committee of one of the Houses of Congress. In this instance, it seems to me that the privilege should not be waived; to do so would be to establish an unfortunate precedent, inconsistent with the position taken by my predecessors.[83]

Another forceful assertion of a Constitutionally-based Executive privilege occurred in 1954 during the McCarthy

[82] 43 Cong. Rec. 527-28 (1909) (emphasis supplied).

[83] Power of the President, *supra* note 75, at 23-24, *quoting* from Hearings of the House Select Comm. to Investigate the Federal Communications Commn., 78th Cong., vol. 2, at 2338-39 (1949) (emphasis supplied).

subcommittee probe into the affairs of the Army. In a letter dated 17 May 1954 President Eisenhower instructed the Secretary of Defense to forbid Department of Defense employees to testify or produce documents regarding internal consultations or communications within the Department. The President cited as reasons for his directive the following:

> [I]t is essential to the successful working of our system that the persons entrusted with power in any one of the three great branches of Government shall not encroach upon the authority confided to the others. The ultimate responsibility for the conduct of the executive branch rests with the President.
>
> Within this constitutional framework each branch should cooperate fully with each other for the common good. However, throughout our history the President has withheld information whenever he found that what was sought was confidential or its disclosure would be incompatible with the public interest or jeopardize the safety of the Nation.[84]

As this survey demonstrates, history abounds of instances in which a Presidential claim, that the Constitutional system gives the President discretion to withhold documents from Congress, has prevailed against Congressional demands for Executive papers. These 184 years of Constitutional practice in the context of Congressional-Presidential relations cannot be ignored when, as in this case, the Judiciary confronts the President with a demand for documents "logically indistinguishable"[85] from a Congressional demand in the Constitutional issue raised.

C. *Judicial Demands for Executive Papers—The Trials of Aaron Burr*

Congressional demands for Executive papers are as numerous as autumn leaves, and frequently fall due to a frost between the two ends of Pennsylvania Avenue. In contrast, Judicial demands for Executive documents can be summarized in the drama and legal intricacies of one *cause celebre*, the two trials of Aaron Burr in 1807, the major historical example of the issuance by a federal court of a subpoena *duces tecum* directing the President to produce documents.[86] Although the United States Circuit Court

---

[84] Letter from Dwight D. Eisenhower to the Secretary of Defense, 17 May 1954, *reproduced in* Power of the President, *supra* note 75, at 73-74.

[85] Bishop, *supra* note 3, at 485.

[86] United States v. Burr, 25 Fed. Cas. 30 (No. 14692d) (C.C.D.Va.1807).

for Virginia, per Chief Justice Marshall,[87] issued the subpoena
duces tecum to President Jefferson, the court never directly
decided the question of the scope of the President's asserted
privilege to withhold documents or portions thereof, nor did it
determine who should decide the scope of the privilege.[88]

In the first trial on the charge of treason, the defendant Burr
requested the aid of the court in obtaining a letter written by
General Wilkinson to President Jefferson on 21 October 1806,
the President's response to the letter, and supporting
documents.[89] The Wilkinson letter, Burr alleged in an
affidavit,[90] would be of great importance in his proof of his
innocence, for Wilkinson was an essential witness against
him.[91] "Great importance" was hardly an overstatement of
Burr's need for the letter; it had been mentioned in President
Jefferson's message to Congress on the horrendous conspiracy, it
probably formed the foundation of the Executive's charges
against Burr, and Jefferson's message to Congress summed up his
opinion—Burr's "guilt is placed beyond question."[92]

The United States Attorney, however, contended that it would
be improper to require the President to produce the letter, that
the letter was private, confidential communication, and that it
might contain vital state secrets.[93] This contention reflected the
views of President Jefferson, who forcefully wrote United States
Attorney Hay on 12 June 1807 that

Reserving *the necessary right of the President of the U.S. to
decide, independently of all other authority,* what papers,
coming to him as President, the public interests permit to be
communicated, & to whom, I assure you of my readiness
under that restriction, voluntarily to furnish on all occasions,
whatever the purposes of justice may require I

---

[87] The United States Chief Justice and a District Judge Griffin comprised the court
hearing the case. District Judge Griffin appears to have made few recorded comments.

[88] Also at issue was the question whether the President could be compelled to
testify in person, but this was not decided either.

[89] *See* 3 A. Beveridge, The Life of John Marshall 433 (1919).

[90] 25 Fed. Cas. at 31.

[91] *Id.* at 36.

[92] 3 A. Beveridge, *supra* note 89, at 341.

[93] 25 Fed. Cas. at 31. MacRae, one of the prosecutors assisting Hay, argued on 10
June 1807 that a subpoena might issue against the President as any other, but that he
was not bound to disclose "confidential communications." Marshall himself had ruled
on that very point in Marbury v. Madison, 5 U.S. (1 Cranch) 137, at 143-145, 2 L.Ed.
60, when he had so advised Attorney General Lincoln. 3 A. Beveridge, *supra* note 89,
at 437-38; E. Corwin, *supra* note 72, at 111-12.

. . . devolve on you the exercise of that discretion which it would be my right & duty to exercise, by withholding the communication of any parts of the letter which are not directly material for the purposes of justice.[94]

The accused, however, argued that a subpoena should issue notwithstanding the possibility of confidential communications not relating to the case or state secrets, but suggested that the President might point out the confidential passages, which need not be read in open court.[95]

After consideration of these arguments, Marshall held that a subpoena *duces tecum* could issue to the President. He reasoned that an accused has a right to the compulsory process of the court, notwithstanding the position of the person to whom the subpoena was directed, so long as the document or paper itself was proper for production. Chief Justice Marshall wrote,

The propriety of introducing any paper into a case, as testimony, must depend on the character of the paper, not on the character of the person who holds it.[96]

and further stated that any exception to this rule of general obligation to compulsory process must be sought in the law of evidence.[97] Marshall thus seemed to rely on the evidentiary nature of the asserted privilege, and did not refer to a possible Constitutional basis.

Thus, considering the question on customary rules of evidence, Marshall found no exception therein for the President, "The court [could] perceive no legal objection to issuing a subpoena duces tecum to any person whatever, provided the case be such as to justify the process," although he carefully distinguished the issuance of a subpoena from the subsequent step of compelling compliance with the subpoena (a distinction made validly in the case at bar):

[W]hatever difference may exist with respect to the power to compel the same obedience to the process, as if it had been directed to a private citizen, there exists no difference with

[94] 9 Writings of Jefferson, *supra* note 1, at 44 (emphasis supplied).

[95] 25 Fed. Cas. at 31.

[96] *Id.* at 34.

[97] *Ibid.* Marshall wrote,
   In the provisions of the constitution, and of the statute, which give to the accused a right to the compulsory process of the court, there is no exception whatever.

respect to the right to obtain it.[98]

The court anticipated that objections of the President to compliance with the subpoena could and should be shown on the return of the subpoena, but should not be taken into account in the decision to issue the subpoena.[99]

Marshall admittedly was troubled by the possibility that the letter might contain "matter which ought not be disclosed."[100] He acknowledged that this was a "delicate question," but stated that

> At the present it need only be said that the question does not occur at this time. There is certainly nothing before the court which shows that the letter in question contains any matter the disclosure of which would endanger the public safety. If it does contain such matter, the fact may appear before the disclosure is made. If it does contain any matter which it would be imprudent to disclose, such matter, if it be not immediately and essentially applicable to the point, will, of course, be suppressed . . . . Everything of this kind, however, will have its due consideration on the return of the subpoena.[101]

Later in the opinion the court reiterated this point, with respect to the written response of the President to the Wilkinson letter.[102]

The court noted that it had great respect for the President. Yet it felt that the reputation of the court would be tarnished if it refused to aid an accused in procuring papers which he deemed essential for his defense.[103]

President Jefferson attacked this decision as violating the Constitutional principle of independence of the Branches of Government, a point to which Marshall nowhere directly adverted at any time in his opinions in the Burr trials.[104] In a

[98] *Ibid.*

[99] *Ibid.*

[100] *Id.* at 37.

[101] *Ibid.*

[102] "If it contains matter not essential to the defense, and the disclosure be unpleasant to the executive, it certainly ought not to be disclosed. This is a point which will appear on the return . . . . If they contain matter interesting to the nation, the concealment of which is required by the public safety, the matter will appear upon the return. If they do not, and are material, they may be exhibited." *Ibid.*

[103] *Ibid.*

[104] The closest which Marshall came to recognizing any separation of powers issue was at the end of his opinion allowing the issuance of the subpoena for the 21 October

letter to Hay on 20 June 1807 Jefferson wrote,

> The leading principle of our Constitution is the independence
> of the Legislature, executive and judiciary of each other, and
> none are more jealous of this than the judiciary. But would the
> executive be independent of the judiciary, it he were subject
> to the *commands* of the latter, & to imprisonment for
> disobedience . . . ?[105]

It is highly significant that President Jefferson, himself a lawyer
with more formal legal training than Marshall,[106] had, at the
very outset of the matter, gone to the very root of the
Constitutional question from the point of view of the Executive.
Anticipating that at some point in the great drama, taking place
in the Richmond courtroom ninety miles to the south of the
White House, there would be a confrontation between the
Executive and Judicial powers on 2 June 1807 Jefferson had
written to Hay:

> *The Constitution intended* that the three great branches of
> the government should be co-ordinate, and independent of
> each other.[107]

When notified of the issuance of the subpoena, Jefferson on 12
June immediately replied: "Sir,—Your letter of the 9th is this
moment received. Reserving the necessary right of the President
of the U.S. to decide, independently of all other authority, what
papers, coming to him as President, the public interests permit to
be communicated, & to whom, . . .". (As quoted at p.782,
supra.) The acquittal of Burr for treason came many weeks later,
but the battle over the subpoena was to go on.

In the second part of the Burr litigation, when Burr was on
trial for a misdemeanor (beginning a military expedition against
the territory of Spain), the Burr request for the Wilkinson letter

---

letter. 25 Fed. Cas. at 37. Here Marshall discussed the problem of disrespect for the
President which might be thought to arise from the decision. Marshall simply stated
that his respect for the President was as great as it could be, given his duties on the
Court. Even here, however, he did not deal directly with any Constitutional principle
of the independence of Executive and Judiciary.

[105] 9 Writings of Jefferson, *supra* note 1, at 60 (emphasis original).

[106] Both Jefferson and Marshall received their formal legal training under George
Wythe. Jefferson studied for five years in Whthe's law office and was admitted to the
bar in 1767. 12 Encyclopedia Britannica 985 (1968). Marshall, on the other hand,
simply attended a short series of lectures given by Wythe at William and Mary College
in 1780, and he was licensed to practice in August 1780. 14 Encyclopedia Britannica
959 (1968).

[107] 9 Writings of Jefferson, *supra* note 1, at 53 (emphasis supplied).

of 21 October 1806 again drew the attention of the court.[108]   In the course of argument Burr referred to the letter and noted that it had not yet been produced.[109] The U.S. District Attorney Hay indicated that he could produce a copy of the letter, but not the original.[110]   The court, per Justice Marshall, then stated that a copy would not be admissible unless the loss of the original were proved.[111]

During later argument the same day, 3 September 1807, Burr made a new request, for a letter from General Wilkinson to President Jefferson written on 12 November 1806, which he also felt was material to his defense.[112] Hay then proposed to produce the 12 November letter and let the clerk of the court in confidence copy those parts of the letters which were relevant and which could be made public. Burr's counsel, however, demanded the whole of the letters. Hay next suggested that Burr's counsel should examine the letters; Hay would rely on their integrity not to disclose confidential passages, and if any disagreement arose, Hay would let the court decide.[113]   Burr's counsel refused to inspect anything which Burr himself could not inspect.

Hay finally responded to the Burr demands by asserting the ultimate position that the President had kept for himself the power to decide what portions of the letter should be made public, but that he wished to make all but the most confidential sections public,[114] as the President had specifically stated in his letters to Hay.[115]   President Jefferson maintained that he found the source of his powers in both the common practice of all nations' executives and in the Constitution.[116]

While Jefferson had been willing earlier to comply substantially with the subpoena,[117] he now felt that Burr had

[108] United States v. Burr, 25 Fed. Cas. 187 (No. 14694) (C.C.D.Va.1807).

[109] *Id.* at 189.

[110] President Jefferson had written on 23 June 1807 to Hay, indicating that Wilkinson probably had copies of his letters, and that the General had expressed a willingness to furnish them to the court. 9 Writings of Jefferson, *supra* note 1, at 61.

[111] 25 Fed. Cas. at 189.

[112] *Id.* at 190.

[113] *Ibid.*

[114] *Ibid.*

[115] Jefferson's letter to Hay of 12 June 1807 had so indicated. *See* text accompanying note 94 *supra*.

[116] Letter of President Jefferson to Hay of 17 June 1807, in 9 Writings of Jefferson, *supra* note 1, at 57.

[117] *Id.* at 56.

converted the trial into a contest between the Executive and the Judiciary. He was disappointed that Justice Marshall had allowed this, but he hoped that Marshall would not press on with the conflict. If Marshall did continue, however, Jefferson noted that the powers given the Executive by the Constitution would enable him to prevail.[118] Jefferson was determined to resist the execution of the process and was willing to use force if necessary, although he hoped that Marshall would not push the issue to a head.

On 4 September 1807 Burr again demanded the letters of General Wilkinson written to President Jefferson on 21 October and on 12 November 1806. Burr stated in court that the President was in contempt for failure to comply with the subpoena issued for the 21 October letter, but he hoped that the President would produce the letters without the necessity of resorting to contempt proceedings.[119] Burr indicated he might accept a copy of the 21 October letter, the original of which had apparently been mislaid, but only if the copy were properly authenticated.[120]

After a lengthy debate, the court issued a second subpoena *duces tecum*, to the United States Attorney, which was returned with a copy of the 12 November 1806 letter, the copy excepting the parts not material or relevant in Hay's opinion. Hay indicated

---

[118] Draft letter of President Jefferson to Hay in 9 Writings of Jefferson, *supra* note 1, at 62. Ford, and others, are not sure if this letter was ever received by Hay. Nonetheless, the draft is important as an expression of Jefferson's views:
    That Burr & his counsel should wish to . . . .convert his Trial into a contest between the judiciary & Exve Authorities was to be expected. But that the Ch. Justice should lend himself to it, and take the first step to bring it on, was not expected. Nor can it be now believed that his prudence or good sense will permit him to press it. But should he contrary to expectation, proceed to issue any process which should involve any act of force to be committed on the persons of the Exve or heads of depmts, I must desire you to give me instant notice, & by express if you find that can be quicker done than by post; and that moreover you will advise the marshall on his conduct, as he will be critically placed between us. His safest way will be to take no part in the exercise of any act of force ordered in this case. The powers given to the Exve by the constn are sufficient to protect the other branches from Judiciary usurpation of preeminence, & every individual also from judiciary vengeance, and the marshal may be assured of its effective exercise to cover him. I hope however that the discretion of the C. J. will suffer this question to lie over for the present, and at the ensuing session of the legislature he may have means provided for giving to individuals the benefit of the testimony of the Exve functionaries in proper cases, without breaking up the government. *See* note 1 *supra.*

[119] 25 Fed. Cas. at 190.

[120] The record of the case reveals no further action taken concerning the 21 October letter. Nor do the histories which we have consulted indicate whether Burr ever received a full copy of the letter.

that this power of selection of the passages to be made public
had been delegated to him by the President.[121] However, the
United States Attorney was willing to submit the original letter
to the court so that it could test the accuracy of his opinion, and
he also certified that the deleted parts contained opinions about
certain persons which would not be admissible in court.[122] Burr
still was not satisfied, and the court apparently would be
required to resolve the issue.

Chief Justice Marshall recognized that while the President was
subject to the general rule requiring compliance with a subpoena,
nevertheless the President may have "sufficient motives for
declining to produce a particular paper, and those motives may
be such as to restrain the court from enforcing its
production."[123] He continued by stating that

> The occasion for demanding it ought, in such a case, to be very
> strong, and to be fully shown to the court before its
> production could be insisted on. I admit, that in such a case,
> much reliance must be placed on the declaration of the
> president; and I do think that a privilege does exist to
> withhold private letters of a certain description.[124]

This expression of acknowledgement of some kind of Executive
privilege for confidential communications, made by Marshall on
4 September 1807, is reminiscent of Marshall's statement four
years earlier in Marbury v. Madison, that Attorney General
Lincoln need not disclose anything which had been
communicated to him in confidence.[125]

Marshall was troubled, however, by the possibility of denying

---

[121] *See* text accompanying note 94 *supra*. President Jefferson later wrote Hay on
7 September 1807 on this subject:

I received, late last night, your favor of the day before, and now re-enclose you
the subpoena. As I do not believe that the district courts have a power of *commanding*
the executive government to abandon superior duties & attend on them at whatever
distance, I am unwilling, by any notice of the subpoena, to set a precedent which
might sanction a proceeding so preposterous. I enclose you, therefore, a letter, public
& for the court, covering substantially all they ought to desire. If the papers which
were enclosed in Wilkinson's letter may, in your judgment, be communicated without
injury, you will be pleased to communicate them. I return you the original letter.

9 Writings of Jefferson, *supra* note 1, at 63. This letter was thought by Beveridge to
indicate that the President had received a second subpoena. 3 A. Beveridge, *supra* note
89, at 522. The record of the case does not show that another subpoena was issued to
Jefferson himself.

[122] 25 Fed. Cas. at 190.

[123] *Id. at 191.*

[124] *Id. at 192.*

[125] Marbury v. Madison, 5 U.S. (1 Cranch) 137, 144-145, 2 L.Ed. 60 (1803).

the accused information which might be of aid in his defense. He indicated that the court would give great deference to the reasons of the President for withholding the information, and would require the accused to show that the material was essential to the defense.[126] Here, however, it had been Hay, rather than the President, who had decided which specific passages should be withheld. This gave Marshall still another opportunity to avoid the direct Constitutional clash:

> Had the President, when he transmitted it, subjected it to certain restrictions, and stated that in his judgment the public interest required certain parts of it to be kept secret, and had accordingly made a reservation of them, all proper respect would have been paid to it; but he has made no such reservation . . . . In regard to the secrecy of these parts which it is stated are improper to give out to the world, the court will take any order that may be necessary. I do not think that the accused ought to be prohibited from seeing the letter; but, if it should be thought proper, I will order that no copy of it be taken for public exhibition, and that no use shall be made of it but what is necessarily attached to the case.[127]

The great Chief Justice had finessed the issue.

Hay immediately sought instructions from the President, and on 9 September he presented the court with " a certificate from the president, annexed to a copy of Gen. Wilkinson's letter, excepting such parts as he deemed he ought not permit to be made public."[128] The president's certificate, dated 7 September 1807, noted that

---

[126] Marshall wrote,

I cannot precisely lay down any general rule for such a case. Perhaps the court ought to consider the reasons which would induce the president to refuse to exhibit such a letter as conclusive on it, unless such letter could be shown to be absolutely necessary in the defense. The president may himself state the particular reasons which may have induced him to withhold a paper, and the court would unquestionably allow their full force to those reasons. At the same time, the court could not refuse to pay proper attention to the affidavit of the accused. But on objections being made by the president to the production of a paper, the court would not proceed further in the case without such an affidavit as would clearly show the paper to be essential to the justice of the case . . . .In no case of this kind would a court be required to proceed against the president as against an ordinary individual. (Emphasis supplied.) 25 Fed. Cas. at 192.

25 Fed. Cas. at 192.

[127] Ibid. (emphasis supplied).

This is as far as my colleagues discuss the Burr trials supra at 716 n. 74). They rest with Marshall's language re the United States Attorney's assertion of privilege; they do not discuss President Jefferson's final assertion of 7 September 1807—and neither did Marshall.

[128] Id. at 193 (emphasis supplied).

On re-examination of a letter of Nov. 12, 1806, from Genl. Wilkinson to myself, . . . I find in it some passages entirely confidential, given for my information in the discharge of my executive functions, and which my duties & the public interest forbid me to make public. I have therefore given above a correct copy of all those parts which I ought to permit to be made public. *Those not communicated are in nowise material for the purposes of justice* on the charges of treason or misdemeanor depending against Aaron Burr; *they are on subjects irrelevant to any issues which can arise out of those charges, & could contribute nothing towards his acquittal or conviction.*[129]

The trial proceeded, and Burr was found by the jury to be not guilty.[130] The full Wilkinson to Jefferson letter of 12 November 1806 was never produced.

My colleagues "think the *Burr* case makes clear that application of Executive privilege depends on a weighing of the public interest protected by the privilege against the public interest that would be served by disclosure in a particular case." (*Per Curiam, supra* at 716.) Not so, not by a long shot, not by the difference between a United States Attorney and a President.

Marshall *might* have been willing to pit the Judiciary versus the Executive by a final order to produce the whole letter or else, when only the excerpted letter was furnished and the deletions were done by the judgment of the U.S. Attorney. But when the *President himself* later came forth with his excerpted version and certificate as to what had been deleted and why, Marshall said nothing and he did nothing.

The full 12 November letter was never produced; the 21 October letter was never produced in the first trial for treason, and there is no record that even a copy was produced in the second trial for misdemeanor.

If we go on *what was actually done*, the *Burr* trials prove that the final "weighing of the public interest" is done by the Chief Executive. If we go on what was *said* by Marshall, the *Burr* trials leave the ultimate issue of Who finally decides the public interest completely undecided, for Marshall never faced up, even verbally, to a confrontation with the President himself with the issue drawn on the question of separation of powers.[131]

---

[129] 9 Writings of Jefferson, *supra* note 1, at 64 (emphasis supplied).

[130] 25 Fed. Cas. at 201.

[131] Professor Paul Hardin summarizes the *Burr* case in his article on Executive privilege by stating:

These two great Constitutional and political antagonists—Marshall and Jefferson, Chief Justice and President—had circled each other warily, each maintaining his position, each, out of respect for the other and for the delicate fabric of the Constitution, not forcing the ultimate issue. Who *should* decide the scope and applicability of the Chief Executive's privilege? The *Burr* trials give no definite answer. Who *did* decide the Chief Executive's privilege? The portions of the letter determined by the President to be confidential remained confidential; the full letter was never produced to the court.

III. RELATIONSHIP OF THE GRAND JURY TO THE JUDICIARY AND TO THE EXECUTIVE

In my view, the case at bar presents the same conflict between the Judiciary and the Executive which faced Chief Justice Marshall in the *Burr* trials. I would decide the question the same way Marshall actually left it; my colleagues would decide the question by asserting a Judicial supremacy over the Chief Executive, which Marshall may have hinted he preferred, but which he was too prudent finally to assert.

There is a third position which is argued by the Special Prosecutor, and indeed is relied on by the District Judge, hence must be addressed briefly here. The Special Prosecutor contends, ". . . it is a false conflict to see the present controversy as a struggle between the powers of the Judiciary and the prerogatives of the President. Rather, what is involved is the respondent's refusal to respond to a demand from the people, speaking through their organ, the grand jury."[132] And, ". . . the grand jury's 'authority is derived from none of the three basic divisions of our government, but rather directly from the people

Chief Justice Marshall, sitting as trial judge in the trial of Aaron Burr, subpoenaed information in the hands of President Jefferson. Marshall asserted the power of the court to subpoena the President, examine him as a witness, and require him to produce "any paper in his possession," but later in the same opinion seemed to recognize a restricted legitimate area in which executive discretion might operate. For his part Jefferson avowed that he had the absolute power to withhold documents sought by subpoena, but his eventual cooperation avoided a decisive conflict. This entire paper footnotes the proposition that the *Burr* trial did not provide a final answer to the vexing questions of executive privilege. The case did provide, however, a remarkable example of executive cooperation, considering Jefferson's personal feelings toward Burr, his distaste for the judiciary, and his firm belief that he could resist disclosure if he chose to do so.

Hardin, *supra* note 3, at 899-890 (citations omitted).

[132] Special Prosecutor's Memorandum in Support at 44, In re Subpoena to Nixon, 360 F.Supp. 1 (D.C.D.C. 1973).

themselves.' (Citation omitted.)"[133] Judge Sirica held, "[t]he grand jury derives its authority directly from the people . . . ."[134]

In the first place, it is undeniable that, under the very terms of Judge Sirica's Order and Opinion, the nine tapes are to be turned over to the District *Court,* and the grand jury may never see or hear any of them after the District Judge's review *in camera.* So the Judiciary-Executive confrontation is there at the outset, whatever the character of the grand jury. In the second place, the grand jury is only an appendage of the court under whose direction it operates. When the grand jury functions, it functions within the recognized tripartite divison of powers as an arm of the Judicial Branch.

A. *Background*

The Supreme Court has described the grand jury as "brought to this country by the early colonists and incorporated in the Constitution by the Founders. There is every reason to believe that our constitutional grand jury was intended to operate substantially like its English progenitor."[135] In its formative stages in England, the jury[136] was "a body of neighbors summoned by some public officer to give, upon oath, a true answer to some question."[137] In the twelfth century Henry II made extensive use of the jury as a source of general information necessary for the administration of his centralized government. The jury's role as a source of general information for the Crown diminished when Parliament became the grand inquest of the nation.[138] "So gradually, in the course of the fourteenth century, the use of the jury in connection with the central government came to be chiefly confined to *judicial functions.*"[139]

In the thirteenth century and early part of the fourteenth,

---

[133] Ibid.

[134] In re Subpoena to Nixon, 360 F.Supp. 1, 9 (D.C.D.C. 1973).

[135] Costello v. United States, 350 U.S. 359, 362, 76 S.Ct. 406, 408, 100 L.Ed. 397 (1956).

[136] A clear distinction between the grand and petit jury did not develop until the fourteenth century. *See* notes 140-141 *infra* and accompanying text.

[137] 1 F. Pollock and F. Maitland, History of English Law 138 (2d ed. 1923).

[138] 1 W. Holdsworth, History of English Law 313-14 (6th rev. ed. 1938).

[139] *Id.* at 314. (Emphasis supplied.)

members of the grand jury that accused a person of crime often served on the petit jury that tried him.[140] However, by 1351-52 no indictor could serve on the trial jury if he were challenged for cause by the accused.[141] It seems clear that in early England the grand jury was as much a part of the judicial machinery as the petit jury.

From a tool of the Crown for ferreting out criminals, the grand jury later evolved into a protector of the citizenry against arbitrary prosecution. The grand jury's role as a shield dates from the 1681 case of the Earl of Shaftesbury, in which the grand jury wrote "Ignoramus" ("we ignore it") on the bill of indictment presented by the Crown against Shaftesbury.[142] The protective function of the grand jury was recognized by the drafters of the Bill of Rights when they provided in the Fifth Amendment that "[n]o person shall be held to answer for a capital, or otherwise infamous crime, unless on a presentment or indictment of a Grand Jury . . . ."[143] In Wood v. Georgia the Court emphasized the protective role of the grand jury:

> Historically, this body has been regarded as a primary security to the innocent against hasty, malicious and oppressive persecution; it serves the invaluable function in our society of standing between the accuser and the accused, whether the latter be an individual, minority group, or other, to determine whether a charge is founded upon reason or was dictated by an intimidating power or by malice and personal ill will.[144]

In addition to its historical roles as an accusatory body and as a shield of the innocent, the grand jury has traditionally been accorded broad powers to investigate possible wrongdoing.[145] Thus, a grand jury may initiate an independent

[140] *Id.* at 322.

[141] *Ibid.*

[142] 8 Howell's State Trials 751.

[143] This provision has been held not to apply to the states through the due process clause of the Fourteenth Amendment. Hurtado v. California, 110 U.S. 516, 4 S.Ct. 111, 292, 28 L.Ed. 232 (1884).

[144] 370 U.S. 375, 390, 82 S.Ct. 1364, 1373, 8 L.Ed.2d 569 (1962).

[145] *See generally* Note, The Grand Jury as an Investigatory Body, 74 Harv. L. Rev. 590 (1961); Note, The Grand Jury—Its Investigatory Powers and Limitations, 37 Minn. L. Rev. 586 (1953).
The Supreme Court described the inquisitorial function of the grand jury in Blair v. United States, 250 U.S. 273, 282, 39 S.Ct. 468, 471, 63 L.Ed. 979 (1919):

investigation and request that charges be made against those whose wrongdoing was discovered.[146]

B. *Relationship of the Grand Jury to the Judiciary*

From the above survey of the history and traditional functions of the grand jury, it should be clear that the grand jury operates within the judicial sphere of Government. The Supreme Court has so treated it: "The grand jury is an arm of the court and its *in camera* proceedings constitute 'a judicial inquiry.' "[147] Perhaps the fullest exposition of the judicial nature of the grand jury's activities is contained in *In re National Window Glass Workers:*

A grand jury has no existence aside from the court which calls it into existence and upon which it is attending. A grand jury does not become, after it is summoned, impaneled, and sworn, an independent planet, as it were, in the judicial system, but still remains an appendage of the court on which it is attending. No grand jury shall be summoned to attend any District Court unless the judge thereof, in his own discretion or upon a notification by the district attorney that such jury will be needed, orders a venire to issue therefor. [Citation omitted.] The District Court may discharge a grand jury whenever in its judgment it deems a continuance of the sessions of such a jury unnecessary. [Citation omitted.] All indictments or presentments of a grand jury become effective only when presented in court and a record is made of such action. A grand jury is not, therefore, and cannot become, an independent, self-functioning, uncontrollable agency. It is and remains a grand jury attending on the court, and does not, after it is organized, become an independent body, functioning at its uncontrolled will, or the will of the district attorney or special assistant.[148]

[The grand jury] is a grand inquest, a body with powers of investigation and inquisition, the scope of whose inquiries is not to be limited narrowly by questions of propriety or forecasts of the probably result of the investigation, or by doubts whether any particular individual will be found properly subject to an accusation of crime. *See also* Hale v. Henkel, 201 U.S. 43, 26 S. Ct. 370, 50 L.Ed. 652 (1906).

[146] United States v. Smyth, 104 F.Supp. 283, 295 (N.D.Cal. 1952).

[147] Levine v. United States, 362 U.S. 610, 617, 80 S.Ct. 1038, 1043, 4 L.Ed.2d 989 (1960).

[148] 287 F. 219, 225 (N.D. Ohio 1922). *See also* Branzburg v. Hayes, 408 U.S. 665, 688, 92 S.Ct. 2646, 2660, 33 L.Ed.2d 626 (1972) ("the powers of the grand jury are not unlimited and are subject to the supervision of the judge."); Brown v. United States, 359 U.S. 41, 49, 79 S.Ct. 539, 3 L.Ed.2d 609 (1959) ("A grand jury is clothed

Although a court has no authority to order the grand jury to return an indictment (or to refuse to do so),[149] it may exercise control over the grand jury in several significant respects.[150] The court summons and empanels the grand jury[151] and apparently has broad discretion to discharge it for any reason.[152] The grand jury's jurisdiction to investigate is limited to that of the presiding court.[153] In making its inquiries, the grand jury must rely on the process of the court to procure evidence and summon witnesses and must look to the power of the court to enforce its subpoenas.[154] "Unreasonable or oppressive" subpoenas may be quashed or modified by the court on motion.[155] The court has considerable discretion to instruct the grand jury and to prescribe rules for the conduct of its proceedings.[156] In summary, the court has broad supervisory authority with respect to the activities of the grand jury.

The nature of the grand jury's functions and its subordination to the supervisory authority of the court place it squarely within the Judicial Branch. Moreover, in order to perform its protective function,[157] the grand jury must remain detached from and

with great independence in many areas, but it remains an appendage of the court . . . ."); Hammond v. Brown, 323 F.Supp. 326, 344-345 (N.D. Ohio), aff'd, 450 F.2d 480 (6th Cir. 1971); United States v. Smyth, 104 F. Supp. 283 (N.D. Cal. 1952); 1 L.Orfield, Criminal Procedure Under the Federal Rules 475 (1966).

[149] United States v. United States District Court, 238 F.2d 713, 722 (4th Cir. 1956), cert. denied, 352 U.S. 981, 77 S.Ct. 382, 1 L.Ed.2d 365 (1957). But note that the court can prevent indictment by summary discharge. United States v. Smyth, 104 F. Supp. 283, 292 (N.D. Cal. 1952).

[150] *See generally* United States v. Smyth, 104 F.Supp. 283, 289, 292, 293; 1 L.Orfield, *supra* note 148, at 476-77.

[151] Fed. R. Crim. P. 6(a). However, "the tenure and powers of a grand jury are not affected by the beginning or expiration of a term of court." Fed. R. Crim. P. 6(g).

[152] Fed. R. Crim. P. 6(g); United States v. Smyth, 104 F.Supp, 283, 292 (N.D. Cal. 1952).

[153] In re United Electrical, Radio & Machine Workers of America, 111 F.Supp. 858, 864 (S.D.N.Y.1953); 1 L. Orfield, *supra* note 148, at 472, 483.

[154] Brown v. United States, 359 U.S. 41, 49, 79 S.Ct. 539, 3 L.Ed.2d 609 (1959). Apparently, however, the court has no discretion to refuse the grand jury process on the ground that the evidence sought is immaterial to its investigation. United States v. United States District Court, 238 F.2d 713 (4th Cir. 1956), cert. denied, 352 U.S. 981, 77 S.Ct.382, 1 L.Ed.2d 365 (1957).

[155] Fed.R.CrimP. 17(c).

[156] United States v. Smyth, 104 F.Supp. 292 (N.D.Cal.1952). For examples of instructions to grand juries see Charge to the Grand Jury, 12 F.R.D. 495 (N.D.Cal.1952); Charge to the Grand Jury, 30 Fed.Cas. 992, No. 18,255 (C.C.D.Cal.1872) (Field, J.).

[157] *See* notes 142-44 *supra* and accompanying text.

independent of the Executive Branch. Therefore, the grand jury is under no compulsion to follow the orders of the prosecutor.[158] Its power to investigate and return a presentment based on its findings is not impaired by the prosecutor's discretion to decide whether or not to proceed with a prosecution.[159]

Thus, for purposes of applying the doctrine of separation of powers, the grand jury must be aligned with the Judicial Branch. As one court stated in Hammond v. Brown,

> The grand jury in its inquest of crimes and offenses is part of the judicial branch of government. Like other branches of

---

[158] United States v. Smyth,104 F.Supp. 283, 294 (N.D.Cal.1952). *See generally* Note, 37 Minn.L.Rev., *supra* note 145, at 599-600.

[159] United States v. Cox, 342 F.2d 167 (5th Cir.), cert. denied, 381 U.S. 935, 85 S.Ct. 1767, 14 L.Ed.2d 700 (1965), is not to the contrary. In *Cox* the court reversed a contempt order against a United States Attorney who had refused to sign an indictment tendered by a grand jury despite an order by the supervising court that he do so. A majority of the appeals court held that the prosecutor must help the grand jury draw up the indictment papers, but that he need not give the indictment effect by signing it. The four dissenting judges argued that signing the indictment was a mere ministerial function of the United States Attorney, whose only vehicle for termination of a prosecution is a motion to dismiss the indictment under Fed.R.Crim.P. 48(a). Thus, *Cox* does establish that the Executive branch has complete control over the indictment process; the prosecutor can prevent the grand jury from returning an effective indictment by refusing to sign the indictment papers as required by Fed.R.Crim.P. 7(c).

However, *Cox* is relevant only to the accusatorial function of the grand jury. As Judge Wisdom pointed out in his concurring opinion:

The decision of the majority does not affect the inquisitorial power of the grand jury. No one questions the jury's plenary power to inquire, to summon and interrogate witnesses, and to present either findings and a report on an accusation in open court by presentment.

342 F.2d at 189. Judge Wisdom's distinction between the grand jury's "presentment" function, see notes 145-46 *supra* and accompanying test, and its "indictment" function is supported by the cases. In re Miller, 17 Fed.Cas. 295, No. 9,552 (C.C.Ind. 1878), the President ordered the district attorney to terminate an embezzlement prosecution under investigation by the grand jury. The supervising court instructed the jury as follows:

If you believe the president's instructions to the district attorney were intended to prevent you from making the fullest investigation into the matter now before you, and from returning an indictment against the accused if the evidence should warrant it, you should be inspired with additional determination to do your duty. The moment the executive is allowed to control the action of the courts in the administration of criminal justice their independence is gone.

In Sullivan v. United States, 348 U.S. 170, 75 S.Ct. 182, 99 L.Ed. 210 (1954), the Court held that an Executive Order fixing responsibility for bringing tax law prosecutions with the Attorney General's office could not affect the power of the grand jury to investigate, even on the basis of evidence presented by the United States Attorney without the Attorney General's approval. These cases illustrate that the Executive cannot control the scope and nature of a grand jury's investigation, even if the Executive has no intention of going forward with any indictment returned by the grand jury as a result of its inquiries.

government the judicial branch is subject to the doctrine of separation of powers. [Citation omitted.] The grand jury is part of the judicial branch of government and is separate and distinct from the legislative and executive branches of government; and the grand jury, therefore, may not "impinge upon the authority or rights of the others" . . . . [Citation omitted.] [160]

IV. AMENABILITY OF THE PRESIDENT TO JUDICIAL PROCESS—AN ILLUSORY ISSUE IN THE INSTANT CASE

My colleagues have decided an "immunity" issue, which, in my humble judgment, is a non-issue in this case—both from the majority view and my own.

A. If the President has the power and responsibility to decide where lies the public interest in disclosure or non-disclosure, as I believe, what business does any court have issuing any "Order"? Apparently none, for the *Per Curiam* opinion states: "If the Constitution or the laws of evidence confer upon the President the absolute discretion to withhold material subpoenaed by a grand jury, then of course we would vacate, rather than approve with modification, the order entered below." (*Per Curiam, supra* at 712.)

B. If the court has the power to weigh and balance the public interest in the confidentiality of Executive records, but the court has no physical power to enforce its subpoena should the President refuse to comply—as my colleagues apparently recognize full well (*Per Curiam, supra* at 708 and notes 32-33)—then what purpose is served by determining whether the President is "imune" from process?

It can hardly be questioned that in any direct confrontation between the Judiciary and the Executive, the latter must prevail. Therefore, the "issue" of whether the President is amenable to court process is an illusory one. No one questions that the court can issue to the President a piece of paper captioned "Subpoena" and that the President owes some obligation at least to inform the court of how he intends to respond. But our history is full of examples of situations in which direct confrontations between two or more of the co-equal Branches were avoided by one of the Branches deciding not to push its position to the limit.

It should be crystal clear from the detailed account of the

[160] *323 F.Supp. 326, 344-345 (N.D.Obio), aff'd, 450 F.2d 480 (6tb Cir. 1971).*

trials of Aaron Burr (II.C. *supra*) that *Burr* provides no support for my colleagues' deciding this "issue" as they do, for Chief Justice Marshall never came to the final confrontation with President Jefferson. Since the Burr trials represent the sole[161] example in our history of a court subpoena *duces tecum* to an incumbent President, it is with some astonishment that I read the majority's confident assertion: "The courts' assumption of legal *power to compel production of evidence* within the possession of the Executive surely stands on firm footing. Youngstown Sheet & Tube v. Sawyer, . . ." (*Per Curiam, supra* at 709) (emphasis supplied).

Youngstown[162] involved no documents, no tapes, no Presidential conversations—no assertion of a Constitutional privilege of any kind. *Youngstown* represents the Judicial power, by compulsory process or otherwise, to prohibit the Executive from engaging in actions contrary to law. *Youngstown* represents the principle that no man, cabinet minister or Chief Executive himself,[163] is above the law; *Youngstown* says nothing about

[161] In 1818 a subpoena was issued to President James Monroe, but it summoned him merely to appear personally, not to produce any documents. The subpoena was satisfied when the President answered the court's interrogatories. *See Per Curiam, supra* at 710 n. 42; *supra* note 25. In United States v. Cooper, 25 Fed.Cas. 631 (No. 14,865, C.C.D.Pa. 1800), Justice Chase refused to permit "a subpoena to issue directed to the president of the United States." 25 Fed. Cas. at 933. No reasons for his refusal are recorded. In a related case, No. 14,861, Justice Chase stated:

The constitution gives to every man, charged with an offense, the benefit of compulsory process, to secure the attendance of his witnesses. I do not know of any privilege to exempt members of *congress* from the service, or the obligations, of a subpoena, in such cases. (25 Fed.Cas. at 626).

Thus, Justice Chase seemed to be establishing a different standard for members of Congress than for the President. For an interpretation of the *Cooper* cases favorable to the President, see Power of the President *supra* note 75, at 36-37.

[162] 343 U.S. 579, 72 S.Ct. 863, 96 L.Ed. 1153 (1952).

[163] That the President has taken personal custody of the tapes and is himself a party to the action is, in my view as well as the majority's, immaterial. "There is not slightest hint in any of the *Youngstown* opinions that the case would have been viewed differently if President Truman rather than Secretary Sawyer had been the named party," as Justice Black made clear. The authorities relied on by my colleagues here are simply not applicable because no Constitutional privilege of the Executive regarding documents was involved.

It is arguable that judicial process may issue ordering the President to perform a *purely ministerial* act. The basis for such an argument is language contained in Mississippi v. Johnson, 71 U.S. (4 Wall.) 475, 18 L.Ed. 437 (1867):

A ministerial duty, the performance of which may, in proper cases, be required of the head of a department, by judicial process, is one in respect to which nothing is left to discretion. It is a simple, definite duty, arising under conditions admitted or proved to exist, and inposed by law.

71 U.S. (4 Wall.) at 498. *Johnson* held that a court could not order the President to cease enforcement of the Reconstruction Acts on the ground that enforcement of Congressional enactments is purely discretionary with the President and thus not

Which Branch Decides a Constitutional privilege based on separation of powers.

Nor are the other authorities cited by the majority opinion to decide the unnecessary question of Presidential "immunity" any more relevant. United States v. United States District Court[164] involved a Fourth Amendment violation by wiretapping, and the consequent required disclosure or dismissal in the well-known adversary litigation situation. Kendall v. United States ex rel. Stokes[165] was a mandamus to a cabinet officer to comply with an act of Congress, with no privileged communicaitons whatsoever involved. State Highway Commission v. Volpe[166] involved an injunction against a cabinet officer, with no privileged communications asserted.

Thus, the real issue, even by the analysis in other parts of the *Per Curiam* opinion, is whether it is appropriate for the court to determine the legal validity of a claim of privilege by the President, or whether the Constitutional principle of separation of powers requires the court to yield to the President's judgment as to where the public interest lies. My answer would be the latter. But taking the answer given by the *Per Curiam* as correct and at the broadest, the proper role of the court is to decide the legal issue of the nature and extent of the President's privilege, and, given the court's admitted lack of physical power to enforce compliance, express such conclusions in a declaratory judgment form. The court need not issue any process to be served on the President, so the question of "immunity" need never arise. If the court's decision is adverse to the President, he must decide whether to comply or risk adverse political consequences.

---

subject to judicial process. Therefore, even if a court could order the President to perform a "ministerial" act, the issue is whether the Presidential action sought is ministerial or discretionary.

In the case at bar, that issue turns on whether the privilege asserted by the President is a mere evidentiary one, as the *Per Curiam* contends, or is grounded on the Constitutional doctrine of separation of powers, as I believe. If the privilege were a qualified, evidentiary one, the President arguably would have a ministerial duty to turn over evidence in his possession when ordered to do so by a judicial subpoena. However, I have endeavored to show that the President has an *unqualified, Constitutional privilege* to decide whether it is in the public interest to disclose records in his possession to a co-equal Branch of Government. The decision whether to disclose or not to disclose the evidence sought in this case is thus a *discretionary* one for the President and not subject to judicial process under Mississippi v. Johnson. As with many of the other subsidiary issues in the case at bar, resolution of the ministerial versus discretionary question rests on the basic Constitutional issue, *Who Decides?*

[164] 407 U.S. 297, 92 S.Ct. 2125, 32 L.Ed.2d 752 (1972).

[165] 37 U.S. (12 Pet.) 524, 9 L.Ed. 1181 (1828).

[166] 479 F.2d 1099 (8th Cir., 1973).

Whatever the court's decision here, whichever rationale is followed, it seems clear that any issue of Presidential "immunity" or amenability to court process is totally illusory.

V. APPLICATION OF THE CONSTITUTIONAL TRIPARTITE PRIVILEGE

A. *Procedures and Practicalities— Statutes and the Constitution*

Parts V and VI of the *Per Curiam* opinion suggest certain procedures to be followed by the District Court on remand, derived from Environmental Protection Agency v. Mink[167] and our own opinions in Vaughn v. Rosen[168] and Cuneo v. Schlesinger.[169] The procedures themselves are irreproachable, and might well be workable, if we were dealing with a usual statutory privilege and the ordinary papers of the bureaucracy.

We are not; whence arise two great objections to the *Per Curiam* recommended solution: (1) the Constitutional barrier of separation of powers, which means that neither the authorities nor the techniques relied on are applicable here; and (2) certain practical problems inherent in the Judiciary dealing with the most confidential communications of the Chief Executive.

1. *The Authorities*

Mink, Vaughn, and *Cuneo* all dealt with statutory exemptions from disclosure specifically defined in the Freedom of Information Act.[170] No Constitutional privilege was ever invoked. The same can be said of Carl Zeiss[171] and Soucie v. David.[172] In these cases the "courts appropriately examine[d] a disputed item *in camera*" (*Per Curiam, supra* at 720), because the statute provided the indispensable *guidelines* for District Court examination and decision; *i. e.*, the statute specifically defined and described the *categories* of information which were to be exempt from disclosure.

---

[167] 410 U.S. 73, 93 S.Ct. 827, 35 L.Ed.2d 119 (1973).

[168] U.S. App.D.C.–, 484 F.2d 820 (1973).

[169] U.S.App.D.C.–, 484 F.2d 1086 (1973).

[170] 5 U.S.C. § 552 (1970).

[171] Carl Zeiss Stiftung v. V.E.B. Carl Zeiss, Jena, 40 F.R.D. 318 (D.C.D.C. 1966), aff'd on opinion below, 128 U.S.App.D.C. 10, 384 F.2d 979, cert. dismissed, 389 U.S. 952, 88 S.Ct. 334, 19 L.Ed.2d 361 (1967).

[172] 145 U.S.App.D.C. 144, 448 F.2d 1067 (1971)

In this situation the task of the District Judge is clear and definite; he is to look at the confidential material (properly segmented for intelligent decision-making) *in camera*, and make a *factual* determination[173] as to whether the subject matter fits within or without the statutorily exempted categories. If within any defined exemption, the information is kept confidential; if not within any of seven categories, the information is disclosed to the demanding party.

The District Judge does no "balancing" or "weighing of conflicting public interests"; the balancing and weighing has already been done by the Congress in the statute itself. In category "(1) specifically required by Executive order to be kept secret in the interest of the national defense or foreign policy," the undisputed fact of an Executive order categorizing a document as secret precludes even *in camera* inspection by the District Judge, as the Supreme Court held in *Mink*. There is no *factual* question left for the judge to determine, so no inspection violating Executive secrecy is permissible. With regard to other claimed categories of exemption in *Mink* as in *Vaughn* and *Cuneo*, *in camera* inspection was needed to determine the *fact* of the proper classification.

This is comparable to United States v. Reynolds,[174] which antedates the Freedom of Information Act. There the Supreme Court, after determining as a fact from the showing made by the Government that the material related to important national defense secrets, forbade even *in camera* inspection. And, as my colleagues correctly point out, ". . . the Court formally reserved decision on the Government's claim that the Executive has an absolute discretion constitutionally founded in separation of powers to withhold documents." (*Per Curiam*, *supra* at 714.[175])

If we look at Part VI of the *Per Curiam* spelling out the procedure prescribed for the District Judge, aside from the category of national defense or foreign relations (*supra* at 721-722), by what criteria, by what guidelines, with reference to what categories of information communicated to or in the presence of the President, will the District Judge decide what is to be disclosed to and what kept from the Special Prosecutor and grand jury? By what standards is the District Judge to weigh or balance the conflicting claims of the Chief Executive and the

[173] Vaughn v. Rosen, –– U.S.App.D.C. ––, 484 F.2d 820 (1973).

[174] 345 U.S. 1, 73 S.Ct. 528, 97 L.Ed. 727 (1953).

[175] *Citing Id.,* at 6 & n. 9, 73 S.Ct. 528.

Special Prosecutor? By the amorphous standard of "the public interest"? With all due respect to Chief Judge Sirica, why is any one of 400 District Judges better equipped than the Chief Executive of the Nation to determine "the public interest"?

There is missing completely from the situation here the absolutely indispensable ingredient which made the techniques of classification and *in camera* inspection feasible in *Mink, Vaughn,* and *Cuneo, i. e.,* categories of information previously specifically defined by statute as disclosable or confidential. In the situation here, what the District Judge must do is to make the value judgment as to disclosure or confidentiality, which was made by Congress on material subject to statutory mandate, and which here constitutionally belongs to the Chief Executive himself, not to a District Judge, under the doctrine of separation of powers.

2. *Pragmatic Considerations*

The first problem is that of security, an omnipresent consideration when the office of the President is concerned. If *in camera* examination involved only *one* United States District Judge, the violation of Executive privacy might be tolerable. Such restricted access is remote as a practical prospect. There is the process of assembling, classifying, and furnishing the tapes to the court, necessarily involving counsel and other persons who previously have had no access to this stored information. There is the legal and clerical assistance the District Judge must require. There are the probable demands of prospective defendants to be confronted, which may call for access by the Special Prosecutor beyond what he originally required.[176]

After the District Court's decision, then will arise the question of appeal. It is too much to expect any decree of the District Court to have either the wisdom or finality of Solomon's. A *non*-appealable Order of a District Judge, either suppressing or exposing the most confidential recorded conversations of the President, will satisfy no one. The alternative is equally unattractive. Appeal will involve three to nine (in some Circuits, more) judges in the Court of Appeals, with a minimum of clerical and legal staff assistance. Then will come the nine members of the Supreme Court with appropriate supporting personnel.

As a member of the Federal Judiciary, the writer means no disrespect to its members or staff assistants. As the circle of

---

[176] Indeed, the interest in and impact of the court's decision in this case already extend well beyond the parties and legal rights directly involved. Several third parties have sought to assert their interests and views by moving to file briefs as *amici curiae.*

"secrecy" widens, it will dissolve and vanish. All human experience teaches this—particularly in Washington, D.C.

Nor is *in camera* inspection of Presidential material without danger to the Judiciary. The judge who suppresses eagerly sought information can never adequately justify his decision by a public explanation of his rationale in the usual opinion. The judge's decision may in truth be unjustifiable, grossly in error, because federal judges are not necessarily equipped with the type of information on which to base an intelligent decision on confidentiality. By the nature of the problem, the places the judge can turn for assistance are limited or nonexistent. The needed background information may be political in nature, as may the sought after information, and willy-nilly, whatever his decision, the judge may have injected himself and the whole Judiciary into what is basically part of the political process.

B. *A Healthy Tension*

Many speak as if all answers to all conceivable problems of our Government are to be found in specific Constitutional provisions. They imagine that somewhere in that magnificent document there must be the answer to how a conflict between the

1. *The Senate Select Committee on Presidential Campaign Activities.* The Committee is seeking to enforce its own subpoena *duces tecum* against the President in the District Court for the District of Columbia. Select Committee on Presidential Campaign Activities, et al. v. Nixon, — F.Supp. —. In its brief, the Committee takes the position that its case "like the one at bar, presents important constitutional issues relating to the refusal of Richard M. Nixon, President of the United States, to comply with lawfully issued subpenas for vital evidence relating to possible criminal conduct by high executive officials. In both cases, the President's noncompliance with the subpenas is grounded on the claim that material requested is protected by the doctrine of executive privilege." (Brief of Amicus Curia at 3.)

2. *American Civil Liberties Union.* The ACLU sought leave to file as *amicus curiae* in order to vindicate "the public's right to know how the government is discharging its duties." The ACLU also raised doubts about whether the Special Prosecutor should have access to the tapes for use against persons who did not consent to the recording of their conversations with the President.

3. *Louis Schroder, et al.* These movants are plaintiffs-appellants in Schroeder, et al. v. Richardson, No. 73-1265, currently pending in this court. The plaintiffs-appellants allege that they have an interest in this case because one of the issues raised by the briefs is to what extent officials of the Executive Branch can control the investigative functions of federal grand juries.

4.5. Two other *amicus* motions were made that might be characterized as frivolous, charitably speaking.

6. In addition to these *amicus curiae* motions the appellees in Nader v. Butz, No. 73-1935 (D.C.Cir.), moved to schedule the oral arguments on their motion for summary affirmance at the same time as the oral arguments in this case (11 Sept. 1973). In Nader v. Butz, District Judge Jones ordered *in camera* inspection of White House records in the face of a claim of Executive privilege similar to the claim made here. Thus, appelless in *Nader* asserted that the decision in this case would be dispositive of *Nader*.

Executive and the Judiciary (or Executive and Legislative), each claiming to act within the powers of its Branch, should be resolved. I suggest that this is one of several major areas in which the Constitutional Convention deliberately provided no specific answer.

I suggest that the best (and historically only) answer is that judgment on the proper exercise of the Executive and Judicial powers ultimately rests, and was intended to rest, with the American people. Having created three co-equal separate Branches, the Constitutional Convention did not foul up the grand design by providing that one Branch was to be superior and prevail over another, nor did the grand scheme entrust the decision between two conflicting Branches to the third Branch. This was graphically demonstrated by the Constitutional theory on which Washington and his cabinet first acted, that the Executive himself should determine what papers in the public interest could be furnished to another Branch.

It was and is the President's right to make that decision initially, and it is the American people who will be the judge as to whether the President has made the right decision, i. e., whether it is or is not in the public interest that the papers (tapes) in question be furnished or retained. If his decision is made on visibly sound grounds, the people will approve the action of the Executive as being in the public interest. If the decision is not visibly on sound grounds of national public interest, in political terms the decision may be ruinous for the President, but it is his to make. The grand design has worked; the separate, independent Branch remains in charge of and responsible for its own papers, processes and decisions, not to a second or third Branch, but it remains *responsible* to the American people.

This may seemingly frustrate the role of the Special Prosecutor in part of his work, it may frustrate what a Congressional investigative committee conceives to be its role, but in my judgment this was the way the Constitution was intended to work. The Constitution was not designed as an all-powerful efficient instrument of government. The primary concern in the minds of the Founding Fathers of 1787 was to devise a reasonably efficient method of government that above all did not have the inbuilt capacity to become oppressive.[177] And to that

---

[177] This was their concern, but the Framers were not confident they had completely achieved it: " . . . a mere demarcation on parchment of the constitutional limits on parchment of the constitutional limits of the several departments is not a sufficient guard against those encroachments which led to a tyrannical concentration of all the

end they first designed the separation of powers, making each Branch independent, and then left inherent in the structure they had designed the possibility of irreconcilable conflict.[178] But in their view, the possibility of irreconcilable conflict was not necessarily bad, because above all this would guarantee that the National Government could never become an efficient instrument of oppression of the people.

The Founding Fathers were not looking for the *most efficient* government design. After all, they had been subject to and rebelled against one of the most efficient governments then existing.[179] What the Founding Fathers designed was *not efficiency, but protection against oppression.*[180] Leaving the three Branches in an equilibrium of tension was just one of their devices to guard against oppression.[181]

This healthy equilibrium of tension will be destroyed if the result reached by the *Per Curiam* is allowed to stand. My colleagues cannot confine the effect of their decision to Richard M. Nixon. The precedent set will inevitably have far-reaching implications on the vulnerability of any Chief Executive to judicial process, not merely at the behest of the Special Prosecutor in the extraordinary circumstances of Watergate, but at the behest of Congress. Congress may have equally plausible needs for similar information. The fact that Congress is usually or frequently locked in political battle with the Chief Executive cannot mean that Congress' need or right to information in the hands of the Chief Executive is any less than it otherwise would

powers of government in the same hands." The Federalist No. 47 (J. Madison), *Cf.* Mr. Justice Frankfurter: "[T]he doctrine of separation of powers was not mere theory; it was a felt necessity." Youngstown Sheet & Tube Co. v. Sawyer, 343 U.S. 579, 593, 72 S.Ct. 863, 889, 96 L.Ed. 1153 (1952) (concurring opinion).

[178] "The same rule which teaches the propriety of a partition between the various branches of power, teaches us likewise that this partition ought to be so contrived as to render the one independent of the other." The Federalist No. 70 (A. Hamilton).

[179] From Queen Anne's reign in the early 1700's, the time of Marlborough and Godolphin, the English had enjoyed the most efficient government in the western world, with the possible exception of France for a time under Louis XIV or Prussia under Frederick the Great.

[180] Compare the devices enumerated by Hamilton in The Federalist No. 50, "On Maintaining a Just Partition of Power Among the Necessary Departments."

[181] The reason for the separation of powers was well put by Mr. Justice Brandeis:
The doctrine of the separation of powers was adopted by the Convention of 1787, not to promote efficiency but to preclude the exercise of arbitrary power. The purpose was, not to avoid friction, but, by means of the inevitable friction incident to the distribution of governmental powers among three departments, to save the people from autocracy.
Myers v. United States, 272 U.S. 53, 293, 47 S.Ct. 21, 85, 71 L.Ed. 160 (1926) (dissenting opinion).

be. The courts will have been enlisted on one side of what would be even more undeniably and fundamentally a political question.

The *Per Curiam* notes (at 722) that "[w]hat the courts are now called upon primarily to decide, . . . is how to reconcile the need of the United States, by its grand jury, with the legitimate interest of the President in not disclosing those portions of the tapes that may deal with unrelated matters." This is indeed revelatory. One would have thought that the President, not a Special Prosecutor or grand jury, should best determine "the need of the United States." One would have thought that when "the need of the United States" was to be evaluated, the President, not one of 400 District Judges, would be the most fitted to determine where the overall public interest lies. It is thus all too clear that, to reach the result achieved by the *Per Curiam,* somehow, subconsciously, it is essential to assume implicitly that the President no longer represents the United States or is qualified to determine where the overall public interest lies. Without that implicit assumption, the majority here would be powerless to reach the result it does.

At an earlier point the *Per Curiam* defines the position of the Chief Executive here as "The President claims that, at least with respect to conversations with his advisers, the privilege is absolute, since he, rather than the courts, has final authority to decide . . . ." (*Per Curiam, supra* at 713.) My colleagues reject this claim on the basis that "The President's privilege cannot, therefore, be deemed absolute . . . . [A]pplication of Executive privilege depends on a weighing of the public interests . . . ." (*Per Curiam, supra* at 716.)

In the first place, that answer represents the balancing test applicable to the ancient common sense-common law source of all Government privilege; it ignores totally the Constitutional source of the Chief Executive's privilege, separation of powers, which creates the basic question in this case: Under the Constitution, Who Decides?

In the second place, the Constitutional principle also means this: with "absolute" privilege goes *absolute responsibility.* When we reach the level of the Chief Executive, this can only mean responsibility to the American people. I think the Framers meant it that way.

Yet, my colleagues' answer doubtless has appeal to those who theoretically would reject a theoretical absolute. So, in the third place, whatever our answer in theory should be, we must realize both the question and the answer also ignore history. If the same question is phrased in regard to the holder of office in Congress, or the holder of office in the Judiciary, where privilege in regard to the private papers, documents, and deliberations of the Congress and the Judiciary are concerned, the answer is clear—the holder of the office has *always* been the absolute determinant of the privilege.

Has a court ever refused to accept the determination of one House of Congress that its papers were privileged from judicial subpoena, and insisted on compliance with a subpoena *duces tecum? Never. (E. g., Brewster, Calley, Hoffa*, etc., etc.)[182] Has Congress ever refused to accept the determination of the Chief Executive that his papers were privileged from a Congressional committee demand, and sought to enforce it either by its own process or by judicial process? *Never. (E. g.*, the Jay Treaty in Washington's administration, corporate bureau antitrust papers in Theodore Roosevelt's administration, etc., etc.)[183]

To put the theoretical situation and possibilities in terms of "absolute" privilege sounds somewhat terrifying—*until one realizes that this is exactly the way matters have been for 184 years of our history*, and the Republic still stands. The practical capacity of the three independent Branches to adjust to each other, their sensitivity to the approval or disapproval of the American people, have been sufficient guides to responsible action, without imposing the authority of one co-equal Branch over another.[184]

The American Constitutional design may look like sloppy craftmanship, it may upset the tidy theoreticians, but it has worked—a lot better than other more symmetrical models.

At the least, this is a point in favor of its continuance unchanged; at the most, this may be all the answer we need.

---

[182] *See* notes 40-45 *supra* and accompanying text.

[183] *See* notes 75-85 *supra* and accompanying text.

[184] Hamilton began his essay "On Maintaining a Just Partition of Power Among the Necessary Departments" by posing the question:

To what expedient, then, shall we finally resort, for maintaining in practice the necessary partition of power among the several departments, as laid down in the Constituiton? The only answer that can be given is that as all these exterior provisions are found to be inadequate, the defect must be supplied, by so contriving the interior structure of the government as that its several constitutent parts may, by their mutual relations, be the means of keeping each other in their proper places.

He then first referred to that

due foundation for that separate and distinct exercise of the different powers of government which to a certain extent is admitted on all hands to be essential to the preservation of liberty. . . .

The Federalist No. 50.

III
JUDGE SIRICA'S
OPINION IN
UNITED STATES
v.
NIXON

After the Court of Appeals decision in Nixon v. Sirica, *a number of Presidential tapes were submitted to the Special Prosecutor's office. However the dispute between the President and the Special Prosecutor flared up again after the indictment of the President's chief aides (H.R. Haldeman, John Ehrlichman, John N. Mitchell and others) on March 1, 1974 for conspiring to obstruct justice in the Watergate cover-up. Leon Jaworski, the new Special Prosecutor, subpoenaed 64 additional presidential tapes, which he claimed he would need to prepare for the criminal trial. Judge Sirica once again upheld the subpoena.*

IN THE UNITED STATES DISTRICT COURT FOR
THE DISTRICT OF COLUMBIA

Criminal No. 74-110

United States of America

v.

JOHN N. MITCHELL, et al.

(Filed: May 20, 1974, James F. Davey, Clerk)

OPINION AND ORDER

This matter comes before the Court on motion of President
Richard M. Nixon to quash a subpoena *duces tecum* issued to
him by the Watergate Special Prosecutor with leave of this Court.
On April 16, 1974, Special Prosecutor Leon Jaworski moved
the Court for an order, pursuant to Rule 17(c),[1] Federal Rules
of Criminal Procedure, directing the issuance of a subpoena for
the production of specified materials prior to trial in the case of
United States v. *John N. Mitchell, et al.*, CR 74-110, DDC.[2] The
proposed subpoena, prepared by the Special Prosecutor and
directed to the President "or any subordinate officer, official, or
employee with custody or control of the documents or objects"
described, listed in 46 paragraphs the specific meetings and
telephone conversations for which tape recordings and related
writings were sought. Relying on the legal memorandum and
affidavit of the Special Prosecutor in support of the motion, the

---

[1] Rule 17. Subpoena: "(c) For Production of Documentary Evidence and of
Objects. A subpoena may also command the person to whom it is directed to produce
the books, papers, documents or other objects desginated therein. The court on motion
made promptly may quash or modify the subpoena if compliance would be
unreasonable or oppressive. The court may direct that books, papers, documents or
objects designated in the subpoena be produced before the court at a time prior to the
trial or prior to the time when they are to be offered in evidence and may upon their
production permit the books, papers, documents or objects or portions thereof to be
inspected by the parties and their attorneys."

[2] The motion asked that the subpoenaed materials be ordered produced before the
Court with permission granted to Government attorneys to inspect them. Three of the
seven defendants in United States v. Mitchell have filed motions joining in that of
the Special Prosecutor with the stipulation that materials produced be made available
to the defendants in full. A fourth defendant filed a response in support of the
subpoena, but in opposition to the Special Prosecutor's motion insfar as it failed to
assure defendants access to the materials upon production.

Court on April 18, 1974, ordered that the subpoena issue forthwith to the President commanding production before the Court.

Prior to the May 2, 1974 return date of the subpoena, the President filed a Special Appearance and Motion to Quash (eo nomine) which included a formal claim of privilege against disclosure of all subpoenaed items generally as "confidential conversations between a President and his close advisors that it would be inconsistent with the public interest to produce."[3] Thereafter, within time limits fixed by the Court, the Special Prosecutor and five defendants filed papers opposing the President's motion to quash on various grounds.[4] The Government's submission, containing a lengthy and detailed showing of its need for the subpoenaed items and their relevance, has been placed under seal as have the various reply briefs and motions for protective orders and to expunge that were subsequently filed.[5] The matter came on for oral argument *in camera* on May 13, 1974.

In entering a special appearance, the President contends that the Court lacks jurisdiction to enforce the instant subpoena on two grounds: First, courts are without authority to rule on the scope or applicability of executive privilege when asserted by the President, and Second, a dispute between the President and Special Prosecutor regarding the production of evidence is an intra-branch controversy wholly within the jurisdiction of the executive branch to resolve. The first contention, as the President admits, is without legal force in this Circuit.[6] See *Nixon* v. *Sirica*, — U.S. App. D.C. — 487 F. 2d 700 (1973).

The second argument, whatever its merits in the setting of a disagreement between the President and a cabinet officer, for example, has no application to the present situation. The current

---

[3] The document noted, however, that "[p]ortions of twenty of the conversations described in the subpoena have been made public and no claim of privilege is advanced with regard to those Watergate-related portions of those conversations."

[4] Defendant Strachan also filed a motion for an order directing the issuance of a subpoena identical to that of the Special Prosecutor in the event that enforcement of the government subpoena is abandoned.

[5] Although initially accepted under the seal, the Court has released those portions of briefs relating to the jurisdictional issue of "intra-executive controversy" discussed in the text below.

The Court has granted a motion of the Special Prosecutor made pursuant to Rule 6(e), Federal Rules of Criminal Procedure, for leave to disclose grand jury proceedings as necessary in support of the subpoena with the proviso urged by defense counsel that, for the present, such disclosures not be made public.

[6] The President has asserted the point to preserve it, in his words, "should it be necessary for this case to reach a court in which *Nixon* v. *Sirica* is not a controlling precedent."

Special Prosecutor is vested with the powers and authority conferred upon his predecessor pursuant to regulations which have the force of law.[7] Among other prerogatives, the Special Prosecutor has "full authority" to determine "whether or not to contest the assertion of 'Executive Privilege' or any other testimonial privilege." The Special Prosecutor's independence has been affirmed and reaffirmed by the President and his representatives,[8] and a unique guarantee of unfettered operation accorded him: "the jurisdiction of the Special Prosecutor will not be limited without the President's first consulting with such Members of Congress [the leaders of both Houses and the respective Committees on the Judiciary] and ascertaining that their consensus is in accord with his proposed action."[9] The President not having so consulted, to the Court's knowledge, his attempt to abridge the Special Prosecutor's independence with the argument that he cannot seek evidence from the President by court process is a nullity and does not defeat the Court's jurisdiction.

The President advances three principal arguments on the merits supporting his motion to quash. Primary among these is his assertion that the subpoena, together with the Special Prosecutor's showing of relevancy and evidentiary value filed May 10, 1974, fails to comply with the requirements of Rule 17(c). It is conceded by all parties that Rule 17(c) cannot be employed as a vehicle for discovery, and that a showing of good cause is necessary. The landmark cases interpreting Rule 17(c), *Bowman Dairy Company* v. *United States*, 341 U.S. 214 (1951) and *United States* v. *Iozia*, 13 F.R.D. 335 (SDNY 1952), are cited and relied upon by both sides. Basically, good cause under Rule 17(c) requires a showing that (1) subpoenaed materials are evidentiary and relevant; (2) they are not otherwise procurable reasonably in advance of trial; (3) the party cannot properly

---

[7] *Nader* v. *Bork*, 366 F. Supp. 104 (DDC 1973). Former Special Prosecutor Archibald Cox received a delegation of powers and responsibilities from the Attorney General acting by authority of 28 U.S.C. § § 509, 510 and 5 U.S.C. § 301. The terms of this delegation were promulgated by Department of Justice Order No. 517-73, 38 Fed. Reg. 14,688 (June 4, 1973) and reaffirmed as to Mr. Jaworski in Department of Justice Order No. 551-73, 38 Fed. Reg. 30, 738 (November 7, 1973)

[8] *See, e.g., The President's News Conference of October 26, 1973*, 9 Weekly Compilation of Presidential Documents, p. 1289 (Oct. 29, 1973); Letter of Acting Attorney General Robert H. Bork to Leon Jaworski, Esq. dated November 21, 1973; and Hearings Before the Senate Committee on the Judiciary on the Special Prosecutor, 93rd Cong., 1st Sess., pt. 2, pp. 571-573.

[9] Department of Justice Order No. 554-73, 38 Fed. Reg. 32,805 (November 27, 1973).

prepare for trial without them, and failure to obtain them may delay the trial; and (4) the application is made in good faith, and does not constitute a "fishing expedition." See *United States* v. *Iozia, supra,* 13 F.R.D. at 338. It is the Court's position that the Special Prosecutor's May 10, 1974 memorandum correctly applies the Rule 17(c) standards, particularly in the more unusual situation of this kind where the subpoena, rather than being directed to the government by defendants, issues to what, as a practical matter, is a third party. It is the Court's conclusion as well, supported again by reference to the Special Prosecutor's memorandum and appendix, that the requirements of Rule 17(c) are here met.[10]

With regard to the confidentiality privilege interposed by the President, the Court agrees that his claim is presumptively valid. The Special Prosecutor's submissions, however, in the Court's opinion, constitute a *prima facie* showing adequate to rebut the presumption in each instance, and a demonstration of need sufficiently compelling to warrant judicial examination in chambers incident to weighing claims of privilege where the privilege has not been relinquished.[11] In citing relinquishment of privilege, the Court has reference to the portions of subpoenaed recordings which the President has caused to be reduced to transcript form and published. For such, the Court finds the privilege claimed non-existent since the conversations are, to that extent at least, no longer confidential. See *Nixon* v. *Sirica, supra,* 487 F. 2d at 718.

The President's third argument on the merits speaks to the defendant's contention that the subpoenaed materials are

[10] The *Nixon* v. *Sirica* case, arising out of the grand jury investigation which produced the indictment herein, presented circumstances warranting the Court's *in camera* inspection of subpoenaed items, 487 F. 2d at 718, 719. The need for evidence presented here is, if anything, more compelling since the matter has developed into a criminal trial where the standard of proof is not simply probable cause but proof beyond a reasonable doubt, and where defendants confront a more direct threat to their reputations and liberty. The President contends that because the Special Prosecutor would not have commenced this case without evidence sufficient, in his opinon, to convict the defendants, the need for other evidence is insubstantial. Such an argument, however, ignores the fact not only that it is the Special Prosecutor alone, in this instance, who has the duty to determine the quantity and quality of evidence necessary to prosecute, but that the Prosecutor has an obligation to obtain and present *all* the relevant evidence. It has never been the law that once an indictment issues, evidence beyond that at hand is unneccessary and should not be sought.

[11] In this connection, it is significant that although the Special Prosecutor is forced in part to rest his showing on circumstantial evidence, having been denied access to the material solicited, in the approximately 20 instances where contents of subpoenaed tapes have been made public, the Prosecutor's assertions that "Watergate" was discussed have been shown accurate without exception. Counsel for the President is unable to state that other subpoenaed items are or are not relevant to this case because

necessarily producible to them under the principles enunciated in *Brady* v. *Maryland* 373 U.S. 83 (1963) and its progeny, the Jencks Act, 18 U.S.C. § 3500, and rules of discovery for criminal proceedings. The President maintains instead that defendants cannot require production under *Brady* of material in the possession of a non-investigatory government agency or items made unavailable because of their privileged character. The Court finds it unnecessary, due to its disposition of the motion to quash, to reach this question. Under Rule 17(c), the Court "may permit" the materials produced "to be inspected by the parties or their attorneys." The Court intends to supply defense counsel with any and all exculpatory matter that may be found in the items produced, and to deliver any and all non-privileged matter to the Special Prosecutor. It is, of course, the Special Prosecutor's continuing obligation to furnish defendants with *Brady* material that comes into his possession. Defendant's requests for access to the whole of materials produced will be more appropriately considered in conjunction with their pretrial discovery motions.

In requiring compliance with the subpoena, that is, production before the Court, and in ruling on claims of privilege, the Court adopts in full the procedures and criteria established by the United States Court of Appeals for this Circuit in *Nixon* v. *Sirica, supra,* 487 F. 2d at 716-721 (parts IV, V, and VI of the majority opinion). Thus, adequate time will be allowed for preparation of an index and analysis detailing particular claims of privilege the President wishes to make. The originals of all subpoenaed items will accompany the index and analysis when transmitted to the Court. In addition, a separate tape recording, copies from the originals, containing only those portions of conversations since transcribed and made public should be prepared and delivered along with the subpoenaed materials.

he has not seen or heard them. (Transcript of Proceedings In Camera, May 13, 1974, pp. 61, 62.) Nevertheless, he cites the President's April 29, 1974 public characterization of edited transcripts produced from tape recordings including some those here subpoenaed:

"They include all the relevant portions of all of the subpoenaed conversations that were recorded—that is, all portions that relate to the question of what I knew about Watergate or the cover-up, and what I did about it. They also include transcripts of other conversations which were not subpoenaed, but which have a significant bearing on the question of Presidential action with regard to Watergate.

*   *   *   *   *

"As far as what the President personally knew and did with regard to Watergate and the cover-up is concerned, these materials—together with those already made available—will tell it all."

Be that as it may "what the President personally knew and did" is not dispositive of the issue in this case.

To protect the rights of individuals, various of the proceedings and papers concerning this subpoena have been sealed. Such matters will remain under seal, and all persons having knowledge of them will remain subject to restrictions of confidentiality imposed upon them pending further order of the Court. The foregoing, of course, does not affect the transmittal of such materials to appellate courts under seal as a necessary part of the record in this matter. The Court sees no need to grant more extensive protective orders at this time or to expunge portions of the record. Matter sought to be expunged is relevant, for example, to a determination that the presumption of privilege is overcome.

Now, therefore, it is by the Court this 20th day of May, 1974,

ORDERED that the President's motion to quash be, and the same hereby is, denied; and it is

FURTHER ORDERED that on or before May 31, 1974, the President or any subordinate officer, official, or employee with custody or control of the documents or objects subpoenaed by the Special Prosecutor with leave of Court on April 18, 1974, shall deliver to the Court the originals of all subpoenaed items together with an index and analysis and copy tape recording as described in the foregoing opinion; and it is

FURTHER ORDERED that motions for protective orders and to expunge filed or raised orally in this matter, except to the extent already granted by the Court in proceedings heretofore, be, and the same hereby are, denied; and it is

FURTHER ORDERED that should the President initiate appellate review of the Court's order prior to 4:00 p.m., Friday, May 24, 1974, the Court's order shall be stayed pending the completion of such review.

JOHN J. SIRICA
United States District Judge.

IV
THE PETITIONS TO THE SUPREME COURT

After Judge Sirica's order was issued, the President's lawyer filed a notice of appeal to the Court of Appeals. In order to short-cut the appeal procedure, Jaworski petitioned the Supreme Court to take the case immediately before any decision was rendered by the Court of Appeals. This highly unusual procedure—technically a "petition for certiorari before judgment"—had been followed by the Supreme Court in the Steel Seizure case in 1952 (Youngstown Sheet & Tube Co. v. Sawyer), the last great Supreme Court Decision on the scope of the President's constitutional powers. James St. Clair, the President's lawyer, objected to accelerating the case, calling it an ill-advised "rush to judgment." But the Supreme Court agreed to hear argument before the Court of Appeals acted. At that point, St. Clair asked the Supreme Court to review another question: Did the Watergate grand jury have the power to name President Nixon an unindicted co-conspirator for his actions in the Watergate cover-up? The Supreme Court agreed to examine that question. Additional legal papers relating to the secrecy of the grand jury deliberations and transmission of the grand jury records were also filed by the parties and are included below:

IN THE SUPREME COURT OF THE UNITED STATES

October Term, 1973

No. 73-1766

UNITED STATES OF AMERICA, PETITIONER

v.

RICHARD M. NIXON, PRESIDENT OF
THE UNITED STATES, ET AL.,
RESPONDENTS

PETITION FOR A WRIT OF CERTIORARI TO THE
UNITED STATES COURT OF APPEALS FOR THE
DISTRICT OF COLUMBIA CIRCUIT AND
SUGGESTION FOR EXPEDITED SCHEDULE

The Special Prosecutor, on behalf of the United States, petitions for a writ of certiorari before judgment to the United States Court of Appeals for the District of Columbia Circuit.[1]

If the petition is granted, the Special Prosecutor suggests, in view of the imperative public importance that the issues herein be resolved during the present Term of the Court, that the Court expedite the schedule for briefing and argument. In this regard, the Special Prosecutor would suggest that the brief for petitioner be filed on June 7, 1974, and any briefs for respondents on June 7, 1974—all briefs to be filed initially in typewritten form, but to be replaced as soon as possible with printed briefs. The Special Prosecutor further would suggest that the Court hear argument in this case as soon after the filing of briefs as is consistent with the Court's calendar.

---

[1] Under 28 U.S.C. 510, 517, and 518, and Department of Justice Order No. 551-73, 28 C.F.R. § 0.37 *et seq.* (App. B, pp. 26-34, *infra*), The Special Prosecutor has authority, in lieu of the Solicitor General, to conduct litigation before this Court on behalf of the United States in cases within his jurisdiction.

OPINION BELOW

The district court's opinion and order of May 20, 1974, denying the motion to quash the subpoena and enforcing compliance with it (Appendix A, *infra*, pp. 15-23) are not yet officially reported.

JURISDICTION

The order of the district court sought to be reviewed was entered on May 20, 1974, in *United States* v. *Mitchell, et al.* (D.D.C. Crim. No. 74-110). On May 24, 1974, respondent Richard M. Nixon, President of the United States, filed a timely notice of appeal from that order in the district court,[2] and that same day the certified record from the district court was docketed in the United States Court of Appeals for the District of Columbia Circuit (No. 74——). The jurisdiction of this Court to review the instant case, which is now pending in the court of appeals (see *Gay* v. *Ruff*, 292 U.S. 25, 30), is invoked under 28 U.S.C. 1254(1) and 2101(e). See *Youngstown Sheet & Tube Co.* v. *Sawyer*, 343 U.S. 579; *United States* v. *United Mine Workers*, 330 U.S. 258, 269. In both *Youngstown Sheet & Tube Co.* v. *Sawyer* and *United States* v. *United Mine Workers* a writ of certiorari was granted before final judgment in the court of appeals at the instance of the party that had prevailed in the district court.

---

[2] *Nixon* v. *Sirica*, 487 F. 2d 700, 707 n. 21 (D.C. Cir. 1973), the court of appeals stated that an order of this type directed to the President is appealable under 28 U.S.C. 1291. In any event, the court of appeals has jurisdiction pursuant to the All Writs Act, 28 U.S.C. See 687 F. 2d at 706-707.

QUESTIONS PRESENTED

1.   Whether the President, when he has assumed sole personal and physical control over evidence demonstrably material to the trial of charges of obstruction of justice in a federal court, is subject to a judicial order directing compliance with a subpoena *duces tecum* issued on the application of the Special Prosecutor in the name of the United States.

2.   Whether a federal court is bound by the assertion by the President of an absolute "executive privilege" to withhold demonstrably material evidence from the trial of charges of obstruction of justice by his own White House aides and party leaders, upon the ground that he deems production to be against the public interest.

3.   Whether a claim of executive privilege based on the generalized interest in the confidentiality of government deliberations can block the prosecution's access to evidence material and important to the trial of charges of criminal misconduct by high government officials who participated in those deliberations, particularly where there is a *prima facie* showing that the deliberations occurred in the course of the criminal conspiracy charged in the indictment.

4.   Whether any executive privilege that otherwise might have been applicable to discussions in the offices of the President concerning the Watergate matter has been waived by previous testimony pursuant to the President's approval and by the President's public release of 1,216 pages of edited transcript of forty-three Presidential conversations relating to Watergate.

5.   Whether the district court properly determined that a subpoena *duces tecum* issued to the President satisfies the standards of Rule 17(c) of the Federal Rules of Criminal Procedure because an adequate showing has been made that the subpoenaed items are relevant to issues to be tried and will be admissible in evidence.

CONSTITUTIONAL PROVISIONS, STATUTES, RULE, AND REGULATIONS INVOLVED

The constitutional provisions, statutes, rule and regulations involved, which are set forth in Appendix B, *infra*, pp. 24-38, are:

Constitution of the United States:
Article II, Section 1
Article II, Section 2
Article II, Section 3
Article III, Section 2
Statutes of the United States:
5 U.S.C. 301
28 U.S.C. 509, 510, 515-519
Rule:
Rule 17(c) Federal Rules of
Criminal Procedure
Regulations:
Department of Justice Order No. 551-73
(November 2, 1973), 38 Fed. Reg. 30, 738,
adding 28 C.F.R. § § 0.37, 0.38, and
Appendix to Subpart G-1
Department of Justice Order No. 554-73
(November 19, 1973), 38 Fed. Reg. 32,
805, amending 28 C.F.R. Appendix to
Subpart G-1

STATEMENT

This case presents for review the denial of a motion filed on behalf of the respondent Richard M. Nixon, President of the

United States, pursuant to Rule 17(c) of the Federal Rules of Criminal Procedure, seeking to quash a subpoena *duces tecum* issued in a criminal case, directing the President to produce "tapes and other electronic and/or mechanical recordings and reproductions, and any memoranda, papers, transcripts, and other writings" relating to sixty-four specifically described conversations (Appendix C, *infra*, pp. 39-46).

1. On March 1, 1974, a grand jury of the United States District Court for the District of Columbia returned an indictment charging respondents John N. Mitchell, H.R. Haldeman, John D. Ehrlichman, Charles W. Colson, Robert C. Mardian, Kenneth W. Parkinson and Gordon Strachan with various offenses relating to the Watergate matter, including a conspiracy to defraud the United States and to obstruct justice.[3] The subpoena *duces tecum* in question was issued by the district court on April 18, 1974, upon the motion of the Special Prosecutor as Attorney for the United States and was made returnable on May 2, 1974. (Appendix D, *infra*, pp. 47-48). The subpoena called for production of the evidence in advance of the September 9, 1974 trial date in order to allow time for any litigation over the subpoena and for transcription and authentication of any tape recordings produced. Several defendants joined in the subpoena.

On May 1, 1974, President Nixon, through his White House counsel, filed a "special appearance" and motion to quash the subpoena. Subsequent proceedings, at the joint suggestion of counsel for the President and the Special Prosecutor and with the approval of counsel for the defendants, were held *in camera* because of some especially sensitive matters submitted to the district court by the Special Prosecutor in opposition to the motion to quash. Although only defendants Colson, Mardian and Strachan formally joined in the Special Prosecutor's motion for issuance of the subpoena, all seven defendants (respondents herein) argued in opposition to the motion to quash at the hearing in the district court. At that hearing, further motions to expunge and for protective orders, relating to the information submitted by the Special Prosecutor, were filed or raised orally

---

[3] At some or all of the times in question, respondent Mitchell, a former Attorney General of the United States, was Chairman of the Committee for the Re-election of the President. Respondent Haldeman was Assistant to the President and chief of staff. Respondent Ehrlichman was Assistant to the President for Domestic Affairs. Respondent Colson was Counsel to the President. Respondent Mardian, a former Assistant Attorney General, was an official of the President's re-election campaign. Respondent Parkinson was an attorney for the re-election committee. And respondent Strachan was Staff Assistant to the President.

by counsel for the President.

2. In its opinion and order of May 20, 1974, the district court denied the motion to quash and the motions to expunge and for protective orders. It further ordered "the President or any subordinate officer, official or employee with custody or control of the documents or objects subpoenaed" to deliver to the court on or before May 31, 1974 the originals of all subponaed items as well as an index and analysis of those items, together with the tape copies of those portions of the subpoenaed recordings for which transcripts had been released to the public by the President on April 30, 1974. The district court stayed its order pending appellate review on the condition that appellate review was sought before 4:00 p. m. on May 24, 1974, and further provided that matters filed under seal remain under seal when transmitted as part of the record.

In requiring compliance with the subpoena *duces tecum*, the district court rejected the contention by counsel for the President that it had no jurisdiction because the proceeding allegedly involved solely an intra-executive dispute. The court ruled that this argument lacked substance in light of jurisdictional responsibilities and independence with which the Special Prosecutor has been vested by regulations that have the force and effect of law and that had received the explicit concurrence of the President.[4] The court emphasized the "unique guarantee of unfettered operation" given to the Special Prosecutor and noted that under these regulations, as amended and explained by the Acting Attorney General (App. B, *infra*, pp. 37-38), the Special Prosecutor's jurisdiction, which includes express authority to contest claims of executive privilege, cannot be limited without the President's first consulting with the leaders of both Houses of Congress and the respective Committees on the Judiciary and securing their consensus. In these circumstances, the court found that there exists sufficient independence to provide the court with a concrete legal controversy between adverse parties and not simply an intra-agency dispute over policy.[5]

---

[4] The validity of these regulations establishing the authority of the Special Prosecutor has been upheld in three other cases, in additon to the decision below, See *Nader* v. *Bork*, 366 F. Supp. 104 (D.D.C. 1973); *United States* v. *Ehrlichman*, —— F. Supp. —— (D.D.C. Crim. No. 74-116) (May 21, 1974); *United States* v. *Andreas*, —— F. Supp. —— (D. Minn. No. 4-73-Cr. 201) (March 12, 1974).

The regulations are reprinted in Appendix B, *infra*, pp. 29-38.

[5] The court later held that as the recipient of a subpoena in this criminal case, the President "as a practical matter, is a third party" (Appendix A, *infra*, p. 19).

As this Court noted in *Berger* v. *United States*, 295 U.S. 78, 88, the prosecuting

On the merits, and relying on the *en banc* decision in *Nixon* v. *Sirica*, 487 F. 2d 700 (D.C. Cir. 1973), the district court held that in the circumstances of this case, the courts, and not the President, are the final arbiter of the applicability of a claim of executive privilege for the subpoenaed items. Here, the court ruled, the presumptive privilege for documents and materials reflecting executive deliberations was overcome by the Special Prosecutor's *prima facie* showing that the items are relevant and important to the issues to be tried in the Watergate cover-up case and that they will be admissible in evidence.[6]

Finally, the district court held that the Special Prosecutor, in his memorandum and appendix below, satisfied the requirements of Rule 17(c) that the subpoenaed items be relevant and evidentiary. See *Bowman Dairy Co.* v. *United States*, 341 U.S. 214.

3. The President has sought review of this decision in the court of appeals and the Special Prosecutor, on behalf of the United States, seeks certiorari before judgment.

REASONS FOR GRANTING THE WRIT

1. It is the position of the Special Prosecutor that the decision of the district court, relying on *Nixon* v. *Sirica, supra,* is fully in accord with constitutional principles first enunciated in *Marbury* v. *Madison,* 1 Cranch 137, and *United States* v. *Burr,* 25 Fed. Cas. 30 (No. 14,692d) (C.C.D. Va. 1807), and repeatedly reaffirmed by this Court, as recently as the decision in *Environmental Protection Agency* v. *Mink,* 410 U.S. 73. See also *United States* v. *Reynolds,* 345 U.S. 1; *Youngstown Sheet & Tube Co.* v. *Sawyer, supra.* We believe these authorities support the principle that the President is amenable to judicial orders directing the performance of legal duties. Furthermore, we submit that they also demonstrate that, when a claim of executive privilege is interposed in a lawsuit, the courts have the ultimate power to decide whether that privilege has been properly invoked and whether, under all the circumstances, it should be accepted. The Executive's determination is not conclusive.[7]

attorney in a federal criminal case represents the United States as a sovereign government.

[6] As to the claims by defendants that they are entitled to the subpoenaed items under Rule 17(c), the court withheld ruling, stating that defendants' requests for access will be more appropriately considered in conjunction with their pretrial discovery motions.

[7] It is possible that the President is now foreclosed from contesting in this case the issues finally decided in *Nixon* v. *Sirica, supra,* a related proceeding between essentially

Nevertheless, the constitutional issues involved in this case are exceedingly important, both in their own right and in the context of the litigation in which they arise. The case involves basic constitutional issues arising out of the doctrine of the separation of powers and the powers of the Judiciary and the prerogatives of the Chief Executive. Perhaps more fundamentally, this case also presents a question of overriding concern to the full and impartial administration of justice—is our constitutional system of government sufficiently resilient to permit the Executive Branch to establish an independent prosecutor fully capable of investigating and prosecuting allegations of criminal misconduct by officials in the Executive Office of the President, and validly authorized to resort to the judicial process to secure physical evidence from the President himself.

Whether the President is amenable to the judicial process, whether the President or the courts have the ultimate authority to determine the applicability of "executive privilege" to material evidence for judicial proceedings, whether executive privilege can be invoked in the face of a *prima facie* showing that the conversations at issue involved a criminal enterprise, whether any confidentiality privilege for Watergate-related conversations has been irretrievably waived by the President, and whether the President has been properly ordered to comply with the instant subpoena—are all issues worthy of review by this Court.

2. Moreover, it is of imperative public importance that this case be resolved as quickly as possible to permit the trial in the "Watergate cover-up case," *United States* v. *Mitchell, et al.,* to proceed as scheduled on September 9, 1974. If the decision below were to proceed through normal appellate processes, it is likely that there would be no final decision in the court of appeals prior to the end of the current Term of this Court. Assuming that this Court thereafter were not to convene a Special Term to hear this case, the case then could not be heard and disposed of by this Court until the late Fall of this year. Accordingly, the trial could not proceed until the spring of 1975, particularly if the district court's decision is upheld and the district court must conduct *in camera* proceedings to determine which items, if any, are to be produced to the government or defense. In addition, the trial would have to await the transcription of any recordings produced for use at trial. All in

the same parties, See, *e.g., Sunshine Anthracite Coal Co.* v. *Adkins,* 310 U.S. 381, 402-404.

all, at a minimum there would be a delay of six months in the start of the trial.

Immediate consideration of the case by this Court during the present Term would not sacrifice any benefits of intermediate appellate review. The Court of Appeals for the District of Columbia Circuit previously has considered and ruled at length on the principal constitutional issues presented for review by this petition. See *Nixon* v. *Sirica, supra.* Indeed, in his Memorandum in Support of the President's Motion to Quash Subpoena Duces Tecum filed in the district court, counsel for the President stated (pp.1-2): "We recognize that at the present stage of this case these [constitutional] contentions are foreclosed by the decision in *Nixon* v. *Sirica,*—U.S. App. D.C.—487 F. 2d 700 (1973). Thus we do not now press these points, but mention them here in order that they may be preserved should it be necessary for this case to reach a court in which *Nixon* v. *Sirica* is not controlling precedent."

Thus, this case satisfies the standards of Rule 20 of this Court's rules for granting certiorari before judgment as those standards have been articulated in the cases therein cited.

CONCLUSION

For the foregoing reasons, the petition for a writ of certiorari should be granted and the case set for briefing and argument this Term.

Respectfully submitted.

> LEON JAWORSKI,
> *Special Prosecutor.*
>
> PHILIP A. LACOVARA,
> *Counsel to the*
> *Special Prosecutor.*
>
> JAMES F. NEAL,
> *Special Assistant to*
> *the Special Prosecutor*

May 1974.

IN THE SUPREME COURT OF THE UNITED STATES
October Term, 1973

No. 73-1766

UNITED STATES OF AMERICA, PETITIONER

v.

RICHARD M. NIXON, PRESIDENT OF
THE UNITED STATES, ET. AL.,
RESPONDENTS

BRIEF IN OPPOSITION TO PETITION
FOR WRIT OF CERTIORARI BEFORE JUDGMENT

STATEMENT OF THE CASE

In documents filed May 24, 1974, the Special Prosecutor has
asked this Court to grant certiorari before judgment in the Court
of Appeals to review the decision of the District Court for the
District of Columbia on May 20, 1974, denying the President's
motion to quash a subpoena duces tecum. The Special Prosecutor
further suggests to the Court that his brief be filed on June 7,
1974, and that the President file his brief on June 14, 1974, and
requests that argument be heard "as soon after the filing of briefs
as is consistent with the Court's calendar." The President opposes
the petition for certiorari before judgment and he further
opposes the suggestion for an expedited schedule.

REASON FOR DENYING THE WRIT

At page 9 of his Petition, the Special Prosecutor asserts that

the constitutional issues involved in this case are exceedingly
important, both in their own right and in the context of the
litigation in which they arise. The case involves basic
constitutional issues arising out of the doctrine of the
separation of powers and the powers of the Judiciary and the
prerogatives of the Chief Executive.

Of course, we agree with that characterization. But it is precisely
because of the importance of these issues that the President
opposes any attempt to shortcut the usual judicial process.
Prompt judicial action is important in this case but "prompt
judicial action does not mean unjudicial haste." *New York Times
Co.* v. *United States*, 403 U.S. 713, 749 (1971) (Burger, C. J.,

dissenting). When a case raises the most fundamental issues of the allocation of power among the three branches of the federal government, it is more important that it be decided wisely than that it be decided hurriedly.

This is both a "great case" and a "hard case." If the unfortunate result of which Justice Holmes warned in a famous passage, *Northern Securities Co.* v. *United States*, 193 U.S. 197, 400—401 (1904), is to be avoided, it is imperative that this Court consider the case under those conditions that are essential to the judicial process at its best. This means that the Court must be assisted to the greatest possible extent by the lower courts and by counsel and that the Court must have the opportunity for careful reflection and deliberation that wise decision requires.

> The indispensable condition for the discharge of the Court's responsibility is adequate time and ease of mind for research, reflection, and consultation in reaching a judgment, for critical review by colleagues when a draft opinion is prepared, and for clarification and revision in light of all that has gone before. [*Report of the Study Group on the Caseload of the Supreme Court* 1 (1972).]

Those conditions are hardly likely to exist in the closing days of a busy term, when the Court is already under grueling pressure to complete its action on difficult cases argued months before.

Attempts in the past by the Court to make a hurried disposition of an important case arising in the dying days of a term have not been among the proudest chapters in the history of the Court. *New York Times Co.* v. *United States*, 403 U.S. 713 (1971), is but the most recent example. Without commenting on the result in that case, it is hardly likely that any member of the Court found the conditions under which decision was made optimum or that the multiplicity of opinions that issued from the Court represent the best of which the Court was capable. What Justice Harlan said there, at 753, is applicable here as well:

> Due regard for the extraordinarily important and difficult questions involved in these litigations should have led the Court to shun such a precipitate timetable.

An earlier example were the cases of the war brides, *Reid* v. *Covert*, 351 U.S. 487 (1956), and *Kinsella* v. *Kruger*, 351 U.S. 470 (1956), although the pace there was less frenzied than what the Special Prosecutor apparently contemplates for the present case. In those cases review was granted on March 12th oral argument was heard on May 3rd, and the decisions were announced on the last day of the term, June 11th. Even so, only a bare majority of the

Court was prepared to rush to judgment. Justice Frankfurter reserved his vote, because the time had not been sufficient for adequate study and reflection. 351 U.S. at 485. Chief Justice Warren and Justices Black and Douglas announced that they would dissent but said "we need more time than is available in these closing days of the Term in which to write our dissenting views." 351 U.S. at 486.

The hasty decision in those cases bore bitter fruit. When the Court reconvened in the fall, it granted, on November 5, 1956, a petition for rehearing, and when the cases were finally decided on June 10, 1957, 354 U.S. 1 (1957), the Court, by a vote of six to two, accepted the constitutional proposition that it had rejected the preceding spring. Justice Harlan explained his change of vote:

> The petitions for rehearing which were filed last summer afforded an opportunity for a greater degree of reflection upon the difficult issues involved in these cases than, at least for me, was possible in the short interval between the argument and decision of the cases in the closing days of last Term. As a result I became satisfied that this court-martial jurisdiction could in any event not be sustained upon the reasoning of our prior opinion. [354 U.S. at 65.]

If a further example be needed, *A. L. A. Schechter Poultry Corp.* v. *United States*, 295 U.S. 495 (1935), will serve as well as any. In *Schechter* certiorari was granted on April 15th, argument heard May 2nd and 3rd, and the decision announced on May 27th. History has long since pronounced its verdict on that unfortunate decision.

A case as important as the present one deserves better handling from this Court than was given the cases of the sick chickens, the war brides, or the Pentagon Papers. It is unreasonable to expect more from the Court, however, if it is asked to act under the conditions suggested by the Special Prosecutor.

Hasty decision is inappropriate in this case not only because of the importance of the issues involved but also because of their difficulty and their novelty. The issues raised in the Petition for Certiorari have never before been decided in this Court. Indeed the only precedents anywhere, which bear more than a remote analogy to what must be decided here, are the inconclusive rulings of Chief Justice Marshall sitting at circuit in the trial of Aaron Burr, *United States* v. *Burr*, 25 F. Cas. 187 (No. 14, 694) (C.C.D. Va. 1807), the decisions of the Court of Appeals for the District of Columbia Circuit in *Nixon* v. *Sirica*, 487 F. 2d 700 (D.C. Cir. 1973), and *Senate Select Committee* v. *Nixon*, No. 74—1258 (D.C. Cir., May 23, 1974), and the decision of the

District Court that the Special Prosecutor is asking this Court to review.

Moreover, there are other substantial constitutional issues presently pending before the court of appeals in this proceeding concerning the district court's denial of the President's motions to expunge and for a protective order as well as the application of *Brady* v. *Maryland*, 373 U.S. 83 (1963) to privileged material not in the possession of the prosecution. Those issues, under seal by order of that court, are issues of first impression equally critical and significant to the outcome of the present litigation. Thus, it is even more imperative that all the issues involved in this proceeding receive careful consideration, reflection and deliberation at the intermediate appellate level prior to ultimate review by this Court.

This is not to underestimate the importance to the nation, and to the parties, of a prompt resolution of the present controversy to say that the urgency here is considerably less than in the steel seizure case, involving as it did the seizure of a basic industry in a time of war. However, the urgency of what is at issue here, the trial of persons charged with crimes, cannot be equated with the magnitude and irreparable effect to the Nation that was involved in the steel seizure case. Even under the more exigent conditions surrounding the steel seizure case, Justice Burton, speaking for himself and Justice Frankfurter, voted against bypassing the court of appeals.

> The constitutional issue which is the subject of the appeal serves for its solution all of the wisdom that our judicial process makes available. The need for soundness in the result outweighs the need for speed in reaching it. The Nation is entitled to the substantial value inherent in an intermediate consideration of the issue by the Court of Appeals. Little time will be lost and none will be wasted in seeking it. The time taken will be available also for constructive consideration by the parties of their own positions and responsibilities. [*Youngstown Sheet & Tube Co.* v. *Sawyer*, 345 U.S. 937 (1952).]

All that Justice Burton wrote in that case is true here. There have been suggestions in the press that an opinion from the Court of Appeals would not be of benefit here because that court has already spoken on these issues in *Nixon* v. *Sirica*, 487 F. 2d 700 (D.C. Cir. 1973). Nevertheless it can only be of value to this Court to have the advantage of a decision by the Court of Appeals applying the rules it announced in the earlier case to the very different facts of the present case. The decision by the

Court of Appeals last Thursday in the *Senate Select Committee* case—of which the District Court did not have the benefit when it made the order that it is sought to have reviewed here—shows that *Nixon* v. *Sirica* did not deal the death blow to executive privilege that some had imagined. The doctrine remains alive and well—and even if the limitations put on it in the *Sirica* case should ultimately be accepted as the law, the application of the doctrine as limited, is a sensitive question that requires hard judicial thinking. That thinking should be done in the first instance by the Court of Appeals. When the appropriate time comes, we shall of course argue to this Court that it ought not to accept the standard set out in *Nixon* v. *Sirica* but on that issue—as on the other issues that will remain should we be unpersuasive on that point—it will be illuminating to see how the court that decided the *Sirica* standard thinks it applies to the present set of facts.

It should also be noted that there has been no assertion by either the defendants or the Special Prosecutor that the operation of the judicial process within the normal time frame would adversely affect the orderly administration of justice or the rights of the defendants in this case.[1]   Thus, the purported need advanced by the Special Prosecutor for a hasty determination of the issues by avoiding the normal channels of appellate review is clearly outweighed by the actual need for a thorough and carefully considered review of the substantial constitutional issues involved in this litigation. In addition, it is at least questionable whether it is in the best interest of all parties involved to rush to judgment in this case in the midst of an impeachment inquiry involving intrinsically related matters.

Finally, the ability of counsel to assist the Court in the resolution of the issues in this case in such a short time frame is compounded by the concurrency of an impeachment inquiry in the Committee on the Judiciary, United States House of Representatives, which requires a full time effort by the President's Special Counsel and his staff.

To allow the judicial process to run its orderly course will cause some delay, but though speedy justice is an important aim of the law it can never take precedence over just justice. "We all crave speedier judicial processes but when judges are pressured as

---

[1] In fact, on May 1, 1974, a motion with respect to *inter alia*, a continuance, was filed on behalf of defendant Ehrlichman. Defendant Haldeman moved the district court to adopt that request on the same date.

in these cases the result is a parody of the judicial function." *New York Times Co.* v. *United States*, 403 U.S. 713, 752 (1971) (Burger, C. J., dissenting).

CONCLUSION

For all of the foregoing reasons the petition for certiorari before judgment ought to be denied.

Respectfully submitted

> Charles Alan Wright,
>   2500 Red River Street,
>   Austin, Texas 78705
> James D. St. Clair,
> Michael A. Sterlacci,
> Jerome J. Murphy,
> Jean A. Staudt,
> *Attorneys for the President*,
>   The White House,
>   Washington, D.C. 20500

IN THE SUPREME COURT OF THE UNITED STATES
October Term, 1973

No. 73-1834

RICHARD M. NIXON, PRESIDENT OF
THE UNITED STATES, PETITIONER

v.

UNITED STATES OF AMERICA, RESPONDENTS

CROSS-PETITION FOR WRIT OF CERTIORARI
BEFORE JUDGMENT

Richard Nixon, President of the United States, through his counsel, cross-petitions for a writ of certiorari before judgment in the United States Court of Appeals for the District of Columbia Circuit.

OPINIONS

The district court's opinion and order of May 20, 1974, denying the motions to quash the subpoena and to expunge are not yet officially reported.

JURISDICTION

The jurisdictional statement filed by the Special Prosecutor in his Petition for Writ of Certiorari is hereby incorporated by reference.

QUESTIONS PRESENTED

In addition to those questions presented by the Special Prosecutor in his Petition for Writ of Certiorari the following question is presented for review:

Whether, under the Constitution, a grand jury has the authority to charge an incumbent President as an unindicted co-conspirator in a criminal proceeding.

CONSTITUTIONAL PROVISIONS

The additional provisions of the United States Constitution are relevant to the question presented.

STATEMENT OF THE CASE

The statement filed by the Special Prosecutor in his Petition adequately presents the factual development of this case.

REASONS FOR GRANTING WRIT

It is our belief that the issue presented for review by this Cross-Petition is already before the Court.[2] The Special Prosecutor has understandably not identified this issue with particular clarity because of its prejudicial nature, and in an exercise of caution to insure that this critical issue is properly presented for review, we are filing this Cross-Petition.[3]

It is essential that the Court grant this Cross-Petition in order that the respondent not be divested of his right to appeal an adverse decision of a district court by at least one court of appellate jurisdiction. Moreover, this is an issue of first impression concerning a question of grave constitutional magnitude and import that should not be determined with finality by a single district court. If the decision of the district court on this issue is allowed to stand, we believe it seriously impinges upon the constitutional grant of authority vested in the United States House of Representatives by Article I. In addition, such a decision could be interpreted to mean that a President would be subject to similar action by any grand jury throughout the United States. The prejudicial nature and irreparable effect of such a grand jury finding cannot be seriously questioned. If the Court, however, deems it advisable for this issue to be severed and heard in the first instance in the United States Court of Appeals, due to the summary disposition of this issue by the district court, respondent has no objection. Moreover, in the course of this proceeding, if this Court finds it unnecessary to resolve this issue, for any reason, we request that the Court frame its order in such a manner as to preserve the appealability of this issue in a subsequent proceeding, if necessary.

---

[2] See Letter from Counsel to the Special Prosecutor to Clerk, Supreme Court of the United States, dated June 3, 1974. We are in agreement with the Special Prosecutor that because of the grand jury matters involved, it is imperative that the Joint Appendix or portions thereof be placed under seal.

[3] See e.g., *National Labor Relations Board* v. *International Van Lines*, 409 U.S. 48, 52 n.4 (1972) where respondent was precluded from seeking review of an adverse issue where no timely cross-petition for certiorari was filed. See also, *Brennan* v. *Arnheim & Neely, Inc.*, 410 U.S. 512, 516 (1972).

CONCLUSION

For the reasons stated above, the cross-petition for certiorari should be granted, or in the alternative, the issue should be certified to the United States Court of Appeals.

Respectfully submitted,

James D. St. Clair,
Michael A. Sterlacci,
Jerome J. Murphy,
Jean A. Staudt,
James R. Prochnow,
Attorneys for the President,
The White House,
Washington, D.C. 20500.

IN THE SUPREME COURT OF THE UNITED STATES
October Term, 1973

No. 73-1766

UNITED STATES OF AMERICA,
Petitioner

v.

RICHARD M. NIXON, PRESIDENT OF
THE UNITED STATES, ET AL.,
Respondents

No. 73-1834

RICHARD M. NIXON, PRESIDENT OF
THE UNITED STATES,
Petitioner

v.

UNITED STATES OF AMERICA

MEMORANDUM OF THE UNITED   STATES IN
OPPOSITION TO MOTION FOR DISCLOSURE AND
TRANSMITTAL OF GRAND JURY MATTERS

The United States submits this memorandum in opposition to
the motion by the President to disclose to the President and his
counsel and to transmit to this Court all transcripts, tape
recordings, grand jury exhibits and any and all other matters
occurring before the June 5, 1972 Grand Jury which pertain to
the grand jury's action in naming the President as an unindicted
co-conspirator in *United States* v. *Mitchell, et al.*, D.D.C. Crim
No. 74—110.

We do not address various procedural objections that could be
raised to the filing of this motion. We do note, however, that this
same relief was sought by motion filed in the district court on
June 11, 1974. By order entered on June 18, 1974, the district
court denied that motion. (A copy of that order is annexed as
Exhibit A.) Thus, the present motion is necessarily an application
for a writ of mandamus to review that decision by District Judge
John J. Sirica.

INTRODUCTION

On May 31, 1974, this Court granted the government's petition for a writ of certiorari (No. 73—1766) and agreed to review the portion of the district court's order of May 20, 1974, that had denied the President's motion to quash a subpoena *duces tecum* on the ground of executive privilege. The President, on June 10, 1974, filed a cross-petition for a writ of certiorari (No. 73—1834), seeking review of that portion of the May 20th order that denied his motion to expunge from the record the grand jury's action in naming him as an unindicted co-conspirator in *United States* v. *Mitchell, et al.* The relevant portions of the record that were before the district court when it acted on the President's motion were duly transmitted to this Court on May 28, 1974.

On June 11, 1974, the President moved in the district court for an order disclosing to him and transmitting to this Court all of the materials on which the grand jury had acted in taking the course it did, and attached to his motion various extracts from the grand jury evidence that was submitted to the Committee on the Judiciary of the House of Representatives pursuant to the district court's order of March 18, 1974 (D.D.C. Misc. No. 74—21). These extracts evidently have been made available to counsel for the President by the Committee in connection with the impeachment inquiry. The government opposed the motion and on June 18, 1974, the district court denied it. See Exhibit A, *infra.*

In this Court, counsel for the President is equally selective in attaching material made available to him by the House Judiciary Committee in attempting to support his rather startling assertion that the "evidence presented [to the grand jury] was and is totally insufficient to support the action taken" by the grand jury in identifying the President, among others, as an unindicted co-conspirator. St. Clair Aff. ¶ 4. That decision was reached by a randomly selected panel of citizens regularly impanelled in the district court and was reached by a vote of 19-0 after hearing scores of witnesses during an eighteen-month investigation.

The President's present contention seems based on an attack upon the significance of one tape-recorded conversation he was ordered to produce under subpoena. etc.

The President's present contention seems based on an attack upon the significance of one tape-recorded conversation he was ordered to produce under subpoena. *Nixon* v. *Sirica*, 487 F.2d

700 (D.C. Cir. 1973).[1] Of course, the grand jury's decision was not based on any particular item of evidence, and as counsel for the President well knows, the grand jury, pursuant to the order of the district court on March 18, 1974, transmitted to the House Judiciary Committee a vast amount of evidence it considered "material" to the President's role in Watergate. We are advised, furthermore, that under the Committee's rules, counsel for the President has access to all the evidence that is presented to the Committee by its Impeachment Inquiry Staff in executive session, and that this includes the overwhelming majority of the volume of evidence furnished by the grand jury. Thus, to the extent that counsel seeks access directly to the grand jury minutes in connection with the cases pending in this Court, claiming some due-process right to know the evidence against him in the House, the argument seems not only directed to the wrong forum but unwarranted by the facts.

Coming to the specifics of the President's motion, we submit that it is governed by undisputed legal principles which have repeatedly been applied by the courts, and should be denied for two distinct but related reasons: First, a challenge to the factual sufficiency of the grand jury's finding was not raised in the President's motion to expunge and therefore was not passed upon by the district court's decision of May 20, 1974, and this issue is not now before this Court upon review of that order. Second, the courts have unanimously rejected an invitation to determine *de novo* whether a grand jury's finding of probable cause was supported by adequate evidence, and the circumstances of the present application make it especially inappropriate for this Court to assume that function. Thus, there is no compelling reason under Rule 6(e) of the Federal Rules of Criminal Procedure for disclosing directly to counsel for the President the evidence relied on by the grand jury in its decision to name the President as an unindicted co-conspirator.[2]

---

[1] The contention on p. 1 of the President's memorandum in support of his motion in this Court that he "voluntarily" provided "the grand jury with numerous documents and other materials" in order to "assist that grand jury" hardly reflects the way in which, the record shows, the grand jury acquired evidence from him.

[2] The materials sought by the President would include substantially more than those transcripts and exhibits forwarded by the grand jury to the House Judiciary Committee. In addition to the evidence directly relating to involvement of the President, there exists a large amount of materials indirectly relevant to the grand jury's decision to name Richard Nixon, among others, as a co-conspirator in this case.

ARGUMENT

I

It is significant — indeed controlling — that counsel for the President is unable to show that the materials to which he wants access and wants transmitted to this Court relate to any of the issues before the Court. A brief review of these proceedings shows why this is so.

In the President's motion to expunge, filed in the district court on May 13, 1974, counsel challenged only the legal authority of the grand jury to take any action suggesting criminal complicity by an incumbent President. The argument presented was solely one of law: that an incumbent President could not be indicted; that it follows "with equal if not more force" that "a grand jury cannot authorize the naming of the President as an unindicted co-conspirator" (President's Reply Memorandum, p. 19); and that the court was therefore obliged to expunge its action from the record. The government countered that it is far from certain that an incumbent President is immune to indictment but that in any event the practical arguments in support of such a proposition in no way suggest immunity from being named an *unindicted* co-conspirator when it is necessary and appropriate to do so in conjunction with an independent criminal prosectuion. We argued that the court was in no sense, therefore, obliged to expunge the grand jury's action.[3]

In its opinion of May 20th, the court refused to expunge the grand jury's action, finding: "Matter sought to be expunged is relevant, for example, to a determination that the presumption of [executive] privilege is overcome." It is clear that at no time was the district court invited by counsel for the President to inquire into the evidentiary support for the grand jury's action, that the court did not purport to do so, and that the material on which the grand jury may have relied was not before that court. In denying the President's motion seeking the relief now sought by the instant motion, the district court expressly noted that "the evidentiary grounds for the jury's action . . . have never been raised" in the district court. Exhibit A, *infra*, p. 2.

Accordingly, none of the grand jury transcripts of this lengthy investigation was certified to the court of appeals as part of the record on the President's appeal from the district court's May

---

[3] We note that the President would not automatically be entitled to expungement even if the grand jury had overstepped its precise functions, since the courts have discretion to consider the overall public interest. See generally *In re Grand Jury Proceedings*, 479 F.2d 458, 460 n.2 (5th Cir. 1973); *Application of Johnson*, 484 F.2d 791, 797 (7th Cir. 1973).

20th ruling, and that is the record that was transmitted to this Court before it granted the petition and cross-petition for certiorari before judgment.

The material that counsel for the President now wishes to insert in the record and have transmitted to this Court, therefore, is not properly part of the record, and indeed would not even be relevant to the issue posed by the President's cross-petition for certiorari. The only question presented by the President's cross-petition is (p. 2):

> Whether, under the Constitution, a grand jury has the authority to charge an incumbent President as an unindicted co-conspirator in a criminal proceeding.

Thus, this Court is called upon to decide only the question of constitutional power, not the evidentiary basis for the grand jury's finding. Under Rule 23(1)(c) of the Supreme Court Rules, only the questions specifically set forth in the petition for certiorari or fairly comprised therein will be considered by the Court. *Andrews* v. *Louisville & N. R. Co.*, 406 U.S. 320, 324-25; *Namet* v. *United States*, 373 U.S. 179, 190. See generally R. Stern & E. Gressman, *Supreme Court Practice* 297-98 (4th ed. 1969). Neither the question presented to the Court by the President nor those presented in the Special Prosecutor's petition for certiorari (which deal solely with the amenability of a President to a subpoena *duces tecum* and with the validity of the claim of executive privilege in the context of this case) fairly include, as a necessary determination, an evaluation of the *factual* justification for the grand jury's naming of the President as an unindicted co-conspirator. This is well demonstrated by the fact that neither brief or argue the factual questions in connection with the briefing of the legal question decided by the district court.

Moreover, an inquiry into this factual question, involving the weighing of vast amounts of testimony and documentary evidence, certainly would not be a "plain error" which the Court might reach despite Rule 23(1) (c). That power, sparingly used, may be exercised "only in clear cases of an exceptional circumstances." *Kessler* v. *Strecker*, 307 U.S. 22, 34, See, *e. g.*, *Sibbach* v. *Wilson & co.*, 312 U.S. 1, 16.

In his Appendix C in Support of the pending Motion, "Memorandum — The Evidence Establishes that the President Did Not Authorize the Payment of Howard Hunt's Attorney Fees," which counsel for the President has submitted under seal, counsel argues at length, as he might to a jury, why the selected items of evidence with which he deals do not establish that the

President was a co-conspirator. We reiterate what we noted above: the grand jury's action cannot be reduced to dependence on the excerpts discussed by counsel. Moreover, the grand jury's finding of probable cause — even if it were premised wholly on tapes the President explained to Senator Ervin: "The tapes are entirely consistent with what I know to be the truth and what I have stated to be the truth. However, as in any verbatim recording of informal conversations, they contain comments that persons with different perspectives and motivations would inevitably interpret in different ways." Letter from Richard Nixon to Chairman Sam J. Ervin, Jr., July 23, 1973, *Hearings Before the Senate Select Committee on Presidential Campaign Activities*, Book 6, p. 2479 (1973). The grand jury, with its perspective shaped by sondieration of numerous witnesses and exhibits, was certainly free to draw an inference against which counsel for an interested party argues.

Since these factual issues were neither argued to nor decided by the district court, whose decision is to be reviewed, it is especially inappropriate for this Court to be called upon to make the inquiry. *Bivens* v. *Six Unknown Agents of Federal Bureau of Narcotics*, 403 U.S. 388, 397-98; *United States* v. *Martin D. Eby Constr. Co.*, 386 U.S. 317, 330.

II

Furthermore, in considering the application by counsel for the President to have access to the material on which the grand jury acted in order to litigate the evidentiary basis for its judgment, two points should be kept in mind: First, the grand jury's action regarding the President was merely incidental to its indictment of seven other persons in this case, and he was not the focus or target of its action. Second, there is already available to the President another forum in which to litigate the weight of the evidence before the grand jury, since the evidence the grand jury considered directly material to the President has been transmitted to the House Judiciary Committee where, it is apparent from counsel's papers in support of the pending motion, this evidence is being made fully available to counsel in accordance with the Committee's procedures.[4]

[4] On pp. 11-12 of his Memorandum in support of the pending motion, counsel suggests that as a result of the "screening" by the grand jury and the Special Prosecutor, some "exculpatory materials could have been deleted." This speculation is unfounded. As shown by counsel's own exhibits and the sealed argumentative memorandum based on them, all material evidence was furnished to the Committee, including, for example, the testimony of persons who denied any wrong-doing on their part or the President's.

The President's status as an alleged co-conspirator is significant in the posture of the cases pending in this Court for one reason, and that is the reason it was brought to the attention of the district court: executive privilege cannot be invoked by a party to an illegal enterprise to suppress the evidence of that conspiracy. For this reason the district court below found that the grand jury's finding was relevant to determining whether the subpoenaed items are covered by a valid privilege. As we shall argue more fully in our main brief, it is settled law that a privilege designed to promote candor, like executive privilege, is inapplicable once there has been a *prima facie* showing that what would ordinarily have been a privileged or confidential relationship has been abused and tainted. See, *e.g., Clark* v. *United States,* 289 U.S. 1, 14; *United States* v. *Aldridge,* 484 F.2d 655, 658 (7th Cir. 1973); *Pfizer, Inc.* v. *Lord,* 456 F.2d 545 (8th Cir. 1972); *United States* v. *Friedman,* 445 F.2d 1076 (9th Cir. 1971), cert. denied, 404 U.S. 958. This Court need not look beyond that *prima facie* showing.

Here, the grand jury's finding is sufficient to make that *prima facie* showing and is not to be litigated on the facts. The kind of inquiry counsel for the President seeks to open is one that is traditionally eschewed by the courts. In *Ex Parte United States,* 287 U.S. 241, 250, this Court held that the vote of "a properly constituted grand jury conclusively determines the existence of probable cause." The Court had earlier explained, in a similar holding, that "an indictment found by a proper grand jury should be accepted everywhere through the United States as at least *prima facie* evidence of the existence of probable cause." *Beavers* v. *Henkel,* 194 U.S. 73, 85. And in *Ewing* v. *Mytinger & Casselberry, Inc.,* 339 U.S. 594, 599, the Court observed that, even though the "impact of judicial proceedings is often serious" for the "reputation or liberty of a man," the grand jury's determination "whether there is probable cause to believe he is guilty" is "conclusive on the issue of probable cause." The Court then explained: "Yet it has never been held that the hand of the government must be stayed until the courts have had an opportunity to determine whether the government is justified in instituting suit in the courts." Accord, *United States* v. *King,* 482 F. 2d 768, 776 (D.C. Cir. 1973).

Hence, challenges to an indictment, valid on its face, on the ground that the grand jury acted on the basis of inadequate or incompetent evidence, have been summarily disallowed. See *United States* v. *Calandra,* — U.S. — , (42 U.S.L.W. 4104, 4105, January 8, 1974); *Coppedge* v. *United States,* 311 F.2d 128

(D.C. Cir. 1962), cert. denied, 373 U.S. 946; *United States* v. *Birmingham*, 454 F.2d 706, 709 (10th Cir. 1971), cert. denied, 406 U.S. 969; *Reyes* v. *United States*, 417 F.2d 916, 918-19 (9th Circ. 1969). One reason behind this rule has been articulated by this Court:

> If indictments were to be held open to challenge on the ground that there was inadequate or incompetent evidence before the grand jury, the resulting delay would be great indeed. The result of such a rule would be that before trial on the merits a defendant could always insist on a kind of preliminary trial to determine the competency and adequacy of the evidence of the grand jury. This is not required by the Fifth Amendment.

Costello v. *United States*, 350 U.S. 359, 363. See also *Lawn* v. *United States*, 355 U.S. 339, 348-50. Moreover, there is no requirement that grand jury proceedings be transcribed. 8 *Moore's Federal Practice* ¶ 6.02[2][d] (1973). In addition, the scope of information the grand jury may properly consider is extremely broad, see *United States* v. *Dionisio*, 410 U.S. 1, 15; *Branzburg* v. *Hayes*, 408 U.S. 665, 701, and thus judicial re-examination of the grand jury's determination is generally not feasible in any event.

Counsel for the President states that the general rule that a grand jury finding of probable cause is not subject to challenge on the ground that it was reached on the basis of inadequate evidence is subject to an exception for instances in which "an abuse of the grand jury function" is alleged. Even if this were the law, however, an abuse of the grand jury function is not shown by a bald charge of insufficient evidence. If the President has no constitutional immunity to being named an unindicted co-conspirator — and that is purely a question of law — a properly constituted grand jury which hears evidence and returns an accusation for crimes within the jurisdiction of the court acts in accordance with the law, regardless of the weight of the evidence. [5]

---

[5] Moreover, it is clear that no such exception exists. In *In re Grand Jury Investigation*, 32 F.R.D. 175, appeal dismissed, 318 F.2d 533 (2d Cir. 1963), cert. denied, 374 U.S. 802, on which the President relies, General Motors Corporation alleged that a grand jury was being misused by the government for the purpose of discovery in connection with a pending prosecution. Even there, however, in the face of a strong claim of a true abuse of the grand jury, Judge Edelstein refused to grant General Motors access to secret grand jury materials, stating that any abuse could be remedied without violating grand jury secrecy.

The reasoning which refuses to allow a defendant to challenge the adequacy of the facts supporting a grand jury's finding applies with even more force in the case of an unindicted co-conspirator, who is not a party to the action initiated by the indictment and who suffers no direct legal burden because of it. Indeed, since an indictment need not list the name of every co-conspirator, *Rogers* v. *United States*, 340 U.S. 367, 375; *Cross* v. *United States*, 392 F.2d 360, 362 (8th Cir. 1968), even if his identity is known to the grand jury, *United States* v. *Gasoline Retailers Ass'n, Inc.*, 285 F.2d 688, 692 (7th Cir. 1961), an unindicted co-conspirator might not be aware of his status until the eve of trial, thus compounding the difficulties that would arise if a challenge to that finding were allowed. Significantly, counsel for the President has not cited a single case in which *any* person named as an unindicted co-conspirator has been allowed to litigate the sufficiency of the evidence available to the grand jury to support that charge.

Even if a challenge to the grand jury's finding might be permitted under special or unusual circumstances, counsel for the President has made no showing which would tend to support his assertion that the grand jury's action in this case was unjustified by the facts. The affidavit of the President's counsel states only that he has heard part of the evidence submitted to the grand jury (and in turn furnished to the House Judiciary Committee) and that, in his opinion, that evidence is insufficient to warrant a finding of probable cause. There is no contention, however, that he has been advised that the grand jury acted only on the basis of the materials annexed to his affidavit (although we do not concede that, standing alone, that evidence would be insufficient to infer probable cause), and indeed the grand jury's submission to the House of Representatives contained additional evidence.[6] In any event, the opinion of any lawyer that the evidence against his client is not persuasive cannot be accepted as a sufficient reason for granting unrestricted access to grand jury proceedings and exhibits.

In sum, the courts will conclusively presume that a grand jury's finding of probable cause is supported by adequate evidence, and will not permit litigation over the factual basis for that determination. Yet the President now seeks release of these voluminous grand jury materials for the very purpose of asking

---

[6] Moreover, as noted earlier, the grand jury heard and considered evidence indirectly relevant to the President's complicity which was not forwarded to the House Judiciary Committee.

this Court to undertake that task *de novo*. The request must be denied as unwarranted.

Finally, as counsel for the President concedes, the courts have been extremely chary of intruding into "the indispensable secrecy of grand jury proceedings," *United States* v. *Johnson*, 319 U.S. 503, 513, and have done so only upon a strong and persuasive showing of a great need.

> [Grand jury secrecy] must not be broken except where there is a compelling necessity. There are instances when that need will outweigh the countervailing policy. But they must be shown with particularity.

United States v. *Proctor & Gamble Co.*, 356 U.S. 677, 682. The burden, of course, is on the person seeking disclosure. *Pittsburgh Plate Glass Co.* v. *United States*, 360 U.S. 395, 400. The less restrictive "particularized need" standard of *Dennis* v. *United States*, 384 U.S. 855, is based upon the notion of fair play for criminal defendants, who must prepare for trial, and is thus not applicable to the present situation, where disclosure is sought — we assume — "in connection with a judicial proceeding" (the cases pending before this Court) which in no sense require access to that material as a matter of fundamental fairness. See Rule 6(e), Federal Rules of Criminal Procedure; 1 Wright, *Federal Practice and Procedure* § 109 (1969).

CONCLUSION

We submit, therefore, that the President has failed to meet the high standards imposed by the courts before grand jury materials will be released. The President is not a direct party to this criminal prosecution, and hence does not require access to the grand jury transcripts and exhibits to aid in preparing a defense. To the extent he wishes access to these materials in order to deal with the impeachment inquiry, such a request is not properly made in the context of the present proceedings, and seems unwarranted in any event in light of the Judiciary Committee's apparent practice of making all evidence submitted to the Committee available to the President's counsel.

Accordingly, the President's pending motion should be denied. Respectfully submitted.

LEON JAWORSKI,
Special Prosecutor

PHILIP A. LACOVARA,
*Counsel to the Special
Prosecutor.*

Watergate Special Prosecution Force,
Department of Justice,
1425 K Street, N. W.,
Washington, D. C. 20005.

Attorneys for the United States.

June 20, 1974

IN THE UNITED STATES DISTRICT COURT
FOR THE DISTRICT OF COLUMBIA

UNITED STATES OF AMERICA

v.   Criminal Case No. 74—110

JOHN N. MITCHELL, et al

ORDER

This matter comes before the Court on the Special Appearance and Motion to Disclose and to Transmit Grand Jury Matters (eo nomie) of the President filed June 11, 1974. The President and his counsel seek access to "any and all transcripts, tape recordings of Presidential conversations, grand jury minutes and exhibits and any and all other matters occurring before the Grand Jury which pertain to the Grand Jury action in naming and/or authorizing the Special Prosecutor to identify Richard Nixon as an unindited co-conspirator," and also move to "transmit this material as a part of the certified record of the above captioned case to the United States Supreme Court." The motion is made in connection with litigation now before the Supreme Court relating to this Court's denial of motions to quash and to expunge in the instant criminal matter.

The Special Prosecutor filed a Memorandum in opposition to the President's Motion on June 14, 1974. In ruling on the President's Motion, the Court adopts the Argument of the Special Prosecutor with particular emphasis on the fact that the question earlier before this Court and now before the Supreme Court regarding the naming of President Richard M. Nixon as an unindicted co-conspirator in CR 74-110 is a question of law, to wit: Whether, under the Constitution, a grand jury has the authority to name an incumbent President as an unindicted co-conspirator in a criminal proceeding. It is not a question of evidentiary support for such grand jury action. The Court cannot discern any need or basis for lifting the traditional secrecy of grand jury proceedings where the evidentiary grounds for the jury's action are not at issue, have never been raised in the lower court and probably could not be attacked in any event.

Now, therefore, it is this 18th day of June, 1974,
ORDERED that the Motion to Disclose and Transmit Grand
Jury Matters be, and the same hereby is, denied.

JOHN J. SIRICA
United States District Judge

IN THE SUPREME COURT OF THE UNITED STATES

OCTOBER TERM, 1973

No. 73—1766

UNITED STATES OF AMERICA, PETITIONER

v.

RICHARD M. NIXON, PRESIDENT OF THE UNITED STATES
ET AL., RESPONDENTS

No 73—1834
RICHARD M. NIXON, PRESIDENT OF THE UNITED STATES,
PETITIONER

v.

UNITED STATES OF AMERICA

MEMORANDUM ON BEHALF OF THE PRESIDENT IN
REPLY TO THE MEMORANDUM OF THE SPECIAL
PROSECUTOR IN OPPOSITION TO MOTION TO
DISCLOSE AND TO TRANSMIT GRAND JURY MATTERS

STATEMENT

On June 19, 1974, the President of the United States, through
his counsel, filed in this Court a Motion for Disclosure and
Transmittal of Grand Jury Matters to complete the record for
review in the above-styled cause. On June 20, 1974, the Special
Prosecutor filed a Memorandum in Opposition to the President's
motion. This memorandum will reply to the Special Prosecutor's
opposition.

ARGUMENT

I. Newly Discovered Evidence Is Basis For Motion

The Special Prosecutor argues that this motion should be
denied because:

A challenge to the factual sufficiency of the grand jury's
finding was not raised in the President's motion to expunge
and therefore was not passed upon by the district court's
decision of May 20, 1974. Memorandum of the United States

in Opposition to Motion for Disclosure and Transmittal of Grand Jury Matters [hereinafter 'Memo in Opposition'] at 4

This reason cannot be used to deny this motion because the grand jury excerpts, which we use as the basis for our claim that the grand jury was acting outside its authority, were only released by the House Judiciary Committee to the President's Counsel on May 21, 1974, one day *after* the district court's decision of May 20, 1974, and can be considered legally as "newly discovered evidence." As we have already pointed out to this court, this material only recently came into our possession. Memorandum in Support of Motion for Disclosure and Transmittal of Grand Jury Matters [hereinafter Memo in Support] p. 7; Memo in Support, Appendix A, p. 1. After receipt and subsequent analysis of this new evidence, the President's counsel proceeded in the district court to seek full disclosure of the grand jury material. The district court without holding an evidentiary hearing denied the President's Fed. R. Crim P. 6(e) motion.

Under Fed. R. Crim P. 33, courts have developed criteria to evaluate a claim that "newly discovered evidence" entitles a defendant to a new trial. If this court were to consider the instant motion under the criteria developed under Rule 33, our claim unquestionably satisfies all requirements. The criteria for "newly discovered evidence" under Rule 33 utilized in most courts is as stated in *Thompson* v. *United States*, 188 F. 2d 652 (D.C. Cir. 1951) (new trial motion following robbery conviction denied when defendant made an insufficient showing of "newly discovered evidence") which sets out a five-pronged test:

> To obtain a new trial because of newly discovered evidence (1) the evidence must have been discovered since the trial; (2) the party seeking the new trial must show diligence in the attempt to procure the newly discovered evidence; (3) the evidence relied on must not be merely cumulative or impeaching; (4) it must be material to the issues involved; and (5) of such nature that in a new trial it would probably produce an acquittal." 188 F. 2d at 653. (emphasis added) *Accord: U.S.* v. *Gordon*, 246 F. Supp. 522 (D.D.C. 1965); *U.S.* v. *Rodriquez*, 437F. 2d 940 (5th Cir. 1971).

In the instant case, these requirements are met. The grand jury excerpts were given to the President's Counsel by the House Judiciary Committee in executive session after the district court order of May 20, 1974. Due to the nature of the material, it could not have been discovered earlier, and thus it was impossible to advance this argument before the district court rendered its decision. This newly discovered evidence is relevant to the issue of whether the grand jury was acting outside its authority in naming the President. It stands to reason that the grand jury passed that which it considered the most incriminating evidence of the President's role to the House Judiciary Committee. Yet that material which has been presented to the House Judiciary Committee and which we have attached as a sealed appendix to our motion could not justify probable cause in naming the President as an unindicted co-conspirator and does form the basis of our motion for limited disclosure in the instant case.

II. The Grand Jury Matter Is Relevant to the Issues
Before This Court

The Special Prosecutor at page six of the Memo in Opposition urges that the material requested in the instant motion "would not even be relevant to the issue posed by the President's cross-petition for certiorari." It is not for the Special Prosecutor to determine the relevancy of this motion. This court will perform that function. The issues of this case pertain to whether the grand jury was acting within its authority in naming the President as an unindicted co-conspirator and whether the grand jury determination in this regard made out a *prima facie* case of criminal activity. The Special Prosecutor astutely has focused on the legal aspects of these issues, but has blithely ignored that there is a basic factual consideration inherent in an analysis of the issues. A grand jury or any judicial body can overstep its authority by crossing over the legal bounds of its jurisdiction *or* by making determinations of fact without any factual basis.

In this regard, it is significant to note that the material forwarded to the House Judiciary Committee by the grand jury was that quantum of material deemed to be relevant to the Committee's inquiry. If the Special Prosecutor now contends that there is additional "indirectly relevant" evidence available that justified the grand jury's action, then it is noteworthy that the grand jury did not at that time deem it of sufficient substance to merit transmittal. On the other hand, if there is no other evidence, then the grand jury was outside its authority in reaching a determination without a factual basis. The affidavit and the appendices attached to the Motion to Disclose demonstrate a sufficient showing to warrant this limited release of the grand jury materials to resolve the question of whether the grand jury acted outside its authority.

Furthermore, it is possible that this Court, in its analysis of the grand jury's action, would desire to examine the purported factual basis for the grand jury's action. A grand jury may indict only on competent evidence. E.g., *United States* v. *Smyth*, 104 F. Supp. 283, 287 n. 1 (N.D. Cal. 1952). A grand jury may act only upon knowledge acquired either from its own observations or upon the evidence of witnesses given before it. *Hale* v. *Henkel*, 201 U.S. 43, 65-66 (1906). The purpose of our motion is to allow this court to have a full record so a complete analysis of the grand jury's determination is possible.

Furthermore, this Court may decide to view the factual basis for the grand jury's action in relation to the issue of whether the grand jury's determination pertaining to the President constituted a *"prima facie"* showing of criminal activity sufficient to overcome the claim of executive privilege. The Special Prosecutor apparently would limit the focus of this Court in its resolution of the above-captioned case. It is in the interest of justice to insure that this Court has the fullest record possible in order to not dampen the breadth of its analysis.

More basically, what the Special Prosecutor has failed to demonstrate in his opposition to this motion is what harm will occur if the grand jury material is released under seal to the Supreme Court to the President. Certainly the purposes of Fed. R. Crim. P. 6(e) will not be frustrated by this limited disclosure to the highest Court in the land. The historic function of the grand jury it would seem would be in consonance with our motion. As the Supreme Court in *Woods* v. *Georgia*, 370 U.S. 375, 390 (1962) said:

Historically, this body [grand jury] has been a primary security to the innocent against hasty, malicious and oppressive prosecution.

In the instant case, the showing we made in our motion warrants an inquiry into the grand jury itself to prevent the oppressive persecution of the President without a trial in an adversary forum where he can rebut the grand jury's charge that he is an unindicted co-conspirator. The Special Prosecutor in his opinion completely fails to assert any reason for denying the motion other than his obvious self-serving desire to limit the argument pending in this Court, and perhaps his fear that factual analysis by an impartial body will not support the grand jury's action.

III. The Motion to Disclose Is not a Request for a De Novo Review of the Grand Jury's Finding

Another reason why the Special Prosecutor would have this

court deny the instant motion is because:

> Courts have unanimously rejected an invitation to determine *de novo* whether a grand jury's finding of probable cause was supported by the evidence and the circumstances of the present application make it especially inappropriate for this Court to assume that function. Memo in Opposition at 4.

This reason is patently insufficient to use as the basis for a denial of the motion to disclose. In the first place, *de novo* means "anew; afresh; a second time." *Black's Law Dictionary* (Rev. 4th Ed.) at 483. In the instant case there has been no judicial review of the grand jury's action. The court below never had an evidentiary hearing on our motion to disclose the grand jury matter. The Special Prosecutor himself, in his haste in attempting to enforce the subpoena upon the President, has chosen this Court as the forum in which to test the grand jury's action.

The Special Prosecutor contends that:

> The grand jury's action regarding the President was *merely incidental* to its indictment of seven other persons in this case, and he was not the focus or target of its action. Memo in Opposition at 8-9. (emphasis added).

Such action and its effect on a President undergoing impeachment proceedings in Congress can hardly be called "merely incidental." It has been reported that the grand jury originally wished to indict the President, but they were informed that an incumbent President could not be indicted.[1] Apparently, the grand jury then decided to name the President as an unindicted co-conspirator and to forward evidence showing the President's alleged complicity to Congress.

The Special Prosecutor contends that the House Judiciary Committee is a forum available to the President "to litigate the weight of the evidence before the grand jury" and that "the evidence is being fully available to counsel" in that proceeding. Memo in Opposition at 9. Contrary to the Special Prosecutor's suggestion, Counsel for the President has not had full access to the evidence through the Judiciary Committee. Only a portion of the evidence has been made known to the President. In addition, the evidence made available to the President has been screened by two independent bodies—the grand jury and the Special Staff of the Committee on the Judiciary. The first screening was conducted by the grand jury which forwarded to the Judiciary

---

[1] See, *New York Times*, March 12, 1974 p. 1.

Committee evidence of the President's alleged involvement in the conspiracy.[2]

There has been no showing nor assertion by the Special Prosecutor to the effect that the Judiciary Committee has received any exculpatory material. Moreover, the Special Prosecutor acknowledges in his opposition memorandum that "indirectly relevant" material was not forwarded. (Memo in opposition at 4n.2).

The second screening was undertaken by the Special Staff of the Judiciary Committee which attached only a limited number of documents to its presentation. In addition, the Special Staff Presentation only included portions of the testimony for each witness. Thus, counsel for the President has been given no access to the complete materials held by the Judiciary Committee. In either of the screenings, exculpatory materials could have been deleted.

Lastly, it should be noted that the Special Prosecutor leaves us confused as to whether we have seen all the relevant material in this matter. At page 13 n. 6, of his Memo in Opposition, the Special Prosecutor claims there is "evidence indirectly relevant[3] to the President's complicity[4] which was not forwarded to the House Judiciary Committee." Yet at page nine, the Special Prosecutor suggests that we have seen all material when he says since the evidence the grand jury considered directly material to the President has been transmitted to the House Judiciary Committee where, it is apparent from counsel's papers in support of the pending motion, this evidence is being made fully available to counsel in accordance with the Committee's procedures."

IV. This Motion Is Justified by the Extraordinary Nature of This Case.

The Special Prosecutor, citing authority in this Court, suggests that an inquiry into factual questions is required only in

---

[2] The proceedings pursuant thereto are styled *In Re Report and Recommendation of June 5, 1972, Grand Jury Concerning Transmission of Evidence to the House of Representatives,* 370 F. Supp. 1219 (D.D.C. 1974).

[3] How relevant material can be categorized as "indirectly relevant" adds greatly to our confusion.

[4] In this regard we are confident that the Special Prosecutor's oversight in failing to modify "complicity" with the necessary adjective "alleged" was unintentional. Yet, that the omission was inadvertent, does not reduce the prejudicial effect.

"exceptional circumstances." Memo in Opposition at 7. If the action of a federal grand jury in naming the President as an unindicted co-conspirator is not an "exceptional circumstance," we are at a loss to know what is. The Special Prosecutor chides us for "not citing a single case in which *any* person named as an unindicted co-conspirator has been allowed to litigate the sufficiency of the evidence." Memo in Opposition at 12. Yet the Special Prosecutor, in spearheading numerous attempts to overturn the doctrine of executive privilege, has failed to cite any precedent which authorizes the grand jury's action in naming the President as an unindicted co-conspirator. The reason for his failure to offer any support for the unauthorized, impermissible action of the grand jury is starkly simple. There is no such authority in the annals of American jurisprudence.

We agree with the Special Prosecutor's claim at page 4 of Memo in Opposition that court's uniformly do not consider "whether a grand jury's finding of probable cause was supported by adequate evidence." . . . However, our agreement abruptly ends when he continues "and the circumstances of the present application make it especially inappropriate for this Court to assume that function." We submit that the circumstances in this case demand that this Court require judicial scrutiny and vindication. The Special Prosecutor's statement conveniently ignores the rationale for courts declining to review grand jury's findings. In an ordinary case any error committed by the grand jury may be offset in the adversary forum with the full panoply of constitutional safeguards available, and will, of course, be remedied by a petit jury's acquittal. More importantly, in an ordinary case, the adversely affected party is not the President of the United States, a putative respondent in an ongoing impeachment inquiry, who has been and continues to be irremediably prejudiced unless this Court provides "Equal Justice Under Law."

CONCLUSION

For the foregoing reasons, we respectfully request that the Motion to Disclose and to Transmit the Grand Jury Matters be granted.

Respectfully submitted,

James D. St. Clair
Michael A. Sterlacci
Jerome J. Murphy
Eugene R. Sullivan
*Attorneys for the
President*

The White House
Washington, D.C. 20500
Telephone No. 456-1414

V
SPECIAL PROSECUTOR'S MAIN BRIEF IN UNITED STATES v. NIXON

The Special Prosecutor's brief before the Supreme Court is as much a study of political science and constitutional history as it is a legal document. It examined in detail the power of the grand jury to cite the President, the Court's authority over the Executive and the scope of executive privilege.

IN THE SUPREME COURT OF THE UNITED STATES
October Term, 1973

No. 73-1766

UNITED   STATES OF AMERICA, PETITIONER

v.

RICHARD M. NIXON, PRESIDENT OF THE
UNITED   STATES, ET AL., RESPONDENTS

No. 73-1834

RICHARD M. NIXON, PRESIDENT OF THE
UNITED STATES, PETITIONER

v.

UNITED STATES OF AMERICA

*ON WRITS OF CERTIORARI TO THE UNITED STATES
COURT OF APPEALS
FOR THE DISTRICT OF COLUMBIA CIRCUIT*

BRIEF FOR THE UNITED STATES

OPINION AND ORDERS BELOW

The district court's order of April 18, 1974 (Pet. App. 47[1])
issuing the subpoena *duces tecum* in question is unreported. The
district court's opinion and order of May 20, 1974, denying the
motion to quash the subpoena, enforcing compliance therewith,
and denying the motion to expunge (Pet. App. 15) is not yet
officially reported.

JURISDICTION

The order of the district court (Pet. App. 23) was entered on
May 20, 1974. On May 24, 1974, Richard M. Nixon, President of
the United States, filed a timely notice of appeal from that order

---

[1] "Pet. App." refers to the Appendix to the Petition in No. 73-1766. "A." refers
to the printed joint Appendix.

in the district court, and the certified record was docketed in the United States Court of Appeals for the District of Columbia Circuit that same day (D.C. Cir. No. 74-1534). Also on May 24, 1974, the President filed a petition for a writ of mandamus in the court below seeking review of the district court's order (D.C. Cir. No. 74-1532).[2]

On May 24, 1974, the Special Prosecutor filed a petition for a writ of certiorari before judgment on behalf of the United States (No. 73-1766),[3] and certiorari was granted on May 31, 1974. On June 6, 1974, President Nixon filed a cross-petition for a writ of certiorari before judgment (No. 73-1834), which was granted on June 15, 1974. The jurisdiction of this Court rests on 28 U.S.C. 1254(1), 1651, and 2101(e).

In response to the Court's order of June 15, 1974, two jurisdictional questions are being discussed in our Supplemental Brief.

QUESTIONS PRESENTED

In No. 73-1766:

1. Whether a federal court must determine itself if executive privilege is properly invoked in a criminal proceeding or whether it is bound by the President's assertion of an absolute "executive privilege" to withhold demonstrably material evidence from the trial of charges of conspiracy to defraud the United States and obstruct justice by his own White House aides and party leaders, upon the ground that he deems production to be against the public interest.

2. Whether the President is subject to a judicial order directing compliance with a subpoena *duces tecum* calling for production of evidence, under his sole personal control, that is demonstrably material to a pending federal criminal prosecution.

3. Whether the President's claim of executive privilege based on the generalized interest in the confidentiality of government deliberations can block the prosecution's access to material evidence for the trial of criminal charges against the former

---

[2] In *Nixon* v. *Sirica*, 487 F. 2d 700, 707 n. 21 (D.C. Cir. 1973), the court of appeals stated that an order of this type directed to the President is appealable under 28 U.S.C. 1291. In any event, the court also asserted jurisdiction pursuant to the All Writs Act, 28 U.S.C. 1651. See 487 F. 2d at 706-707.

[3] Under 28 U.S.C. 510, 517, and 518, and Department of Justice Order No. 551-73, 28 C.F.R. § 0.37 *et seq.* (Appendix pp. 143-50, *infra*), the Special Prosecutor has authority, in lieu of the Solicitor General, to conduct litigation before this Court on behalf of the United States in cases within his jurisdiction.

officials who participated in those deliberations, particularly where there is a *prima facie* showing that the President is a co-conspirator and that the deliberations occurred in the course of and in furtherance of the conspiracy.

4. Whether any executive privilege that otherwise might have been applicable to discussions between the President and alleged co-conspirators concerning the Watergate matter has been waived by previous testimony given pursuant to the President's approval and by the President's public release of edited transcripts of forty-three such conversations.

5. Whether the district court properly determined that the subpoena *duces tecum* issued to the President satisfied the standards of Rule 17(c) of the Federal Rules of Criminal Procedure because an adequate showing had been made that the subpoenaed items are relevant to issues to be tried and will be admissible in evidence.

In No. 73-1834:

6. Whether the district court acted within its discretion in declining to expunge the federal grand jury's naming of the President as an unindicted co-conspirator in offenses for which the grand jury returned an indictment.

The two questions the parties were requested to brief and argue by the Court's order of June 15, 1974, are discussed in our Supplemental Brief.

CONSTITUTIONAL PROVISIONS, STATUTES, RULE, AND REGULATIONS INVOLVED

The constitutional provisions, statutes, rule, and regulations involved, which are set forth in the Appendix, *infra*, pp. 141-53, are:

Constitution of the United States:

> Article II, Section 1
> Article II, Section 2
> Article II, Section 3
> Article III, Section 2

Statutes of the United States:

> 5 U.S.C. 301
> 28 U.S.C. 509, 510, 515-519

Rule:

> Rule 17(c), Federal Rules of Criminal Procedure

Regulations:

Department of Justice Order No. 551-73 (November 2,

1973), 38 Fed. Reg. 30,738, adding 28 C.F.R. §§ 0.37, 0.38, and Appendix to Subpart G-1

Department of Justice Order No. 554-73 (November 19, 1973), 38 Fed. Reg. 32,805, amending 28 C.F.R. Appendix to Subpart G-1

STATEMENT

This case presents for review the denial of a motion filed on behalf of respondent Richard M. Nixon, President of the United States, pursuant to Rule 17(c) of the Federal Rules of Criminal Procedure, seeking to quash a subpoena *duces tecum* issued in a criminal case, directing the President to produce tape recordings and documents relating to sixty-four specifically described Presidential conversations. This subpoena (Pet. App. 39) issued on behalf of the United States at the request of the Special Prosecutor convers evidence which is demonstrably material to the trial of charges of conspiracy to defraud the United States and obstruct justice by former aides and associates of the President.

1. *Appointment of a Special Prosecutor*

On May 25, 1973, Attorney General Elliot L. Richardson established the Office of the Watergate Special Prosecution Force, to be headed by Special Prosecutor Archibald Cox, with "full authority for investigating and prosecuting offenses against the United States arising out of the unauthorized entry into Democratic National Committee headquarters at the Watergate."[4] The appointment of the Special Prosecutor, together with his specific duties and responsibilities, including full authority for determining whether or not to contest the assertion of "executive privilege," was settled in connection with the hearings of the Senate Judiciary Committee on the nomination of Mr. Richardson to be Attorney General.[5]

2. *Enforcement of the 1973 Grand Jury Subpoena Duces Tecum*

On July 16, 1973, Alexander Butterfield, formerly chief administrative officer at the White House, testified before the

[4.] Department of Justice Order No. 517-73, 38 Fed. Reg. 14,688, adding 28 C.F.R. § 0.37 and Appendix to Subpart G-1.

[5.] See *Hearings Before the Senate Judiciary Committee on the Nomination of Elliot L. Richardson to be Attorney General*, 93rd Cong., 1st Sess. 144-46 (1973).

Senate Select Committee on Presidential Campaign Activities that at the President's direction the Secret Service as a matter of course had been recording automatically all conversations in the President's offices in the White House and Old Executive Office Building.[6] Because there had been sharply contradictory testimony regarding the relationship between several Presidential meetings and telephone conversations and an alleged conspiracy to conceal the identity of the persons responsible for the Watergate break-in, the Special Prosecutor issued a grand jury subpoena *duces tecum* to the President, who had assumed sole personal control over the recordings,[7] requiring him to produce the recordings of these meetings.

When the President refused to comply with the subpoena, the grand jury unanimously instructed the Special Prosecutor to apply for a court order requiring production. After a hearing, the court ordered the President to produce the subpoenaed items for *in camera* inspection, rejecting the President's contentions that he is immune from compulsory process and that he has absolute, unreviewable discretion to withhold evidence from the courts on the ground of executive privilege. *In re Grand Jury Subpoena Duces Tecum Issued to Richard M. Nixon*, 360 F. Supp. 1 (D.D.C. 1973). The Court of Appeals for the District of Columbia Circuit upheld this order, with modifications, in an *en banc* decision denying the President's petition for a writ of mandamus. *Nixon* v. *Sirica*, 487 F. 2d 700 (1973). The Court of Appeals *sua sponte* then stayed its order to permit the President to seek review by this Court.

3. *Dismissal of the Special Prosecutor*

The President decided, however, not to seek review by this Court, and instead proposed a "compromise" to the Special Prosecutor which would have supplied edited transcripts of the subpoenaed recordings for use before the grand jury and at any subsequent trial. At the same time the President issued an order to Special Prosecutor Cox forbidding him ever again to resort to the judicial process to seek evidence from the President. The Special Prosecutor refused to accept this compromise or to accede to the order that would have barred him from exercising

---

[6.] *Hearings Before the Senate Select Committee on Presidential Campaign Activities*, 93rd Cong., 1st Sess., Book 5, at 2074-81 (1973).

[7.] Letter from Richard M. Nixon to Senator Sam J. Ervin, Chairman of the Senate Select Committee on Presidential Campaign Activities, July 23, 1973, *id.*, Book 6, at 2479.

his discretion to seek evidence necessary for prosecutions within his jurisdiction. When the President then ordered Attorney General Richardson to dismiss the Special Prosecutor, the Attorney General resigned rather than obey, and Deputy Attorney General William Ruckelshaus was fired when he too refused to carry out the President's order.[8] On the night of October 20, 1973, Solicitor General Robert H. Bork, upon whom the responsibilities of Acting Attorney General devolved, elected to obey the President's instruction and peremptorily discharged Special Prosecutor Cox and abolished the Watergate Special Prosecution Force.[9]

On October 23, 1973, after considerable congressional and public reaction, counsel for the President announced to the district court that the President would comply with the district court's order as modified by the court of appeals.[10] Counsel for the President subsequently disclosed for the first time that two of the subpoenaed conversations were not recorded, and that eighteen and one-half minutes of the subpoenaed recording of the meeting between the President and H.R. Haldeman on June 20, 1972, had been obliterated.[11]

4. Appointment of a New Special Prosecutor

In response to the discharge of Special Prosecutor Cox, both the Senate Judiciary Committee and the House of Representatives Judiciary Subcommittee on Criminal Justice began hearings on legislation to establish a court-appointed Special Prosecutor independent of control by the President.[12] Both committees reported out such bills for action

[8] See generally Congressional Quarterly, Inc., *Historic Documents 1973,* at 859-78.

[9] The United States District Court for the District of Columbia later ruled that the Special Prosecutor's firing was illegal because Acting Attorney General Bork had relied simply upon instructions from the President and had not purported to find any "extraordinary impropriety," as had been specified by the regulations extablishing the Office of the Watergate Special Prosecutor as the sole ground for dismissal. *Nader* v. *Bork,* 366 F. Supp. 104 (1973), appeal pending.

[10] Hearing on October 23, 1973, *In re Grand Jury Subpoena Duces Tecum Issued to Richard M. Nixon,* D.D.C. Misc. No. 47-73.

[11] An Advisory Panel of experts, nominated jointly by the Special Prosecutor and counsel for the President, and appointed by the district court, has concluded that the only "completely plausible explanation" of the 18½ minute "buzz" section is a set of from five to nine erasures caused by manual operation of a recording machine. "Report on a Technical Investigation Conducted for the U.S. District Court for the District of Columbia by the Advisory Panel on White House Tapes," filed June 4, 1974. *In re Grand Jury Subpoena Duces Tecum Issued to Richard M. Nixon,* D.D.C. Misc. No. 47-73. 47-73.

[12] See *Hearings Before the Senate Judiciary Committee on the Special Prosecutor,*

by the House and Senate.[13]

Neither House considered the legislation on the floor, however, because on October 26, 1973, the President announced that Acting Attorney General Bork would appoint a new Special Prosecutor. The President explained that he had no greater interest than seeing that the Special Prosecutor has "the independence that he needs" to prosecute the guilty and clear the innocent.[14]

On November 2, 1973, the Acting Attorney General re-established the Watergate Special Prosecution Force and appointed Leon Jaworski as Special Prosecutor, vesting in him the same powers and authority possessed by his predecessor, including "full authority" to "contest the assertion of 'Executive Privilege' or any other testimonial privilege" (Appendix pp. 146-51, *infra*).[15] The only change in the regulations relevant to this Court's consideration was the addition of a provision, in "accordance with assurances given by the President to the Attorney General," that the President would not limit the jurisdiction of the Special Prosecutor or effect his dismissal without first consulting with the Majority and Minority Leaders of both Houses of Congress and their respective Committees on the Judiciary (Appendix pp. 151-52), *infra*).[16] Thereafter both Houses tabled the legislation for court appointment of an independent Special Prosecutor, but the bills remain on their respective calendars.

5. *The Indictment in This Case and the Naming of the President as a Co-Conspirator*

On March 1, 1974, a grand jury of the United States District Court for the District of Columbia returned an indictment (A.

93rd Cong., 1st Sess. (1973); *Hearings Before the House Judiciary Subcommittee on Criminal Justice*, 93rd Cong., 1st Sess. (1973).

[13] The Senate Committee on the Judiciary reported out S. 2611 (S. Rep. 93-595) and S. 2642 (S. Rep. 93-596). See 119 Cong., Rec. D. 1324 (daily ed. Nov. 21, 1973). The House Committee on the Judiciary reported out H.R. 11401 (H. Rep. 93-660), which was rewritten as H.R. 11555 by the House Rules Committee. See 119 Cong. Rec. D. 1371 (daily ed. Dec. 3, 1973). All three bills remain on the calendars of each House, subject to being called up on the floor without further hearings or committee action. See House Calendar, 93rd Cong., 2d Sess., for June 5, 1974, at 138, 139 (Senate bills), 92 (House bill).

[14] 9 Weekly Compilation of Presidential Documents 1289 (October 29, 1973).

[15] Department of Justice Order No. 551-73, 38 Fed. Reg. 30,738.

[16] See also letter from the Acting Attorney General to the Special Prosecutor explaining this amendment (Appendix pp. 152-53, *infra*).

5A) charging respondents John N. Mitchell, H. R. Haldeman, John D. Ehrlichman, Charles W. Colson, Robert C. Mardian, Kenneth W. Parkinson and Gordon Strachan with various offenses relating to the Watergate matter, including a conspiracy to defraud the United States and to obstruct justice. *United States* v. *Mitchell, et al.*, D.D.C. Crim. No. 74-110. At some or all of the times in question, respondent Mitchell, a former Attorney General of the United States, was Chairman of the Committee for the Re-Election of the President; respondent Haldeman was Assistant to the President and his chief of staff; respondent Ehrlichman was Assistant to the President for Domestic Affairs; respondent Colson was Special Counsel to the President; respondent Mardian, a former Assistant Attorney General, was an official of the President's re-election campaign; respondent Parkinson was an attorney for the re-election committee; and respondent Strachan was Staff Assistant to the President.

In the course of its consideration of the indictment, the grand jury, by a vote of 19-0, determined that there is probable cause to believe that respondent Richard M. Nixon (among others) was a member of the conspiracy to defraud the United States and to obstruct justice as charged in the indictment, and the grand jury authorized the Special Prosecutor to identify President Nixon (among others) as an unindicted co-conspirator in connection with subsequent legal proceedings.

6. *Issuance of the Trial Subpoena to the President*

In order to obtain additional evidence which the Special Prosecutor has reason to believe is in the custody of the President and which would be important to the government's proof at the trial in *United States* v. *Mitchell, et al.*, the Special Prosecutor, on behalf of the United States, moved on April 16, 1974, for the issuance of the subpoena *duces tecum* in question (Pet. App. 39). On April 18, 1974, the district court ordered the subpoena to issue, returnable on May 2, 1974 (Pet. App. 47). The subpoena called for production of the evidence in advance of the September 9, 1974, trial date in order to allow time for any litigation over the subpoena and for transcription and authentication of any tape recordings produced.

On April 30, 1974, the President released to the public and submitted to the House Judiciary Committee conducting an impeachment inquiry 1,216 pages of edited transcripts of forty-three conversations dealing with Watergate. Portions of twenty subpoenaed conversations were included. On May 1, 1974, President Nixon, through his White House counsel, filed in the district court a "special appearance," a "formal claim of privilege," and a motion to quash the subpoena. (A. 47A) At the suggestion of counsel for the President and the Special Prosecutor and with the approval of counsel for the defendants, subsequent proceedings were held *in camera* because of the sensitive nature of the grand jury's finding with respect to the President, which was submitted to the district court by the Special Prosecutor as a ground for denying the motion to quash. Defendants Colson, Mardian, and Strachan formally joined in the Special Prosecutor's motion for issuance of the subpoena, and all seven defendants (respondents herein) argued in opposition to the motion to quash at the hearing in the district court. At that hearing, counsel for the President also moved to expunge the grand jury's finding and to enjoin all persons, except for the President and his counsel, from ever disclosing the grand jury's action.

7. *The Decision Below*

In its opinion and order of May 20, 1974 (Pet. App. 15), the district court denied the motion to quash and the motion to expunge and for protective orders. It further ordered "the President or any subordinate officer, official or employee with custody or control of the documents or objects subpoenaed" to deliver to the court the originals of all subpoenaed items as well as an index and analysis of those items, together with tape copies of those portions of the subpoenaed recordings for which transcripts had been released to the public by the President on April 30, 1974. The district court stayed its order pending prompt application for appellate review and further provided that matters filed under seal remain under seal when transmitted as part of the record (Pet. App. 22-23).[17]

In requiring compliance with the subpoena *duces tecum*, the district court rejected the contention by counsel for the President that it had no jurisdiction because the proceeding allegedly involved solely an "intra-executive" dispute (Pet. App. 18). The court ruled that this argument lacked substance in light of jurisdictional responsibilities and independence with which the Special Prosecutor had been vested by regulations that have the force and effect of law and that had received the explicit concurrence of the President. The court noted the "unique guarantee of unfettered operation" given to the Special

---

[17] By order entered on June 7, 1974, the district court rescinded its orders sealing portions of the record. On June 15, 1974, this Court denied a motion to unseal the record except as it related to an extract concerning the grand jury's finding with respect to the President.

Prosecutor and emphasized that under these regulations the Special Prosecutor's jurisdiction, which includes express authority to contest claims of executive privilege, cannot be limited without the President's first consulting with the leaders of both Houses of Congress and the respective Committees on the Judiciary and securing their consensus (Pet. App. 18-19). In these circumstances, the court found that there exists sufficient independence to provide the court with a concrete legal controversy between adverse parties and not simply an intra-agency dispute over policy. Moreover, the court later noted that as a recipient of a subpoena in this criminal case, the President "as a practical matter, is a third party" (Pet. App. 19).

On the merits, and relying on the *en banc* decision in *Nixon* v. *Sirica, supra*, the district court held that in the circumstances of this case, the courts, and not the President, are the final arbiter of the applicability of a claim of executive privilege for the subpoenaed items (Pet. App. 17). Here, the court ruled, the presumptive privilege for documents and materials reflecting executive deliberations was overcome by the Special Prosecutor's *prima facie* showing that the items are relevant and important to the issues to be tried in the Watergate cover-up case and that they will be admissible in evidence (Pet. App. 20-21).[18]

Finally, the district court held that the Special Prosecutor, in his memorandum and appendix submitted to the court, satisfied the requirements of Rule 17(c) that the subpoenaed items be relevant and evidentiary (Pet. App. 19-20).

The President has sought review of this decision in the court of appeals, and the case is now before this court on writs of certiorari before judgment granted on May 31, 1974, and June 15, 1974, on the petition of the United States and the cross-petition of the President, respectively.

SUMMARY OF ARGUMENT

The narrow issue presented to this Court is whether the President, in a pending prosecution against his former aides and associates being conducted in the name of the United States by a Special Prosecutor not subject to Presidential directions, may

---

[18] As to claims by defendants that they are entitled to the subpoenaed items under Rule 17(c), the court withheld ruling, stating that defendants' requests for access will be more appropriately considered in considered in conjunction with their pre-trial discovery motions (Pet. App. 21-22). Accordingly, the court refused to decide whether *Brady* v. *Maryland*, 373 U.S. 83, applies to "privileged" evidence not in the possession of the prosecutor.

withhold material evidence from the court merely on his assertion that the evidence involves confidential governmental deliberations. The Court clearly has jurisdiction to decide this issue. The pending criminal prosecution in which the subpoena *duces tecum* was issued constitutes a "case or controversy," and the federal courts naturally have the duty and, therefore, the power to determine what evidence is admissible in that prosecution and to require that that evidence be produced. This is only a specific application of the general but fundamental principle of our constitutional system of government that the courts, as the "neutral" branch of government, have been allocated the responsibility to resolve all issues in a controversy properly before them even though this requires them to determine authoritatively the powers and responsibilities of the other branches.

Any notion that this controversy, arising as it does from the issuance of a subpoena *duces tecum* to the President at the request of the Special Prosecutor, is not justiciable is wholly illusory. In the context of the most concrete and vital kind of case—the federal criminal prosecution of former White House officials—the Special Prosecutor, as the attorney for the United States, has resorted to a traditional mechanism to procure evidence for the government's case at trial. In objecting to the enforcement of the subpoena, the President has raised a classic question of law—a claim of privilege—and the United States, through its counsel and in its sovereign capacity, is opposing that claim. Thus, viewed in practical terms, it would be hard to imagine a controversy more appropriate for judicial resolution.

The fact that this concrete controversy is presented in the context of a dispute between the President and the Special Prosecutor does not deprive this Court of jurisdiction. Congress has vested in the Attorney General, as the head of the Department of Justice, the exclusive authority to conduct the government's civil and criminal litigation, including the exclusive authority for securing evidence. The Attorney General, with the explicit concurrence of the President, has vested that authority with respect to Watergate matters in the Special Prosecutor. These regulations have the force and effect of law and establish the functional independence of the Special Prosecutor. Accordingly, the Special Prosecutor, representing the sovereign authority of the United States, and the President appear before the Court as adverse parties in the truest sense. The President himself has ceded any power that he might have had to control the course of the pending prosecution, and it would stand the Constitution on its head to say that this arrangement, if respected and given effect by the courts, violates the "separation of powers."

I

Throughout our constitutional history the courts, in cases or controversies before them, consistently have exercised final authority to determine whether even the highest executive officials are acting in accordance with the Constitution. In fulfilling this basic constitutional function, they have issued appropriate decrees to implement those judicial decisions. The courts have not abjured this responsibility even when the most pressing needs of the Nation were at issue.

In applying this fundamental principle, the courts have determined for themselves not only what evidence is admissible in a pending case, but also what evidence must be produced, including whether particular materials are appropriately subject to a claim of executive privilege. Indeed, this Court has squarely rejected the claim that the Executive has absolute, unreviewable discretion to withhold documents from the courts.

The unbroken line of precedent establishing that the courts have the final authority for determining the applicability and scope of claims of executive privilege is supported by compelling arguments of policy. The Executive's legitimate interests in secrecy are more than adequately protected by the qualified privilege defined and applied by the courts. But as this Court has recognized, an absolute privilege which permitted the Executive to make a binding determination would lead to intolerable abuse. This case highlights the inherent conflict of interest that is presented when the Executive is called upon to produce evidence in a case which calls into question the Executive's own action. The President cannot be a proper judge of whether the greater public interest lies in disclosing evidence subpoenaed for trial, when that evidence may have a material bearing on whether he is impeached and will bear heavily on the guilt or innocence of close aides and trusted advisors.

In the framework of this case, where the privilege holder is effectively a third party, the interests of justice as well as the interests of the parties to the pending prosecution require that the courts enter a decree requiring that relevant and unprivileged evidence be produced. The "produce or dismiss" option that is sometimes allowed to the Executive when a claim of executive privilege is overruled merely reflects a remedial accommodation of the requirements of substantive justice and thus has never been available to the Executive where the option could not satisfy these requirements. This is particularly true where the option would make a travesty out of the independent institution of the Special Prosecutor by allowing the President to accomplish indirectly what we cannot do directly: secure the abandonment of the Watergate prosecution.

II

There is nothing in the status of the President that deprives the courts of their constitutional power to resolve this dispute. The power to issue and enforce a subpoena *duces tecum* against the President was first recognized by Chief Justice Marshall in the *Burr* case in 1807, in accordance with two fundamental principles of our constitutional system: First, the President, like all executive officials as well as the humblest private citizens, is subject to the rule of law. Indeed, this follows inexorably from his constitutional duty to "take Care that the Laws be faithfully executed." Second, in the full and impartial administration of justice, the public has a right to every man's evidence. The persistent refusal of the courts to afford the President an absolute immunity from judicial process is fully supported by the deliberate decision of the Framers to deny him such a privilege.

Although it would be improper for the courts to control the exercise of the President's constitutional discretion, there can be no doubt that the President is subject to a judicial order requiring compliance with a clearly defined legal duty. The crucial jurisdictional factor is not the President's office, or the physical power to secure compliance with judicial orders, but the Court's ability to resolve authoritatively, within the context of a justiciable controversy, the conflicting claims of legal rights and obligations. The Court is called upon here to adjudicate the obligation of the President, as a citizen of the United States, to cooperate with a criminal prosecution by performing the solely ministerial task of producing specified, unprivileged evidence that he has taken within his sole personal custody.

III

The qualified executive privilege for confidential intra-governmental deliberations, designed to promote the candid interchange between officials and their aides, exists only to protect the legitimate functioning of government. Thus, the privilege must give way where, as here, it has been abused. There has been a *prima facie* showing that each of the participants in the subpoenaed conversations, including the President, was a member of the conspiracy to defraud the United States and to obstruct justice charged in the indictment in the present case, and a further showing that each of the conversations occurred in the course of and in furtherance of the conspiracy. The public purpose underlying the executive privilege for governmental deliberations precludes its application to shield alleged criminality.

But even if a presumptive privilege were to be recognized in this case, the privilege cannot be sustained in the face of the compelling public interest in disclosure. The responsibility of the courts in passing on a claim of executive privilege is, in the first instance, to determine whether the party demanding the evidence has made a *prima facie* showing of a sufficient need to offset the presumptive validity of the Executive's claim. The cases have held that the balance should be struck in favor of disclosure only if the showing of need is strong and clear, leaving the courts with a firm conviction that the public interest requires disclosure.

It is difficult to imagine any case where the balance could be clearer than it is on the special facts of this proceeding. The recordings sought are specifically identified, and the relevance of each conversation to the needs of trial has been established at length. The conversations are demonstrably important to defining the extent of the conspiracy in terms of time, membership and objectives. On the other hand, since the President has authorized each participant to discuss what he and the others have said, and since he repeatedly has summarized his views of the conversations, while releasing partial transcripts of a number of them, the public interest in continued confidentiality is vastly diminished.

The district court's ruling is exceedingly narrow and, thus, almost no incremental damage will be done to the valid interests in assuring future Presidential aides that legitimate advice on matters of policy will be kept secret. The unusual circumstances of this case—where high government officials are under indictment for conspiracy to defraud the United States and obstruct justice—at once make it imperative that the trial be conducted on the basis of all relevant evidence and at the same time make it highly unlikely that there will soon be a similar occasion to intrude on the confidentiality of the Executive Branch.

IV

Even if the subpoenaed conversations might once have been covered by a privilege, the privilege has been waived by the President's decision to authorize voluminous testimony and other statements concerning Watergate-related discussion and his recent release of 1,216 pages of transcript from forty-three Presidential conversations dealing with Watergate. A privilege holder may not make extensive disclosures concerning a subject and then selectively withhold portions that are essential to a complete and impartial record. Here, the President repeatedly has referred to the conversations in support of his own position and even allowed defendant Haldeman access to the recordings after he left public office to aid him in preparing his public testimony. In the unique circumstances of this case, where there is no longer any substantial confidentiality on the subject of Watergate because the President has made far-reaching, but expurgated disclosures, the court may use its process to acquire all relevant evidence to lay before the jury.

V

The district court, correctly applying the standards established by this Court, found that the government's showing satisfied the requirements of Rule 17(c) of the Federal Rules of Criminal Procedure that items subpoenaed for use at trial be relevant and evidentiary. The enforcement of a trial subpoena *duces tecum* is a question for the trial court and is committed to the court's sound discretion. Absent a showing that the finding by the court is arbitrary and had no support in the record, the finding must not be disturbed by an appellate court. Here, the Special Prosecutor's analysis of each of the sixty-four conversations, submitted to the district court, amply supports that court's finding.

INTRODUCTION: THE ISSUES BEFORE THE COURT PRESENT A LIVE, CONCRETE JUSTICIABLE CONTROVERSY

In the district court, counsel for the President, in a sealed reply to the government's papers opposing the motion to quash, raised for the first time the contention that the court lacked "jurisdiction to consider the Special Prosecutor's request of April 16, 1974, relating to the disclosure of certain presidential documents." Counsel was referring to the trial subpoena applied for by the Special Prosecutor on behalf of the United States (Pet. App. 39) and issued by the district court on April 18, 1974 (Pet. App. 47). It was that subpoena that the President moved to quash. The basis for the President's contention that the court lacked jurisdiction to "consider" that "request" for evidence was the assertion that the subpoena involved merely a "dispute between two entities within the Executive Branch."

The district court rejected this contention, ruling that under the circumstances established by applicable statutes and regulations, the President's "attempt to abridge the Special Prosecutor's independence with the argument that he cannot seek evidence from the President by court process is a nullity and does not defeat the Court's jurisdiction" (Pet. App. 19). Before addressing the issues before this Court on the merits, we pause to express the reasons why this litigation between the United States, represented by the Special Prosecutor, and the President presents a live, concrete, justiciable controversy.

A. *This Case Comes Within the Judicial Power of the Federal Courts*

This litigation is not merely a dispute between two executive officers over preferred policy, or even over an interpretation of a statute. The courts have not been called upon to render an advisory opinion upon some abstract or theoretical question. Rather, in the context of the most concrete and vital kind of case—the federal criminal prosecution of former White House officials, styled *United States* v. *Mitchell, et al.*—the Special Prosecutor as the attorney for the United States has resorted to a traditional mechanism to procure evidence for the government's case at trial—a subpoena—in the face of the unwillingness of a distinct party or entity—the President—to furnish the evidence voluntarily. In objecting to the enforcement of the subpoena, the President has raised a classic question of law—a claim of privilege—and the United States, through its counsel, is opposing that claim. Thus, viewed in practical terms, it would be hard to imagine a controversy more appropriate for judicial resolution and more squarely within the jurisdiction of the federal courts. This Court is called upon to review questions that are well "within the traditional role accorded courts to interpret the law." *Powell* v. *McCormack*, 395 U.S. 486, 548; see, *e.g.*, *Roviaro* v. *United States*, 353 U.S. 53; *United States* v. *Reynolds*, 345 U.S.1.

Ever since *Marbury* v. *Madison*, 1 Cranch (5 U.S.) 137, it has been settled that, as long as a federal court is properly vested with subject-matter jurisdiction,[19] it has the judicial power to

[19] The district court's subject-matter jurisdiction over the pending criminal case and over the trial subpoena *duces tecum* issued in this case is clear. See 18 U.S.C. 3231; Rule 17, Federal Rules of Criminal Procedure.

render an authoritative, binding decision on the rights, powers and duties of the other two branches of government. See, *e.g.*, *Youngstown Sheet & Tube Co.* v. *Sawyer*, 343 U.S. 579; *United States* v. *United States District Court*, 407 U.S. 297; *Kendall* v. *United States ex rel. Stokes*, 12 Pet. (37 U.S.) 524; *Kilbourn* v. *Thompson*, 103 U.S. 168; *Doe* v. *McMillan*, 412 U.S. 306. This judicial power extends fully to disputes between representatives of the other two branches, *e.g.*, *United States* v. *Brewster*, 408 U.S. 501; *Gravel* v. *United States*, 408 U.S. 606; *Senate Select Committee on Presidential Campaign Activities* v. *Nixon*, — F. 2d — (D.C. Cir. No. 74-1258) (May 23, 1974), as well as to disputes within one of those other branches, *e.g.*, *Powell* v. *McCormack*, *supra; Service* v. *Dulles*, 354 U.S. 363; *Sampson* v. *Murray*, — U.S. — (42 U.S.L.W. 4221, February 19, 1974).

As we shall discuss below, the fact that the President and the Special Prosecutor (on behalf of the United States) are the legal adversaries in this phase of the controversy in no way undermines the existence of the judicial power to adjudicate the legal rights and duties at issue—namely, the existence *vel non* of a privilege to withhold evidence from a criminal trial pending in the federal court.

B. *The United States, Represented by the Special Prosecutor, Is a Party Distinct From the President*

We begin by making the fundamental point, overlooked by counsel for the President, that federal criminal prosecutions are brought in the name of the United States of America as a sovereign nation. Despite his extensive powers and even his status as Chief Executive and Chief of State, the President, whether in his personal capacity or his official capacity, is distinct from the United States and is decidedly *not* the sovereign. Although the Constitution vests the executive power generally in the President (Art. II, Sec. 1), it expressly contemplates the establishment of executive departments which will actually discharge the executive power, with the President's function necessarily limited to "take Care that the Laws be faithfully executed" by other officers of the government (Art. II, Sec. 3). Thus, Article II, Section 2 expressly provides that, instead of giving the President power to appoint (and, perhaps, remove) "inferior Officers" of the Executive Branch, "Congress may by Law vest the Appointment of such inferior Officers, as they think proper, * * * in the Courts of Law, or in the Heads of Departments."

Congress has organized the Department of Justice and

provided that the Attorney General is its head. 28 U.S.C. 501, 503. Under Article II, Section 2, Congress has vested in him alone the power to appoint subordinate officers to discharge his powers. 28 U.S.C. 509, 510, 515, 533. Among the responsibilities given by Congress to the Attorney General is the authority to conduct the government's civil and criminal litigation (28 U.S.C. 516):

> Except as otherwise authorized by law, the conduct of litigation *in which the United States*, an agency, or officer thereof *is a party*, or is interested, *and securing evidence therefor*, is reserved to officers of the Department of Justice, under the direction of the Attorney General. (Emphasis added.)

As this Court has recognized, this section and companion provisions, see 28 U.S.C. 515-519, "impose on the Attorney General the authority and the duty to protect the Government's interests through the courts." *United States* v. *California*, 332 U.S. 19, 27-28. Under this framework it is not the President who has personal charge of the conduct of the government's affairs in court but, rather, it is the Attorney General acting through the officers of the Department of Justice appointed by him. This Court underscored the special status of the officers of the Department of Justice before the courts in *Berger* v. *United States*, 295 U.S. 78, 88, explaining that the federal prosecutor "is the representative not of an ordinary party to a controversy, but of a sovereignty. * * * As such, he is in a peculiar and a very definite sense the servant of the law, the twofold aim of which is that guilt shall not escape or innocence suffer."

Thus, as the district judge below pointedly recognized (Pet. App. 19), the subpoena *duces tecum* issued by the prosecution to the President is directed to a person who "as a practical matter, is a third party."[20]

---

[20] District Judge Gesell, who is presiding over the trial in *United States* v. *Erlichman, et al.* (D.D.C. Crim. No. 74-116), which involves charges against former White House officials growing out of the break-in at the offices of Dr. Louis Fielding, Daniel Ellsberg's psychiatrist, has recognized the indpendent status of the Special Prosecutor and the peculiar and unique circumstances that surround prosecutions within his jurisdiction:

"In one view of the matter, one portion of the Government is prosecuting another portion of the Government. Thus perhaps very unique circumstances are presented that require trial judges to use common sense to adapt criminal procedures and rules developed under more routine circumstances to the peculiar necessities of this special situation."
Transcript of Hearing on June 3, 1974, at 7-8, *United States* v. *Ehrlichman, et al, supra.*

It was in the capacity as attorney for the United States that the Special Prosecutor invoked the judicial process. Exercising his exclusive authority under 28 U.S.C. 516 to secure evidence for a pending criminal prosecution within his jurisdiction, the Special Prosecutor is seeking evidence from an adverse party—evidence which the Special Prosecutor has reason to believe is highly material to the trial. Under the law, the Special Prosecutor speaks for the United States in conducting this criminal trial, and under the applicable statutes and regulations he has authority, which can be enforced by the courts, to seek evidence even from the President. Not only is this authority expressly included in the Department of Justice regulations defining his powers (Appendix pp. 146-50, *infra*), but the record shows that the President personally acceded to the arrangement whereby his assertion of privilege would not preclude the Special Prosecutor, in a proper case, from invoking the judicial process to litigate the validity of the claim.

Before agreeing to accept appointment as the new Special Prosecutor, Mr. Jaworski obtained an assurance from the President's chief of staff, General Alexander Haig, who had conferred with the President, that there would be no bar to his resorting to judicial process, if necessary, to fulfill his responsibilities as he viewed them.[21] The Acting Attorney

---

[21] Mr. Jaworski testified as follows, under oath, before the Senate Committee on the Judiciary, which was considering legislation concerning establishment of an independent Special Prosecutor's office:

"* * * And when I came to Washington I first met with General Haig for probably an hour or an hour and a half, during which time this matter was discussed in detail. And as a result of that discussion, there eventuated the arrangement that we have mentioned.

"General Haig assured me that he would go and talk with the President, place the matter before him. And he came back and told me after a while, after maybe a lapse of 30 minutes or so, that it had been done, and that the President had agreed.

"The CHAIRMAN. You are absolutely free to prosecute anyone; is that correct?

"Mr. JAWORSKI. That is correct. And that is my intention.

"The CHAIRMAN. And that includes the President of the United States?

"Mr. JAWORSKI. It includes the President of the United States.

* * * *

"Senator McCLELLAN. May I ask you now, do you feel that with your understanding with the White House that you do have the right, irrespective of the legal issues that may be involved—that you have an understanding with them that gives you the right to go to court if you determine that they have documents you want or materials that you feel are essential and necessary in the performance of your duties, and in conducting a thorough investigation and following up with prosecution thereon, *you have the right to go to court to raise the issue against the President and against any of his staff with respect to such documents or materials and to contest the question of privilege.*

"Mr. JAWORSKI. I *have been assured that right.* And I intend to exercise it if necessary." (Emphasis added.)

Hearings Before the Senate Judiciary Committee on the Special Prosecutor, 93d Cong., 1st Sess., pt. 2, at 571, 573 (1973).

General, who appointed the Special Prosecutor, was fully apprised of the understanding. He testified as follows before the Senate Judiciary Committee:

Although it is anticipated that Mr. Jaworski will receive cooperation from the White House in getting any evidence he feels he needs to conduct investigations and prosecutions, it is clear and understood on all sides that *he has the power to use judicial processes to pursue evidence if disagreement should develop.* (Emphasis added.) [22]

He also assured the House Subcommittee on Criminal Justice: "I understand and it is clear to me that Mr. Jaworski can go to court and test out" any refusal to produce documents on the ground of confidentiality.[23]

Similarly, the President's nominee to be Attorney General, William Saxbe, testified that the Special Prosecutor would have "sole discretion" in deciding whether to contest an assertion of executive privilege by the President and stated "he can go to court at any time to determine that."[24] Significantly, neither the President, nor his counsel, nor Acting Attorney General Bork has ever disavowed the assurances given. In fact, in announcing the appointment of a new Special Prosecutor on October 26, 1973, President Nixon stated (9 Weekly Compilation of Presidential Documents (Oct. 29, 1973)):

And I can assure you ladies and gentlemen, and all our listeners tonight, that I have no greater interest than to see that the new special prosecutor has the cooperation from the executive branch *and the independence that he needs to* bring about that conclusion [of the Watergate investigation]. (Emphasis added.)

The regulations governing the Special Prosecutor's jurisdiction and independence, together with the Presidential assurances given to the public directly and to the Special Prosecutor through General Haig, reflect the public demand for an independent prosecutor not subject to the direct or indirect control of the President and not dependent upon the discretion of the President

[22] *Id.*, at 450. See also *id.*, at 470.

[23] *Hearings Before the House Judiciary Subcommittee on Criminal Justice on H.J. Res. 784 and H.R. 10937,* 93d Cong., 1st Sess. 266 (1973).

[24] *Hearings Before the Senate Judiciary Committee on the Nomination of William B. Saxbe to be Attorney General,* 93d Cong., 1st Sess. 9 (1973).

for access to information upon which to base investigations and prosecutions.[25] From the first, the regulations establishing and then reestablishing the Office of the Watergate Special Prosecution Force [26] have had the force and effect of law, e.g., *Vitarelli* v. *Seaton*, 359 U.S. 535; *Service* v. *Dulles, supra; Accardi* v. *Shaughnessy*, 347 U.S. 260; *Nader* v. *Bork, supra*, and empower the Special Prosecutor to contest the assertion of Executive Privilege in any case within his jurisdiction when he, not the President, concludes the assertion is unwarranted. See *Accardi* v. *Shaughnessy, supra*, 347 U.S. at 266-67.

This Court has held that, by virtue of their office, public officials necessarily have a sufficient "personal stake in the outcome" of any litigation that challenges the performance of their duties on constitutional grounds. See, *e.g., Board of Education* v. *Allen*, 392 U.S. 236, 241 n. 5; *Coleman* v. *Miller*, 307 U.S. 433, 437-45. It follows, therefore, that under applicable statutes and regulations the Special Prosecutor has standing to take all necessary steps in court to promote the conduct of the cases under his jurisdiction, including the litigation of claims of "executive privilege" advanced as a reason for withholding evidence considered important to one of those prosecutions.

C. *The Special Prosecutor Has Authority to Seek, and the Federal Courts Have Power to Grant, a Production Order Addressed to the President Even Though the Special Prosecutor Is a Member of the Executive Branch*

What has been shown above makes clear the authority of the Special Prosecutor to bring such prosecutions as are within his jurisdiction and to seek court orders for the production of such evidence as is necessary to the litigation. We have shown that, in so discharging his duties, the Special Prosecutor does not act as the mere agent-at-will of the President. He enjoys an independent authority derived from constitutional delegations of authority by the Congress to the Attorney General and from the Attorney General to him under valid regulations that reflect the solemn

[25] After the appointment of the new Special Prosecutor with these assurances of independent authority, *inter alia*, to contest in court any Presidential claims of executive privilege, both Houses of Congress tabled bills that would have provided for court appointment of a Special Prosecutor pursuant to Article II, Section 2. See note 13, *supra*.

[26] The authority of the Attorney General to issue the regulations is conferred by 28 U.S.C. § § 509, 510 and 5 U.S.C. § 301. The legality of these regulations delegating the authority of the Attorney General has been sustained in *Nader* v. *Bork, supra; United States* v. *Andreas*, – F. Supp. – (D. Minn. No. 4-73-Cr. 201) (March 12, 1974); *United States* v. *Ehrlichman*, – F. Supp. – (D.D.C. Crim. No. 74-116) (May 21, 1974).

commitments of the President himself.

Since the Special Prosecutor has authority to bring prosecutions and to seek production of evidence and does not take such actions in the President's name or at his behest, and since, as we show in Part II of our argument below, the President can, in an appropriate case, be ordered to produce evidence, there would seem to be no obstacle to the Special Prosecutor's seeking an order that the President produce evidence. The proceedings surrounding such an order constitute a justiciable controversy whether or not the President could, through a complicated series of steps, lawfully replace the Special Prosecutor and despite the somewhat unusual appearance on opposite sides of two parties both of whom are members of the Executive Branch.

1. *Whatever Power the President may have to Circumvent an Adverse Ruling by Taking Steps to Abrogate the Special Prosecutor's Independence Cannot Serve to Render the Controversy Non-justiciable*

The mere fact that the President is Chief Executive, with ultimate responsibility to "take Care that the Laws be faithfully executed," does not destroy the Special Prosecutor's independence or standing to sue. Whatever might be the situation in a proceeding conducted by a mere agent of the President, the Special Prosecutor's functional and legal independence empowers him, on behalf of the United States, to seek a subpoena against the President for evidence.

Congress frequently confers powers and duties upon subordinate executive officials, and in such situations the President's function as Chief Executive does not authorize him to displace the designated officer and to act directly in the matter himself. As long as the officer holds his position, the power to act under the law is his alone. A familiar example of this basic principle was illustrated by President Andrew Jackson's legendary battle over the Bank of the United States. Two Secretaries of the Treasury refused to obey the President's command to withdraw deposits from the Bank, a function entrusted to the Secretary by law. The President's only recourse was to seek a third, who complied with Jackson's wish. See generally Van Deusen, *The Jacksonian Era*, 1828-1848, pp. 80-82 (1959). Attorney General Roger Taney gave a similar opinion to President Jackson, advising him that as long as a particular United States Attorney remained in office, he was empowered to conduct a particular litigation as he saw fit, despite the wishes of the President. See 2 Op. Att'y Gen. 482 (1831).

More recently, President Nixon apparently recognized a similar limitation on his powers as Chief Executive when, in order to effect the discharge of the former Special Prosecutor over the refusal of Attorney General Richardson and Deputy Attorney General Ruckelshaus to dismiss him, the President had to procure the removal of those officials and rest upon Acting Attorney General Bork's exercise of their power.

These principles, considered in light of the authority of the Special Prosecutor reviewed above, establish that, short of finding some way to accomplish the removal of the Special Prosecutor, the President has no legal right or power to limit or direct his actions in bringing prosecutions or in seeking the evidence needed for these prosecutions. Any effort to interfere in the Special Prosecutor's decisions is inadmissible and any order would be without legal effect so long as the Attorney General has not effectively rescinded the regulations creating and guaranteeing the Special Prosecutor's independence—a course he may be legally barred from taking without the Special Prosecutor's consent, see *Nader* v. *Bork*, *supra*, 366 F. Supp. at 108. Even then any order would have to come from the Attorney General to satisfy statutory requirements.

The President is bound by duly promulgated regulations even where he has power to amend them for the future. *Accardi* v. *Shaughnessy*, 347 U.S. at 266-67. It is even clearer in the present situation that regulations and statutes which he has no power to modify prevent him from assuming direction of the Watergate prosecutions. Thus, there can be no argument that a case or controversy is lacking because the President could dismiss the prosecution or withdraw the subpoena even if he so desired.

Nor is any valid objection to the concrete reality of this dispute furnished by the hypothesis, *arguendo*, that the President could nullify any adverse ruling by procuring the dismissal of the Special Prosecutor and finding another prosecutor who would not enforce the Court's decision. A similar argument was rejected well over a century ago. In *Kendall* v. *United States ex rel. Stokes*, 12 Pet. (37 U.S.) 524, it was argued that the Judiciary lacked power to issue a mandamus requiring the Postmaster General to credit a sum of money to a contractor on the ground that the President would frustrate performance of the decree by discharging the respondent and appointing a new Postmaster General. The Court rejected the argument and granted mandamus. The federal courts have continued to resolve legal controversies despite the theoretical power of one of the parties to avoid the impact of the judgment by lawful means. See, *e.g.*,

Glidden Co. v. *Zdanok* 370 U.S. 530.

The same argument against jurisdiction fails in the present case, not only on the basis of precedent, but for three other reasons as well.

First, in the present situation, the President does not have the power to remove the Special Prosecutor and to appoint a replacement more to his liking. Under Article II, Section 2 of the Constitution, Congress has vested appointment of officers of the Department of Justice, like the Special Prosecutor, in the Attorney General, not the President.[27] And, the President explicitly has ceded any right and power he may have to restrict the independence of the Special Prosecutor or effect his discharge by agreeing to the issuance of regulations precluding such action unless the "consensus" of eight specified Congressional officials concurs in that course. The regulations establishing this condition precedent to any action by the President have the force of law, and the Special Prosecutor thus stands before the Court independent of any direct control by the Attorney General or the President. In short, the present regulations governing the Special Prosecutor's tenure and independence are even more restrictive of the residual authority of the President and the Attorney General than were the regulations that were held in *Nader* v. *Bork*, *supra*, to have been violated by the dismissal of Special Prosecutor Cox.[28]

Second, even the dismissal of the Special Prosecutor would not nullify a ruling that the evidence must be produced, since the Attorney General and the Solicitor General, as officers of this Court, would be legally obliged to attend to the proper enforcement of a decree by the Court, particularly one in favor of the United States. See *United States* v. *Shipp*, 203 U.S. 563; *United States* v. *Shipp*, 214 U.S. 386 (proceedings for criminal contempt initiated and conducted before this Court by Attorney General for defiance of Court's order); 28 U.S.C. 518 (a).

[27] The locus of the appointment power may also fix the authority to remove, *United States* v. *Perkins*, 116 U.S. 483, although the removal power itself is not absolute. *Humphrey's Executor* v. *United States*, 295 U.S. 602; *Wiener* v. *United States*, 357 U.S. 349; *Myers* v. *United States*, 272 U.S. 52.

[28] The regulations also provide that the Special Prosecutor's office will not be abolished without the consent of the Special Prosecutor and that the Attorney General will not countermand any decisions of the Special Prosecutor (see Appendix pp. 149, 151,   ). Judge Gesell in *Nader* v. *Bork*, *supra*, 336 F. Supp. at 108, indicated that those guarantees are legally binding and not unilaterally revocable.

This Court has recognized, of course, that the President's power to remove subordinate officers of the government, even those in the Executive Branch, is not unlimited, and may be non-existent when the executive official exercises some "duties of a quasi-judicial character." *Myers* v. *United States*, *supra*, 272 U.S. at 135. See also *Humphrey's Executor* v. *United States*, *supra*; *Wiener* v. *United States*, *supra*.

Third, the speculative possibility that something might occur in the future cannot render a presently live controversy moot, when it is hardly inevitable that the Court's decision will be ineffective. Compare *DeFunis* v. *Odegaard*, — U.S. — (42 U.S.L.W. 4578, April 23, 1974). Just as "voluntary cessation of allegedly illegal conduct does not deprive the tribunal of power to hear and determine the case, *i.e.*, does not make the case moot," *United States* v. *W.T. Grant Co.*, 345 U.S. 629, 632, it follows *a fortiori* that the hypothetical—and possible illegal—dismissal of the Special Prosecutor after a decision in his favor by this Court cannot render the present case moot. As this Court noted earlier this Term in rejecting a mootness claim involving a challenge to state welfare benefits to striking workers where the particular strike had ended: "The judiciary must not close the door to the resolution of the important questions these concrete disputes present." *Super Tire Engineering Co.* v. *McCorkle*, — U.S. — (42 U.S.L.W. 4507, 4511, April 16, 1974). In the present case, the precise controversy is still very much alive, and the President has not even threatened to attempt to defeat an adverse ruling by effecting the dismissal of the Special Prosecutor.

2. There is No Lack of a True Case or Controversy Because the Opposing Parties are Both Members of the Executive Branch

In the present matter, there can be no serious contention that this is a feigned or collusive suit or an abstract or speculative debate; the issues are sharply drawn over the production or nonproduction of specific evidence for a pending criminal trial, and the litigants—the United States and President Nixon—have manifestly concrete but antagonistic interests in the outcome, for if the subpoenaed materials are ordered produced the United States can proceed to trial in a major criminal case armed with important evidence, while a contrary decision would leave President Nixon in absolute control over those materials and thereby weaken the government's case against his former aides, whom he has publicly supported in this criminal investigation (see pp. 59-60, *infra*).

Thus, we submit that it is clear beyond peradventure that the Special Prosecutor, as the exclusively authorized attorney for the United States—the prosecuting sovereign in the pending criminal case of *United States* v. *Mitchell, et al.*, for which the instant trial subpoena was issued—has standing to seek enforcement of the subpoena, for the prosecution has "such a personal stake in the outcome of the controversy as to assure that concrete adverseness which sharpens the presentation of issues upon which the court so largely depends for illumination of difficult constitutional questions." *Baker* v. *Carr* 369 U.S. 186, 204. See also *Flast* v. *Cohen*, 392 U.S. 83, 98-100.

Framing this controversy as a mere "intra-executive branch" dispute, as counsel for the President did below, seems to invoke the sterile conceptualism, long ago discarded, that since "no person may sue himself," suits between government officials cannot be maintained. As this Court said when it rejected such an argument in *United States* v. *ICC*, 337 U.S. 426, 430, "courts must look behind names that symbolize the parties to determine whether a justiciable case or controversy is presented."[29] See also *Secretary of Agriculture* v. *United States*, 350 U.S. 162. This practical approach was underscored only this Term, when the Court noted probably jurisdiction and heard argument in two cases in which the United States, represented by the Justice Department, was appealing from two separate district court decisions dismissing the government's complaints attacking bank mergers under Section 7 of the Clayton Act. *United States* v. *Marine Bancorporation, Inc.*, No. 73-38; *United States* v. *Connecticut National Bank*, No. 73-767. The Comptroller of the Currency has responsibility for administering the Bank Merger Act and the National Bank Act, and in each case the Comptroller had approved a merger challenged by the Department of Justice under the Clayton Act. In each case the Comptroller of the Currency, an official of the Treasury Department, 12 U.S.C. § 1, 2, was named as an appellee and filed a brief in opposition to the position taken by the Solicitor General on behalf of the Department of Justice. Although such litigation is relatively rare and typically involves disputes between an executive department and a "quasi-independent" regulatory agency, there is nothing in the "case or controversy" requirement of Article III that denies the federal courts the power to adjudicate concrete controversies between government officials over their respective legal powers and duties, see *e.g.*, *Powell* v. *McCormack*, *supra*, particularly when—as in the present case—the resolution of the legal controversy has direct consequences upon them and private parties.

We do not suggest, of course, that the President or the Department of Justice could confer jurisdiction on the courts where such jurisdiction is constitutionally impermissible. What

[29]. Judge Holtzoff had held that the suit there had to be dismissed because "the United States of America always acts in a sovereign capacity. It does not have separate governmental and proprietary capacities." *United States* v. *ICC*, 78 F. Supp. 580, 583 (D.D.C. 1948). This Court reversed.

we do argue, however, is that the Court must look beyond the President's formalistic objections to the Court's jurisdiction, based as they are on a talismanic incantation of the "intra-executive" nature of the proceeding. By pointing to the mere formality of the Special Prosecutor's status as an executive officer, counsel to the President ignores the substantive concern underlying the "case or controversy" requirement of Article III. A proceeding is justiciable if it presents live, concrete issues between adverse parties that are susceptible of adjudication. See, e.g., O'Shea v. Littleton, — U.S. — (42 U.S.L.W. 4139, January 15, 1974); United States v. SCRAP, 412 U.S. 669, 687; Flast v. Cohen, 392 U.S. 83, 94-101; Baker v. Carr 369 U.S. 186, 204. And it is against these standards that the Court must resolve the objections to its jurisdiction.

Although counsel for the President has argued that somehow the "separation of powers" principle denies to the federal courts the power to decide this controversy between the President and the prosecution in United States v. Mitchell, this argument will not withstand analysis. The inescapable irony of the President's position can only be appreciated by focusing on the fact that the regulations creating a Special Prosecutor's office armed with functional independence and with explicit authority to litigate against Presidential claims of privilege do not reflect a statutory regime imposed by the Legislative Branch; these regulations were promulgated with the President's approval by his Attorney General. This, then, is the President's position—not that Congress has unconstitutionally invaded his sphere, but rather that the doctrine of separation of powers forecloses him from the ability to control his "own" Executive Branch in such a way as to safeguard public confidence in the integrity of the law enforcement process. The Office of the Watergate Special Prosecution Force was established with the approval of the President as an independent entity within the Department of Justice in response to the public demand for an impartial investigation of charges of criminal misconduct by officials in the Executive Office of the President. After Special Prosecutor Cox's dismissal, the Office was re-established amid a public reaction so severe that it has generated the first serious possibility of a Presidential impeachment in more than a century and made enactment of legislation for a court-appointed Special Prosecutor almost certain.[30] Perhaps the most important assurance of independence built into the proposed role of the Special

---

[30] See note 13, supra.

Prosecutor, as reflected in congressional testimony[31] as well as public statements by the President and the Attorney General, was his authority to invoke the judicial process to obtain necessary evidence from the President. It simply stands the doctrine of separation of powers on its head to suggest that it precludes the Judiciary from giving full force and effect to the allocation of authority within the Executive Branch under an arrangement that was designed by the Attorney General and approved by the President as indispensible to forestall a further erosion of faith in the Executive Branch.

D. *The Speculative Possibility that the President*
May Disregard a Valid Court Order Does Not
Deprive the Court of Jurisdiction

A theme advanced earlier by counsel for the President in opposition to enforcement of a grand jury subpoena *duces tecum* in *Nixon* v. *Sirica* was that the President has "the power and thus the privilege to withhold information."[32]   This raw assertion in no way undermines the justiciability of this controversy. The naked power of the Chief Executive, despite a court order to withhold evidence from a judicial proceeding does not deprive the courts of jurisdiction to order its production. To link physical power with legal privilege runs contrary to our entire constitutional tradition. As this Court stated in *Kendall* v. *United States ex rel. Stokes, supra,* 12 Pet. at 613, "[t]o contend that the obligation imposed on the President to see the laws are faithfully executed implies a power to forbid their execution, is a novel construction of the Constitution, and entirely inadmissible." It might as well be said that a Secretary of State, acting upon orders of the President, would have had "the power and thus the privilege" to withhold the signed commission at issue in *Marbury* v. *Madison, supra;* or that a Postmaster General, acting upon instructions of the President, would have had "the power and thus the privilege" to refuse to pay money owed pursuant to a contract, contrary to the decision in *Kendall, supra;* or that the President has "the power and thus the privilege" to seize industrial property in a wartime labor dispute, contrary to *Youngstown Sheet & Tube Co.* v. *Sawyer, supra;* or to conduct warrantless electronic surveillance in domestic

[31] *Hearings Before the Senate Judiciary Committee on the Special Prosecutor,* 93d Cong., 1st Sess., pt. 2, at 571, 573 (1973).

[32] Brief in Opposition p. 3, *In re Grand Jury Subpoena Duces Tecum Issued to Richard M. Nixon,* 360 F. Supp. 1 (D.D.C. 1973).

security investigations, contrary to the Fourth Amendment as interpreted in *United States* v. *United States District Court*, *supra.*

This Court has never allowed doubt about its physical power to enforce its commands to deter the issuance of appropriate orders. In *Worcester* v. *Georgia*, 6 Pet. (31 U.S.) 515, counsel strenuously argued that the Court should not order Georgia to surrender jurisdiction over a prisoner seized in Cherokee Indian territory because the President would not and the Court could not force Georgia to obey the judicial command, but the Court did not abdicate its responsibility to decide the issues. In *McPherson* v. *Blackmer*, 146 U.S. 1, 24, the Court ruled upon the constitutionality of a Michigan statute providing for the choice of Presidential electors by congressional districts despite the argument that the State's political agencies might frustrate the decision, saying:

> The question of the validity of this act, as presented to us by this record, is a judicial question, and we cannot decline the exercise of our jurisdiction upon the inadmissible suggestion that action might be taken by political agencies in disregard of the judgment of the highest tribunal of the state as revised by our own.

Most recently in *Glidden Co.* v. *Zdanok*, *supra*, the Court rejected the argument that a money claim against the United States did not present a justiciable issue because the courts were without power to force execution of a judgment against the United States: "If this Court may rely on the good faith of state governments or other public bodies to respond to its judgments, there seems to be no sound reason why the Court of Claims may not rely on the good faith of the United States." 370 U.S. at 571[33] In conformity with this principle, the court of appeals in *Nixon* v. *Sirica* rejected the attempt to equate physical power to disobey with legal immunity from the judicial process itself: "The legality of judicial orders should not be confused with the legal consequences of their breach; for the courts of his country always assume that their orders will be obeyed, especially when addressed to responsible government officials." *Nixon* v. *Sirica*, *supra*, 487 F. 2d at 711-12.

The effect of a President's physical power to disobey a court order is wholly speculative at this juncture and undoubtedly will

---

[33] See also *Powell* v. *McCormack*, *supra*, 395 U.S. at 517-18; *Baker* v. *Carr*, *supra*, 369 U.S. at 208-37; *South Dakota* v. *North Carolina*, 192 U.S. 286, 318-21; *La Abra Silver Mining Co.* v. *United States*, 175 U.S. 423, 461-62.

remain so. There is no reason to believe that President Nixon would disregard a decision of this Court fixing legal responsibilities, any more than he did the order of the district court, as modified by the court of appeals in *Nixon* v. *Sirica, supra,* requiring him to submit for *in camera* inspection recordings subpoeaed by the grand jury. In announcing that President Nixon would comply with the mandate in *Nixon* v. *Sirica,* counsel for the President stated in open court: "This President does not defy the law, and he has authorized me to say he will comply in full with the orders of the court."[34]

The Court, therefore, can cast aside as wholly illusory any of the obstacles that may be suggested as barring its exercise of the judicial power of the United States to decide the evidentiary privilege issue interposed in this criminal case. The case is within the jurisdiction of the federal courts and is fully justiciable.

[34] Transcript of Hearing on October 23, 1973, *In re Grand Jury Subpoena Duces Tecum Issued to Richard M. Nixon, supra,* D.D.C. Misc. No. 47-73.

I. THE COURTS HAVE BOTH THE POWER AND THE DUTY TO DETERMINE THE VALIDITY OF A CLAIM OF EXECUTIVE PRIVILEGE WHEN IT IS ASSERTED IN A JUDICIAL PROCEEDING AS A GROUND FOR REFUSING TO PRODUCE EVIDENCE

A. *The Courts Have the Power to Resolve All Issues in a Controversy Properly Before Them, Even Though This Requires Determining, Authoritatively, the Powers and Responsibilities of the Other Branches*

Our basic submission, and the one we suggest controls this case, is a simple one—the courts, in the exercise of their jurisdiction under Article III of the Constitution, have the duty and, therefore, the power to determine all issues necessary to a lawful resolution of controversies properly before them. The duty includes resolving issues as to the admissibility of evidence in a criminal prosecution as well as the obligation to produce such evidence under subpoena. This allocation of responsibility is inherent in the constitutional duty of the federal courts, as the "neutral" branch of government, to decide cases in accordance with the rule of law, and it supports rather than undermines the basic separation of powers conceived by the Constitution.

The principle was clear at the very outset of our constitutional history. Since 1803 there has been no question that in resolving any case or controversy within the jurisdiction of a federal court, "[i]t is emphatically the province and the duty of the judicial department to say what the law is." *Marbury* v. *Madison, supra,* 1 Cranch at 177. See *Powell* v. *McCormack, supra,* 395 U.S. at 521. As *Marbury* v. *Madison* firmly establishes, this is true even though the controversy before the courts implicates the powers and responsibilities of a co-ordinate branch. In conformity with this principle the courts consistently have exercised final authority to determine whether even the highest executive officials are acting in accordance with the Constitution and have issued appropriate decrees to implement those judicial decisions. *E.g., Youngstown Sheet & Tube Co.* v. *Sawyer, supra* (alleged right of President to authorize the Secretary of Commerce to seize steel mills); *United States* v. *United States District Court, supra* (alleged power of the President, acting through the Attorney General, to authorize electronic surveillance in internal security matters without prior judicial approval); *Kendall* v. *United States ex rel. Stokes, supra* (alleged power of the President, acting through the Postmaster General, to withhold money owed pursuant to a contract); *Land* v. *Dollar,* 190 F. 2d 623 (D.C. Cir. 1951), vacated as moot, 344 U.S. 806 (alleged right of Secretary of Commerce and Acting Attorney General to obey order of President inconsistent with judicial decree; officials adjudicated in civil contempt).

The courts have not retreated from this responsibility even when the most pressing and immediate needs of the Nation were at issue. President Truman directed the Secretary of Commerce to seize and operate specified steel facilities because of his judgment that a threatened work stoppage at the Nation's steel mills during the Korean War "would immediately jeopardize and imperil our national defense." Executive Order No. 10340 (April 8, 1952). Nevertheless, this Court ruled that the President had exceeded his constitutional powers and upheld a preliminary injunction enjoining the seizure. Justice Jackson's concurring opinion expresses the fundamental principle underlying the Court's decision (343 U.S. at 655):

> With all its defects, delays and inconveniences, men have discovered no technique for long preserving free government except that the Executive be under the law.

Even Justice Frankfurter, one of the most ardent exponents of the separation of powers, who expressed "every desire to avoid judicial inquiry into the powers and duties of the other two branches of government," concurred in the judgment of the Court, albeit "with the utmost unwillingness." He recognized: "To deny inquiry into the President's power in a case like this, because of the damage to the public interest to be feared from upsetting its exercise by him, would in effect always preclude inquiry into challenged power * * *." 343 U.S. at 596.

It is too late in our history to contend that this duty and competence of the Judiciary is inconsistent with the separation of powers, either in general or as applied to questions of evidentiary privilege. As the court of appeals held in *Nixon* v. *Sirica, supra,* 487 F. 2d at 715, such a claim, premised on the contention that the separation of powers prevents the courts from compelling particular action from the President or from reviewing his determinations, mistakes the true nature of our constitutional system. Focusing on the "separation" of functions in our tri-partite system of government obscures a crucial point: the exercise by one branch of constitutional powers within its own competence frequently requires action by another branch within its field of powers. Thus, the Legislative Branch has the power to make the laws. Its enactments bind the Judiciary—unless unconstitutional—not only in the decision of cases and controversies, but in the very procedures through which the Judiciary transacts its business.[35]   Congress, in scores of statutes, regularly imposes legal duties upon the President. [36] The very essence of his constitutional function is the legal duty to carry out congressional mandates by taking "Care that the Laws be faithfully executed." Finally, the President may require action by the courts. The courts, for example, have a legal duty to give—and do give—effect to valid executive orders.[37] Where the President or an appropriate official institutes a legal action in his own name or that of the United States, a judge is compelled to grant the relief requested if in accordance with law.

We enjoy a well-functioning constitutional government because each branch is independent and yet acknowledges its duties in response to the functioning of others. "Checks and balances were established in order that this should be a 'government of laws and not of men.' * * * The doctrine of separation of powers was adopted by the Convention of 1787, not to promote efficiency but to preclude the exercise of arbitrary power." *Myers* v. *United States*, 272 U.S. 52, 292-93 (Brandeis, J., dissenting). At the same time, as Mr. Justice Jackson explained in *Youngstown Sheet & Tube Co.* v. *Sawyer*, *supra*, 343 U.S. at 635 (concurring opinion):

> While the Constitution diffuses power the better to secure liberty, it also contemplates that practice will integrate the dispersed powers into a workable government. It enjoins upon its branches separateness but interdependence, autonomy but reciprocity.

Thus, there is no room to argue that the separation of powers makes each branch an island, alone unto itself. Despite the "separation of powers implications, the separation of powers doctrine has not previously prevented this Court from reviewing the acts" of a coordinate branch of the government when placed in issue in a case within the jurisdiction of the federal courts. *Doe* v. *McMillan*, *supra*, 412 U.S. at 318 n. 12.

[35] See, *e.g.*, 28 U.S.C. 2, 44(c), 45, 47, 48, 134(b), 144, 331, 332, 333, 455, 1731-1745, 1826(b), 1863, 2102, 2554(b), 2284(4), 2403; 18 U.S.C. 2519, 3006A, 3331(a), 6003(a), 6005(a).

[36] See, *e.g.*, *National Treasury Employees Union* v. *Nixon*, 492 F. 2d 587, 603 (D.C. Cir. 1974) holding the President was obliged to submit a federal employee pay increase as required by Congress).

[37] See, *e.g.*, *Environmental Protection Agency* v. *Mink*, 410 U.S. 73 (security classification).

B. *The Judicial Power to Determine the Limits of Executive Authority When Necessary to Resolve a Justiciable Controversy Includes the Power to Resolve Claims of Executive Privilege Made with Regard to Evidence Sought by the Prosecutor for Use in a Pending Criminal Case.*

In applying the fundamental principle that the Judiciary, and not the Executive, has the ultimate responsibility for interpreting and applying the law in any justiciable case or controversy, the courts consistently have determined for themselves not only what evidence is admissible, but also what evidence must be produced, including whether particular materials are appropriately subject to a claim of executive privilege. This issue, like questions of the constitutionality and meaning of statutes or executive orders, is one of the matters that a court has a duty to resolve authoritatively whenever their resolution is an integral part of the outcome of a case or controversy within the court's jurisdiction. [38]

The question was decided squarely in *United States* v. *Reynolds* 345 U.S. 1, where the Executive Branch argued that "department heads have power to withhold any documents in their custody from judicial view if they deem it to be in the public interest," 345 U.S. at 6 (footnote omitted)—a position strikingly similar to the one advanced by counsel for the President. The case involved a Tort Claims Act suit arising out of the crash of a B-29 bomber testing secret electronic equipment. The plaintiffs sought discovery of the Air Force's official accident investigation report and the statements of the surviving crew members. Although this Court agreed that an evidentiary privilege covers military secrets, 345 U.S. at 6-7, 11, it held that "[t]he court itself must determine whether the circumstances are appropriate for the claim of privilege * * *. Judicial control over the evidence in a case cannot be abdicated to the caprice of executive officers." 345 U.S. at 8, 9-10 (footnote omitted). See also *Roviaro* v. *United States, supra,* 353 U.S. at 62.

Since the decision in *Reynolds,* every court of appeals that has confronted the question has rejected a claim of absolute executive privilege to withhold evidence merely upon the assertion by the Executive that disclosure would not be in the public interest. The Court of Appeals for the District of Columbia Circuit, for example, which has had the most frequent occasion to consider and discuss this issue, has noted that "this claim of absolute immunity for documents in the possession of an executive department or agency, upon the bald assertion of its head, is not sound law." *Committee for Nuclear Responsibility, Inc.* v. *Seaborg*, 463 F. 2d 783, 792 (1971). In recently reaffirming the validity of this decision, the court ruled *en banc* that judicial determination "is not only consistent with, but dictated by, separation of powers doctrine." *Nixon* v. *Sirica, supra,* 487 F. 2d at 714.[39]

Even in the first case that firmly recognized a confidentiality privilege for "intra-agency advisory opinions," *Kaiser Aluminum & Chemical Corp.* v. *United States,* 157 F. Supp. 939 (1958),[40] the Court of Claims, in an opinion by Justice Reed, held that documents reflecting executive deliberations "are privileged from inspection as against public interest *but not* absolutely. * * * The power must lie in the courts to determine executive privilege in litigation." 157 F. Supp. at 946-47 (emphasis added). Thus, even in the embryonic stages of

---

[38] Because there is no legislative analogy to the historic judicial duty to determine all questions of law necessarily raised by a case or controversy, rejection of the claim of executive privilege in the present case does not necessarily suggest any answer to the distinct questions of the scope of the President's right to stand on a claim of executive privilege *vis-a-vis* the Congress or of the role, if any, of the courts in such a confrontation. History provides a great variety of opinions on the relative rights of the Executive and the Congress in such a situation. See generally Berger, *Executive Privilege* v. *Congressional Inquiry,* 12 U.C.L.A. L. Rev. 1043, 1078-98 (1965).

The Court of Appeals for the District of Columbia Circuit recently affirmed a decision of the district court refusing a declaratory judgment that a subpoena issued to the President by the Senate Select Committee on Presidential Campaign Activities was valid and enforceable. *Senate Select Committee on Presidential Campaign Activities* v. *Nixon,* – F. 2d – (No. 74-1258) (D.C. Cir. May 23, 1974). By deciding that the Committee's "need" for the subpoenaed recordings was "too attenuated and too tangential to its functions to permit a judicial judgment that the President is required to comply with the Committee's subpoena," thereby reaching the merits of the claim of executive privilege, the court held implicitly that the Committee's action presented a justiciable controversy. Cf. *Powell* v. *McCormack, supra.*

At one time it was generally assumed that a claim of executive privilege *vis-a-vis* the Congress presented a nonjusticiable political question. See, *e.g.,* L. Hand, The Bill of Rights 17-18 (1958). But no one has ever suggested that an application for an order requiring the Executive Branch to produce evidence in the usual course of judicial or grand jury proceedings presents a non-justiciable "political question."

[39] Accord, *Egbyl Corporation* v. *Environmental Protection Agency,* 478 F. 2d 47, 51 (4th Cir. 1973); *Carr* v. *Monroe Manufacturing Co.,* 431 F. 2d 384, 388 (5th Cir. 1970), cert. denied, 400 U.S. 1000; *Sperandeo* v. *Milk Drivers & Dairy Employees Local 537,* 334 F. 2d 381, 384 (10th Cir. 1964); *N.L.R.B.* v. *Capitol Fish Co.,* 294 F. 2d 868, 875 (5th Cir. 1961); *Halpern* v. *United States,* 258 F. 2d 36, 43 (2d Cir. 1958). See also *Pan American World Airways, Inc.* v *Aetna Cas. & Sur. Co.,* 368 F. Supp. 1098, 1139-40 (S.D.N.Y. 1973); *United States* v. *Article of Drug, etc.,* 43 F.R.D. 181, 190 (D. Del. 1967); *O'Keefe* v. *Boeing Co.,* 38 F.R.D. 329, 334 (S.D.N.Y. 1965); *Timken Roller Bearing Co.* v. *United States,* 38 F.R.D. 57, 63 (N.D. Ohio 1964); *Morris* v. *Atchison, Topeka & Santa Fe Ry. Co.,* 21 F.R.D. 155, 157-58 (W.D. Mo. 1957); *Snyder* v. *United States,* 20 F.R.D. 7, 9 (E.D.N.Y. 1956).

[40] See generally R. Berger, *Executive Privilege: A Constitutional Myth* 353-55 (1974).

this relatively recently articulated version of "executive privilege," the courts recognized that the legitimate interests of the Executive do not require unreviewable discretion to shield its decision-making processes from scrutiny by the Judiciary. A similar conclusion has been reached by the courts of almost all other countries following the common law.[41]

In short, the President's assertion in the district court "that it is for the President of the United States, rather than for a court, to decide when the public interest requires that he exercise his constitutional privilege to refuse to produce information" flies in the face of an unbroken line of precedent.[42]

The uniform precedent of allocating to the Judiciary the determination of the applicability and scope of executive claims of privilege not to produce necessary evidence is supported by compelling arguments of policy. Certainly, there are legitimate interests in secrecy. But these interests are more than adequately protected by the qualified privilege defined and applied by the courts.[43] This Court, as we have noted, has adverted to the danger of abdicating objective judicial discernment "to the caprice of executive officers," *United States* v. *Reynolds, supra,* 345 U.S. at 9-10, and stated that "complete abandonment of judicial control would lead to intolerable abuses." 345 U.S. at 8. This is necessarily true because the Executive has an inherent

---

[41] In *Conway* v. *Rimmer,* [1968] 1 All E.R. 874, the House of Lords unanimously overruled the prior English rule that an assertion of executive (or "Crown") privilege is absolute: The House of Lords ruled that the courts may require *in camera* inspection to weigh the competing interests. See generally Cappelletti and Golden, *Crown Privilege and Executive Privilege: A British Response to an American Controversy,* 25 Stanford L. Rev. 836 (1973).

As the court of appeals noted in *Nixon* v. *Sirica, supra,* 487 F. 2d at 713-14, n. 60, judicial power to scrutinize claims of privilege has been recognized in nearly every common law jurisdiction. See, *e.g., Robinson* v. *South Australia* (No. 2), [1931] All E.R. 333 (P.C.); *Gagnon* v. *Quebec Securities Comm'n,* [1965] 50 D.L.R. 2d 329 (1964); *Bruce* v. *Waldron,* [1963] Vict. L.R. 3; *Corbett* v. *Social Security Comm'n,* [1962] N.Z.L.R. 878; *Amar Chand Butail* v. *Union of India,* [1965] 1 India S. Ct. 243.

[42] This Court has not even afforded such status to the Speech or Debate Clause, which is an *express* constitutional privilege for congressmen and their aides similar to the privilege claimed by the President. This Court repeatedly has affirmed that the courts must determine the reach of the Clause. See, *e.g., Gravel* v. *United States, supra; United States* v. *Brewster, supra; United States* v. *Johnson,* 319 U.S. 503.

[43] The courts never have decided whether executive privilege derives implicitly from the constitutional separation of powers, or whether it is merely a common law evidentiary privilege. See, *e.g., United States* v. *Reynolds,* 345 U.S. at 6-7; *Committee for Nuclear Responsibility, Inc.* v. *Seabor, supra,* 463 F. 2d at 793-94. Professor Charles Alan Wright has observed that "[t]he commentators * * * have not found much substance in the constitutional argument, based, as it is, on separation of powers." 8 Wright and Miller, Federal Practice and Procedure, § 2019, at 175 n. 44 (1970 ed.).

conflict of interest when its actions are called into question if it is to decide whether evidence is to remain secret. Thus, in *Committee for Nuclear Responsibility, Inc.* v. *Seaborg, supra,* the Court of Appeals for the District of Columbia Circuit has emphasized a related rationale for denying absolute executive discretion to assert a binding confidentiality privilege: "executive absolutism cannot override the duty of the court to assure that an official has not exceeded his charter or flouted the legislative will." 463 F. 2d at 793. The court presciently stated (463 F. 2d at 794):

> [N]o executive official or agency can be given absolute authority to determine what documents in his possession may be considered by the court in its task. Otherwise the head of any executive department would have the power on his own say so to cover up all evidence of fraud and corruption when a federal court or grand jury was investigating malfeasance in office, and this is not the law.[44]

In a similar vein, the Court of Appeals for the Fifth Circuit recently noted:

> The granting or withholding of any privilege requires a balancing of competing policies, 8 Wigmore, § 2285 at 527-28. The claim of governmental privilege is no exception; in fact, the potential for misuse of government privilege, and the consequent diminution of information about government available to the public, is one more factor which strongly suggests the need for judicial arbitration of the availability of the privilege.

Carr v. *Monroe Manufacturing Co., supra,* 431 F. 2d at 388.

We do not question the need for a qualified privilege to serve as an encouragement to the candid exchange of ideas necessary for the formulation of executive policy. Indeed, as the court of appeals held in *Nixon* v. *Sirica, supra,* 487 F. 2d at 717, such discussions are "presumptively privileged." But this case brings into high relief the dangers that would be posed by unbridled, absolute discretion to invoke executive privilege and underscores

---

[44] The rationale is equally well summarized by Wigmore (§ 2379, at 809-10):
"A court which abdicates its inherent function of determining the facts upon which the admissibility of evidence depends will furnish to bureaucratic officials too ample opportunities for abusing the privilege. The lawful limits of the privilege are extensible beyond any control if its applicability is left to the determination of the very official whose interest it may be to shield a wrongdoing under the privilege. Both principle and policy demand that the determination of the privilege shall be for the court."
See also *United States* v. *Cotton Valley Operators Comm.,* 9 F.R.D. 719, 720-21 (W.D. La. 1949), aff'd by an equally divided Court, 339 U.S. 940.

the wisdom of the rule vesting ultimate power in the courts to rule upon such claims when they are advanced in the context of judicial proceedings. President Nixon cannot be a proper judge of whether the greater public interest lies in disclosing the subpoenaed evidence for use at trial or in withholding it. He is now the subject of an impeachment inquiry by the Committee on the Judiciary of the House of Representatives, and the subpoenaed evidence may have a material bearing on whether he is impeached and, if impeached, whether he is convicted and removed from office. This is an issue to which he can hardly be indifferent. In addition, the Special Prosecutor, as prosecuting attorney for the United States, seeks the subpoenaed evidence in prosecuting the President's highest and closest aides and associates. The President is bound to them by the natural emotions of loyalty and gratitude. Thus, in his Address to the Nation on April 30, 1973, announcing the resignation of defendants Haldeman and Ehrlichman, the President referred to them as "two of the finest public servants it has been my privilege to know." 9 Weekly Compilation of Presidential Documents 434 (May 7, 1973). And during a question-and-answer session between President Nixon and participants at the Associated Press Managing Editors Association annual convention on November 17, 1973, the President stated unequivocally: "* * * Mr. Haldeman and Mr. Ehrlichman had been and were dedicated, fine public servants, and I believe, it is my belief based on what I know now, that when these proceedings are completed that they will come out all right." 9 Weekly Compilation of Presidential Documents 1349 (November 26, 1973).

We call attention to these facts without disrespect to the President or his Office. But even if by extraordinary act of conscience, he could judge impartially the relative public advantages of secrecy and disclosure without regard to the consequences for himself or his associates, confidence in the integrity and impartiality of the legal system as between the high and the lowly still would be impaired through violation of the ancient precept that no man shall be a judge in his own cause. Compare *Ward* v. *Village of Monroeville*, 409 U.S. 57; *Mayberry* v. *Pennsylvania*, 400 U.S. 455; *Offutt* v. *United States*, 348 U.S. 11; 28 U.S.C. 455.

C. Courts Have the Power to Order the Production of Evidence from the Executive When Justice So Requires

When the court's duty to decide a case or controversy requires the court to determine the validity of a claim of executive privilege, the court has the concomitant power to order the production of the evidence from the Executive Branch when justice so requires. This Court's decision last Term in *Environmental Protection Agency* v. *Mink*, 410 U.S. 73, clearly establishes the proposition that the constitutional separation of powers does not give the Executive any constitutional immunity from judicial orders for the production of evidence. The plaintiffs there had sought access under the Freedom of Information Act to a report prepared for the President by the Undersecretaries Committee of the National Security Council on the proposed underground nuclear test on Amchitka Island. The government opposed the request partly upon the ground that the documents were exempt from disclosure as "inter-agency memorandums or letters,"[45] arguing that the need to avoid disclosure of communications with the President was "particularly important." Brief for the Petitioners 39-40. Nevertheless, this Court remanded for a judicial determination of the claim of privilege; the opinion states explicitly that in opposing disclosure the government carried the burden of establishing "to the satisfaction of the District Court" that the documents were exempt from disclosure. 410 U.S. at 93. Significantly, the Freedom of Information Act expressly provides that "[i]n the event of noncompliance with the order of the court" to disclose material found unprivileged, the court may punish the responsible executive officer "for contempt." 5 U.S.C. 552 (a) (3). Neither in *Mink* nor in any other decision has any doubt been expressed about the constitutional power of the court to enter a mandatory order for the production of evidence after a claim of executive privilege has been overruled by the court.

Other precedents confirm the existence of judicial power to require the production of evidence by executive officials when the court determines the evidence to be material and unprivileged. *United States* v. *Burr*, 25 Fed. Cas. 30 (No. 14,692d) (C.C.D. Va. 1807), of course, is an early and clear example involving evidence in the possession of the President sought for use in a federal criminal case. In *Bowman Dairy Co.* v. *United States*, 341 U.S. 214, 221, this Court treated contempt as a proper sanction against government counsel if he refused to

---

[45] Although the Court dealt within the framework of the Freedom of Information Act, 5 U.S.C. 552(b) (5), it recognized that Congress simply had incorporated the common law executive privilege. 410 U.S. at 85-89. The exemption was defined with specific reference to the court decisions that had developed the privilege at issue here.

obey a subpoena for the production of documents after the court rejected a claim of privilege. Similarly, while holding that an FBI agent could not properly be held in contempt for refusing to obev a subpoena to produce information for use in a state prisoner's habeas corpus action without permission from the Attorney General, the Court implicitly assumed, and Justice Frankfurter explicitly stated in his concurring opinion, that the Attorney General himself could be required to litigate the underlying claim of privilege in court. *United States ex rel. Touhy* v. *Ragen*, 340 U.S. 462, 473. In private litigation the lower courts consistently have assumed the existence of power to enforce a subpoena for documents in the Executive Branch over a claim of privilege.[46]

Thus, Professor Charles Alan Wright, after explaining that—

The determination whether to allow the claim of [executive] privilege is then for the court * * *

goes on to say that—

In private litigation refusal of a government officer to comply with a court order overruling a claim of executive privilege and ordering disclosure could lead to conviction for contempt * * *.

8 Wright and Miller, Federal Practice and Procedure § 2019, at 171-72 (1970) (footnotes omitted).

In some cases, it is true, the Executive Branch has been left free to decline to produce information if it is willing to suffer the loss of litigation in which it is a party. See, *e.g.*, *Alderman* v. *United States*, 394 U.S. 165, 184; *Jencks* v. *United States*, 353 U.S. 657, 672; *Roviaro* v. *United States*, *supra*, 353 U.S. at 60-61; cf. *Reynolds* v. *United States*, *supra*, 345 U.S. at 12. But the existence of this remedial alternative in some cases does not support the proposition that the Executive rather than the courts has the final authority for determining whether, legally, a claim

---

[46] See, *e.g.*, *Westinghouse Electric Corp.* v. *City of Burlington*, 351 F. 2d 762 (D.C. Cir. 1965); *Machin* v. *Zuckert*, 316 F. 2d 336 (D.C. Cir. 1963), cert. denied, 175 U.S. 896; *Boeing Airplane Co.* v. *Coggeshall*, 280 F. 2d 654 (D.C. Cir. 1960); *Pan American World Airways, Inc.* v. *Aetna Cas. & Sur. Co.*, 368 F. Supp. 1098 (S.D.N.Y. 1973); *Pilar* v. *SS Hess Petrol*, 55 F.R.D. 159 (D. Md. 1972); *Hancock Bros., Inc.* v. *Jones*, 293 F. Supp. 1229 (N.D. Cal. 1968), *Cooney* v. *Sun Shipbuilding & Drydock Co.*, 288 F. Supp. 708 (E.D. Pa. 1968); *McFadden* v. *Avco Corp.*, 278 F. Supp. 57 (M.D. Ala. 1967); *O'Keefe* v. *Boeing Co.*, 38 F.R.D. 329 (S.D.N.Y. 1965); *Rosee* v. *Board of Trade*, 35 F.R.D. 512 (N.D. Cal. 1964); *Morris* v. *Atchison, Topeka & Sante Fe Ry. Co.*, 21 F.R.D. 155 (W.D. Mo. 1957); cf. *Garland* v. *Torre*, 259 F. 2d 545 (2d Cir. 1958) (Stewart, J.), cert. denied, 358 U.S. 910.

of privilege is well founded or not. Moreover, those decisions do not mark the limits of judicial power, for the underlying rationale in each was that the remedial "choice" fully protected the rights of the opposing party, the interests of the Executive and the integrity of the judicial process. In each case this Court recognized that the courts had the ultimate responsibility for passing upon the claim of privilege; only after the courts made the decisive determination could the government elect whether to sacrifice the case or produce the evidence found unprivileged.

In these "produce or dismiss" cases, the requirements of justice could be satisfied without compelling production of particular evidence sought by an adverse party, after judicial rejection of an executive claim of privilege, if the government preferred to accept the "remedy" of losing the case to which it was a party. See generally Rule 16(g), Federal Rules of Criminal Procedure; Rule 37(b), Federal Rules of Civil Procedure. Where dismissal is not an adequate or proper remedy for the parties or is not consistent with judicial integrity, however, the "produce or dismiss" choice cannot be available to the Executive following a judicial ruling rejecting the claim of privilege. As the district court recognized in the present case, the subpoena *duces tecum* to the President here issued to a person who, "as a practical matter, is a third party" (App. 98A). The President has personal custody of evidence sought by the United States, through its attorney, for use in a proceeding in which the President is not a party. Clearly, a person who is not a party to the main lawsuit has no lawful "election" other than to comply with a judicial determination overruling his claim of a privilege to refuse to give material evidence. The cases have so held.[47]

Furthermore, there is no such election when the very object of the legal proceeding is to acquire the information. Thus, for example, in the Freedom of Information Act cases, it could not be seriously contended that the government had some option other than to disclose any information the court finally determines was unprivileged. Indeed, as we observed above, the Act itself specifically provides the sanction of contempt for such an attempt to flout the court's decision.

Most basically, the "produce or dismiss" option reflects a realistic accommodation of the requirements of substantive justice in litigation. But any reliance on an alleged Presidential option to cause dismissal of this criminal prosecution by standing on a claim of privilege, even if overruled by the courts, must be rejected out of hand as plainly insufficient to satisfy the needs of

---

[47] See cases cited in note 46, *supra*.

public justice. The seriousness of the charged offenses and the high offices held by those indicted brand that "solution" as impermissible. The President, himself subject to investigation with respect to the offenses charged in the indictment, is in no position to make the delicate judgment whether the greater public interest lies in producing the evidence and continuing the prosecution or abandoning the prosecution.

As we discussed above (pp. 27-39), under the regulations establishing the Watergate Special Prosecution Force as a quasi-independent office within the Department of Justice, the President has no authority directly—or through the Attorney General—to decide that the Watergate prosecution, *United States v. Mitchell, et al.*, should be abandoned. It would make a travesty out of the independent institution of the Special Prosecutor if the President could accomplish this objective by indirection—by claiming that the courts have no power to order the production of evidence in this criminal prosecution and insisting that the courts be content with posing the dilemma of "produce or dismiss."

Counsel for the President previously argued that "[i]n the exercise of his discretion to claim executive privilege the President is answerable to the Nation but not the courts."[48] This assertion merely highlights the salutary effect of requiring the Executive to make its choice *after* the courts have adjudicated the relevant rights and obligations. Public responsibility cannot be fixed, however, until the alternatives are defined. Only then can the people, as the ultimate rulers, know who controlled the course of events and who took what decisions. The President cannot have it both ways: he cannot suggest that he could abort this investigation rather than comply with an order overruling his claim of privilege and use that hypothetical course to prevent the Court from ruling on the validity of the privilege claim itself. Unless and until the President attempts to exercise whatever powers he might have under the Constitution as Chief Executive to intervene directly in the conduct of this prosecution by the Department of Justice, as represented by the Special Prosecutor, and to procure the Special Prosecutor's dismissal and the countermanding of his conduct of the case, the President must allow the Special Prosecutor and the courts to conduct the prosecution in accordance with the regular processes of the law and without regard to any *potential* executive power to frustrate the administration of justice.

[48] Brief in Opposition 4, *In re Grand Jury Subpoena Duces Tecum Issued to Richard M. Nixon, supra.*

II. THE PRESIDENT IS NOT IMMUNE FROM JUDICIAL ORDERS REQUIRING THE PRODUCTION OF MATERIAL EVIDENCE FOR A CRIMINAL TRIAL

There is nothing in the position of the President, despite his status as Chief Executive, that deprives the courts of their constitutional power to resolve this dispute. The power to decide this case simply cannot differ because the President elected to take personal control of the subpoenaed evidence. The Framers of our Constitution concerned as they were about the abuses of royal prerogative, were very careful to provide for a Presidency with defined and limited constitutional powers and not the prerogatives and immunities of a sovereign. Under our Constitution, the people are sovereign, and the President, though Chief Executive and Chief of State, remains subject to the law.[49] Indeed, it is the very essence of the Presidential Office that it is subject to the commands of the law, for the President's basic governmental function is that of Chief Executive—whose duty it is to "take Care that the Laws be faithfully executed." It follows inexorably that in our system *even the President* is under the law.

No one would deny that every other officer of the executive branch is subject to judicial process,[50] and there is little basis in logic, policy or constitutional history for concluding that a matter becomes walled off from judicial authority simply because the President has elected to become personally involved in it. More basically, however, a true regard for the constitutional separation of powers compels the conclusion that the President himself is appropriately subject to judicial orders. It is the function of the courts to determine rights and obligations of public officers within the context of a justiciable controversy, including those of the President, and it is hiw sworn duty to "execute" those decisions. See *Cooper* v. *Aaron*, 358 U.S. 1, 12.

---

[49] Alexander Hamilton explained the posture of the President in our constitutional system in *The Federalist* Number 69 (B.F. Wright ed. 1961):

"The President of the United States would be an officer elected by the people for *four* years; the king of Great Britain is a perpetual and *hereditary* prince. The one would be amenable to personal punishment and disgrace; the person of the other is sacred and inviolable." (Emphasis in original.)

[50] See, *e.g., Panama Canal Co.* v. *Grace Lines, Inc.,* 356 U.S. 309, 317-18; *Wilbur* v. *United States ex rel. Kadrie,* 281 U.S. 206, 218-22; *Work* v. *United States ex rel. Rivers,* 267 U.S. 175, 177-78; *Ballinger* v. *United States ex rel. Frost,* 216 U.S. 240, 249; *Garfield* v. *United States ex rel. Goldsby,* 211 U.S. 249, 262; *Roberts* v. *United States ex rel. Valentine,* 176 U.S. 221, 229-31; *United States ex rel. McBride* v. *Schurz,* 102 U.S. 378; *Kendall* v. *United States ex rel. Stokes, supra,* 12 Pet. at 609 *et seq.; Marbury* v. *Madison, supra,* 1 Cranch at 164-66.

It must follow that the courts have the power in appropriate cases to order even the President to perform a legal duty.

A. *The Power of the Courts to Issue Subpoenas to the President, Long Recognized by the Courts, Flows from the Fundamental Principle That No Man Is Above the Law*

At the heart of the court's power to issue and enforce a subpoena *duces tecum* directed to the President of the United States lies the "longstanding principle 'that the public * * * has a right to every man's evidence.' " *Branzburg* v. *Hayes*, 408 U.S. 665, 688;[51] *cf. Watkins* v. *United States*, 354 U.S. 178, 187. This power, which in the context of the Watergate investigation and prosecution has proved essential to the full and impartial administration of justice, was upheld in *Nixon* v. *Sirica*, *supra*, 487 F. 2d at 708—12, a decision with which President Nixon willingly complied, rather than seek review in this Court. As the court of appeals recognized, "incumbency does not relieve the President of the routine legal obligations that confine all citizens." 487 F. 2d at 711. "The clear implication [of the *Burr* case] is that the President's special interests may warrant a careful judicial screening of subpoenas after the President interposes an objection, but that some subpoenas will nevertheless be properly sustained by judicial orders of compliance." 487 F. 2d at 710.

The holding of the court in *Nixon* v. *Sirica* is hardly a newfound principle wrought from the exigencies of Watergate. The authority to issue a subpoena *duces tecum* to a sitting President was recognized as early as 1807 by Chief Justice Marshall in *United States* v. *Burr*, 25 Fed. Cas. 30 (No. 14,692d) (C.C.D. Va.).[52] This landmark decision was noted with approval

[51] This Court in *Branzburg* quoted Jeremy Bentham's vivid illustration:

"Are men of the first rank and consideration—are men high in office—men whose time is not less valuable to the public than to themselves—are such men to be forced to quit their business, their functions, and what is more than all, their pleasure, at the beck of every idle or malicious adversary, to dance attendance upon every petty cause? Yes, as far as it is necessary, they and everybody . . . Were the Prince of Wales, the Archbishop of Canterbury, and the Lord High Chancellor, to be passing by in the same coach while a chimneysweeper and a barrow-woman were in dispute about a halfpennyworth of apples, and the chimneysweeper or the barrow-woman were to think proper to call upon them for their evidence, could they refuse it? No, most certainly."

See 4 The Works of Jeremy Bentham 320-21 (Bowring ed. 1843).

See also *United States* v. *Dionisio*, 410 U.S. 1, 9; *Blackmer* v. *United States*, 284 U.S. 421, 438; *Blair* v. *United States*, 250 U.S. 273, 280-281; 8 Wigmore, Evidence § 2192 (McNaughton rev. 1961) [hereinafter cited as "Wigmore"].

[52] For a complete exposition of the decisions in the *Burr* cases based upon the original record of the Burr trials, see Berger, *The President, Congress, and the Courts*, 83 Yale L.J. 1111-22 (1974).

by this Court in *Branzburg* v. *Hayes, supra,* 408 U.S. at 689 n. 26. Although Chief Justice Marshall acknowledged that the power was one to be exercised with attention both to the convenience of the President in performing his arduous duties and to the possibility that the public interest might preclude coercing particular disclosures, he utterly rejected any suggestion that the President, like the King of England, is absolutely immunte from judicial process (25 Fed. Cas. at 34):

Although he [the King] may, perhaps, give testimony, it is said to be incompatible with his dignity to appear under the precess of the court. Of the many pants of difference which exist between the first magistrate in England and the first magistrate of the United States, in respect to the personal dignity conferred on them by the constitutions of their respective nations, the court will only select and mention two. It is a principle of the English constitution that the king can do no wrong, that no blame can be imputed to him, that he cannot be named in debate. By the constitution of the United States, the president, as well as any other officer of the government, may be impeached, and may be removed from office on high crimes and misdemeanors. By the constitution of Great Britain, the crown is hereditary, and the monarch can never be a subject. By that of the United States, the president is elected from the mass of the people, and, on the expiration of the time for which he is elected, returns to the mass of the people again. How essentially this difference of circumstances must vary the policy of the laws of the two countries, in reference to the personal dignity of the executive chief, will be perceived by every person. In this respect the first magistrate of the Union may more properly be likened to the first magistrate of a state; at any rate, under the former Confederation; and it is not known ever to have been doubted, but that the chief magistrate of a state might be served with a subpoena and testificandum.

The decisions in the *Burr* case and *Nixon* v. *Sirica* are premised on the theory that every citizen, no matter what his station or office, has an enforceable legal duty not to withhold evidence the production of which the courts determine to be in the public interest. Stated more broadly, and in more familiar terms, they flow from the premise that this is a government of laws and not of men. This Court summed up this fundamental precept of our republican form of government nearly a century ago in *United States* v. *Lee,* 106 U.S. 196,220:

No man in this country is so high that he is above the law.

No officer of the law may set that law at defiance with impunity. All the officers of the government, from the highest to the lowest, are creatures of the law and are bound to obey it. It is the only supreme power in our system of government, and every man who by accepting office participates in its functions is only the more strongly bound to submit to that supremacy, and to observe the limitations which it imposes upon the exercise of the authority which it gives.

The Steel Seizure Case is perhaps the most celebrated instance where this Court has reviewed the assertion of Presidential power. *Youngstown Sheet & Tube Co.* v. *Sawyer, supra.* As we noted above, President Truman concluded that a work stoppage at the Nation's steel mills during the Korean War "would immediately jeopardize and imperil our national defense." In directing the Secretary of Commerce to seize certain of the mills, the President asserted that he "was acting within the aggregate of his constitutional powers as the Nation's Chief Executive and the Commander in Chief of the Armed Forces of the United States." 343 U.S. at 582. District Judge Holtzoff denied a temporary restraining order on the ground that what was involved was the action of the President and that the courts could not enjoin Presidential action. Judge Pine, however, granted a preliminary injunction. This Court, deciding "whether *the President* was acting within his constitutional power" (343 U.S. at 582, emphasis added), upheld the preliminary injunction. In doing so, there was no doubt expressed that the Court could adjudicate the claim that the President had no constitutional power to issue the Executive Order. Nor, after reading the opinions of the Court, can there be any question that the Court would have granted relief against the President if he had directly ordered the seizure of the mills rather than acting through the Secretary of Commerce.[53] See, *e.g.*, 343 U.S. at 585.

[53.] It is true that custom dictates that legal process should not be addressed to the President of the United States whenever a Cabinet member or lesser official is available, even though the subordinate official is acting upon direct order of the President. *E.g.*, *Youngstown Sheet & Tube Co.* v. *Sawyer, supra*, 343 U.S. 579; *cf. United States Servicemen's Fund* v. *Eastland*, 488 F. 2d 1252, 1270 (D.C. Cir. 1973). It became necessary to seek this evidence from the President only because he elected, by deliberate and affirmative actions, to displace the ordinary custodians of the materials and to assume personal control of them. To allow this device to render the tapes immune from ordinary legal process would exalt form over substance and set a President above the law, contrary to our firm constitutional tradition. As the court of appeals stated in *Nixon* v. *Sirica, supra*, 487 F. 2d at 709, "[t]he practice of judicial review would be rendered capricious—and very likely impotent—if jurisdiction vanished whenever the President personally denoted an Executive action or omission as his own." See also *National Treasury Employees Union* v. *Nixon, supra*, 492 F. 2d at 613.

The Executive's claim of total immunity from judicial decrees is not a new one. In *Land* v. *Dollar, supra,* the Court of Appeals for the District of Columbia Circuit held Secretary of Commerce Sawyer and Acting Attorney General Perlman and subordinate executive officials in civil contempt for failing to comply with a final order requiring them to deliver full and effective possession of certain stock to the prevailing litigant. They attempted to justify their conduct in part on the ground that they were following the directive of the President to Secretary Sawyer "to continue to hold this stock on behalf of the United States" and they further asserted "that, even though the courts determine that a specific action is not within the official capacity of an executive officer, he is immune from compulsion by the courts in respect to that action." 190 F. 2d at 639. The court of appeals rejected the argument in the most emphatic terms (ibid.):

> To claim that the executive has such power [to hold the shares despite the decree] is to claim the total independence of the executive from judicial determinations in justiciable cases and controversies. To characterize such judicial determinations as illegal coercion of the executive is to deny one of the fundamental concepts of our government.

Although there have been a few notorious instances in our history in which Presidents have refused to give appropriate force to judicial decrees, or are reputed to have made disdainful statements about the decisions, none involved direct disobedience of a court order. More importantly, it is the judgment of history that those were essentially lawless departures from the constitututional norm.[54] The responsible constitutional position was expressed by President Truman—a defender of a strong Executive—in announcing that he would comply with an order of this Court in the Steel Seizure Case if it

In addition to the courts below in the present case and in *Nixon* v. *Sirica,* other courts have recognized that compulsory process may issue against the President, when necessary. See *Minnesota Chippewa Tribe* v. *Carlucci,* 358 F. Supp. 973, 975 (D.D.C. 1973) (holding that the President can be sued to compel performance of specific legal duties) (order vacated on grounds of mootness); *Meyers* v. *Nixon,* 339 F. Supp. 1388 (S.D.N.Y. 1972); *Atlee* v. *Nixon,* 336 F. Supp. 790 (E.D. Pa. 1972).

[54] See, *e.g.,* R. Scigliano, *The Supreme Court and the Presidency* 36-37 (1971) and C. Warren, *The Supreme Court in United States History* 759 (rev. ed. 1926). (President Andrew Jackson's failure to take steps to vindicate the Court's decision in the Cherokee Nation case, *Worcester* v. *Georgia,* 6 Pct. (31 U.S.) 515); Scigliano, *supra,* 37-38 (Jackson's vetoing of the national bank bill on consitutional grounds, despite an earlier decision by this Court tending to sustain its validity); Scigliano, *supra,* at 41-43 (President Lincoln's ignoring of several writs of habeas corpus addressed to military commanders during the Civil War). See generally Scigliano, *supra,* 58-59.

went against him, despite his claim of constitutional power to order the seizure. The President's position was stated through Senator Hubert Humphrey, who quoted the President as saying he would "rest his case with the courts of the land." The President was further quoted as saying:

I am a constitutional President and my whole record and public life has been one of defense and support of the Constitution.

New York Times, April 29, 1952, p. 1, col. 3. A report of a later press conference with President Truman on this issue stated:

Asked whether he had been quoted correctly in saying that he would accept the Supreme Court's decision on seizure, the President said certainly—he had no ambition to be a dictator.

New York Times, May 2, 1952, p. 1, col. 5. Of course, when this Court later rejected the constitutional bases for President Truman's action, he complied with the decision, in deference to the principle that even in the gravest matters, the President is under the law.

B. *There Is no Basis Either in the Constitution or in the Intent of the Framers for Conferring Absolute Immunity on the President*

The decisions in the *Burr* case and *Nixon* v. *Sirica* are in accord with settled decisions of this Court and others. They establish principles that faithfully reflect what historical evidence shows was the intent of the Framers. Contrasted with the explicit privileges in Article I for Congress, no comparable privileges or immunities were specified for the President or Executive Branch in Article II, even though they had been commonplace for the King. The Founding Fathers were keenly aware of the dangers of executive power. Even James Wilson, who favored a strong Executive,[55] rejected "the Prerogatives of the British Monarch as a proper guide in defining the Executive powers."[56] He stated at the Pennsylvania Ratification Convention:

The executive power is better to be trusted when it has no

[55.] See E. Corwin, *The President: Office and Powers* 11 (1948).

[56] 1 Farrand, Records of the Federal Convention of 1787, at 65-66 (1911) (hereinafter "Farrand"). See also 4 Elliot's Debates 108-09 (2d ed. 1836) (remarks of Iredell at the North Carolina Ratification Convention).

screen. Sir, we have a responsiblity in the person of our President; he cannot act improperly, and hide either his negligence or inattention; he cannot roll upon any other person the weight of his criminality * * * . Add to all this, that officer is placed high, and is possessed of power far from being contemptible; yet not a *single privilege* is annexed to his character * * * .[57]

One might infer quite plausibly from the specific grant of official privileges to Congress that no other constitutional immunity from normal legal obligations was intended for government officials or papers. Indeed, Charles Pinckney stated in the Senate on March 5, 1800, speaking of the express congressional privilege from arrest:

> They [the Framers] well knew how oppressively the power of undefined privileges had been exercised in Great Britian, and were determined no such authority should ever be exercised here. * * *
>
> *   *   *   *   *
>
> No privilege of this kind was intended for your Executive, nor any except that which I have mentioned for your Legislature.[58]

The teaching of history is thus persuasive against the claim of an absolute Presidential prerogative to be immune from the judicial process. The Court of Appeals for the District of Columbia Circuit recognized this in rejecting President Nixon's claim of absolute immunity from a grand jury subpoena *duces tecum Nixon* v. *Sirica, supra,* 487 F. 2d at 711):

> The Constitution makes no mention of special presidential immunities. Indeed, the Executive Branch generally is afforded none.   *   *   * Lacking textual support, counsel for the President nonetheless would have us infer immunity from the President's political mandate, or from his vulnerability to impeachment, or from his broad discretionary powers. These are invitations to refashion the Constitution, and we reject them.

Similarly, a special panel composed of Senior Circuit Judges Johnsen, Lumbard and Breitenstein, speaking for the Seventh

---

[57] 2 Elliot's Debates 480 (2d ed. 1836).

[58] 3 Farrand at 384-385.

The Founding Fathers were conscious of the "aversion of the people to monarchy." *The Federalist* Number 67 (B. F. Wright ed. 1961). Corwin has explained "that 'the executive magistracy' was the natural enemy, the legislative assembly the natural friend of liberty." E. Corwin, *The President: Office and Powers* 4 (1948).

Circuit in connection with the prosecution of Circuit Judge Otto Kerner, recently rejected his argument, similar to the one made by counsel for the President, that the constitutional provision for impeachment (Art. I, Sec. 3, cl. 7) implicitly confers immunity on civil officers from the criminal process prior to impeachment and removal from office, *United States* v. *Isaacs and Kerner*, 493 F. 2d 1124 (7th Cir. 1974), cert. denied, —— U.S. —— (June 17, 1974). The court concluded (493 F. 2d at 1144):

> [W]hatever immunities or privileges the Constitution confers for the purpose of assuring the independence of the co-equal branches of government they do not exempt the members of those branches "from the operation of the ordinary criminal laws." Criminal conduct is not part of the necessary functions performed by public officials. Punishment for that conduct will not interfere with the legitimate operations of a branch of government.

The fact that the President is the *head* of the Executive Branch does not render these principles inapplicable here.[59] "We have no officers in this government from the President down to the most subordinate agent, who does not hold office under the law, with prescribed duties and limited authority." *The Floyd Acceptances*, 7 Wall. (74 U.S.) 666, 676-77.

C. *The Courts Can Issue Process to the President Where, as Here, It Does Not Interfere with His Exercise of Discretionary Power but Merely Requires Ministerial Compliance with a Legal Duty*

The argument that the President is immune from process is sometimes rested upon a misreading of *Mississippi* v. *Johnson*, 4 Wall. (71 U.S.). 475.[60] In that case the State of Mississippi sought leave to file an original bill to enjoin President Johnson from enforcing the Reconstruction Acts, which provided for reconstitution of the governments of the ertswhile Confederacy. Because the President was named as a defendant in the bill, this Court heard argument upon the question of jurisdiction before

---

[59] We are not dealing in this case, of course, with the question whether, even in the absence of any explicit immunity, an incumbent President is entitled to implicit immunity from having to defend himself against criminal charges lodged against him in an indictment.

[60] Scattered district court opinions seem to have accepted that argument, at least where discretionary executive powers were at issue. See, *e.g., National Ass'n of Internal Revenue Employees* v. *Nixon*, 349 F. Supp. 18, 21 (D.D.C. 1972), rev'd, 492 F. 2d 587 (D.C. Cir. 1974); *Reese* v. *Nixon*, 347 F. Supp. 314, 316-17 (C.D. Cal. 1972).

the bill was filed, instead of reserving the question to a later stage.[61] Attorney General Stanbery argued to the Court that the President is "above the process of any court," asserting that "[he] represents the majesty of the law and of the people as fully and as essentially, and with the same dignity, as does any absolute monarch or the head of any independent government in the world." 4 Wall. at 484.

Faithful to the tradition that in the United States no man and noffice are above the law, this Court refused to accept the Attorney General's claim of royal immunity for the President of the United States (4 Wall. at 498). Rather, it held that it had "no jurisdiction of a bill to enjoin the President in the performance ot his official duties" (4 Wall. at 501), distinguishing the power of the courts to require the President to perform a simple ministerial act from an attempt to control the exercise of his broad constitutional discretion (4 Wall. at 499):

> In each of these cases [involving ministerial duties] nothing was left to discretion. There was no room for the exercise of judgment. The law required the performance of a single specific act; and that performance, it was held, might be required by mandamus.
>
> Very different is the duty of the President in the exercise of the power to see that the laws are faithfully executed, and among these laws the acts named in the bill. * * * The duty thus imposed on the President is in no just sense ministerial. It is purely executive and political.

Mississippi v. *Johnson* arose shortly after the Civil War, when there was a bitter political conflict over the proper national policy to be followed in dealing with the secessionist States. In declining to exercise its original jurisdiction over an equitable suit brought by a State seeking to enjoin the President from enforcing congressional policy, the Court had no occasion to decide that *no* federal court could ever issue *any* order to the President, and the Court was careful to leave open the question of the President's amenability to the judicial process where only a clear legal duty, rather than the exercise of discretionary political judgment, is involved, as in the present case.

Shortly after the decision in *Mississippi* v. *Johnson*, the Court also declined jurisdiction of similar bills naming the Secretary of War or a military commander as respondent. *Georgia* v. *Stanton*, 6 Wall. (73 U.S.) 50. Their disposition is further proof that it was

---

[61] Fairman, *Reconstruction and Reunion 1864-88*, 6 History of the Supreme Court of the United States 379-80, 436-37 (1971).

the character of the question presented and not the identity of the respondent that determined the issue in *Mississippi* v. *Johnson.* In the words of Chief Justice Marshall, "[i]t is not by the office of the person to whom the writ is directed, but the nature of the thing to be done, that the propriety or impropriety of issuing a mandamus is to be determined." *Marbury* v. *Madison, supra,* 1 Cranch at 170.

Later cases have confirmed that *Mississippi* v. *Johnson* did not turn on the fact that the respondent was the President, but was an early expression of the nonjusticiability of "political questions."[62] This Court has cited the decision as an example of instances where the Court has refused "to entertain * * * original actions * * * that seek to embroil this tribunal in 'political questions.' " *Ohio* v. *Wyandotte Chemicals Corp.,* 401 U.S. 493, 496.

The crucial jurisdictional issue, then, is not the identity of the executive officer or the physical power to secure compliance with judical orders,[63] but the Court's ability to resolve authoritatively the conflicting claims of legal rights and obligations. See *Baker* v. *Carr, supra,* 369 U.S. at 208-237. The Judiciary, of course, must be circumspect in issuing process against the President to avoid interference with the proper discharge of his executive functions. For example, it might not be proper, in the absence of strong necessity, to require the President to appear personally before a court if that appearance would interfere with his schedule or the performance of his duties. Similarly, the courts should not saddle the Chief Executive with requests that are administratively burdensome. Compare *United States* v. *Burr,* 25 Fed. Cas. 30, 34 (No. 14,692d) (C.C.D. Va. 1807). The Court's discretionary power to control its own process and grant protective orders provides adequate safeguard against undue imposition on the President's time. Beyond that, there may be some Presidential acts that are beyond the court's ken entirely, such as his exercise of discretionary constitutional powers that implicate "political questions." See *Mississippi* v. *Johnson, supra,* 4 Wall. at 499-501; *Marbury* v. *Madison, supra,* 1 Cranch at 165-66, 170. See also *National Treasury Employees Union* v. *Nixon,* 492 F. 2d 587, 606 (D.C. Cir. 1974).

But the question here is very different. The Court is called

---

[62] See also *Colegrove* v. *Green,* 328 U.S. 549, 556; *Louisiana* v. *McAdoo,* 234 U.S. 627, 633-34; *Wisconsin* v. *Pelican Insurance Co.,* 127 U.S. 265, 296; *National Treasury Employees Union* v. *Nixon, supra,* 492 F. 2d at 613-15.

[63] See pp. 44-47, *supra.*

upon to adjudicate the obligation of the President, as a citizen of the United States, to cooperate with a criminal prosecution by performing the solely ministerial task of producing specified recordings and documentary evidence. This Court has defined "ministerial duty" as "one in respect to which nothing is left to discretion. It is a simple, definite duty, arising under conditions admitted or proved to exist, and imposed by law." *Mississippi* v. *Johnson, supra,* 4 Wall. at 498. Judge Fahy, noting that "the word 'ministerial' is not sufficiently expressive to denote adequately every situation into which the courts may enter," added, however, that "a duty often becomes ministerial only after a court has reached its own judgment about a disputable legal question and its application to a factual situation." *Seaton* v. *Texas Co.,* 256 F. 2d 718, 723 (D.C. Cir. 1958). As we have shown above, the courts, and not the Executive, must decide the existence *vel non* of a privilege for evidence material to a criminal prosecution. A decision overruling the claim will be as fully binding on the President as it would be upon a subordinate executive officer who had custody or control of the subpoenaed evidence.[64]

III. THE CONVERSATIONS DESCRIBED IN THE SUBPOENA RELATING TO WATERGATE LIE OUTSIDE THE EXECUTIVE PRIVILEGE FOR CONFIDENTIAL COMMUNICATIONS

The President, in his Formal Claim of Privilege submitted to the court below, asserted that the items in the subpoena, other than the portions of twenty conversations already made public:

> are confidential conversations between a President and his close advisors that it would be inconsistent with the public interest to produce. Thus I must respectfully claim privilege with regard to them to the extent that they may have been recorded, or that there may be memoranda, papers, transcripts, or other writings relating to them.

The President was relying, of course, on "the longstanding judicial recognition of Executive privilege * * * [for] 'intra-governmental documents reflecting * * * deliberations comprising part of a process by which governmental decisions and policies are formulated.' "[65] *Nixon* v. *Sirica, supra,*

---

[64] The subpoena *duces tecum* is directed to "Richard M. Nixon *or* any subordinate officer" whom he may designate as having custody of the tape recordings and other documents.

[65] We use the term "generalized claim of executive privilege" to cover a claim of

487 F. 2d at 713.

The President made a similar claim in response to the grand jury's subpoena *duces tecum* at issue in the earlier litigation involved in *Nixon* v. *Sirica*.[66] His counsel argued to the court that the "threat of potential disclosure of any and all conversations would make it virtually impossible for President Nixon or his successors in that great office to function."[67] Counsel argued further that the President's absolute prerogative to withold information "reaches any information that the President determines cannot be disclosed consistent with the public interest and the proper performance of his constitutional duties."[68] Within the contours of the instant case, counsel for the President in effect poses the following question for the Court: Shall guilt or innocence in the criminal trials of former White House aides be determined upon full consideration of all the evidence found relevant, competent and unprivileged by due process of law? Or shall the evidence from the White House be confined to what a single person, highly interested in the outcome, is willing to make available?

By urging upon the courts the absolute, unreviewable discretion of the President to withhold evidence from the trial in *United States* v. *Mitchell, et al.*, counsel for the President seemingly ignores the principle, articulated by Justice Reed, that executive privilege is granted "for the benefit of the public." *Kaiser Aluminum & Chemical Corp.* v. *United States, supra*, 157

---

privilege based on an asserted interest in the confidentiality of communications within the Executive Branch, as distinguished from more specific privileges sometimes covered by the term "executive privilege."

Thus, the courts have recognized a specific privilege for "state secrets," covering government information bearing on international relations, military affairs and the national security. See, *e.g.*, *United States* v. *Reynolds, supra*, 345 U.S. at 6-7; *United States* v. *Curtiss-Wright Export Corp.*, 299 U.S. 304, 320-21; 8 Wigmore § 2378. There is also a privilege for "investigative files," including information relating to confidential informants. See, *e.g.*, *Alderman* v. *United States*, 394 U.S. 165, 184-85; *Roviaro* v. *United States*, 353 U.S. 53; *Machin* v. *Zuckert, supra*, 316 F. 2d at 339; 8 Wigmore § § 2374-77; cf. *United States ex rel. Touhy* v. *Ragen*, 340 U.S. 462.

The President has not claimed any such specific type of "executive privilege" for any of the conversations described in the subpoena.

[66] In a letter to Chief Judge Sirica on July 25, 1973, the return date of that subpoena, President Nixon stated:

I have concluded, however, that it would be inconsistent with the public interest and with the Constitutional position of the Presidency to make available recordings of meetings and telephone conversations in which I was a participant and I must respectfully decline to do so.

Special Appearance of Richard M. Nixon, Exh. A, *In Re Grand Jury Subpoena Duces Tecum Issued to Richard M. Nixon, supra*.

[67] Brief in Opposition 2-3, *id*.

[68] Brief in Opposition 12-13, *id*.

F. Supp. at 944. Ultimately, the public interest must govern whether or not particular items are disclosed. When the participants in Presidential conversations are themselves subject to indictment and the subject matter of the conversations is material to the issues to be tried upon the indictment, denying the courts access to recordings of the conversations impedes the due administration of justice.

Moreover, production of the evidence sought, even upon order of the court, does not threaten wholesale disclosure of Presidential documents either now or in the future. It bears repeating that this is a case in which the other participants in the conversations are subject to indictment. The conversations covered by the present subpoena are demonstrably important—as the trial court below found—to defining the extent of the conspiracy in terms of time, membership, and objectives. Surely there will be few instances, if ever, where there are similar concrete circumstances warranting intrusion into an otherwise privileged domain of conversations involving the President and his aides. Thus, any slight risk that future conversations may be disclosable under such a standard hardly will intimidate Presidential aides in giving open and candid advice. Furthermore, the desirable public policy of encouraging frank advice to governmental officials does not and cannot depend on any expectation of absolute confidentiality. It is almost commonplace in our system for former officials, including Presidents, promptly to publish their memoirs, frequently based on documents reflecting governmental deliberations.[69] This is a generally understood phenomenon, and it is unthinkable that the court's entitlement to important evidence must be relegated to a lower priority.

Under these circumstances, the district court properly rejected the claim of privilege (Pet. App. 20), holding that the "Special Prosecutor's submissions * * * constitute a *prima facie* showing adequate to rebut the presumption [of privilege] in each instance, and a demonstration of need sufficiently compelling to warrant judicial examination in chambers incident to weighing claims of privilege where the privilege has not been relinquished." The court followed the "settled rule" that "the court must balance the moving party's need for the documents in the litigation against the reasons which are asserted in defending

---

[69] For example, Executive Order 11,652, "Classification and Declassification of National Security Information and Material," issued by President Nixon on March 8, 1972, provides for access to classified data by persons "who have previously occupied policymaking positions to which they were appointed by the President" (Sec. 12), although publication of the material is not authorized.

their confidentiality." *Committee for Nuclear Responsibility, Inc.* v. *Seaborg, supra,* 463 F. 2d at 791. See also *United States* v. *Reynolds, supra,* 345 U.S. at 11; *Nixon* v. *Sirica, supra,* 487 F. 2d at 716; cf. *Doe* v. *McMillan, supra,* 412 U.S. at 320.

Although the court below followed the "settled rule" of balancing particular need against the specific interest in confidentiality, that rule becomes applicable only where the "presumptive privilege" for the materials has not been vitiated by other factors. In the present case, there are two additional grounds for overruling the asserted privilege, each of which shows that the subpoenaed material has lost its character as "presumptively privileged." First, the interest in confidentiality is never sufficient to support an official privilege where, as here, there is a *prima facie* showing that the subpoenaed materials cover conversations and activities in furtherance of a criminal conspiracy; thus, Watergate-related conversations are not even covered by the presumptive privilege recognized in *Nixon* v. *Sirica, supra,* 487 F. 2d at 717. Second, as we show in Part IV below, to the extent that the subpoenaed conversations relating to Watergate are deemed covered by some presumptive executive privilege, any claim to continued secrecy has been waived as a matter of law by the extensive testimony and public statements of participants, given with the President's consent, concerning these conversations and by the President's recent release of transcripts of forty-three Presidential conversations dealing with these issues.

Before turning to the discussion of the independent grounds for overruling the President's claim of privilege, we briefly mention two basic principles that should guide this Court's determination. First, whether particular documents or other materials are privileged in the context of a criminal prosecution is *for judicial determination*—upon the extrinsic evidence if sufficient, but otherwise *upon in camera* inspection (see Part I(A), *supra*). Second, in making this determination, the Court must construe the privilege strictly. Evidentiary privileges generally are "an obstacle to the administration of justice" (8 Wigmore § 2192, at 73), and, as "so many derogations from [the] positive general rule" that the public has a right to every man's evidence (*id.*, at 70), they must be confined to the narrowest limits justified by their underlying policies.[70] "To hold otherwise would be to invite gratuitous injury to citizens for

---

[70] See 8 Wigmore § 2192, at 73; Morgan, Foreword to ALI Model Code of Evidence 7 (1942).

little if any public purpose." *Doe* v. *McMillan, supra,* 412 U.S. at 316-17. Such strictness in application of executive privilege conforms to the ideas of the Founding Fathers, who were keenly aware of the dangers of Executive secrecy.[71]

A. Executive Privilege Based Upon a Need for Candor in Governmental Deliberations Does Not Apply Where There Is a Prima Facie Showing That the Discussions Were in Furtherance of a Continuing Criminal Conspiracy

As stated above, the only privilege relied upon by the President stems from his assertion that the "items sought are confidential conversations between a President and his close advisors." We freely concede that a qualified or "presumptive" privilege normally attaches to "intra-governmental documents reflecting advisory opinions, recommendations and deliberations comprising part of a process by which governmental decisions are policies are formulated." *Carl Zeiss Stiftung* v. *V.E.B. Carl Zeiss, Jena,* 40 F.R.D. 318, 324 (D.D.C. 1966), aff'd on opinion below, 384 F. 2d 979 (D.C. Cir. 1967), cert. denied, 389 U.S. 952. But there can be no valid public policy affording the protection of executive privilege where there is a *prima facie* showing that the officials participating in the deliberations did so as part of a continuing criminal plan. In this case, where the grand jury has voted the Special Prosecutor the authority to identify the President himself as an unindicted co-conspirator in the events charged in the indictment and covered by the government's subpoena, there is such a *prima facie* showing and the President is foreclosed from invoking a privilege that exists only to protect and promote the legitimate conduct of the Nation's affairs.

The qualified privilege for governmental deliberations is based on "two important policy considerations * * * : encouraging full and candid intra-agency discussion, and shielding from disclosure the mental processes of executive and administrative officers."[72] *International Paper Co.* v. *Federal Power Commission,* 438 F. 2d 1349, 1358-59 (2d Cir. 1971), cert. denied, 404 U.S. 827. The privilege, however, whether in the context of intra-agency communications or in the context of deliberations at the highest level of the Executive Branch, exists only to promote the legitimate functioning of government. It cannot serve as a cloak to protect those charged with criminal wrong-doing. Executive privilege is granted "for the benefit of the public, not of executives who may happen to then hold

---

[71] For a discussion of the intent of the Framers, see pp. 76-80, *supra.*

office." *Kaiser Aluminum & Chemical Corp.* v. *United States, supra,* 157 F. Supp. at 944.

This is a familiar principle in the law of evidentiary privileges generally. For example, a client may not hide behind the attorney-client privilege and prevent his attorney from being required to disclose plans of continuing criminal activity even though told to him in confidence. See, *e.g., United States* v. *Aldridge,* 484 F. 2d 655 (7th Cir. 1973); *United States* v. *Rosenstein,* 474 F. 2d 705 (2d Cir. 1973); *United States* v. *Shewfelt,* 455 F. 2d 836 (9th Cir.) 1972), cert. denied, 406 U.S. 944; *United States* v. *Bartlett,* 449 F. 2d 700 (8th Cir. 1971), cert. denied, 405 U.S. 932; *Garner* v. *Wolfinbarger,* 430 F. 2d 1093 (5th Cir. 1970), cert. denied, 401 U.S. 974. Similarly, the courts have refused to recognize any privilege not to disclose communications by a patient which were not for the legitimate purpose of enabling the physician to prescribe treatment. See 8 Wigmore § 2383; McCormick, *Evidence* § 100 (2d ed. 1972). Even the privilege against disclosing marital communications or jury deliberations has been overruled when such communications were in furtherance of fraud or crime. See, *e.g., United States* v. *Kahn,* 471 F. 2d 191 (7th Cir. 1972), cert. denied, 411 U.S. 986. See generally Note, *Future Crime or Tort Exception to Communications Privileges,* 77 Harv. L. Rev. 730 (1964).

The Speech or Debate Clause provides a compelling illustration of this principle. That clause confers an explicit constitutional privilege on members of Congress in order to promote candid and vigorous deliberations in the Legislative Branch.[73] Like executive privilege, which is based upon the same underlying policies and interests, "[t]he immunities of the Speech or Debate Clause were not written into the Constitution simply for the personal or private benefit of Members of Congress, but to protect the integrity of the legislative process." *United States* v. *Brewster, supra,* 408 U.S. at 507. The purpose of the Clause was to "assure a co-equal branch of the government wide freedom of speech, debate and deliberation without intimidation or threats from the Executive Branch." *Gravel* v. *United States, supra,* 408 U.S. at 616. But even though the Clause protects a legislator in

---

[72] Only the interest in confidentiality as an encouragement to candor is involved in the present case, for there is plainly no challenge to the rationale for any governmental decision or order.

[73] The Speech or Debate Clause, Art. I, Sec. 6, cl. 1, provides that no Senator or Representative may be "questioned in any other Place" for "any Speech or Debate in either House." It prohibits inquiry "into those things generally said or done in the House or the Senate in the performance of official duties and into the motivation for those acts." *United States* v. *Brewster, supra,* 408 U.S. at 512.

the performance of legislative acts, "it does not privilege either Senator or aide to violate an otherwise valid criminal law in preparing for or implementing legislative acts." *Gravel* v. *United States, supra,* 408 U.S. at 626. See also *Tenney* v. *Brandhove,* 341 U.S. 367, 476 (legislative immunity is restricted to "the sphere of legitimate legislative activity"). Thus, both the legislator and his aide may be compelled to give evidence in that situation, notwithstanding the explicit privilege. See also *Doe* v. *McMillan, supra.*

Similarly, discussions within the Executive Branch which are in furtherance of a criminal conspiracy cannot be subsumed within executive privilege. The privilege, which is limited by its underlying public purpose, see, *e.g., Halpern* v. *United States, supra,* 258 F. 2d at 44, does not extend beyond the transaction of legitimate official activities so as to protect conversations that constitute evidence of official misconduct or crime. In *Rosee* v. *Board of Trade,* 36 F.R.D. 684, 690 (N.D. Ill. 1965), for example, the court overruled a claim of executive privilege invoked in the face of a substantiated charge of offical misconduct where the party seeking the evidence showed "(1) that there is a reasonable basis for his request and (2) that the defendant government agents played some part in the operative events."[74] When the governmental processes which are fostered and protected by a privilege of confidentiality are abused or subverted, the reasons for secrecy no longer exist and the privilege is lifted.

Executive privilege compares in this respect to executive immunity. A government official, of course, may not be held liable for damages in a civil action for the consequences of acts within the scope of his official duties. *Barr* v. *Matteo,* 360 U.S. 564. This immunity, like privilege, has been considered necessary to foster "the fearless, vigorous, and effective administration of policies of government." 360 U.S. at 571. But the immunity does not shield him for acts "manifestly or palpably beyond his authority." *Spalding* v. *Vilas,* 161 U.S. 483, 498. See also *Doe* v. *McMillan, supra; Bivens* v. *Six Unknown Federal Bureau of Narcotics Agents,* 456 F. 2d 1339 (2d Cir. 1972). And, as in the present case, the policy underlying executive immunity does not permit it to reach "so far as to immunize criminal conduct.   *   *   * " *O'Shea* v. *Littleton, supra,* —— U.S. at —— (42

---

[74] See also *Black* v. *Sheraton Corp.,* 371 F. Supp. 97 (D.D.C. 1974); *United States* v. *Procter & Gamble Co.,* 25 F.R.D. 485, 490-91 (D.N.J. 1960); *cf. Carl Zeiss Stiftung* v. *V.E.B. Carl Zeiss, Jena, supra,* 40 F.R.D. at 329 (footnotes omitted): "Here, unlike the situation in some cases, no charge of governmental misconduct or perversion of governmental power is advanced."

U.S.L.W. at 4144).

The Court of Appeals for the District of Columbia Circuit vividly highlighted the essence of this principle when it explained why the courts must not feel bound by the assertion of executive privilege but must instead scrutinize the propriety of the claim. "Otherwise," the court said, "the head of any executive department would have the power on his own say so to cover up all evidence of fraud and corruption when a federal court or grand jury was investigating malfeasance in office, and this is not the law." *Committee for Nuclear Responsibility, Inc.* v. *Seaborg, supra,* 463 F. 2d at 794.

Justice Cardozo gave an eloquent statement of why this is not the law in *Clark* v. *United States,* 289 U.S. 1, an analogous case dealing with the secrecy normally attaching to a jury's deliberations. Speaking for a unanimous Court, he recognized that the privilege, based upon a need for confidentiality, is generally valid: "Freedom of debate might be stifled and independence of thought checked if jurors were made to feel that their arguments and ballots were to be freely published to the world." 289 U.S. at 13. But Justice Cardozo also held that such a privilege, like other privileges based on the desirability of encouraging candid discourse and interplay, is subject to "conditions and exceptions" when there are other policies "competing for supremacy. It is then the function of the court to mediate between them." *Ibid.* The Court then held that where there is a "showing of a *prima facie* case" (289 U.S. at 14) that the relation has been tainted by criminal misconduct, the interest in confidentiality must yield. The Court held that the jury's privilege of confidentiality is dissipated if there is "evidence, direct or circumstantial, that money has been paid to a juror in consideration of his vote" (289 U.S. at 14). Justice Cardozo reasoned (*ibid.*):

> The privilege takes as its postulate a genuine relation, honestly created and honestly maintained. If that condition is not satisfied, if the relation, honestly created and honestly main- juror may not invoke a relation dishonestly assumed as a cover and cloak for the concealment of the truth.

The Court then drew an analogy to the attorney-client privilege, one of the most venerable privileges in the law, and emphasized: "The privilege takes flight if the relation is abused." 289 U.S. at 215.[75]

---

[75] Recently the Court of Appeals for the Seventh Circuit held that the attorney-client privilege must yield upon a *"prima facie"* showing that the

1. The Grand Jury's Finding Is Valid and Is Sufficient to Show Prima Facie That the President Was a Co-Conspirator

The present case is governed by these principles, as articulated in cases like *Clark*. On February 25, 1974, in the course of its consideration of the indictment in *United States* v. *Mitchell, et al.*, the grand jury, by a vote of 19—0, determined that there is probable cause to believe that Richard M. Nixon (among others) was a member of the conspiracy to defraud the United States and to obstruct justice charged in Count I of the indictment. The grand jury authorized the Special Prosecutor to identify Richard M. Nixon (among others) as an unindicted co-conspirator in connection with subsequent proceedings in *United States* v. *Mitchell, et al.* The district court below, denying the President's motion to expunge the grand jury's finding, ruled that this finding is relevant "to a determination that the presumption of privilege is overcome" (Pet. App. 23).

The grand jury's authorization to the Special Prosecutor constitutes the requisite *prima facie* showing to negate any claim of executive privilege for the subpoenaed conversations relating to Watergate and is binding on the courts at this stage of the proceedings in *United States* v. *Mitchell, et al.* As this Court held in *Ex Parte United States*, 287 U.S. 241, 250, the vote of a "properly constituted grand jury conclusively determines the existence of probable cause   * * * ."[76] Despite the

communications were made in furtherance of a continuing or future fraud or crime. *United States* v. *Aldridge, supra*, 484 F. 2d at 658. Other circuits agree that a *prima facie* showing that some fraud or criminal misconduct may have attained what would otherwise have been a privileged, confidential relationship is sufficient to require that the privilege yield. See, *e.g., Pfizer, Inc.* v. *Lord*, 456 F. 2d 545 (8th Cir. 1972); *United States* v. *Friedman*, 445 F 2d 1076 (9th Cir. 1971), cert. denied, 404 U.S. 958; *United States* v. *Bob*, 106 F. 2d 37 (2d Cir. 1939), cert. denied, 308 U.S. 589. See also *O'Rourke* v. *Darbishire*, [1920] A.C. 581 (H.L.), establishing the same standard.

[76] Accord, *Ewing* v. *Mytinger & Casselberry*, 339 U.S. 594, 599; *United States* v. *King*, 482 F. 2d 768, 776 (D.C. Cir. 1973); *United States* v. *Kysar*, 459 F. 2d 422, 424 (10th Cir. 1972). The grand jury's finding cannot be challenged on the ground that it was based upon inadequate evidence. See, *e.g., United States* v. *Calandra*, — U.S. —, — (42, U.S.L.W. 4104, 4106, Jan. 8, 1974); *Costello* v. *United States*, 350 U.S. 359, 363 (1956).

The above decisions, of course, concern findings of probable cause which appear on the face of the indictment. The June 5, 1972 grand jury could likewise have listed every known co-conspirator in the indictment, in which case that finding of complicity in the conspiracy would have been conclusive in these pre-trial proceedings. Out of deference to the President's public position, however, the grand jury instead decided to vote *in camera* upon a finding of probable cause against each alleged co-conspirator, but not to name any formally in the indictment. The grand jury further authorized the Special Prosecutor to disclose and rely upon its determination of probable cause if and when such action became necessary. There is no reason why the same conclusive effect should not be given to the grand jury's

President's contention in No. 73—1834, therefore, the district court properly refused to expunge this finding.[77]

Each of the principal participants in the subpoenaed conversations has been identified by the grand jury as a co-conspirator, and, as demonstrated by the showing in the Appendix submitted to the district court below in opposition to the President's motion to quash, it is probable that each of the subpoenaed conversations includes discussions in furtherance of the conspiracy charged in the indictment. Thus, there is no room to argue that the subpoenaed conversations are subject to a

determination in this case as would have been accorded if the grand jury had been less solicitous of the President's position.

[77] There is no reason to believe that the grand jury's finding is unconstitutional or in any sense an abuse of the grand jury's power. In the district court, the President premised the motion to expunge on the contention that the President is not subject to indictment prior to removal from office. The Constitution, however, contains no explicit Presidential immunity from the ordinary process of the criminal law prior to impeachment and removal, and there are substantial arguments that an implicit immunity is likewise not warranted by the Constitution. See Berger, "The President, Congress, and the Courts," 83 Yale L.J. 1111, 1123-36 (1974); Rawle, *A View of the Constitution of the United States of America* 215 (2d ed. 1829). See also, *United States* v. *Isaacs and Kerner, supra,* holding that an impeachable officer is liable to criminal prosecution prior to impeachment and removal.

Here, however, the grand jury did not indict the President, but only named him as an unindicted co-conspirator. Therefore, the broader question of whether an indictment of a sitting President is constitutionally permissible need not be reached. None of the practical difficulties incident to indicting an incumbent President and requiring him to defend himself while still conducting the affairs of state exists when the grand jury merely names the President as an unindicted co-conspirator. This action does not constitute substantial interference with the President's ability to perform his official functions. For example, an unindicted co-conspirator need not spend time and effort in preparing his defense, time which a President may need to devote to carrying out his constitutional duties. Nor is there any inherent unfairness in such a course since an incumbent President has at his command all of the Nation's communications facilities to convey his position on the events in question. Thus, whatever may be the case with respect to indictment, there are no substantial arguments for creating an immunity for the President even from being identified as a co-conspirator when a grand jury finds it necessary and appropriate to do so in connection with an independent criminal prosecution of others.

Furthermore, even assuming *arguendo* that the grand jury's action was without legal effect, the district judge had ample discretion to refuse to expunge its finding. See *In re Grand Jury Proceedings,* 479 F. 2d 458, 460 n. 2 (5th Cir. 1973) and *Application of Johnson,* 484 F. 2d 791 (7th Cir. 1973), discussing the criteria to be applied in passing upon motions to expunge grand jury reports. The grand jury's action concerns a subject of legitimate public concern. The President has neither alleged nor established any prejudice from the grand jury's action. The strong public interest in placing before the petit jury what the grand jury believed was the full scope of the alleged conspiracy to obstruct justice which forms the basis for the indictment in *United States* v. *Mitchell, et al.* made it reasonable for the grand jury to designate all participants in the conspiracy as co-conspirators. In deference to the Office of the Presidency, and sensitive to the practical difficulties in indicting an incumbent President, the grand jury named him as an unindicted co-conspirator, and there is no constitutional impediment to such action, and no compelling reason to expunge that determination.

privilege that exists to protect the public's legitimate interests in effective representative government. The grand jury has returned an indictment charging criminal conduct by high officials in the Executive Branch, and the public interest requires no less than a trial based upon *all* relevant and material evidence relating to the charges.

In opposing the grand jury's subpoena *duces tecum,* counsel for the President argued that despite any showing that statements in the course of Presidential conversations were made in furtherance of a conspiracy to obstruct justice, the general principle of confidentiality must be maintained in order to assure the effective functioning of the Presidential staff system. An analogous argument was made in *Clark* and decisively rejected by this Court in a passage we are constrained to quote at length (289 U.S. at 16):

> With the aid of this analogy [to the attorney-client privilege] we recur to the social policies competing for supremacy. A privilege surviving until the relation is abused and vanishing when abuse is shown to the satisfaction of the judge has been found to be a workable technique for the protection of the confidences of client and attorney. Is there sufficient reason to believe that it will be found to be inadequate for the protection of a juror? No doubt the need is weighty that conduct in the jury room shall be untrammeled by the fear of embarrassing publicity. The need is no less weighty that it shall be pure and undefiled. A juror of integrity and reasonable firmness will not fear to speak his mind if the confidences of debate are barred to the ears of mere impertinence or malice. He will not expect to be shielded against the disclosure of his conduct in the event that there is evidence reflecting upon his honor. The chance that now and then there may be found some timid soul who will take counsel of his fears and give way to their repressive power is too remote and shadowy to shape the course of justice. It must yield to the overmastering need, so vital in our polity, of preserving trial by jury in its purity against the inroads of corruption.

It is hard to imagine a stronger need for piercing the cloak of confidentiality than in the present case. Requiring production of the evidence under these circumstances presents only a minimal threat to a President's ability to obtain advice from his aides with complete freedom and candor, for surely there will be few occasions where there is probable cause to believe that conversations in the Executive Office of the President occurred during the course of and in furtherance of a criminal conspiracy. Counsel cannot seriously claim that the aides of any future President will be so "timid" in the face of such a remote danger of disclosure of their advice, or that some small risk of reticence is too great a price to pay to preserve the President's Office "against the inroads of corruption." In light of the grand jury's finding of probable cause to believe that the President was a co-conspirator in the indictment charging a conspiracy to defraud the United States and obstruct justice and the showing by the Special Prosecutor that the subpoenaed conversations in all probability occurred during the course of and in furtherance of the conspiracy, the conversations relating to Watergate cannot be shielded by a privilege designed to protect the objective, candid, and honest formulation of policy in government affairs.[78]

B. *The Public Interest in Disclosure of Relevant Conversations for Use at Trial in This Case Is Greater Than the Public Interest Served by Secrecy*

Even apart from the *prima facie* showing that the President and the other participants in the subpoenaed conversations were co-conspirators, the claim of privilege cannot stand here. Executive privilege, unlike personal privileges (for example, the privilege against self-incrimination) is an official privilege, granted for the benefit of the public, not of executives who may happen to hold office. Thus, when this privilege is asserted in a judicial proceeding as a reason for refusing to produce evidence, the overall public interest, as determined by the Judiciary, must control. It is now settled law "that application of Executive

[78] Executive privilege still may attach, of course, to any subpoenaed material irrelevant to the issues to be tried in *United States* v. *Mitchell, et al.* The district court, in accordance with the procedures established in *Nixon* v. *Sirica, supra,* 487 F. 2d at 716-21, and followed thereafter, has ordered the President or any subordinate officer to submit the originals of the subpoenaed items to that court. Briefly, under these procedures, the President or his designee must submit an "analysis" itemizing and indexing those segments of the materials for which he asserts a particularized claim of privilege (*e.g.,* items subject to a claim of "national security") and those segments which he asserts are irrelevant to Watergate. The President may decline initially to submit for *in camera* inspection those items which he contends relate to "national defense or foreign relations." If there are any such claims, the district judge must hold a hearing to determine whether to sustain the claim of particularized privilege. As to all items for which there is no claim of particularized privilege or as to which the district judge rejects such a claim, the judge must inspect them *in camera* to determine which segments relate to Watergate and thus are not privileged. The judge may consult with the parties in determining relevancy.

These procedures are fully consistent with the principles set forth by this Court in *Environmental Protection Agency* v. *Mink, supra,* 410 U.S. at 92-94, and *United States* v. *Reynolds, supra,* 345 U.S. at 7-10.

privilege depends on a weighing of the public interest protected by the privilege against the public interests that would be served by disclosure in a particular case." *Nixon* v. *Sirica, supra,* 487 F. 2d at 716. See, *e.g., United States* v. *Reynolds, supra,* 345 U.S. at 11; *Carr* v. *Monroe Manufacturing Co., supra,* 431 F. 2d at 388; cf. *Doe* v. *McMillan, supra,* 412 U.S. at 320.

Where the courts are left with the firm and abiding conviction that the public interest requires disclosure, particularly where disclosure does not pose any discernible threat to the interests protected by secrecy, the privilege must give way. Accordingly, even if the subpoenaed conversations here remain "presumptively privileged," despite the *prima facie* showing of the President's complicity, the privilege must yield. There is a compelling public interest in the availability of all relevant and material evidence for the trial of the charges in *United States* v. *Mitchell, et al.,* involving as they do a conspiracy to defraud the United States and obstruct justice by high government officials. The subpoenaed conversations consist of discussions by the defendants or other co-conspirators about the subject matter of the alleged conspiracy: Watergate. Such evidence is obviously of fundamental importance. Moreover, the public interest in continued secrecy is vastly diminished, if not nonexistent, in the wake of the extensive testimony on this subject permitted by the President and of the President's recent release of transcripts of parts of forty-three Presidential conversations relating to Watergate, including parts of twenty of the subpoenaed conversations.

1. *The Balancing Process Followed by the District Court Accords with Decisions of This Court*

In holding that the applicability of executive privilege depends upon a weighing of competing interests, the court in *Nixon* v. *Sirica* relied upon Chief Justice Marshall's decision in the misdemeanor trial of Aaron Burr. *United States* v. *Burr,* 25 Fed. Cas. 187 (No. 14,694) (C.C.D. Va. 1807). The Chief Justice, at the request of Burr, issued a subpoena *duces tecum* to the United States Attorney, who had possession of a letter written to President Jefferson by General Wilkinson.[79] In his return, the

---

[79] This was a different letter than the one for which the Chief Justice had issued a subpoena to the President in connection with the grand jury inquiry. *United States* v. *Burr,* 25 Fed. Cas. 30 (No. 14,692d) (C.C.D. Va. 1807).

United States Attorney surrendered a copy of the letter "excepting such parts thereof as are, in my opinion, not material for the purposes of justice, for the defence of the accused, or pertinent to the issue now about to be joined." 25 Fed. Cas. at 190. In ruling that only the President could assert "motives for declining to produce a particular paper" in such a situation, the Chief-Justice did recognize "that the president might receive a letter which it would be improper to exhibit in public, because of the manifest inconvenience of its exposure." 25 Fed. Cas. at 191-92. The Chief Justice, however, clearly contemplated that the court could require production even though the President's showing was entitled to "much reliance": "The occasion for demanding it ought, in such a case, to be very strong, and to be fully shown to the court before its production could be insisted on." 25 Fed. Cas. at 192.[80]

Similarly, this Court in *Reynolds, supra*, held that a claim of privilege may be rejected upon a sufficient showing (345 U.S. at 11):

> Where there is a strong showing of necessity, the claim of privilege should not be lightly accepted.

In reversing the lower court decisions which would have required *in camera* inspection to determine whether the privilege should be upheld, this Court held merely that there had only been a "dubious" showing of necessity for access to confidential investigative reports on the crash of a bomber testing secret equipment.[81] Since state secrets were involved, the party seeking the evidence had not made the requisite threshold showing to overcome the presumptive privilege even to justify *in camera* inspection.

More recently the Court considered the government's privilege

---

[80] The Chief Justice continued: "The president may himself state the particular reasons which may have induced him to withhold a paper, and the court would unquestionably allow their full force to those reasons. At the same time, the court could not refuse to pay proper attention to the affidavit of the accused."

[81] Justices Black, Frankfurter and Jackson dissented from the decision of the Court, relying on the opinion of Judge Maris below. 192 F. 2d 987 (3d Cir. 1951). Judge Maris, as did this Court, rejected the government's contention that the determination of the executive officer claiming the privilege must be accepted. Although Judge Maris recognized a privilege for "state secrets," he rejected the availability of a "housekeeping" privilege in an instance where the government had consented to be sued. Judge Maris predicted (192 F. 2d at 995): "[W]e regard the recognition of such a sweeping privilege against any disclosure of the internal operations of the executive departments of the Government as contrary to a sound public policy. * * * It is but a small step to assert a privilege against any disclosure of records merely because they might prove embarrassing to government officers. * * *"

to withhold the identity of informants. *Roviaro* v. *United States, supra.* This privilege, like the privilege for government deliberations, encourages candor through secrecy. Persons are thought to be more likely to provide information to law enforcement agencies if they can remain anonymous. But the privilege is not absolute. "Where the disclosure of an informer's identity, or of the contents of his communication, is relevant and helpful to the defense of an accused, or is essential to a fair determination of a cause, the privilege must give way." 353 U.S. at 60-61. See also *Hodgson* v. *Charles Martin Inspectors of Petroleum, Inc.*, 459 F. 2d 303, 305 (5th Cir. 1969).

2. *There Is a Compelling Public Interest in Trying
the Conspiracy Charged in* United States *v.* Mitchell, et al.,
upon All Relevant and Material Evidence

Whether one views the President's assertion of privilege as entitled to "much reliance," see *United States* v. *Burr, supra,* 25 Fed. Cas. at 192, or "presumptively" valid, see *Nixon* v. *Sirica, supra,* 487 F. 2d at 717, the privilege is overcome here. In upholding the district court's order enforcing the grand jury's subpoena *duces tecum,* the court of appeals held that the "presumption of privilege * * * must fail in the face of the uniquely powerful showing made by the Special Prosecutor in this case." *Nixon* v. *Sirica, supra,* 487 F. 2d at 717. According to the court, this showing was made possible by the "unique intermeshing of events unlikely soon, if ever, to recur." 487 F. 2d at 705. It is clear that the "unique" circumstances which led to the rejection of the President's claim of privilege in the context of a grand jury investigation have continued applicability. Indeed, now that the grand jury has returned an indictment charging a conspiracy to defraud the United States and obstruct justice, the need for full disclosure is, if anything, greater.

At the time *Nixon* v. *Sirica* was decided, the grand jury was investigating mere allegations of criminal wrongdoing by high government officials. That investigation has resulted in a finding of probable cause to believe that some of those officials have committed offenses which strike at the very essence of a "government of laws." It is precisely this type of situation where this Court has spoken of the "over-mastering" need for preserving our institutions against "the inroads of corruption," even to the extent of overcoming a privilege of confidentiality. *Clark* v. *United States, supra,* 289 U.S. at 16. The warning of the court of appeals in *Committee for Nuclear Responsibility, Inc.* v. *Seaborg, supra,* 463 F. 2d at 794, bears repeating:

But no executive official or agency can be given absolute authority to determine what documents in his possession may be considered by the court in its task. Otherwise the head of an executive department would have the power on his own say so to cover up all evidence of fraud and corruption when a federal court or grand jury was investigating malfeasance in office, and this is not the law.

That the privilege must yield regardless of the President's involvement is easily demonstrated by analogy. Justice Cardozo's opinion in *Clark* indicated that if there were direct or substantial evidence that a juror had accepted a bribe, the veil of secrecy ordinarily surrounding a jury's deliberations would be dissipated and the arguments and votes of even the unsuspected jurors would be admissible as evidence upon whether the putatively guilty juror had in fact taken a bribe. 289 U.S. at 16. It would seem clear that, if there were a *prima facie* showing that a high executive official had accepted a bribe in consideration of his fraudulently inducing the President to grant a pardon or take other executive action favorable to the one giving the bribe, executive privilege would not be allowed to bar proof of the official's representations to the President even though the President was totally ignorant of the wrongdoing and had acted innocently in exercising his constitutional powers. So here, regardless of the President's wish, the law cannot and does not recognize a privilege that would shield a miscreant adviser from prosecution for a criminal offense in violation of the President's confidence as well as his public trust.

It is thus immaterial whether the President was actually aware that other participants in the conversations were discussing criminal activities in which they themselves were involved. The district court below found that the Special Prosecutor had made a sufficient showing of relevancy and evidentiary value with respect to the subpoenaed conversations (Pet. App. 19-20), since the conversations are material to defining the scope, membership, and objects of the conspiracy. The public interest in laying this evidence before a jury, therefore, must be considered compelling.

The President himself emphasized this interest, albeit in the context of impeachment, in discussing the factors that persuaded him to release transcripts of portions of forty-three conversations dealing with Watergate—

I believe all the American people, as well as their Representatives in Congress, are *entitled to have not only the facts, but also the evidence that demonstrates these facts.*[82]

[82] The President's Address to the Nation, April 29, 1974, 10 Weekly Compilation of Presidential Documents 452 (May 6, 1974).

This judgment is highly relevant to any balance drawn by the courts. See *Nixon* v. *Sirica, supra,* 487 F. 2d at 717-18.

Counsel for the President, in his memorandum in support of the motion to quash, argued that because the Special Prosecutor signed the indictment, he must have been satisfied that there was sufficient evidence available to him to make a *prima facie* showing of guilt, thereby suggesting that the Special Prosecutor should be content with the evidence now available to him. The indictment, of course, rests upon the requisite finding of probable cause. The standard that the government now bears, however, is proof beyond a reasonable doubt, and the public is entitled to the most effective presentation of its case that can be made. Justice will be done here only if the jury hears the whole story and not just the excerpted evidence the President chooses to make available.

This is not a case where the government is seeking incriminating evidence which is merely cumulative or corroborative. The analysis of the released transcripts in the Appendix submitted to the district courts shows that conversations not previously available to the Special Prosecutor in fact contain evidence extremely important to material issues in the indictment—evidence that would not otherwise be available to the Special Prosecutor. See *Nixon* v. *Sirica, supra,* 487 F. 2d at 717.[83] Two of the principal areas are discussions relating to the

---

[83] The recordings themselves are necessary for trial, and the President's release of portions of some transcripts cannot be considered adequate compliance with the subpoena. As this Court is well aware, the recordings themselves, and not the transcripts, constitute the most reliable evidence of what actually transpired. In *Lopez* v. *United States,* 373 U.S. 427, 439-40, the Court acknowledged that recordings of admissible conversations are "highly useful evidence" and the "most reliable evidence possible of a conversation." Cf. *United States* v. *White,* 401 U.S. 745, 753. In addition to providing the most accurate reflection of what was actually spoken, the recordings also are important because they reveal tone and inflection often necessary to evaluate the meaning of spoken words.

Furthermore, a comparison of the transcripts prepared by the White House and the transcripts prepared by the Watergate Special Prosecution Force of recordings previously produced by the President reveals material differences. In some cases, the transcripts differ as to the words spoken. In other cases, a comparison indicates that the White House has failed to transcribe portions without indicating that material has been deleted or is unintelligible. A number of these discrepancies were called to the attention of the district court. See Memorandum for the United States in Opposition to the Motion to Quash Subpoena Duces Tecum 40-43. The White House transcripts also indicate that "material unrelated to Presidential actions" has been deleted. The reasonable inference to be drawn is that material has been deleted that relates to other persons' actions concerning Watergate. Clearly, such material is important to the prosecution of defendants in *United States* v. *Mitchell et al.*

Finally, there is some question whether the transcripts, without the underlying recordings, would be admissible under the "best evidence" rule. Generally stated,

future testimony of White House officials and campaign aides and discussions of how to handle executive clemency and other benefits for various individuals as charged in the indictment. As the analysis in the Appendix shows, it is likely that the forty-four subpoenaed conversations for which no transcripts have been released include additional evidence which also is not merely cumulative or corroborative. When one is considering an on-going conspiracy, evidence of each link in the conspiracy, either in terms of time or in terms of objectives, may be crucial to a successful prosecution.[84]

We note that there has been not as much as a suggestion from counsel for the President that any of the subpoenaed conservations are *not* relevant to the criminal trial. Moreover, we emphasize that neither the President nor his counsel is in a position to make the refined judgments as to what evidence is necessary to the Special Prosecutor's case in chief or for use on cross-examination. Neither is familiar with the evidence in the possession of the government or with the theory on which the government's case will be prosecuted. In our adversary system, the judgments of what evidence to offer and how to use that evidence must be left to the advocates. See, *e.g., Dennis* v. *United States*, 384 U.S. 855, 874-75.

The court of appeals in *Nixon* v. *Sirica* also emphasized the impact of existing contradictory testimony. *E.g.,* 487 F. 2d at 705. Since that decision, the debate over the credibility of witnesses has heightened. On May 4, 1974, during the pendency of the present motion, the White House released a memorandum based on its expurgated transcripts, attacking the credibility of a prospective government witness, John W. Dean. 32 Congressional

---

that rule provides that where a party seeks to prove the terms of a "writing," the original writing must be produced unless it is shown to be unavailable. See McCormick, *Evidence* § 230, at 560 (1972). "The danger of mistransmitting critical facts which accompanies the use of written copies or recollection, but which is largely avoided when an original writing is presented to prove its terms, justifies preference for the original documents." *Id.,* § 231, at 561. Although recordings do not fall within the strict confines of the rule, "sound recordings, where their content is sought to be proved, so clearly involve the identical considerations applicable to writings as to warrant inclusion within the rule." *Id.,* § 232, at 563.

[84] In *Senate Select Committee on Presidential Campaign Activities* v. *Nixon, supra,* the court of appeals ruled that the Committee's "need" for the five recordings it had subpoenaed "is too attenuated and too tangential to its functions to permit a judicial judgment that the President is required to comply with the Committee's subpoena" (slip op. at 17). The question the court asked was whether the recordings were "demonstrably critical to the responsible fulfillment of the Committee's functions" (slip op. at 13). Highly specific factfinding, of course, is rarely, if ever, "demonstrably critical" to the legislative function, whereas it is the very essence of the determination a trial jury is called upon to make beyond a reasonable doubt.

Quarterly 1154 (May 11, 1974). Conflicts in testimony continue. The tape recordings of Presidential conversations will be critical to resolving these conflicts and weighing the credibility of trial witnesses.

3. *Disclosure of the Subpoenaed Recordings will not Significantly Impair the Interests Protected by Secrecy*

It is axiomatic, of course, that once privileged communications are no longer confidential, the privilege no longer applies and the public interest no longer is served by secrecy. See, *e.g.*, *Roviaro* vs. *United States, supra,* 353 U.S. at 60. In *Nixon* v. *Sirica,* the court of appeals considered important to its calculus that "the public testimony given consequent to the President's decision [on May 22, 1973, to waive executive privilege] substantially diminishes the interest in maintaining the confidentiality of conversations pertinent to Watergate." 487 F. 2d at 718. We argue in Part IV below that, as a matter of law, the President, as a result of his May 22, 1973, statement and the recent release of transcripts of portions of forty-three Presidential conversations, has waived executive privilege with respect to any Watergate-related conversations. There simply is no confidentiality left in that subject and no justification in terms of the public interest in keeping from public scrutiny the best evidence of what transpired in Watergate-related conversations. Whether or not this Court agrees that there has been a waiver as a matter of law, the "diminished interest in maintaining the confidentiality of conversations pertinent to Watergate" is an important consideration in this case in drawing any balance.

The enforcement of the subpoena in this case marks only the most modest and measured displacement of presumptive privacy for Presidential conversations, and augurs no general assault on the legitimate scope of that privilege. This is not a civil proceeding between private parties or even between the United States and a private party, where masses of confidential communications might be arguably relevant in wide-ranging civil discovery. The more rigorous standards applicable in a criminal case have been satisfied here, and they sharply narrow the scope of possible future demands for such evidence. Nor is this one of a long history of congressional investigations seeking to expose to the glare of publicity the policies and activities of the Executive Branch. In such instances the evidence is often sought in order to probe the mental processes of the Executive Office in a review of the wisdom or rationale of official Executive action. Compare *Morgan* v. *United States,* 304 U.S. 1, 18; *United States* v.

Morgan, 313 U.S. 409, 422. The threat to freedom and candor in giving advice is probably at the maximum in such proceedings; they invite bringing to bear upon aides and advisors the pressures of publicity and political criticism, the fear of which may discourage candid advice and robust debate.

The charges to be prosecuted here involve high Presidential assistants and criminal conduct in the Executive Office. Such involvement is virtually unique. Because its is—hopefully—unlikely to recur, production of White House documents in this prosecution will establish no precedent to cause unwarranted fears by future Presidents and their aides or to deter them from full, frank and vigorous discussion of legitimate governmental issues. Indeed, future aides may well feel that the greatest danger they face in engaging in free and trusting discussion is the type of partial, one-sided revelations that the President has encouraged in this case.

4. The Balance in This Case Overwhelmingly Mandates in Favor of Disclosure

Certainly, courts should not lightly override the assertion of executive privilege. But the privilege is sufficiently protected if it yields only when the courts are left with the firm and abiding conviction that the public interest requires disclosure. The factors in this case overwhelmingly support a ruling that Watergate-related Presidential conversations are not privileged in response to a reasonable demand for use at the trial in *United States* v. *Mitchell, et al.* There is probable cause to believe, based upon the indictment, that high Executive officers engaged in discussions in furtherance of a criminal conspiracy in the course of their deliberations. The veil of secrecy must be lifted; the legitimate interests of the Presidency and the public demand this action.

IV. ANY PRIVILEGE ATTACHING TO THE SUBPOENAED CONVERSATIONS RELATING TO WATERGATE HAS BEEN WAIVED AS A RESULT OF PERVASIVE DISCLOSURES MADE WITH THE PRESIDENT'S EXPRESS CONSENT

Even if the conversations described in the subpoena could be regarded as covered by a privilege for executive confidentiality, the privilege cannot be claimed in the face of the President's decision to authorize voluminous testimony and other statements concerning Watergate-related discussions and his recent release of 1,216 pages of transcript from forty-three Presidential conversations, including twenty covered by the present subpoena. In his Formal Claim of Privilege submitted to the district court, the President stated that because "[p]ortions of twenty of the conversations described in the subpoena have been made public, no claim of privilege is advanced with regard to those Watergate-related portions of those conversations." This concession reflects inevitable recognition that there can be no generalized claim of executive privilege based upon confidentiality where, in fact, no confidentiality exists. "[T]he moment confidence ceases, privilege ceases." *Parkhurst* v. *Lowten*, 36 Eng. Rep. 589, 596 (Ch. 1819). But as we show below, the waiver in this case extends beyond those transcripts released publicly, since a privilege holder may not make extensive but selective disclosures concerning a subject and then withhold portions that are essential to a complete and impartial record. The circumstances of this case compel the conclusion that, as a matter of law, the President has waived executive privilege with respect to *all* Watergate-related conversations described in the subpoena.

The rule that voluntary disclosure eliminates any privilege that would otherwise attach to confidential information has been applied in cases dealing with claims of governmental privilege, *Roviaro* v. *United States, supra*, 353 U.S. 53; *Westinghouse Electric Corp.* v. *City of Burlington*, 351 F. 2d 762 (D.C. Cir. 1965), as well as in cases dealing with attorney-client privilege, *Hunt* v. *Blackburn*, 128 U.S. 464; *United States* v. *Woodall*, 438 F. 2d 1317, 1325 (5th Cir. 1970); physician-patient privilege, *Munzer* v. *Swedish American Line*, 35 F. Supp. 493 (S.D.N.Y. 1940); and marital privilege, *Pereira* v. *United States*, 347 U.S. 1, 6. The general principles governing waiver are stated concisely and forcefully in Rule 37 of the Uniform Rules of Evidence.[85]

A person who would otherwise have a privilege to refuse to disclose or to prevent another from disclosing a specified matter has no such privilege with respect to that matter if the judge finds that he * * * without coercion and with the knowledge of his privilege, made disclosure of any part of the matter or consented to such a disclosure made by any one.

This is precisely the situation here. In his statement of May 22, 1973, the President announced, in light of the importance of the "effort to arrive at the truth," that "executive privilege will not be invoked as to any testimony concerning possible criminal

---

[85] This rule was approved by the Court of Appeals for the District of Columbia Circuit in *Ellis* v. *United States*, 416 F. 2d 791, 801 n. 26 (1969). See also *United States* v. *Cote*, 456 F. 2d 142, 145 (8th Cir. 1972).

conduct or discussions of possible criminal conduct, in the matters presently under investigation, including the Watergate affair and the alleged cover-up."[86] As the Court can judicially notice, in the months following that statement there has been extensive testimony in several forums concerning the substance of the recorded conversations now sought for use at the trial in *United States* v. *Mitchell, et al.* The testimony, as the Court is also aware, is quite often contradictory and is pervaded by hazy recollections. See also *Nixon* v. *Sirica, supra,* 487 F. 2d at 705.

It could be argued that the express waiver of May 22, 1973, coupled with the subsequent testimony of participants in the conversations, is itself sufficient to preclude a claim of executive privilege based upon confidentiality for Watergate-related conversations. There has been a supervening event, however, which as a matter of law removes any vestige of confidentiality in the President's discussions of Watergate with Messrs. Colson, Dean, Ehrlichman and Haldeman. On April 30, 1974, the President submitted to the Committee on the Judiciary of the House of Representatives and released to the public 1,216 pages of transcript from forty-three Watergate-related Presidential conversations.[87] The conversations range over the period from September 15, 1972, until April 27, 1973.

In his address on live television and radio on the evening prior to releasing the transcripts, the President explained that he was seeking "[t]o complete the record." He further explained: "As far as what the President personally knew and did with regard to Watergate and the cover-up is concerned, these materials—together with those already made available, will tell it all."[88] This statement is not literally accurate, but it is true that the broad outlines of the President's conversations and conduct throughout the relevant period may be portrayed by the transcripts that have been publicly released. These disclosures are sufficient to cede any privilege to conceal from production pursuant to the subpoena either the original tapes from which the publicly released transcripts were purportedly made or the tapes of other relevant conversations which necessarily complete the picture the public and the jury are entitled to see.

A privilege holder who opens the door to an area that was

[86] 9 Weekly Compilation of Presidential Documents 697 (May 28, 1973).

[87] *Submission of the Recorded Presidential Conversations to the Committee on the Judiciary of the House of Representatives by President Richard Nixon, April 30, 1974.* This document was before the district court. See Transcript of Hearing on May 13, 1974.

[88] 10 Weekly Compilation of Presidential Documents 451-52 (May 6, 1974).

once confidential can no longer control the fact-finder's search for the whole truth by attempting to limit the ability to discern the interior fully. The boundaries of the disclosure are legally no longer within his exclusive control. For example, in cases involving the analogous privileges accorded to attorney-client and physician-patient communications, it is clear that once testimony has been received as to a particular communication, either with the consent of the holder of the privilege or without his objection, the privilege is lost. There can be no assertion of the privilege to block access to another version of the conversation. See, *e.g.*, *Hunt* v. *Blackburn, supra,* 128 U.S. at 470-71; *Rosenfeld* v. *Ungar,* 25 F.R.D. 340, 342 (S.D. Iowa 1960); *Munzer* v. *Swedish American Line, supra,* 35 F. Supp. at 497-98; *In re Associated Gas & Electric Co.,* 59 F. Supp. 743, 744 (S.D. N.Y. 1944); 8 Wigmore § § 2327, 2389, at 636 and 855-61.

The same principles apply to the Fifth Amendment's privilege against self-incrimination. Once the privilege holder elects to disclose his version of what happened, a due "regard for the function of courts of justice to ascertain the truth" requires further disclosure "on the matters relevantly raised by that testimony." *Brown* v. *United States,* 356 U.S. 148, 156, 157. Once the privilege holder has opened the door, "he is not permitted to stop, but must go on and make a full disclosure." *Brown* v. *Walker,* 161 U.S. 591, 597.

There is still another dimension that the Court should consider. The President in the past has used the recordings of Presidential conversations to aid in the presentation of the White House interpretation of relevant events. For example, in June 1973, the White House transmitted a memorandum to the Senate Select Committee on Presidential Campaign Activities listing "certain oral communications" between the President and John W. Dean. Subsequently, but prior to Mr. Dean's testimony before the Committee, J. Fred Buzhardt, Special Counsel to the President, telephoned Fred D. Thompson, to relate to him Mr. Buzhardt's "understanding as to the substance" of twenty of the meetings.[89]

The President also has allowed, indeed requested, the recordings to be used in preparing public testimony. Defendant H. R. Haldeman, one of the respondents in the case before the Court and hardly a disinterested witness, was allowed to take home the tapes of selected conversations even after he had

[89] Affidavit of J. Fred Thompson dated August 9, 1973, *Hearings before the Senate Select Committee on Presidential Campaign Activities.* 93d Cong. 1st Sess., Book 4, at 1794-1800 (1973).

resigned his position as Assistant to the President and to use them in preparing his testimony.[90]

The general principle that the privilege holder's offer of his own version of confidential communications constitutes a waiver as to all communications on the same subject matter governs under these circumstances. "This is so because the privilege of secret consultation is intended only as an incidental means of defense, and not as an independent means of attack, and to use it in the latter character is to abandon it in the former." 8 Wigmore § 2327, at 638. The President time and again—even before the existence of the recordings was publicly known—has resorted to the recordings in support of his position.[91] In short, the President cannot have it both ways. He cannot release only those portions he chooses and then stand on the privilege to conceal the remainder. No privilege holder can trifle with the judicial search for truth in this way.

The high probability that the yet undisclosed conversations include information which will be important to resolving issues to be tried in *United States* v. *Mitchell, et al.* provides a compelling reason for disclosure. As the President himself recognized, the public interest demands the complete story based upon the impartial sifting and weighing of all relevant evidence. That is emphatically the province of the judicial process for it is "the function of a trial * * * to sift the truth from a mass of contradictory evidence. * * *" *In the Matter of Michael*, 326 U.S. 224, 227. And in the unique circumstances of this case, where there is no longer any substantial confidentiality on the subject of Watergate because the President has chosen to make far-reaching but expurgated disclosures, the Court must use its process to acquire all revelant evidence to lay before the jury. In the present context it can do so with the least consequences for confidentiality of other matters and future deliberations of the Executive Branch by ruling that there has been a waiver with respect to this entire affair.

---

[90] *Id.*, Book 7, at 2888-89; Book 8, at 3101-02.

[91] See, *e.g.*, Letter from President Richard M. Nixon to Senator Sam J. Ervin, Chairman of the Senate Select Committee on Presidential Campaign Activities, July 23, 1973, *id*, Book 6, at 2479:
"Before their existence became publicly known, I personally listened to a number of them. The tapes are entirely consistent with what I know to be the truth and what I have stated to be the truth."

V. THE DISTRICT COURT PROPERLY DETERMINED THAT THE SUBPOENA "DUCES TECUM" ISSUED TO THE PRESIDENT SATISFIED THE STANDARDS OF RULE 17(C), BECAUSE AN ADEQUATE SHOWING HAD BEEN MADE THAT THE SUPOENAED ITEMS ARE RELEVANT AND EVIDENTIARY

Once the privilege issues are passed,[92] the only remaining question before the Court is whether the district judge properly found (Pet. App. 19-20) that the government's subpoena satisfied the standards generally applied under Rule 17(c) of the Federal Rules of Criminal Procedure. The district court held that the standards of Rule 17(c) had been satisfied by the Special Prosecutor's submission of a lengthy and detailed specification setting out with particularity the relevance and evidentiary value of each of the tape recordings and other material being sought. This showing was submitted as a forty-nine page Appendix to the Memorandum for the United States in Opposition to the Motion to Quash Subpoena Duces Tecum included in the record before this Court.[93]

Enforcement of a trial subpoena *duces tecum* is pre-eminently a question for the trial court and is committed to the court's sound discretion. For this reason, the district court's determination should not be disturbed absent a finding by the reviewing court that it was arbitrary and had no support in the record. See *Covey Oil Co.* v. *Continental Oil Co.*, 340 F. 2d 993, 999 (10th Cir. 1965), cert. denied, 380 U.S. 964; *Sue* v. *Chicago Transit Authority*, 279 F. 2d 416, 419 (7th Cir. 1960); *Schwimmer* v. *United States*, 232 F. 2d 855, 864 (8th Cir. 1956), cert. denied, 352 U.S. 833; *Shotkin* v. *Nelson*, 146 F. 2d 402 (10th Cir. 1944). This is especially true where, as here, the

---

[92] In the Formal Claim of Privilege which was submitted along with the Motion to Quash, the President expressly stated that he was not asserting any privilege with respect to the twenty conversations for which partial transcripts already have been released publicly by the White House. Since no privilege was asserted as to these conversations, no further inquiry was necessary by the district court into whether there would otherwise have been any privilege, or whether the government had a strong need for the evidence, or whether the government's need outweighed any available privilege. Thus, the Special Prosecutor's showing of relevancy and evidentiary value as to these conversations, which was held adequate to satisfy Rule 17(c), warranted enforcement of the subpoena (at least as to the portions of the tapes for which transcripts have been released) without more.

[93] Some of the material contained in the Appendix, and additional material relating to conversations of June 4, 1973, being sought by Item 46 of the subpoena, were also discussed at oral argument before the district court on May 13, 1974.

assessment of the relevancy and evidentiary value of the items sought is primarily a determination of fact and the district judge is intimately familiar with the grand jury's investigation and the indictment in the case. Since the district court's findings are amply supported by the record and reflect the application of the proper legal criteria, those findings should not be disturbed by this Court. Indeed, in the absence of any dispute between the parties on the correctness of the legal principles applied by the district court under Rule 17(c), this essentially factual determination ordinarily would not merit review by this Court at all. In the interest of final disposition of the case, however, we urge the Court to uphold the lower court's action on this aspect of the case as well.

A. Rule 17(C) Permits the Government to Obtain Relevant, Evidentiary Material Sought in Good Faith for Use at Trial

Rule 17(c) provides:

A subpoena may also command the person to whom it is directed to produce the books, papers, documents or other objects designated therein. The court on motion made promptly may quash or modify the subpoena if compliance would be unreasonable or oppressive. The court may direct that books, papers, documents or objects designated in the subpoena be produced before the court at a time prior to the trial or prior to the time when they are to be offered in evidence and may upon their production permit the books, papers, documents or objects or portions thereof to be inspected by the parties and their attorneys.

As all parties and the district court recognized (Pet. App. 19), the leading cases establishing the criteria for satisfaction of Rule 17(c) are *Bowman Dairy Co.* v. *United States, supra,* 341 U.S. 214, and *United States* v. *Iozia,* 13 F.R.D. 335 (S.D.N.Y. 1952). See generally 8 Moore, Federal Practice ¶ 17.07 (1973). In *Bowman Dairy,* the Court held that the government properly had been ordered, under Rule 17(c), to produce to the defendant prior to trial all documents, books, records, and objects gathered by the government during its investigation or preparation for trial which were either presented to the grand jury or would be offered as evidence at trial. The Court upheld the order to produce even though the defendant's subpoena did not further specify particular items sought.

In *Iozia,* the question presented was whether defendant properly could obtain material from the government under Rule

17(c) upon a mere showing that it might be material to the preparation of the defense. The district court, elaborating upon the *Bowman Dairy* standard, declared that a mere showing of possible use in pre-trial preparation was insufficient: the defendant must show (1) that the material was evidentiary and relevant, (2) that it was not otherwise procurable reasonably in advance of trial, (3) that the party seeking it could not properly prepare for trial without it and failure to obtain it might delay trial, and (4) that the request was made in good faith and did not constitute a general "fishing expedition." These were the tests the district court below stated it was applying when it found that "the requirements of Rule 17(c) are here met" (Pet. App. 20).

The standard of relevancy established by these cases is clear. Material being sought under Rule 17(c) is relevant if it is "related to the charges" in the indictment, *United States* v. *Gross* 24 F.R.D. 138, 140, (S.D.N.Y. 1959), or "closely related to the subject matter of the indictment," *United States* v. *Iozia, supra,* 13 F.R.D. at 339, even though it might not, for example, "serve to exonerate this defendant of the crime charge * * *." *Ibid.*

In contrast, the requirement that the material sought be "evidentiary" has not been as well defined in the case law. See 8 Moore, *supra* § 17.07, at 17-19. In the district court, counsel for the President asserted that under Rule 17(c) the government must show that the items sought would be admissible at trial in its case in chief. The reported decisions, however, show that the purpose of the "evidentiary" requirement articulated in *Bowman* and *Iozia* is to oblige the party seeking production to show that the items sought are of a character that they could be used in the trial itself, not simply for general pre-trial preparation. Thus, a subpoena can seek not only evidence that would be admissible in the party's direct case but can also demand material that could be used for impeachment purposes. "Rule 17(c) is applicable only to such documents or objects as would be admissible in evidence at the trial, or which may be used for impeachment purposes." *United States* v. *Carter,* 15 F.R.D. 367, 371 (D.D.C. 1954) (Holtzoff, J.). See also 8 Moore, *supra,* ¶ 17.07, n. 16 ("the documents sought must be admissible in evidence (at least for the purpose of impeachment)").[94] For example, evidentiary

---

[94] In his Reply Memorandum below, counsel for the President argued that the Special Prosecutor's reliance on *Carter* and related cases was misleading because in some of those cases *pretrial* production of material admissible for impeachment of witness was in fact denied. In the instant case, of course, the necessity of pre-trial production is predicated on the government's showing—apparently not contested by counsel for the President—that delaying production of the recordings until trial would

material sought by the government such as prior inconsistent statements by defendants, even if not pertinent in the government's case in chief, would be admissible for purposes of impeachment if a defendant took the stand or in the government's rebuttal case.

Moreover, the "evidentiary" requirement of *Bowman Dairy* and *Iozia* has developed almost exclusively in cases in which defendants sought material prior to trial from the government in addition to that to which they were entitled by the comprehensive pre-trial discovery provisions of Rule 16 of the Federal Rules of Criminal Procedure. Courts have, therefore, taken special care, as the *Bowman* and *Iozia* opinions show, to insure that Rule 17(c) not be used as a device to circumvent the limitations on criminal pre-trial discovery embodied in Rule 16. Rule 16 provides only for discovery from the parties. By contrast, in the instant case the government seeks material from what is in effect, as the district court observed, a third party. As applied to evidence in the possession of third parties, Rule 17(c) simply codifies the traditional right of the prosecution or the defense to seek evidence for trial by a subpoena *duces tecum.* Whether the stringent standards developed in *Bowman Dairy* and *Iozia* for Rule 17(c) subpoenas between the prosecution and the defense should be applied to subpoenas to third parties is a question the Court need not reach, however, since the court below correctly found that the Special Prosecutor had fully met even the higher standards.

The final requirement enunciated in *Iozia*, that the application be made "in good faith" and not "as a general fishing expedition," appears to be simply a requirement that the materials sought be sufficiently identifiable that the court can make a determination that they exist, that they are relevant, and that they would have some evidentiary use at trial. Indeed, the standard most often applied after *Iozia* in determining enforceability of subpoenas under Rule 17(c) appears to be a combination of the *Iozia* requirements of relevancy, evidentiary value, and good faith: the subpoena must be an "honest effort to obtain evidence for use on trial." *United States* v. *Gross, supra,* 24 F.R.D. at 141; *United States* v. *Solomon,* 26 F.R.D. 397, 407 (S.D. Ill. 1960); *United States* v. *Jannuzio,* 22 F.R.D. 223 (D. Del. 1958).

In the district court, counsel for the President took the position that a subpoena should be considered a "fishing

---

not allow adequate time for testing, enhancement, transcription, and preparation of the evidence that would be required for actual use at trial.

expedition" unless the party seeking its enforcement can make a *conclusive* showing that each and every item sought is, beyond doubt, both relevant and evidentiary. As to the majority of conversations involved in the subpoena, this standard is satisfied by consideration of the transcripts made public by the White House, uncontradicted testimony, and other evidence. As to the remaining conversations, there is strong and unrebutted circumstantial evidence—the inferences from which are not denied—indicating that the standard is met.

But the position urged by counsel for the President is not supported and indeed is contradicted by the reported decisions. For instance, the subpoena held enforceable in *Bowman Dairy* was directed to all material in the government's possession that had been presented to the grand jury in the course of the investigation or that would be presented at trial, without further specificity. The subpoena held enforceable in *Iozia* was directed at certain documents, correspondence, and files of a former associate of the defendant. The defendant alleged that he had reason to believe that certain activities may have been engaged in by still other persons and that the former associate was "in the best position to know" about these if they indeed occurred. The cases realistically recognize that the party seeking production often cannot know precisely what is contained in the material sought until he has the opportunity to inspect it. The Court in *Bowman Dairy*, for example, quoted with approval the statement of a member of the Advisory Committee on the Criminal Rules, to the effect that the purpose of Rule 17(c) was to permit a court to order production in advance of trial "for the purpose of course of enabling the party to see whether he can use it or whether he wants to use it." 341 U.S. at 220 n. 5. Common sense dictates that the party seeking production cannot tell what it "can or will use until it has had the opportunity to see the documents." *United States* v. *Gross, supra,* 24 F.R.D. at 141. As Chief Justice Marshall observed in considering a trial subpoena *duces tecum* directed to President Jefferson in *United States* v. *Burr, supra,* 25 Fed. Cas. at 191: "It is objected that the particular passages of the letter which are required are not pointed out. But how can this be done while the letter itself is withheld?"

Because the Special Prosecutor has been denied even preliminary access to the subpoenaed materials, it is obviously impossible for him to demonstrate *conclusively* with respect to a small number of the conversations that they are relevant and evidentiary. But Rule 17(c) and the cases interpreting it do not require that this be done. Rather, they require only that an adequate showing of relevancy and evidentiary value be made, based upon the evidence available. In short,

A predetermination of the admissibility of the subpoenaed material is not the criterion of the validity of the process. It need only appear that the subpoena is being utilized in good faith to obtain evidence * * * [citing *Bowman Dairy*]. *United States* v. *Jannuzio, supra*, 22 F.R.D. at 226.

B. *There was Ample Support for the Finding of the District Court that the Government's Showing of Relevancy and Evidentiary Value was Adequate to Satisfy Rule 17(C)*

1. *Relevance*

Transcripts released to the public by the White House, uncontradicted testimony concerning the subject matter of certain conversations, and other evidence compiled in the Special Prosecutor's showing establish beyond any question the relevancy of the vast majority of the subpoenaed conversations.[95] Indeed, the White House transcripts that have been released of twenty of the subpoenaed conversations not only show conclusively the relevancy of those conversations but also tend to prove the relevancy of the rest of the sixty-four conversations sought by the subpoena.[96]

With respect to some of the conversations, particularly those listed in Items 32-40 of the subpoena, relevancy can be established at this time only by circumstantial and indirect evidence. Nevertheless, the available evidence that these conversations—all of which took place in the three days from April 18 to April 20, 1973—in fact concerned Watergate is strong. The evidence, set forth in detail in the government's Appendix below, shows that the primary subject of concern to the participants in the meetings sought over those three days—the President and defendants Haldeman and

---

[95] In some instances tape recordings already obtained by the Special Prosecutor contain strong evidence of the relevancy of additional conversations sought under this subpoena. For example, it was pointed out in oral argument in the district court that the June 4, 1973, recording of the President listening to prior recordings indicates why the March 13, 1973, telephone conversations sought by Item 46 of the subpoena are important. See Transcript of Hearing on May 13, 1974, at 57.

[96] As pointed out below, the transcripts in some instances provide circumstantial evidence concerning what happened at meetings for which no transcripts were released. In addition, the Court certainly may take notice of the fact that each and every subpoenaed conversation for which a transcript was subsequently released did in fact substantially concern Watergate.

Ehrlichman—was Watergate; that Haldeman and Ehrlichman had withdrawn from their regular White House duties to work exclusively on a Watergate defense; and that meetings between these three persons very probably could have concerned only Watergate. Furthermore, with respect to these conversations, the evidence that is available is unrebutted. The Special Prosecutor argued below that since only the President was in a position to make more informed representations about the relevancy of the subpoenaed conversations, the showing made by the Special Prosecutor was at least sufficient to shift the burden to the President to demonstrate any alleged irrelevancy to the district court by providing the appropriate recordings for *in camera* inspection. In subsequent oral argument in the district court counsel to the President, responding to direct questions from the court, stated that he could make no representations whatever concerning the relevancy *vel non* of any of the subpoenaed conversations.[97]

2. *Evidentiary Nature*

Tape recordings of conversations are admissable as evidence upon the laying of a proper and adequate foundation showing that "the recording as a whole [is] accurate and sufficiently complete."[98] This foundation may be laid by the testimony of one of the participants in the conversation that the recording accurately represents the conversation that was' held.[99] Alternatively, the government could introduce a recording in its direct case even if none of the participants were available as a prosecution witness by showing the circumstances and method by which the recording was made and the chain of custody of the particular recording sought to be introduced.[100]

There can be no doubt that the tape recordings sought by the subpoena here, covering conversations of co-conspirators relating to the subject matter of the alleged conspiracy, are of an evidentiary character. In *Nixon* v. *Sirica, supra,* in upholding enforcement of an earlier subpoena for Presidential tapes, the court squarely held: "Where it is proper to testify

---

[97] Transcript of Hearing, May 13, 1973, at 61-62.

[98] *Stubbs* v. *United States,* 428 F. 2d 885, 888 (9th Cir. 1970), cert. denied, 400 U.S. 1009; *United States* v. *McKeever,* 160 F. Supp. 426 (S.D.N.Y. 1958).

[99] *United States* v. *Madda,* 345 F. 2d 400, 403 (7th Cir. 1965).

[100] See *Stubbs* v. *United States, supra; cf. United States* v. *Sutton,* 426 F. 2d 1202, 1207 (D.C. Cir. 1969) (authentication of writings); Proposed Federal Rules of Evidence, Rule 901 (b) (9).

about oral conversations, taped recordings of those conversations are admissible as probative and corroborative of the truth concerning the testimony." 487 F. 2d at 718 (footnote omitted). The same principle would apply to use of such recordings for impeachment purposes. Such materials are, therefore, amenable to a trial subpoena. In *Monroe* v. *United States*, 234 F. 2d 49, 55 (D.C. Cir. 1956), cert. denied, 352 U.S. 873, the court of appeals held that tape recordings made by a police officer of conversations between himself and defendants were "admissible as independent evidence of what occurred" and that they "were evidentiary, and therefore under the interpretation of Rule 17(c) adopted by the Supreme Court [in *Bowman Diary*] and already followed by this Court, the trial court in its discretion could have required pre-trial production."[101] See also *United States* v. *Lemonakis*, 485 F. 2d 941 (D.C. Cir. 1973), cert. denied, —— U.S. —— (42 U.S.L.W. 3541, March 26, 1974).

Statements recorded on tapes sought by the instant subpoena, while hearsay for some purposes, but see *Anderson* v. *United States*, —— U.S. —— (42 U.S.L.W. 4815, June 3, 1974), would be admissible into evidence in the government's case in chief under one or more of the traditional exceptions to the hearsay rule.

First, it is settled that extra-judicial admissions made by one conspirator in the course of and in furtherance of a conspiracy are admissible against his fellow co-conspirators. *Dutton* v. *Evans*, 400 U.S. 74, 81 (1970); *Myers* v. *United States*, 377 F. 2d 412, 418-19 (5th Cir. 1967), cert. denied, 390 U.S. 929. Each of the principal participants in the subpoenaed conversations either has been indicted as a conspirator or will be named as an unindicted co-conspirator in the government's bill of particulars. As the Special Prosecutor demonstrated in his showing, the transcripts released by the White House, together with both direct and circumstantial evidence, establish a very strong probability that substantial portions of each and every one of the subpoenaed conversations occurred in the course of and in furtherance of the conspiracy alleged in the indictment. Subject to proof of this fact at trial, any recorded statements in furtherance of the conspiratorial objectives made by any one of the conspirators in the course

---

[101] The court upheld the district court's exercise of discretion not to compel production prior to trial because the government had already played the recordings for defendant and his counsel over a period of several days.

of these conversations would be admissible under the co-conspirator exception to the hearsay rule.

Second, even absent proof *aliunde* that each and every subpoenaed conversation was held in the furtherance of the conspiracy, any relevant taped extra-judicial statements made by defendants Haldeman or Ehrlichman would be admissible in the government's case in chief against that particular defendant. *On Lee* v. *United States*, 343 U.S. 747, 756; *United States* v. *Lemonakis, supra*, 485 F. 2d at 949.

Furthermore, other recorded statements made during these conversations may be useful to the government for the purpose of impeaching defendants Haldeman or Ehrlichman should they elect to testify in their own behalf. *E.g., Calumet Broadcasting Corp.* v. *FCC*, 160 F. 2d 285, 288 (D.C. Cir. 1947); *United States* v. *McKeever*, 169 F. Supp. 426, 430 (S.D.N.Y. 1958). And statements on the tapes by government witnesses would be admissible to show the witnesses' prior consistent statements, should the defense attack the witnesses' credibility or the truth of their testimony on cross-examination.[102]

The Special Prosecutor's showing submitted to the district court listed, by individual subpoenaed conversation, the admissions and other statements that are contained in the recordings (according to the White House transcripts released to the public) or should be found therein (according to sworn testimony and other evidence) which would be admissible for one or more of the above-stated reasons. With respect to those conversations in late April 1973 about which there has not been detailed testimony and for which transcripts have not been made public by the White House, the Special Prosecutor argued below that the rich evidentiary vein running through the conversations already released constituted a sufficient showing that similar statements are likely to be contained in those not yet disclosed. Again, this showing was at least sufficient to shift the burden to the President to demonstrate, by submission of tape recordings of these conversations to the Court for *in camera* inspection or at least by certification of counsel, that no evidentiary material was in fact contained therein.

---

[102] See *Monroe* v. *United States, supra*. Prior consistent statements have traditionally been admissible only to rebut charges of recent fabrication or improper influence or motive, but the Proposed Federal Rules of Evidence, Rule 801(d) (1) (B), would permit use of such statements as substantive evidence as well.

3. *Need for the evidence prior to trial*

In his affidavit in connection with the Motion of the United States for issuance of the subpoena, the Special Prosecutor stated that based on experience with other Presidential recordings a considerable amount of time would be necessary to analyze and transcribe the tapes sought by the instant subpoena and that pre-trial production of the tapes was therefore warranted under Rule 17(c). At no point below has counsel for the President sought to contest this showing. A considerable amount of time is required to listen and re-listen to recordings and filter or enhance them where necessary, to make accurate transcripts, to select and prepare relevant portions for trial, and to make copies for defendants where appropriate under the discovery rules. Moreover, much of this work can be performed only by attorneys knowledgeable about the case who must simultaneously prepare all other aspects of the case for trial. The Court should be advised that the Special Prosecutor's staff originally estimated that the simple physical process described above of preparing the recordings sought for trial would require at least two months.

For these reasons, the district court correctly held that the subpoenaed items were genuinely needed prior to trial for preparation of the case and to avoid delay of the trial itself.

CONCLUSION

Settled principles of law, therefore, lead inevitably to the conclusion that the order of the district court, denying the President's motion to quash the subpoena *duces tecum* and directing compliance with it, and denying the motion to expunge the grand jury's action listing him as an unindicted co-conspirator, should be affirmed in all respects.

Respectfully submitted.

Leon Jaworski,
Special Prosecutor.
Philip A. Lacovara,
Counsel to the Special Prosecutor.

Attorneys for the United States.

June 1974.

APPENDIX

APPLICABLE PROVISIONS OF CONSTITUTION, STATUTES, RULES, AND REGULATIONS

1. The Constitution of the United States provides in pertinent part—

Article II, Section 1:

The executive Power shall be vested in a President of the United States of America. He shall hold his Office during the Term of four Years, and, together with the Vice President, chosen for the same Term, be elected, as follows

* * * * *

Article II, Section 2:

The President shall be Commander in Chief of the Army and Navy of the United States, and of Militia of the several States, when called into the actual Service of the United States; he may require the Opinion, in writing, of the principal Officer in each of the executive Departments, upon any Subject relating to the Duties of their respective Offices, and he shall have Power to grant Reprieves and Pardons for Offences against the United States, except in Cases of Impeachment.

He shall have Power, by and with the Advice and Consent of the Senate, to make Treaties, provided two thirds of the Senators present concur; and he shall nominate, and by and with the Advice and Consent of the Senate, shall appoint Ambassadors, other public Ministers and Consuls, Judges of the supreme Court, and all other Officers of the United States, whose Appointments are not herein otherwise provided for, and which shall be established by Law: but the Congress may by Law vest the Appointment of such inferior Officers, as they think proper, in the President alone, in the Courts of Law, or in the Heads of Departments.

* * * * *

Article II, Section 3:

* * * he shall receive Ambassadors and other public Ministers; he shall take Care that the Laws be faithfully executed, and shall Commission all the Officers of the United States.

Article III, Section 2:

The judicial Power shall extend to all Cases, in Law and

Equity, arising under this Constitution, the Laws of the United States, and Treaties made, or which shall be made, under their Authority;—to all Cases affecting Ambassadors, other public Ministers and Consuls;—to all Cases of admiralty and maritime Jurisdiction;—to Controversies to which the United States shall be a Party;—to Controversies between two or more States;—between a State and Citizens of another State;—between Citizens of different States;—between Citizens of the same State claiming Lands under Grants of different States, and between a State, or the Citizens thereof, and foreign States, Citizens of Subjects.

  *   *   *   *   *

2. Title 5, United States Code, provides in pertinent part—

§ 301. Departmental Regulations.

The head of an Executive department or military department may prescribe regulations for the government of his department, the conduct of its employees, the distribution and performance of its business, and the custody, use, and preservation of its records, papers, and property. This section does not authorize withholding information from the public or limiting the availability of records to the public.

Title 28, United States Code, provides in pertinent part—

§ 509. Functions of the Attorney General.

All functions of other officers of the Department of Justice and all functions of agencies and employees of the Department of Justice are vested in the Attorney General except the functions—

(1) vested by subchapter II of chapter 5 of title 5 in hearing examiners employed by the Department of Justice;

(2) of the Federal Prison Industries, Inc.;

(3) of the Board of Directors and officers of the Federal Prison Industries, Inc.; and

(4) of the Board of Parole.

§ 510. Delegation of Authority.

The Attorney General may from time to time make such provisions as he considers appropriate authorizing the performance by any other officer, employee, or agency of the Department of Justice of any function of the Attorney General.

§ 515. Authority for Legal Proceedings; Commission, Oath, and Salary for Special Attorneys.

(a) The Attorney General or any other officer of the Department of Justice, or any attorney specially appointed by the Attorney General under law, may, when specifically directed by the Attorney General, conduct any kind of legal proceeding, civil or criminal, including grand jury proceedings and proceedings before committing magistrates, which United States attorneys are authorized by law to conduct, whether or not he is a resident of the district in which the proceeding is brought.

* * * * *

§ 516. Conduct of Litigation Reserved to Department of Justice.

Except as otherwise authorized by law, the conduct of litigation in which the United States, an agency, or officer thereof is a party, or is interested, and securing evidence therefor, is reserved to officers of the Department of Justice, under the direction of the Attorney General.

§ 517. Interests of United States in Pending Suits.

The Solicitor General, or any officer of the Department of Justice, may be sent by the Attorney General to any State or district in the United States to attend to the interests of the United States in a suit pending in a court of the United States, or in a court of a State, or to attend to any other interest of the United States.

§ 518. Conduct and Argument of Cases.

(a) Except when the Attorney General in a particular case directs otherwise, the Attorney General and the Solicitor General shall conduct and argue suits and appeals in the Supreme Court and suits in the Courts of Claims in which the United States is interested.

(b) When the Attorney General considers it in the interests of the United States, he may personally conduct and argue any case in a court of the United States in which the United States is interested, or he may direct the Solicitor General or any officer of the Department of Justice to do so.

§ 519. Supervision of Litigation.

Except as otherwise authorized by law, the Attorney General shall supervise all litigation to which the United States, an agency, or officer thereof is a party, and shall direct all United States attorneys, assistant United States attorneys, and special attorneys appointed under section 543 of this title in the discharge of their respective duties.

3. Rule 17, Federal Rules of Criminal Procedure, provides in pertinent part—

SUBPOENA

* * * * *

(c) For Production of Documentary Evidence and of Objects. A subpoena may also command the person to whom it is directed to produce the books, papers, documents or other objects designated therein. The court on motion made promptly may quash or modify the subpoena if compliance would be unreasonable or oppressive. The court may direct that books, papers, documents or objects designated in the subpoena be produced before the court at a time prior to the trial or prior to the time when they are to be offered in evidence and may upon their production permit the books, papers, documents or objects or portions thereof to be inspected by the parties and their attorneys.

* * * * *

4. Department of Justice Order No.551-73 (Nov. 2, 1973) 38 Fed. Reg. 30,738 adding 28 C.F.R. § § 0.37, and 0.38, and Appendix to Subpart G-1, provides

TITLE 28—JUDICIAL ADMINISTRATION

Chapter 1—Department of Justice

Part O—Organization of the Department of Justice

Order No. 551-73

Establishing the Office of Watergate Special Prosecution Force

By virtue of the authority vested in me by 28 U.S.C. 509, 510 and 5 U.S.C. 301, there is hereby established in the Department of Justice, the Office of Watergate Special Prosecution Force, to be headed by a Director. Accordingly, Part O of Chapter I of Title 28, Code of Federal Regulations, is amended as follows:

1. Section 0.1(a) which lists the organization units of the Department, is amended by adding "Office of Watergate Special Prosecution Force" immediately after "Office of Criminal Justice."

2. A new Subpart G-1 is added immediately after Subpart G,

to read as follows:

"Subpart G-1—Office of Watergate Special Prosecution Force

§ 0.37 General Functions

The Office of Watergate Special Prosecution Force shall be under the direction of a Director who shall be the Special Prosecutor appointed by the Attorney General. The duties and responsibilities of the Special Prosecutor are set forth in the attached appendix which is incorporated and made part hereof.

§ 0.38 Specific Functions.

The Special Prosecutor is assigned and delegated the following specific functions with respect to matters specified in this Subpart:

(a) Pursuant to 28 U.S.C. 515(a), to conduct any kind of legal proceeding, civil or criminal, including grand jury proceedings, which United States Attorneys are authorized by law to conduct, and to designate attorneys to conduct such legal proceedings.

(b) To approve or disapprove the production or disclosure of information or files relating to matters within his cognizance in response to a subpoena, order, or other demand of a court or other authority. (See Part 16(B) of this chapter.)

(c) To apply for and to exercise the authority vested in the Attorney General under 18 U.S.C. 6005 relating to immunity of witnesses in Congressional proceedings.

The listing of these specific functions is for the purpose of illustrating the authority entrusted to the Special Prosecutor and is not intended to limit in any manner his authority to carry out his functions and responsibilities."

Robert H. Bork,
Acting Attorney General.

Date: November 2, 1973.

APPENDIX

Duties and Responsibilities of the Special
Prosecutor

The Special Prosecutor

There is appointed by the Attorney General, within the Department of Justice, a Special Prosecutor to whom the Attorney General shall delegate the authorities and provide the staff and other resources described below.

The Special Prosecutor shall have full authority for investigating and prosecuting offenses against the United States arising out of the unauthorized entry into Democratic National Committee Headquarters at the Watergate, all offenses arising out of the 1972 Presidential Election for which the Special Prosecutor deems it necessary and appropriate to assume responsibility, allegations involving the President, members of the White House staff, or Presidential appointees, and any other matters which he consents to have assigned to him by the Attorney General.

In particular, the Special Prosecutor shall have full authority with respect to the above matters for:

—conducting proceedings before grand juries and any other investigations he deems necessary;
—reviewing all documentary evidence available from any source, as to which he shall have full access;
—determining whether or not to contest the assertion of "Executive Privilege" or any other testimonial privilege;
—determining whether or not application should be made to any Federal court for a grant of immunity to any witness, consistently with applicable statutory requirements, or for warrants, subpoenas, or other court orders;
—deciding whether or not to prosecute any individual, firm, corporation or group of individuals;
—initiating and conducting prosecutions, framing indictments, filing informations, and handling all aspects of any cases within his jurisdiction (whether initiated before or after his assumption of duties), including any appeals;
—coordinating and directing the activities of all Department of Justice personnel, including United States Attorneys;
—dealing with and appearing before Congressional committees having jurisdiction over any aspect of the

above matters and determining what documents, information, and assistance shall be provided to such committees.

In exercising this authority, the Special Prosecutor will have the greatest degree of independence that is consistent with the Attorney General's statutory accountability for all matters falling within the jurisdiction of the Department of Justice. The Attorney General will not countermand or interfere with the Special Prosecutor's decisions or actions. The Special Prosecutor will determine whether and to what extent he will inform or consult with the Attorney General about the conduct of his duties and responsibilities. In accordance with assurances given by the President to the Attorney General that the President will not exercise his Constitutional powers to effect the discharge of the Special Prosecutor or to limit the independence that he is hereby given, the Special Prosecutor will not be removed from his duties except for extraordinary improprieties on his part and without the President's first consulting the Majority and the Minority Leaders and Chairmen and ranking Minority Members of the Judiciary Committees of the Senate and House of Representatives and ascertaining that their consensus is in accord with his proposed action.

Staff and Resource Support

1. *Selection of Staff.*—The Special Prosecutor shall have full authority to organize, select, and hire his own staff of attorneys, investigators, and supporting personnel, on a full or part-time basis, in such numbers and with such qualifications as he may reasonably require. He may request the Assistant Attorneys General and other officers of the Department of Justice to assign such personnel and to provide such other assistance as he may reasonably require. All personnel in the Department of Justice, including United States Attorneys, shall cooperate to the fullest extent possible with the Special Prosecutor.

2. *Budget.*—The Special Prosecutor will be provided with such funds and facilities to carry out his responsibilities as he may reasonably require. He shall have the right to submit budget requests for funds, positions, and other assistance, and such requests shall receive the highest priority.

3. *Designation and Responsibility.*—The personnel acting as the staff and assistants of the Special Prosecutor shall be known as the Watergate Special Prosecution Force and shall be responsible only to the Special Prosecutor.

Continued Responsibilities of Assistant Attorney General,

Criminal Division.—Except for the specific investigative and prosecutorial duties assigned to the Special Prosecutor, the Assistant Attorney General in charge of the Criminal Division will continue to exercise all of the duties currently assigned to him.

Applicable Department Policies.—Except as otherwise herein specified or as mutually agreed between the Special Prosecutor and the Attorney General, the Watergate Special Prosecution Force will be subject to the administrative regulations and policies of the Department of Justice.

Public Reports.—The Special Prosecutor may from time to time make public such statements or reports as he deems appropriate and shall upon completion of his assignment submit a final report to the appropriate persons or entities of the Congress.

Duration of Assignment.—The Special Prosecutor will carry out these responsibilities, with the full support of the Department of Justice, until such time as, in his judgment, he has completed them or until a date mutually agreed upon between the Attorney General and himself.

5. Department of Justice Order No. 554-73 (Nov. 19, 1973), 38 Fed. Reg. 32,805, amending 28 C.F.R. Appendix to Subpart G-1, provides—

TITLE 28—JUDICIAL ADMINISTRATION

Chapter I—Department of Justice

Part O—Organization of the Department of Justice

Subpart G-1—Office of Watergate Special Prosecution Force

Order No. 554-73

Amending the Regulations Establishing the Office of Watergate Special Prosecution Force

By virtue of the authority vested in me by 28 U.S.C. 509, 510 and 5 U.S.C. 301, the last sentence of the fourth paragraph of the Appendix to Subpart G-1 is amended to read as follows: "In accordance with assurances given by the President to the Attorney General that the President will not exercise his Constitutional powers to effect the discharge of the Special Prosecutor or to limit the independence that he is hereby given, (1) the Special Prosecutor will not be removed from his duties except for extraordinary improprieties on his part and without the President's first consulting the Majority and the Minority Leaders and Chairmen and ranking Minority Members of the Judiciary Committees of the Senate and House of Representatives and ascertaining that their consensus is in accord with his proposed action, and (2) the jurisdiction of the Special Prosecutor will not be limited without the President's first consulting with such Members of Congress and ascertaining that their consensus is in accord with his proposed action."

Robert H. Bork,
Acting Attorney General.

Date: November 19, 1973.

6. The letter from the Acting Attorney General to the Special Prosecutor on November 21, 1973, stating the intention of Department of Justice Order No. 554-73, is as follows—

Office of the Solicitor General,
Washington, D.C., 20530, November 21, 1973.

Leon Jaworski, Esq.,
Special Prosecutor,
Watergate Special Prosecution Force,
1425 K Street, N.W.,
Washington, D.C. 20005

Dear Mr. Jaworski: You have informed me that the amendment to your charter of November 19, 1973 has been questioned by some members of the press. This letter is to confirm what I told you in our telephone conversation. The amendment of November 19, 1973 was intended to be, and is, a safeguard of your independence.

The President has given his assurance that he would not exercise his constitutional powers either to discharge the Special Prosecutor or to limit the independence of the Special Prosecutor without first consulting the Majority and Minority leaders and chairmen and ranking members of the Judiciary Committees of the Senate and the House, and ascertaining that their consensus is in accord with his proposed action.

When that assurance was worked into the charter, the draftsman inadvertently used a form of words that might have been construed as applying the President's assurance only to the subject of discharge. This was subsequently pointed out to me by an assistant and I had the amendment

of November 19 drafted in order to put beyond question
that the assurance given applied to your independence
under the charter and not merely to the subject of
discharge.

There is, in my judgment, no possibility whatever that
the topics of discharge or limitation of independence will
ever be of more than hypothetical interest. I write this letter
only to repeat what you already know: the recent
amendment to your charter was to correct an ambiguous
phrasing and thus to make clear that the assurances
concerning congressional consultation and consensus apply
to all aspects of your independence.

Sincerely,

Robert H. Bork,
Acting Attorney General.

VI
SPECIAL PROSECUTOR'S
SUPPLEMENTAL BRIEF IN
UNITED STATES
v.
NIXON

After the Supreme Court granted review in the case, it asked the parties to submit briefs on two procedural questions: (1) was Judge Sirica's order of May 20, 1974 appealable at that stage of the proceedings, and (2) did the Court have jurisdiction to review the petition for mandamus filed by the President in the Court of Appeals as a device to appeal Judge Sirica's order. These technical questions were examined in a supplemental brief filed by the Special Prosecutor.

IN THE SUPREME COURT OF THE UNITED STATES

OCTOBER TERM, 1973

No. 73—1766

UNITED STATES OF AMERICA, PETITIONER

v.

RICHARD M. NIXON, PRESIDENT OF THE
UNITED STATES, ET AL., RESPONDENTS

No. 73—1834

RICHARD M. NIXON, PRESIDENT OF THE
UNITED STATES, PETITIONER

v.

UNITED STATES OF AMERICA

*ON WRITS OF CERTIORARI TO THE
UNITED STATES COURT OF APPEALS
FOR THE DISTRICT OF COLUMBIA CIRCUIT*

SUPPLEMENTAL BRIEF FOR THE UNITED STATES
ON APPELLATE JURISDICTION

QUESTIONS PRESENTED

1. Whether the District Court order of May 20, 1974, requiring the President to submit certain evidence to the court for *in camera* inspection, is an appealable order.

2. Whether this Court has jurisdiction to entertain and decide the petition for mandamus, seeking review of the district court's order requiring the President to submit certain evidence to the court for *in camera* inspection, transmitted to this Court by the Court of Appeals.

CONSTITUTIONAL PROVISION AND
STATUTES INVOLVED

Article III, Section 2 of the Constitution of the United States provides in pertinent part—

The judicial Power shall extend to all Cases, in Law and

Equity, arising under this Constitution, the Laws of the United States, and Treaties made, or which shall be made, under their Authority;—to all Cases affecting Ambassadors, other public Ministers and Consuls;—to all Cases of admiralty and maritime Jurisdiction;—to Controversies to which the United States shall be a Party;—to Controversies between two or more States;—between a State and Citizens of another State;—between Citizens of different States,—between Citizens of the same State claiming Lands under Grants of different States, and between a State, or the Citizens thereof, and foreign States, Citizens or Subjects.

In all Cases affecting Ambassadors, other public Ministers and Consuls, and those in which a State shall be Party, the Supreme Court shall have original jurisdiction. In all the other Cases before mentioned, the supreme Court shall have appellate Jurisdiction, both as to Law and Fact, with such Exceptions, and under such Regulations as the Congress shall make.

* * * * * *

Section 1254 of Title 28 of the United States Code provides in pertinent part—

Cases in the courts of appeals may be reviewed by the Supreme Court by the following methods:

(1) By writ of certiorari granted upon the petition of any party to any civil or criminal case before or after rendition of judgment or decree;

* * * * *

Section 1651(a) of Title 28 of the United States Code provides—

The Supreme Court and all courts established by Act of Congress may issue all writs necessary or appropriate in aid of their respective jurisdictions and agreeable to the usages and principles of law.

Section 2101(e) of Title 28 of the United States Code provides—

An application to the Supreme Court for a writ of certiorari to review a case before judgment has been rendered in the court of appeals may be made at any time before judgment.

INTRODUCTION

The United States files this Supplemental Brief on Appellate Jurisdiction in response to the order of this Court of June 15, 1974, requesting the parties to brief and argue, in addition to the questions presented by the petition for certiorari (No. 73—1766), the cross-petition for certiorari (No. 73—1834) and the petition for a writ of mandamus filed in the court of appeals (D.C. Cir. No. 74—1532), the following questions:

(a) Is the District Court order of May 20, 1974, an appealable order?

(b) Does this Court have jurisdiction to entertain and decide the petition for mandamus transmitted by the Court of Appeals to this Court?

The United States respectfully submits that both questions must be answered affirmatively and that the jurisdiction of this Court to review the decision of the district court rests alternatively on 28 U.S.C. 1254(1) and 1651.

STATEMENT

On May 24, 1974, pursuant to 28 U.S.C. 1651 and Rule 21(a) of the Federal Rules of Appellate Procedure, the President filed in the court of appeals a petition for a writ of mandamus seeking an order directing the district court to vacate its order of May 20, which had denied the President's motion to quash the subpoena *duces tecum* and his motion to expunge the grand jury's naming of him as an unindicted co-conspirator and which had ordered compliance with the subpoena. The petition was duly docketed in the court of appeals and assigned Docket Number 74—1532. On the same day, the President filed a notice of appeal from the district court's order and the district court record was docketed in the court of appeals under Docket Number 74—1534.

Later on May 24, the United States filed a petition for certiorari before judgment (No. 73—1766) seeking review of those cases in the court of appeals and describing five questions presented by those cases, including questions that covered the issues raised by Issue (b) of the President's mandamus petition in the court of appeals, relating to the district court's order overruling the claim of privilege and ordering compliance with the subpoena. The President's cross-petition for a writ of certiorari before judgment (No. 73—1834), filed on June 6, 1974, raises the question presented as Issue (d) in the mandamus petition, involving the district court's refusal to expunge the grand jury's finding concerning the President. Issue (a) of the mandamus petition, relating to the jurisdiction of the district court to decide an "intraexecutive dispute," was not explicitly presented as a question in either certiorari petition, but is being addressed in the briefs in this Court as a jurisdictional issue.

Issue (c) of the mandamus petition, relating to the application of *Brady* v *Maryland*, 373 U.S. 83, to privileged material not in the prosecutor's possession, is not raised separately in either petition. The district court expressly refused to pass upon that question as a ground for ordering compliance with the subpoena, and it is doubtful that it was properly before the court of appeals. Thus, the three viable issues raised in the President's petition for mandamus are "fairly comprised" within the questions framed by the parties in seeking certiorari before judgment. See Sup. Ct. Rule 23(c).

It is our contention that the May 20 order of the district court is properly before this Court for review on two distinct, independent grounds. First, we believe the order of the district court is appealable under 28 U.S.C. 1291, and since an appeal had been taken to the court of appeals, this Court has jurisdiction under 28 U.S.C. 1254(1) to review the order before judgment in the court of appeals. Second, this Court also has jurisdiction under 28 U.S.C. 1254(1) to consider the President's petition for a writ of mandamus, which was pending in the court of appeals, and is fairly comprehended by the questions presented in the petition and cross-petition for certiorari.

In any event, the Court has adequate jurisdiction to resolve the issues presented under the All Writs Act, 28 U.S.C. 1651, which empowers this Court to issue common law writs of certiorari or writs of mandamus to review directly decisions of district courts in extraordinary cases.

ARGUMENT

I. THE ORDER OF THE DISTRICT COURT REQUIRING THE PRESIDENT TO PRODUCE EVIDENCE FOR IN CAMERA INSPECTION IS APPEALABLE

Ordinarily, of course, an order like the one presented for review—requiring the production of evidence pursuant to a subpoena *duces tecum* and denying a motion to quash—is not considered a final order appealable under 28 U.S.C. 1291. In such cases, the person to whom the subpoena is directed "must either obey its commands or refuse to do so and contest the validity of the subpoena if he is subsequently cited for contempt on account of his failure to obey." *United States* v. *Ryan*, 402 U.S. 530, 532. See also *Cobbledick* v. *United States*, 309 U.S. 323; *Alexander* v. *United States*, 201 U.S. 117. As this Court held in *Cohen* v. *Beneficial Industrial Loan Corp.*, 337 U.S. 541, 546, however, Section 1291 must be given a "practical rather than a technical construction." The compelling circumstances of this case—where the person to whom the subpoena is directed is the President of the United States—require an exception to this judically constructed rule that normally governs the timeliness of an appeal from the enforcement of a subpoena. See *Nixon* v. *Sirica*, 487 F. 2d 700, 707 n. 21 (D.C. Cir. 1973) (*en banc*).

Even though an order enforcing a subpoena *duces tecum* issued to a third-party witness in a criminal proceeding effectively determines that party's interests in a matter collateral to the prosecution and, as a practical matter, is a final order, the interests in the orderly administration of justice have led this Court to hold that such an order is not appealable. There can be no question that if such orders were routinely appealable, there would be interminable delays in nearly every criminal case while third-party witnesses litigated their obligation to provide evidence. Thus, "the necessity for expedition in the administration of the criminal law justifies putting one who seeks to resist the production of desired information to a choice between compliance with a trial court's order to produce prior to any review of that order, and resistance to that order with the concomitant possibility of an adjudication of contempt if his claims are rejected on appeal." *United States* v. *Ryan, supra*, 402 U.S. at 533. In the circumstances of this case, however, that "choice" not only would be wholly inappropriate, but most likely would defeat the very purpose of Ryan—expedition of the criminal process. There is certainly no statutory obstacle to treating the ordinary timeliness rule as inapplicable here, since as this Court reaffirmed quite recently, the final order rule of 28 U.S.C. 1291 "does not limit appellate review to 'those final judgments which terminate an action.'" *Eisen* v. *Carlisle & Jacquelin*, — U.S. — (42 U.S.L.W. 4804, 4808, May 28, 1974), citing *Cohen* v. *Beneficial Loan Corp., supra*, 337 U.S. at 545.

Although it is an open question whether the President is legally and constitutionally subject to citation for civil or criminal contempt of court,[1] no one would question that such a course would be radical and, even if constitutionally feasible, should be avoided if at all possible while still maintaining the integrity of the courts and the administration of justice. This was the crucial factor in leading the Court of Appeals for the District of Columbia Circuit to state that despite *Ryan*, an order

---

[1] But see *Land* v. *Dollar*, 190 F. 2d 623 (D.C. Dir. 1951), vacated as moot, 344 U.S. 806 (cabinet officers held in contempt for refusing on directions of the President to obey court order); *United States* v. *Isaacs and Kerner*, 493 F. 2d 1194 (7th Cir. 1974), cert. denied, - U.S. - (June 17, 1974) (impeachable officer liable to criminal conviction prior to impeachment and removal).

requiring the President to submit evidence for *in camera* inspection under a subpoena is appealable. "In the case of the President, contempt of a judicial order—even for the purpose of enabling a constitutional test of the order—would be a course unseemly at best." *Nixon* v. *Sirica, supra,* 487 F. 2d at 707 n.21.[2] The courts simply as a matter of comity between the Branches should not place the President in the position of having to suffer a contempt citation—itself an inevitable subject of constitutional litigation—in order to secure review of such an order directed to him. Nor, as a matter of discretion, should they invite a situation where they will be called upon to decide whether the President in fact can be held in contempt if he declines to obey the lower court order.

It goes without saying that this is one of that "small class" of cases where the issues finally determined by the district court are "too important to be denied review and too independent of the cause itself to require that appellate consideration be deferred until the whole case is adjudicated." *Cohen* v. *Beneficial Industrial Loan Corp., supra,* 337 U.S. at 546. Unlike the ordinary litigation concerning a subpoena *duces tecum,* the basic constitutional issues involved in this case have not been decided definitively by this Court. Since the evidence sought in the subpoena, as we demonstrate in Parts III(B) and V of our Brief, is highly material to the prosecution in *United States* v. *Mitchell, et al.,* these issues require prompt resolution by this Court. Finally, it would be hard to envision a case which belongs to a smaller class—a case where a subpoena has issued to *and* compliance ordered against the President.

The rule established by *Ryan* and *Cobbledick,* every bit as much as the *Cohen* rule or the recent holding in *Eisen,* reflects an "evaluation of the competing considerations underlying all questions of finality—'the inconvenience and costs of piecemeal review on the one hand and the danger of denying justice by delay on the other.'" *Eisen* v. *Carlisle and Jacquelin, supra,* 42 U.S.L.W. at 4808. The "evaluation" here shows that this case is clearly distinguishable even from the cases where third-party witnesses are ordered to produce evidence and mandates clearly that the order of the district court be construed as a final order appealable under 28 U.S.C. 1291.

---

[2] In an *en banc* order entered on June 18, 1974, the court of appeals held that a district court order, entered in the interim, overruling a Presidential claim of executive privilege for a specific subpoenaed item is appealable, and ordered the President's mandamus petition, seeking review of that order, docketed as an appeal. *Nixon* v. *Sirica* (D.C. Cir. No. 74-1618).

II. THIS COURT HAS JURISDICTION TO ENTERTAIN AND DECIDE THE PETITION FOR MANDAMUS TRANSMITTED BY THE COURT OF APPEALS TO THIS COURT

By its order of June 15, 1974, this Court also directed the parties to address the question whether it has "jurisdiction" to entertain and decide the petition for a writ of mandamus transmitted by the court of appeals as part of the record on certiorari. In our view, this Court unquestionably has such jurisdiction.

A. *Review of the Mandamus Petition Is Authorized by 28 U.S.C. 1254(1)*

We begin by noting that under the All Writs Act, 28 U.S.C. 1651(a), the court of appeals (like this Court) has jurisdiction to issue "all writs necessary or appropriate in aid of " the court's jurisdiction and "agreeable to the usages and principles of law." In view of the extraordinary nature of proceedings seeking to order the President to comply with a subpoena *duces tecum*, the court of appeals held in *Nixon* v. *Sirica, supra,* 487 F. 2d at 706—07, that the normal predicate for seeking review of such an order—suffering a contempt adjudication—was inappropriate, and that, to the extent an appeal could not be supported, immediate exercise of the court's "review power under the All Writs Act" was warranted, "particularly in light of the great public interest in prompt resolution of the issues that his petition presents." 487 F. 2d at 707 (footnotes omitted). That ruling, based on the court's review of the numerous decisions of this Court dealing with mandamus, was unquestionably within the Court's statutory power and reflects a legitimate exercise of discretion. See generally *Will* v. *United States,* 389 U.S. 90; *Schlagenhauf* v. *Holder,* 379 U.S. 104; *Roche* v. *Evaporated Milk Ass'n,* 319 U.S. 21; *United States* v. *United States District Court,* 444 F. 2d 651, 655-56 (6th Cir. 1971) aff'd, 407 U.S. 297, 301 n.3. In seeking review of the May 20, 1974 order by mandamus, the President was following the course marked out by the court of appeals, and that court had statutory jurisdiction to entertain the petition.

This Court's jurisdiction to review that mandamus case on certiorari is similarly clear. Under 28 U.S.C. 1254(1) the Court has jurisdiction to review "cases in the court of appeals":

> By writ of certiorari granted under the petition of *any* party to *any* civil or criminal case, before or after rendition of judgment or decree. (Emphasis added.)

This congressional vesting of jurisdiction under Article III of the Constitution is plainly sufficient. We see no room to doubt that a duly docketed petition for mandamus comes within the scope of "any case" pending in the court of appeals. As the Court stated in *Gay* v. *Ruff*, 292 U.S. 25, 30, the power given to review cases before judgment in the court of appeals is "unaffected by the condition of the case as it exists in the circuit court of appeals; * * * the sole essential of this Court's jurisdiction to review is that there be a case pending in the circuit court of appeals." There is no reason to believe that when Congress used the term "any civil or criminal case" in Section 1254(1) it intended to limit the Court's power to reviewing district court cases that were brought to the court of appeals by the way of appeal and to exclude cases involving mandamus applications to review those cases. The language of the statute covers mandamus cases, and the policy reasons for authorizing expedited review apply with at least equal force to such applications. See Sup. Ct. Rule 20.

Although issue had not been joined in the court of appeals by a request for a response to the mandamus petition under Rule 21(b), Federal Rules of Appellate Procedure, the certiorari petitions were timely. Section 2101(e) provides that an application for certiorari before judgment has been rendered by a court of appeals may be made "at any time" before judgement, and the cases in which this expedited procedure has been followed typically are in the most preliminary stages of docketing when review is applied for and granted by this Court.[3]

As we pointed out in our petition for a writ of certiorari, the statutory authority to grant review before judgment on the application of "any party" to the case in the court of appeals has been used on prior occasions to bring a case up for review on the application of the party that had prevailed in the district court, as in the present case. See *Youngstown Sheet & Tube Co.* v. *Sawyer*, 343 U.S. 579; *United States* v. *United Mine Workers*, 330 U.S. 258, 269; *United States* v. *Bankers Trust Co.*, 294 U.S. 240.[4]

B. *The Court Has Appellate Jurisdiction Under Article III*

Nor is there any doubt that this statutory authority is a valid

---

[3] See Stern & Gressman, *Supreme Court Practice* ¶ 2.3, at 28 (4th ed. 1969).

[4] The application of this statute to a petition by the party prevailing in the district court was demonstrated in the government's petition in *Bankers Trust*. No. 471, O.T. 1934, at 11-16.

exercise of the Congressional power to regulate the *appellate* jurisdiction of this Court under Article III of the Constitution. Although a petition for a writ of mandamus—whether applied for in the court of appeals or in this Court—is in a sense a new proceeding, it has been settled since *Marbury* v. *Madison*, 1 Cranch 137, that mandamus to review the action of an inferior court is an exercise of the Court's *appellate* jurisdiction. In that case, Chief Justice Marshall stated, as the "essential criterion of appellate jurisdiction, that it revises and corrects the proceedings in a cause already instituted, and does not create that cause." 1 Cranch at 175. As Justice Harlan explained in his lengthy concurring opinion, discussing similar issues, in *Chandler* v. *Judicial Council of the Tenth Circuit*, 398 U.S. 74, 96:

> Beyond cavil, the issuance of a writ of mandamus to an inferior *court* is an exercise of appellate jurisdiction. In re Winn, 213 U.S. 458, 465—466. (Emphasis in original.)

For this reason, the Court regularly has entertained and decided "original petitions for writs of mandamus directed to district courts in the exercise of what is, under Article III, the Court's appellate jurisdiction. See, *e.g.*, *McCullough* v. *Cosgrave*, 309 U.S. 634 (per curiam); *Ex parte Peru*, 318 U.S. 578, 582-83; *Ex parte United States*, 287 U.S. 241, 245-49. Indeed, Rule 30 of this Court's Rules expressly recognizes the Court's power to issue extraordinary writs like mandamus, which necessarily involve a valid exercise of appellate jurisdiction when review of a lower court's decision is sought thereby. It follows, *a fortiori*, that this Court has constitutional jurisdiction to exercise the authority conferred by Section 1254(1) to consider, before judgment, the mandamus case filed in the court of appeals, since the object of the Court's review is identical: to set aside, modify or leave undisturbed the district court's order. See 28 U.S.C. 2106.[5]

C. *Alternatively, Jurisdiction Can Be Rested on the All Writs Act, 28 U.S.C. 1651(a)*

Finally, we note that, if for some reason the Court concludes that the mandamus petition was not properly a "case" pending "in" the court of appeals, so as to fit within the statutory certiorari-before-judgment provision in Section 1254(1), this

[5] Whether Section 1254(1) applies to petitions filed in courts of appeals for direct review of administrative agency decisions and whether review of such petitions before judgment of the court of appeals would come within this Court's appellate jurisdiction under Article III are distinct questions that need not be addressed in this case, where the Court is being called upon to review an order of a lower federal court. See generally Stern & Gressman, *supra*, ¶ 2.3, at 29-30.

Court would still have ample jurisdiction to entertain and decide the issues raised and briefed by the parties. All of the same issues, of course, are raised by the President's duly docketed appeal to the court of appeals. In addition, even if there is some defect with that appeal (but see Part I, above), the Court still has an adequate basis for jurisdiction. As expressly recognized by this Court's Rule 31(2), the All Writs Act, 28 U.S.C. 1651(a), authorizes the Court to issue extraordinary writs like the "common law writ of certiorari" to a lower court, and this power has been used when cases were found not to be pending "in" a court of appeals. See, *e.g.*, *House* v. *Mayo*, 324 U.S. 42, 44; *Matter of 620 Church St. Building Corp.*, 299 U.S. 24, 26. See also *United States Alkali Export Ass'n* v. *United States*, 325 U.S. 196; *DeBeers Consolidated Mines Ltd.* v. *United States*, 325 U.S. 212. In addition, the Court could treat the President's cross-petition for certiorari before judgment as an application for an "original" writ of mandamus to review the district court's order directly. See *McCullough* v. *Cosgrave, supra; Ex parte Peru, supra; Ex parte United States, supra.* Since review of an order of a district court is sought, such review comes within the "appellate" jurisdiction under Article III. The circumstances of the present case, as measured by the criteria followed by the Court in other cases, certainly show that the use of an extraordinary writ, if necessary, is warranted to resolve promptly the major constitutional issues raised by this important litigation.

CONCLUSION

The Court has jurisdiction over the issues raised in the petitions for writs of certiorari before judgment, and the judgment of the district court should be affirmed on the merits for the reasons set forth in our main brief.

Respectfully submitted.

> Leon Jaworski,
> *Special Prosecutor.*
> Philip A. Lacovara,
> *Counsel to the Special Prosecutor.*
> *Attorneys for the United States.*

June 1974.

VII
THE PRESIDENT'S
MAIN BRIEF IN
UNITED STATES
v.
NIXON

The President's brief in the Supreme Court took two absolutist positions with respect to the subpoena. First, Mr. St. Clair argued that the courts were without power to intervene in the dispute between two entities of the Executive branch. Secondly, he claimed that assertions of executive privilege by the President were not reviewable by the courts. Finally, he urged that the Special Prosecutor had failed to demonstrate a compelling need for the tapes in question. He also argued his point on the inability of the grand jury to name the President as a co-conspirator.

IN THE SUPREME COURT OF THE UNITED STATES

OCTOBER TERM, 1973

Nos. 73-1766 and 73-1834

UNITED STATES OF AMERICA, PETITIONER

v.

RICHARD M. NIXON, PRESIDENT OF THE
UNITED STATES, ET AL., RESPONDENTS

RICHARD M. NIXON, PRESIDENT OF THE
UNITED STATES, CROSS-PETITIONER

v.

UNITED STATES OF AMERICA, RESPONDENT

*ON WRITS OF CERTIORARI BEFORE JUDGMENT
TO THE UNITED STATES COURT OF APPEALS FOR THE
DISTRICT OF COLUMBIA CIRCUIT*

**BRIEF FOR THE RESPONDENT, CROSS-PETITIONER
RICHARD M. NIXON, PRESIDENT OF THE UNITED STATES**

OPINIONS BELOW

The opinion and order of the district court (P. A. 15)[1] has not yet been reported. The United States Court of Appeals for the District of Columbia circuit has neither considered nor rendered an opinion in this case.

JURISDICTION

The opinion and order of the district court was entered on May 20, 1974 (P.A. 15). On May 24, 1974, the President filed both a timely notice of appeal in the district court and a petition for a writ of mandamus in the United States Court of Appeals for the District of Columbia Circuit. Upon the filing of the appeal, the order of the district court was stayed. On May 24, 1974, appellee, United States of America, filed in this Court a petition

---

[1] The reference "P.A." is to the Appendix to the Petition in No. 73-1766. The reference "J.A." is to the unsealed joint appendix filled in this case.

for writ of certiorari before judgment, which was granted on May 31, 1974. (No. 73-1766) On June 6, 1974, the President filed a cross-petition for writ of certiorari before judgment which was granted on June 15, 1974. (No. 73-1834) At that time, both cases were consolidated. The jurisdiction of this Court is invoked under 28 U.S.C. 1254(1).

1. Whether the Court has jurisdiction to review the order of the district court on the grounds that either:
   a. the district court's order of May 20, 1974, was an appealable order, or
   b. The Court has jurisdiction to entertain and decide a petition for mandamus transmitted by a court of appeals to this Court.

2. Whether the Judiciary has jurisdiction to intervene in an internal dispute of a co-equal branch.

3. Whether a court can substitute its judgment for that of the President, when he exercises his discretion, in determining that disclosures of presidential records would not serve the public interest.

4. Whether a court has authority to enforce a subpoena against a President of the United States by ordering him to produce for *in camera* inspection, records demanded by a subpoena when the President has interposed a valid and formal claim of privilege.

   Whether, under the Constitution, a grand jury has the authority to charge an incumbent President of the United States as an unindicted co-conspirator in a criminal proceeding.

6. Whether the Special Prosecutor has made the necessary showing required to obtain materials under Rule 17(c), Federal Rules of Criminal Procedure, and *Nixon* v. *Sirica*, 487 F.2d 700 (D.C. Cir. 1973).

CONSTITUTIONAL PROVISIONS, STATUTES, RULES AND REGULATIONS

The constitutional provisions, statutes, rules, and regulations involved are set forth in the Appendix, *infra*, pp. 138-164, are:

Constitution of the United States:

    Article I, section 2, clause 2.
    Article I, section 3, clause 7.
    Article I, section 5, clause 2.

Article I, section 6.
Article II, section 1.
Article II, section 1, clause 1.
Article II, section 1, clause 8.
Article II, section 2, clause 1.
Article II, section 2, clause 7.
Article II, section 3.
Article II, section 3, clause 1.
Article II, section 3, clause 7.
Article III, section 2.

Statutes of the United States:

18 U.S.C. 371; 62 Stat. 701.
18 U.S.C. 1001; 62 Stat. 749.
18 U.S.C. 1503; 82 Stat. 1115.
18 U.S.C. 1621; 78 Stat. 995.
18 U.S.C. 1623; 84 Stat. 932.
Jencks Act, 18 U.S.C. 3500; 84 Stat. 926.
18 U.S.C. 3731; 84 Stat. 1890.
28 U.S.C. 44; 82 Stat. 183.
2 U.S.C. 133; 85 Stat. 742.
28 U.S.C. 1254; 62 Stat. 928.
28 U.S.C. 1291; 72 Stat. 348.
28 U.S.C. 1651; 63 Stat. 102.
Presidential Libraries Act, 44 U.S.C. 2107;
82 Stat. 1288.
44 U.S.C. 2108(c); 82 Stat. 1289.

Rules:

Rule 26, Federal Rules of Civil Procedure. Rule 6(e),
Federal Rules of Criminal Procedure. Rule 17(c), Federal
Rules of Criminal Procedure.

Regulations:

Department of Justice Order No. 551-73 (November 2,
1973), 38 Fed. Reg. 30, 738, adding 38 C.F.R. ss 0.37,
0.38, and Appendix to Subpart G-1.
Department of Justice Order No. 554-73 (November 19,
1973), 38 Fed. Reg. 32, 805, amending 38 C.F.R.
Appendix to Subpart G-1.

STATEMENT

This case presents for review an opinion and order of a federal
district court holding that it has jurisdiction to intervene in a
dispute between the President and the Special Prosecutor,
jurisdiction to review a claim of privilege asserted by the

President as to various executive materials, and jurisdiction to order the President, by compulsory process, to produce subpoenaed items for *in camera* review. Review is also sought of the lower court's order denying, without opinion, the President's motion to expunge from the record any finding by a grand jury that he was an unindicted co-conspirator in a criminal proceeding.

A. *The Indictment*

On June 5, 1972, a federal grand jury of the United States District Court for the District of Columbia was empanelled. To assist that grand jury, the President voluntarily waived all claim of privilege as to the personal testimony of his advisors and aides on all Watergate-related matters. Following the decision in *Nixon v. Sirica*, 487 F. 2d 700 (D.C. Cir. 1973), the President provided the grand jury with numerous documents and other materials including tape recordings.

On March 1, 1974, the grand jury returned an indictment charging seven individuals with one count each of conspiracy, 18 U.S.C. 371 (J.R. 5a-39a).[2] Four of the defendants were also charged with counts of obstruction of justice, 18 U.S.C. 1503; making false statements to agents of the Federal Bureau of Investigation, 18 U.S.C. 1001; perjury, 18 U.S.C. 1621; and making false declarations to a grand jury or court, 18 U.S.C. 1623.[3]

On March 1, 1974, the grand jury also lodged a report with the district court which it filed under seal. In its accompanying report and recommendation, the grand jury stated that it had heard evidence bearing on matters within the primary jurisdiction of the Committee of the Judiciary of the House of Representatives and recommended that the sealed materials be submitted to the Committee. This material was subsequently transmitted to the Committee by order of the court dated March 18, 1974.[4]

---

[2] Those charged were Charles Colson, John Ehrlichman, H.R. Haldeman, Robert C. Mardian, John Mitchell, Kenneth W. Parkinson and Gordon Strachan.

[3] The validity of the entire indictment is presently being challenged by defendant Haldeman in the district court on the ground that the grand jury had been improperly continued past its term, and therefore had no authority at the time the indictment was returned. See H.R. Haldman "Motion to Dismiss Indictment" filed May 1, 1974, in *United States* v. *Mitchell*, et al., (D.D.C. Cr. No. 74-110).

[4] The President declined to express his views on the propriety of the transmittal because in his view, such matters were within the court's own discretion. In its decision authorizing the transmittal of this material, however, the court noted that the grand jury report drew no accusatory conclusions, deprived no individual of an official forum

Subsequently, it was learned that the grand jury in a separate report named, among others, Richard M. Nixon as an "unindicted co-conspirator."

B. *The Special Prosecutor's Subpoena*

On April 16, 1974, the Special Prosecutor, Leon Jaworski, moved the district court for an order pursuant to Rule 17(c), Federal Rules of Criminal Procedure, directing the issuance of a subpoena to Richard Nixon, President of the United States, for the production and inspection of certain presidential material. This material consists of tapes and other electronic and mechanical recordings or reproductions and any memoranda, papers, transcripts, and other writings, relating to 64 confidential conversations between the President and his closest advisors. (J.A. 42a-46a). This motion was subsequently joined in by three of the defendants, Robert C. Mardian, John D. Ehrlichman, and Charles W. Colson, who is no longer a defendant in this proceeding.[5]

On May 1, 1974, the President, through his counsel, entered a special appearance and moved to quash the subpoena *duces tecum* (J.A. 47a) A formal claim of privilege was filed by the President regarding the subpoenaed presidential materials with the exception of those portions of the conversations which had already been made public by the President. (J.A. 48a) On May 3, 1974, the Special Prosecutor moved the district court for an order pursuant to Rule 6(e) of the Federal Rules of Criminal Procedure, authorizing the disclosure of matters occurring before the grand jury to the extent necessary to prepare its memorandum in response to the President's motion to quash. At an *in camera* hearing on May 6, 1974, the district court ruled that the grand jury material could be filed with the court under seal. On May 10, 1974, the Special Prosecutor submitted a memorandum in opposition to the motion to quash, accompanied by an appendix to support a claim of relevancy for the particular subpoenaed materials. (S.P.S.A.)[6] In part, the

---

in which to respond, was not a substitute for indictments where such indictments might properly issue, and contained no recommendations, advice, or statements that infringed on the prerogatives of the other branches of the government. *In Re Report and Recommendations of the June 5, 1972 Grand Jury Concerning Transmission of Evidence to the House of Representatives,* 370 F. Supp. 1219 (D.D.C. 1974).

[5] On June 3, 1974, Charles Colson pleaded guilty to the felony of obstruction of justice in violation of 18 U.S.C. 1503 in the case of *United States* v. *Ehrlichman et al.,* (D.D.C. Cr. No. 74-116).

[6] The reference "S.P.S.A." is to the Special Prosecutor's Sealed Appendix.

Special Prosecutor in this memorandum relied upon the finding by the grand jury that the President was an unindicted co-conspirator to establish the relevancy of many of the subpoenaed items and to overcome the presumptively privileged nature of the material as required by *Nixon* v. *Sirica*, 487 F. 2d 700 (D.C. Cir. 1973).

On May 13, 1974, the President, through his counsel, filed a special appearance and motion to expunge the grand jury finding on the ground that such a finding was beyond the authority of the grand jury. (J.A. 3a) The President also submitted a point-by-point response to the Special Prosecutor's analysis of the relevancy of the subpoenaed materials. (P.S.A. 1-7)[7] Following oral arguments heard *in camera* on May 13, 1974, the Special Prosecutor filed a further memorandum under seal on May 17, 1974.

C. *District Court's Opinion*

On May 20, 1974, the district court entered its opinion and order denying the President's motion to quash and his motion to expunge. The court further ordered the President to produce the subpoenaed materials together with an index and analysis of each item, and a copy of the tape of each portion of those conversations previously transcribed and published. (J.A. 3a)

Regarding its jurisdiction, the district court held that under *Nixon* v. *Sirica*, 487 F. 2d 700 (D.C. Cir. 1973), the court had the authority to rule on the scope and applicability of executive privilege and that its jurisdiction was not affected by the intra-executive nature of the dispute, for the President was required to consult with congressional leaders prior to attempting to abridge the independence and authority granted to the Special Prosecutor. In the absence of such action, the court found it had jurisdiction to entertain this suit. The district court did not, however, address itself to the question of whether the President had ever delegated to the Special Prosecutor his authority as Chief Executive to determine what materials would not be available to a federal prosecutor upon request, and in the absence of such a delegation on what basis the court had jurisdiction to intervene in the prosecutorial discretion of the President.

On the merits, the court ruled that the requirements of Rule 17(c) had been met and that the Special Prosecutor had demonstrated the "compelling need" required under *Nixon* v. *Sirica* to overcome the presumptively privileged nature of the

[7] The reference "P.S.A." is to the President's Sealed Appendix.

presidential communications. Therefore, the court ordered the President or any subordinate officer with custody or control of the materials to deliver the subpoenaed items to the court on April 18, 1974. The district court denied, without opinion, the President's motion to expunge the finding of the grand jury that the President was an unindicted co-conspirator. (J.A. 3a)

D. *Subsequent Events*

On May 24, 1974, the President filed a notice of appeal in the district court, docketed the appeal in the Court of Appeals for the District of Columbia Circuit (D.C. Cir. No. 74-1534), and filed therein under seal, a petition for a writ of mandamus (D.C. Cir. No. 74-1532). On May 24, 1974, the Special Prosecutor filed in this Court a petition for a writ of certiorari before judgment which was granted with expedited briefing schedule, by order of May 31, 1974.[8] The President, through his counsel, on June 6, 1974, filed under seal a cross-petition for a writ of certiorari before judgment which was granted by order of June 15, 1974.

On June 6, 1974, the President, through his counsel, also entered a special appearance and moved the district court to lift its protective order regarding the grand jury's naming of certain individuals as co-conspirators and to any additional extent deemed appropriate by the court on the grounds that public disclosure by the news media made the reaons for continuance of the protective order no longer compelling. By order of June 7, 1974, the district court removed its protective order. On June 10, 1974, the Special Prosecutor and counsel for the President jointly moved this Court to unseal those portions of the briefs and oral argument in the lower court which related to the action of the grand jury regarding the President. This Court denied that motion on June 15, 1974, except for the grand jury's immediate finding relating to the status of Richard M. Nixon as an unindicted co-conspirator.

The President's cross-petition for a writ of certiorari raised the issue of a grand jury's authority to charge an incumbent President as an unindicted co-conspirator in a criminal proceeding. In conjunction therewith, the President, through his counsel, on June 10, 1974, entered a special appearance and pursuant to Rule 6(e), Federal Rules of Criminal Procedures, moved the district court to disclose to the President any and all transcripts, tapes and recordings of Presidential conversations,

---

[8] Unfortunately, the accelerated schedule under which this case is being argued has not permitted the kind of time for the precise and detailed preparation of briefs that Counsel feel the historic nature of both the case and occasion requires.

grand jury minutes and exhibits, and any and all other matters occurring before the grand jury which pertained to the grand jury action in naming or authorizing the Special Prosecutor to identify Richard M. Nixon as an unindicted co-conspirator. It was requested that this material be transmitted as part of the record to this Court. This motion was denied by the district court on June 18, 1974.

On June 19, 1974, the President moved this Court to have the materials disclosed and transmitted to this Court in order that both the President and the Court would have the entire record upon which to present and decide this case.

INTRODUCTION

In a very real sense, every case that comes before this Court is unique; but few in the Nation's history have cut so close to the heart of the basic constitutional system in which our liberties are rooted.

Thus the stakes are enormously high, from a constitutional standpoint. At the same time, and making the Court's judgment more difficult, the case comes wrapped in the passions of a dramatic conflict which has dominated the Nation's headlines for more than a year. This is a conflict which now has involved all three branches of Government, and pits their constitutional rights and responsibilities one against another.

Just as the first allegiance of this Court is to the Constitution, the first responsibility of this Court must now be to decide the case before it in a way which preserves the balances that are central to the Constitution.

At its core, this is a case that turns on the separation of powers.

All other considerations are secondary, because preserving the integrity of the separation of powers is vital to the preservation of our Constitution as a living body of fundamental law. If the arguments of the Special Prosecutor were to prevail, the constitutional balance would be altered in ways that no one alive today could predict or measure.

The questions presented reach beyond the exigencies of the moment; beyond the needs of any particular criminal prosecution; beyond the interests of any particular Administration.

The extraordinary nature of this case stems partly from the issues directly presented, and partly from the coloration placed on those issues by the surrounding circumstances.

It would do justice neither to the parties nor to the issues if this were treated as just another case, or simply as an appeal from a discovery procedure in a criminal action against private individuals. It is, in fact, an extraordinary proceeding intrinsically related to the move now pending in the Congress to impeach the President of the United States.

In effect, court process is being used as a discovery tool for the impeachment proceedings—proceedings which the Constitution clearly assigns to the Congress, not to the courts. This is so because of the particular relationship which has evolved among the Special Prosecutor, the district court and the House Judiciary Committee, and because of the impact which any presidential action with regard to the subpoenas issued would inevitably have on the impeachment proceedings. As a result of the history of the so-called Watergate cases in the district court, the Special Prosecutor is well aware that the district court feels obligated to turn over to the Judiciary Committee any information that might bear on the pending congressional action. Thus the effect, whatever the intent, of the discovery procedures being pressed by the Special Prosecutor would be to produce evidence for the Congress that the Congress could not obtain by its own procedures.

As a result, there has been a fusion of two entirely different proceedings: one, the criminal proceeding involving various individual defendants, and the other the impeachment proceeding involving the President. The first lies in the courts; the second lies in the Congress. The Special Prosecutor strengthens this fusion by utilizing the unsubstantiated, unprecedented and clearly unconstitutional device of naming the President as an unindicted co-conspirator in the criminal cases, with the apparent purpose of strengthening his claim to recordings of presidential conversations as potential evidence in the criminal cases.

Two processes—each with an entirely different history, function and structure—have become intertwined, and the resulting confusion, both conceptual and procedural, is manifestly unfair to the President as an individual and harmful to the relationship between his office and the legislative branch.

To place the present events in perspective, it is useful to reflect on how this case would have been viewed in normal times. If there were no impeachment pending, and if the Special Prosecutor used the device of naming the President as an unindicted co-conspirator in order to obtain recordings of private presidential conversations, on which the President had interposed a claim of executive privilege, the Special Prosecutor's request would be given short shrift.

If this procedure were allowed to go forward, inevitably affecting the impeachment inquiry, it would represent an expansion of the Court's jurisdiction into the impeachment process that the Constitution assigns solely to the House of Representatives. Whatever the combination of circumstances producing it, the result would be clear: an expansion of the Court's jurisdiction into a realm that the Constitution clearly prohibits. It follows necessarily that the courts may not be used, either deliberately or inadvertently, as a back-door route to circumvent the constitutional procedures of an impeachment inquiry, and thus be intruded into the political thicket in this most solemn of political processes.

Anyone who has practiced before this Court is familiar with the observation of Justice Holmes that "(g)reat cases, like hard cases, make bad law." This is true if the pressures of the moment allow the courts to be swayed from their rigid adherence to great principles; if remedies for the perceived passing needs of the moment are allowed at the expense of those enduring constitutional doctrines that have preserved our system of ordered liberty through the ages. Of those doctrines, none is more fundamental to our government structure itself than the separation of powers—with all of its inherent tensions, with all of its necessary inability to satisfy all people or all institutions all of the time, and yet with the relentless and saving force that it generates toward essential compromise and accommodation over the longer term even if not always in the shorter term. Often a price has to be paid in the short term in order to preserve the principle of separation of powers, and thereby to preserve the basic constitutional balances, in the longer term. The preservation of this principle, the maintenance of these balances, are at stake in the case now before this Court.

SUMMARY OF ARGUMENT

The district court order of May 20, 1974, is an appealable order under 28 U.S.C. 1291, for unless review is granted now the President's claimed right will be irremediably lost. This Court also has jurisdiction to entertain and decide the petition for mandamus transmitted by the Court of Appeals under 28 U.S.C. 1651 because the lower court's decision exceeded that court's jurisdiction.

Under the doctrine of separation of powers, the Judiciary is without jurisdiction to intervene in the intra-branch dispute between the President and the Special Prosecutor. The duty to determine whether disclosure of confidential presidental communications is in the public interest has not been, and cannot be, delegated to the Special Prosecutor.

Under the standards set forth in *Baker* v. *Carr*, 369 U.S. 186 (1962), this intra-branch dispute raises a political question which the federal courts lack jurisdiction to decide. The district court does not have the power to substitute its judgment for that of the President on matters exclusively within the President's discretion.

Inherent in the executive power vested in the President under Article II of the Constitution is executive privilege, generally recognized as a derivative of the separation of powers doctrine. The powers traditionally asserted by the other branches support the validity of the claim of confidentiality invoked by the President.

Even if this Court were to determine that a presidential privilege is subject to judicial supervision, the lower court erred in refusing to quash the subpoena since the Special Prosecutor failed to demonstrate the "unique and compelling need" required by *Nixon* v. *Sirica*, 487 F.2d 700 (D.C. Cir. 1973), to overcome the presumptively valid claim of presidential privilege.

However, even before a determination can be made as to whether the President's assertion of executive privilege is overcome, the Special Prosecutor has the burden of proving that his subpoena meets the requirements of Rule 17(c), Federal Rules of Criminal Procedure. An analysis of the showing made by Special Prosecutor in the court below demonstrates that he failed to meet the case law criteria developed to prevent abuse of Rule 17(c). For this reason alone the district court erred in refusing to quash the subpoena.

The President is not subject to the criminal process whether that process is invoked directly or indirectly. The only constitutional recourse against a President is by impeachment and through the electoral process. The naming of the President as an unindicted co-conspirator by an official body is a nullity which both prejudices the ongoing impeachment proceeding and denies due process to the President. The grand jury's action does not constitute a *prima facie* showing of criminality and is without legal effect to overcome a presidential claim of executive privilege.

ARGUMENT

I. THIS COURT MAY REVIEW THE MAY 20, 1974, ORDER OF THE DISTRICT COURT BY EITHER ONE OF TWO ALTERNATIVE METHODS:

A. *By Appeal Pursuant to 28 U.S.C. 1291*

The district court order of May 20, 1974, denying the motion of Richard Nixon, President of the United States, to quash a subpoena *duces tecum* directed to him at the request of the Special Prosecutor is an appealable order under 28 U.S.C. 1291.[9]

28 U.S.C. 1291 provides:

The courts of appeals shall have jurisdiction of appeals from all final decisions of the district courts of the United States, the United States District Court for the District of the Canal Zone, the District Court of Guam, and the District Court of the Virgin Islands, except where a direct review may be had in the Supreme Court.

Under the criteria established by this Court for determining finality, it is clear that this order should be considered a "final order" and therefore subject to an immediate appeal. In *Cohen* v. *Beneficial Industrial Loan Corp.*, 337 U.S. 541 (1949), the Court held that a denial of defendant-corporation's motion to compel the plaintiff-shareholder to produce security for payment of reasonable expenses incurred by the corporation in defense of the shareholder's derivative suit, should the plaintiff's claim fail, constituted an appealable order under 28 U.S.C. 1291. Justice Jackson explained the rationale of the Court:

[T]his order of the District Court did not make any step toward final disposition of the merits of the case and will not be merged in final judgment. When that time comes, it will be too late effectively to review the present order, and the rights conferred by the statute, if it is applicable, will have been lost, probably irreparably. (337 U.S. at 546).

Following this decision, the Court in *Gillespie* v. *United States Steel Corp.*, 379 U.S. 148 (1964), reiterated its previous approach in this area and held appealable an order granting a

---

[9] Although this particular action springs from a criminal proceeding, it is a collateral matter of sufficient independence to warrant civil treatment under 28 U.S.C. 1291 and applicability of the reasoning of *Cohen* v. *Beneficial Loan Corp.*, 337 U.S. 541 (1949), a civil case, and its progeny. See *Carroll* v. *United States*, 354 U.S. 394, 403, (1957). See also *United States* v. *Ryan*, 402 U.S. 530, 532 (1971).

motion to strike a particular cause of action (a second cause of action survived). In discussing appealability, Justice Black emphasized that "this Court has held that the requirement of finality is to be given a 'practical rather than a technical construction.'" 379 U.S. at 152. He further noted that "in deciding the question of finality the most important competing considerations are 'the inconvenience and costs of piecemeal review on the one hand and the danger of denying justice by delay on the other.'" 379 U.S. at 152-153.

In light of the foregoing judicial precedent, this Court, on May 28, 1974, decided *Eisen* v. *Carlisle & Jacquelin*,—U.S.—(42 U.S.L.W. 4804, May 28, 1974). In *Eisen*, the plaintiff filed a class action on behalf of himself and all other odd-lot traders on the New York Stock Exchange charging various brokerage firms with numerous breaches of federal antitrust and securities laws. After a myriad of battles over the class action aspect, the district court finally held the suit maintainable as such an action. The brokerage firms appealed to the United States Court of Appeals for the Second Circuit pursuant to 28 U.S.C. 1291, over the plaintiff's vigorous objection of non-appealability. The Court of Appeals, for reasons irrelevant to this case, dismissed the suit as a class action. On further review, this Court met the issue of appealability head-on.

This Court, in concluding that the Court of Appeals had possessed jurisdiction under 28 U.S.C. 1291, relied upon *Cohen* v. *Beneficial Loan Corp.*, 337 U.S. 541 (1949). Justice Powell, speaking for the Court, called attention to two dispositive elements: (1) The order of the district court had *conclusively* determined, by rejection, the claim of the brokerage firms on the class action issue, and (2) That order was "a final disposition of a claim of right which is not an ingredient of the cause of action and does not require consideration with it," i.e. "it concerned a collateral matter that could not be reviewed effectively on appeal from the final judgment." 42 U.S.L.W. at 4808-4809.

Applying these tests to the facts of this particular case is not difficult; neither is the result. The district court's order rejected the President's position, both on jurisdictional grounds and on the merits, and ordered the production of all subpoenaed items for an *in camera* inspection.[10] Therefore unless review is granted at this stage of the proceeding, the President's claimed right will be irremediably lost[11] because, as a non-party to the primary

---

[10] *United States* v. *Mitchell* Cr. No. 74-110 (D.D.C. May 20, 1974) at pp. 3-7.

[11] In *North Dakota State Board of Pharmacy* v. *Snyder's Drug Stores, Inc.*, 414 U.S. 156, 159, 162 (1973), Justice Douglas, speaking for a unanimous Court, held a

suit, he will not be able to appeal from the criminal judgment.[12] Moreover, if the materials requested are absolutely privileged, the irreparable nature of the injury resulting from disclosure cannot be questioned.

In a closely analogous case also involving the appealability of a ruling by a district court on a motion to quash a subpoena *duces tecum*, the Court of Appeals for the Fifth Circuit in *Caswell* v. *Manhattan Fire and Marine Insurance Co.*, 399 F. 2d 417, 422 (5th Cir. 1968), stated the following:

> Manhattan contends we are without jurisdiction to review this question. We disagree. Although an order granting or denying a motion to quash a subpoena is normally considered interlocutory and not subject to review by immediate appeal, such an order, like other discovery orders, may be assigned as error on appeal from a final judgment on the merits. See "Developments in the Law—Discovery," 74 Harv. L. Rev. 940, 992 (1961). A nonparty may appeal an order denying his motion to quash when under the circumstances he would be otherwise denied an effective mode of review. *Carter Products, Inc.* v. *Eversharp, Inc.*, 360 F. 2d 868 (7th Cir. 1966); *Covey Oil Co.* v. *Continental Oil Co.*, 340 F. 2d 993 (10th Cir.), cert. *denied*, 380 U.S. 964, 85 S. Ct. 1110, 14 L. Ed. 2d 155 (1965). Compare *Robinson* v. *Bankers Life & Cas. Co.*, 226 F. 2d 834 (6th Cir. 1965). *An order requiring a nonparty to produce documents often will be final insofar as the nonparty is concerned.* Moreover in many cases substantial prejudice may result from denying immediate appellate review. 399 F 2d at 422 (emphasis added).

For the above reasons, the same conclusion is mandated here. More recently, the Court of Appeals for the District of Columbia Circuit in *Nixon* v. *Sirica*, 487 F. 2d 700 (D.C. Cir. 1973), held judgment of the Supreme Court of North Dakota to be "final" even though that court remanded the case to a state administrative board for further hearings; to do otherwise would have deprived the petitioner of a constitutional issue which would have been lost. Although decided under 28 U.S.C. 1254, dealing with review of state judgments, the decision and language reflected the traditional requirements of 28 U.S.C. 1291, set out in *Cohen, supra.* See *United States* v. *Ryan*, 402 U.S. 530, 532 (1971).

[12] In addition, the observation by the court in *Nixon* v. *Sirica*, 487 F. 2d 700, 721 n. 100 (D.C. Cir. 1973) is instructive: since the subpoenaed recordings will already have been submitted to the District Court, the opportunity to test the court's ruling in contempt proceedings would be foreclosed. Any ruling adverse to the Special Prosecutor would clearly be a pretrial "decision or order . . . suppressing or excluding evidence . . . in a criminal proceeding. . . ." Thus the District Court's rulings on particularized claims would be appealable by the President. as final judgments under 28 U.S.C. 1291 (1970), and by the Special Prosecutor under 18 U.S.C. 3731 (1970). See also the Order of June 18, 1974), in *Nixon* v. *Sirica* and *Jaworski,* (D.C. Cir. No. 74-1618).

that the district court's denial of the President's motion to quash a grand jury subpoena was reviewable under the All Writs Act, although the court did not discard "direct appeal as an alternative basis for review in the particular situation before us." 487 F. 2d at 707 n. 21. In addition, the court made particular reference to the unusual circumstances arising in an action involving the President, which further emphasize the critical need for appellate review at this stage of the proceeding:

> The final-order doctrine, as a normal prerequisite to a federal appeal, is not a barrier where it operates to leave the suitor "powerless to avert the mischief of the order." *Perlman* v. *United States*, 247 U.S. 7, 13, 38, S. Ct. 417, 419, 62 L. Ed. 950 (1918). In the case of the President, contempt of a judicial order—even for the purpose of enabling a constitutional test of the order—would be a course unseemly at best. (487 F. 2d at 707 n. 21).

Although there is, as a general rule, a need to avoid piecemeal litigation which may unduly hamper the efficient administration of the courts, *Alexander* v. *United States*, 201 U.S. 117 (1906), this practical consideration has always given way when the rights of an individual will be irreparably affected by the delay. *Gillespie* v. *United States Steel Corp.*, 379 U.S. 148, 152-153 (1964).

Under the circumstances presented, the district court's denial of the President's motion to quash is a final order, and is therefore appealable under 28 U.S.C. 1291.

B. *By Entertaining and Deciding a Petition for Writ of Mandamus Transmitted by a Court of Appeals*

We also submit that this Court has jurisdiction to entertain and decide the petition for mandamus transmitted by the court of appeals to this Court under 28 U.S.C. 1651. Pursuant to this Court's order granting the Special Prosecutor's petition for certiorari and the President's cross-petition for certiorari, the entire record before the court of appeals has been transmitted to this Court under the mandate of Rule 25 of the Rules of the Supreme Court of the United States.

The All Writs Statute of the Judicial Code of 1948, 28 U.S.C. 1651, provides that:

> (a) The Supreme Court and all courts established by Act of Congress may issue all writs necessary or appropriate in aid of their respective jurisdiction and agreeable to the usages and principles of law.

(b) An alternative writ or *rule nisi* may be issued by a justice or judge of a court which has jurisdiction.

It is appropriate in the present case that this Court entertain and decide the petition for mandamus, because the order entered by the trial court demanding *in camera* inspection of the tape recordings is clearly erroneous and beyond that court's jurisdiction in that it purports to intervene in a wholly intra-executive dispute. In addition, this Court's discretion to issue this extraordinary writ should be exercised at this stage of the proceedings because judicial action which would necessitate presidential involvement in a criminal contempt proceeding would be action totally insensitive to the role of the Office of the Presidency in our framework of government, without judicial benefits to be gained.

This Court in *LaBuy* v. *Howes Leather Co.*, 352 U.S. 249, 259-260 (1957), recognized that there are instances when a judgment that is not final and appealable under 28 U.S.C. 1291 must be subject to further review so as not to result in an injustice, and Congress via 21 U.S.C. 1651 has provided an effective remedy. In determining what is "necessary or appropriate" within the scope of 21 U.S.C. 1651, it is clear that this section operates in aid of this Court's appellate jurisdiction, for in *Ex parte Peru*, 318 U.S. 578 (1943), this Court considered this question in relationship to the Judiciary Act of 1925, the predecessor of this Act, and concluded that:

> The jurisdiction of this Court to issue common law writs in aid of its appellate jurisdiction has been consistently sustained. The historic use of writs of prohibition and mandamus directed by an appellate to an inferior court has been to exert the revisory appellate power over the inferior court. The writs thus afford an expeditious and effective means of confining the inferior court to a lawful exercise of its prescribed jurisdiction, or of compelling it to exercise its authority when it is its duty to do so. Such has been the office of the writs when directed by this Court to district courts, both before the Judiciary Act of 1925 and since. (318 U.S. at 582-583).

This Court also stated that:

> The jurisdiction of this Court to issue such [common law writs], like its jurisdiction to grant certiorari, is discretionary. The definite aim of the 1925 Act was to enlarge, not to destroy, the Court's discretionary jurisdiction. That aim can hardly give rise to an inference of an unexpressed purpose to amend or repeal the statutes of the United States conferring jurisdiction on the Court to issue the writs, or an inference

that such would have been the purpose had repeal been proposed. The exercise of that jurisdiction has placed no undue burden on this Court. (318 U.S. at 585).

Once having the power to grant this writ, we submit this is a most appropriate instance to exercise that power, for the above reasons. In its recent statement this Court reviewed many of the instances where the writ of mandamus has been used; however, none are as timely and imperative as the present case. In *Will* v. *United States*, 389 U.S. 90 (1967), Chief Justice Warren, speaking for the Court, stated:

> The peremptory writ of mandamus has traditionally been used in the federal courts only 'to confine an inferior court to a lawful exercise of its prescribed jurisdiction or to compel it to exercise its authority when it is its duty to do so.' *Roche* v. *Evaporated Milk Assn.*, 319 U.S. 21, 26 (1943). While the courts have never confined themselves to an arbitrary and technical definition of 'jurisdiction,' it is clear that only exceptional circumstances amounting to a judicial 'usurpation of power' will justify the invocation of this extraordinary remedy, *DeBeers Consol. Mines, Ltd.* v. *United States*, 325 U.S. 212, 217 (1945). Thus, the writ has been involved where unwarranted judicial action threatened 'to embarrass the execution arm of the Government in conducting foreign relations,' *Ex parte Peru*, 318 U.S. 578, 588 (1943), where it was the only means of forestalling intrusion by the federal judiciary on a delicate area of federal-state relations, *Maryland* v. *Soper*, 270 U.S. 9 (1926), where it was necessary to confine a lower court to the terms of an appellate tribunal's mandate, *United States* v. *United States Dist. Court*, 344 U.S. 258 (1948), and where a district judge displayed a persistent disregard of the Rules of Civil Procedure promulgated by this Court, *LaBuy* v. *Howes Leather Co.*, 352 U.S. 249 (1957); see *McCullough* v. *Cosgrave*, 309 U.S. 634 (1940); *Los Angeles Brush Mfg. Corp.* v. *James*, 272 U.S. 701, 706, 707 (1927) (dictum).
> (389 U.S. at 95).

Thus, we submit that it is an appropriate exercise of jurisdiction under 28 U.S.C. 1651 for this Court to entertain a writ of mandamus transmitted to it by a Court of Appeals.

II. THE COURT LACKS JURISDICTION OVER AN INTERNAL DISPUTE OF A CO-EQUAL BRANCH[13]

Under the firmly established doctrine of separation of powers, the Judiciary is without jurisdiction to intervene in the solely intra-executive dispute presented here. This entire dispute, between two entities within the executive branch of the government, concerns the prosecutorial discretion vested in the executive branch and involves only the issue of what executive materials should be available to aid in a criminal prosecution. In this respect, this case differs fundamentally from *Nixon* v. *Sirica* 487 F.2d 700 D.C. (Cir. 1973), which involved a grand jury subpoena directed to the President and as such represented an inter-branch dispute.

The ultimate authority over all executive branch decisions is, under Article II of the Constitution, vested exclusively in the President of the United States. The President has neither waived nor delegated to the Special Prosecutor his duty to determine what confidential presidential documents shall be made available to another executive officer. Therefore in the absence of a delegation of this duty, the President, as the chief executive officer, and not the Special Prosecutor or the Judiciary, is and remains the final authority as to what presidential material may be utilized in the furtherance of any prosecution. Because the President has not delegated this duty and responsibility to the Special Prosecutor, it is unnecessary for this Court to even consider whether such a delegation of responsibility is constitutionally permissible. *United States* v. *Burr*, 25 F. Cas 187, 192 No. 14694 (C.C.D. Va. 1807).[14] See also *Williams* v. *United States*, 1 How. (14 U.S.) 290, 297 (1843); *Runkle* v.

---

[13] The Court should be advised that a difference of opinion exists between the Special Prosecutor and Special Counsel to the President as to the propriety of presenting this argument. The Special Prosecutor contends that as an inducement to his accepting his position, he was provided free access to the courts to resolve any dispute with the President involving the claim of executive privilege. Special Counsel to the President has not been able to confirm that the President at any time agreed to forego any legal remedies available to him in opposing the efforts of the Special Prosecutor to obtain materials over which the President claimed executive privilege. Be that as it may, the jurisdiction of the court cannot be stipulated by the parties and counsel have a duty to call the attention of the court to the possible lack of jurisdiction. See discussion *infra* at pp. 43-44. See also the excellent discussion of this jurisdictional question published by Professor Bickel at an earlier stage of the Special Prosecutor's efforts to obtain presidential tape recordings. *The Tapes, Cox, Nixon*, The New Republic (September 29, 1973).

[14] In *Burr*, the Court specifically stated:

"In this case, however, the President has assigned no reason whatever for withholding the paper called for. The propriety of withholding it must be decided by himself, not by another for him." (25 F. Cas. at 192.)

United States, 122 U.S. 543, 557 (1887); *United States* v. *Fletcher*, 148 U.S. 84, 88 (1893); *French* v. *Weeks*, 259 U.S. 326, 334 (1922); 38 Op. Att'y. Gen. 457 (1936). Accordingly, this entire dispute is intra-executive in nature and beyond the jurisdiction of this Court.[15]

At the outset, we wish to make clear to the Court that we do not question the jurisdiction of the Court to resolve any disagreement or conflict between the various independent but co-equal branches of the government, *Marbury* v. *Madison*, 1 Cranch (5 U.S.) 137 (1803). Nor do we challenge the jurisdiction of the court to negate an act performed by one branch in excess of its constitutionally delegated authority. *Youngstown Sheet & Tube Co.* v. *Sawyer*, 343 U.S. 579 (1952). However, under the clearly enunciated doctrine of separation of powers adopted by the Framers of the Constitution, we do challenge the authority of the court or any branch of the government to intervene in a solely intra-branch dispute, even at the request of a disputant, whether an individual member of that branch, an established committee, or a recognized department. Certainly, an intra-branch dispute, regardless of the context in which it arises, is within the exclusive jurisdiction of that body alone and can properly be resolved, if necessary, only by the constitutionally designated official or body vested with the ultimate responsibility for that branch of government.

The concept of separation of government powers is deeply rooted in the history of political theory, finding its early expression in the works of Aristotle[16] who recognized the fundamental distinction between the legislative, executive and judicial functions.[17]

Although subsequently elaborated upon by many historians and scholars, the principle of separation of the branches of government was most familiar to colonial America in the writings of Locke[18] and Montesquieu.[19]

In the most influential political work of its day, Montesquieu in *The Spirit of Laws* wrote:

[15] We do not challenge the jurisdiction to a court to entertain a properly documented request by a defendent for exculpatory materials. *Brady* v. *Maryland*, 373 U.S. 83 (1963).

[16] *Aristotle's Politics*, 197-198 (B. Jowett transl. 1943).

[17] The early history of the doctrine of separation, as set forth above, is from Forkosch, *Separation of Powers* 41 U. Colo. L. Rev. 529 (1969).

[18] J. Locke, *An Essay Concerning the True Original Extent and End of Civil Government* (J. W. Gough, ed.1947).

[19] Montesquieu, *The Spirit of Laws* (38 Great Books of the Western World, 1900).

In every government there are three sorts of power: the legislative, the executive * * * the judiciary * * * When the legislative and executive powers are united in the same person, or in the same body of magistrates, there can be no liberty; * * * Again, there is no liberty if the judicial power be not separated from the legislative and executive. Were it joined with the legislative, the life and liberty of the subject would be exposed to arbitrary control; for the judge would then be legislator. Were it joined to the executive power, the judge might behave with violence and oppression. There would be an end of everything were the same men or the same body, whether of nobles or of the people to exercise all three powers, that of enacting laws, that of executing the public resolutions, and of trying the causes of individuals.[20]

It was this philosophy that influenced the Framers of the Constitution as they began their task of developing a form of government that would survive change and crisis over the long future.[21]

Even prior to the opening days of the Constitutional Convention, the doctrine of separation had been accepted by the states. This is exemplified by the Constitution of the State of Massachusetts, adopted in 1780, which provided:

Article XXX: In the government of this commonwealth, the legislative department shall never exercise the executive and judicial powers, or either of them; the executive shall never exercise the legislative and judicial powers or either of them; the judicial shall never exercise the legislative and executive powers or either of them; to the end it may be a government of laws and not of men.[22]

At the Constitutional Convention, the theory of separation was not seriously questioned. The tripartite form of government introduced by the Virginia proposal[23] was adopted in principle by the Convention[24] and referred to the Committee for Detail

---

[20] *Id.* Bk.XI, ch. 6 at 70.

[21] *The Federalist* No. 47 (J. Madison).

[22] At the present time 40 state constitutions expressly provide for a separation of powers and the remaining states have provisions substantially identical to the United States Constitution, W. Dodd, *State Government,* 58 (2d ed. 1928); See also: Constitutions of Hawaii (1959) and Alaska (1959).

[23] 1 Farrand, *Records of the Federal Convention of 1787,* 20-21 (rev. ed. 1966); [hereinafter cited as *Farrand*].

[24] 1 *Farrand* 30-31.

for implementation.[25] As described by the notes of James Wilson, the Committee set forth the tripartite principle and specifically stated that the legislative power of the United States shall be vested in Congress, the executive power in a single person, and the judicial power in a Supreme Court.[26] Following the submission of the Committee report to the full Convention, the structure and organization of the three branches were extensively debated but not the principle of separation itself. The separation doctrine as submitted by the Committee on Detail emerged from the debates intact and remained substantially unchanged by the Committee on Style.[27]

Although it is clear that a system of checks and balances was incorporated into the structure to avoid a domination or usurpation of power by any one branch, it was equally clear that each branch would be free to carry on its own delegated functions free from interference by a coordinate branch. James Madison eloquently stated the sentiment, which pervaded the Convention: "If it be essential to the preservation of the liberty that the Legislative, Executive and Judiciary powers be separate, it is essential to the maintenance of the separation, that they should be independent of each other."[28] In further emphasizing this concept of separation and independence, James Wilson wrote that the independence of each department requires that its proceedings "shall be free from the remotest influence, direct or indirect of either of the other two."[29]

The doctrine of separation of powers, as a vital and necessary element of our democratic form of government, has long been judicially recognized. *United States* v. *Klein*, 13 Wall (80 U.S.) 128 (1872). As early as 1879, this Court stressed the integrity and independence of each branch of the government, when it stated: "One branch of the government cannot encroach on the domain of another without danger." The safety of our institutions depends in no small degree on a strict observance of this salutary rule." *Sinking Fund Cases*, 99 U.S. 700, 718 (1879). Since that time, the Court has continually reaffirmed this doctrine in an unbroken line of decisions. In *O'Donoghue* v. *United States*, 289 U.S. 516 (1933) Justice Sutherland speaking for the Court stated:

[25] 2 *Farrand* 129.

[26] 2 *Farrand* 152, 171, 172.

[27] 2 *Farrand* 590, 597, 600.

[28] 2 *Farrand* 34.

[29] Andrews, 1 *The Works of James Wilson*, 367 (1896).

If it be important thus to separate the several departments of government and restrict them to the exercise of their appointed powers, it follows, as a logical corollary, equally important, that each department should be kept completely independent of the others—independent not in the sense that they shall not co-operate to the common end of carrying into effect the purposes of the Constitution, but in the sense that the acts of each shall never be controlled by, or subjected, directly, or indirectly, to, the coercive influence of either of the other departments. (289 U.S. at 530).

Again two years later, the Court added:

The fundamental necessity of maintaining each of the three general departments of government, entirely free from the control or coercive influence, direct or indirect, of either of the others, has often been stressed and is hardly open to serious question. So much is implied in the very fact of the separation of the powers of these departments by the Constitution; and in the rule which recognizes their essential co-equality. *Humphrey's Executor* v. *United States,* 295 U.S. 602, 629-630 (1935) (emphasis added). See also: *Monaco* v. *Mississippi,* 292 U.S. 313 (1934); *National Ins. Co.* v. *Tidewater Co.,* 337 U.S. 582 (1949); *Marshall* v. *Gordon,* 243 U.S. 521 (1917).

It is this constitutional principle which establishes the most fundamental jurisdictional limitation on each of the three branches and prohibits each from intervening in the discretionary powers constitutionally vested in another coordinate branch.

In specifically referring to the jurisdiction of the Judiciary, Chief Justice Warren stated in *Flast* v. *Cohen,* 392 U.S. 83 (1968),

the jurisdiction of federal courts is defined and limited by Article III of the Constitution . . . [I]n part [that article] defines the role assigned to the judiciary in a tripartite allocation of power to assure that the federal courts will not intrude into areas committed to the other branches of the government. (392 U.S. at 94-95).

Stated more simply by Justice Story, neither of the departments in reference to each other "ought to possess directly or indirectly an overwhelming influence in the administration of their respective powers."[30]

[30] *The Federalist* No. 48 (J. Madison) cited in 1 Story, *The Constitution* 530 (4th ed).

This concept was elaborated by the Court in *Springer* v. *Philippine Islands*, 277 U.S. 189 (1927):

> Some of our state constitutions expressly provide in one form or another that the legislative, executive and judicial powers of the government shall be forever separate and distinct from each other. Other constitutions, including that of the United States, do not contain such an express provision. But it is implicit in all, as a conclusion logically following from the separation of the several departments. See *Kilbourn* v. *Thompson*, 103 U.S. 168, 190-191 and this separation and the consequent exclusive character of the powers conferred upon each of the *three departments is basic and vital—not merely a matter of government mechanism* . . .
>
> It may be stated then, as a general rule inherent in the American constitutional system, that, unless otherwise explicitly provided or incidental to the powers conferred, the legislature cannot exercise either executive or judicial power; the executive cannot exercise either legislative or judicial power; the judiciary cannot exercise either executive or legislative power. The existence in the various constitutions of occasional provisions expressly giving to one of the departments powers which by their nature or otherwise would fall within the general scope of the authority of another department emphasizes, rather than casts doubts upon, *the generally inviolate character of this basic rule.* 277 U.S. at 201-202 (emphasis added).

It is therefore evident that the district court had no jurisdiction to settle or intervene in an intra-executive disagreement relating to the evidentiary material to be made available from one executive department to another. The settlement of such a dispute in all circumstances is within the exclusive jurisdiction of the chief executive officer, for as this Court stated in *Humphrey's Executor* v. *United States*, 295 U.S. 602 (1935):

> So much is implied in the very fact of the separation of powers of these departments by the Constitution, and in the rule which recognizes the essential co-equality. The sound application of the principle that makes one master in his own house precludes him from imposing his control in the house of another who is master there. (295 U.S. at 629-630).

The district court's lack of jurisdiction here is illustrated by a simple analogy. If two congressional committees simultaneously claim jurisdiction over a particular bill, it is unlikely that anyone would question that their sole recourse is an appeal to the congressional committee designated to resolve such disputes, or in its absence, to the Speaker of the House. It is inconceivable that any court would conclude that it had jurisdiction to resolve the matter, even if one or both of the disputants were to appeal to the Judiciary.

Similarly, within the executive branch, if an Assistant United States Attorney seeking information to bolster his case against an individual, were denied access to executive documents by either the Attorney General or the President, he could not properly seek assistance from the Judiciary, for a court would have no jurisdiction in the matter. The same result is mandated here, for as this Court clearly stated in *Kilbourn* v. *Thompson*, 103 U.S. 168, 190 (1880):

> It is also essential to the successful working of this system that the persons entrusted with power in any of these branches shall not be permitted to encroach upon the powers confided to the others, but that each shall by the law of its creation be limited to the exercise of the powers appropriate to its own department and no other.

In attempting to negate this fundamental jurisdictional limitation, the Special Prosecutor relies heavily upon this Court's decision in *United States* v. *Interstate Commerce Commission*, 337 U.S. 426 (1949) for the proposition that the Judiciary does have jurisdiction to intervene in this dispute. However, that case is plainly inapplicable for it did not involve an intra-branch dispute. On the contrary, there the Department of Justice, on behalf of the executive branch, brought suit against various independent railroads, and on appeal the Commission, a creation of the legislative branch, was joined as a party defendant. Under those circumstances, this Court had jurisdiction to resolve the dispute, for the ICC has been firmly recognized as an administrative body created by Congress to carry into effect its legislative policies and, like the Federal Trade Commission, "cannot in any proper sense be characterized as an arm or eye of the executive. Its duties are performed without executive leave and, in the contemplation of the statute, must be free from executive control." *Humphrey's Executor* v. *United States*, 295 U.S. 602, 628 (1935). Consequently, that dispute was plainly inter-branch in nature, and therefore within the Court's jurisdiction to resolve controversies arising among the various branches. That case does not, however, in any way support the proposition that the court has jurisdiction to entertain a solely intra-executive dispute for the Office of Special Prosecutor, unlike the Commission, was created by the executive branch, within the executive branch, and performs solely executive functions.

In this instance, there can be no question that under the doctrine of separation of powers, the Court lacks jurisdiction to intervene in an intra-executive dispute concerning the availability and use of executive documents to assist in the prosecution of any individual charged with criminal conduct. As the Judiciary has long recognized, under Article II, Section 3 of the Constitution, it is the exclusive prerogative of the executive branch, not the Judiciary, to determine whom to prosecute, on what charges, and with what evidence or information. *Confiscation Cases* 7 Wall (74 U.S.) 454 (1869); *United States* v. *Cox 342 F. 2d 167 (5th Cir.)*, cert. denied, 381 U.S. 935 (1965); *Smith* v. *United States*, 375 F. 2d 243, 247 (5th Cir. 1967); *District of Columbia* v. *Buckley*, 128 F. 2d 17 (1942); *Pugach* v. *Klein*, 193 F. Supp. 630 (S.D.N.Y. 1961); and *In Re Grand Jury January 1969*, 315 F. Supp. 662 (D. Md. 1970). Under the Constitution, the President, as the highest executive officer, was expressly delegated all prosecutorial authority when he alone was vested with the responsibility "to take care that the laws be faitfhfully executed." In *Marbury* v. *Madison*, 1 Cranch (5 U.S.) 137, 164-166 (1803), Chief Justice Marshall expressed the views of the Court as to its jurisdiction to intervene in the authority constitutionally delegated to the President.

By the Constitution of the United States, the President is invested with certain important political powers, in the exercise of which he is to use his own discretion, and is accountable only to his country in his political character and to his own conscience. To aid him in the performance of these duties, he is authorized to appoint certain officers, who act by his authority and in conformity with his orders.

In such cases, their acts are his acts; and whatever opinion may be entertained of the manner in which executive discretion may be used, still there exists, and can exist, no power to control that discretion. *The subjects are political: they respect the nation, not individual rights, and being instrusted to the executive, the decision of the executive is conclusive.* (1 Cranch at 165-166) (emphasis added).

Thus, the courts have uniformly recognized that under the Constitution, the Judiciary was given no role in determining any matters within the executive's prosecutorial discretion. As demonstrated in *United States* v. *Cox*, 342 F. 2d 167 (5th Cir.) *cert. denied*, 381 U.S. 935 (1965), even when the executive branch determines, in the face of a grand jury finding of probable cause, that it will not prosecute a particular individual, the courts lack jurisdiction to intervene. In discussing the "absolute and exclusive discretion" of the executive branch in such matters, Judge Wisdom of the United States Court of Appeals for the Fifth Circuit stated in *United States* v. *Cox:*

[W]hen, within the context of law-enforcement, national policy is involved, because of national security, conduct of foreign policy, or a conflict between two branches of government, the appropriate branch to decide the matter is the executive branch. The executive is charged with carrying out national policy on law-enforcement and, generally speaking, is informed on more levels than the more specialized judicial and legislative branches. In such a situation, a decision not to prosecute is analogous to the exercise of executive privilege. The executive's absolute and exclusive discretion to prosecute may be rationalized as an illustration of the doctrine of separation of powers, but it would have evolved without the doctrine and exists in countries that do not purport to accept this doc doctrine (concurring opinion). (342 F. 2d at 193).

A fortiori, if it is solely an executive decision to prosecute, it follows that the courts are equally powerless to determine what material within the executive branch must be used in the case. Such a decision is exclusively within the power delegated by the Constitution to the Chief Executive; and the right of the Chief Executive to determine what presidential material shall or shall not be used in the furtherance of this or any prosecution has not been delegated to the Special Prosecutor.

If the President were interfering with a power that had been delegated to the Special Prosecutor, the conclusion of the district court that the President must, under 38 Fed. Reg. 30,738, first consult congressional leaders before taking such action might have been correct. However, it is absolutely clear from the regulation governing the authority of the Special Prosecutor, that the President has not delegated to the Special Prosecutor or any subordinate official, his duty to determine the privileged nature and use of executive material. Therefore, the district court plainly erred in asserting that it had jurisdiction to intervene in this suit on the ground that the President was abridging the independence of the Special Prosecutor over matters that were delegated to him. Moreover, it is unnecessary for this Court to speculate on the jurisdictional basis for this suit if the President, had, in fact, delegated his right and responsibilities concerning executive materials to the Special Prosecutor.

On November 27, 1973, Acting Attorney General Bork recreated the Office of Special Prosecutor and delegated to it his authority over all Watergate-related matters. The terms of this delegation are set forth in 38 Fed. Reg. 30,738 (November 7, 1973) and the letter of Acting Attorney General Bork to Mr. Leon Jaworski, dated November 21, 1973. In accordance with that agreement, the President has not in the past nor does he here challenge those powers that were given to the Special Prosecutor in Watergate-related matters, including the right to conduct grand jury and other investigations, review documentary evidence available, and determine within the confines of the Constitution whom to prosecute and on what charges. Moreover, all decisions relating to the procedural aspects of prosecution including the right to request immunity for any witness are within the scope of his authority. In these and other areas delegated to him, the Special Prosecutor has had and continues to have complete independence.

However, as the agreement clearly shows on its face, the President has neither waived nor delegated to the Special Prosecutor the President's duty to claim privilege as to all materials, confidential in nature, which fall within the President's inherent authority to refuse to disclose to any executive officer. Nor did Acting Attorney General Bork attempt to delegate such authority to the Special Prosecutor.[31] On the contrary, the authority granted to the Special Prosecutor by then Acting Attorney General Bork in this regard was specifically limited to at most: "determin[ing] whether or not to contest the assertion of executive privilege or any other testimonial privilege." 38 Fed. Reg. 30,739 (1973).

From this provision, it is abundantly clear that the President has not waived or delegated to the Special Prosecutor his duty to determine within his discretion what executive materials were privileged. Since this decision was retained by the President and falls within the normal scope of his prosecutorial discretion over all criminal cases, the courts are powerless to intervene, even at the request of the Special Prosecutor.

Moreover, the court's fundamental lack of jurisdiction to intervene in the President's prosecutorial discretion or any other executive decision within the realm of his constitutionally

---

[31] It should be noted that had Acting Attorney General Bork attempted to delegate this right to the Special Prosecutor such a grant of authority would have been void, for the Attorney General himself has never had authority to override or challenge a decision by the Chief Executive and therefore could not delegate such authority to another.

delegated authority, was not altered by the arrangement between Acting Attorney General Bork and Mr. Jaworski allowing the Special Prosecutor to determine what testimonial privileges to challenge. It is an elementary rule of jurisdiction, that where the courts constitutionally lack jurisdiction to intervene in a decision, as they do in all decisions concerning prosecutorial discretion, such jurisdiction can neither be waived nor conferred by an agreement between the parties. *Mitchell* v. *Maurer*, 293 U.S. 237, 244 (1934); *Industrial Addition Association* v. *I.R.S.*, 323 U.S. 310 (1945). Accordingly, even a decision by Mr. Jaworski that he wishes to contest a claim of privilege, either executive or testimonial, will not confer jurisdiction on the court.

Therefore, because the President in all criminal proceedings has the right to determine what confidential or sensitive material should not be used to assist a federal prosecutor, as this right was not delegated to the Special Prosecutor, the court remains without jurisdiction to intervene in his prosecutorial decision by the Chief Executive.

III. THIS INTRA-BRANCH DISPUTE DOES NOT PRESENT A JUSTICIABLE CASE OR CONTROVERSY WITHIN THE MEANING OF ARTICLE III, SEC. 2 OF THE CONSTITUTION

We submit that the prior argument is dispositive of those questions presented to this Court by the Special Prosecutor and mandates that the district court order be vacated. However, should the Court determine that it does have jurisdiction to entertain this suit, it should of its own authority decline to do so, for a resolution of the fundamental issue as to whether it best serves the public interest to disclose presidential material, if not absolutely privileged, would require the Court to resolve a political question.

Underlying the doctrine of political question, is the fundamental notion that many controversies brought before the Court are best resolved by another branch of the government which possesses the necessary familiarity and expertise. This dispute raises a question of justiciability because it involves a political dispute solely between two officials of the executive branch—the President and a lesser official, the Special Prosecutor. Under Article III, Section 2 of the Constitution, the judicial branch does not have the constitutional power to resolve such a political question.

Courts have struggled to establish criteria that would enable them to identify and uniformly deal with political questions.

Such criteria have been elusive. *Marbury* v. *Madison*, 1 Cranch (5 U.S.) 137, 164—166 (1803); *Coleman* v. *Miller*, 307 U.S. 433, 454—455 (1939);*Poe* v. *Ullman*, 367 U.S. 497, 508 (1961); and *Flast* v. *Cohen*, 392 U.S. 83 (1968).

It was not until *Baker* v. *Carr*, 369 U.S. 186 (1962), however, that the Court finally succeeded in isolating and articulating a set of criteria for identifying an issue that presents a political question. The Court said:

> Prominent on the surface of any case held to involve a political question is found a textually demonstrable constitutional commitment of the issue to a coordinate political department; or a lack of judicially discoverable and manageable standards for resolving it; or the impossibility of deciding without an initial policy determination of a kind clearly for non-judicial discretion; or the impossibility of a court's undertaking independent resolution without expressing lack of the respect due coordinate branches of government; or an unusual need for unquestioning adherence to a political decision already made; or the potentiality of embarrassment from multifarious pronouncements by various departments on one question. (369 U.S. at 217).

It is very clear that the Special Prosecutor's request that the district court overrule the legitimate invocation of executive privilege posed a nonjusticiable political question that meets the criteria established in *Baker*. There are no judicially discoverable standards or manageable criteria by which the courts could resolve this political question. The court below was asked to make an initial policy determination that the President has improperly or mistakenly invoked executive privilege against the Special Prosecutor. Such a determination by the lower court is constitutionally impermissible and violates the basic tenets of the separation of powers. Moreover, it is a determination beyond judicial abilities since the Court simply cannot substitute its judgment for that of the President. *Baker* is clear and compelling on this proposition and requires, in this case, recognition that the indicia of nonjusticiability are present.

Moreover, the matter before this Court is a nonjusticiable political question because it arises out of a President exercising a textually demonstrable grant of power from Article II of the Constitution.[32]

---

[32] Textually demonstrable grants of power are both explicit and implied in Article II of the Constitution. The Supreme Court has stated:

"It is true, that such a power, if it exists, must be derived from implication, and the genius and spirit of our institutions are hostile to the exercise of implied powers. Had

Any determination concerning the disclosure of presidential documents necessarily requires the exercise of the unique discretion and expertise of the Chief Executive, for such a decision involves "considerations of policy, considerations of extreme magnitude, and certainty, entirely incompetent to the examination and decision of a court of justice." *Ware* v. *Hylton*, 3 Dall. (3 U.S.) 199, 260 (1796). Only the President is in a position to determine which communications must be maintained in confidence, for the public interest in this matter is a judgment only the President can make. It involves a complex blend of policy, perspective, and knowledge uniquely within the province of the President and the executive branch. Neither the courts nor Congress can claim for themselves the elements of knowledge and perspective necessary to examine and review such a decision.

Gilligan v. *Morgan*, 413 U.S. 1 (1972), confirms the continuing validity of the concept of justiciability; in that case Chief Justice Burger said:

> . . . because this doctrine has been held inapplicable to certain carefully delineated situations, it is no reason for federal courts to assume its demise. The voting rights cases, indeed, have represented the Court's efforts to strengthen the political system by assuring a higher level of fairness and responsiveness to the political processes, not the assumption of a continuing judicial review of substantive political judgments entrusted expressly to the coordinate branches of government. (413 U.S. at 11).

Indeed, in recent political cases with political overtones such as *Powell* v. *McCormick*, 395 U.S. 486 (1969) and *Committee For Nuclear Responsibility* v. *Seaborg*, 463 F. 2d 788 (D.C. Cir. 1971), the issues related to the court's traditional role of interpreting the Constitution or legislation, vis-a-vis the constitutional rights of individuals, and thus are distinguishable from cases which concern discretionary decision-making by a coordinate branch of government.

the faculties of man been competent to the framing of a system of government which would have left nothing to implication, it cannot be doubted that the effort would have been made by the framers of the Constitution. But what is the fact? There is not in the whole of that admirable instrument a grant of powers which does not draw after it others, not expressed, but vital to their exercise; not substantive and independent, indeed, but auxiliary and subordinate." (*Anderson v. Dunn*, 6 Wheat [19 U.S.], 204, 225-226 [1821].) See also, *New York Times* v. *United States*, 403 U.S. 713, 752 n.3 (1971) (Burger, C. J. dissenting).

[33] Cf. E. Corwin, *Introduction to Congressional Research Service, The Constitution of the United States of America* XII (1973).

This Court's resolution of this constitutional confrontation should not restrict the powers of the President by superimposing the decision of a subordinate in the executive branch over the Chief Executive through the impermissible intervention of the judicial branch. Rather, if any action is taken at all, the sole appropriate procedure for the consideration of alleged abuses is by way of impeachment. See *Ex Parte Grossman*, 267 U.S. 87, 121 (1925).

IV. A PRESIDENTIAL ASSERTION OF PRIVILEGE IS NOT REVIEWABLE BY THE COURT

A. *The Separation of Powers Doctrine Precludes Judicial Review Of The Use Of Executive Privilege By A President*

Justice Douglas, at the threshold of his dissent in *Environmental Protection Agency* v. *Mink*, 410 U.S. 73, 105 (1973), remarked that "The starting point of a decision usually indicates the result." In this case, the foundation for the President's assertion of executive privilege is the Constitution.

The Constitution as the embodiment of the grand design of our political system was described in *Kilbourn* v. *Thompson*, 103 U.S. 168, 190—191 (1880), as follows:

It is believed to be one of the chief merits of the American system of written constitutional law that all powers entrusted to government, whether state or national, are divided into the three grand departments, the executive, the legislative, and the judicial. That the functions appropriate to each of these branches of government shall be vested in a separate body of public servants, and that the perfection of the system requires that the lines which separate and divide these departments shall be broadly and clearly defined.

The doctrine of the separation of powers, inherent in the nature of our government,[33] was reflected in the Constitution by the definitive expression of the Framers of each of the separate, co-equal branches. In the case at hand, Art.II, Sec. 1, Cl. 1 is in focus:

The executive Power shall be vested in a President of the United States of America.

Inherent in that executive power, as part and parcel of the separation of powers, is executive privilege; in this case, more accurately described as presidential privilege. Unless this is so, the full panoply of power embodied in the executive power, would be, in reality, greatly diluted, a concept at odds with the intent of the Framers of the Constitution.[34, 35]

A second parallel source of presidential privilege lies in the common law and its embodiment of the concept of confidentiality as a prerequisite to the effective administration of government. Rather than sapping vitality from our constitutional position, the common law, as described, adds increased force and dimension to it.[36]

This case is important, both to the parties involved and the citizenry at large. "The men and issues were large"[37] in 1807 when the Aaron Burr cases[38] were before Chief Justice Marshall and they are equally so here. Significantly, the precise issue of the "absoluteness" of executive privilege, as applied to presidential communications, has never been squarely confronted and definitively resolved by this Court. This Court's thoughtful consideration of the issues presented is of particular importance because the foundation of the district court's decision,[39] *Nixon v. Sirica,* 487 F. 2d 700 (D.C. Cir. 1973), rested upon a surface assessment that purely social or public policy considerations, as opposed to the Constitution, constituted the rationale for the privilege. 487 F. 2d at 712. As a result, the dimensions of presidential privilege have been miscalculated and its integrity impaired.

[34] Unlike its companion privilege attendant upon the Congress by virtue of the Speech and Debate Clause, executive privilege was not meticulously delineated by the Framers of our Constitution. Its nature as a constitutional privilege, however, is not undermined by that fact. See *Kilbourn v. Thompson,* 103 U.S. 168, 189 (1880); see also *Inland Waterways v. Young,* 309 U.S. 517, 525 (1940); *United States v. Midwest Oil,* 236 U.S. 459, 483, 505 (1915).

[35] We suggest an additional constitutional source of presidential privilege resides in Article II, Sec. 1, cl. 8;

Before he enter on the Execution of his Office, he shall take the following or Affirmation: 'I do solemnly swear (or affirm) that I will faithfully execute the Office of the President of the United States, and will to the best of my Ability, preserve, protect and defend the Constitution of the United States.

The duty of the holder of the Office of the President to preserve, protect, and defend the Constitution compels care that Article II, sec. 1, cl. 1 be fully defended from encroachment.

[36] Judge Wilkey, dissenting in *Nixon v. Sirica,* 487 F. 2d 700, 763 (D.C. Cir. 1973), succinctly stated:

"The oldest source of Executive Branch privilege, the common sense-common law privilege of confidentiality, existed long before the Constitution of 1789, and might be deemed an inherent power of any government."

[37] See dissenting opinion of Judge Wilkey in *Nixon v. Sirica,* 487 F. 2d 700, 768 (D.C. Cir. 1973).

[38] *United States v. Burr,* 25 F. Cas. 187, No. 14694 (C.C.D. Va. 1807). *United States v. Burr,* 25 F. Cas. 187, No. 14694 (C.C.D. Va. 1807).

[39] *United States v. Mitchell,* Cr. No. 74-110 (D.D.C. 1974) at 3, 7.

The Presidency, as the repository of the executive power of the United States, was forged out of intense controversy during the Constitutional Convention.[40] The debate is well-described by Clinton Rossiter:

> The progress of the Convention toward this decision was labored and uncertain, however, and it often seemed that the hard lessons of the previous decade would be wasted on a majority of the delegates. Persistent voices were raised against almost every arrangement that eventually appeared in Article II and Wilson and his colleagues were able to score their final success only after a series of debates, decisions, reconsiderations, references to committees, and private maneuvers that will leave the historian befuddled. I have followed the tortuous progress of the incipient Presidency through Madison's *Notes* four times, and I am still not sure how the champions of the strong executive won their smashing victory. It can be said for certain, however, that at least eight decisions on the structure and powers of the executive were taken at different stages of the proceedings, and that out of these arose the Presidency. Everyone of these decisions, with one partial exception that history was shortly to remedy, was taken in favor of a strong executive.[41]

The result of these deliberations was to create an officer who is Chief of State, Chief Executive, Chief Diplomat and Commander-in-Chief.[42] Because of the great role entrusted to the Presidency by the Constitution and because the President alone is representative of the whole country,[43] there are important respects in which he is not treated by the law in the same fashion as are others.[44] The President is not above the law—but he is responsible to the law in a specific fashion that the

[40] See Congressional Research Service, *The Constitution of the United States of America* 429-433 (1974).

[41] C. Rossiter, *The American Presidency* 55 (1956).

[42] *Id.* at 16.

[43] Lest the President's position be misunderstood, it must be stressed we do not suggest that the President has the attributes of a king. *Inter alia*, a king rules by inheritance and for life. See A. Hamilton, *The Federalist*, No 69; 3 *Farrand* 301-301; Letter of Pierce Butler, dated May 5, 1788, to Weedon Butler, an English subject.

[44] This fact was recognized by Justices Warren and Douglas, in dissent, in *Barr* v. *Matteo*, 360 U.S. 564, 582-583 (1959), a controversy involving issues of executive immunity:
Spalding v. *Vilas, supra*, presents another situation in which absolute privilege may be justified. There the Court was dealing with the Postmaster General—a Cabinet Officer personally responsible to the President of the United States for the operation of one of

Framers, with utmost care, wrote into the Constitution. That historical perspective serves to define the stark language of Article II, Section 1, Clause 1, that "the executive Power shall be vested in a President * * * " Judge MacKinnon, in his dissenting opinion in *Nixon* v. *Sirica*, 487 F. 2d 700, 750 (D.C. Cir. 1973), described the relationship between the exercise of that executive power and the doctrine of executive privilege:

> The effective discharge of the presidential duty faithfully to execute the laws requires a privilege that preserves the integrity of the deliberative processes of the executive office. It would be meaningless to commit to the President a constitutional duty and then fail to protect and preserve that which is essential to its effective discharge. Thus the term "effective" is the *sine qua non* that imbues the presidential decisional process with a constitutional shield. The genius of our Constitution lies, perhaps as much as anywhere, in the generality of its principles which makes it susceptible to adaptation to the changing times and the needs of the country. But this much is explicit: '[The President] shall take Care that the Laws be faithfully executed. . . .' U.S. Const. art. II § 3. Is it plausible that the Framers should have charged the President with so basic a responsibility, one upon which every ordered society is premised, and yet left him without that ability effectively to satisfy the high charge? Emphatically, the answer must be, 'No.' The duty and the means of its discharge coalesce and each, the one explicit and the other implicit, finds its source in the Constitution.

Executive privilege as claimed by this President, has been asserted by Presidents beginning with George Washington, just as the legislative and judicial branches have continually asserted and jealously guarded their respective "privileges." The initial invocation occurred when in 1792, the House of Representatives passed a resolution requesting military papers pertaining to the

the major departments of government. Cf. *Glass* v. *Ickes*, 73 App. D.C. 3, 117 F.2d 273; *Mellon* v. *Brewer*, 57 App. D.C. 126, 18 F.2d 168. The importance of their positions in government as policymakers for the Chief Executive and the fact that they have the expressed trust and confidence of the President who appointed them and to whom they are personally and directly responsible suggest that the absolute protection partakes of presidential immunijy. Perhaps the *Spalding* v. *Vilas* rationale would require the extension of such absolute immunity to other government officials who are appointed by the President and are directly responsible to him in policy matters even though they do not hold Cabinet positions. But this extension is not now before us. since it is clear that petitioner Barr was not appointed by the President nor was he directly responsible to the President. Barr was exercising powers originally delegated by the President to the Director of Economic Stabilization who redelegated them to the Director of Rent Stabilization (footnote omitted).

campaign of Major General St. Clair. Although the papers were apparently produced,[45] the consideration given to that request is illustrative:[46]

> First, that the House was an inquest, and therefore might institute inquiries. Second that it might call for papers generally. Third, that the Executive ought to communicate such papers as the public good would permit, and ought to refuse those, the disclosure of which would injure the public: *consequently were to exercise a discretion.* Fourth, that neither the commitee nor House had a right to call on the Head of a Department, who and whose papers were under the President alone; but that the committee should instruct their chairman to move the House to address the President. (emphasis added).

Since then, Presidents [47] and Attorneys General have asserted

[45] 1 P. Ford, *The Writings of Thomas Jefferson* 303-305 (1893).

[46] 3 *Annals of Congress* 493; 1 P. Ford, at 303-304.

[47] In 1948, President Truman, railing against an anticipated bill from a Republican Congress that would have required every President might consider compliance to be contrary to the public interest, had a Memorandum prepared to demonstrate the bill's unconstitutionality. Part of that Memorandum follows:

Resume and Conclusions

A bird's-eye-view of the refusals by seventeen of our Presidents, and their heads of departments, to comply with congressional requests for informatin and papers from the Executive, beginning with 1796 to the present time, follows:

President	Date	Type of Information Refused
George Washington	1796	Instruction to U.S. Minister concerning Jay Treaty.
Thomas Jefferson	1807	Confidential information and letters relating to Burr's conspiracy.
James Monroe	1825	Documents relating to conduct of naval officers.
Andrew Jackson	1833	Copy of paper ready by President to heads of departments relating to removal of bank deposits.
	1835	Copies of charges against removed public official.
	1835	List of all appointments made without Senate's consent, since 1829, and those receiving salaries, without holding office.
John Tyler	1842	Names of Members of 26th and 27th Congress who applied for office.

the privilege. Even more important is the fact that Presidents
have always acted on the assumption that it is discretionary with
them alone, to determine whether the public interest permits

	1843	Report to War Department dealing with alleged frauds practiced on Indians, and Col. Hitchcock's view of personal characters of Indian delegates.
James K. Polk	1846	Evidence of payments made through State Department, on President's certificates, by prior administration.
Millard Fillmore	1852	Official information concerning proposition made by King of Sandwich Islands to transfer Islands to U.S.
James Buchanan	1860	Message of Protest to House against Resolution to investigate attempts by executive to influence legislation.
Abraham Lincoln	1861	Dispatches of Major Anderson to the War Department concerning defense of Fort Sumter.
Ulysses S. Grant	1876	Information concerning executive acts performed away from Capitol.
Rutherford B. Hayes	1877	Secretary of Treasury refused to answer questions and to produce papers concerning reasons for nomination of Theodore Roosevelt as Collector of Port of New York.
Grover Cleveland	1886	Documents relating to suspension and removal of Federal officials.
Theodore Roosevelt	1909	Attorney General's reasons for failure to prosecute U.S. Steel Corporation, Department of Commerce.
Calvin Coolidge	1924	List of companies in which Secretary of Treasury Mellon was interested.
Herbert Hoover	1930	Telegrams and letters leading up to London Naval Treaty.
	1932	Testimony and documents concerning investigations made by Treasury Department.
Franklin D. Roosevelt	1941	Federal Bureau of Investigation reports.
	1943	Director, Bureau of the Budget, refused to testify and to produce files.
	1943	Chairman, Federal Communications Commission, and Board of War Communications refused records.
	1943	General Counsel, Federal Communications Commission, refused to produce records.
	1943	Secretaries of War and Navy refused to furnish documents, and permission for Army and Naval officers to testify.

production of presidential papers, and the other branches of Government have until recently accepted this position. *Senate Select Committee on Presidential Campaign Activities* v. *Richard M. Nixon.* Slip Op. No. 74—1258 (D.C. Cir. May 23, 1974); *Nixon* v. *Sirica*, 487 F. 2d 700 (D.C. Cir. 1973). The opinions over a long period of years by the highest legal officer[48] in the Government cannot be lightly disregarded. The fact that the litigation arising out of the Watergate investigations is the first time that a subpoena has been directed to force production of presidential papers since Colonel Burr's abortive attempt to subpoena documents from President Jefferson is because it has been universally accepted that there is no power to compel the President in the exercise of his discretion. Uninterrupted usage continued from the early days of the Republic is weighty evidence of the proper construction of any clause of the Constitution. *Inland Waterways Corp.* v. *Young*, 309 U.S. 517, 525 (1940). Justice Lamar, in *United States* v. *Midwest Oil Co.*, 236 U.S. 459, 472—473 (1915), observed:

> Both officers, lawmakers and citizens naturally adjust themselves to any long continued action of the Executive Department—on the presumption that unauthorized acts would not have been allowed to be so often repeated as to crystallize into regular practices. That presumption is not

	1944	J. Edgar Hoover refused to give testimony and to produce President's directive.
Harry S. Truman	1945	Issued directions to heads of executive departments to permit officers and employees to give information to Pearl Harbor Committee.
	1945	President's directive did not include any files or written material.
	1947	Civil Service Commission records concerning applicants for positions.

Note: Truman Memorandum at 44 a, b, c (1948).

In the bird's-eye picture, reference is made to the refusals of Presidents Monroe, Fillmore, Lincoln, and Hayes[;] Monroe's refusal may be found in a message dated January 10, 1825, 2 Richardson, *Messages and Papers of Presidents*, p. 278' [sic] Fillmore's in 5 Richardson, p. 159; Lincoln's in 6 Richardson p. 12, and the refusal in Hayes' administration is dealt with in 17 Cong. Rec. 2332 and 2618.

(In addition, it appears President Kennedy exercised executive privilege four times, the Johnson Administration twice, and, through March 28, 1973, the Nixon Administration fifteen times, four of which were actually claimed by the President. 119 Cong. Rec. 2244-2245 (daily ed. March 28, 1973).

[48] See 11 Op. Att'y Gen. 137, 142-143 (1865) (Atty. Gen. Speed); 20 Op. Att'y Gen. 557, 558 (1893) (Atty. Gen. Olney); 25 Op. Att'y Gen. 45, 49 (1941) (Atty. Gen., later Justice Jackson).

reasoning in a circle but the basis of a wise and quieting rule that in determining the meaning of the statute or the exercise of a power, weight should be given to the usage itself—even when the validity of the practice is itself the subject of investigation.

The significance and rationale for this uninterrupted assertion of privilege by holders of the Office of the Presidency, are underscored by reference to the way in which the other co-equal branches of government have regarded the need for confidentiality. Chief Justice Burger, in *New York Times* v. *United States*, 403 U.S. 713, 752 n. 3 (1971), in his dissent, revealed his assessment of privilege:

> With respect to the question of inherent power of the Executive to classify papers, records, and documents as secret, or otherwise unavailable for public exposure, and to secure aid of courts for enforcement, there may be an analogy with respect to this Court. No statute gives this Court express power to establish and enforce the utmost security measures for the secrecy of our deliberations and records. Yet I have little doubt as to the inherent power of the Court to protect the confidentiality of its internal operations by whatever judicial measures may be required.

Although Professor Arthur Selwyn Miller and a collaborator have recently argued to the contrary, Miller & Sastri, *Secrecy and the Supreme Court: On The Need For Piercing the Red Velour Curtain*, 22 Buff. L. Rev. 799 (1973), it has always been recognized that judges must be able to confer with their colleagues, and with their law clerks, in circumstances of absolute confidentiality. Justice Brennan has written that Supreme Court conferences are held in "absolute secrecy for obvious reasons." Brennan, *Working at Justice*, in *An Autobiography of the Supreme Court* 300 (Westin ed. 1963). Justice Frankfurter had said that the "secrecy that envelops the Court's work" is "essential to the effective functioning of the Court." Frankfurter, *Mr. Justice Roberts*, 104 U. Pa. L. Rev. 311, 313 (1955).

Congress, too, has seen fit to hold to such a privilege. It is a long established practice of each House of Congress to regard its own private papers as privileged. No court subpoena is complied with by the Congress or its committees without a vote of the House concerned to turn over the documents. *Soucie* v. *David*, 448 F. 2d 1067, 1081—1082 (D.C. Cir. 1971). This practice is insisted on by Congress even when the result may be to deny relevant evidence in a criminal proceeding either to the prosecution or to the accused person.[49]

Similarly, when President Kennedy refused to disclose to a Senate Subcommittee the names of Defense Department speech reviewers, the Subcommittee, speaking through Senator Stennis, relied on the privilege of confidentiality Congress enjoys in upholding the President's claim of privilege:

> We now come face to face and are in direct conflicts with the established doctrine of separation of powers * * *.
>
> I know of no case where the Court has ever made the Senate or the House surrender records from its files, or where the Executive has made the Legislative Branch surrender records from its files—and I do not think either one of them could. So the rule works three ways. Each is supreme within its field, and each is responsible within its field. (Committee on Armed Servies, U.S. Senate, *Military Cold War Escalation* and *Speech Review Policies*, 87th Congress, 2d Sess., 512 [1962].)

On June 12, 1974, the United States Senate emphatically reiterated its position on privilege by deed, as well as by word. Senator Eastland, Chairman of the Judiciary Committee, urged, at the request of the Special Prosecutor, passage of a resolution permitting a staff attorney to file a trial affidavit with the Special Prosecutor. Without objection, S. Res. 338 was passed.

It reads in part:

> *Resolved*, That by the privilege of the Senate of the United States no evidence under the control and in the possession of the Senate of the United States can, by the mandate of process of the ordinary courts of justice, be taken from such control or possession, but by its permission.
>
> * * * (Sections 2—4) * * *
>
> SEC. 5. The said Peter Stockett, Junior, may provide information with respect to any other matter material and relevant for the purposes of identification of any document or documents in such case, if any such document has previously

---

[49] See e.g., 108 Cong. Rec. 3626 (1962), showing Senate adoption of a resolution permitting staff members and former staff members of a Senate Committee to appear and to testify in a criminal proceeding against James Hoffa but forbidding them from taking any documents or records in the custody of the Senate and from testifying about information that they gained while employed in the Senate. In explaining the resolution to the Senate, Senator McClellan said in part: "The Senate recognizes it has certain privileges as a separate and distinct branch of Government, which it wishes to protect." *Id.* at 3627.

On July 16, 1970, counsel for 1st Lt. William L. Calley, Jr., moved in his court-martial proceeding for production of testimony concerning the My Lai incident that has been presented to a subcommittee of the House Committee on Armed Services in executive session. Calley claimed that his testimony would be exculpatory of him and would help him establish his defense in the court-martial. The subcommittee

been made available to the public, but he shall respectfully decline to provide information concerning any and all other matters that may be based on knowledge acquired by him in his official capacity either by reason of documents and papers appearing in the files of the Senate or by virtue of conversations or communications with any person or persons.

The considerations of public policy that required the deliberations of the Constitutional Convention be held in confidence for half a century[50] and made it imperative that judges and members of Congress be permitted to work under conditions of absolute confidentiality are particularly compelling when applied to presidential communications with his advisers. As stated by the President on July 6, 1973, in his letter to Senator Sam J. Ervin:

No President could function if the private papers of his office, prepared by his personal staff, were open to public scrutiny. Formulation of sound public policy requires that the President and his personal staff be able to communicate among themselves in complete candor, and that their tentative judgments, their exploration of alternatives, and their frank

---

Chairman, Rep. F. Edward Hebert, refused to make the testimony available, advising defense counsel on July 17, 1970, that Congress is "an independent branch of the Government, separate from and equal to the Executive and Judicial branches," and that accordingly only Congress can direct the disclosure of legislative records. He concluded from this that the material requested by the defense was not within the rule of *Brady* v. *Maryland,* 373 U.S. 83 (1963), nor subject to the requirements of the Jencks Act, 18 U.S.C. 3500. Subsequently the military court issued a subpoena to the Clerk of the House of Representatives. The Speaker laid this before the House on November 17, 1970, 116 Cong. Rec. 37652 [1970] but to date the House has taken no action nor given any indication that it will supply the information sought.

On October 4, 1972, the United States Senate bluntly refused, via Senate Resolution, a judicial subpoena for *inter alia,* documentary evidence in the criminal case of *United States* v. *Brewster,* then pending in the federal district court, District of Columbia. 118 Cong. Rec. S. 16, 766 (92d Cong., 2d Sess).

[50] The Framers understood perfectly well that enlightened decision-making requires the kind of frank and free discussion that can only be had when confidentiality is absolutely assured. On May 29, 1787, one of the first acts of the Constitutional Convention was the adoption of the following rule: "That nothing spoken in the House be printed, or otherwise published, or communicated without leave." 1 *Farrand* XV. It was not until 1819, that the Journal of the Convention, a mere skeleton of motions and votes, was made public. The fullest record of the proceedings of the Convention is in Madison's *Notes.* As late as 1831, 44 years after the Convention, Madison thought it was not yet appropriate for those *Notes* to be made public, 3 *Farrand* 497, and they were not published until 1840, four years after his death. 1 *Farrand* xv. President Madison thus anticipated the view of the most distinguished modern student of the Constitution, Paul Freund, who has said: "I sometimes wonder irreverently whether we would have had a Constitution at all if the Convention had been reported by daily columnists." Hughes, *The Living Presidency* 33n. (1973).

comments on issues and personalities at home and abroad remain confidential.

This has been the position of every President in our history, and it has been specifically stated by President Nixon's immediate predecessors.

Writing his memoirs in 1955, President Truman explained that he had found it necessary to omit certain material, and said: "Some of this material cannot be made available for many years, perhaps for many generations." 1 Truman, *Memoirs* x (1955). President Eisenhower stated the point with force on July 6, 1955, in connection with the Dixon-Yates controversy:

> But when it comes to the conversations that take place between any responsible official and his advisers or exchange of little, mere slips of this or that, expressing personal opinions on the most confidential basis, those are not subject to investigation by anybody, and if they are, will wreck the Government. There is no business that could be run if there would be exposed every single thought that an adviser might have, because in the process of reaching an agreed position, there are many, many conflicting opinions to be brought together. And if any commander is going to get the free, unprejudiced opinions of his subordinates, he had better protect what they have to say to him on a confidential basis. *Public Papers of Presidents of the United States: Dwight D. Eisenhower* 1955 at 674 (1959).

Congress recognized the high degree of confidentiality that must attach to presidential papers for many years when it enacted the Presidential Libraries Act of 1955, Pub. L. 84–373, 69 Stat. 695 (1955), now codified in 44 U.S.C. 2107, 2108. That statute encourages Presidents to give their papers to a presidential library, and provides that papers, documents, and other historical materials so given "are subject to restrictions as to their availability and use stated in writing by the donors or depositors * * * The restrictions shall be respected for the period stated, or until revoked or terminated by the donors or depositors or by persons legally qualified to act on their behalf." 44 U.S.C. 2108(c); *Nichols* v. *United States*, 460 F. 2d 671 (10th Cir.), *cert. denied*, 409 U.S. 966 (1972.) Since that Act was passed, the gifts of presidential papers of President Eisenhower, Kennedy, and Johnson have all specified that "materials containing statements made by or to" the President are to be kept "in confidence" and are to be held under seal and not revealed to anyone except the donors or archival personnel until "the passage of time or other circumstances no longer require such materials being kept under restriction." See letter of April 13, 1960, from President Dwight D. Eisenhower to the Administrator of General Services; Agreement of February 25, 1965, between Mrs. Jacqueline B. Kennedy and the United States and Letter of August 13, 1965, from President Lyndon B. Johnson to the Administrator of General Services. In addition, the letters from President Eisenhower and from President Johnson specifically prohibit disclosure to "public officials" and state, as the reason for these restrictions, that "the President of the United States is the recipient of many confidences from others, and * * * the inviolability of such confidence is essential to the functioning of the constitutional office of the Presidency * * *."

The need to preserve the confidentiality of the Oval Office has been recognized from without as well as by those who have borne the burdens of service there. What Justice Stewart, who was joined by Justice White, said in his concurring opinion in *New York Times Co.* v. *United States*, 403 U.S. 713, 728 (1971), has particular force here.

And within our own executive departments, the development of considered and intelligent international policies would be impossible if those charged with their formulation could not communicate with each other freely, frankly, and in confidence. * * *
[I]t is clear to me that it is the constitutional duty of the Executive—as a matter of sovereign prerogative and not as a matter of law as the courts know law—through the promulgation and enforcement of executive regulations, to protect the confidentiality necessary to carry out its responsibilities in the fields of international relations and national defense. (403 U.S. at 728—730).

Of course, international relations and national defense have very special claims to secrecy, but the importance of the President being able to speak with his advisers "freely, frankly, and in confidence" is not confined to those matters. It is just as essential that the President be able to talk openly with his advisers about domestic issues as about military or foreign affairs. The wisdom that free discussion provides is as vital in fighting inflation, choosing Supreme Court Justices, deciding whether to veto a large spending bill, and dealing with the myriad other important questions that the President must confront in his roles as Chief of State and Chief Executive, as it is when he is acting as Chief Diplomat or as Commander-in-Chief. Any other view would fragment the executive power vested in him and would assume that some of his constitutional responsibilities are more important than others. It is true that the President has more substantive freedom to act in foreign and military affairs than he does in domestic affairs, but his need for candid advice is no different in the one situation than in the other.

We submit, with all respect, that if the decision below were allowed to stand it could no longer fairly be contended that the President of the United States is "master of his own house." The confidences of that house would be open for disclosure to the Special Prosecutor—and thus ultimately to defendants—whenever one of 400 district judges chose not to accept the President's claim of privilege.[51] Judge MacKinnon, in his dissent, in *Nixon* v. *Sirica*, 487 F. 2d 700, 752 (D.C. Cir. 1973), laid his finger on the pulse:

> But the greatest vice of the decision sought by the Special Prosecutor is that it would establish a precedent that would subject every presidential conference to the hazard of eventually being publicly exposed at the behest of some trial judge trying a civil or criminal case. It is this precedential effect which transforms this case from one solely related to the recordings sought here, to one which decides whether this President, and all future Presidents, shall continue to enjoy the independency of executive action contemplated by the Constitution and fully exercised by all their predecessors.

B. *The Right of Privacy And Freedom of Expression Support The Absolute Confidentiality of Presidential Communications with His Advisers*

The President's sole discretion to decide what presidential communications he will disclose, and to control the circumstances of disclosure, is independently grounded in the

---

[51] In *Nixon* v. *Sirica*, 487 F. 2d 700 (D.C. Cir. 1973), the court emphatically stated, at 705: "The strength and particularity of this showing were made possible by a unique intermeshing of events, unlikely soon, *if ever*, to recur." It said at 722: "We end, as we began by emphasizing the extraordinary nature of this case. We have attempted to decide no more than the problem before us—a problem that takes its unique shape from a grand jury's compelling showing of need." Since that decision, the President has received more than two dozen subpoenas emanating from various courts throughout the country, calling for the production of voluminous amounts of privileged materials. Indeed, the crippling effect on the Executive Branch, generated by that decision, was correctly predicted by Judge MacKinnon in his dissent. Thus, the impairment of the Executive function is no longer just an unverified, theoretical proposition. A further denial of the President's claim of privilege, as asserted, can only foreshadow further destruction of the Office of the Presidency. As Justice Rehnquist recognized in *State of Michigan* v. *Tucker*, No. 73-482 (June 10, 1974): "The pressure of law enforcement and the vagaries of human nature would make such an expectation [no errors by policeman in investigating serious crimes] unrealistic."

right of privacy[52] and the constitutionally protected freedom of expression[53] possessed by the President, his advisers and others with whom he confers in the course of carrying out his official responsibilities. The relationship among these "rights" was summarized by Judge Wilkey, dissenting in *Nixon* v. *Sirica*, 487 F. 2d 700, 767 (D.C. Cir. 1973):

> Certainly the Chief Executive's right to be fully, frankly, and confidentially informed is equal to that of any other citizen in the land; his need is undeniably greater. To breach his privacy would unquestionably have a 'chilling effect' on those who otherwise would counsel and confide in the President with complete candor and honesty.

In *Eastern Railroad Presidents Conference* v. *Noerr Motor Freight, Inc.*, 365 U.S. 127 (1961) this Court acknowledged the broad scope of the First Amendment rights when it held immune from Sherman Act prosecution the attempts of railroads to influence legislation, the enforcement of laws, and the exercise of the veto power by the Governor of Pennsylvania, even though the railroads' efforts had been conducted fraudulently, unethically, and with an intent to injure or destroy competitors. This Court's interpretation of the Act was influenced heavily by the realistic assessment that the effective functioning of representative government depends on the most generous support for First Amendment values. Justice Black, for a unanimous Court, stated that the application of the Sherman Act to the conduct in question—

> would substantially impair the power of government to take actions through its legislature and executive that operate to restrain trade. In a representative democracy such as this, these branches of government act on behalf of the people and, to a very large extent, the whole concept of representation depends

[52] See *Griswold* v. *Connecticut*, 381 U.S. 479, 483-484 (1965), wherein Justice Douglas etched these words:

In other words, the First Amendment has a penumbra where privacy is protected from governmental intrusion.

* * * * *

The foregoing cases suggest that specific guarantees in the Bill of Rights have penumbras, formed by emanations from those guarantees that help give them life and substance.

[53] Article II, Section 2, Clause 1, of the Constitution, states, in part:

[H]e may require the Opinion, in writing, of the principal Officer in each of the executive Departments, upon any Subject relating to the Duties of their respective Offices.

upon the ability of the people to make their wishes known to their representatives. (365 U.S. at 137).

The Court, therefore, refused to find that

the government retains the power to act in this representative capacity and yet hold, at the same time, that the people cannot freely inform the government of their wishes * * * . (365 U.S. at 137).

In *N.A.A.C.P.* v. *Alabama*, 357 U.S. 449 (1958), this Court quashed Alabama's discovery attempt to obtain N.A.A.C.P.'s membership lists,[54] thus preserving the organization from the "chilling effect" that disclosure would have wrought. The court emphasized:

that the immunity from state scrutiny of membership lists which the Association claims on behalf of its members is here so related to the right of the members to pursue their lawful private interests privately and to associate freely with others in so doing as to come within the protection of the Fourteenth Amendment. And we conclude that Alabama has fallen short of showing a controlling justification for the deterrent effect on the free enjoyment of the right to associate which disclosure of membership lists is likely to have. (357 U.S. at 466).

See also *Dombrowski* v. *Pfister*, 380 U.S. 479, 488—489 (1965).

As illustrated by the *Noerr* and *N.A.A.C.P.* cases, the problem of protecting political communications and the right of petition is a recurring issue involving a wide variety of factual settings. The ramifications for the effective functioning of the Presidency are of course virtually endless. Congressmen or their staff members must be able to give the President candid assessments of the political situation in the country, including the likely reactions of the House of Representatives and the Senate to legislative proposals and to suggest presidential action. A legislator may wish to urge a course of action as wise, while warning that in a legislative battle he could not be counted on because of pressure from his constituents. Private persons and groups, too, may come to present points of view, offer support, warn of political retaliation, or suggest trade-offs. Contemporaneous memoranda prepared by or for the President and designed to preserve the details of such meetings are a vital

---

[54] Alabama's objective was to ensure compliance by the N.A.A.C.P. with the state's corporate registration laws, an objective uncontested by the N.A.A.C.P. The N.A.A.C.P.'s objection was to the *means* to obtain the end.

part of the working and historical record. Knowledge that such records might be made public, under compulsion, in a future litigation would not only inhibit the expression of opinion but would dry up sources of indispensable information. The President would be denied the raw materials he needs to function effectively and responsibly.

The other side of this coin is that unless a President has the power to protect records of his private conversations from public disclosure, he himself would be seriously fettered. He would be less likely to seek out a broad range of advice and advisors; he would be constrained in his discourse or disabled from maintaining a record of his actions and conversations. Instead of concerning himself solely with shaping policy, a President would be driven to striking poses for the record, for history, or for his own personal protection.

C. *The Judicial Branch Cannot Compel Production of Privileged Material from the President*

The doctrine of the separation of powers embodies the concept that each branch is independent of the others, except where some form of interaction flows from the regular operation of the government or where the Constitution or statutes explicitly provide to the contrary. The doctrine necessarily includes the right of the holder of the privilege to decide when it is to be exercised. It means, in this case, that compulsory process cannot issue against the President.

Chief Justice Taft in *Myers* v. *United States*, 272 U.S. 106, 116 (1926), provided the classic judicial statement of one separation of powers doctrine:

> Montesquieu's view that the maintenance of independence as between the legislative, the executive and the judicial branches was a security for the people had [the Framers'] full approval. Madison in the Convention, 2 Farrand, Records of the Federal Convention, 56 *Kendall* v. *United States*, 12 Pet. 524, 610, 9 L. ed. 1181, 1215. Accordingly the Constitution was so framed as to vest in the Congress all legislative powers therein granted, to vest in the President the executive power, and to vest in one Supreme Court and such inferior courts as Congress might establish the judicial power. From this division on the principle, the reasonable construction of the Constitution must be that the branches should be kept separate in all cases in which they were not expressly blended, and the Constitution should be expounded to blend them no more than it affirmatively requires. Madison, 1 Annals of Congress,

497. This rule of construction has been confirmed by this court in *Meriwether* v. *Garrett*, 102 U.S. 472, 515, 26 L. ed. 197, 205; *Kilbourn* v. *Thompson*, 103 U.S. 168, 190, 26 L. ed. 377, 386; *Mugler* v. *Kansas*, 123 U.S. 623, 662, 8 S. Ct. 273, 31 L. ed. 205, 210.

Although the specific holding of the *Myers* case was narrowed to some extent in *Humphrey's Executor* v. *United States*, 295 U.S. 602 (1935), that narrowing was on a point that does not bear on the present issue. The later case was at pains to reaffirm the vigor with which the constitutional separation of powers must be protected and preserved. Justice Sutherland, writing for a unanimous Court, said:

> The fundamental necessity of maintaining each of the three general departments of government entirely free from the control of coercive influence, direct or indirect, of either of the others, has often been stressed and is hardly open to serious question. So much is implied in the very fact of the separation of the power of these departments by the Constitution; and in the rule which recognizes their essential co-equality. The sound application of a principle that makes one master in his own house precludes him from imposing his control in the house of another who is master there. (295 U.S. at 629–630).

The President's assertion of his privilege as a functioning of his role as the head of an independent branch of government is supported by the basic case law. In *Marbury* v. *Madison, 1 Cranch* (5 U.S.) 137 (1803), William Marbury, a Federalist and recipient of a "lame duck" judicial appointment, i.e., justice of the peace, from President John Adams in the post-election days of 1800, sought, in early 1801, to secure from James Madison, the new Secretary of State under President Jefferson, the actual commission of his appointment. When Madison declined, Marbury sought mandamus relief in the Supreme Court pursuant to Section 13 of the Judiciary Act of 1789. On February 24, 1803, after a fourteen month "recess," Chief Justice John Marshall, a fellow Federalist, denied all relief, holding that although only a ministerial duty on Madison's part was involved, the statute bestowing the judicial power on the Supreme Court in such a case was unconstitutional.[55] In the course of ascertaining

---

[55] M. R. Cohen, *The Supreme Court in United States History*, 178-180 (1946) states that Marshall's decision was motivated by fear of impeachment from the newly-elected Republican Congress. Charles Warren, *The Supreme Court in United States History* 206-265 (1922), indicates the Republicans had been incensed at Adams' post-election appointments. This controversy eventually led to the fourteen month involuntary recess of the Court.

whether the particular factual situation excluded Marbury from obtaining legal redress, the Chief Justice examined the relationship between the official position of the defendant and the nature of his act. Significantly, he stated:

By the Constitution of the United States, the President is invested with certain important political powers, in the exercise of which he is to use to his own discretion, and is accountable only to his country in his political character and to his own conscience. To aid him in the performance of these duties, he is authorized to appoint certain officers, who act by his authority and in conformity with his orders.

In such cases their acts are his acts; and *whatever opinion may be entertained of the manner in which executive discretion may be used, still there exists, and can exist, no power to control that discretion.* The subjects are political. They respect the nation, not individual rights, and being intrusted to the executive, *the decision of the executive is conclusive.* 1 Cranch (5 U.S.) at 165 (emphasis added).

The exchange between the Chief Justice and Mr. Lincoln, the Attorney General, during the hearing of the case foreshadowed his decision:

The questions being written, were then read and handed to him. He repeated the ideas he had before suggested, and said his objections were of two kinds.

1st. He did not think himself bound to disclose his official transactions while acting as secretary of state; and, 2d. He ought not be compelled to answer any thing which might tend to criminate himself.

Mr. Lincoln thought it was going a great way to say that every Secretary of State should at all times be liable to be called upon to appear as a witness in a court of justice, and testify to facts which came to his knowledge officially. He felt himself delicately situated between his duty to this court, and the duty he conceived he owed to an executive department; and hoped the court would give him time to consider of the subject.

The court said that if Mr. Lincoln wishes time to consider what answers he should make, they would give him time; but they had no doubt he ought to answer. *There was nothing confidential required to be disclosed. If there had been he was not obliged to answer it; and if he thought that any thing was communicated to him in confidence he was not bound to disclose it;* nor was he obliged to state any thing which would criminate himself; but that the fact whether such commissions had been in the office or not, could not be a confidential fact; it is a fact which all the world have a right to know. 1 Cranch (5 U.S.) at 143—145 (emphasis added).

Four years later, the *Burr* cases[56] came before Chief Justice Marshall. Three subpoenaes *duces tecum, in toto*, were sought and issued during the course of the intensely-contested trials, although only two were directed to President Jefferson. The first was requested on June 11, 1807, by Colonel Burr to obtain an October 21, 1806, letter from Colonel Wilkinson to the President, and two military orders, thought to be exculpatory on charges raised by a possible treason indictment. Following more than two days of argument on whether the Court had the right, under the circumstances of the case, to issue a subpoena against President Jefferson, the Chief Justice found that it ought to issue. The Court confined its inquiry to the narrow question of whether a subpoena should issue, and not to whether the court could or would compel actual compliance.[57] The Chief Justice said:

If then, as is admitted by the counsel for the United States, a subpoena may issue to the President the accused is entitled to it of course; and whatever difference may exist with respect to the power to compel the same obedience to the process, as if it had been directed to a private citizen, there exists no difference with respect to the right to obtain it. The guard, furnished to this high officer, to protect him from being harrassed by vexatious and unnecessary subpoenas, is to be looked for in the conduct of a court after those subpoenas have issued; not in any circumstances which is to precede their being issued. (25 Fed. Cas. at 34).

At best as can be determined from an ambiguous history, President Jefferson never complied with that subpoena. President Jefferson did transmit to the United States Attorney, George Hay, certain records from the offices of the Secretaries of the Army and Navy that were covered by the subpoena. This was done, however in apparent ignorance of the fact that the subpoena had issued because his transmittal letter contains a

---

[56] *United States* v. *Burr* 25 Fed. Cas. 30, No. 14692d (C.C.D. Va 1807); *United States* v. *Bur*, 25 Fed. Cas. 187, No. 14694 (C.C.D. Va. 1807).

[57] The cautious reference to the *Burr* ruling in *Branzburg* v. *Hayes*, 408 U.S. 665, 689 n. 26 (1972), goes no further than to note that Chief Justice Marshall had "opined" that a subpoena might issue. In *Branzburg*, itself, this Court recognized that ordinarily a grand jury has the right to every man's evidence, but immediately qualified that statement by adding "except for those persons protected by a constitutional, common-law, or statutory privilege." *Branzburg* v. *Hayes*, 408 U.S. 665, 688 (1972).

well-stated argument why a subpoena should not issue, 9 Ford, *Writings of Jefferson* 56—57 (1899). President Jefferson did not transmit the described letter from General Wilkinson, although that document was specifically designated by the subpoena. It appears Burr was forced to trial for treason without the benefit of the letter, for on the convening of his subsequent trial for misdemeanor on September 3, 1807, he again demanded that letter, and another.

If President Jefferson did fully comply with that first subpoena, this is unknown to Marshall's biographer. See 3 Beveridge, *The Life of John Marshall* 518—522 (1919). The letters called for were not produced and Colonel Burr asserted that the President was in contempt of court, since a subpoena was outstanding. Jefferson was nervous about what Chief Justice Marshall might do, and threatened to use force against the execution of the process of the court. A subpoena *duces tecum* then issued against Hay, who had one of the letters Colonel Burr was seeking. Hay produced a part of the letter but refused to give passages that the President deemed confidential. After Mr. Hay made his return, unsatisfactory to Mr. Burr, Chief Justice Marshall, noting that the President had not personally assigned any reasons for nonproduction of the item sought, cautiously opined that the President could not lawfully delegate to his attorney presidential discretion concerning what matters required continued secrecy and ordered that the letter be produced.[58] Five days later, President Jefferson responded with his certificate and the letter, "excepting such parts as he deemed he ought not to permit to be made public." *United States* v. *Burr*, 25 F. Cas. 187, 193 No. 14,694 (C.C.D. Va. 1807). As Beveridge relates it:

> A second subpoena *duces tecum* seems to have been issued against Jefferson, and he defiantly refused to "sanction a proceeding so preposterous," by "any notice" of it. And there

---

[58] One writer has asserted that "in fact [Jefferson] *fully complied* with the subpoena." Berger, *Executive Privilege* v. *Congressional Inquiry,* 12 U.C.L.A. L. Rev. 1043, 1107 (1965) (emphasis in original). The author's footnote at that point, however, fails to support the statement in the test. Indeed, that same writer has retreated, since then, from his earlier categorical position. He now says: "In fact Jefferson went a *long way* toward full compliance." R. Berger, *Executive Privilege: A Constitutional Myth* 188 (1974). See 60 A.B.A.J., Irwin Rhodes, *What Really Happened to the Jefferson Subpoena* 52 (January, 1974) for an additional, contemporary analysis of the *Burr* cases, which concludes: "It is eminently clear that President Jefferson never submitted the contents of the withheld material to the Court or Burr and that his claim to an exclusive exercise of executive privilege, unreviewed by the courts, was upheld by Chief Justice Marshall." (At 54).

this heated and dangerous controversy appears to have ended. *Id.* at 522.

At this point, Beveridge adds in a footnote:

For some reason the matter was not again pressed. Perhaps the favorable progress of the case relieved Burr's anxiety. It is possible that the "truce" so earnestly desired by Jefferson was arranged. *Id.* at 522 n. 4.

Other historians have read the evidence the same way. Rossiter expresses doubt whether Jefferson was a great President but thinks that one act that remains "to his lasting credit" was his "first declaration of presidential independence in his rejection of Marshall's subpoena in the Burr trial." Rossiter, *The American Presidency* 70 (1956). At another point Rossiter says:

Jefferson's rejection of Marshall's subpoena *duces tecum* in the Burr trial and Chase's opinion in *Mississippi* v. *Johnson* (1867), which spared Andrew Johnson the necessity of answering a writ of injunction, make clear that the judiciary has no power to enjoin or mandamus or even question the President. *Id.* at 39.[59]

The Court in *Mississippi* v. *Johnson* refuted the state's request to enjoin President Johnson from enforcing two Reconstruction Act statutes because "the duty thus imposed on the President (to see that the laws are faithfully executed) is in no sense ministerial. It is purely executive and political."[60] 4 Wall. (7 U.S.) at 499. The Court noted that the "fact that no such application was ever before made in any case indicates the general judgment of the profession that no such application should be entertained," 4 Wall. at 500, and summarized the thrust of the case in these terms:

It is true that in the instance before us the interposition of the court is not sought to enforce action by the Executive under constitutional legislation, but to restrain such action under legislation alleged to be unconstitutional. But we are unable to

[59] Actually, in *United States* v. *Cooper*, 25 Fed. Cas. 631, 633, No. 14865 (C.C. Pa. 1800), Justice Chase, sitting as a Circuit Justice, refused to direct a subpoena to President Adams stating that "it was a very improper and very indecent request." Cooper, *Account of the Trial of Thomas Cooper* 10 (1800).

[60] See *Kendall* v. *United States* ex rel *Stokes*, 12 Pet. (37 U.S.) 524, 609 (1838), and *Nat'l Treasury Employees Union* v. *Nixon*, 492 F 2d 587 (D.C. Cir. 1974), for cases where purely ministerial duties were involved. While the courts are unable to compel a President to act or restrain him from acting, his act, when performed, is in proper cases subject to judicial review and disallowance. *Youngstown Sheet & Tube Co.* v. *Sawyer*, 343 U.S. 579 (1952).

perceive that this circumstance takes the case out of the general principles which forbid judicial interference with the exercise of executive discretion.

* * * * *

The Congress is the Legislative Department of the government, the President is the Executive Department. Neither can be restrained in its action by the Judicial Department; though the acts of both, when performed, are, in proper cases, subject to its cognizance. The impropriety of such interference will be clearly seen upon consideration of its possible consequences. 4 Wall. at 499—500).

Without exception, the basic precedents support our contention that it is for the President to decide whether to disclose confidential presidential communications, and that his discretion is not subject to judicial review. Otherwise, the "essential co-equality" of the three branches, as the Court described it in *Humphrey's Executor* v. *United States*, 295 U.S. 602, 630 (1935), would be ended, and we would have taken a long—and probably irreversible—step toward government by Judiciary. Today it would be the Presidency that would be lessened and crippled in its ability to function. Tomorrow it could be Congress, for if presidential privacy must yield to a judicial determination, it is difficult to think of any ground on which congressional privacy could continue to stand.[61]

D. *An Allegation of Criminal Activity Does Not Overcome the Assertion of Presidential Privilege*

Even if the Special Prosecutor were able to make an evidentiary showing that the requested conversations were in furtherance of an alleged criminal conspiracy, such a showing could not overcome a presidential assertion of executive privilege. Executive privilege, unlike the attorney-client privilege, the husband-wife privilege, and other personal and evidentiary privileges, is a constitutional privilege which runs to the benefit of the public, rather than to the benefit of a particular individual. *Kaiser Aluminum and Chemical Corp.* v. *United States*, 157 F. Supp. 939, 944 (Ct. Cl. 1958). Current case law supports the view that proof of criminality will allow the defeat of an assertion of individual privilege. *United States* v. *Aldridge*, 484 F.

[61] Some measure of congressional privacy would remain under the Speech or Debate Clause of Article I, Sec. 6, but it is clear that Congress has long claimed a right of privacy, based on separation of powers, that goes far beyond what is protected by the Speech or Debate Clause.

2d 655, 658 (7th Cir. 1973).[62]

The issue of whether this Court should allow an allegation of criminality to defeat a presidential assertion of privilege should be reached only after thorough and careful consideration of the applicable constitutional principles. The separation of powers doctrine is obviously vital to this determination, since this Court's consideration of the issue must necessarily include the broadest logical extensions that could result from denying the validity of the privilege. The Special Prosecutor argued successfully to the district court that the public interest to be served by disclosure of presidential conversations is the interest in seeing that "a trial is based upon all relevant and material evidence relating to the charges." (Memorandum of the Special Prosecutor, May 10, 1974, at p. 24). This finite interest in one criminal case must be weighed against the public interest in preserving the Presidency as a co-equal branch of government. The district court's construction of the exective privilege should not be allowed to stand merely to satisfy the desire to insure that "a criminal trial [is] based upon *all* relevant and material evidence relating to the charges." (Memorandum of the Special Prosecutor, May 10, 1974, at 24.)

Executive privilege, inherent in the separation of powers doctrine, extends to an entire branch of government. It is not an individual privilege. The right of confidentiality of executive communications is not a right established for the personal benefit of any one President. Consequently, even an abuse of that right by a President should not affect the validity or vitality of the privilege. If a President abuses the privileges and powers of his office, the proper remedy is not to reduce the office, but to deal with the offense, and to do so in accordance with the Constitution, *Marbury* v. *Madison*, 1 Cranch (5 U.S.) 137, (1803); *Kendall* v. *United States* ex rel. *Stokes*, 12 Peters (37 U.S.) 524, 609 (1838).

The Framers of the Constitution were aware of the potential abuse by a President of a right or privilege accorded to his office. Nevertheless, it was made clear that the privilege was not affected. Only two days before the adoption of the Constitution,

---

[62] It is interesting to note in *Aldridge* that the individual privilege was held to fail only after the government, by producing evidence *at trial*, has established a *prima facie* case that the defendants had been involved in both securities and mail-fraud. 484 F. 2d at 658. It would be incongruous to allow a pre-trial showing of a grand jury's determination developed in a non-adversary forum, namely, that the President had an undefined role in a conspiracy, to overcome a constitutional privilege vital to the separation of powers doctrine. To do so would give the individual privilege a preferred classification over a constitutional privilege.

the question of presidential abuse of power or personal involvement in criminal actions was discussed. To protect against a President who had committed treason from being able to pardon co-offenders, Gouvenor Randolph made a motion to except cases of treason from the presidential pardon power.[63] He argued that:

> The prerogative of pardon in these cases was too great a trust. The President may himself be guilty. The Traitors may be his own instruments. (2 *Farrand* 626—627).

In opposing the motion, James Wilson stressed the impropriety of limiting the applicability of a privilege accorded to the executive office because of the potential for abuse by an individual holding that office for a term. Should the officeholder be involved in the conspiracy, he argued, procedures were available in the Constitution other than the limitations or destruction of the privilege, that would deal with such abuse.

The Framers' rationale for not limiting the privileges and powers vested in the Presidency is equally applicable here. The right of confidentiality of the executive office, which has been recognized for the past 187 years, cannot be diminished, disregarded, or destroyed by the alleged criminal activities of the officeholder. Should any incumbent abuse the office, the sole remedy is impeachment, not judicial limitations or exceptions to the privileges or rights vested in the Presidency itself. *Mississippi v. Johnson*, 4 Wall (71 U.S.) 475 (1867); *Marbury v. Madison*, 1 Cranch (5 U.S.) 137 (1803); *Ex Parte Grossman*, 267 U.S. 87, 121 (1925). An allegation of criminal involvement on the part of a President, therefore, does not affect the right of confidentiality which inheres in his office.

V. THE SPECIAL PROSECUTOR HAS FAILED TO DEMONSTRATE A UNIQUE AND COMPELLING NEED REQUIRED UNDER *NIXON* V. *SIRICA* TO OVERCOME A VALID CLAIM OF PRESIDENTIAL PRIVILEGE

As we have shown above, the assertion of privilege by a President is necessarily absolute and unreviewable. However, under different factual circumstances, in *Nixon v. Sirica*, 487 F. 2d 700 (D.C. Cir. 1973), the United States Court of Appeals for the District of Columbia Circuit held, that presidential

---

[63] Describing the President's power to grant pardons, the United States Constitution, Art II, Section 2, Clause 1, provides: "... he shall have the power to Grant Reprieves and Pardons for Offenses against the United States, except in cases of Impeachment."

conversations are "presumptively privileged," 487 F. 2d at 717, and may be overcome only by a "uniquely powerful showing," 487 F. 2d at 717, that the material subpoenaed was "critical," 487 F. 2d at 706, and contain[ed] evidence peculiarly necessary . . . for which no effective substitute is available. 487 F. 2d at 717.

A. Privilege Generally

Thus, even if an evidentiary showing as required by Rule 17(c) had been made as to each of the requested items, the Special Prosecutor must demonstrate a unique and compelling need to overcome the privileged nature of the materials. He has not done so, nor is he able to do so in this case. Although a party seeking production of material pursuant to Rule 17(c) may establish that the requested items are both relevant and evidentiary, a subpoena will not issue if the requested material is subject to a valid claim of privilege. In *Mackey* v. *United States*, 351 F. 2d 794, 795 (D.C. Cir. 1965), the court of appeals acknowledged the defense of "privilege" and held that "the government may be required to produce documents in its possession unless it makes a valid claim of privilege." Courts have long recognized that the public interest in maintaining state secrets of a diplomatic or military nature will override the interests in continuing litigation. See e.g. *Totten* v. *United States*, 92 U.S. 105, 107 (1875); *United States* v. *Reynolds* 345 U.S. 1, 11 (1953). The Judiciary has also responded to executive pleas to protect "intra-governmental documents reflecting * * * deliberations comprising part of a process by which governmental decision and policies are formulated." *Cary Zeiss Stiftung* v. *V. E. B. Carl Zeiss, Jena*, 40 F.R.D. 318, 324 (D.D.C. 1966), aff'd on the opinion below, 128 U.S. App. D.C. 10, 384, F. 2d 979, *cert. denied* 389 U.S. 952 (1967); *Kaiser Aluminum & Chemical Corp.* v. *United States*, 157 F. Supp. 939, 946 (Ct. Cl. 1958).

Similarly, in *Continental Oil Co.* v. *United States*, 330 F. 2d 347 (9th Cir. 1964), the existence of a valid claim of attorney client privilege as to the various documents requested by a grand jury was sufficient alone to quash a subpoena *duces tecum*. See also *United States* v. *White*, 322 U.S. 694, 699 (1944) (privilege against self-incrimination), *United States* v. *Jacobs*, 322 F. Supp. 1299 (C.D. Cal. 1971) (attorney-client privilege) and *United States* v. *Judson*, 322 F. 2d 460 (9th Cir. 1963) (privilege against self-incrimination). Moreover, if even a portion of a requested document is not subject to a valid claim of confidentiality, the privileged portions should nevertheless not be subject to disclosure by subpoena. Cf. *Magida* v. *Continental Can Co.*, 12 F.R.D. 74, 77 (S.D. N.Y. 1951).

B. *Applicability of Executive Privilege*

Under *Nixon v. Sirica*, 487 F. 2d 700 (D.C. Cir. 1973), the same rationale for individual privileges is equally applicable to a valid claim of executive privilege. The peculiar circumstances of the decision in *Nixon* v. *Sirica* should be outlined in order to better understand the scope of the court's treatment of executive privilege. In that case, the Special Prosecutor's showing in support of a grand jury subpoena was held to be sufficient to overcome the assertion of executive privilege. The court observed: "[t]he strength and particularity of this showing were made possible by a unique intermeshing of events unlikely soon, if ever, to recur." 487 F. 2d at 705. Based on sworn testimony before the Senate Committee investigating the Watergate incident and the testimony before the grand jury investigating the Watergate incident, the Special Prosecutor was able to demonstrate to the court's satisfaction that significant inconsistencies in the sworn testimony of presidential advisors relating to the content of conversations of these advisors raised a distinct possibility that perjury had been committed before the Senate Committee, and, perhaps, before the grand jury itself. 487 F. 2d at 705. This is the context in which *Nixon* v. *Sirica* must be read.

In that case, the court of appeals expressly "acknowledge[d] the longstanding judicial recognition of executive privilege," 487 F. 2d at 713, and agreed that the conversations involved were "presumptively privileged" 487 F. 2d at 717. The court noted that the presumption of privilege premised on the public interest in confidentiality may "fail in the face of the uniquely powerful showing made by the Special Prosecutor in this case." *Id.* at 713. Simple logic dictates, however, that if a presumption is not to be merely illusory, then a certain quantum of evidence is needed to overcome it. In this regard, the court stated that a claim of executive privilege is entitled to "great weight." 487 F. 2d at 715. Thus, the quantum of evidence to overcome the privilege must necessarily be even greater. It must at least be "uniquely powerful" since the court's holding in *Nixon* v. *Sirica* was premised on a "particularized showing of the grand jury's need for each of the several subpoenaed tapes," a need that both the District Court, 360 F. Supp. at 11 n. 7, and the majority of the court of appeals called "well documented and imposing." 487 F. 2d at 705.

It is important to recognize that the decision of the majority of the court of appeals in *Nixon* v. *Sirica* was based on the unique need of the grand jury, and not that of a prosecutor in a post-indictment setting. Indeed, the special function of the grand jury was the predicate for the court's finding that the "presumption of privilege premised on the public interest in confidentiality must fail in the face of the uniquely powerful showing made by the Special Prosecutor in this case." 487 F. 2d at 717. The court said:

> The function of the grand jury mandated by the Fifth Amendment for the institution of federal criminal prosecutions for capital or other serious crimes, is not only to indict persons when there is probable cause to believe they have committed crime, but also to protect persons from prosecution when probable cause does not exist. As we have noted, the Special Prosecutor has made a strong showing that the subpoenaed tapes contain evidence peculiarly necessary to the carrying out of this vital function—*evidence for which no effective substitute is available.* (487 F. 2d at 717) (emphasis added).

The court of appeals continually reaffirmed this limitation of its holding by speaking in terms of the grand jury's access and emphasizing that "we limit our decision strictly to that required by the precise and entirely unique circumstances of the case." 487 F. 2d at 704. See also 487 F. 2d at 722.

The fundamental distinction between a grand jury's need for evidence and that of a prosecutor in a post-indictment setting is significant here. The Special Prosecutor's position in requesting information for trial is not analogous to, and indeed is essentially different from, that of a grand jury seeking "evidence critical to [its] decision as to whether and whom to indict." 487 F. 2d at 706. By the very nature of the grand jury's function, the scope of its need for evidence is much broader than that of a prosecutor in a post-indictment setting. The standards of relevancy and materiality are thus necessarily much narrower in a trial setting than that of a grand jury investigation. This undisputed fact was recognized in *Schwimmer* v. *United States*, 332 F. 2d 855 (8th Cir.), *cert. denied*, 352 U.S. 833 (1956) when the court stated. "[R]elevance and materiality necessarily are items of broader content in their use as to a grand jury investigation than in their use as to the evidence of a trial." 232 F. 2d at 862. The rationale for having this stricter standard at the trial stage was explained by the court *In Re Grand Jury Subpoena Duces Tecum*, 203 F. Supp. 575 (S.D.N.Y. 1961). "[B]ecause the grand jury may have to develop evidence for the first time, the requirements of relevance and materiality are certainly less strict on a grand jury investigation than at trial." 203 F. Supp. at 579. The district court in this case totally failed to address this distinction.

In *Nixon* v. *Sirica*, the Special Prosecutor was able to show that the nine tapes he requested "were each directly relevant to the grand jury's task" and they contained "evidence critical to the grand jury's decision as to whether and whom to indict," 487 F.2d at 706, "evidence for which no effective substitute is available." 487 F. 2d at 717. No such descriptions can be used to justify the Special Prosecutor's need in this case. There has been no allegation that the requested materials are essential or even necessary to the trial. Nor has there been any attempt to demonstrate what relevant and admissible evidence is lacking that the subpoenaed material will fulfill. For all that is known, the material sought, to the extent that it may exist, may not contain any relevant evidence or the evidence it may contain may be wholly cumulative of matters than can be otherwise proved. In addition a large volume of evidence, both documentary and testimonial, is already available to the Special Prosecutor, including a very significant amount of material furnished him by the President.[64]

We submit that the public interest that would be served by disclosure in a post-indictment context is substantially less compelling than it is in a grand jury context, a rationale recognized by the court in *Schwimmer* v. *United States*, 232 F. 2d 855 (8th Cir.), *cert. denied*, 352 U.S. 833 (1956). The presumption of privilege remains the same in both contexts. However, after a grand jury's finding of probable cause, the prosecutor's ability to make a showing of compelling need for the production of evidence is greatly enhanced because of evidence already available to him. Thus, in a post-indictment setting his burden of showing compelling need must necessarily be greater and factually more difficult, if it is to overcome the presumption of privilege. This conclusion is further enhanced by the fact that the Special Prosecutor signed the indictment returned by the grand jury in this case, which indeed could not have been returned without his assent. *United States* v. *Cox*, 372 F. 2d 167 (5th Cir.), *cert. denied*, 381 U.S. 935 (1965). Therefore, the Special Prosecutor must have been satisfied that sufficient competent evidence of criminality was available to

---

[64] Subsequent to the issuance of this subpoena, the President made available voluminous transcripts of numerous privileged conversations regarding Watergate-related matters to both the Special Prosecutor and the general public.

warrant the proceeding to trial against the persons indicted. The need for additional incriminating evidence, even if the items presently sought were in fact evidentiary, is bound to be cumulative or corroborative—certainly not a clear and compelling necessity.

C. *Balancing Test*

The court of appeals in *Nixon* v. *Sirica,* in deciding whether to quash a grand jury subpoena *duces tecum,* indicated that "the application of executive privilege depends on a weighing of the public interest protected by the privilege against the public interests that could be served by disclosure in a particular case." 487 F. 2d at 716. The court also acknowledged, "[t]hat the President's special interests may warrant a careful judicial screening of subpoenas . . . ," 487 F. 2d at 710, and if this "judicial screening" is to be meaningful, it must occur before a court engages in the balancing process. The court of appeals recognized this when it quoted with approval, the statement of Chief Justice Marshall in *United States* v. *Burr,* 25 F. Cas. 187, No. 14, 694 (C.C.D. Va. 1807):

> The President, although subject to the general rules which apply to others, may have sufficient motives for declining to produce a particular paper, and those motives may be such as to restrain the court from enforcing its production * * *. I can readily conceive that the President might receive a letter which it would be improper to exhibit in public * * *. The occasion for *demanding* it ought, in such a case, to be very strong and to be fully shown to the court before its production could be *insisted* on. 25 F. Cas. at 190-192. (emphasis in original) (487 F. 2d at 710).

Other cases also clearly demonstrate that in order for a court to balance countervailing public interest, the party seeking disclosure must make a threshold showing of compelling need or "uniquely powerful" need. In *United States* v. *Reynolds,* 345 U.S. 1 (1953), a case relied upon in *Nixon* v. *Sirica,* this court stated:

> In each case, the showing of necessity which is made will determine how far the court should probe in satisfying itself that the occasion for invoking the privilege is appropriate. Where there is a strong showing of necessity, the claim of privilege should not be lightly accepted, but even the most compelling necessity cannot overcome the claim of privilege if the court is ultimately satisfied that military secrets are at stake. *A fortiori,* where necessity is dubious, a formal claim of

privilege . . . will have to prevail. (345 U.S. at 11).

At another point in *Reynolds* this Court stated:

[W]e will not go so far as to say that the court may automatically require a complete disclosure to the judge before the claim of privilege will be accepted in any case. *Id.*

This point is further illustrated by *Committee for Nuclear Responsibility, Inc.* v. *Seaborg*, 463 F. 2d 788, 792 (D.C. Cir. 1971). There the court held:

Of course, the party seeking discovery must make a preliminary showing of necessity to warrant even *in camera* disclosure, . . .

Certainly, this well-documented principle supports the proposition that, before a court can even engage in balancing, the party seeking disclosure must show a compelling need to overcome a presumption of privilege. *Senate Select Committee on Presidential Campaign Activities* v. *Richard M. Nixon*, Slip Op. No. 74-1258 (D.C. Cir. May 23, 1974). Since that showing has not been made in this case, it was incumbent upon the district court to grant the President's motion to quash.

It is clear that the Special Prosecutor has failed to make the requisite showing of compelling need necessary to activate the balancing test. Nor has he made a sufficient showing to establish that each of the requested materials is relevant and admissible and that it is not an attempt to discover additional evidence already known. Therefore under well-established case law, the subpoena should have been quashed in all respects by the court below.

VI. AN INCUMBENT PRESIDENT CANNOT LAWFULLY BE CHARGED WITH A CRIME BY A GRAND JURY

A. *The President Cannot Be Indicted While He Is Serving as President*

It has never been seriously disputed by legal scholars, jurists, or constitutional authorities that a President may not be indicted while he is an incumbent. The reasons for the President's non-indictability bear directly on the question of whether he may be named as an unindicted co-conspirator by a grand jury. The reasons are obvious and compelling. They are particularly relevant in the light of the ongoing proceedings in the House of Representatives.

The Presidency is the only branch of government that is vested exclusively in one person by the Constitution. Art. II, Section 1, Clause 1 states:

The executive Power shall be vested in a President of the United States of America. He shall hold his Office during the Term of four years   *   *   *

Article II then details the powers and functions that the President shall personally have and perform. The functioning of the executive branch ultimately depends on the President's personal capacity: legal, mental and physical. If the President cannot function freely, there is a critical gap in the whole constitutional system established by the Framers.

The President, personally, as no other individual, is necessary to the proper maintenance of orderly government. Thus, in order to control the dangerous possibility of any incapacity affecting the President, and hence the executive branch, the Constitution specifically limits and provides for all those events that could incapacitate a President.[65]

The necessary reason for the great concern and specificity of the Constitution in providing for a President at all times capable of fulfilling his duties, is the fact that all three branches of government must have the capacity to function if the system is to work. While the capacity to function is assured to the legislative and judicial branches by the numbers of individuals who comprise them, the executive branch must depend on the personal capacity of a single individual, the President. Since the executive's responsibilities include the day-to-day administration of the government, including all emergency functions, his capacity to function at any hour is highly critical. Needless to say, if the President were indictable while in office, any prosecutor and grand jury would have within their power the ability to cripple an entire branch of the national government and hence the whole system.

Further analysis makes it even more clear that a President may not be indicted while in office. The President is vested under Art. II, section 3, clause 1, with the power "that the Laws be faithfully executed" and he has under Art. II, section 2, clause 1, the power of granting "Pardons for Offenses against the United States, except in Cases of Impeachment." Under that same clause, he shall appoint the "Judges of the Supreme Court" with "the Advice and Consent of the Senate." The President has also been granted by Congress the same power to appoint all Article III judges. 28 U.S.C. 44 and 28 U.S.C. 133. Since the President's powers include control over all federal prosecutions, it is hardly

---

[65] U.S. Const., Amend. 25, ratified on February 23, 1967. See Congressional Research Service, United States Congress, *The Constitution of the United States* at 42-43.

reasonable or sensible to consider the President subject to such prosecution. This is consistent with the concept of prosecutorial discretion, the integrity of the criminal justice system or a rational administrative order. This is particularly true in light of the impeachment clause which makes a President amenable to post-impeachment indictment. Art. I, section 3, clause 7. This clause takes account of the fact that the President is not indictable and recognizes that impeachment and conviction must occur before the judicial process is applicable to the person holding office as President. This section reads: "But the Party convicted shall nevertheless be liable and subject to Indictment, Trial, Judgment and Punishment, according to Law."While out of necessity an incumbent President must not be subject to indictment in order for our constitutional system to operate, he is not removed from the sanction of the law. He can be indicted after he leaves office at the end of his term or after being "convicted" by the Senate in an impeachment proceeding.

The history surrounding the Constitution's adoption further makes it clear that impeachment is the exclusive remedy for presidential criminal misconduct. A very revealing interchange took place on September 15, 1787, only two days before the final adoption of the Constitution. Gouverneur Randolph moved to except cases of treason from the power of the President to pardon offenses against the United States, a power granted by Art. II, section 2, clause 7.

Judgment in Cases of Impeachment shall not extend further than to removal from Office, and disqualification to hold and enjoy any Office of honor, Trust, or Profit under the United States: but the Party convicted shall nevertheless be liable and subject to Indictment, Trial, Judgment, and Punishment, according to Law.

There are several relevant considerations that should be noted about the Convention and the provision that resulted from them. First, it is clear that an incumbent President is not subject to criminal prosecution. He is amenable to the criminal laws, but only after he has been impeached and convicted, and thus stripped of his critical constitutional functions.

The text of Art. I, section 3, clause 7, points so explicitly in that direction that it hardly requires exposition, and the legislative history is wholly in accord. James Wilson noted that if the President himself be a "party to the guilt he can be impeached and prosecuted." 2 *Farrand* 626. And on September 4, 1787, in the recurring debate on whether impeachments should be tried by the Senate or by the Supreme Court, Gouverneur Morris said:

A conclusive reason for making the Senate instead of the Supreme Court the Judge of Impeachments, was that the latter was to try the President after the trial of the impeachment. 2 *Farrand* 500.

The decision to make the Senate, and not the Supreme Court,[66] the ultimate body to decide upon the President's removal, further argues for limiting any court or grand jury from removing a President by way of indictment or other judicial process.

There is literally nothing in all of the records of the Convention to suggest that any delegate had any contrary view. This reading of the language in question was put forward twice by Hamilton when he wrote:

The punishment which may be the consequence of conviction upon impeachment, is not to terminate the chastisement of the offender. After having been sentenced to a perpetual ostracism from the esteem and confidence, and honors and emoluments of his country, he will still be liable to prosecution and punishment in the ordinary course of law. *The Federalist*, No. 65, at 426 (Modern Library ed. 1937).

He returns to the point in the 69th *Federalist*, and uses it there to illustrate an important distinction between a President and a king.

The President of the United States would be liable to be impeached, tried, and, upon conviction of treason, bribery, or other high crimes or misdemeanors, removed from office; and would afterwards be liable to prosecution and punishment in the ordinary course of law. The person of the King of Great Britain is sacred and inviolable; there is no constitutional tribunal to which he is amenable; no punishment to which he can be subjected without involving the crisis of a national revolution.

So far as we are aware, that an incumbent President is not indictable is a proposition that has never been challenged by the

---

[66] In this respect Gouverneur Morris noted:

[N]o other tribunal than the Senate could be trusted [to try the President]. The Supreme Court were too few in number and might be warped or corrupted. He was agst. [sic] a dependence of the Executive on the Legislature, considering the Legislative tyranny the great danger to be apprehended; but there could be no danger that the Senate would say untruly on their oaths that the President was guilty of crimes or facts, especially as in four years he can be turned out. 2 *Farrand 551*.

Special Prosecutor. The proposition is relevant here because of the suggestion that an otherwise valid claim of privilege by the President should be overridden if there is in some manner an alleged showing of a *prima facie* criminal case or a *prima facie* finding of criminal involvement, such as the authorizing of the naming, or the naming of the President as an unindicted co-conspirator. If, however, such facts were true, which they are not, they go not to the evidentiary needs of the grand jury, but to those of the Committee on the Judiciary in the House.

Whatever the grand jury may claim about a President, its only possible proper recourse is to refer such facts, with the consent of the court, to the House and leave the conclusions of criminality to that body which is constitutionally empowered to make them. The grand jury may not indict the President or allege that there is probable cause to find criminal liability on the part of a President. Thus, such a claimed "finding" by the grand jury has no force in overcoming any presidential claim of privilege, as it is a legal nullity, being constitutionally impermissible.

A second important theme that runs through the debates of the Constitutional Convention of 1787 is whether the President should be answerable, in an impeachment proceeding, to the courts or to the Senate. On June 13, 1787, the Committee of the Whole adopted a resolution offered by Messrs. Randolph and Madison to give the national Judiciary jurisdiction of "Impeachments of any national officers." 1 *Farrand* 224. On July 18th, however, the Convention voted unanimously to remove the language giving the courts jurisdiction of impeachments. 2 *Farrand* 39. This did not end the matter. The report of the Committee on Detail, on August 6th, would have given the Supreme Court original jurisdiction "in cases of impeachment." 2 *Farrand* 186. As noted above a subsequent committee, however, recommended on September 4th that the trial of impeachments be by the Senate, 2 *Farrand* 493. This was approved on September 8th by a vote of nine states to two. 2 *Farrand* 547. See the report of the debate on this issue at 2 *Farrand* 551-553.

The significance of the foregoing history is that it is not mere chance or inadvertence that the President is made answerable to the Senate, sitting as a Court of Impeachment. The Framers repeatedly considered making him answerable to the Judiciary, and they twice rejected proposals to this effect, thus further reinforcing the conclusion that it would be wholly inconsistent with the Framer's intent to hold a President indictable.

Finally, it should also be observed that there was no sentiment in the Convention for providing restraints other than impeachment against a President. The argument went quite the other way. There was sentiment in the Convention that a President would not be subject even to impeachment and that it would be enough that he served for a limited term and would answer to the people if he chose to stand for reelection. This point was extensively debated on July 20, 1787, with the motion to strike out the impeachment provision offered by Charles Pinckney and Gouverneur Morris, 2 *Farrand* 64—69. The arguments in favor of the Pinckney motion seem unpersuasive, and in fact during the course of the debate on it, Morris admitted that the discussion had changed his mind. But the debate is interesting because those who opposed the Pinckney motion, and supported retention of impeachment, made it clear that this was the only means by which they considered that the President was subject to law. Thus, Colonel George Mason said:

> No point is of more importance than that the right of impeachment should be continued. Shall any man be above Justice? Above all shall that man be above it, who can commit the most extensive injustice? When great crimes were committed he was for punishing the principal as well as the Coadjutors. (2 *Farrand* 65).

And again Eldridge Gerry—

> urged the necessity of impeachments. A good magistrate will not fear them. A bad one ought to be kept in fear of them. He hoped that maxim would never be adopted here that the Chief Magistrate could do no wrong. (2 *Farrand* 66).

By a vote of eight states to two, the Pinckney motion was defeated and the Convention agreed that the Executive should be removable on impeachment. 2 *Farrand* 69. But it is only conviction in the Senate that leads to this result. On September 14th, the Convention rejected, by a vote of eight states to three, a proposal that an officer impeached by the House be suspended from office until tried and acquitted by the Senate. 2 *Farrand* 612-613.

This examination of the proceedings of the Constitutional Convention of 1787 establishes that the Framers deliberately chose one particular means of guarding against the abuse of the powers they entrusted to a President. He may not be indicted unless and until he has been impeached and convicted by the Senate. Impeachment is the device that ensures that he is not above justice during the term in office, and the trial of impeachment is left to the Senate and not to the courts.

Those principles have been recognized by this Court. In the

early and leading case of *Marbury* v. *Madison* 1 Cranch (5 U.S.) 137, 165 (1803), the Court said:

> By the Constitution of the United States, the President is invested with certain important political powers, in the exercise of which he is to use his own discretion, and is accountable only to his country in his political character, and to his own conscience.

Thirty-five years later, in *Kendall* v. *United States ex. rel. Stokes*, 12 Pet. (37 U.S.) 524, 610 (1838) the Court said:

> The executive power is vested in a President and as far as his powers are derived from the Constitution, he is beyond the reach of any other department, except in the mode prescribed by the Constitution through the impeaching power.[67]

We are wholly mindful of weighty warnings aginst the view that "the great clauses of the Constitution must be confined to the interpretation which the Framers, with the conditions and outlook of their time, would have placed upon them. . . ." *Home Building & Loan Assn.* v. *Blaisdell.* 290 U.S. 398, 443 (1934). But if the provisions of the Constitution that we have been discussing can fairly be said to have taken on new meaning with the passage of years, and with the emergence of new problems, surely any change must be in the direction of strengthening the independence of the Presidency, rather than creating new hobbles on it.

Powell v. *McCormick*, 395 U.S. 486 (1969), reaffirms the extraordinary nature and strictly limited character of the power to remove political officials, particularly those directly elected by the people. That decision held that the Congress could not expand the constitutional limits mandated for expelling or alternatively excluding a Congressman from his seat. U.S. Const., Article I, section 5, clause 2; Article I, section 2, clause 2. The constitutional sanctity of the people's electoral choice, therefore, was considered so important that it required judicial intervention and protection. While judicial action was required in *Powell* to protect the electorate's rights under the Constitution, the reverse is certainly not true. This same power cannot be used to nullify the electorate's decision. This is particularly true in the case of the Presidency when the Constitution explicitly delegates the

---

[67] See also the observations in 1 Bryce, *The American Commonwealth* 89 (1889):

The President is personally responsible for his acts, not indeed to Congress, but to the people, by whom he is chosen. No means exist of enforcing this responsibility, except by impeachment, but as his power lasts for four years only, and is much restricted, this is no serious evil.

power to remove the President under strict conditions to the representatives of the voters who elected him. It seems improbable, at best, to suggest that the Framers felt that any court and grand jury could also remove or even legally incapacitate the Chief Executive. The specificity and grave nature of the impeachment process and the total absence of any discussion of any other method, is an extremely powerful argument for the exclusivity of impeachment as the only method of removing a President.

The *Powell* case emphasizes that while another branch cannot control the Congress in the execution of their peculiar constitutional responsibilities, neither can the Congress, as a whole, control the execution of a particular Congressman's duties via exclusion. Exclusion is an action that the Congress may take solely within the limits of Article I, Section 2, Clause 2. It is not a political tool. Obviously this also applies to the executive branch. If Congressman Powell could not be excluded from his congressional seat by a majority of Congress except by adhering to the requirements of the Constitution, then surely the Chief Executive may not be deprived of his ability to control decisions in the executive branch by a member of the executive department, unless the President has specifically delegated this authority to him. Nor can such an employee control the President through judicial or criminal process.

The decision in *Powell* is also harmonious with the long established principle that the Judiciary may prevent other branches from overstepping their constitutional bounds of responsibility. *Marbury* v. *Madison*, 1 Cranch (5 U.S.) 137 (1803). In *Youngstown Sheet & Tube Co.* v. *Sawyer*, 343 U.S. 579 (1952), this Court made a similar determination that certain actions taken by the executive branch were beyond the scope of the constitutional duties mandated to the branch. If the Judiciary had determined that seizing the steel mills had been within the powers the Constitution and the laws had entrusted to the President, clearly it could not have forced the President to exercise his discretion and seize the mills. Although the Supreme Court has ruled innumerable laws unconstitutional over the last 187 years it has never once mandated that either Congress exercise its descretion to pass a law or the Executive prosecute an individual. The reasons are self-evident.

Today, in our nuclear age, far more than in George Washington's time, the nature of our country and of the world insistently requires a President who is free to act as the public interest requires, within the framework created by the Constitution. The whole Watergate problem has illustrated how truly complex the right decision can be. It is thus all the more necessary that a President have the ability to freely discuss issues, think out loud, play the devil's advocate, and consider alternatives, free from the threat that a probing statement will one day form the basis for an allegation of criminal liability.

B. *The Grand Jury Action of Naming the President as an Unindicted Co-Conspirator Is a Nullity*

The constitutional policy that mandates that the President is not subject to judicial process or criminal indictment while President, clearly shows that the grand jury action naming or authorizing the name of the President as an unindicted co-conspirator contravenes the constitutional power of the grand jury or any court of this country.

The implication by a grand jury on the basis of certain alleged facts, that the President may have violated the law can have only one proper result. As stated above, the grand jury may with the district court's consent, forward the factual material creating the implications, minus any conclusions, to the House of Representatives.[68] That result was fulfilled when the grand jury filed with the court below its factual report and recommended that it be forwarded to the House Judiciary Committee, in March of 1974. The President made no objection to this move because the House of Representatives is the proper body, the only proper body, to impeach a President, as part of the process of removing a President from office. The grand jury's constitutionally impermissible authorization to the Special Prosecutor, permitting the President to be named or naming the President as an unindicted co-conspirator, however, attempts to subvert and prejudice the legitimate constitutional procedure of impeachment.

In its opinion in *In Re Report and Recommendation of the June 5, 1972 Grand Jury Concerning Transmission of Evidence to the House of Representatives,* 370 F. Supp. 1219 (D.D.C. 1974), the district court convincingly demonstrated why the

---

[68] This is the necessary implication of the grand jury's role, as a body with a limited mandate, as opposed to the House of Representatives whose political and constitutional mandate entitles them to consider whether in light of the President's complex responsibilities and political concerns a particular action or statement of his constitutes a crime. While any citizen may clearly express an opinion to his Congressman on the President's guilt, innocence or character, a grand jury, as an official part of our system of justice, with all that implies for its credibility and impact, may not.

June 5, 1972, Grand Jury could not authorize the naming of the President as an unindicted co-conspirator. The very reasons why it was proper to refer the *Report and Recommendation to the House of Representatives* are those that argue against referring the naming or the authorization to name the President as an unindicted co-conspirator to that same body. In fact, these same considerations today require its expungement, because it is a legal nullity that continues to prejudice the President by its purported legal significance and apparent authority. The court below noted of the Report.

The Report here at issue suffers from none of the objectionable qualities noted in *Hammond* and *United Electrical*. It draws no accusatory conclusions. It deprives no one of an official forum in which to respond. It is not a substitute for indictments where indictments might properly issue. *It contains no recommendations, advice or statements that infringe on the prerogatives of other branches of government.* Indeed, its only recommendation is to the Court, and rather than injuring separation of powers principles, the Jury sustains them by lending its aid to the House in the exercise of that body's constitutional jurisdiction. It renders no moral or social judgments. The Report is a simple and straightforward compilation of information gathered by the Grand Jury, and no more. (370 F. Supp at 1226) (emphasis added).

As noted by the district court nothing could be more important to America's future than that the ongoing impeachment be "unswervingly fair." 370 F. Supp at 1230. And nothing could be more clear than that the naming of the President of the United States as an unindicted co-conspirator by a secret grand jury proceeding, which was subsequently leaked to the press, is a direct and damaging assault on the fairness of the House impeachment proceeding. It is the kind of prejudice that a court would certainly be required to remedy or compensate for if it affected the rights of a criminal defendant to a trial, free from the probability of prejudicial pre-trial publicity. *In Re Murchison,* 349 U.S. 133 (1955); *Estes* v. *Texas,* 381 U.S. 532 (1965); *Sheppard* v. *Maxwell,* 384 U.S. 333 (1966).

This unauthorized action of the grand jury that has the appearance of official status, and presently the implicit approval of the lower court may well directly affect the outcome of the House procedure. Yet, the President has no legal recourse against the grand jury's action execpt with this Court. No petit jury, whose obligation is to find guilt "beyond a reasonable doubt" is empowered to adjudicate this charge against the President.[69]

The rigorous adversary format, with that most powerful tool for determining the truth, cross-examination, is not available in the secret grand jury setting. It is now well established that the right of cross-examination is an essential element of due process in any proceeding where an individual's "property" or "reputation" may be adversely affected.[70] The fundamental right to present evidence and to cross-examine witnesses in an impeachment proceeding is manifest. As the experience of our judicial system has demonstrated, the most effective method of establishing the truth of an accusation is to permit the respondent the right to personally cross-examine those presenting adverse testimony. The Supreme Court flatly states in *Greene* v. *McElroy*, 360 U.S. 474 (1959) that:

> Certain principles have remained relatively immutable in our jurisprudence. One of these is that where governmental action seriously injures an individual, and the reasonableness of the action depends on fact findings, the evidence used to prove the Government's case must be disclosed to the individual so that he has an opportunity to show that it is untrue. While this is important in the case of documentary evidence, it is even more important where the evidence consists of the testimony of individuals whose memory might be faulty or who, in fact, might be perjurers or persons motivated by malice, vindictiveness, intolerance, prejudice or jealousy. We have formalized these protections in the requirements of confrontation and cross-examination. They have ancient roots. They find expression in the Sixth Amendment. . . . This Court has been zealous to protect these rights from erosion. It has spoken out only in criminal cases, . . . but also in all types of cases where administrative . . . action was under scrutiny. (360 U.S. at 496-497).

Justice Douglas in the concurring opinion in *Peters* v. *Hobby*, 349 U.S. 331 (1955), emphasized the necessity of permitting a respondent to cross-examine all adverse witnesses.

Under cross-examination [witnesses] stories might disappear

---

[69] While the President, as an individual, might some day vindicate himself before a petit jury, as long as he holds the office of President he could not be vindicated in a court of law.

[70] *Goldberg* v. *Kelly*, 397 U.S. 254 (1970); *Sniadach* v. *Family Finance Corp.*, 395 U.S. 337 (1969); *Fuentes* v. *Shevin*, 407 U.S. 67 (1972); *Bell* v. *Benson*, 402 U.S. 535 (1971); Cf. *Board of Regents* v. *Roth*, 408 U.S. 564, 573 (1972) and *Wisconsin* v. *Constaintineau*, 400 U.S. 433, 437 (1971).

like bubbles. Their whispered confidences might turn out to be yarns conceived by twisted minds or by people who, though sincere, have poor faculties of observation and memory.

Confrontation and cross-examination under oath are essential, if the American ideal of due process is to remain a vital force in our public life. We deal here with the reputation of men and their right to work—things more precious than property itself. We have here a system where government with all its power and authority condemns a man to a suspect class and outer darkness, without the rudiments of a fair trial. (349 U.S. at 351).

There is no way within our judicial system to disprove allegations made against a President. It is because of this and because of the vast impact of this purportedly official criminal implication and charge against a President, on the whole body politic, that the Constitution requires no less a body than the whole House of Representatives to find the President likely enough to be guilty of criminal misconduct that he should be tried by the Senate.

The characterization of the President of the United States as an unindicted co-conspirator, is nothing less than an attempt to nullify the presumption of innocence by a secret, non-adversary proceeding. The presumption of innocence is a fundamental of American justice; the grand jury's procedure is an implication of guilt which corrupts this ideal. To thus allow the Special Prosecutor to use such a constitutionally impermissible device, as an incident to an evidentiary desire, for the purpose of overcoming executive privilege, is wholly intolerable. The American legal system has never allowed the desire for evidence to go beyond the bounds of law. *Boyd* v. *United States*, 116 U.S. 616 (1886); *Weeks* v. *United States*, 232 U.S. 383 (1914); *Silverthorne Lumber Company* v. *United States*, 251 U.S. 385 (1920); *Mapp* v. *Ohio*, 367 U.S. 643 (1961). The President should not be made a hostage of the unwarranted pressure inherent in the grand jury's improper action.

The former Special Prosecutor, Mr. Archibald Cox, was quoted in the *New York Times* on January 5, 1974, as dealing with this exact issue. In response to rumors that he would name the President as an unindicted co-conspirator the newspaper printed this:

Mr. Cox, in the telephone interview from his vacation home in Maine, described such a technique as 'just a backhanded way of sticking the knife in.' *New York Times*, January 6, 1974, p. 1, col. 6; p. 40, col. 1.

A later issue of the *New York Times* dealt with the same basic questions when it stated:

> Leon Jaworski, the Watergate special prosecutor, advised the Federal Grand Jury investigating the Watergate break-in and cover-up that it would not be 'responsible conduct' to move to indict President Nixon, according to a spokesman for the office.
>
> Although Mr. Jaworski's advice to the Grand Jury did not refer to President Nixon by name—the matter was discussed in terms of a factual situation such as exists—it did include the suggestion that the House Judiciary Committee's impeachment inquiry was the proper forum to consider matters of evidence relating to a President.
>
> Although there had been speculation that Mr. Jaworski had tentatively concluded that legal complications militated against a move to indict the President, today's statement was the first direct confirmation of the fact. *New York Times*, March 12, 1974, p. 1.

It is only by impeachment and conviction and then subsequent criminal action that the President may be found to be a member of any criminal conspiracy. To base a desire for evidence on a stratagem which attempts to cripple the Presidency, and thus nullify the President's claim of executive privilege, is unprecedented, but more significantly a grotesque attempt to abuse the process of the judicial branch of government. Under our system of government only the House of Representatives may determine that evidence of sufficient quantity and quality exists to try the President. And, that trial must take place in the Senate with the Chief Justice presiding.

C. Even If It Were Permissible, the Naming of an Incumbent President as an Unindicted Co-Conspirator Does Not Constitute a Prima Facie Showing of Criminal Activity

In the preceding section we have conclusively demonstrated why it is not constitutionally permissible to name an incumbent President as an undicted co-conspirator. However, if such an act had been constitutionally permissible, it would nevertheless not have the effect of constituting a *prima facie* showing of criminality sufficient to overcome the President's constitutional claim of executive privilege.

There is a basic distinction between a finding of "probable cause" and the showing of a *"prima facie"* case which makes the

Special Prosecutor's use of these two terms in the instant case both inaccurate and improper.

Probable cause is a legal concept based on the proposition that a crime "might" have been committed. As such it justifies an inquiry into an individual's guilt. It does not justify any legal effect that would operate to overcome either a presumption of innocence or executive privilege attaching to an otherwise valid claim. On the other hand, *prima facie* evidence is evidence sufficient to have a legal effect, which if unrebutted, is sufficient to go to a jury in a trial setting and sufficient to convict an

individual of a crime before a petit jury. The finding of the grand jury at issue here has none of this sufficiency. It has never been tested in any adversary forum and hence is insufficient to have any legal effect on the rights or privileges of anyone.

This elementary distinction was noted by the Court in *Locke* v.*United States*, 7 Cranch (11 U.S.) 339, 348 (1813);

> It is contended, that probable cause means *prima facie* evidence, or, in other words, such evidence as, in the absence of exculpatory proof, would justify condemnation.
>
> This argument has been very satisfactorily answered on the part of the United States by the observation that this would render the provision totally inoperative. It may be added, that the term "probable cause," according to its usual acceptation, means less than evidence which would justify condemnation; and, in all cases of seizure, has a fixed and well-known meaning. It imports a seizure made under circumstances which warrant suspicion. In this, its legal sense, the court must understand the term to have been used by Congress.

Nothing could make the legal objections to using a probable cause standard to overcome a valid claim of presidential privilege clearer, than this Court in *Brinegar* v. *United States*, 338 U.S. 160, 176 (1949), when it stated:

> The rule of probable cause is a practical, nontechnical conception affording the best compromise that has been found for accommodating these often opposing interests. Requiring more would unduly hamper law enforcement. To allow less would be to leave law-abiding citizens at the mercy of the officers' whim or caprice.

The claim that the grand jury's action is sufficient to constitute a *prima facie* showing of criminality can be seen for what it is: an attempt to use a practical tool of law enforcement as a constitutional bludgeon to batter down the President's rights to due process and his fundamental right to be presumed innocent by the law. Recently this basic point was reaffirmed by the Court in *United States* v. *Ventresca*, 380 U.S. 102, 108 (1965), when in quoting *Brinegar*, this Court stated:

> There is a large difference between the two things to be proved [guilt and probable cause], as well as between the tribunals which determine them, and therefore a like difference in the quanta and modes of proof required to establish them. (338 U.S. at 108).

The *prima facie* showing that the Special Prosecutor claims to have made can only have been made if the President of the United States is to be tried and convicted by a grand jury! Thus the Special Prosecution's argument is a legal absurdity.

An indictment may be returned against an accused upon a grand jury's finding that the "evidence" constituted the existence of probable cause to believe the accused participated in criminal activity. It must always be remembered that this "evidence" is not the type of evidence that in a trial court goes to the question of guilt or innocence. It is not evidence that has ever been tested in an adversary forum, in which an opportunity would have been presented to explore its alternative inferences, to question its credibility by cross examination, and to offer evidence which may rebut the original allegation. All that the evidence weighed by a grand jury can ever be said to show fairly is that there is probable cause to believe someone should be brought to trial. In the instant case, the grand jury could only find "probable cause" of criminal activity on the part of the President and nothing more, if it could even find that. Yet the Special Prosecutor says this finding of probable cause is a *"prima facie"* showing of criminality. *Prima facie* evidence of a fact, however, is such evidence as will establish that fact in a court of law if not rebutted. *Lilienthal's Tobacco* v. *United States*, 97 U.S. 237, 268 (1877); *United States* v. *Wiggins*, 14 Pet. (39 U.S.) 334 (1840). It thus becomes obvious that in a grand jury setting, the kind of *prima facie* showing the Special Prosecutor talks about, cannot occur.

A grand jury finding of probable cause in most cases results in an indictment which is merely an accusation of criminal activity and is not evidence of criminality. In *United States* v. *Cummings*, 468 F. 2d 274, 278 (9th Cir. 1972), the Court of Appeals found serious error and reversed the judgment of the trial court because it allowed counsel for the government in closing argument to suggest that the return of an indictment by a grand jury was an indication of the guilt of the accused. In a criminal trial, the fact that a grand jury heard evidence and, based on that evidence, returned an indictment, does not allow inference of guilt. *United States* v. *Sutton*, 312 F. Supp. 969, 972 (D. Ariz. 1970), *Aff'd* 446 F. 2d 916, 922 (9th Cir. 1971), *cert. denied*, 404 U.S. 1025 (1972). In *Sutton*, the United States Attorney, in his summation, made reference to the fact that the proceeding was by indictment and that at least twelve people have to agree on the indictment after hearing evidence. This comment was objected to and the trial judge sustained the objection and, shortly thereafter, instructed the jury that the indictment is no evidence and it does not create any presumption or inference of guilt. 312 F. Supp. at 972. In this regard the court of appeals found that only the trial judge's timely actions prevented the United States Attorney's improper comment from prejudicing the appellant and eliminated any necessity for a mistrial. 446 F. 2d at 922. Likewise, only this Court's timely action in declaring the invalidity and improper character of the grand jury's action in this case will offset to some degree the prejudice to the President.

Jury instructions are frequently, if not always, used to inform a jury that an indictment is merely a formal method of accusing a defendant of a crime and is not evidence of any kind against the accused.[71] e.g. 1 Federal Jury Practice and Instructions, Devitt & Blackmar, § 11.02 at 208 (1970). Such instructions are universally accepted. See e.g., *Adjmi* v. *United States*, 343 F. 2d 164, 165 (5th Cir. 1965); *Black* v. *United States*, 309 F. 2d 331, 343 (8th Cir. 1962), *cert. denied*, 372 U.S. 934 (1963); *United States* v. *Senior*, 274 F. 2d 613, 617 (7th Cir. 1960). Therefore, since the grand jury's determination of probable cause is not evidence of guilt or criminality in a trial proceeding we submit that the court below was not and could not have been presented with a *prima facie* showing of criminality.

Moreover, in the instant case, even if the Special Prosecutor could, by some strange convolution of law and logic, make an evidentiary showing of criminality on the part of the President, it would still have been necessary for this "showing" to overcome three distinct presumptions in order to allow the trial court to rule properly that the conversations sought here are not privileged. These presumptions are (1) the presumed validity of a claim of executive privilege, (2) the presumption that every man is innocent until proven guilty, beyond a reasonable doubt, in a court of law, and (3) the presumption of regularity applied to the acts of a governmental official.

---

[71] A similar instruction is used when a charge is made by an information rather that an indictment.

Besides the presumption of validity that is inherent in any presidential assertion of executive privilege, *Nixon* v. *Sirica*, 487 F.2d 700, 715, 717 (D.C. Cir. 1973), there exists the presumption of innocence afforded to every man under the law. At the start of a trial, the law presumes an accused innocent with no evidence against him. *United States* v. *Agnew* 165 U.S. 36, 52, (1897); 9 *Wigmore On Evidence* § 2511 (3rd ed. 1940). The President, who is not even involved in a criminal proceeding, is certainly presumed innocent of criminal activity until a proper and sufficient evidentiary showing is made to demonstrate the contrary. Such a showing could only be made in an impeachment proceeding, followed by indictment, trial and conviction in a court of law. In any event, a secret, nonadversary grand jury proceeding, leaked to the public, can hardly cast any legal stones at the President's presumption of innocence. In the instant case, the Special Prosecutor has not made any evidentiary showing of criminality.

The final presumption that must be overcome in order for a judicial determination to be made that the subpoenaed conversations deal with criminal conduct is the presumption of regularity. The law presumes that government officials perform the requirements of legal conditions incumbent to their office. 9 *Wigmore On Evidence*, § 2534 (3rd ed. 1940). The President operates under the constitutionally imposed duty to see "that the Laws be faithfully executed." U.S. Const., Art. II, sec. 3. The presumption of regularity applied to the acts of the President, in the instant case, would require a presumption that, when the President converses with his aides, his action is proper and pertains to the performance of official duties imposed by law. See *F.C.C.* v. *Schreiber*, 381 U.S. 279, 296 (1965). (Administrative agencies of the government are entitled to the presumption that they will act properly and according to law.) The nature and scope of the President's constitutional mandate dictate that the quantum of evidence necessary to overcome the presumption of regularity indeed be substantial. Any other result would severely limit the President's ability to fulfill his wide discretionary responsibilities under the Constitution. Thus, the presumptions of a valid claim of executive privilege, innocence, and the regularity of governmental activities present formidable barriers which the Special Prosecutor has not overcome, and which he certainly cannot overcome behind the closed doors of a grand jury proceeding.

VII. THE SPECIAL PROSECUTOR FAILED TO SATISFY THE REQUIREMENTS FOR A RULE 17(C) SUBPOENA

A. *The Special Prosecutor Has failed to demonstrate that the materials Were Relevant and Evidentiary*

Before a determination can be made that the President's assertion of executive privilege has been overcome, the Special Prosecutor has the burden of proving that his subpoena meets the stringent requirements of Rule 17(c), Federal Rules of Criminal Procedure. The court below in its May 20, 1974, opinion and order reached the conclusion that the requirements of Rule 17(c) were met. Specifically, the court stated:

> It is the Court's position that the Special Prosecutor's May 10, 1974, memorandum correctly applies the Rule 17(c) standards particularly in the more unusual situation of this kind where the subpoena, rather than being directed to the government by defendants, issues to what, as a practical matter, is a third party. *(United States* v. *Mitchell,* Cr. No. 74-110, (D.D.C. filed May 20, 1974) at 5).

This determination of the court below is a conclusion, unsupported by any reference either to the specific requirements of Rule 17(c) or to how the Special Prosecutor's showing has satisfied these requirements. The Court's conclusion is apparently based on the Special Prosecutor's memorandum of May 10, 1974, and the court's finding that the President is a third party. The showing made in the memorandum of May 10, 1974 does not meet the strict requirements of Rule 17(c). Furthermore, the President is not to be judged as a typical third party in a judicial subpoena proceeding.

The Special Prosecutor sought this subpoena pursuant to Criminal Rule 17(c), which provides:

> A subpoena may also command the person to whom it is directed to produce the books, papers, documents or other objects designated therein. The court on motion made promptly may quash or modify the subpoena if compliance would be unreasonable or oppressive. The court may direct that books, papers, documents or objects designated in the subpoena be produced before the court at a time prior to the trial or prior to the time when they are to be offered in evidence and may upon their production permit the books, papers, documents or objects or portions thereof to be inspected by the parties and their attorneys.

The leading case discussing Rule 17(c) is *Bowman Dairy Co.* v. *United States,* 341 U.S. 214 (1951). In *Bowman,* this Court plainly emphasized that "Rule 17(c) was not intended to provide an additional means of discovery." 341 U.S. at 220. On the contrary, its application was specifically limited only to production of "evidentiary" material. 341 U.S. at 219. In this regard this court stated, "[I]n short, any document or other material admissible as evidence . . . is subject to subpoena." 341 U.S. at 221. By utilizing this admissible evidence standard in applying Rule 17(c), this Court rejected a conclusory request by the defendants for materials that "are relevant to the allegations or charges contained in said indictment, whether or not they might constitute evidence with respect to the guilt or innocence of any of the defendants . . ." 341 U.S. at 221, a request that is quite similar to the one sustained by the court below. This Court considered such a "catch-all" request as invalid for it was "not intended to produce evidentiary materials but [was] merely a fishing expedition to see what may turn up." 341 U.S. at 221.

That all subpoenaed materials under Rule 17(c) must be both evidentiary in nature and relevant is uniformly required by the courts, which have recognized that Rule 17(c) is subject to abuse by parties seeking additional pretrial discovery. Consequently, courts have developed criteria that the party seeking a pretrial subpoena must meet before compliance will be ordered. In *United States* v. *Iozia,*·13 F.R.D. 335 (S.D.N.Y. 1952), Judge Weinfeld formulated the following criteria, which have been frequently cited by other courts:

(1) That the documents are evidentiary and relevant;

(2) That they are not otherwise procurable by the defendant reasonably in advance of trial by the exercise of due diligence;

(3) That the defendant cannot properly prepare for trial without such production, and inspection in advance of trial and failure to obtain such inspection may tend reasonably to delay the trial;

(4) That the application is made in good faith and is not intended as a general fishing expedition. 13 F.R.D. at 338.[72]

As to the burden of establishing the validity of a subpoena *duces tecum*, controlling case law recognizes that it is incumbent upon the party seeking disclosure to set forth each request with sufficient specificity to establish that each document is both

[72] This case has been prominently cited in numerous decision. See for example, *United States* v. *Bearden*, 423 F. 2d 805, 810 n. 4, (5th Cir.), *cert. denied*, 400 U.S. 836 (1970); *United States* v. *Garrison*, 168 F. Supp 622, 624 (E.D. Wis. 1958); *United States* v. *Duncan*, 22 F.R.D. 295, 298 (S.D.N.Y. 1958).

"relevant" and "admissible," and that the other *Iozia* criteria have been met. *United States* v. *Palermo*, 21 F.R.D. 11, 13 (S.D.N.Y. 1957). In this regard the court in *United States* v. *Winkler*, 17 F.R.D. 213 (D.R.I. 1955), held:

> [T]he right of a defendant to the production and inspection of documents and objects prior to trial under Rule 17(c) is not absolute but that upon objection thereto good cause for such production and inspection must be first shown by the party seeking the same. (17 F.R.D. at 215).

In *Iozia*, where the defendant sought a subpoena, the court held that "there must be a showing of good cause to entitle the defendant to production and inspection of documents under Rule 17(c)." 13 F.R.D. at 338. "Good cause" as defined by the *Iozia* court, requires a showing by the defendant[73] that all four of the criteria set out above have been met. In the court below there was not even a showing that the material sought "would be admissible in evidence or relevant at trial." See *United States* v. *Winkler*, 17 F.R.D. 213, 215 (D.R.I. 1955).

That the Special Prosecutor has failed to demonstrate that the materials requested are "relevant and evidentiary" is readily apparent from the record of the court below. The original Rule 17(c) motion was supported by the Special Prosecutor's affidavit and memorandum of May 10, 1974. At page two of this affidavit, the Special Prosecutor requested 64 presidential conversations on the bald assertion that each of these materials *"contains or is likely to contain* evidence that will be relevant to the trial of this case." (emphasis added). At page two of his memorandum of May 10, 1974, the Special Prosecutor, in an unsupported allegation, stated: *"In all probability*, many of the subpoenaed items will contain evidence which will be relevant and material to the trial . . . " (emphasis added). Thus, it is evident that the Special Prosecutor was unable to make the necessary showing that each of the requested 64 items was evidentiary. A general allegation that some or a majority of the material sought may be relevant or admissible is not sufficient under *Iozia* to establish that all requested items "are evidentiary and relevant." 13 F.R.D. at 338.

Moreover, even the general assertion made by the Special Prosecutor that some of the materials may be relevant is devoid of any meritorious factual support. As such, it was an

---

[73] That the provisions of Rule 17(c) are applicable to the government as well as to a defendant is not open to serious challenge. See *United States* v. *Gross,* 24 F.R.D. 138, 140 (S.D.N.Y. 1959).

unsupported allegation seeking discovery and Rule 17(c) may not be used for that purpose. It has been firmly established in criminal cases that in seeking discovery, the requirement of a showing of materiality and admissibility is not satisfied, "by a mere conclusory allegation that the requested information is material" to the preparation of a case. *United States* v. *Conder*, 423 F.2d 904, 910 (6th Cir.), *cert. denied*, 400 U.S. 958 (1970). Nor is it sufficient to make a "bare allegation that the requested information would be material in the preparation of the defense." 423 F.2d at 910.

From the Special Prosecutor's statements that the requested materials were "likely to contain evidence" and "in all probability" may contain evidence, it is readily apparent that he was attempting to seek evidence not already known. As the court definitively stated in *United States* v. *Frank*, 23 F.R.D. 145 (D.D.C. 1959), Rule 17(c) "does not permit blunderbuss inspection of the government's evidence in an attempt to learn something not known, it is not a discovery provision." 23 F.R.D. at 147. This same concept was reaffirmed by the court in *United States* v. *Gross*, 24 F.R.D. 138 (S.D.N.Y. 1959), when it stated *"the government* [cannot] use Rule 17(c) to obtain leads as to the existence of additional documentary evidence or seek information relating to the defendant's case." 24 F.R.D. at 141 (emphasis added). Any request designed merely to disclose additional evidence not already known has properly been termed a "fishing expedition," which will not be countenanced under this rule. *Bowman Dairy Co.* v. *United States*, 341 U.S. at 221. The Special Prosecutor is obviously attempting to use Rule 17(c), contrary to established case law, to obtain additional evidence not already known.

In addition, the district court is noticeably silent to the teaching of *United States* v. *Marchisio*, 344 F.2d 653, 669 (2nd Cir. 1965), that a subpoena *duces tecum* in a criminal action is not intended for the purposes of discovery, and that the documents sought must at that time meet the test of relevancy and admissibility.

It is also important to emphasize that there is an essential distinction between disclosure in civil and criminal actions. *United States* v. *Maryland & Virginia Milk Producers, Inc.*, 9 F.R.D. 509 (D.D.C. 1949). In this regard it is interesting to note that contrary to the more limited criminal discovery provisions applicable here, the Special Prosecutor's request in this instance was very similar in both substance and tone to the broader civil discovery provisions of Rule 26 of the Federal Rules of Civil

Procedure.[74]

Additionally, it has been judicially recognized that the test to be met by one seeking material must be met at the time that the items are sought, and the mere "probability" that the items may later become relevant is of no consequence. The court in *United States* v. *Marchisio*, 344 F.2d 653 (2nd Cir. 1965), stated: "Unlike the rule in civil action actions, a subpoena *duces tecum* in a criminal action is not intended for the purpose of discovery; the documents sought must at that time meet the tests of relevancy and admissibility." 344 F.2d at 669. See also *United States* v. *Murray*, 297 F.2d 812, 821-822 (2nd Cir. 1962); *United States* v. *Palermo*, 21 F.R.D. 11, 13 (S.D.N.Y. 1957).

Furthermore, in the Special Prosecutor's conclusion to the first section of his argument, he, in effect, urged the court below to allow him a lesser standard of relevancy and evidentiary showing when "seeking material from third parties the precise contents of which is unknown" (Special Prosecutor's memorandum, May 10, 1974, at 1, 10). This suggestion of a lesser standard than that required by Rule 17(c) case law is not as astonishing as the tacit implication that the Special Prosecutor does not know the contents of the material he is seeking. For without this knowledge, the Special Prosecutor cannot even hope to meet any of the *Iozia* criteria and is obviously on a "fishing expedition" or is attempting to use Rule 17(c) as a discovery device.

It is also readily apparent that since the Special Prosecutor cannot show that the privileged conversations are relevant for the purpose for which he seeks them, he is attempting to formulate a new standard whereby the President should produce the recorded conversations unless the President can establish to the satisfaction of the Special Prosecutor and this Court that the subpoenaed conversations are not relevant. This attempt to shift the burden of establishing relevancy from the party seeking material under Rule 17(c) to the party being subpoenaed is unsupported by any case law and flies in the face of established precedent. In this regard the court in *United States* v. *Winkler*, 17 F.R.D. 213 (D.R.I. 1955), held:

[74] Rule 26, F.R.C.P. provides, in part:

(b) Scope of Discovery. Unless otherwise limited by order of the court in accordance with these rules, the scope of discovery is as follows:

(1) In General. Parties may obtain discovery regarding any matter, *not privileged*, which is relevant to the subject matter involved in the pending action ... It is not ground for objection that the information sought will be inadmissible at the trial if *the information sought appears reasonably calculated to lead to the discovery of evidence.* (emphasis added).

The right of a defendant to the production and inspection of documents and objects prior to trial under Rule 17(c) is not absolute but that upon objection thereto good cause for such production and inspection must be first shown by the party seeking the same. (17 F.R.D. at 215).

As a further attempt to demonstrate admissibility, the Special Prosecutor proffers at pages 15-16 of his memorandum of May 10, 1974, that "statements made during conversations may be useful to the Government for the purpose of impeaching defendants Haldeman, Ehrlichman, and Colson should they elect to testify in their own behalf." The Special Prosecutor's suggestion that he is entitled to materials useful for impeachment conceals the fact that courts hold that impeachment materials cannot be obtained in advance of trial and one must wait to see if the person to be impeached actually testifies. *United States* v. *Carter*, 15 F.R.D. 367, 371 (D.D.C. 1954) (Holtzoff, J.); *United States* v. *Murray*, 297 F.2d 812, 821-822 (2nd Cir.) *cert denied*, 369 U.S. 828 (1962); *United States* v. *Brockington*, 21 F.R.D. 104, 106 (E.D. Va. 1957); *United States* v. *Hiss*, 9 F.R.D. 515, 516-517 (S.D.N.Y. 1949).

In light of the lower court's conclusion that the President was, in essence, a third party, it should be noted that in criminal proceedings, because of the respective roles of the parties, it is much easier for a defendant to factually satisfy the *Iozia* requirements when seeking items from the government than it is for the government or defendant to do so against a third party. This is because a defendant may make conclusive statement as to relevancy and admissibility without knowing the precise nature of the materials. Prosecutors by presenting evidence to a grand jury and intending to use evidence at trial, necessarily classify such items as relevant and evidentiary. Thus, it follows that a defendant may utilize conclusive assertions regarding the quality of material he seeks. Obviously, the government does not have this same advantage of utilizing unsupported statements and must therefore justify in greater specificity the items it is seeking.

B. *The President should not be judged as a "TYPICAL" Third Party.*

The Special Prosecutor has attempted to ease his "relevant and evidentiary" burden under Rule 17(c) by pointing out at page 7 of his memorandum of May 10, 1974, that "in the instant case the Government seeks to obtain evidentiary items from a third party." The President, however, is not a normal third party. But even if he were, it is well established that a typical third party has rights which protect him from burdensome subpoenas. *Application of Magnus*, 299 F.2d 335, 337 (2nd Cir.), *cert. denied*, 370 U.S. 918 (1962) (third party corporation has standing to object to an IRS subpoena which would infringe constitutional rights); *Amsler* v. *United States*, 381 F.2d 37, 51 (9th Cir. 1967) (Rule 17 subpoena to third party quashed when court held subpoena was oppressive and unreasonable). As Judge Moore stated in *In Re Magnus, Mabee & Reynard, Inc.*, 311 F.2d 12 (2nd Cir.), *cert. denied*, 373 U.S. 902 (1962):

> Third parties have the protection always accorded to them by the courts which limit burdensome subpoenas, restrict them to relevant materials and refuse to permit unwarranted searches and seizures. (311 F.2d at 16).

Thus, even judicial subpoenas directed to third parties have been restricted to *relevant* materials, not materials which have a "likelihood of relevancy" as the Special Prosecutor suggests. Even as a normal third party responding to a judical subpoena, the President should be afforded, at a minimum, the full range of rights afforded by the Fourth Amendment. As this Court observed in *Oklahoma Press Publishing Co.* v. *Walling*, 327 U.S. 186 (1946), a subpoena is, in many ways, like a search warrant and as such it must meet the constitutional requirements of the Fourth Amendment. In the instant case, the Special Prosecutor's inadequate showing of relevancy can be likened to the lack of definiteness and overbreadth which are abuses guarded against by the Fourth Amendment. In this context, the Court in *Oklahoma Press* held, "[t]he gist of the protection is in the requirement, expressed in terms, that the disclosure sought shall not be unreasonable." 327 U.S. at 208.

The district court's finding that the Special Prosecutor was merely seeking "evidentiary items from a third party" is clearly erroneous. The Constitution states, "The executive Power shall be vested in a President of the United States of America." U.S. Const., Article II, section 1. To allow this constitutionally mandated power to be challenged and overcome by a district court subpoena issued under the standards governing subpoenas to third parties, is an action that would erode and ultimately destroy the "separation of powers" concept that has existed since 1787.

CONCLUSION

Last fall, the United States Court of Appeals for the District of

Columbia circuit observed in *Nixon* v. *Sirica*, 487 F.2d 700 (D.C. Cir. 1973):

> We acknowledge that wholesale public access to Executive deliberations and documents would cripple the Executive as a co-equal branch. (487 F.2d at 715).

The velocity with which the confidentiality of presidential communications has eroded in the short time since the quoted words were written is demonstrated by the vast scope of the Special Prosecutor's pending subpoena, by the meager grounds offered to support it, and by the district court's casual disposition of the President's motion to quash. This circumstance—and the escalating confusion and torrent of prejudicial leaks generated by the concurrent involvement of the President in criminal proceedings as a so-called "third party" and in an impeachment investigation as the putative respondent—recalls the introductory words of the brief filed on behalf of the President in *Nixon* v. *Sirica*. Those words are relevant here because they analyze the dynamics of this case and the course it will take in terms that continue to be valid for this and other Presidents in their effort to maintain the confidentiality upon which the effective functioning of the Presidency so crucially depends.

> Great cases like hard cases make bad law. For great cases are called great, not by reason of their real importance in shaping the law of the future, but because of some accident of immediate overwhelming interest which appeals to the feelings and distorts the judgment. These immediate interests exercise a kind of hydraulic pressure which makes what previously was clear seem doubtful, and before which even well settled principles of law will bend.

Holmes, J., dissenting in *Northern Securities Co.* v. *United States*, 193 U.S. 197, 400-401 (1904). This case is a classic illustration of the danger against which Justice Holmes warned.

The District Court, in a decision utterly without precedent, has held that it is for it, and not for the President, to decide whether the public interest requires that private Presidential conversations be kept confidential, and it has held that it may, by compulsory process, order the President to produce recordings of these conversations if the Court determines to do so.

As recently as a year ago such a ruling would have been unthinkable. The universal view of the legal community, as reflected in the literature, was that the courts lacks power to substitute their judgment for that of the President on an issue of this kind and that they lack power to compel a President to make production. It was, quite literally, hornbook law that "confidential communications to and from the President are inviolate to a judicial request * * *." Forkosch, *Constitutional Law* 131 (1963).

The change in the climate of legal and popular opinion that has made a ruling such as that of the District Court possible is the result of Watergate. The hydraulic force arising out of that sordid and unhappy episode has led men of great distinction to suppose that the Constitution means something different today than it meant throughout all of our history and to contend that the need to exhaust every avenue of factual inquiry concerning Watergate ranks so high in our national priorities that it must be served, even if the cost is to impair markedly the ability of every President of the United States from this time forward to perform the Constitutional duties vested in him.

It is no exaggeration to say that the revelations of Watergate have so sharpened the public appetite for more revelations that the claim of a Presidential right and responsibility under the Constitution to maintain the confidentiality of Presidential conversations must run the gamut of a broadly held popular sentiment that the claim is probably unjust and is therefore presumably unsound. The President's assertion of a right to maintain this confidentiality, a right relied on by every President since George Washington, is likened to the absolute claim of kings. His stand on an important Constitutional principle is viewed in many places with suspicion or even hostility. Despite his unprecedented cooperation with the investigations by allowing his advisers to testify about relevant portions of the conversations in question, he stands accused in some quarters of obstructing rather than facilitating the investigations.

Our submission on this appeal must acknowledge this Watergate phenomenon since it is an operative factor, though it is one that courts, judging in calmness and not moved by the passions of the moment, should be expected to ignore. We conceive it to be our task to demonstrate that the decision below was reached by casting the Constitution in the mold of Watergate rather than by applying Constitutional practices and restraints to the facts of Watergate. It is our further responsibility to show that what may seem inevitably just in the heat and excitement of an unprecedented political scandal may prove inexorably corrosive to the principles and practices of a Constitution that must stand the test of a long and uncertain future and serve the needs of a changing culture and polity.

With all respect, the decision below did not harmlessly walk the "middle ground" between an overbroad claim of privilege and an excessive demand for discovery. We do not doubt at all but that this was the well-intentioned aim of the distinguished judge of the court below. But in result, the ruling below, in decisive terms, came down squarely on the side of breaching the wall of confidentiality of Presidential communications. If sustained, that decision will alter the nature of the American Presidency profoundly and irreparably. If sustained, it will alter, equally irreparably, the delicate balance that has existed between three heretofore separate and co-equal branches of government. * * *

For the foregoing reasons, the decision of the district court denying the President's motions to quash and expunge should be reversed.

Respectfully submitted.

JAMES D. ST. CLAIR,
MICHAEL A. STERLACCI,
JEROME J. MURPHY,
LOREN A. SMITH,
JAMES R. PROCHNOW,
EUGENE R. SULLIVAN,
JEAN A. STAUDT,
THEODORE J. GARRISH,
JAMES J. TANSEY,
LARRY G. GUTTERRIDGE,
Attorneys for the President.

The White House,
Washington, D.C. 20500,
Telephone Number: 456-1414

(APPENDIX)

APPLICABLE 'PROVISIONS OF CONSTITUTION,
STATUTES, RULES, AND REGULATIONS'

1. The Constitution of the United States provides in pertinent part—

Article I, Section 2:

The House of Representatives shall be composed of Members chosen every second Year by the People of the several States, and the Electors in each State shall have the

Qualifications requisite for Electors of the most numerous Branch of the State Legislature.

No person shall be a Representative who shall not have attained to the Age of twenty-five Years, and been seven Years a Citizen of the United States, and who shall not, when elected, be an Inhabitant of that State in which he shall be chosen.

[Representatives and direct Taxes shall be apportioned among the several States which may be included within this Union, according to their respective Numbers, which shall be determined by adding to the whole Number of free Persons, including those bound to Service for a Term of Years, and excluding Indians not taxed, three fifths of all other persons.] The actual Enumeration shall be made within three Years after the first Meeting of the Congress of the United States, and within every subsequent Term of ten Years, in such Manner as they shall by Law direct. The Number of Representatives shall not exceed one for every thirty Thousand, * * but each State shall have at Least one Representative; and until such enumeration shall be made, the State of New Hampshire shall be entitled to chuse three, Massachusetts eight, Rhode-Island and Providence Plantations one, Connecticut five, New-York six, New Jersey four, Pennsylvania eight, Delaware one, Maryland six, Virginia ten, North Carolina five, South Carolina five, and Georgia three.

When vacancies happen in the Representation from any State, the Executive Authority thereof shall issue Writs of Election to fill such Vacancies.

The House of Representatives shall chuse their Speaker and other Officers; and shall have the sole Power of Impeachment.

*   *   *   *   *

The Senate of the United States shall be composed of two Senators from each State, [chosen by the Legislature thereof,] ***for six Years; and each Senator shall have one Vote.

Immediately after they shall be assembled in Consequence of the first Election, they shall be divided as equaly as may be into three Classes. The Seats of the Senators of the first Class shall be vacated at the Expiration of the second Year, of the second Class at the Expiration of the fourth Year, and of the third Class at the Expiration of the sixth Year, so that one-third may be chosen every second Year; [and if Vacancies happen by Resignation, or otherwise, during the Recess of the Legislature of any State, the Executive thereof may make temporary Appointments until the next Meeting of the Legislature, which shall then fill such Vacancies.]*

No Person shall be a Senator who shall not have attained to the Age of thirty years, and been nine Years a Citizen of the United States, and who shall not, when elected, be an Inhabitant of that State for which he shall be chosen.

The Vice President of the United States shall be President of the Senate, but shall have no Vote, unless they be equally divided.

The Senate shall chuse their other Officers, and also a President pro tempore, in the absence of the Vice President, or when he shall exercise the Office of President of the United States.

The Senate shall have the sole Power to try all Impeachments. When sitting for that purpose, they shall be on Oath or Affirmation. When the President of the United States is tried, the Chief Justice shall preside: And no Person shall be convicted without the Concurrence of two thirds of the Members present.

Judgment in Cases of Impeachment shall not extend further than to removal from Office, and disqualification to hold and enjoy any Office of honor, Trust or Profit under the United States: but the Party convicted shall nevertheless be liable and subject to Indictment, Trial, Judgment and Punishment, according to Law.

*   *   *   *   *

Article I, Section 5:

Each House shall be the Judge of the Elections, Returns and Qualifications of its own Members, and a Majority of each shall constitute a Quorum to do Business; but a smaller number may adjourn from day to day, and may be authorized to compel the Attendance of absent Members, in such Manner, and under such Penalties as each House may provide.

Each House may determine the Rules of its Proceedings, punish its Members for disorderly Behavior, and, with the Concurrence of two thirds, expel a Member.

Each House shall keep a Journal of its Proceedings, and from time to time publish the same, excepting such Parts as may in their Judgment require Secrecy; and the Yeas and Nays of the Members of either House on any questions shall, at the Desire of one fifth of those Present, be entered on the Journal.

Neither House, during the Session of Congress, shall, without the Consent of the other, adjourn for more than three days, nor to any other Place than that in which the two Houses shall be sitting.

*　　*　　*　　*　　*

Article I, Section 6:

Section 6. The Senators and Representatives shall receive a Compensation for their Services, to be ascertained by Law, and paid out of the Treasury of the United States. They shall in all Cases, except Treason, Felony and Breach of the Peace, be privileged from Arrest during their Attendance at the Session of the respective Houses, and in going to and returning from the same; and for any Speech or Debate in either House, they shall not be questioned in any other Place.

No Senator or Representative shall, during the time for which he was elected, be appointed to any civil Office under the Authority of the United States, which shall have been created, or the Emoluments whereof shall have been encreased during such time; and no Person holding any Office under the United States, shall be a Member of either House during his Continuance in Office.

*　　*　　*　　*　　*

Article II, Section 1:

The executive power shall be vested in a President of the United States of America. He shall hold his Office during the Term of four Years, and, together with the Vice-President, chosen for the same Term, be elected, as follows.

Each State shall appoint, in such Manner as the Legislature thereof may direct, a Number of Electors, equal to the whole Number of Senators and Representatives to which the State may be entitled in the Congress: but no Senator or Representative, or Person holding an Office of Trust or Profit under the United States, shall be appointed an Elector.

[The Electors shall meet in their respective States, and

vote by Ballot for two persons, of whom one at least shall not be an Inhabitant of the same State with themselves. And they shall make a List of all the Persons voted for, and of the Number of Votes for each; which List they shall sign and certify, and transmit sealed to the Seat of the Government of the United States, directed to the President of the Senate. The President of the Senate shall, in the Presence of the Senate and House of Representatives, open all the Certificates, and the Votes shall then be counted. The Person having the greatest Number of Votes shall be the President, if such Number be a Majority of the whole Number of Electors appointed; and if there be more than one who have such Majority, and have an equal Number of Votes, then the House of Representatives shall immediately chuse by Ballot one of them for President; and if no Person have a Majority, then from the five highest on the List the said House shall in like Manner chuse the President. But in chusing the President, the Votes shall be taken by States, the Representation from each State having one Vote; a quorum for this Purpose shall consist of a Member or Members from two thirds of the States, and a Majority of all the States shall be necessary to a Choice. In every Case, after the Choice of the President, the Person having the greatest Number of Votes of the Electors shall be the Vice President. But if there should remain two or more who have equal Votes, the Senate shall chuse from them by Ballot the Vice-President.]

The Congress may determine the Time of chusing the Electors, and the Day on which they shall give their Votes; which Day shall be the same throughout the United States.

No person except a natural born Citizen, or a Citizen of the United States, at the time of the Adoption of this Constitution, shall be eligible to the Office of President; neither shall any Person be eligible to that Office who shall not have attained to the Age of thirty-five Years, and been fourteen Years a Resident within the United States.

[In Case of the Removal of the President from Office, or of his Death, Resignation, or Inability to discharge the Powers and Duties of the said Office, the same shall devolve on the Vice President, and the Congress may by Law, provide for the Case of Removal, Death, Resignation or Inability, both of the President and Vice President, declaring what Officer shall then act as President, and such Officer shall act accordingly, until the Disability be removed, or a President shall be elected.

The President shall, at stated Times, receive for his Services, a Compensation, which shall neither be encreased nor diminished during the Period for which he shall have been elected, and he shall not receive within that Period any other Emolument from the United States, or any of them.

Before he enter on the Execution of his Office, he shall take the following Oath or Affirmation:—"I do solemnly swear (or affirm) that I will faithfully execute the Office of President of the United States, and will to the best of my Ability, preserve, protect and defend the Constitution of the United States."

*   *   *   *   *

Article II, Section 2:

The President shall be Commander in Chief of the Army and Navy of the United States, and of the Militia of the several States, when called into the actual Service of the United States; he may require the Opinion in writing, of the principal Officer in each of the executive Departments, upon any subject relating to the Duties of their respective Offices, and he shall have Power to Grant Reprieves and Pardons for Offenses against the United States, except in Cases of Impeachment.

He shall have Power, by and with the Advice and Consent of the Senate, to make Treaties, provided two-thirds of the Senators present concur; and he shall nominate, and by and with the Advice and Consent of the Senate, shall appoint Ambassadors, other public Ministers and Consuls, Judges of the supreme Court, and all other Officers of the United States, whose Appointments are not herein otherwise provided for, and which shall be established by Law: but the Congress may by Law vest the Appointment of such inferior Officers, as they think proper, in the President alone, in the Courts of Law, or in the Heads of Departments.

The President shall have Power to fill up all Vacancies that may happen during the Recess of the Senate, by granting Commissions which shall expire at the End of their next Session.

*   *   *   *   *

Article II, Section 3:

He shall from time to time give to the Congress Information of the State of the Union, and recommend to their Consideration such Measures as he shall judge necessary and expedient; he may, on extraordinary

Occasions, convene both Houses, or either of them, and in Case of Disagreement between them, with Respect to the Time of Adjournment, he may adjourn them to such Time as he shall think proper; he shall receive Ambassadors and other public Ministers; he shall take Care that the Laws be faithfully executed, and shall Commission all the Officers of the United States.

* * * * *

Article III, Section 2:

The judicial Power shall extend to all Cases, in Law and Equity, arising under this Constitution, the Laws of the United States, and Treaties made, or which shall be made, under their Authority;—to all Cases affecting Ambassadors, other public Ministers and Consuls;—to all Cases of admiralty and maritime Jurisdiction;—to Controversies to which the United States shall be a Party;—to Controversies between two or more States;—between a State and Citizens of another State;—between Citizens of different States;—between Citizens of the same State claiming Lands under Grants of different States, and between a State, or the Citizens thereof, and foreign States, Citizens or Subjects.

In all Cases affecting Ambassadors, other public Ministers and Consuls, and those in which a State shall be Party, the supreme Court shall have original Jurisdiction. In all other Cases before mentioned, the supreme Court shall have appellate Jurisdiction, both as to Law and Fact, with such Exceptions, and under such Regulations as the Congress shall make.

The trial of all Crimes, except in Cases of Impeachment, shall be by Jury; and such Trial shall be held in the State where the said Crimes shall have been committed; but when not committed within any State, the Trial shall be at such Place or Places as the Congress may by Law have directed.

* * * * *

2. Title 18, United States Code, provides in pertinent part:

§ 371. Conspiracy to commit offense or to defraud United States—

If two or more persons conspire either to commit any offense against the United States, or to defraud the United States, or any agency thereof in any manner or for any purpose, and one or more of such persons do any act to effect the object of the conspiracy, each shall be fined not more than $10,000 or imprisoned not more than five years, or both.

If, however, the offense, the commission of which is the object of the conspiracy, is a misdemeanor only, the punishment for such conspiracy shall not exceed the maximum punishment provided for such misdemeanor. June 25, 1948, c. 645, 62 Stat. 701.

* * * * *

§ 1001. Statements or entries generally—

Whoever, in any matter within the jurisdiction of any department or agency of the United States knowingly and willfully falsifies, conceals or covers up by any trick, scheme, or device a material fact, or makes any false, fictitious or fraudulent statements or representations, or makes or uses any false writing or document knowing the same to contain any false, fictitious or fraudulent statement or entry, shall be fined not more than $10,000 or imprisoned not more than five years, or both. June 25, 1948, c. 645, 62 Stat. 749.

* * * * *

§ 1503. Influence or injuring officer, juror or witness generally—

Whoever corruptly or by threats or force, or by any threatening letter or coomunication, endeavors to influence, intimidate, or impede any witness, in any court of the United States or before any United States magistrate or other committing magistrate, or any grand or petit juror, or officer in or of any court of the United States, or officer who may be serving at any examination or other proceeding before any United States magistrate or other committing magistrate, in the discharge of his duty, or injures any party or witness in his person or property on account of his attending or having attended such court or examination before such officer, commissioner, or other committing magistrate, or on account of his testifying or having testified to any matter pending therein, or injures any such grand or petit juror in his person or property on account of any verdict or indictment assented to by him, or on account of his being or having been such juror, or injures any such officer, magistrate, or other committing magistrate in his person or property on account of the performance of his official duties, or corruptly or by threats or force, or by any threatening letter of communication, influences, obstructs, or impedes, or endeavors to influence, obstruct, or impede, the due administration of justice, shall be fined not more than $5,000 or imprisoned not more than five years, or both.

As amended Oct. 17, 1968, Pub. L. 90-578, Title III, § 301(a) (1), (3), 82 Stat. 1115.

§ 1621. Perjury generally—

Whoever, having taken an oath before a competent tribunal, officer, or person, in any case in which a law of the United States authorizes an oath to be administered, that he will testify, declare, depose, or certify truly, or that any written testimony, declaration, deposition, or certificate by him subscribed, is true, willfully and contrary to such oath states or subscribes any material matter which he does not believe to be true, is guilty of perjury, and shall, except as otherwise expressly provided by law, be fined not more than $2,000 or imprisoned not more than five years, or both. This section is applicable whether the statement or subscription is made within or without the United States. June 25, 1948, c. 645, 62 Stat. 733; Oct. 3, 1964, Pub. L. 88-619, § 1, 78 Stat. 995.

* * * * *

§ 1623. False declarations before grand jury or court—

(a) Whoever under oath in any proceeding before or ancillary to any court or grand jury of the United States knowingly makes any false material declaration or makes or uses any other information, including any book, paper, document, record, recording, or other material, knowing the same to contain any false material declaration, shall be fined not more than $10,000 or imprisoned not more than five years, or both.

(b) This section is applicable whether the conduct occurred within or without the United States.

(c) An indictment or information for violation of this section alleging that, in any proceedings before or ancillary to any court or grand jury of the United States, the defendant under oath has knowingly made two or more declarations, which are inconsistent to the degree that one of them is necessarily false, need not specify which declaration is false if—

(1) each declaration was material to the point in question, and

(2) each declaration was made within the period of

the statute of limitations for the offense charged under this section.

In any prosecution under this section, the falsity of a declaration set forth in the indictment or information shall be established sufficient for conviction by proof that the defendant while under oath made irreconcilably contradictory declarations material to the point in question in any proceeding before or ancillary to any court or grand jury. It shall be a defense to an indictment or information made pursuant to the first sentence of this subsection that the defendant at the time he made each declaration believed the declaration was true.

(d) Where, in the same continuous court or grand jury proceeding in which a declaration is made, the person making the declaration admits such declaration to be false, such admission shall bar prosecution under this section if, at the time the admission is made, the declaration has not substantially affected the proceeding, or it has not become manifest that such falsity has been or will be exposed.

(e) Proof beyond a reasonable doubt under this section is sufficient for conviction. It shall not be necessary that such proof be made by any particular number of witnesses or by documentary or other type of evidence.

Added Publ. L. 91-452, Title IV, § 401(a), Oct. 15, 1970, 84. Stat. 932.

§ 35.00. Demands for production of statements and reports of witnesses—

(a) In any criminal prosecution brought by the United States, no statement or report in the possession of the United States which was made by a Government witness or prospective Government witness (other than the defendant) shall be the subject of subpoena, discovery, or inspection until said witness has testified on direct examination in the trial of the case.

[See main volume for text of (b) and (c)]

(d) If the United States elects not to comply with an order of the court under subsection (b) or (c) hereof to deliver to the defendant any such statement, or such portion thereof as the court may direct, the court shall strike from the record the testimony of the witness, and the trial shall proceed unless the court in its discretion shall determine that the interests of justice require that a mistrial be declared.

(e) The term "statement", as used in subsections (b), (c), and (d) of this section in relation to any witness called by the United States, means—

(1) a written statement made by said witness and signed or otherwise adopted or approved by him;

(2) a stenographic, mechanical, electrical, or other recording, or a transcription thereof, which is a substantially verbatim recital of an oral statement made by said witness and recorded contemporaneously with the making of such oral statement; or

(3) a statement, however taken or recorded, or a transcription thereof, if any, made by said witness to a grand jury.

As amended Pub. L. 91-452, Title I, § 102, Oct. 15, 1970, 84 Stat. 926.

* * * * *

§ 3731. Appeal by United States—

In a criminal case an appeal by the United States shall lie to a court of appeals from a decision, judgment, or order of a district court dismissing an indictment or information as to any one or more counts, except that no appeal shall lie where the double jeopardy clause of the United States Constitution prohibits further prosecution.

An appeal by the United States shall lie to a court of appeals from a decision or order of a district courts suppressing or excluding evidence or requiring the return of seized property in a criminal proceeding, not made after the defendant has been put in jeopardy and before the verdict or finding on an indictment or information, if the United States attorney certifies to the district court that the appeal is not taken for purpose of delay and that the evidence is a substantial proof of a fact material in the proceeding.

The appeal in all such cases shall be taken within thirty days after the decision, judgment or order has been rendered and shall be diligently prosecuted.

Pending the prosecution and determination of the appeal in the foregoing instances, the defendant shall be released in accordance with chapter 207 of this title.

The provisions of this section shall be liberally construed to effectuate its purposes. As amended Jan. 2,

1971, Pub. L. 91-644, Title III,§14(a), 84 Stat. 1890.

Title 28, United States Code, provides in pertinent part:

§ 44. Appointment, tenure, residence and salary of circuit judges—

(a) The President shall appoint, by and with the advice and consent of the Senate, circuit judges for the several circuits as follows:

Circuits	Number of Judges
District of Columbia	Nine
First	Three
Second	Nine
Third	Nine
Fourth	Seven
Fifth	Fifteen
Sixth	Nine
Seventh	Eight
Eighth	Eight
Ninth	Thirteen
Tenth	Seven

(b) Circuit judges shall hold office during good behaviour.

(c) Except in the District of Columbia, each circuit judge shall be a resident of the circuit for which appointed at the time of his appointment and thereafter while in active service.

(d) Each circuit judge shall receive a salary of $33,000 a year. As amended Aug. 3, 1949, c. 387, § 1, 63 Stat. 493; Feb. 10, 1954, c. 6, § 1, 68 Stat. 8; Mar. 2, 1955, c. 9, § 1 (b), 69 Stat. 10; May 19, 1961, Pub. L. 87-36, § 1(b), 75 Stat. 80; Aug. 14, 1964, Pub. L. 88-426, Title IV,§403(b), 78 Stat. 434; Mar. 18, 1966, Pub. L. 89-372, § 1(b), 80 Stat. 75; June 18, 1968, Pub. L. 90-347, § 3, 82 Stat. 183.

* * * * *

§ 133. Appointment and number of district judges—

The President shall appoint, by and with the advice and consent of the Senate, district judges for the several judicial districts, as follows:

As amended June 2, 1970, Pub. L. 91-272, § 1(c), (d), 84 Stat. 294, 295; Dec. 18, 1971, Pub. L. 92-208, § 3(d)

85 Stat. 742.

§ 1254. Courts of appeals; certiorari; appeal; certified questions—

Cases in the courts of appeals may be reviewed by the Supreme Court by the following methods:

(1) By writ of of certiorari granted upon the petition of any party to any civil or criminal case, before or after rendition of judgment or decree;

(2) By appeal by a party relying on a State statute held by a court of appeals to be invalid as repugnant to the Constitution, treaties or laws of the United States, but such appeal shall preclude review by writ of certiorari at the instance of such appellant, and the review on appeal shall be restricted to the Federal questions presented;

(3) By certification at any time by a court of appeals of any question of law in any civil or criminal case as to which instructions are desired, and upon such certification the Supreme Court may give binding instructions or require the entire record to be sent up for decision of the entire matter in controversy. June 25, 1948, c. 646, 62 Stat. 928.

* * * * *

§ 1291. Final decisions of district courts—

The courts of appeals shall have jurisdiction of appeals from all final decisions of the district courts of the United States, the United States District Court for the District of the Canal Zone, the District Court of Guam, and the District Court of the Virgin Islands, except where a direct review may be had in the Supreme Court. June 25, 1948, c. 646, 62 Stat. 929; Oct. 31, 1951, c. 655, § 48, 65 Stat. 726; July 7, 1958, Pub. L. 85-508, § 12(e), 72 Stat. 348.

* * * * *

§ 1651 Writs—

(a) The Supreme Court and all courts established by Act of Congress may issue all writs necessary or appropriate in aid of their respective jurisdictions and agreeable to the usages and principles of law.

(b) An alternative writ or rule nisi may be issued by a justice or judge of a court which has jurisdiction. June 25, 1948, c. 646, 62 Stat. 944; May 24, 1949 c. 139,

§ 90, 63 Stat. 102.

Title 44, United States Code, provides in pertinent part:

§ 2107. Material accepted for deposit—

When the Administrator of General Services considers it to be in the public interest he may accept for deposit—

(1) the papers and other historical materials of a President or former President of the United States, or other official or former official of the Government, and other papers relating to and contemporary with a President or former President of the United States, subject to restrictions agreeable to the Administrator as to their use; and

(2) documents including motion-picture films, still pictures, and sound recordings, from private sources that are appropriate for preservation by the Government as evidence of its organization, functions, policies, decisions, procedures, and transactions.   Pub. L. 90-620, Oct. 22, 1968, 82 Stat. 1288.

*   *   *   *   *

§ 2108. Presidential archival depository—

(c) When the Administrator considers it to be in the public interest, he may exercise, with respect to papers, documents, or other historical materials deposited under this section, or otherwise, in a Presidential archival depository, all the functions and responsibilities otherwise vested in him pertaining to Federal records or other documentary materials in his custody or under his control. The Administrator, in negotiating for the deposit of Presidential historical materials, shall take steps to secure to the Government, as far as possible, the right to have continuous and permanent possession of the materials. Papers, documents, or other historical materials accepted and deposited under section 3106 of this title and this section are subject to restrictions as to their availability and use stated in writing by the donors or depositors, including the restriction that they shall be kept in a Presidential archival depository. The restrictions shall be respected for the period stated, or until revoked or terminated by the donors or depositors or by persons legally qualified to act on their behalf. Subject to the restrictions, the Administrator may dispose by sale, exchange, or otherwise, of papers, documents, or other materials which the Archivist determines to have no permanent value or historical interest or to be surplus to the needs of a Presidential archival depository. Pub. L. 90-620, Oct. 22, 1968, 82 Stat. 1289.

3. Rule 26, Federal Rules of Civil Procedure, provides in pertinent part:

(b) Scope of Discovery. Unless otherwise limited by order of the court in accordance with these rules, the scope of discovery is as follows:

(1) *In General.* Parties may obtain discovery regarding any matter, not privileged, which is relevant to the subject matter involved in the pending action, whether it relates to the claim or defense of the party seeking discovery or to the claim or defense of any other party, including the existence, description, nature, custody, condition and location of any books, documents, or other tangible things and the identity and location of persons having knowledge of any discoverable matter. It is not ground for objection that the information sought will be inadmissible at the trial if the information sought appears reasonably calculated to lead to the discovery of admissible evidence.

*　*　*　*　*

(3) *Trial Preparation: Materials.* Subject to the provisions of subdivision (b)(4) of this rule, a party may obtain discovery of documents and tangible things otherwise discoverable under subdivision (b)(1) of this rule and prepared in anticipation of litigation or for trial by or for another party or by or for that other party's representative (including his attorney, consultant, surety, indemnitor, insurer, or agent) only upon a showing that the party seeking discovery has substantial need of the materials in the preparation of his case and that he is unable without undue hardship to obtain the substantial equivalent of the materials by other means.

*　*　*　*　*

Rule 6, Federal Rules of Criminal Procedure, provides in pertinent part:

(e) Secrecy of Proceedings and Disclosure. Disclosure of matters occurring before the grand jury other than its deliberations and the vote of any juror may be made to the attorneys for the government for use in the performance of their duties. Otherwise a juror, attorney, interpreter, stenographer, operator of a recording device, or any typist who transcribes recorded testimony may disclose matters occurring before the grand jury only when so directed by the court preliminarily to or in connection with a judicial proceeding or when permitted by the court at the request of the defendant upon a showing that grounds may exist for a motion to dismiss the indictment because of matters occurring before the grand jury. No obligation of secrecy may be imposed upon any person except in accordance with this rule. The court may direct that an indictment shall be kept secret until the defendant is in custody or has given bail, and in that event the clerk shall seal the indictment and no person shall disclose the finding of the indictment except when necessary for the issuance and execution of a warrant or summons.

*　　*　　*　　*　　*

Rule 17, Federal Rules of Criminal Procedure, provides in pertinent part:

(c) For Production of Documentary Evidence and of Objects. A subpoena may also command the person to whom it is directed to produce the books, papers, documents or other objects designated therein. The court on motion made promptly may quash or modify the subpoena if compliance would be unreasonable or oppressive. The court may direct that books, papers, documents or objects designated in the subpoena be produced before the court at a time prior to the trial or prior to the time when they are to be offered in evidence and may upon their production permit the books, papers, documents or objects or portions thereof to be inspected by the parties and their attorneys.

*　　*　　*　　*　　*

4. Department of Justice Order No. 551-73 (Nov. 2, 1973) 38 Fed. Reg. 30,738 adding 28 C.F.R. § § 0.37, and 0.38, and Appendix to Subpart G-1, provides:

Title 28—Judicial Administration

Chapter I—Department of Justice

Part O—Organization of the Department of Justice

Order No. 551—73

*Establishing the Office of Watergate Special
Prosecution Force*

By virtue of the authority vested in me by 28 U.S.C.
509, 510 and 5 U.S.C. 301, there is hereby established in
the Department of Justice, the Office of Watergate
Special Prosecution Force, to be headed by a Director.
Accordingly, Part O of Chapter I of Title 28, Code of
Federal Regulations, is amended as follows:

1. Section 0.1(a) which lists the organization units of
the Department, is amended by adding "Office of
Watergate Special Prosecution Force" immediately after
"Office of Criminal Justice."

2. A new Subpart G-1 is added immediately after
Subpart G, to read as follows:

*"Subpart G-1—Office of
Watergate Special Prosecution Force*

§ 0.37. General Functions

The Office of Watergate Special Prosecution
Force shall be under the direction of a Director who
shall be the Special Prosecution Force shall be under
the direction of The duties and responsibilities of the
Special Prosecutor are set forth in the attached
appendix which is incorporated and made a part
hereof.

§ 0.38. Specific Functions

The Special Prosecutor is assigned and delegated the
following specific functions with respect to matters
specified in this Subpart:

(a) Pursuant to 28 U.S.C. 515(a), to conduct any kind
of legal proceeding, civil or criminal, including grand jury
proceedings, which United States attorneys are
authorized by law to conduct, and to designate attorneys
to conduct such legal proceedings.

(b) To approve or disapprove the production or
disclosure of information or files relating to matters
within his cognizance in response to a subpoena, order, or
other demand of a court or other authority. (See Part
16(B) of this chapter.)

(c) To apply for and to exercise the authority vested
in the Attorney General under 18 U.S.C. 6005 relating to
immunity of witnesses in Congressional proceedings.

The listing of these specific functions is for the purpose of illustrating the authority entrusted to the Special Prosecutor and is not intended to limit in any manner his authority to carry out his functions and responsibilities."

ROBERT H. BORK,
Acting Attorney General.

Date: November 2, 1973.

APPENDIX

DUTIES AND RESPONSIBILITIES OF THE SPECIAL PROSECUTOR

The Special Prosecutor

There is appointed by the Attorney General, within the Department of Justice, a Special Prosecutor to whom the Attorney General shall delegate the authorities and provide the staff and other resources described below.

The Special Prosecutor shall have full authority for investigating and prosecuting offenses against the United States arising out of the unauthorized entry into Democratic National Committee Headquarters at the Watergate, all offenses arising out of the 1972 Presidential Election for which the Special Prosecutor deems it necessary and appropriate to assume responsibility, allegations involving the President, members of the White House staff, or Presidential appointees, and any other matters which he consents to have assigned to him by the Attorney General.

In particular, the Special Prosecutor shall have full authority with respect to the above matters for:

—conducting proceedings before grand juries and any other investigations he deems necessary;

—reviewing all documentary evidence available from any source, as to which he shall have full access;

—determining whether or not to contest the assertion of "Executive Privilege" or any other testimonial privilege;

—determining whether or not application should be made to any Federal court for a grant of immunity to any witness, consistently with applicable statutory requirements, or for warrants, subpoenas, or other court orders;

—deciding whether or not to prosecute any individual, firm, corporation or group of individuals;

—initiating and conducting prosecutions, framing indictments, filing informations, and handling all aspects of any cases within his jurisdiction (whether initiated before or after his assumption of duties), including any appeals;

—coordinating and directing the activities of all Department of Justice personnel, including United States Attorneys;

—dealing with and appearing before Congressional committees having jurisdiction over any aspect of the above matters and determining what documents, information, and assistance shall be provided to such committees.

In exercising this authority, the Special Prosecutor will have the greatest degree of independence that is consistent with the Attorney General's statutory accountability for all matters falling within the jurisdiction of the Department of Justice. The Attorney General will not countermand or interfere with the Special Prosecutor's decisions or actions. The Special Prosecutor will determine whether and to what extent he will inform or consult with the Attorney General about the conduct of his duties and responsibilities. In accordance with assurances given by the President to the Attorney General that the President will not exercise his Constitutional powers to effect the discharge of the Special Prosecutor or to limit the independence that he is hereby given, the Special Prosecutor will not be removed from his duties except for extraordinary improprieties on his part and without the President's first consulting the Majority and the Minority Leaders and Chairmen and ranking Minority Members of the Judiciary Committees of the Senate and House of Representatives and ascertaining that their consensus is in accord with his proposed action.

Staff and Resource Support

1. *Selection of Staff.*—The Special Prosecutor shall have full authority to organize, select, and hire his own staff of attorneys, investigators, and supporting personnel, on a full or part-time basis, in such numbers and with such qualifications as he may reasonably require. He may request the Assistant Attorneys General and other officers of the Department of Justice to assign such personnel and to

provide such other assistance as he may reasonably require. All personnel in the Department of Justice, including United States Attorneys, shall cooperate to the fullest extent possible with the Special Prosecutor.

2. *Budgets.*—The Special Prosecutor will be provided with such funds and facilities to carry out his responsibilities as he may reasonably require. He shall have the right to submit budget requests for funds, positions, and other assistance, and such requests shall receive the highest priority.

3. *Designation and Responsibility.*—The personnel acting as the staff and assistants of the Special Prosecutor shall be known as the Watergate Special Prosecution Force and shall be responsible only to the Special Prosecutor.

Continued Responsibilities of Assistant Attorney General, Criminal Division.—Except for the specific investigative and prosecutorial duties assigned to the Special Prosecutor, the Assistant Attorney General in charge of the Criminal Division will continue to exercise all of the duties currently assigned to him.

Applicable Departmental Policies.—Except as otherwise herein specified or as mutually agreed between the Special Prosecutor and the Attorney General, the Watergate Special Prosecution Force will be the subject to the administrative regulations and policies of the Department of Justice.

Public Reports.—The Special Prosecutor may from time to time make public such statements or reports as he deems appropriate and shall upon completion of his assignment submit a final report to the appropriate persons or entities of the Congress.

Duration of Assignment.—The Special Prosecutor will carry out these responsibilities with the full support of the Department of Justice, until such time as, in his judgment, he has completed them or until a date mutually agreed upon between the Attorney General and himself.

5. Department of Justice Order No. 554-73 (Nov. 19, 1973), 38 Fed. Reg. 32,805, amending 28 C.F.R. Appendix to Subpart G-1, provides—

Title 28—Judicial Administration

CHAPTER I—DEPARTMENT OF JUSTICE

Part O—Organization of the Department of Justice

Subpart G-1—Office of Watergate Special Prosecution Force

Order No. 554-73

Amending the Regulations Establishing the Office of Watergate Special Prosecution Force

By virtue of the authority vested in me by 28 U.S.C. 509, 510 and U.S.C. 301, the last sentence of the fourth paragraph of the Appendix to Subpart G-1 is amended to read as follows: "In accordance with assurances given by the the President to the Attorney General that the President will not exercise his Constitutional powers to effect the discharge of the Special Prosecutor or to limit the independence that he is hereby given, (1) the Special Prosecutor will not be removed from his duties except for extraordinary improprieties on his part and without the President's first consulting the Majority and the Minority Leaders and Chairmen and ranking Minority Members of the Judiciary Committees of the Senate and Houses of Representatives and ascertaining that their consensus is in accord with his proposed action, and (2) the jurisdiction of the Special Prosecutor will not be limited without the President's first consulting with such Members of Congress and ascertaining that their consensus is in accord with his proposed action."

ROBERT H. BORK,
Acting Attorney General.

Date: November 19, 1973.

6. The letter from the Acting Attorney General to the Special Prosecutor on November 21, 1973, stating the intention of Department of Justice Order No. 554-73, is as follows—

OFFICE OF THE SOLICITOR GENERAL,
Washington, D.C. 20530,
November 21, 1973.

LEON JAWORSKI, *Esq.*,
Special Prosecutor,
Watergate Special Prosecution Force,
1425 K Street, N.W.,
Washington, D.C. 20005

Dear Mr. Jaworski: You have informed me that the amendment to your charter of November 19, 1973 has been questioned by some members of the press. This letter is to confirm what I told you in our telephone conversation. The amendment of November 19, 1973 was intended to be, and is, a safeguard of your independence. The President has given his assurance that he would not exercise his constitutional powers either to discharge the Special Prosecutor or to limit the independence of the Special Prosecutor without first consulting the Majority and Minority leaders and chairmen and ranking members of the Judiciary Committees of the Senate and the House, and ascertaining that their consensus is in accord with his proposed action.

When that assurance was worked into the charter, the draftsman inadvertently used a form of words that might have been construed as applying the President's assurance only to the subject of discharge. This was subsequently pointed out to me by an assistant and I had the amendment of November 19 drafted in order to put beyond question that the assurance given applied to your independence under the charter and not merely to the subject of discharge.

There is, in my judgment, no possibility whatever that the topics of discharge or limitation of independence will ever be of more than hypothetical interest. I write this letter only to repeat what you already know: the recent amendment to your charter was to correct an ambiguous phrasing and thus to make clear that the assurances concerning congressional consultation and consensus apply to all aspects of your independence.

Sincerely,

ROBERT H. BORK,
Acting Attorney General.

VIII
SPECIAL PROSECUTOR'S REPLY BRIEF IN UNITED STATES
v.
NIXON

The Special Prosecutor's reply brief focused on the grand jury's power to name the President as a co-conspirator. It also discussed the "political question" doctrine, and the scope of executive privilege.

IN THE SUPREME COURT OF THE UNITED STATES

OCTOBER TERM, 1973

No. 73—1766

UNITED STATES OF AMERICA, PETITIONER

v.

RICHARD M. NIXON, PRESIDENT OF THE
UNITED STATES, ET AL., RESPONDENTS

No. 73—1834

RICHARD M. NIXON, PRESIDENT OF THE
UNITED STATES, PETITIONER

v.

UNITED STATES OF AMERICA

*ON WRITS OF CERTIORARI TO THE UNITED STATES
COURT OF APPEALS FOR THE
DISTRICT OF COLUMBIA CIRCUIT*

REPLY BRIEF FOR THE UNITED STATES

The Special Prosecutor, on behalf of the United States, submits this Reply Brief in response to the brief submitted by counsel for the President on June 21, 1974.

ARGUMENT

I. THE GRAND JURY'S ACTION IN DESIGNATING THE
PRESIDENT AS ONE OF THE UNINDICTED
CO-CONSPIRATORS WAS A RESPONSIBLE EXERCISE
OF ITS CONSTITUTIONAL POWERS

In the district court, counsel for the President premised his motion to expunge the grand jury's action concerning the President on the argument that an incumbent President could not be indicted. In this Court, counsel also challenges the motives that led to that action. These are false issues that should be dismissed at once so that the Court can address on the merits the question on which certiorari was granted in No. 73—1834.

A. *The Grand Jury's Action Was Taken and Disclosed in Good Faith and Was Unrelated to the Impeachment Inquiry before the House of Representatives*

One of the contentions that is repeated throughout the President's brief in this Court is that "court process is being used as a discovery tool for the impeachment proceedings" now pending before the Committee on the Judiciary of the House of Representatives (P. Br. 13[1]). The argument is advanced that the courts are being used "as a back-door route to circumvent the constitutional procedures of an impeachment inquiry, and thus [being] intruded into the political thicket in this most solemn of political processes" (P. Br. 15). Later, counsel charges that our submissions, relying in part on the grand jury's finding, "base a desire for evidence on a stratagem which attempts to cripple the Presidency" and constitute "a grotesque attempt to abuse the process of the judicial branch of government" (P. Br. 114). These assertions are unfounded.

The grand jury's determination that there is evidence that the President was one of the conspirators involved in the conspiracy alleged in the indictment in *United States* v. *Mitchell, et al.,* D.D.C. No. 74—110 (A. 5a—14a), and the government's reliance on that action in opposing the President's motion to quash the subpoena *duces tecum* were made in good faith, within the legitimate sphere of constitutional authority. We shall discuss below the reasons why the President can be identified constitutionally as an unindicted co-conspirator by a federal grand jury (see pp. 16—23, *infra*), but we consider it important to set the record straight on the reasons for its action and the context of the disclosure of that action. The record shows that both the grand jury and the Special Prosecutor have been sensitive to the President's position and have endeavored to avoid unnecessary interference with the constitutional processes being pursued simultaneously by the House Judiciary Committee.

By the time it returned the conspiracy indictment in this case on March 1, 1974, the grand jury had been in session since June 5, 1972, and had first heard Watergate-related evidence shortly after the June 17, 1972 break-in.[2] It resumed its investigation in

---

[1] "P. Br." refers to the printed brief submitted by counsel for the President on June 25 in substitution for the brief filed on June 21. "Br." refers to the main brief for the United States.

[2] Counsel for the President notes (P. Br. 6 n. 3) that the validity of the indictment has been challenged by the defendants in this case on the ground that the grand jury's term had expired under Rule 6(g), Fed. R. Crim. P. However, by act of Congress (Pub. L. 93-172, 87 Stat. 691), the term of the grand jury was extended until June 4, 1974,

March 1973 after the trial and conviction of the seven Watergate burglars and pursued this inquiry virtually full-time until the return of the indictment. During the course of its investigation, it received a considerable amount of information concerning the President's role in the alleged conspiracy to obstruct justice and to defraud the United States charged in Count I. As we pointed out in our principal brief, out of "deference to the President's public position" (Br. 98 n. 76), the grand jury elected to take no action publicly that would cause needless embarrassment to the President at the time the Judiciary Committee was conducting its inquiry.

But as an independent constitutional institution with grave public responsibilities, the grand jury was not free to ignore the evidence it had heard. Hence, it decided to recommend to the chief judge of the district court that the material evidence concerning the President be transmitted to the Judiciary Committee. The Special Prosecutor, as the grand jury's counsel, notified the chief judge of this intended action, and, at the time the indictment was received, the chief judge received and sealed the grand jury's "Report and Recommendation" together with the accompanying evidence. The "Report and Recommendation" stated that the grand jury was "deferring" to the "primary jurisdiction" of the House. Before taking any action, the court gave counsel for the President and counsel for the defendants (as well as counsel for the Judiciary Committee) an opportunity to submit written memoranda and to argue the matter orally at a hearing. Counsel for the President was allowed to inspect the "Report and Recommendation" and stated that the President had no objection to the court's granting the grand jury's request that the evidence be transmitted. See *In re Report and Recommendation of June 5, 1972 Grand Jury Concerning Transmission of Evidence to House of Representatives*, 370 F. Supp. 1219, 1221 & nn. 1, 2 (D.D.C. 1974), narrating these developments. In fact, at the hearing before the district court, counsel stated that it was the President's own decision to make available to the House directly any evidence he had furnished to the grand jury. Transcript of Hearing, March 6, 1974, at 3 (D.D.C. Misc. No. 74—21).

(subject to further extension by the court) to allow it to continue and conclude this investigation. This legislation was unquestionably valid. See *United States* v. *Johnson*, 319 U.S. 503, 507-513; *Stillman* v. *United States*, 177 F. 2d 607, 611 n. 2 (9th Cir. 1949). Cf. *Government of Virgin Islands* v. *Parrott*, 476 F. 2d 1058, 1060-61 (3d Cir. 1973), cert. denied, 414 U.S. 871 (later statute prevails over rule).

In determining that he would exercise his discretion under Rule 6(e) of the Federal Rules of Criminal Procedure and would transmit the grand jury evidence to the House, the judge found that the grand jury's report "draws no accusatory conclusions. It deprives no one of an official forum in which to respond." 370 F. Supp. at 1226.[3] The court also noted (*ibid*):

It contains no recommendation, advice or statements that infringe on the prerogatives of other branches of government. Indeed, its only recommendation is to the Court, and rather than injuring separation of powers principles, the Jury sustains them by lending its aid to the House in the exercise of that body's constitutional jurisdiction. It renders no moral or social judgments. The Report is a simple and straightforward compilation of information gathered by the Grand Jury, and no more.

When several defendants filed petitions for writs of mandamus or prohibition to preclude the transmission of the evidence, the court of appeals called for the "Report and Recommendation" and the accompanying evidence. With the materials before the court *en banc*, the court of appeals denied the petitions, noting that "the President of the United States, who is described by all parties as the focus of the report and who presumably would have the greatest interest in its disposition, has interposed no objection to the District Court's action." *Haldeman* v. *Sirica*, —F.2d—, — (Nos. 74—1364, 74—1368) (D.C. Cir. March 27, 1974). The court did not challenge the district court's finding that the grand jury's proposed submission to the House was not accusatory and involved merely a compilation of evidence. When no further review was sought, the evidence thereafter was transmitted to the House.

The grand jury's action identifying the President as a co-conspirator, now at issue before this Court, is entirely unrelated. This determination was made as an integral part of the grand jury's performance of its own constitutional functions. In making its determination, the grand jury was not focusing on the President *qua* President. Rather, it was discharging its sworn duty to determine "whether a crime has been committed and who has committed it." *United States* v. *Dionisio*, 410 U.S. 1, 15. It decided to indict seven persons and to state in the indictment simply its belief that there were other co-conspirators "to the

---

[3] The President's motion and exhibits before this Court concerning the grand jury evidence show that the House Judiciary Committee is giving counsel for the President access to the grand jury materials placed on the record before the Committee.

Grand Jury known and unknown" (A. 7a), but without publicly identifying those who were known. At the same time, however, the grand jury recorded for later disclosure in connection with the criminal trial its determination of the identity of each of the known co-conspirators, including "Richard M. Nixon." It takes no extended discussion to show that this action, while unquestionably painful for all parties concerned, was in furtherance of legitimate and, indeed, compelling purposes.

Counsel for the President is simply wrong in alleging that the naming of the President was a "stratagem" or "device" to "nullify the President's claim of executive privilege" (P. Br. 113, 114). This claim ignores the basic principle that the grand jury's function is to return a "true bill" that fully and fairly alleges what it believes the evidence shows. Moreover, in light of the apparent thrust of the evidence here, the naming of the President at some stage prior to trial was virtually inevitable. While it is not mandatory that unindicted conspirators be named in the indictment, see *Rogers* v. *United States*, 340 U.S. 367, 375, such information commonly must be furnished by the prosecution in its bill of particulars. See, *e.g.*, *United States* v. *Pilnick*, 267 F. Supp. 791, 801 (S.D.N.Y. 1967); cf. *United States* v. *Debrow*, 346 U.S. 374, 378.

A specific finding by the grand jury on the identity of the known but unindicted co-conspirators was especially important here to furnish additional protection against the possibility of unfounded accusations, particularly when one of the persons seemingly involved was the President. This course makes it clear that the grand jury—the "conscience of the community"—and not merely the prosecutor, made this important determination in the first instance.

Furthermore, the identification of each co-conspirator—regardless of his station—is a prerequisite to making his declarations in furtherance of the conspiracy admissible against the other conspirators. See *Lutwak* v. *United States*, 344 U.S. 604, 617—19; *Anderson* v. *United States*, — U.S. — (42 U.S.L.W. 4815, June 3, 1974). This will be an essential consideration in assuring a trial upon all material and important evidence. It is well within a prosecutor's proper discharge of his duties to pursue a case to trial by relying on the grand jury's *prima facie* determination of the membership in the alleged conspiracy, and unless good reason exists to the contrary, he is obligated to do so. It is for these reasons that the grand jury properly made its judgments on the question, and that the Special Prosecutor was authorized to disclose its action to the court and the parties to this case in connection with the post-indictment proceedings.

Nor is there any foundation for the insinuation that the grand jury's determination regarding President Nixon was intended to prejudice the President's position before the country or before the Judiciary Committee. As noted above, when the grand jury transmitted the material evidence concerning the President to the Judiciary Committee, it carefully disavowed any assessment of its significance insofar as the President's official status was concerned, and, as the district court and court of appeals agreed, the grand jury abstained from offering the House its views on the thrust of the evidence. In discharging its own constitutional functions and in appraising the involvement of "Richard M. Nixon" (and other unindicted co-conspirators) in the offenses for which it returned an indictment, it also endeavored to respect the President's official position by maintaining its determination as to *all* unindicted co-conspirators in secret. That vote was taken on February 25, 1974. It was anticipated that disclosure of the identity of the co-conspirators, including Richard M. Nixon, would be deferred many months, at least until pre-trial discovery proceedings were under way and a bill of particulars filed, by which time the impeachment proceedings might have been concluded.

When, however, the President refused to comply with the instant subpoena for evidence to be used at the trial on the indictment and on May 1, 1974, moved to quash it, claiming "executive privilege," it became appropriate, if not obligatory, to invoke the grand jury's finding in order to permit the court to make an informed determination whether the President could lawfully invoke that public privilege to withhold the evidence sought. As the record before the Court reflects, counsel for the President was advised of the grand jury's action before any answering papers were filed by the Special Prosecutor and, again out of regard for the President's position, the Special Prosecutor suggested to the President's counsel that the matter should be handled *in camera*.[4] The President's counsel then joined in the Special Prosecutor's motion to seal all pleadings reflecting the grand jury's action and to hold oral argument *in camera*. The district court, after an *in camera* hearing with defense counsel present, accepted this suggestion, and further proceedings were conducted in this extraordinary way—to avoid, insofar as possible, having the proceedings in this important criminal

---

[4] Counsel for the President commended the Special Prosecutor for suggesting this procedure. Transcript of *In Camera* Hearing on May 8, 1974, at 4.

prosecution affect the concurrent proceedings before the House.

In denying the President's motion to quash, the district court's opinion was carefully guarded in referring to the significance of the sealed material (Pet. App. 22—23). Because of the number of persons who were necessarily privy to this information, however, news media were able to piece together the essentials of what had been disclosed and litigated *in camera*, and on June 6, 1974, counsel for the President publicly confirmed the reports about the grand jury's action. But the record shows that the grand jury, the district court and the Special Prosecutor successfully maintained the grand jury's determination in strict confidence for several months in order to avoid unnecessary impact upon the Judiciary Committee's inquiry. It is hardly fair to say, therefore, as counsel for the President does, that the grand jury and Special Prosecutor were attempting "to subvert and prejudice the legitimate constitutional procedure of impeachment" (P. Br. 108).

B. *A Federal Grand Jury Has the Constitutional Power to Identify an Incumbent President as an Unindicted Co-Conspirator in Connection with Its Return of an Indictment Against Other Persons*

Upon analysis of the merits, the Court will conclude, we believe, that counsel's assertions that an incumbent President cannot be named an unindicted co-conspirator are unpersuasive. The federal grand jury's constitutional powers and responsibilities are sweeping. Although it is by no means clear that a President is immune from indictment prior to impeachment, conviction, and removal from office, the practical arguments in favor of that proposition cannot fairly be stretched to confer immunity on the President from being identified as an *unindicted* co-conspirator, when it is necessary to do so in connection with criminal proceedings against persons unquestionably liable to indictment. Since the naming of unindicted co-conspirators is a fair and common practice and was required here to outline the full range of the alleged conspiracy, the district court's refusal to expunge its determination was fully justified.[5]

---

[5] Even assuming, for some legal reason, that the grand jury's naming of the President as an unindicted co-conspirator is ineffective, it does not follow that the court below abused its discretion in denying the motion to expunge. Expunction of a formal finding by a grand jury, whose existence and powers are constitutionally established, is a drastic remedy, to be granted only after a careful weighing of the legitimacy of the grand jury's action, the strength of the public interest in an accurate

1. The grand jury has broad and important powers as an independent institution of our government

Only a brief discussion is required to establish the unique and important role of the grand jury in the American judicial system. Though an arm of the court, *Levine v. United States*, 362 U.S. 610, 617, the grand jury has an independent constitutional basis in the Fifth Amendment and has functions and prerogatives which are "rooted in long centuries of Anglo-American history." *Hannah v. Larche*, 363 U.S. 420, 490 (Frankfurter, J., concurring). The adoption of the grand jury "in our Constitution as the sole method for preferring charges in serious criminal cases shows the high place it held as an instrument of justice." *Costello v. United States*, 350 U.S. 359, 362. See also *Branzburg v. Hayes*, 408 U.S. 665, 687.

Like its English progenitor, the American grand jury is designed to reflect the conscience of the community. 2 Pollock & Maitland, *History of the English Law* 642 (2d ed. 1909). Its members are "selected from the body of the people"[6] and are "pledged to indict no one because of prejudice and to free no one because of special favor." *Costello v. United States, supra*, 350 U.S. at 362.[7] Its first and only obligation is to the truth—to

public record of proceedings, and the degree of prejudice to those persons affected by full disclosure. See *Application of Johnson*, 484 F. 2d 791, 797 (7th Cir. 1973); *In re Grand Jury Proceedings*, 479 F. 2d 458, 460 n. (5th Cir. 1973).

The President's principal argument below was the expunction was necessary because of the damage which disclosure would cause to the fairness of the impeachment inquiry being conducted by the House of Representatives. *Reply to Memorandum in Opposition to the Motion to Quash Subpoena Duces Tecum* 25-27 (D.D.C. May 13, 1974) (Crim. No. 74-100). That concern has now become academic because of the public disclosure of the grand jury's action. Any resulting harm to him before the House or in the eyes of the public is now unfortunately an "accomplished fact." *Application of Johnson, supra*, 484 F. 2d at 797. See also *United States v. Connelly*, 129 F. Supp. 786, 787 (D. Minn. 1955) (refusal to expunge grand jury report that had already been widely publicized).

The listing of specific co-conspirators pursuant to the finding and return of an indictment was clearly within the traditional confines of grand jury power. The grand jury here did not go beyond this function by making merely gratuitous expressions of views about a general societal condition; or concerning matters outside its area of expertise. Compare *Application of United Electrical, Radio & Machine Workers*, 111 F. Supp. 858 (S.D.N.Y. 1953). Cf. *Hammond v. Brown*, 323 F. Supp. 326, 337 (N.D. Ohio), affirmed, 450 F. 2d 480 (6th Cir. 1971). Certainly the grand jury's action here is not clearly *ultra vires*. There is, in addition, a legitimate public purpose in reporting the fact that serious criminal charges against a government official have been made. *In re Presentment of Special Grand Jury, January 1969*, 315 F. Supp. 662, 678 (D. Md. 1970).

The district judge, therefore, did not abuse his discretion in refusing to expunge the finding.

[6] See the Jury Selection and Service Act of 1968, 28 U.S.C. 1861-1871.

[7] Immediately after the President procured the dismissal of Special Prosecutor Cox when he refused to obey the President's instruction not to seek enforcement of the

determine, unhindered by external influence or supervision, "whether a crime has been committed and who has committed it." *United States* v. *Dionisio, supra,* 410 U.S. at 15. See also *Wood* v. *Georgia,* 370 U.S. 375, 390; *Ex parte Bain,* 121 U.S. 1, 11.

Reflecting this "special role in insuring fair and effective law enforcement," *United States* v. *Calandra,* 414 U.S. 338, 343 (1974), the grand jury's powers of inquiry are extremely broad. It has a right to every man's evidence, and proceeds unhindered by the various evidentiary and exclusionary rules which apply at trial. *Branzburg* v. *Hayes, supra; Lawn* v. *United States,* 355 U.S. 339; *Costello* v. *United States, supra;Holt* v. *United States,* 218 *U.S.245. See also Gravel* v. *United States,* 408 U.S. 606, 628, where this Court allowed wide scope to a grand jury's investigation involving a United States Senator, despite claims that such matters were immune from inquiry under the Speech or Debate Clause. As the courts have frequently noted, society's interests are best served by a grand jury investigation which is "thorough and extensive." *Wood* v. *Georgia, supra,* 370 U.S. at 392.

grand jury subpoena *duces tecum* that had been upheld by the court of appeals in *Nixon* v. *Sirica,* 487 F. 2d 700 (D.C. Cir. 1973), Chief Judge Sirica summoned the two grand juries that were then conducting investigations with the assistance of the Special Prosecutor, including the grand jury that took the action now being challenged by the President. In open court on October 23, 1973, the chief judge instructed them:

"You are advised first, that the grand juries on which you serve remain operative and intact. You are still grand jurors, and the grand juries you constitute still function. In this regard you should be aware that the oath you took upon entering this service remains binding. You must all be especially careful at this time to fully and strictly adhere to that oath which states:

"You and each of you as a member of the grand jury for the District of Columbia, do solemnly swear that you will diligently, fully, and impartially inquire into and true presentment make of all offenses which shall come to your knowledge and of which the United States District Court for the District of Columbia has cognizance; that you will present no one from hatred or malice nor leave anyone unpresented from fear, favor, affection, reward, or hope of reward; that the counsel of the Attorney of the United States, your fellows and your own, you will keep secret and that you will to the best of your ability perform all the duties enjoined upon you as a grand juror, so help you God.

*　　*　　*　　*　　*　　*　　*

"This brings me to my second point; these two grand juries *will* continue to function and pursue their work. You are not dismissed and will not be dismissed except as provided by law upon the completion of your work or the conclusion of your term. Your service to date, I realize, has occasioned personal sacrifices for many of you and inconvenience for all of you. You did not choose this assignment; it is an obligation of citizenship which it fell your lot to bear at this time, and you have borne it well. The Court and the country are grateful to you. Nevertheless, you must be prepared to press forward. We rely on your continued integrity and perseverance." (Emphasis in original.)

The grand jury has the unreviewable independence to refuse to return an indictment requested by the prosecution. *Gaither* v. *United States*, 413 F. 2d 1061, 1066 (D.C. Cir. 1969). Conversely, even direct instructions from the President cannot prevent the grand jury "from making the fullest investigation into the matter" and "from returning an indictment against the accused if the evidence should warrant it * * *." *In re Miller*, 17 Fed. Cas. 295 (No. 9,552) (C.C.D. Ind. 1879). For as the court instructed the grand jury in that case, it was free to disregard the instructions from President Hayes to the prosecutor to restrict its inquiry:"The moment the executive is allowed to control the action of the courts in the administration of criminal justice their independence is gone." See also *United States* v. *Cox*, 342 F. 2d 167, 174 80 (5th Cir. 1965), cert. denied, 381 U.S. 935 (opinion of Rives, Gewin, and Bell, JJ.); *United States* v. *Smyth*, 104 F. Supp. 283, 293–295 (N.D. Calif. 1952).

Thus, in our jurisprudence this body of citizens, randomly selected, beholden neither to court nor prosecutor, trusted historically to protect the individual against unwarranted governmental charges, but sworn to ferret out criminality by the exalted and powerful as well as by the humble and weak, must be able to take cognizance of *all* possible violators of the laws of the United States.

2. *An incumbent President may be named as an unindicted co-conspirator*

Although we shall indicate below why it is not at all clear that an incumbent President may not be named as a *defendant* in a criminal indictment, this case does not turn on that issue and the Court need not decide it. Even assuming *arguendo* that an incumbent President has some implicit constitutional immunity that prevents a federal grand jury from indicting him, he nevertheless may be named as an *unindicted* co-conspirator under the traditional grand jury power to investigate and charge conspiracies that include co-conspirators who are not legally indictable. This power is part of the constitutional power to return indictments in the form and scope the grand jury determines is proper.[8] It includes the authority to indict a person and charge him with conspiring with a person who, for one reason or another, is immune from prosecution.

It is not disputed, of course, that a grand jury has the power to

[8] *Gaither* v. *United States, supra*, 413 F. 2d at 1069; *United States* v. *Cox, supra*, 342 F. 2d at 181, 182.

name persons other than a President as unindicted co-conspirators. While no case in this Court has directly considered the existence of such power, it has long been commonplace for persons to be identified in this way in a conspiracy indictment. See, *e.g.*, *Kotteakos* v. *United States*, 328 U.S. 750, 752 n. 1; *United States* v. *Agueci*, 310 F. 2d 817, 820 (2d Cir. 1962), cert. denied, 372 U.S. 959; *United States* v. *Edwards*, 366 F. 2d 853, 858 (2d Cir. 1966). Indeed, it has been held proper to refuse to strike the names of 37 unindicted co-conspirators from an indictment. *United States* v. *Penney*, 416 F. 2d 850, 852 (6th Cir. 1969), cert. denied, 398 U.S. 932.

The grand jury has the right to decide whether to indict or not to indict particular persons and to decide what charge or charges such person or persons shall face. It may decline to indict a person in the face of sufficient evidence because of mitigating circumstances. In addition, some persons believed to be criminally involved may be immune from prosecution, legally or practically, for any one of numerous reasons: transactional or use immunity; prior acquittal or conviction; diplomatic immunity; incompetence; flight to a foreign sanctuary; pardon; expiration of a statute of limitations; or death. Accordingly, the grand jury has the right to charge some of the participants as defendants and to name others as unindicted co-conspirators. Even where some of the participants enjoy constitutional, legal, or practical immunity from being criminally prosecuted, neither the grand jury nor the prosecution at trial is obliged to suppress all evidence of their complicity.

For example, in *Farnsworth* v. *Zerbst*, 98 F. 2d 541 (5th Cir. 1938), cert. denied, 307 U.S. 642, and *Farnsworth* v. *Sanford*, 115 F. 2d 375 (5th Cir. 1940), cert. denied, 313 U.S. 586, the court of appeals ruled that a person may be convicted and punished for a conspiracy even though his fellow conspirators were immune from prosecution because of the immunity attaching to representatives of foreign governments. There, the defendant, a naval officer, was charged with conspiring with two *named* Japanese diplomats to transmit defense secrets to a foreign government. He argued that the indictment was defective because he was charged with conspiring with persons who had diplomatic immunity from prosecution. In rejecting this argument, the court said (98 F. 2d at 544):

> If such persons in the United States join with a citizen of the United States in a conspiracy to commit a crime, though it be conceded that the foreign diplomat would not be indicted in the District Court, or even that he could not be, his

immunity will not excuse the local citizen. At least two persons must join in an unlawful enterprise to constitute it a conspiracy. The statute expressly so says. But both need not be prosecuted, or prosecutable. One may die, may escape, or obtain a pardon; but the other remains guilty.

Later the court held that the case had not "affected" the diplomats in such a way as to deprive the lower federal courts of jurisdiction over the matter, reasoning (115 F. 2d at 379):

[W]e think that when the Japanese defendants were not arrested and Farnsworth was arraigned alone there was as complete a severance of the case against him as though he alone had been indicted. The case to be tried then in no substantial way affected the ex-attaches in Japan, or the Japanese Ambassador. Each of course would be concerned as the trial might involve reflections on the character and conduct of the ex-attaches, but the case in its results would not touch the person or goods or servants of any of them. * * * The ambassador's feelings, his integrity as a witness, and his standing as a man might all be involved, but he is held not affected.

In *United States* v. *Johnson*, 337 F. 2d 180 (4th Cir. 1964), aff'd and remanded, 383 U.S. 169, the court of appeals expressly held that the government could prosecute private individuals for conspiring to defraud the United States by bribing a Congressman to make a speech on the floor of the House, even though the prosecution required exploration of the Congressman's motivation for the speech and even though the Congressman himself was immune under the Speech or Debate Clause from prosecution on that theory. This Court also has implied that third-party witnesses may be questioned about the legislative acts of congressmen, despite the Speech or Debate Clause, where third-party crimes are the "proper concern of the grand jury or the Executive Branch" in its prosecutive capacity. *Gravel* v. *United States*, 408 U.S. 606, 629, n. 18. Thus, the mere fact that an official has a personal immunity from prosecution does not bar the prosecution from alleging and proving his complicity as part of a case against persons who have no such immunity.

In short, the jurisdiction of the grand jury to name unindicted co-conspirators is a necessary part of the power to charge defendants in a conspiracy case and is not restricted by any immunity a co-conspirator may enjoy not to be brought personally before the bar of justice to answer for the offense.

There is, we submit, no reason to make an exception for an

incumbent President. We realize that the President is entrusted with awesome powers and responsibilities requiring his full attention. While indictment would require the President to spend time preparing a defense and, thus, would interfere to some extent with his attention to his public duties, the course the grand jury has followed here in naming the President as an unindicted co-conspirator cannot be regarded as equally burdensome. It is regrettable that the thrust of the evidence in the grand jury's view encompasses an incumbent President, but it would not be fair to our legal system or to the defendants and other unindicted co-conspirators to blunt the sweep of the evidence artificially by excluding one person, however prominent and important, while identifying all others.

We concede that any person—President or "ordinary" citizen—may suffer adverse consequences if he is named as an unindicted co-conspirator, whether in an indictment, in a bill of particulars or in testimony at a trial. But such consequences are an inevitable part of the judicial process and do not justify prior judicial screening or complete silence. As Justice Douglas observed for the Court in *Ewing* v. *Mytinger & Casselberry, Inc.*, 339 U.S. 594, 599:

> The impact of the initiation of judicial proceedings is often serious. Take the case of the grand jury. It returns an indictment against a man without a hearing. * * * As a result the defendant can be arrested and held for trial. See *Beavers* v. *Henkel*, 194 U.S. 73, 85; *Ex parte United States*, 287 U.S. 241, 250. The impact of an indictment is on the reputation or liberty of a man. The same is true where a prosecutor files an information charging violations of the law. The harm to property and business can also be incalculable by the mere institution of proceedings. Yet it has never been held that the hand of government must be stayed until the courts have an opportunity to determine whether the government is justified in instituting suit in the courts.

Similar considerations apply to the interests of persons who are brought into criminal proceedings collaterally, as unindicted co-conspirators. For example, in *United States* v. *General Motors Corp.*, 352 F. Supp. 1071 (S.D. Mich. 1973), the court denied a motion of the defendants in a conspiracy case under the Sherman Act to suppress a bill of particulars on the ground that numerous unindicted prominent persons named in the bill would be subjected to adverse publicity and embarrassment.[9]

---

[9] Unindicted co-conspirators have sometimes been afforded relief from being

This does not mean that a person has no protection against being named unfairly as a co-conspirator. His primary protection is in the finding of the grand jury that there is sufficient evidence to believe that the conspiracy as charged in the indictment existed. It also lies in the conscience of each member of a grand jury, the same protection that is applicable to an indicted defendant. As this Court stated in *Wood* v. *Georgia, supra,* 370 U.S. at 390:

> Historically, this body has been regarded as a primary security to the innocent against hasty, malicious and oppressive persecution; it serves the invaluable function in our society for standing between the accuser and the accused, whether the latter be an individual, minority group, or other, to determine whether a charge is founded upon reason or was dictated by an intimidating power or by malice and personal ill will.

The scope of the indictment itself as returned by the grand jury and the duty of the United States Attorney to refrain from improper methods also afford protection to an individual from being wrongfully accused as a co-conspirator in the bill of particulars or the evidence. See *Berger* v. *United States,* 295 U.S. 78, 88.

While we readily concede that the naming of an incumbent President as an unindicted co-conspirator is a grave and solemn step and may cause public as well as private anguish, we submit that such action is not constitutionally proscribed. The answer to the constitutional question must be shaped by two postulates of our free society: that grand juries are ordinarily responsible[10] and that, in the public market place of ideas, the people can

---

named in an indictment *after* a trial where the evidence showed that they were *not* in fact involved in the conspiracy charged. See *Application of American Society for Testing and Materials,* 231 F. Supp. 686 (E.D. Pa. 1964); *Application of Turner & Newall, Ltd.,* 231 F. Supp. 728 (E.D. Pa. 1964). See also *Beverly* v. *United States,* 5th Cir., No. 73-2027, pending on appeal, where persons named as unindicted co-conspirators are contending that their names should be expunged from a conspiracy indictment.

It is not unusual for persons tangentially involved in criminal proceedings to suffer adverse consequences. In many instances, an innocent witness may suffer some injury as a result of his testimony. As this Court explained in *United States* v. *Calandra, supra,* 414 U.S. at 345:

"The duty to testify may on occasion be burdensome and even embarrassing. It may cause injury to a witness' social and economic status. Yet the duty to testify has been regarded as 'so necessary to the administration of justice' that the witness' personal interest in privacy must yield to the public's overriding interest in full disclosure."

[10] See, *e.g., Wood* v. *Georgia, supra.*

be trusted to assess the worth of charges and counter-charges, particularly where the acts of a public official are in dispute.[11] There is little reason to fear either that grand juries will accuse an incumbent President maliciously, or that, if they do, their charges will receive credit they do not deserve.

In light of the foregoing principles, we submit that the grand jury's action here was constitutionally legitimate.

3. It is an open and substantial question whether an incumbent president is subject to indictment

Counsel for the President bases his argument against the constitutionality of the grand jury's action here on the premise that an incumbent President cannot be indicted (P. Br. 107—108). We believe we have just shown that the Court's consideration of the issue actually before the Court—whether a President can be named as an *unindicted* co-conspirator—does not require consideration of the assertion by counsel for the President that it cannot be "seriously disputed" that "a President may not be indicted while he is an incumbent" (P. Br. 95). Nevertheless, we cannot allow the assertion to stand uncontroverted. Thus, we outline the reasons why the President's major premise may be unsound, even though the Court need not decide the issue in order to reject the contention that the district court erred in refusing to expunge the grand jury's finding.

Resort to constitutional interpretation, history, and policy does not provide a definitive answer to the question of whether a sitting President enjoys absolute immunity from the ordinary processes of the criminal law. What we believe is clear is that nothing in the text of the Constitution or in its history—including close scrutiny of the background of relevant Constitutional provisions and of the intent of the Framers—imposes any bar to indictment of an incumbent President. Primary support for such a prohibition must be found, if at all, in considerations of constitutional and public policy including competing factors such as the nature and role of the Presidency in our constitutional system, the importance of the administration of criminal justice, and the principle that under our system no person, no matter what his station, is above the law. Whether these factors compel a conclusion that as a matter of constitutional interpretation a sitting President cannot be indicted for violations of federal criminal laws is an issue about

---

[11] See, *e.g., Garrison* v. *Louisiana,* 379 U.S. 64, 76-77; *Monitor Patriot Co.* v. *Roy,* 401 U.S. 265, 273-277.

which, at best, there is presently considerable doubt involved by the Senate. A contemporary student of the subject of impeachment suggests, on the basis of his study of the relevant materials, that the purpose of the "nevertheless" clause was only to preclude the expelled civil officer from avoiding later criminal prosecution by claiming "double jeopardy." Berger, *The President, Congress, and the Courts,* 83 Yale L.J. 1111, 1124 (1974).[12]

Significantly, the clause in question applies to all civil officers who are subject to impeachment, and not solely to the President. Yet, from the earliest days of the Republic, civil officers liable to impeachment have been dealt with in the criminal courts without first being impeached, convicted, and removed. Recently, as this Court is well aware, a panel of the Seventh Circuit composed of three distinguished Senior Circuit Judges specially designated to review the appeal of United States Circuit Judge Otto Kerner rejected the textual argument relied on by counsel for the President and observed that "[t]he purpose of the phrase may be to assure that after impeachment a trial on criminal charges is not foreclosed by the principle of double jeopardy, or it may be to differentiate the provisions of the Constitution from the English practice of impeachment." *United States* v. *Isaacs and Kerner,* 493 F. 2d 1125, 1142 (7th Cir.), cert. denied, — U.S. — (June 17, 1974). In accordance with the plain thrust of the language of this clause, the court expressly refused to construe it to imply that a sitting federal judge, who is liable to impeachment under the same clause that is applicable to the President, may not be

---

[12] Berger in this article surveys the historical material relevant to the indictability of an incumbent President and finds that the Framers did not intend to clothe a President with immunity from criminal process. Berger, *supra,* at 1123-1136.

Luther Martin, a delegate to the Constitutional Convention, stated during the impeachment proceedings against Justice Chase that the "nevertheless' clause was designed to eliminate any double jeopardy argument. 14 Annals of Congress 431 (8th Cong., 2d Sess., 1805). Our research has failed to locate any other statement by a delegate to the Constitutional Convention explicitly stating that the purpose of the "nevertheless" clause was either to avoid the double jeopardy problem or to immunize a President or civil officers from criminal prosecution.

Delegates during the North Carolina debates spoke at length about whether impeachment was the exclusive remedy against miscreant federal officials. 4 Elliot, *The Debates of the Several State Conventions on the Adoption of the Federal Constitution* 32-50 (2d ed. 1836) [hereinafter cited as Elliot's Debates] . At one point Iredell stated that "[h]e [the government official] may be tried in such a court for common-law offenses, whether impeached or not." 4 Elliot's Debates 37. But Governor Johnston was seemingly of the view "that men who were in very high offices could not be come at by the ordinary course of justice; but when called before this high tribunal and convicted, they would be stripped of their dignity, and reduced to the rank of their fellow citizens, and then the courts of common law might proceed against them." *Ibid.*

indicted and tried prior to removal from office.[13] In language equally applicable to a federal judge or a President, the court wrote (493 F. 2d at 1144):

> We conclude that whatever immunities or privileges the Constitution confers for the purpose of assuring the independence of the co-equal branches of government they do not exempt the members of those branches "from the operation of the ordinary criminal laws." Criminal conduct is not part of the necessary functions performed by public officials. Punishment for that conduct will not interfere with the legitimate operations of a branch of government. Historically, the impeachment process has proven to be cumbersome and fraught with political overtones.

The panel made no effort to distinguish the President from the sweep and force of this statement.

The President also refers to the views expressed by the Framers as evidencing at least a clear *intent* to immunize the President from criminal prosecution. While there are some statements cited in the President's brief indicating that criminal indictment was expected to follow impeachment, these few statements cannot support the conclusion that the Framers unambiguously intended to immunize an incumbent President from criminal prosecution. They were made by the delegates to the Convention while discussing the issues of executive power, checks on Presidential prerogatives, and the relationship between the impeachment remedy and the President's independence. The precise issue of Presidential immunity was not confronted by those who wrote and debated the Constitution.[14]

The President relies heavily on Gouverneur Morris' opinion articulated at the federal Convention:

> A conclusive reason for making the Senate instead of the Supreme Court the Judge of impeachment, was that the latter was to try the President after the trial of the impeachment. 2 Farrand, *Records of the Federal Convention of 1787* at 550

---

[13] The same clause in the Constitution provides for the impeachment of the "President, the Vice President and all civil Officers of the United States" (Article II, Section 4), and Article I, Section 3, Cluse 7, relied on so heavily by the President, does not distinguish among the President, Vice President and other civil officers.

[14] When the Framers were debating what privileges should be accorded the legislators, James Madison suggested that the Convention consider "what privileges ought to be allowed to the Executive." The Convention adjourned at that point, however, and did not return to the topic in its later proceedings. 2 Farrand at 502-03. See also statement of Charles Pinckney in the Senate on March 5, 1800 (Br. 77-78).

(1911) [hereinafter cited as Farrand].

All this view contemplates is that a President may commit an act which constitutes *both* an impeachable offense and an indictable crime, and it would be anomalous for the same people who try his impeachment to participate later in the adjudication of his guilt or innocence in a different proceeding but involving the same basic activity. The statement does not imply that Morris considered it mandatory that impeachment precede indictment. Moreover, there was some concern about the possible partiality of judges who had been appointed by the President. Madison, *Debates in the Federal Convention* 536 (1920 ed.). One commentator has suggested that this was the prime reason for having the Senate rather than this Court serve as the tribunal for an impeachment trial. 1 Curtis, *Constitutional History* 482 (1889).

We do not claim that any of the actual debates provide any definitive insight into the Framer's intention on the question of the President's amenability to criminal indictment. While counsel for the President states that "there is literally nothing in all of the records of the Convention to suggest that any delegate had any contrary view (P.Br. 100), the simple fact is that the Framers never confronted the issue at all."

It is significant in this context that unlike congressmen, who were afforded an explicit, limited immunity in the Constitution with respect to their legislative duties, see *Gravel* v. *United States, supra; United States* v. *Brewster*, 408 U.S. 501; *United States* v. *Johnson*, 383 U.S. 169, the President was provided none.[15] And, as we show in our main brief (pp. 67—80), the

---

[15] We do not believe that the failure to provide explicitly for executive immunity was a mere oversight. The debates indicate that much time was spent debating the specifics of the impeachment clause, the powers of the President, and the checks on executive power. A desire to place the Chief Executive above the ordinary processes of law until his term is completed most surely would have been expressly enunciated in the text of the Constitution or at least explicitly recognized during the debates. In our main brief, moreover, we have cited the passages showing that the Framers were careful *not* to give the Executive any sweeping privileges or immunity (Br. 76-79).

There is a dearth of scholarly treatment of the question whether an incumbent President can be indicted. One nineteenth century commentator believed that "the ordinary tribunals, as we shall see, are not precluded, either before or after an impeachment, from taking cognizance of the public and official delinquency." Rawle, *A View of the Constitution of the United States of America* 215 (2d ed. 1929). See also 1 Curtis, *Constitutional History* 481 (1889). A contemporary scholar is of the view that an incumbent President can be indicted and he has concluded that "[i]t was because the Founders had learned this lesson from history that presidential powers were enumerated and limited, and that immunity from arrest was altogether withheld." Berger, *The President, Congress and the Courts,* 83 Yale L.J. 1111, 1136 (1974).

separation of powers doctrine does not result in an absolute immunity.

The President offers the additional argument that "[s]ince the President's powers include control over all federal prosecutions, it is hardly reasonable or sensible to consider the President subject to such prosecution" (P. Br. 97).[16] As we have explained in the introduction to our main brief (pp. 27—44), however, the Special Prosecutor, under applicable regulations, has final control over the position the United States, as sovereign, asserts in cases under his defined jurisdiction. Indeed, as we discussed in our main brief (pp. 20—33), the President personally agreed here to the Attorney General's promulgation of regulations (a) giving the Special Prosecutor "full authority for investigating and prosecuting * * * allegations involving the President," (b) specifying that "the Attorney General will not countermand or interfere with the Special Prosecutor's decisions or actions," and (c) pledging that "the President will not exercise his Constitutional powers to effect the discharge of the Special Prosecutor," or to "limit the independence that he is hereby given" or to limit "the jurisdiction of the Special Prosecutor" unless the consensus of eight Legislative leaders approves the President's "proposed action." (See pp. 148, 149, 151—153 of the Appendix to our main brief.) Evidently, therefore, neither the President nor the Attorney General considered prosecution of a President by an independent Special Prosecutor constitutionally inconceivable. It is hardly inevitable, therefore, that future Presidents must be left with personal control over the decision whether they—or their friends and associates—should be prosecuted.

Counsel for the President suggests that the President may have a unique immunity because the "Presidency is the only branch of government that is vested exclusively in one person by the Constitution" (P. Br. 96). Thus, it is argued: "The functioning of the executive branch ultimately depends on the President's personal capacity: legal, mental and physical. If the President cannot function freely, there is a critical gap in the whole constitutional system established by the Framers." (*Ibid.*) This is a weighty argument and it is entitled to great respect. But whether it is conclusive is uncertain and need not be decided

---

[16] The force of the President's argument here could lead to the conclusion that the Attorney General who under 28 U.S.C. 516 and 519 is authorized to conduct and supervise all litigation in which the United States is a party would likewise be immune from federal indictment, as would the United States Attorney for crimes committed in his district. 28 U.S.C. 547. The Constitution could not intend such a result.

here. It is fair to note, however, that our constitutional system has shown itself to be remarkably resilient. Our country has endured through periods of great crises, including several when our Presidents have been personally disabled for long periods of time. Furthermore, although the executive power is constitutionally vested in the President, it cannot escape notice that, in practical terms, the governmental system that has evolved since 1789 depends for the day-to-day management of the Nation's affairs upon the operation of the several cabinet departments and independent regulatory agencies, without direct Presidential guidance. In addition, the Twenty-fifth Amendment to the Constitution now expressly provides for interim leadership whenever a President is temporarily disabled or incapable of discharging the responsibilities of his office. And it is by no means inevitable, in any event, that the lodging of an indictment against an incumbent President would "cripple an entire branch of the national government and hence the whole system" (P. Br. 97).

Finally, there are very serious implications to the President's position that he has absolute immunity from criminal indictment and to his insistence that under "our system of government only the House of Representatives may determine that evidence of sufficient quantity and quality exists to try the President" (P. Br. 114—15). It is conceded that while the King can do no wrong, a President, in the eyes of the law, is not impeccable. But while there is currently a great debate about whether "impeachable offenses" under the Constitution include *non-criminal* abuses of official power,[17] it appears that not *every* crime would justify impeachment. As both the House Judiciary Committee staff and the attorneys for the President seem to agree, there must be some nexus between the impeachable misconduct and the office held. As one early commentator explained about the phrase "high Crimes and Misdemeanors":

> They can only have reference to public character and official duty. * * * In general those offenses which may be committed equally by a private person as a public officer are not the subjects of impeachment. Murder, burglary, robbery and indeed all offences not immediately connected with

[17] Compare *Constitutional Grounds for Presidential Impeachment: Report by the Staff of the Impeachment Inquiry,* House Judiciary Committee, 93d Cong., 2d Sess. (Comm. Print February 1974), with *An Analysis of the Constitutional Standard for Presidential Impeachment: Analysis Submitted to the House Committee on the Judiciary by Attorneys for the President,* 10 Weekly Compilation of Presidential Documents 270 (March 4, 1974).

office, except the two expressly mentioned [treason and bribery], are left to the ordinary course of judicial proceeding * * *. Rawle, *A View of the Constitution of the United States of America* 215 (2d ed. 1829).

In his submission to the House Judiciary Committee, counsel for the President therefore argued that he is impeachable only for "great crimes against the state." 10 Weekly Compilation of Presidential Documents 271 (March 4, 1974). If counsel for the President is correct that a President is amenable to impeachment only for certain grave public offenses and that he is absolutely immune from criminal prosecution, then indeed the Constitution has left a *lacuna* of potentially serious dimensions.[18]

Because of this purported gap and because of the virtually universal application of statutes of limitations, a President who shared complicity in such "private" crimes as burglary or assault might well be beyond the reach of the law, partaking at least in part of the royal immunities associated with a King. Perhaps this is the design of the Constitution, or a regrettable corollary of it, but we urge caution before such a proposition is accepted as inevitable.

II. THIS DISPUTE BETWEEN THE UNITED STATES, REPRESENTED BY THE SPECIAL PROSECUTOR, AND THE PRESIDENT—TWO DISTINCT PARTIES—PRESENTS A JUSTICIABLE CONTROVERSY

Principles of "separation of powers," frequently quoted in the President's brief, show why on the facts of the present case there are *no* obstacles to the Court's authority to entertain and decide this controversy. This Court's jurisdiction to consider and resolve this dispute on the merits stems from the fundamental role of the courts in our tri-partite constitutional system—the courts, as the "neutral" branch of government, have been allocated the responsibility to resolve all issues in a controversy properly before them, even though this requires them to determine authoritatively the powers and responsibilities of the other branches (Br. 25—27, 48—52).

---

[18] It is not surprising, therefore, that James Wilson, in the Pennsylvania ratification debates, observed that "far from being above the laws, he [the President] is amenable to them in his private character as a citizen, and in his public character by *impeachment.*" 2 Elliot's Debates 480 (emphasis in original). James Iredell, during the North Carolina debates stated:

"If he [the President] commits any misdemeanor in office, he is impeachable, removable from office, and incapacitated to hold any office of honor, trust, or profit. If he commits any crime, he is punishable by the laws of his country, and in capital cases may be deprived of his life." 4 Elliot's Debates 109.

This is true even when the dispute presented for resolution implicates intra-branch relationships. Thus, this Court has entertained cases challenging the right of Congress to exclude a duly-elected representative, see *Powell* v. *McCormack*, 395 U.S. 486, and cases brought by an executive officer challenging the propriety of his dismissal by his executive superiors, see, *e.g.*, *Sampson* v. *Murray*, — U.S. — (42 U.S.L.W. 4221, February 19, 1974; *Service* v. *Dulles*, 354 U.S. 363. Indeed in *Marbury* v. *Madison*, 1 Cranch (5 U.S.) 137, Chief Justice Marshall recognized that a federal court could determine whether the Secretary of State improperly withheld Marbury's commission. Contrary to the implications of the argument by counsel for the President (P. Br. 74—76), the case was not dismissed because it involved the "political" powers of the President. Rather, it was dismissed because the statute conferring original jurisdiction on this Court in that case was not consonant with the provisions of Article III narrowly circumscribing the Court's original jurisdiction.

The present controversy arises in the midst of a criminal prosecution pending in the federal courts. At issue is the enforceability of a subpoena for allegedly privileged evidence. The questions for this Court, then, are whether the judicial process is validly invoked by the Special Prosecutor on behalf of the United States and whether the issue presented for review—the validity of the claim of executive privilege—is justiciable.

A. The Special Prosecutor has independent authority to maintain the prosecution in United States V. Mitchell, et al.

There is no need here to review again the history that led to the regulations establishing the Office of the Watergate Special Prosecution Force or the exclusive authority that the Special Prosecutor has to maintain prosecutions within his jurisdiction (Br. 5—6, 9—11, 27—33). What is important to note here, however, is that counsel for the President, by accepting the proposition that the President and Attorney General can delegate certain Executive functions to subordinate officers (P. Br. 10, 41, 106), implicitly has conceded the validity of the regulations, promulgated with the President's consent, delegating specific

See also *Langford* v. *United States*, 101 U.S. 341, 343, suggesting in dictum that indictment of a President is an alternative to impeachment "if the wrong amounts to a crime."

prosecutorial duties and powers to the Special Prosecutor.[19]

There can be no question that the Attorney General, with the concurrence of the President, has delegated to the Special Prosecutor "full authority" to prosecute the present criminal case and "full authority" to contest claims of executive privilege made during that prosecution. In exercising this authority, the Special Prosecutor has the "greatest degree of independence that is consistent with the Attorney General's statutory accountability." More specifically, the regulations provide that the "Attorney General will not countermand or interfere with the Special Prosecutor's decisions or actions." The only control the Attorney General retains is to dismiss the Special Prosecutor for "extraordinary improprieties." (Br. 146—49.)

Thus, it wholly misses the point for counsel to the President to say that the separation of powers precludes the courts from entertaining this action because "it is the exclusive prerogative of the executive branch, not the Judiciary, to determine whom to prosecute, on what charges, and with what evidence" (P. Br. 39).[20] To the extent this prerogative is exclusively Executive, it now lies with the Special Prosecutor with respect to the prosecution of *United States* v. *Mitchell, et al.*, and not with the Attorney General or the President. In a very real sense, therefore, the Office of the Watergate Special Prosecution Force is a quasi-independent agency. It is an agency intended and designed to be "independent of executive authority, *except in its selection*, and free to exercise its judgment without the leave or hindrance of any other official or any department of the government." *Humphrey's Executor* v. *United States,* 295 U.S. 602, 625—26 (emphasis in original).[21]

---

[19] The delegation of specific and limited powers by the President or by cabinet officers is constitutional. See generally *Jay* v. *Boyd,* 351 U.S. 345, 351 n. 8; *Rose* v. *McNamara,* 375 F. 2d 924, 925 n. 2 (D.C. Cir. 1967), cert. denied, 389 U.S. 856; *Sardino* v. *Federal Reserve Bank,* 361 F. 2d 106, 110 (2d Cir. 1966), cert. denied, 385 U.S. 898.

As we establish in our main brief (32-33), the regulations delegating authority to the Special Prosecutor have the force and effect of law.

[20] The implication that this "prerogative" resides ultimately with the President in this case directly contradicts the position of former counsel for the President at oral argument before the court of appeals in *Nixon* v. *Sirica, supra,* on September 11, 1973 (p. 15):

"Now, in this instance we have a division of function within the Executive in that my friend, Mr. Cox, has been given absolute independence. It is for him to decide whom he will seek to indict. It is for him to decide to whom he will give immunity—decision[s] that ordinarily would be made at the level of the Attorney General, or in an important enough case at the level of the President."

[21] Indeed, even absent the specific delegation to the Special Prosecutor, the President may not have the same unbridled discretion over the Department of Justice,

This case, therefore, is wholly unlike the case of a subordinate executive officer, subject to the direct control of his superior, suing that superior. Rather, it is analogous to independent governmental agencies or departments, each pursuing its respective responsibilities, on opposite sides of a case within the courts' jurisdiction. Thus, for example, as this Court noted in its recent decision in *United States* v. *Marine Bancorporation, Inc.,* — *U.S.* —(June 26, 1974), the Comptroller of the Currency, an officer of the Treasury Department, "intervened in support of the merger as a party defendant" (slip op. at 10) in opposing a suit brought by the Department of Justice in the name of "the United States," challenging a merger the Comptroller had approved under his official powers. The Comptroller was heard in this Court in opposition to the Solicitor General. See also *Secretary of Agriculture* v. *United States,* 350 U.S. 162; *United States* v. *ICC,* 337 U.S. 426. The Special Prosecutor in accordance with his independent responsibilities signed the indictment and initiated the prosecution in the present case. In connection with that prosecution, now properly before the courts, the Special Prosecutor, as attorney for the United States and an officer of the court, is seeking evidence from the President that is relevant and material to the prosecution. The President, acting pursuant to what he views as his responsibilities, has interposed a claim of executive privilege. Fully consistent with the regulations empowering him to contest such a claim, as well as with the expectations of all those who were parties to the establishment of the Office of the Watergate Special Prosecution Force (Br. 29—32), the Special Prosecutor challenged that claim by subpoena, as he is authorized to do without restriction by the President or the Attorney General.

which enforces the law through the courts and whose officers have duties and responsibilities owed to the courts, as he does, for example, over the State Department or the Department of Defense. Cf. *Myers* v. *United States,* 272 U.S. 52, 135. In *Berger* v. *United States, supra,* this court noted (295 U.S. at 88):

"The United States Attorney is the representative not of an ordinary party to a controversy, but of a sovereignty whose obligation to govern impartially is as compelling as its obligation to govern at all; and whose interest, therefore, in a criminal prosecution is not that it shall win a case, but that justice shall be done. As such, he is in a peculiar and very definite sense the servant of the law, the twofold aim of which is that guilt shall not escape or innocence suffer."

It should be emphasized that the Special Prosecutor's independence flows from an arrangement established *by the Executive.* Compare *Humphrey's Executor* v. *United States, supra,* 295 U.S. at 629; *Myers* v. *United States,* 272 U.S. 52. Thus, although the Congress was about to enact legislation to provide for an independent Special Prosecutor and has implicitly ratified the current status of the Special Prosecutor's Office under the Department of Justice regulations by special funding, the Court is not faced with the "separation of powers" issue that would be presented if the Special Prosecutor derived his authority from a regime designed solely by Congress.

Counsel for the President repeatedly stresses that the President has not delegated to the Special Prosecutor his "duty" to claim executive privilege when he sees fit, suggesting that his retention of that power somehow deprives the courts of jurisdiction (*e.g.*, P. Br. 28—29, 43). We fully agree that the President's power to assert a claim of privilege for presidential papers has not been delegated to the Special Prosecutor. Indeed, it is precisely that power, when it comes into conflict with the independent power of the Special Prosecutor in the context of a pending criminal prosecution to contest the claim of privilege, that creates the live, concrete controversy before the courts.[22]

B. *The Assertion of Executive Privilege as a Ground for Refusing to Produce Evidence in a Criminal Prosecution Does Not Present a Political Question and the Validity of Such a Claim Must Be Resolved by the Courts*

In arguing that the Judiciary, and not the Executive, ultimately must determine the validity of a claim of executive privilege when it is asserted in a judicial proceeding, we rely on the fundamental principle that the courts have the power and the duty to resolve all issues necessary to a lawful resolution of controversies properly before them (Br. 48—52). Although

---

[22] Even if the Special Prosecutor were to be dismissed, the Office of the Watergate Special Prosecution Force abolished, and the prosecution of *United States* v. *Mitchell, et al.* placed under the control of the Criminal Division of the Department of Justice, such action would not render moot a decision by this Court upholding enforcement of the subpoena or deprive the Court's ruling of finality.

First, several defendants are asserting rights under *Brady* v. *Maryland,* 373 U.S. 83, and its progeny, to obtain access to the subpoenaed material, and they could pursue independently any decision enforcing the subpoena.

Second, although prosecution is generally considered an executive function, even the Attorney General—still assuming hypothetically that the Special Prosecutor is legally ousted from this case—would not have *carte blanche* to dismiss the prosecution here except by leave of court. See Rule 48(a), Federal Rules of Criminal Procedure. And as we pointed out in our main brief, the Attorney General and Solicitor General would be obliged to see to the enforcement of the Court's mandate.

Third, as long as the prosecution remains pending, the district court itself, under its established power to summon "court witnesses," could insist on compliance with the subpoena. See, *e.g.*, Rule 614(a), Proposed Federal Rules of Evidence; *United States* v. *Lutwak,* 195 F. 2d 748 (7th Cir. 1952), affirmed, 344 U.S. 604; *Troublefield* v. *United States,* 372 F. 2d 912, 916 n. 8 (D.C. Cir. 1966); *Estrella-Ortega* v. *United States,* 423 F. 2d 509 (9th Cir. 1970). As Justice Frankfurter explained in *Johnson* v. *United States,* 333 U.S. 46, 54 (dissenting opinion): "A trial is not a game of blind man's buff; and the trial judge * * * need not blindfold himself by failing to call an available vital witness simply because the parties, for reasons of trial tactics, choose to withhold his testimony"——"Federal judges are not referees at prize-fights but functionaries of justice."

counsel for the President virtually has ignored all the relevant cases, this principle has been applied squarely to cases involving claims of executive privilege. See *Environmental Protection Agency* v. *Mink*, 410 U.S. 73; *Roviaro* v. *United States*, 353 U.S. 53; *United States* v. *Reynolds*, 345 U.S. 1. As those cases demonstrate, the validity *vel non* of a claim of executive privilege presents a justiciable issue. The duty to produce relevant and material evidence for a criminal prosecution, a duty that reaches all citizens, is a duty that "can be judicially identified," and "its breach judicially determined," and the remedy for any breach "can be judicially molded." *Baker* v. *Carr*, 369 U.S. 186, 198.

Counsel for the President nevertheless asserts that this controversy presents a non-justiciable "political question" (P. Br. 44). It was long ago established, however, that the mere fact that a case has "political overtones" (P. Br. 48) does not mean it involves a "political question." See, *e.g.*, *Nixon* v. *Herndon*, 273 U.S. 536. This case involves no "political question" as that concept is correctly understood under the criteria articulated in *Baker* v. *Carr*, *supra*, 369 U.S. at 217. See also *Powell* v. *McCormack*, *supra*, 395 U.S. at 518—19.

Perhaps the principal hallmark of a "political question" beyond the power of the federal courts to decide is its commitment by the text of the Constitution to another branch of government for final resolution. Counsel for the President concedes, with considerable understatement, that "[u]nlike its companion privilege attendant upon the Congress by virtue of the Speech and Debate Clause, executive privilege was *not meticulously delineated* by the Framers of our Constitution" (P. Br. 50 n. 34) (emphasis added). Such a privilege is not "delineated" at all in the text of the Constitution and it is still a matter of dispute whether "executive privilege" is a true constitutional privilege at all or simply a common law evidentiary privilege (Br. 57 n. 43). At the very least it is evident that it has been the courts that have fashioned "executive privilege" to promote unfettered and robust debate on matters of policy and they have done so without reliance on any specific clause in the text of the Constitution. Certainly there is nothing in the text of the Constitution that commits the final determination of the privilege to the Executive. On the contrary, in recognizing this privilege in the context of litigation, the courts from the outset have assumed and asserted that it is for them and not the Executive to determine the validity of a particular claim in the context of the pending case (Br. 54—56).

Moreover, the decisions of this Court, including *Clark* v. *United States*, 289 U.S. 1, as well as *Mink*, *Reynolds* and *Roviaro*, demonstrate that there are "judicially discoverable and manageable standards" for resolving claims of privilege. And thus, there is no basis for invoking the "political question" doctrine on that ground. Indeed, the common law development of evidentiary privileges generally, even those now embodied explicitly in the Constitution, belies any claim that the courts are not suited for such determinations. While in cases where military secrets or foreign affairs are involved, the courts may not be able to make the delicate judgment whether the national interest requires continued secrecy, the generalized executive privilege for confidential deliberations does not implicate any such sensitive matters properly entrusted to the discretion of the Executive. Compare *Gilligan* v. *Morgan*, 413 U.S. 1, 10—11.

Finally, this Court's decision in *Powell* v. *McCormack*, *supra*, 395 U.S. at 549, dispels any notion that the courts are precluded by the political question doctrine from overriding a determination by the President:

> Our system of government requires that federal courts on occasion interpret the Constitution in a manner at variance with the construction given the document by another branch. The alleged conflict that such an adjudication may cause cannot justify the courts' avoiding their constitutional responsibility.

Nothing about the present litigation over a subpoena for allegedly privileged evidence, issued in a pending criminal prosecution, renders it a "political question" beyond the jurisdiction of the federal courts.

III. THE EXECUTIVE BRANCH DOES NOT HAVE AN ABSOLUTE PRIVILEGE TO WITHHOLD EVIDENCE OF CONFIDENTIAL COMMUNICATIONS FROM A CRIMINAL PROSECUTION

A. The Valid Interests of the Executive Branch in Promoting Candid Intra-Agency Deliberations Are Fully Protected by the Qualified Executive Privilege Regularly Recognized and Applied by the Courts

We share the desire of counsel for the President to maintain a strong and viable Executive. And we do not deny that wholesale access to evidence of confidential governmental deliberations by every congressional committee and by every private litigant, no matter what the context of the request for information or the need for information, might "chill" the interchange of ideas necessary for the successful administration of the Executive Branch. But this Court is not confronted with the alternatives seemingly posed by counsel for the President: this case does not present a choice between recognizing an absolute privilege on the one hand, or exposing the Executive to repeated unwarranted intrusions on its confidentiality on the other hand. The narrow issue before the Court is whether the President, in a pending prosecution against his former aides and associates, may withhold material evidence from the court merely on his assertion that the evidence involves confidential communications.

We emphasize at this point that we are not concerned in this case with the "sovereign prerogative" of the Executive "to protect the confidentiality necessary to carry out its responsibilities in the fields of international relations and national defense." *New York Times Co.* v. *United States*, 403 U.S. 713, 729—30 (Stewart, J., concurring). There has been no claim that any of the subpoenaed conversations involves "state secrets" or that disclosure of any of them will "result in direct, immediate, and irreparable damage to our Nation or its people." 403 U.S. at 730.[23] We deal instead solely with deliberations regarding a domestic crime. Thus, the concerns of Justice Stewart and Justice White do not have "particular force here" (P.Br. 66), and there can be no question that in the context of this case, the qualified executive privilege long recognized and applied by the courts fully protects the Executive's legitimate interests in secrecy.

Neither Presidents nor their aides ever have been assured that their communications will be maintained absolutely confidential, and they certainly cannot confer with that expectation.[24] More

---

[23] In oral argument before the district court on the enforceability of the grand jury's subpoena, counsel representing the President stated that "the President has told me that in one of the tapes that is the subject of the present subpoena there is national security material so highly sensitive that he does not feel free even to hint to me what the nature of it is." Transcript of Hearing on August 22, 1973, at 56, *In re Grand Jury Subpoena Duces Tecum Issued to Richard M. Nixon,* 360 F. Supp. 1. (D.D.C. 1973). Nevertheless, when the recordings were submitted to the district court in compliance with later orders of that court and the court of appeals, counsel for the President no longer asserted that any of the subpoenaed conversations included matters relating to the national security and no such information was found.

[24] Counsel for the President states that "Presidents have always acted on the assumption that it is discretionary with them, and with them alone, to determine whether the public interest permits production of presidential papers, and the other branches of Government have until recently accepted this position" (P. Br. 55-56). He relies solely on examples, set forth in a table on pp. 55-58 of his brief, where Presidents have refused to submit evidence to *Congress or congressional committees.*

often than not, Presidents and their aides voluntarily disclose communications when it serves their purposes. There is no better example than the extensive disclosures by President Nixon with respect to Watergate.

Counsel for the President points to the alleged "crippling effect" of the decision in *Nixon* v. *Sirica*, relying solely on the fact that the President "has received more than two dozen subpoenas emanating from various courts throughout the country, calling for the production of voluminous amounts of privileged materials" (P. Br. 68 n. 51). Significantly, counsel for the President does not tell the Court how many of these subpoenas have been quashed. Nor does he indicate in how many instances courts have ordered compliance with the subpoena.[25]

As counsel for the President himself notes (P. Br. 77–78), however, Chief Justice Marshall held in *United States* v. *Burr*, 25 Fed. Cas. 30, 34 (No. 14,692d) (C.C.D. Va. 1807), that subpoenas may issue to the President and that the "guard, furnished to this high officer, to protect him from being harassed by vexatious and unnecessary subpoenas, is to be looked for in the conduct of a court after those subpoenas have issued." While counsel for the President apparently rejects the notion that the courts are equipped to protect the Executive Branch against burdensome and oppressive subpoenas, there is no evidence that the courts have failed in this duty. Indeed, the expectation that the courts are incapable of protecting the legitimate interests of the Executive strikes at the very core of the concept of principled adjudication which is reflected in *Reynolds*, *Roviaro* and the lower court cases which hold that executive privilege is not absolute and is subject to determination by the courts (see our main brief at 52–60). The plain fact is that, as far as we are aware, with the exception of a few subpoenas issued to the

Those examples are wholly inapposite to the case at hand. Congressional oversight responsibilities continually place the Congress and Executive in conflict. On many occasions, probing into the mental processes of Executive decision-making results from essentially political considerations. It is in this context, where executive officers are held up to public ridicule, that there is the greatest danger to the policies underlying executive privilege. We emphasize, as we did in our main brief (53-54, n. 38), that determining the validity of a claim of privilege in a pending criminal prosecution in no way requires this Court to determine whether a claim of privilege asserted against Congress presents a justiciable issue. Thus, a decision in this case will not affect the relationship between the President and Congress that until now has depended largely on political factors.

[25] A number of these have been issued at the request of defendants seeking purportedly exculpatory materials in the President's possession. As counsel for the President concedes (P. Br. 29 n. 15): "We do not challenge the jurisdiction of a court to entertain a properly documented request by a defendant for exculpatory materials."

President at the request of his former aides who are now awaiting criminal trial, all of the other subpoenas to which counsel refers have been quashed by the courts, including several quashed at the Special Prosecutor's urging. Thus, just as with subpoenas to cabinet officers, the courts should be solicitous to avoid *unwarranted* interference with the performance of executive functions, but it is for the courts to decide whether enforcement of process is necessary in each particular case. See *Citizens to Preserve Overton Park, Inc.* v. *Volpe*, 401 U.S. 402, 420.

It is true that in the past it has been rare for subpoenas to be issued against the President. This is hardly surprising, because there have been few occasions on which there has been reason to believe that the President has had in his *personal* possession evidence directly material to a criminal prosecution. Counsel for the President cites (P. Br. 80 n. 59) Justice Chase's refusal to issue a subpoena *ad testificandum* to President Adams during the criminal trial of Thomas Cooper for seditious libel against the President, *United States* v. *Cooper*, 25 Fed. Cas. 631, 633 (No. 14,865) (C.C.D. Pa. 1800). But, despite the implication of counsel's assertion, Justice Chase did *not* refuse the subpoena because he viewed the President as immune from process or as having an absolute privilege not to testify. Rather, the court apparently considered it irrelevant and improper on a charge of criminal libel to call the alleged victim to ask him whether he had done the acts he was maliciously accused of. See Cooper, *Account of the Trial of Thomas Cooper of Northumberland* 10 (1800). Indeed, Cooper at first understood that the subpoena had been refused on grounds of privilege, but Justice Chase was categorical in disabusing him of that notion (*ibid.*):

> [Y]ou have totally mistaken the whole business. It is not upon the objection of privilege that we have refused this subpoena: This court will do its duty against any man however elevated his situation may be. You have mistaken the ground.

It was in that context, when Cooper, who was appearing *pro se*, sought to argue the matter further that Justice Chase interjected: "The Court will not hear you after they have given their decision: It was a very improper and a very indecent request." *Ibid.* That case hardly advances the President's claim here.[26]

---

[26] In fact, William Rawle, who was the United States Attorney for the District of Pennsylvania who personally handled the Cooper prosecution, later wrote in his treatise that the President *is* subject to process, explaining:

"* * * The law makes no distinction of persons, and the maxim that the king can do no wrong, so much admired in England, exists by no analogy in a republican government.

The two most notable instances where subpoenas have been issued to the President include the *Burr* cases and the court martial of Dr. William Barton. As we discussed at length in our main brief, Chief Justice Marshall was unequivocal in upholding the judicial power to issue a subpoena to the President. While there has been dispute over whether President Jefferson complied with the subpoenas, Raoul Berger, after a thorough study of the original reports of the *Burr* trial, has concluded that Jefferson fully intended to comply with the first subpoena, including that part which called for the Wilkinson letter of October 21, 1806. Moreover, after some delay in locating the letter, a copy apparently was submitted to the clerk. See Berger, *The President, Congress, and the Courts,* 83 Yale L.J. 1111, 1115 (1974). As to the second Wilkinson letter, which was in the possession of United States Attorney Hay, the record remains unclear. President Jefferson had claimed privilege with respect to specific portions, asserting that they were irrelevant to the issues at trial. There is no indication whether Chief Justice Marshall ever ruled whether the requirements of Burr's defense to the misdemeanor charge were sufficient to overcome the assertion of privilege. Nor does it appear whether, as the trial developed, Burr's counsel had any occasion to offer the letter into evidence. *Id.,* at 1118—20.

In the Barton court martial, President Monroe was subpoenaed by the defendant.[27] Heeding the advice of his Attorney General that under the *Burr* case such a subpoena may "be properly awarded to the President of the U.S.,"[28] President Monroe indicated on the return that although his official duties precluded a personal appearance at the time, he was prepared to testify by

"It may not be improper to consider why such a rule is admitted in monarchies, and why it cannot take place in a well constituted republic. In every monarchy, a quality termed prerogative, is attached to the monarch. * * * But the principle which thus shields and protects the monarch; the sovereignty resident in himself, creates the distinction between him and the elected, though supreme, magistrate of a republic, where the sovereignty resides in the people. All its officers, whether high or low, are but agents, to whom a temporary power is imparted, and on whom no immunity is conferred. An exemption from the power of the law, even in a small particular, except upon special occasions, would break in upon this important principle, and the freedom of the people, the great and sacred object of republican government, would be put in jeopardy. The exception adverted to, is that already noticed, of members of the legislature * * * but no other officer of government is entitled to the same immunity in any respect."
Rawle, *A View of the Constitution of the United States of America* 168-170 (2d ed. 1829).

[27] See Attorney General's Papers: Letters received from the State Department, January 12, 1818, Record Group 60, National Archives.

[28] Letter from Attorney General William Wirt to Secretary of State John Quincy Adams, January 13, 1818, in Attorney General's Opinions, Book A, at 21, Record Group 60, National Archives.

deposition.[29] President Monroe subsequently submitted answers to the interrogatories forwarded him by the court martial.[30]

In support of an absolute executive privilege, counsel for the President analogizes to the secrecy of internal court deliberations and refusals by Congress to afford evidence for criminal prosecutions. Certainly, we do not question the views of either the Chief Justice or Justice Brennan, quoted in the President's brief at pp. 59—60, that as a general rule the deliberations of judges, either among themselves or with their law clerks, must be kept secret. But nowhere has there been the suggestion that the secrecy is impenetrable, regardless of the reasons mandating in favor of disclosure. For example, consider the *Manton* case, where Circuit Judge Manton was convicted of a conspiracy to obstruct justice and defraud the United States arising out of bribes Manton accepted to influence his decision of cases. See *United States* v. *Manton*, 107 F. 2d 834 (2d Cir. 1939), cert. denied, 309 U.S. 664. We cannot believe that if judicial colleagues of Judge Manton or his law clerk had been in a position to give material testimony on the elements of the crimes charged that they would have been excused because of general notions of confidentiality. Indeed, such a decision would fly in the face of this Court's decision in *Clark* v. *United States, supra.*[31]

Moreover, congressional refusals to supply evidence offer no aid at all to the President's position. On each occasion when Congressmen have refused to testify or when committees have refused to supply documents for use at a trial, there has been an explicit constitutional privilege at issue. These privileges include: (1) the Speech or Debate Clause (Art. I, Sec. 6, cl. 1), which prohibits inquiry "into those things generally said or done in the House or Senate in the performance of official duties and into the motivation for those acts," *United States* v. *Brewster, supra,* 408 U.S. at 512; (2) the Freedom from Arrest Clause (Art. I, Sec. 6, cl. 1);[32] and (3) Article I, Section 5, clause 3, which

---

[29] Records of General Courts Martial and Courts of Inquiry of the Navy Department, Record Group 125, National Archives, Microfilm Publication M273, roll 10, frame 0834.

[30] *Id.,* at frames 0799-0806.

[31] In fact, Circuit Judges Learned Hand, Augustus Hand, and Thomas Swann did testify at the trial (for the defense) about their participation in court conferences with Judge Manton concerning the cases at issue. They stated they had observed nothing unusual about Manton's behavior. Trial Transcript pp. 792-93.

[32] Even that clause does not provide absolute immunity from service of process in a criminal proceeding. See *Gravel* v. *United States, supra; United States* v. *Cooper,* 4 Dall. (4 U.S.) 341.

empowers each House to maintain Journals which must be published, "excepting such Parts as may *in their Judgment* require Secrecy" (emphasis added).[33]

If there is anything to be learned from the congressional refusals to produce evidence, it is that they are justified from the explicit privileges accorded Congress—privileges that are noticeably absent from Article II. Unlike Congress, the President has no explicit privileges, and if any inference is to be drawn, it is that the Framers intended that he have none. See *Anderson v. Dunn*, 6 Wheat. (19 U.S.) 204, 223. Accordingly, examples of congressional refusals to provide evidence in no way imply that the "separation of powers" doctrine would otherwise have justified an absolute congressional privilege and certainly do not support the creation of an absolute executive privilege in the face of the silence of the Constitution on the subject.

B. *The First Amendment Erects No Absolute Privilege for the President to Withhold Relevant Evidence*

For the first time, in this Court, counsel for the President advances the novel argument that the President's rights as an ordinary citizen to privacy and freedom of expression support his claim of an absolute privilege to withhold physical evidence determined to be relevant to the trial of criminal prosecutions.[34]

Viewing this argument as a claim of the President's right as a citizen to free speech, we have an initial difficulty in identifying

---

[33] This clause was discussed in the recent decision in *United States* v. *Richardson*, — U.S. — (June 25, 1974), where Mr. Justice Douglas observed in his dissenting opinion: "Secrecy has of course some constitutional sanction" (pp. 2-3).

In the Calley court martial, cited by counsel for the President (P. Br. 61 n. 49), Calley attempted to subpoena secret testimony which had been given before a subcommittee of the House Armed Services Committee. When the subcommittee chairman refused to supply the testimony, the military court recognized that this was proper under Article I, Section 5. See 116 Cong. Rec. 37,652 (1970).

[34] While the President's chief reliance is on the First Amendment, he also invokes Article II, Section 2, clause 1 of the Constitution:

"[The President] may require the Opinion, in writing, of the principal Officer in each of the executive Departments, upon any Subject relating to the Duties of their respective Offices."

Unfortunately, this provision is cited without elaboration or explanation and its relevance to the claim of privilege in this case is not otherwise readily apparent. With the single exception of one meeting on April 17, 1973, at which then-Secretary of State Rogers was present for part of the time, the subpoenaed tape recordings do not relate to meetings between the President and members of his Cabinet concerning their official duties, but rather to conversations between the President and members of his personal staff concerning the Watergate coverup. To the extent the meeting of April 17 may have included discussionf of Secretary Rogers' official responsibilities, not related to Watergate, the possibility of excising such portions can most appropriately be considered when the full tapes are presented to the district judge for his *n camera* examination.

precisely how the President's freedom of expression would be violated by compliance. There can be no suggestion that enforcement of the subpoena would burden or chill his ability to communicate with the public. This is particularly true in light of the fact that the White House recording system was established in the first place at government expense by government personnel expressly to create an accurate "historical" record of the President's conduct of his office—to create "a complete, accurate record of conversations held by the President." See Transcript of Hearing on November 6, 1973, at 906, *In re Grand Jury Subpoena Duces Tecum Issued to Richard M. Nixon*, D.D.C. Misc. No. 47—73 (testimony of witness Haldeman). As shown by his unilateral action of April 30, 1974, in releasing a great quantity of edited transcripts of Watergate-related conversations, he is free at any time to disclose as much of the recorded material in his possession as he chooses. The thrust of the President's position, however, is to *prevent* any dissemination of the subpoenaed material. Consequently, the interests asserted cannot realistically be those of freedom of expression, but rather solely the converse—the right to refuse to disclose what has been expressed.

But any claim that a constitutional right to privacy bars disclosure here will not withstand analysis. Of course, we do not quarrel with the proposition that the Constitution protects the rights of privacy and freedom of association. These are values at the center not only of the First Amendment, *e.g. Griswold* v. *Connecticut*, 381 U.S. 479, 483; *NAACP* v. *Alabama*, 357 U.S. 449, but also of the Fourth Amendment and the Self-Incrimination Clause of the Fifth Amendment, *Couch* v. *United States*, 409 U.S. 322; *Katz* v. *United States*, 389 U.S. 347; *Hale* v. *Henkel*, 201 U.S. 43; *Boyd* v. *United States*, 116 U.S. 616. The President at no time has claimed to rely on either the Fourth or Fifth Amendment. The subpoena is narrowly and specifically framed, and the President has not resisted disclosure on the ground that the tape recordings in his possession would tend to incriminate him; on the contrary, the President has consistently maintained his innocence of any wrongdoing. Indeed, the edited transcripts were released publicly on April 30 in an effort to demonstrate "that the President has nothing to hide in this matter." 10 Weekly Compilation of Presidential Documents 452 (May 6, 1974).

Nor does the First Amendment shield the President or any other citizen from "the longstanding principle that 'the public . . . has a right to every man's evidence,' "—that was the precise holding in *Branzburg* v. *Hayes*, 408 U.S. 665, 688, where the Court made perfectly clear that even reliance upon the explicit First Amendment freedom of the press creates no absolute privilege to withhold evidence in criminal prosecutions. In *Branzburg*, which involved a grand jury subpoena for testimony by reporters concerning information received from confidential informants, the claim of the newsmen was virtually identical to that of the President here—that "the flow of news will be diminished by compelling reporters to aid the grand jury in a criminal investigation," 408 U.S. at 693. This Court considered and decisively rejected the claim of privilege in a setting where the reporter was asked to provide information concerning possible criminal activities by his informants. The parallel between that situation and this case is obvious, for the subpoenaed conversations here all involve persons (including the President) charged by the grand jury to have been members of a conspiracy to obstruct justice. Entirely aside from the issue of the President's own alleged complicity,[35] the fact that there is reason to believe that these conversations record or reflect criminal conduct by the other participants is sufficient to override any claim of First Amendment privilege that might otherwise apply. As this Court stated in *Branzburg* (408 U.S. at 692):

> Thus, we cannot seriously entertain the notion that the First Amendment protects a newsman's agreement to conceal the criminal conduct of his source, or evidence thereof, on the theory that it is better to write about crime than to do something about it. Insofar as any reporter in these cases undertook not to reveal or testify about the crime he witnessed, his claim of privilege under the First Amendment presents no substantial question. The crimes of news sources are no less reprehensible and threatening to the public interest when witnessed by a reporter than when they are not.

This analysis applies equally to the Executive Office of the President.

The Court also considered the case of a reporter subpoenaed to provide information received from confidential sources about third-party crime. Although it recognized that it was "not irrational" to fear that compelling such testimony would burden freedom of the press, 408 U.S. at 693, it held that such a burden

---

[35] While dissenting from the majority opinion in *Branzburg*, Justice Douglas agreed that even a reporter would have no First Amendment privilege to refuse to testify if he were himself implicated in a crime (although of course he could invoke the Fifth Amendment). 408 U.S. at 712.

is justifiable when the government's purpose is the vindication of the "compelling" and "paramount" public interest in the enforcement of the criminal laws. That test was satisfied as to the reporters' testimony since, on the record,

> it was likely that they could supply information to help the government determine whether illegal conduct had occurred and, if it had, whether there was sufficient evidence to return an indictment. 408 U.S. at 701.

A fortiori, the evidence sought from the President is this case is producible, since the grand jury has already found reason to believe that crimes—involving the President—have been committed, and the tape recordings have been found to be material to the guilt or innocence of defendants already indicted.

First Amendment concepts, therefore, cannot bolster the President's refusal to honor this subpoena for important evidence, whether or not he is regarded as personally implicated in the conspiracy.

IV. THE SUBPOENAED CONVERSATIONS ARE UNPRIVILEGED BECAUSE A PRIMA FACIE SHOWING HAS BEEN MADE THAT THEY OCCURRED IN THE COURSE OF A CRIMINAL CONSPIRACY INVOLVING THE PRESIDENT

We have argued that under cases like *Clark* v. *United States, supra*, the qualified privilege accorded to executive deliberations is inapplicable in this case because of the *prima facie* showing made by the Special Prosecutor below that the subpoenaed conservations were part of a continuing criminal conspiracy involving the President himself (Br. 90—102). Indeed, former counsel for the President conceded in *Nixon* v. *Sirica, supra*, that "[e]xecutive privilege cannot be claimed to shield executive officials from prosecution for crime" (Brief of Petitioner 69). Counsel for the President now responds by challenging the sufficiency of our *prima facie* showing, claiming that the grand jury's naming of the President as an unindicted co-conspirator is proof only of probable cause, which is alleged to be something less than the *prima facie* showing of criminality necessary to overcome the privilege.[36] The President's position, however, not

---

[36] The President also contends that a claim of executive privilege, unlike claims of oter privileges concerning confidential communications, cannot be defeated by a showing that the discussions were in furtherance of a conspiracy because the privilege exists for the benefit of the public rather than the individual asserting it. We freely concede, indeed we emphasize, that executive privilege is not a personal or "individual" privilege. But the recognition that the privilege exists to promote the legitimate functioning of government in no way warrants the conclusion that it must

only misconceives the meaning of the grand jury's action, but also ignores the weighty evidentiary presentation, based upon statements supplied by the President himself or by others under oath, which was submitted to the district court.

Relying upon cases which hold that there is a distinction between a *prima facie* showing of guilt beyond a reasonable doubt and a determination of "probable cause," the President suggests that the grand jury's decision that the evidence before it warranted the return of an indictment represents only · a determination that a crime "might" have been committed (P. Br. 115). This suggestion, however, fundamentally misconstrues the standard applied by a grand jury in determining whether an indictment should issue. A grand jury indictment may not rest on mere suspicion. Thus, as long ago as 1836, Chief Justice Roger B. Taney, sitting as circuit justice in the District of Maryland, instructed a grand jury that it could not indict unless "the evidence before you is sufficient, in the absence of any other proof, to justify the conviction of the party accused." *Charge to Grand Jury*, 30 Fed. Cas. 998, 999 (No. 18, 257) (C.C.D. Md. 1836). This is the settled standard. Sufficient evidence to indict exists "only when there is competent evidence, direct or circumstantial, before you which leads you, as reasonable persons, to believe that the defendant is guilty of the offense charged." Yankwich, *Charge to Grand Jury*, 16 F.R.D. 93, 94 (1955). Indeed, Chief Judge Sirica specifically instructed the grand jury which voted the indictment in *this* case and which alleged that President Nixon was a co-conspirator:

> You ought not to find an indictment unless in your judgment the evidence before you, unexplained and uncontradicted, would warrant a conviction by a petit jury. (Transcript of June 5, 1972).

Thus, the grand jury's naming of the President and others as participants in a conspiracy to obstruct justice constitutes a determination by an independent body, based upon more than eighteen months of evidence, that substantial evidence exists of sufficient strength "to cause a person of ordinary prudence and caution to conscientiously entertain a reasonable belief of the

---

stand as a shield in the face of evidence that it has been abused by the officeholder. Indeed, *Clark* v. *United States, supra,* unmentioned by the President's brief, conclusively rebuts any such notion. The "public" rather than "individual" nature of the privilege demonstrates that it cannot be maintained to conceal the criminal activity of a miscreant officeholder. See our main brief at 90-97.

accused's guilt," *Coleman* v. *Burnett*, 477 F. 2d 1187, 1202 (D.C. Cir. 1973), and was not an expression of a mere suspicion of possible criminality.

To the extent that the President suggests that the *prima facie* showing which the government must make to overcome the privilege is equivalent to proof of the conspiracy and its participants beyond a reasonable doubt (P. Br. 120), his position is clearly erroneous. The absurdity of requiring the government to prove an individual's guilt beyond a reasonable doubt in order to obtain evidence relevant to a conclusive jury determination of that guilt is obvious. See *United States* v. *Matlock*, —— U.S. —— (42 U.S.L.W. 4252, February 20, 1974); *Lego* v. *Twomey*, 404 U.S. 477, 489. Such a rule would put the government to its proof twice, in an enormous expenditure of time and energy, particularly in a case as complex as the present. Indeed, that very rule has been rejected in the analogous context of the co-conspirator-admissions exception to the hearsay rule. See, *e.g.*, *United States* v. *Geaney*, 417 F. 2d 1116, 1120 (2d Cir. 1969), cert. denied, 397 U. S. 1028; *Carbo* v. *United States*, 314 F. 2d 718, 736 (9th Cir. 1963), cert. denied, 377 U.S. 953.

The type of showing which must be made to negate the attorney-client privilege on the ground the relationship was used to further crime is discussed in McCormick, *Evidence*, § 95, at 200 (2d ed. 1972), in terms which are patently relevant here:

> Must the judge, before denying the claim of privilege on [the ground that the communication was made in furtherance of a crime or fraud] find as a fact, after a preliminary hearing if contested, that the consultation was in furtherance of crime or fraud? This would be the normal procedure in passing on a preliminary fact, on which the admissibility of evidence depends, *but here this procedure would facilitate too far the use of the privilege as a cloak for crime*. (Emphasis added.)

Faced with this consideration, McCormick notes that many courts including this Court in *Clark* v. *United States, supra,*

> have cast the balance in favor of disclosure by requiring only that the one who seeks to avoid the privilege bring forward evidence from which the existence of an unlawful purpose could reasonably be found.

In maintaining that we have made a sufficient showing that the subpoenaed conversations were in furtherance of a continuing criminal conspiracy so as to overcome the presumptive privilege, we have not relied, as the President's brief appears to suggest, solely upon the fact that the grand jury has named all of the principal participants in those conversations as conspirators in a conspiracy to obstruct justice. We do maintain that the grand jury's findings as to the existence of the conspiracy and as to its members are conclusive at this stage of the proceedings, and represent a *prima facie* determination that the conspiracy did exist and that the participants in the subpoenaed conversations were among its members. The credit given to grand jury determinations in such similarly important settings, see *Ewing* v. *Mytinger & Casselberry, Inc.*, 339 U.S. 594, 599; *Ex parte United States*, 287 U.S. 241, 250; *Beavers* v. *Henkel*, 194 U.S. 73, 85; justifies acceptance of its considered judgment as an adequate *prima facie* showing here for rejecting a claim of executive privilege.

In addition to these findings, however, we presented to the court below a detailed factual submission which demonstrated at least *prima facie* that each of the 64 subpoenaed conversations was in furtherance of the conspiracy charged in the indictment. See *Appendix to Memorandum for the United States in Opposition to the Motion to Quash Subpoena Duces Tecum.* The district judge expressly held that these submissions, when viewed in light of the grand jury's findings, "constitute a *prima facie* showing adequate to rebut the presumption [of privilege] in each instance" (Pet. App. 20).

In sum, the indictment, the grand jury's finding concerning the President and the evidence presented to the district judge regarding each specific subpoenaed conversation were clearly sufficient to warrant the conclusion that the claim of executive privilege must give way and that "the light should be let in." *Clark* v. *United States, supra*, 289 U.S. at 14.

V. THERE IS A COMPELLING PUBLIC INTEREST IN TRYING THE CONSPIRACY CHARGED IN UNITED STATES V. MITCHELL, ET AL. UPON RELEVANT AND MATERIAL EVIDENCE

In our main brief, in addition to showing that the subpoenaed recordings no longer remain presumptively privileged because they were part of a continuing criminal conspiracy (Br. 90—102) and because any privilege has been waived as a matter of law (Br. 116—123), we demonstrated that, in any event, any qualified privilege must yield in the face of the compelling public interest in trying the conspiracy charged in *United States* v. *Mitchell, et al.*, upon all relevant and material evidence.[37] Counsel for the President now asserts that we have not shown sufficient need to overcome the privilege.

The simple answer to that contention, however, is that after analyzing our submission below in light of *Nixon* v. *Sirica* and the relevant decisions of this Court, the district court found that the submissions "constitute a *prima facie* showing adequate to rebut the presumption in each instance, and a demonstration of need sufficiently compelling to warrant judicial examination in chambers incident to weighing claims of privilege where the privilege has not been relinquished" (Pet App. 20).[38] This finding of the district court, arising from a mixed question of law and fact, is amply supported by the record.

The integrity of the administration of justice demands that all persons—no matter what their station or official status—be answerable to the law. In the context of the indictment in *United States* v. *Mitchell, et al.*, which charges former high government

---

[37] Respondents Ehrlichman and Strachan, defendants in *United States* v. *Mitchell, et al.*, have filed briefs in this Court asserting that they are entitled to the subpoenaed material under *Brady* v. *Maryland, supra*, the Jencks Act, 18 U.S.C. 3500, and Rules 16 and 17(c) of the Federal Rules of Criminal Procedure. The district court withheld ruling on these contentions, stating that defendants' request for access will be more appropriately considered in conjunction with their pre-trial discovery motions (Pet. App. 21-22).

There is no question that the prosecution will make available to defendants any material within its control to which they are entitled under *Brady* or relevant statutes and rules. Beyond that, despite the question raised in the President's mandamus petition, it is clear that the government's obligations under *Brady* extend even to "privileged" evidence. See, *e.g.*, *Roviaro* v. *United States, supra; United States* v. *Andolschek*, 142 F. 2d 503 (2d Cir. 1944). Moreover, *Brady* in all likelihood is applicable to materials within the possession of the President, even though the prosecution has no direct access to them. See *United States* v. *Deutsch*, 475 F. 2d 55, 57 (5th Cir. 1973); *United States* v. *Ehrlichman*, Crim. No. 74-116 (D.D.C. June 14, 1974).

Nevertheless, although *Brady* imposes an affirmative obligation on the government not to suppress exculpatory evidence and to make available to defendants any such evidence of which it is aware, it does not obligate the government to undertake a fishing expedition without any reason to believe exculpatory evidence will be uncovered. See, *e.g.*, *Ross* v. *Texas*, 474 F. 2d 1150, 1153(5th Cir. 1973), cert. denied, 414 U.S. 850. Here, no defendant has specifically identified any of the subpoenaed material he believes to be exculpatory, and the Special Prosecutor has no reason to believe that the subpoenaed conversations will exculpate any of the defendants.

[38] Counsel for the President asserts that because of executive privilege, "the subpoena should have been quashed in all respects by the court below" (P. Br. 95). So that the record is perfectly clear, we emphasize that the President in his Formal Claim of Privilege expressly stated that he was *not* advancing any "claim of privilege" with respect to the portions of twenty of the subpoenaed conversations for which transcripts have been made public (A. 48A). Nowhere in his brief before this Court does counsel advance any reason why the tapes of those portions of the conversations for which the President himself expressly disclaims privilege can be lawfully withheld.

officials with a conspiracy to obstruct justice and defraud the United States, the demands of public justice require a trial based on all relevant and material evidence, particularly where, as here, evidence within the personal possession of the President demonstrably bears on the scope, membership and duration of the conspiracy.

CONCLUSION

For the reasons stated above and in our main brief, the order of the district court should be affirmed in all respects.

Respectfully submitted.

LEON JAWORSKI,
Special Prosecutor.

PHILIP A. LACOVARA,
Counsel to the Special Prosecutor.

Attorneys for the United States.

JULY 1974.

IX
THE PRESIDENT'S REPLY BRIEF IN UNITED STATES v. NIXON

The President's lawyers answered the contentions of the Special Prosecutor point by point in their reply brief. Once again the problems of the Court's jurisdiction, executive privilege and the prosecutor's need for the material were examined.

IN THE SUPREME COURT OF THE UNITED STATES

OCTOBER TERM, 1973

Nos. 73-1766 and 73-1834

UNITED STATES OF AMERICA, PETITIONER

v.

RICHARD M. NIXON, PRESIDENT OF THE UNITED STATES
ET AL., RESPONDENTS

RICHARD M. NIXON, PRESIDENT OF THE UNITED STATES
CROSS-PETITIONER

v.

UNITED STATES OF AMERICA, RESPONDENT

*ON WRITS OF CERTIORARI BEFORE JUDGMENT TO THE
UNITED STATES COURT OF APPEALS FOR THE
DISTRICT OF COLUMBIA CIRCUIT*

**REPLY BRIEF FOR THE RESPONDENT, CROSS-
PETITIONER RICHARD M. NIXON, PRESIDENT OF THE
UNITED STATES**

INTRODUCTION

The vitally important considerations that must control
decision of this case, and that require reversal of the district
court, were expressed in the opinion of Chief Justice Chase, for a
unanimous Court, in *Mississippi* v. *Johnson*, 4 Wall. (71 U.S.)
475, 500-501 (1867).

The Congress is the Legislative Department of the government;
the President is the Executive Department. Neither can be
restrained in its action by the Judicial Department; though the
acts of both, when performed, are, in proper cases, subject to
its cognizance.
The impropriety of such interference will be clearly seen upon
consideration of its possible consequences.
Suppose the bill filed and the injuction prayed for allowed. If
the President refuse obedience, it is needless to observe that
the court is without power to enforce its process. If, on the
other hand, the President complies with the order of the court
and refuses to execute the acts of Congress, is it not clear that
a collision may occur between the Executive and Legislative

Departments of the Government? May not the House of Representatives impeach the President for such refusal? And in that case could this Court interfere in behalf of the President, thus endangered by compliance with its mandate, and restrain by injunction the Senate of the United States from sitting as a court of impeachment? Would the strange spectacle be offered to the public wonder of an attempt by this court to arrest proceedings in that court? These questions answer themselves.

It will not do to say, as the Special Prosecutor does, that "the President is the *head* of the Executive Branch. . . . " (S.P.Br. 79) (emphasis in original).[1] Instead, as the Court said in *Johnson*, "the President is the Executive Department." Or, as Chief Justice Taft, also speaking for a unanimous Court, said in *Ex parte Grossman*, 267 U.S. 87, 120 (1925): "The executive power is vested in a President."

Johnson is important also for its recognition of the utter impropriety of this Court becoming involved in the constitutional process of impeachment. Surely this Court can judicially notice the fact that proceedings are underway in the House Judiciary Committee looking to possible impeachment of the President. The late Thomas Reed Powell is said to have defined the legal mind as a mind that can think of one of two things that are inescapably interrelated without thinking about the other. Only those who would accept this cynical view of the legal process would suppose that this case and the investigation in the Judiciary Committee are wholly unrelated, or that this Court can render a decision in this case without that decision having a heavy impact, one way or the other, in the impeachment process that is so clearly committed exclusively to the House and the Senate.

We shall contend, as we did in our initial brief, that, as it was so powerfully put by Judge Wilkey in his dissent in *Nixon* v. *Sirica*, 487 F. 2d 700, 763-799 (D.C. Circ. 1973), the critical issue is "Who Decides?", and that this Court should affirm the proposition, not seriously challenged for the first 184 years of our constitutional history, that it is for the Chief Executive, not for the judicial branch, to decide when the public interest permits disclosure of Presidential discussions.

It was and is the President's right to make that decision

---

[1] "Pres. Br." refers to the President's brief filed with this Court on June 21, 1974. "S.P. Br." refers to the Special Prosecutor's brief filed on the same date. "P.S.A." refers to the President's Sealed Appendix. These references are followed by appropriate pagination.

initially, and it is the American people who will be the judge as to whether the President has made the right decision, i.e., whether it is or is not in the public interest that the papers (tapes) in question be furnished or retained. If his decision is made on visibly sound grounds, the people will approve the action of the Executive as being in the public interest. If the decision is not visibly on sound grounds of national public interest, in political terms the decision may be ruinous for the President, but it is his to make. The grand design has worked; the separate, independent Branch remains in charge of and responsible for its own papers, processes and decisions, not to a second or third Branch, but it remains *responsible* to the American people. (487 F. 2d at 797) (emphasis in original).

The central point at issue here is not whether the President's judgment in this particular instance is right or wrong, but that it is his judgment. In exercising the discretion vested in him, and in him alone, the President may make a mistaken assessment of what best serves the public interest—but courts also on occasion make mistakes. The President in this exercise of discretion may make a decision that is unpopular—but if so he must suffer the political consequences. The President may even take such action that would constitute a high crime or misdemeanor, but to quote again from Chief Justice Taft in *Ex parte Grossman*, 267 U.S. 87, 121 (1925): "Exceptional cases like this, if to be imagined at all, would suggest a resort to impeachment rather than to a narrow and strained construction of the general powers of the President."

These are the themes we will develop in the balance of this Reply Brief.[2]

---

[2] Having already submitted a 137-page brief, we regret burdening the Court with so lengthy a reply. We have endeavored so far as possible to avoid repetition, and do not, by failing to renew all of the points made in our initial brief, withdraw any of those. But the case is both important and unique, and because of the briefing schedule ordered by the Court this is the first opportunity we have had to respond to the arguments of the petitioner.

We agree with the statement of the Special Prosecutor (Supplemental Brief, June 31, 1974 at 5) that the application of *Brady* v. *Maryland,* 373 U.S. 83 (1963) to privileged materials not in the prosecutor's possession is not properly before this Court. See Sup. Ct. Rule 23(1) (c); *Andrews* v. *Louisville & Nashville R. Co.,* 406 U.S. 320, 324-325 (1972); *Namet* v. *United States,* 373 U.S. 179, 190 (1963); *Mazer* v. *Stein,* 347 U.S. 201, 206 n. 5 (1954); see generally R. Stern & E. Gressman, *Supreme Court Practice* 297-298 (4th ed. 1969).

I. THE SPECIAL PROSECUTOR HAS
FAILED TO ESTABLISH ANY BASIS
FOR THE JURISDICTION OF
THE DISTRICT COURT

In our initial submission we argued that the courts lack jurisdiction over an internal dispute of a co-equal branch of government (Pres. Br. 27—44) and that such an intra-branch dispute is preeminently a political question and outside the scope of Article III. (Pres. Br. 44—48).

Primarily, the Special Prosecutor appears to allege jurisdiction on two grounds: (1) that this is not an intra-branch dispute, for in all criminal proceedings, the Attorney General does not represent the executive branch but rather the United States as a sovereign entity; and (2) even if the Special Prosecutor is an inseparable part of the executive branch, the delegation of authority and independence given to him by Acting Attorney General Bork is, in itself, sufficient to create jurisdiction in this matter. (S.P. Br. 24—47). As we now show however, both arguments fail to withstand analysis.

In an attempt to negate the intra-executive nature of this dispute, the Special Prosecutor repeatedly asserts that he, as the alter ego of the Attorney General, does not represent the President or the executive branch in a criminal proceeding but rather the United States as a distinct sovereign entity. (S.P. Br. 27—29).[3] Such an argument is without merit for there is no sovereign entity distinct from the three recognized branches of the government. Nor, as a practical matter, is the Attorney General unique in his capacity to act in the name of the United States, for most, if not all federal actions are performed in the name of "the United States," the ultimate symbol of this nation's sovereignty. To suggest that a governmental action is not a judicial, executive or legislative action, simply because it is taken in the name of the United States, is to confuse the basic symbol of the government with the functional divisions of its authority. The term "United States" does not refer to a separate entity but is a composite description of the three independent and co-equal branches of the government. Within their respective roles, each coordinate branch acts in the name of the United States. Thus, it

---

[3] This argument is premised upon 28 U.S.C. 516 which provides:

Except as otherwise authorized by law, the conduct of litigation in which the United States, an agency, or officer there is a party, or is interested, and securing evidence therefor, is reserved to officers of the Department of Justice, under the direction of the Attorney General.

is of no distinguishing consequence that the Attorney General or the Special Prosecutor invokes the name of the United States in conducting a criminal prosecution. Nor does this invocation divest the Attorney General or the Special Prosecutor of their status as subordinate officers within the executive branch of government.[4]

To accept the Special Prosecutor's position that there is, in essence, an independent branch of the government known as the United States, would make meaningless the delegation of authority and balance of power existing between the three branches, and destroy the tripartite form of government established by the Framers. It would create an additional fourth branch of the government with its own independently derived authority, entitled to its own representation in court and responsible to none of the other branches. Such a proposition is without logical or constitutional merit.

Alternatively, by tracing the statutory authority of the Attorney General, the Special Prosecutor at pp. 27-29, 35-36, 40-42 of his Brief appears to be suggesting to this Court that there may be some legislative basis for his authority akin to a legislative regulatory agency,[5] which would nullify the claim that the present dispute is intra-executive in nature. He summarizes his position as follows: in discharging his responsibilities, "the Special Prosecutor does not act as a mere agent-at-will of the President. He enjoys an independent authority derived from constitutional delegations of authority by the Congress to the Attorney General and from the Attorney General to him . . . " (S.P. Br. 34).

We do not contest the Special Prosecutor's assertion that his authority is derived from the Attorney General, but it is precisely this derivation of authority that conclusively establishes the executive nature of the office he holds. The Attorney General can only delegate to a subordinate officer the same authority and status he himself possesses. Thus, even as the alter

---

[4] The Special Prosecutor's assertion that he acts not "in the President's name or at his behest" (S.P. Br. 34) is effectively negated in his own statement of facts where he acknowledges that on October 26, 1973, the President announced that a new Special Prosecutor would be appointed and emphasized that he, the President, had no greater interest than seeing that the Special Prosecutor has the independence he needs to prosecute the guilty and clear the innocent. (S.P. Br. 10)

[5] *United States* v. *Interstate Commerce Commission*, 337 U.S. 426 (1949). This case has been fully discussed by us (Pres. Br. 37-38) and that discussion is equally applicable to *Secretary of Agriculture* v. *United States*, 350 U.S. 163 (1956), which also involves a suit by an executive department against the Interstate Commerce Commission.

ego of the Attorney General in a particular matter, the Special Prosecutor is necessarily vested with the same executive status, and no more. To assert that either the Attorney General, an executive cabinet member, or any subordinate officer within the Department of Justice, acts in a legislative or even quasi-legislative capacity when conducting a criminal prosecution is so contrary to the settled law as not to warrant further comment. It remains only to be said that all executive departments exist with some statutory basis, but this does not in anyway alter the exclusively executive nature of their duties and responsibilities. As we point out at the beginning, "the President is the Executive Department." The Attorney General is but "the hand of the President." *Ponzi* v. *Fessenden*, 358 U.S. 254, 262 (1922). He is the agent of the President, and any direction given by him is but a direction by the President. *Confiscation Cases*, 7 Wall. (74 U.S.) 454 (1869). Article II, section 3, imposes on the President the duty to "take Care that the Laws be faithfully executed," and though the President ordinarily acts through the Attorney General and his subordinates, they are acting for the President, not for the legislative branch.[6] Consequently, the Special Prosecutor, like the Attorney General, must be considered an executive officer engaged in the exclusive performance of an executive function, namely the prosecution of individuals charged with criminal activities. Thus, neither under the legislative theory nor the sovereign entity theory proposed by the Special Prosecutor has he demonstrated that the present dispute is anything more than an intra-executive dispute beyond the jurisdiction of the district court.[7]

[6] In *Runkle* v. *United States*, 122 U.S. 543, 557 (1886), this Court stated:

There can be no doubt that the President, in the exercise of his executive power under the Constitution, may act through the head of the appropriate executive department. The heads of departments are his authorized assistants in the performance of his executive duties, and their official acts, promulgated in the regular course of business, are presumptively his acts. That has been many times decided by this court. *Wilcox* v. *Jackson*, 13 Pet. 498, 513; *United States* v. *Eliason*, 16 Pet. 291, 302; *Confiscation Cases*, 20 Wall. 92, 109; *United States* v. *Farden*, 99 U.S. 10, 19; *Wolsey* v. *Chapman*, 101 U.S. 755, 769.

In addition, the Court of Appeals for the Fifth Circuit in *Smith* v. *United States*, 375 F. 2d 243, 246 (5th Cir. 1967) stated:

The President of the United States is charged in Article 2, Section 3, of the Constitution with the duty to "take care that the laws be faithfully executed. . ." The Attorney General is the President's surrogate in the prosecution of all offenses against the United States.

[7] The Special Prosecutor erroneously cites this Court's decision in *Sampson* v. *Murray*, 414 U.S. 904 (1974), for the proposition that the district court has jurisdiction to intervene in an intra-branch dispute. That case is however totally inapplicable for it involved a suit by a private citizen against the United States Civil Service Commission alleging that the individual had been erroneously discharged from federal employment.

Finally, the Special Prosecutor alleges that the delegation of authority to him by Acting Attorney General Bork, combined with the repeated assurances that he would be free to carry out his responsibilities, confers jurisdiction upon the court to resolve the instant dispute.[8] Such an argument fails for three fundamental reasons. First, the Judiciary has never had jurisdiction to review or determine what evidence the executive branch shall or shall not use in the furtherance of its own case in a criminal proceeding. See, e.g., *United States* v. *Cox*, 342 F. 2d 167 (5th Cir), *cert. denied*, 381 U.S. 935 (1965). The responsibility for making this determination has always been within the executive branch, and includes the power to balance and determine what confidential govermental materials would, if disclosed, be detrimental to the public interest. A decision by the executive branch not to use a particular document, even one which tends to support its own burden of proof in a criminal prosecution, has not been and is not a proper subject for judicial review. (Pres. Br. 39-41).

Second, such a decision is exclusively within the duties and responsibilities delegated by the Constitution to the Chief Executive, for he alone was vested with the obligation to see "that the Laws be faithfully executed." U.S. Const. Article II, section 3. Unless the President has delegated his authority to a subordinate officer, the President's decision in such matters is final, and an improper subject for judicial review.[9]

Third, there has been no delegation of this responsibility by the President to the Attorney General or the Special Prosecutor

---

[8] The Special Prosecutor correctly asserts, at some length, that a federal regulation has the force and effect of law and is therefore binding upon the parties. *Accardi* v. *Shaughnessy*, 347 U.S. 260, 266-267 (1954). However, by raising the question of the jurisdictional basis for the district court's action. Counsel for the President cannot be said to be acting in violation of the Special Prosecutor's rights under 38 Fed. Reg. 30, 738 (1973), nor interfering with the independence granted to the Special Prosecutor to carry out those responsibilities delegated to him, for both parties are under an independent obligation to this Court to discuss the jurisdictional aspects of the present proceeding.

[9] There is no merit to either the contention that the President is without authority to direct or control the actions of a subordinate officer or that his control is limited to his ability to discharge an executive employee. (S.P. Br. 35). Even the authority relied upon by the Special Prosecutor, 2 Op. Att'y. Gen. 483 (1831) acknowledges the President's right to direct the actions of a subordinate officer.

Upon the whole, I consider the district attorney as under the control and direction of the President, in the institution and prosecution of suits in the name and on behalf of the United States; and that it is within the legitimate power of the President to direct him to institute or to discontinue a pending suit, and to point out to him his duty, whenever the interest of the United States is directly or indirectly concerned. 2 Op. Att'y Gen. 487 (1831).

in the instant case.[10] Nor has the Attorney General attempted to delegate this authority to the Special Prosecutor.[11] This conclusion is fully supported by the brief filed by the Special Prosecutor before this Court, for there is a notable absence of any claim by the Special Prosecutor that he was, in fact, delegated the President's responsibility to weigh the public interest in determining what presidential material shall or shall not be used in this proceeding. Since this responsibility was retained by the President, there can be no basis for a claim that the President acted beyond the scope of his constitutional authority in determining not to use certain presidential material in this case. In so doing, as Professor Bickel pointed out, he is simply "exercising the lawful powers of his office, which he may do until removed upon impeachment and conviction." *New York Times*, June 3, 1974, p. 30. Because this decision is clearly within the prosecutorial discretion vested in the executive branch, and in particular in the Chief Executive, the district court is without jurisdiction to review this determination.

The district court's lack of jurisdiction was not altered, as the Special Prosecutor suggests, merely because he may "determine whether or not to contest the assertions of executive privilege or any other testimonial privilege." 38 Fed. Reg. 30, 738 (1973). In this suit, the Special Prosecutor is merely asking this Court to determine whether the Chief Executive was correct in determining that certain executive materials should not, in the public interest, be used to further this prosecution. However, neither the President, the Attorney General, or the Special Prosecutor, by agreement or otherwise, can foist upon the courts the executive branch's own responsibility for determining the advisability of using certain executive materials in the furtherance of its own case. Nor, through judicial review, can the executive branch compel the court to resolve or determine the wisdom of a discretionary decision made by the Chief Executive when it is within the bounds of his constitutional authority. Therefore, not even through the mechanism of a lesser official like the Special Prosecutor, can the executive or the legislative branch confer jurisdiction upon the courts to review any discretionary determinations, solely within their respective spheres. In this regard, even the Special Prosecutor is forced to concede that neither "the President nor the Department of Justice could

[10] See Pres. Br. 29 n. 14.

[11] See Pres. Br. 43 n. 31.

confer jurisdiction on the courts when such jurisdiction is constitutionally impermissible." (S.P. Br. 42). In all circumstances it is constitutionally impermissiable for a district court to review a decision by the executive branch, especially the Chief Executive, that it will not use a particular document even to the benefit of its own case. Accordingly, the Special Prosecutor has failed to establish any basis for the district court's jurisdiction to intervene in this intra-branch dispute for the purpose of reviewing a prosecutorial decision made by the Chief Executive in the course of a criminal proceeding.[12]

II. A CONSTITUTIONAL ASSERTION OF A PRESIDENTIAL PRIVILEGE IS NOT REVIEWABLE BY THIS COURT

We deem it important to emphasize three points: (1) The issue at stake is presidential privilege, founded in the Constitution, relating to conversations of the President with his closest advisors, not the concept of executive privilege as it may be generally applicable to persons in the executive branch and under other circumstances; (2) The resolution of this issues lies in an analysis of the design of our government as a whole and its development, including but not limited to that of judicial precedents[13] (pres. Br. 54-68); and (3) We repeat: "Significantly, the precise issue of the 'absoluteness' of executive privilege, as applied to presidential communications, has never been squarely confronted and definitely resolved by this Court." (Pres. Br. 51). To the extent there exists relevant judicial precedent, it supports the President's position. (Pres. Br. 74—82).

Because of the nature of the privilege asserted by the President, the bald statement of the Special Prosecutor that "... this Court has squarely rejected the claim that the

---

[12] We find no necessity to repeat our position as to the power of the Court to entertain and determine a political question. (Pres. Br. 44-48). However, there is one point that must be emphasized. Since *Mississippi* v. *Johnson*, 4 Wall. (71 U.S.) 475 (1867), this Court has correctly been reluctant to intervene in political questions involving discretionary decisions that are properly the sole prerogative of a coordinate branch of government. No dispute could more clearly entangle this Court in a "political question" than the present dispute, which unquestionably affects the ongoing impeachment inquiry, and thus would be an intrusion by the Judiciary on the Legislature as well as the Executive. Only last week the Court refused to "distort the role of the Judiciary in its relationship to the Executive and the Legislature. . . ." *Schlesinger* v. *Reservists Committee to Stop the War*. — U.S. —, No. 72-1188, Slip Op. p. 19 (June 25, 1974).

[13] See Winter, *Watergate and The Law* 54-55 (American Enterprise Institute for Public Policy Research 1974).

Executive has absolute, unreviewable discretion to withhold documents from the courts" (S.P. Br. 18) is unsound. The mainstay of the Special Prosecutor's position, *United States* v. *Reynolds*, 345 U.S. 1 (1953), sustained, without the necessity of judicial inspection, a claim of privilege made on national security grounds by the Secretary of the Air Force.[14] Regardless of what principles may be extracted from that case, one thing is clear: the Court did not decide any constitutional issues. In summarizing *Reynolds*, (S.P. Br. 54), the Special Prosecutor omitted the language of Chief Justice Vinson, which reveals the true nature of the case:

> Both positions have constitutional overtones which we find it unnecessary to pass upon, there being a narrower ground for decision. . . .
> . . . Since Rule 34 compels production only of matters 'not privileged,' the essential question is whether there was a valid claim of privilege under the Rule. . . . We think it should be clear that the term 'not privileged' as used in Rule 34, refers to 'privileges' as that term is understood in the law of evidence. (345 U.S. at 6).

With the exception of *Committee for Nuclear Responsibility, Inc.* v. *Seaborg*,[15] 463 F.2d 788 (D.C. Cir. 1971), the other cases relied upon by the Special Prosecutor are for the same reason not relevant to this Court's disposition of the present dispute.

Roviaro v. *United States*, 353 U.S. 53 (1957), turned on the nature of the "informer's privilege," a government privilege arising out of an interest in effective law enforcement. *Carr* v. *Monroe Manufacturing Company*, 431 F.2d 384 (5th Cir. 1970), a racial discrimination case against private and state defendants, dealt with an absolute privilege claim based on a state statute.[16] *Kaiser Aluminum & Chemical Corp.* v. *United States*, 157 F. Supp. 939 (Ct. Cl. 1958), a breach of contract case,

[14] It should also be noted that the Court felt the necessity for the evidence sought was dubious. 345 U.S. at 11. In circumstances strikingly similar to those of the present case, it was noted that the Government had offered to make available, for testimony, the flight crew whose written statements were a prime object of the plaintiffs' discovery motions.

[15] In *Seaborg*, the court stated that in *United States* v. *Reynolds, supra*, the issue of executive privilege based, on the constitutional doctrine of separation of powers, had been noted, but not decided. 463 F. 2d at 793.

[16] The court utilized *Reynolds*, as an analogy, to buttress its decision against absolute privilege. 431 F. 2d at 388.

involved a claim of executive privilege by the Administrator of the General Services Administration. In language echoing that of this Court in *Reynolds*, the court defined the privilege claimed solely in terms of the law of evidence, with its foundation in custom or statute.[17] The *Seaborg* case involved an attempt by environmentalists to enjoin the explosion of a nuclear underground test by the Atomic Energy Commission. In response to discovery efforts to ascertain whether the requirements of the National Environmental Policy Act had been met, the government through five agency heads, asserted a claim of executive privilege based on constitutional grounds. That claim was summarily rejected by the court of appeals without reference to any judicial precedent or historical analysis.[18] That fact, coupled with the realization that presidential communications were not involved, deprives the holding of that case from exerting any meaningful influence on the precisely-drawn issue which is before this Court.

Our position, contrary to that apparently assumed by the Special Prosecutor (S.P. Br. 49-50), is not at odds with this Court's decision in *Youngstown Sheet and Tube Co.* v. *Sawyer*, 343 U.S. 579 (1952). The touchstone of that holding was that President Truman's action in directing the seizure of the steel mills was not supported by any statutory or constitutional provision or concept; it exceeded all express and inherent power of the Presidency. In contrast, President Nixon's action, i.e., his assertion of executive privilege, is based squarely on the Constitution.[19] All the foregoing cases are examples where the Judiciary has reviewed, in varying degrees, claims of privilege exerted by lesser officers in the executive branch of government.

---

[17] In *Kaiser*, the court held, without judicial review of the documents requested, that no production was required.

[18] 463 F. 2d at 793. Three of the judges of the United States Court of Appeals for the District of Columbia Circuit who were part of the majority in *Nixon* v. *Sirica*, 487 F. 2d 700 (D.C. Cir. 1973) comprised the unanimous Court *Seaborg*.

[19] See *Soucie* v. *David*, 448 F. 2d 1067, 1071 n. 9 (D.C. Cir. 1971); (Pres. Br. 49-50). We call the Court's attention to S.P. Br. 57 n. 43, where the Special Prosecutor notes Professor Wright's summary of commentators' skeptical attitude toward the belief that executive privilege is rooted in the Constitution. This Court should be aware of the actual setting of that observation. Professor Wright, in the text, was discussing governmental privileges covered by the proposed Rules of Evidence. He observed: "There [in the proposed rules] is no mention of the general executive privilege and it is to be abolished except to whatever extent it may be *required by the Constitution*. 8 Wright & Miller, *Federal Practice and Procedure: Civil* § 2019 at 175 (1970) (emphasis added). The footnote that elaborates that textural statement and that encompasses the language cited by the Special Prosecutor has the following remark as its initial thrust:

The Supreme Court has said that the claim of an executive privilege has "constitutional overtones." *U.S.* v. *Reynolds*, 1953, 73 S. Ct. 528, 531, 345 U.S. 1, 6,
* * *

Although, as we have shown, they are readily distinguishable from the case at bar, we recognize that a court will necessarily be confronted with similar issues and must review and determine them. In fulfilling its duty to resolve all the issues before it, a court, at times, must exercise its authority in a manner consistent with competing interests, e.g. a claim of privilege against self-incrimination.[20] However, in this case the court's duty and authority of review is complete when it determines that the President of the United States has asserted privilege.

Environmental Protection Agency v. *Mink*, 410 U.S. 73 (1973), deserves comment because of the Special Prosecutor's allusion to it. There the controversy centered around the government's asserted right of non-disclosure of certain documents under a provision of the Freedom of Information Act, a statute exempting from disclosure non-factual intra-agency advisory material. This Court fashioned a method of examination whereby the trial court could separate factual data from exempt material.[21] In remanding the case, in part thereby reversing the decision of the court of appeals for the plaintiffs, this Court held that "in camera inspection" was not automatic since the agency may be able to show, by affidavit, that the items sought are, in fact, exempt. 410 U.S. at 93. The Special Prosecutor has attempted to utilize this case for the proposition that "the constitutional separation of powers does not give the Executive any constitutional immunity from judicial orders for the production of evidence." (S.P. Br. 61). In this regard, Justice Stewart at the outset of his concurring opinion noted that no constitutional claim was involved, and there was no issue regarding the nature or scope of executive privilege. 410 U.S. at 94. The second point to be noted in the *Mink* case is that no one was compelled to do anything. The Court did not discuss what might legally occur if the claim of privilege was ultimately rejected and noted the difficulty in analogizing Freedom of Information Act cases to ordinary litigation because of the non-availability of the option to dismiss or strike a defense which exists in the latter.

Lastly, *United States* ex rel. *Touhy* v. *Ragen*, 340 U.S. 462 (1951), has been cited in support of the Special Prosecutor's

---

[20] See discussion in *United States* v. *Reynolds,* 345 U.S. 1, 8-9 (1953).

[21] It also held that certain documents could not be subjected to any "in camera" inspection. 410 U.S. at 81-85. As to documents concerned with national defense, Justices Marshall and Brennan felt the need for secrecy was a decision solely for the Executive. 410 U.S. at 99-100.

contention that the Judiciary has the power to compel production of evidence from the executive. (S.P. Br. 63). This case, once again, involved a decision in which the production of documents was not ordered. This Court upheld the validity of a Department of Justice regulation, which constituted the basis for the FBI agent's refusal to comply with a subpoena *duces tecum.* In the holding, this Court specifically stated:

> Petitioner challenges the validity of the issue of the order under a legal doctrine which makes the head of a department rather than a court the determinator of the admissibility of evidence. In support of his argument that the Executive should not invade the Judicial sphere, petitioner cites Wigmore, Evidence (3 ed.), § 2379, and *Marbury* v. *Madison*, 1 Cranch 137. *But under this record we are concerned only with the validity of Order No. 3229.* The constitutionality of the Attorney General's exercise of a determinative power as to whether or on what conditions or subject to what disadvantages to the Government he may refuse to produce government papers under his charge must await a factual situation that requires a ruling. (340 U.S. at 468-469) (emphasis added).

Immediately following his reference to *Ragen*, the Special Prosecutor quotes (S.P. Br. 63) certain language from a work of Professor Wright in an attempt to emphasize his contention concerning the judicial power of enforcement in this case. The entire text of the partially quoted statement of Professor Wright now follows:

> In private litigation refusal of a government officer to comply with a court order overruling a claim of executive privilege and ordering disclosure could lead to conviction of contempt,[22] but there is a natural reluctance to invoke this sanction and the extraordinary writs of mandamus and prohibition have been held available to review contempt citations. If the government is a party, the court may penalize it for its failure to comply with a disclosure order by invoking any of the sanctions set forth in Rule 37(b) (2). In this way the court can achieve fairness in the case before it without actually compelling production of the information that the government is determined to keep confidential. 8 Wright and Miller, *Federal Practice and Procedure: Civil*, § 2019, at 172-173 (1970).

---

[22] The Special Prosecutor's recitation of Professor Wright's language ends here.

When holdings, as opposed to random language, command our attention, it becomes evident that such judicial precedent as does exist in fact supports the President's concept of executive privilege rather than that urged by the Special Prosecutor.

The Special Prosecutor cites *Conway* v. *Rimmer*, (1968) 1 All E.R. 874, in support of his argument that the Executive cannot be given unreviewable discretion in these matters. (S.P. Br. 56 n. 41). *Conway*, far from supporting the Special Prosecutor's view, is in fact wholly consistent with the position we are advancing. It is true that in *Conway* the House of Lords overruled what had been the English rule that a claim of privilege, no matter how routine or unimportant the document, is binding on the courts. Their Lordships, however, were at great pains to distinguish the kind of low-level routine papers there involved from papers at the highest level of government. Every one of the speeches drew this distinction and made it clear that when high-level documents, of the sort we have in the present case, are sought, the court must accept the Executive's claim of privilege without further inquiry. Thus in the principal speech Lord Reid said that "there are certain classes of documents which ought not to be disclosed whatever their content may be." He then referred to "cabinet minutes and the like" as an example of a class of documents that ought not be be disclosed until they "are only of historical interest." [1968] 1 All E.R. at 888. Lord Hodson instanced "cabinet minutes, despatches from ambassadors abroad and minutes of discussions between heads of departments" as among those that are absolutely protected by a claim of Crown privilege. [1968] 1 All E.R. at 902, and see also his remark at 905. Lord Pearce said:

Obviously, production would never be ordered of fairly wide classes of documents at a high level. To take an extreme case, production would never be ordered of cabinet correspondence, letters or reports on appointments to offices of importance and the like; but why should the same yardstick apply to trivial documents and correspondence with or within a ministry. [1968] All E.R. at 910.

The observation of Lord Upjohn was in a similar vein:

No doubt there are many cases in which documents by their very nature fall into a class which requires protection such as, only by way of example, cabinet papers, foreign office despatches, the security of the State, high-level inter-departmental minutes and correspondence, and documents pertaining to the general administration of the naval, military and air force services. . . . So, too, high-level inter-departmental communications, to take, only as an example on establishment matters, the promotion or transfer of reasonably high-level personnel in the service of the Crown; but no catalogue can reasonably be compiled. The reason for this privilege is that it would be quite wrong and entirely inimical to the proper functioning of the public service if the public were to learn of these high-level communications, however innocent of prejudice to the State the actual contents of any particular document might be; that is obvious. [1968] 1 All E.R. at 914-915.

Only Lord Morris of Borth-Y-Gest did not attempt to specify particular kinds of documents that are absolutely privileged, but he too noted that "[i]n many cases it will be plain that documents are within a class of documents which by their very nature ought not to be disclosed." [1968] 1 All E.R. at 901.

This recognition that there are some kinds of documents on which the decision of the Executive must be final, and not subject to review by the courts, is wholly consistent with what was held in *United States* v. *Reynolds*, 345 U.S. 1, 10 (1953), and indeed the *Reynolds* opinion was quoted in the principal speech in *Conway* of Lord Reid. [1968] 1 All E.R. at 887. It is consistent also with this Court's disclaimer in *Marbury* v. *Madison*, 1 Cranch (5 U.S.) 137, 170 (1803) of any judicial power to order "an intrusion into the secrets of the cabinet. . . . "

The distinction insisted upon so vigorously by all of the judges in *Conway* is the distinction that should control here. Decisions concerning material in the lower echelons of government or material of a routine, everyday nature, are not in point. The subpoena here in issue calls for recordings and notes of conversations between the President of the United States and his closest advisers.

We referred in our initial brief to "[t]he velocity with which the confidentiality of presidential communications has eroded. . . . " (Pres. Br. 133). Demands for presidential recordings or papers or even for presidential testimony have come from judges and defendants all over the country, both state and federal.[23] In his letter of July 23, 1973, to Senator Ervin, the President observed that "the tapes could be accurately understood only by reference to an enormous number of other documents and tapes,

[23] See Pres. Br. 68 n. 51.

so that to open them at all would begin an endless process of disclosure and explanation of private Presidential records. . . . " The accuracy of that observation is now a matter of common knowledge. Initially Special Prosecutor Cox subpoenaed tapes and notes of nine conversations. His successor has been furnished all existing material covering those conversations and the President has voluntarily given Special Prosecutor Jaworski tapes of many other conversations. Now the Special Prosecutor seeks to require production of 64 more conversations. Should he be successful in that attempt, only a very foolhardy person would dare to predict that this would be the end of the matter and that the demand for private presidential material would not continue to grow insatiably.

All that we have said on this point was succinctly put by a distinguished constitutional lawyer, Charles L. Black, Jr., who has observed that refusal to disclose communications of the kind involved in this litigation is not only the President's lawful privilege

> but his duty as well, for it is a measure necessary to the protection of the proper conduct of his office, not only by him but, much more importantly, by his successors for all time to come.
>
> * * * * *
>
> It is hard for me to see how any person of common sense could think that those consultative and decisional processes that are the essence of the Presidency could be carried on to any good effect, if every participant spoke or wrote in continual awareness that at any moment any Congressional committee, or any prosecutor working with a grand jury, could at will command the production of the verbatim record of every work written or spoken. Black, "Mr. Nixon, the Tapes, and Common Sense" *New York Times*, August 3, 1973, page 31.[24]

Although the Presidency will survive if the lower court's decision is allowed to stand, it will be different from the office contemplated by the Framers and occupied by Presidents, from George Washington through today.

---

[24] See the fuller expression of Professor Black's view in Cong. Rec. E5320-E5322 (daily ed. August 1, 1973); see also Carr, Bernstein, Morrison, Snyder, & McLean, *American Democracy in Theory and Practice* 609-610 (1956); Winter, *Watergate and The Law* 55 (American Enterprise Institute for Public Policy Research 1974).

III. THE CONSTITUTIONAL PRIVILEGE HAS NOT BEEN WAIVED

The Special Prosecutor purports to offer the Court an easy solution to the hard problems of this case when he says:

the Court must use its process to acquire all relevant evidence to lay before the jury. In the present context it can do so with the least consequences for confidentiality of other matters and future deliberations of the Executive Branch by ruling that there has been a waiver with respect to this entire affair. (S.P. Br. 123).

The Court is offered three theories on which the Special Prosecutor thinks a holding of waiver can be justified. These are the President's statement of May 22, 1973, authorizing his aides to testify about Watergate-related matters (S.P. Br. 119), the President's release to the public of transcripts from 43 Watergate-related Presidential conversations (S.P. Br. 119),[25] and the fact that H. R. Haldeman has been permitted to hear tapes of selected conversations (S.P. Br. 122). Neither singly nor together do any of these waive the President's privilege not to disclose other conversations that are still confidential.

It is of course a truism that ordinary evidentiary privileges can be waived, as the cases discussed by the Special Prosecutor indicate. (S.P. Br. 117-121). But the separation-of-powers notions that underlie what is commonly referred to as "executive privilege" are such that ordinary common law notions of waiver are wholly inapplicable here. The privilege refers to the power of the President to decide whether or not the public interest permits disclosure of particular information. Because the President determines that the public interest permits making public certain information or because he determines that it is in the public interest to disclose other information to those persons in and out of government in whom he has confidence and from whom he seeks advice, he is not thereby precluded from determining that still other information must, in the public interest, be kept in confidence. The matter was well put by Professor Alexander Bickel:

Again, the issue is not whether the President has waived his privilege to keep the tapes secret. To the extent that it exists

---

[25] The President stated in his Formal Claim of Privilege (J.A. 48a) that he advanced no claim of privilege with respect to those portions of 20 tape recorded conversations for which transcripts have been made public. Accordingly, those portions of the 20 tapes are not at issue in this case as the President has no objection to judicial authentication.

and with respect to matter that it covers, I do not see how the privilege can be waived. Naturally, if a document or a tape is no longer confidential because it has been made public, it would be nonsense to claim that it is privileged, and nobody would trouble to subpoena it either, since it would be available.

But nature and reason of the privilege are rather to repose in the President and in him along the subjective judgment whether to maintain privacy or release information—and which, and how much, and when, and to whom. Far from being waived, the privilege, it seems to me, is as much exercised when information is released as when it is withheld. Bickel, "Wretched Tapes (cont.)," *New York Times*, August 15, 1973, p.33.

A constitutionally-based privilege, which exists only so that the President, like the courts and like Congress, can function effectively hardly vanishes because, in Professor Black's phrase, "little mousetraps of 'waiver' are sprung." Letter of Prof. Charles L. Black, Jr., Cong. Rec. E5320, E5323 (daily ed. August 1, 1973).

Nor is there any merit in the argument that by allowing his aides to testify on Watergate matters, the President waived privilege as to tape recordings. There is an inherent distinction between testimonial evidence and tape recorded conversations. This distinction is emphasized and evidenced by the very existence of the present dispute. It should be obvious—and the published transcripts that have been released vividly confirm—that recordings are the raw material of life. By their very nature they contain spontaneous, informal, tentative, and frequently pungent comments on a variety of subjects inextricably intertwined into one conversation. It is precisely with that distinction in mind, and with a strong desire that the truth about Watergate be brought out, that the President has not aserted a presidential privilege with regard to *testimony* about possible criminal conduct or discussions of possible criminal conduct. But testimony can be confined to the relevant portions of the conversations and can be limited to matters that do not endanger other privileged matters. Recordings cannot be so confined and limited, *Alderman* v. *United States*, 394 U.S. 165, 182 (1969), and thus the President has concluded that to produce recordings would do serious damage to presidential privacy and to the ability of that office to function effectively.

The distinction between testimonial evidence and other forms of tangible evidence is not only recognized by the executive branch, as there is a common congressional practice in waiving congressional privilege and authorizing oral testimony by congressional staff members in court, but refusing to permit submission of related tangible material. See *Nixon* v. *Sirica*, 487 F.2d 700, 772 (D.C. Cir. 1973) (Wilkey, J., dissenting), citing *United States* v. *Brewster*, 408 U.S. 501 (1972), and 118 Cong. Rec. S. 16,766, 92nd Cong. 2nd Sess. (October 4, 1972) See also S. Res. 338, 120 Cong. Rec. 4973, 93rd Cong., 2nd Sess. (daily ed., June 12, 1974).

The distinction has been recognized also in this Court. Indeed the short answer to the Special Prosecutor's claim of waiver with regard to the materials now sought may be found in *United States* v. *Reynolds*, 345 U.S. 1 (1953). In that case the United States refused to produce an Air Force investigation report of an airplane crash as well as written statements by survivors of the crash. It offered to allow the survivors to give depositions and to testify as to all matters except those of a "classified nature." The Supreme Court sustained the claim of privilege with regard to the documents sought. The offer to allow the witnesses to testify, far from being a waiver of privilege as to the documents, was expressly relied on by the Supreme Court as a reason for upholding the claim of privilege. 345 U.S. at 11. Similarly, the court of appeals in *Senate Select Committee on Presidential Campaign Activities* v. *Nixon*, No. 74-1258 (D.C. Cir., May 23, 1974), regarded an identical waiver argument, offered by the plaintiffs in that case, as so lacking in substance that it did not merit discussion in the opinion.

Finally, there is much weight in a point made by Judge MacKinnon in his dissent in *Nixon* v. *Sirica*, 487 F.2d 700, 758-759 (D.C. Cir. 1973). He wrote:

> There has been no waiver. This conclusion rests upon three factors: the strict standards applied to privileges of this nature to determine waiver; the distinction between oral testimony and tape recordings; and, most important, considerations of public policy that argue persuasively for a privilege that permits the Chief Executive to disclose information on topics of national concern without that which properly ought to be withheld in the public interest.

Like Judge MacKinnon, we think that the most important of these points is the one last stated. Plainly the country is best served when there is the maximum disclosure possible from the Executive, consistent with the requirements of the public interest. This President, like his predecessors, has always acted on that principle. Disclosure has been the rule and claim of privilege the rare exception. But if this Court were to accept the Special Prosecutor's beguiling suggestion that this case can be decided on a narrow ground of waiver, the inevitable long-term consequence must be less disclosure, not more, since Presidents will be reluctant to make public even those things that can be released without harm to the public interest, if by doing so they may be held to have waived their constitutional privilege to withhold related information that the nation's interests require be kept confidential.

IV. THE SPECIAL NATURE OF THE PRESIDENCY

The Special Prosecutor states an obvious and important truth when he reminds us that "in our system *even the President* is under the law." (S.P. Br. 68) (emphasis in original). A fundamental error that permeates his brief, however, is his failure to recognize the extraordinary nature of the Presidency in our system and that the Framers, who fully understood this, provided an extraordinary mechanism for making a President subject to the law.

The President is not merely an individual, to be treated in the same way as any other person who has information that may be relevant in a criminal prosecution. He is not, as the Special Prosecutor erroneously suggests, merely "the *head* of the Executive Branch." (S.P. Br. 79) (emphasis in original). Instead, as we pointed out at the beginning of this brief, it was announced by this Court more than a century ago, and since reiterated, that "the President is the Executive Department." *Mississippi* v. *Johnson*, 4 Wall. (71 U.S.) 475,500 (1867). So much is apparent from the Constitution itself. Article II begins with the simple but sweeping declaration: "The executive Power shall be vested in *a* President of the United States of America" (emphasis added). In addition, the President, as this Court has recognized, is, more than any other officer of government the representative of all of the people. *Myers* v. *United States*, 272 U.S. 52, 123 (1926). Chief Justice Taft went on to say that

as the President is elected for four years, with the mandate of the people to exercise his executive power under the Constitution, there would seem to be no reason for construing that instrument in such a way as to limit and hamper that power beyond the limitations of it, expressed or fairly implied.

It was no mere happenstance that all executive power was vested in a single person, the President. This was a subject of recurring debate at the Constitutional Convention. Suggestions of a multi-member Executive were repeatedly pressed and as repeatedly rejected. It was seen, as Dr. Franklin said, as "a point of great importance." 1 *Farrand* 65.

In this respect the Executive differs from the other two great branches of government. The legislative power is vested by Article I in "a Congress of the United States," divided into two bodies and composed now of 535 members. The judicial power is, by Article III, spread among the nine Justices of this Court and the hundreds of judges of the inferior courts that Congress has seen fit to ordain and establish. But one person, and one person alone, is entrusted by Article II with the awesome task of exercising the executive power of the United States. "The President is the Executive Department." This difference, as we shall develop below, has important consequences. It serves to distinguish many of the cases relied on by the Special Prosecutor, involving as they do individual members of the legislative and judicial branches. Specifically, the particular position the President occupies in our constitutional scheme means that the courts cannot issue compulsory process to compel him to exercise powers entrusted to him in a certain way, that, so long as he is President, he is not subject to criminal process, and that, as a logical corollary, he may not, while President, be named as an unindicted co-conspirator.

Of course, as we have already pointed out (Pres. Br. 52 n. 45), the Framers did not want a king, and Hamilton devoted all of the 69th *Federalist* to demonstrating that the Presidency, as created in the Constitution, bore no resemblance to the monarchy from which the colonists had successfully rebelled. The term of the President is limited to four years. The legislative branch controls the national purse strings, the war power, and the general policy direction of government. The President is given only a limited veto, subject to being overridden, over legislative acts. He is given no role whatever in the process of constitutional amendment. Finally, and most important for present purposes, the President may be removed from office by conviction on impeachment, and after he has left office, either through expiration of his term or by conviction on impeachment, he is subject to prosecution for crimes that he may have committed.

We have already developed in detail the process by which the impeachment provisions of the Constitution took form. (Pres. Br. 95-104). The language of Article I, section 3, clause 4, can hardly be read in any other way than that indictment of a President can only follow his conviction on impeachment. This was certainly the understanding of the delegates at Philadelphia, of the contemporary expositors of the Constitution, and of students of constitutional law from 1787 until today.

There is nothing in *United States* v. *Isaacs*, 493 F.2d 1124 (7th Cir. 1974), *cert. denied* ——U.S.——, (June 17, 1974), that is contrary to what we have just said. A judge of a court of appeals is not the judicial branch. He is a part of that branch, but the Judiciary can function uninterrupted during those rare occasions when a single judge is forced to stand trial on a criminal charge. The Presidency cannot function if the President is preoccupied with the defense of a criminal case, and the thought of a President exercising great powers from jail boggles the mind.[26]

The President, as we have noted, *is* the Executive Department. If he could be enjoined, restrained, indicted, arrested, or ordered by judges, grand juries, or marshals, these individuals would have the power to control the executive branch. This would nullify the separation of powers and the co-equality of the Executive.

The conclusion that the President is not subject to indictment while in office is consistent also with a proper ordering of government. When this principal national leader, elected by all of the people, is to be removed, it is proper that the removal be considered and accomplished only by a body that, like the President, is politically representative of the whole Nation. Impeachment is a process designed to deal with the problem of criminal conduct by the President and yet still preserve the majoritarian character of the Republic. Criminal indictments or judicial orders cannot provide the tools to remove or limit a whole branch of government, and were not contemplated by the Founders for such a purpose. Only the branch of government that represents the people who elected the President, the legislative branch, can take actions that will in any way remove or tend to remove a President from office. This is the function of Congress, not of a grand jury.

For reasons that we have already fully developed (Pres. Br. 107-115), it follows *a fortiori* from the non-indictability of an incumbent President that he cannot be named as an unindicted co-conspirator, and that the action of the grand jury in this case must be ordered expunged. The ability of a President to function is severely crippled if a grand jury, an official part of the judicial branch, can make a finding that a President has been party to a criminal conspiracy and make this in a form that does not allow that finding to be reviewed or contested and disproved.[27] To allow this would be a mockery of due process and would deny to

[26] It is also worthwhile noting that at the Convention the discussion of impeachment was wholly in terms of a remedy against the President. Berger, *Impeachment: The Constitutional Problems* 100 (1973). The inclusion in Article II, section 4, of the "Vice President, and all Civil Officers of the United States" was made without discussion in the closing hours of the Convention. 2 *Farrand* 575.

[27] And to suggest that the naming of a President as a criminal co-conspirator, even if unindicted, is not an "impeachment" of the President is, we submit, to play games with common words and common sense.

Presidents of the United States even those minimal protections that the Constitution extends to prison inmates subject to disciplinary proceedings. *Wolff* v. *McDonnell*, ——U.S.——, No. 73-679 (June 26, 1974).

If the grand jury had before it evidence, competent or otherwise, *United States* v. *Calandra*, 414 U.S. 338 (1974), that led it to think that the President had been party to a crime, its only permissible course of action was to transmit that evidence to the House Judiciary Committee, rather than to make a gratuitous, defamatory, and legally impermissible accusation against the President.

Presumably the Special Prosecutor advised the grand jury to make this finding, and did so with the thought that it would strengthen his hand in litigation such as the present case (P.S.A. 8). If the President could be considered a co-conspirator, then all of his statements would arguably come within the exception to the hearsay rule and would meet the requirement of Rule 17(c) that subpoenaed material must be evidentiary in nature. In addition, this impermissible finding is relied on by the Special Prosecutor for his argument (P.S. Br. 90-102) that executive privilege vanishes if there is a *prima facie* showing of criminality. But even if the grand jury were empowered to make this finding—and as a matter of law it cannot—we have already shown that an allegation of criminal activity does not overcome the assertion of presidential privilege (Pres. Br. 82-86), and that a grand jury finding, based as it is only on a showing of probable cause, falls far short of the *prima facie* showing of criminality that is required to defeat even the usual evidentiary privileges. (Pres. Br. 115-122).[28]

---

[28] The cases relied on by the Special Prosecutor (S.P. Br. 98) are not to the contrary. Such cases as *Ex parte United States,* 287 U.S. 241, 250 (1932), *Ewing* v. *Mytinger & Casselberry,* 339 U.S. 594, 599 (1950), and the others cited stand only for the proposition that a grand jury indictment conclusively establishes that there is probable cause to hold the person named for trial. They do not hold that the grand jury's action is an evidentiary showing of a *prima facie* case.

Again the Special Prosecutor is not helped by *United States* v. *Aldridge,* 484 F. 2d 655, 658 (7th Cir. 1973); *United States* v. *Bob,* 106 F. 2d 37 (2d Cir. 1939), *cert. denied,* 308 U.S. 589 (1940); or the other cases he cites with regard to attorney-client privilege. In those cases the privilege was held to vanish only after the government by proof at trial, had made a *prima facie* showing of criminal involvement.

Finally, the Special Prosecutor's heavy reliance on *Clark* v. *United States,* 289 U.S. 1 (1933) (S.P. Br. 95-97, 100-101, 108-109), is misplaced. Quite aside from the very different nature of the "privilege," or, more properly, rule of competency, there in issue, Justice Cardozo was quick to point out that "[i]t would be absurd to say that the privilege could be got rid of merely by making a charge of fraud," 289 U.S. at 15, and that "there must be a showing of a *prima facie* case sufficient to satisfy the judge that the light should be let in." 289 U.S. at 14.

The Special Prosecutor makes the suprising suggestion that the President enjoys no privileges or immunities. One might infer quite plausibly from the specific grant of official privileges to Congress that no other constitutional immunity from normal legal obligations was intended for government officials or papers. (S.P. Br. 77).

But it is quite clear that the privileges given to individual members of the legislative branch by Article I section 6, were given them for a specific and well-understood purpose. This was to protect the legislators "against possible prosecution by an unfriendly executive and conviction by a hostile judiciary . . . " United States v. Johnson, 383 U.S. 169, 179 (1966). It was "designed to assure a co-equal branch of government wide freedom of speech, debate, and deliberation without intimidation or threats from the Executive Branch." Gravel v. United States, 408 U.S. 606, 616 (1972).

The Executive needed no protection from himself. As chief of state, chief executive, commander-in-chief, and chief prosecutor, he had no need to fear intimidation by a hostile executive or prosecution by an unfriendly executive. In addition, he was protected further by the elaborate procedure for impeachment, and by his immunity from criminal process until he had been convicted on impeachment. Thus the Constitution says nothing about immunities of the Executive comparable to what it says about members of the legislative branch because to have done so would have been to guard against an evil that could never come to pass.

Even members of the executive branch do have to fear damage actions brought by private citizens, and this Court has not been slow to read into the Constitution an implied immunity to protect the Executive in this situation. The leading case is Spalding v. Vilas, 161 U.S. 583 (1896), frequently relied on in this Court and always with approval. E.g., Barr v. Matteo, 360 U.S. 564, 570 (1959);[29] Scheuer v. Rhodes, 413 U.S. 919, 927 n. 8 (1974).

---

[29] In the Barr case this Court relied heavily, in discussing immunity for executive officers, on the well-known opinion of Judge Learned Hand in Gregoire v. Biddle, 177 F. 2d 579 (2d Cir. 1949), where judicial immunity was at issue. Several of Judge Hand's insights in that case are applicable here. Thus he says:

it can be argued that official powers, since they exist only for the public good, never cover occasions where the public good is not their aim, and hence that to exercise a power dishonestly is necessarily to overstep its bounds. A moment's reflection shows, however, that this cannot be the meaning of the limitation without defeating the whole doctrine. What is meant by saying that the officer must be acting within his power cannot be more than that the occasion must be such as would have justified the act, if he had been using his power for any of the purposes on whose account it was vested in him . . . (177 F. 2d at 581).

The Special Prosecutor would have the Court believe that the discretion about production of documents, which it has always been recognized that Presidents have, shrinks to a mere ministerial duty to produce what is demanded whenever a court disagrees with the Chief Executive's assessment of what the public interest requires. The argument seems little more than a play on words, intended to avoid the decisions, from *Marbury* on, that the courts may compel ministerial acts but that they cannot interfere with discretionary decisions of high executive officers.

Nothing could be clearer than that the decision to disclose or to withhold the most intimate conversations of the President with his chief advisers involves the gravest and most far-reaching possible considerations of public policy. Who can say what the long term, or even short term, public effects of the President's decision to make public transcripts of tapes of his conversations about Watergate will be? It was a difficult and monumental decision, and no man living can predict with assurance how ultimately the history of this country, and indeed of the world, may be influenced by it. It was a discretionary decision in the most important sense, and it is nonsense to call such a disclosure "ministerial" merely because the final action of disclosure can be accomplished by a messenger.

A presidential decision to release the confidential tapes or written memoranda of his meetings with his advisers involves the same basic discretion as his initial decision to make such records. Surely neither the courts nor Congress could require Presidents to make such recordings on the ground that they would then be available should there be charges of misconduct against aides to some future President.

This case must be viewed in the light that the President is the executive branch, co-equal to the multi-membered legislative and judicial branches. If that co-equality is to be preserved, the President cannot be subject to the vagaries of a grand jury nor deprived of his power to control disclosure of his most confidential communications. If he misuses his great powers, he must be proceeded against by the remedy that the Constitution has provided.

Again Judge Hand observed that "[t] here must indeed be means of punishing public officers who have been truant to their duties . . ." 177 F. 2d at 581. But the Constitution provides three sanctions against a truant President. He is subject to the political sanction of being defeated for reelection and to the legal sanctions of conviction on impeachment and of criminal punishment after he has been removed from office.

V. THE SPECIAL PROSECUTOR HAS NOT DEMONSTRATED A UNIQUE AND COMPELLING NEED FOR THIS MATERIAL

The Special Prosecutor makes the casual suggestion that "[t]here is a compelling public interest in trying the conspiracy charged in *United States* v. *Mitchell*, et al., upon all relevant and material evidence." (S.P. Br. 107). Doubtless every prosecutor in history has thought the same thing. The genius of the law, happily, has rejected that course, and in this case the Special Prosecutor's suggestion begs every important question before the Court. A prosecutor has the right to every man's evidence "except for those persons protected by a constitutional, common-law, or statutory privilege." *Branzburg* v. *Hayes*, 408 U.S. 665, 688, (1972). If, as we have argued, the materials at issue are subject to a valid privilege, based both on the Constitution and on the common law, the Special Prosecutor may not have them, no matter how relevant or material he thinks they may be, any more than he could require the defendants in this case to produce relevant and material evidence based on what they told their attorneys or based on confidential communications with their wives.

Our argument, of course, has been that the great question is, as Judge Wilkey put it, "Who Decides?", and that the answer to that question is that the President decides. But even if we are wrong on that, and the courts play a limited role under unusual circumstances, as held by the majority in *Nixon* v. *Sirica*, 487 F.2d 700 (D.C. Cir. 1973), the showing made by the Special Prosecutor falls far short of the requirements that the court of appeals announced in that case. The court there used the terms "critical," 487 F.2d at 706, "peculiarly necessary," 487 F.2d 717, and evidence "for which no effective substitute is available," 487 F.2d at 717, to describe the grand jury's need for the tapes there under subpoena. We predicted in our initial submission that the Special Prosecutor could make no similarly compelling showing in this case (Pres. Br. 86-95), and his brief has confirmed that fact. There is not one statement in the Special Prosecutor's Brief that suggests or even implies that if he is unable to obtain the material sought, the prosecution of this case will not be successful.[30]

---

[30] It is significant that on June 3, 1974, Charles W. Colson pleaded guilty to the felony of obstructing justice, 18 U.S.C. § 1503, in the case of *United States* v. *Ehrlichman, et al.*, (D.D.C. Cr. No. 74-116) and subsequently all other charges against him were dismissed. Thus, assuming *arguendo* the Special Prosecutor does have a need

The Special Prosecutor claims "that the 'unique' circumstances which led to the rejection of the President's claim of privilege in the context of a grand jury investigation have continued applicability." (S.P. Br. 107-108). He, of course, finds it convenient to ignore other salient portions of the opinion in *Nixon* v. *Sirica* that are adverse to his position. It must be remembered that the court of appeals went to great lengths in that case to limit its holding "strictly to that required by the precise and entirely unique circumstances of the case," 487 F.2d at 705, and specifically acknowledged that "we have attempted to decide no more than the problem before us—a problem that takes its unique shape from the grand jury's compelling show of need." 487 F.2d at 722.

The Special Prosecutor cites *Committee for Nuclear Responsibility* v. *Seaborg*, 463 F.2d 788 (D.C. Circ. 1971)., to illustrate the possible consequences of not overcoming a privilege. (S.P. Br. 108). For "[o]therwise the head of an executive department would have the power on his own say-so to cover up *all* evidence of fraud and corruption when a federal court or grand jury was investigating malfeasance in office, and this is not the law." 463 F.2d at 794. (emphasis added). But such a consequence is obviously not possible in our present situation[31] where the President has already permitted his closest aides and advisors to give public and grand jury testimony. In addition, voluminous documents and materials have been submitted to the Special Prosecutor, to the congressional committees investigating Watergate, and to the public at large. As a result, grand jury indictments have been returned, and a number of convictions have already been obtained. There can be no valid assertion that if the privilege is not overcome in the present case, the consequences states in *Seaborg* would result. The *Seaborg* case, rather than supplying reasons for overcoming the privilege in this case, illustrates the absence of any reason for doing so.

We have previously argued that the Special Prosecutor has failed to satisfy the requirements of Criminal Rule 17(c) for

for the subpoenaed items, the fact that Colson is no longer a defendant, certainly diminishes considerably, if not obviates completely, any need the Special Prosecutor may have ever had for subpoenaed items numbered: 1, 4, 5, 6, 13 and 17.

[31]This fact is conceded by the Special Prosecutor, who in order to support his waiver theory freely admits that the President has "authorized voluminous testimony and other statements concerning Watergate-related discussions and his recent release of 1216 pages of transcript . . ." (S.P. Br. 116-117), and that "there has been extensive testimony in several forums concerning the substance of the recorded conversations now sought for use at the trial in *United States* v. *Mitchell, et al.*" (S.P. Br. 118-119).

subpoenaed material. (Pres. Br. 122-133). We continue to believe that. Although in general we do not disagree with the propositions of law advanced by the Special Prosecutor on this issue,[32] we take serious issue with his application of the law to the facts of this case, and particularly to his attempt, implicit in his discussion of the facts, to shift the burden on the issue of relevancy to the President. The Special Prosecutor is seeking the materials. He must show that the documents are evidentiary and relevant. It is not for the President to prove that they are not.

But even if there is enough in the Special Prosecutor's conclusory statements to turn the color of legal litmus paper with regard to Rule 17(c), in its application to ordinary documents, he has failed to show the critical and compelling need that is required to overcome a claim of presidential privilege even under what we think to be the too permissive standard of *Nixon* v. *Sirica.*

CONCLUSION

Two years of Watergate have left their mark on America. Apart from its impact on the lives of the many men and women involved in the events, Watergate will affect practices, attitudes, and values in our political life in ways that are diverse and lasting and, it is to be hoped, for the good. Without the passage of another law or the imposition of another sentence Watergate will have wrought a great change in American life. But the processes of the law that have been set in motion by that set of events must run their course. What remains to be seen is whether the tides that surge about Watergate will alter the relationship among the branches of government; whether, in short, the complex and sensitive balance of our constitutional structure will be impaired.

Our last word is therefore essentially a neutral one. In choosing this closing note we do not abandon our expectations for success or our conviction that we are right. We simply recognize that there has been enough argument about the powers

32 We do take issue with the suggestion that the subpoena upheld in *Bowman Dairy Co.* v. *United States,* 341 U.S. 214 (1951), was much less particular than the subpoena in the present case. (S.P. Br. 126). The subpoena in *Bowman* was specifically limited to the documents, books, records, and objects "which were either presented to the grand jury or would be offered as evidence at trial." 341 U.S. at 217. This was a much more particularized showing of relevance and admissibility than the Special Prosecutor has made.

His reference to *United States* v. *Carter,* 15 F.R.D. 367, 371 (D.D.C. 1954), for the proposition that Rule 17(c) reaches materials useful for impeachment (S.P. Br. 128) is misleading, since that case, and many others we have cited (Pres. Br. 130), hold that impeachment materials cannot be obtained in advance of trial and one must wait to see if the person in question actually testifies.

and privileges of particular individuals who happen to occupy high office in the three branches and exercise their authority temporarily and in a representative capacity. For in the final analysis it is the Constitution we are all analyzing, arguing, expounding, and, in a sense of mutuality, undertaking to protect for the long life of the Nation.

In this setting the terminal question is: What decision best defends the constitutional structure of American government? What decision lifts the resolution of this case above the passions of this moment in history and safeguards the strengths and integrity of the Constitution against the exigencies of an unknown and unknowable future? There is no doubt about the power, indeed the responsibility, of the Court to answer justiciable questions that are appropriately posed about the meaning of the Constitution. Nor, in our submission, is there any question but that the central idea of the Constitution is the distribution of power among the separate branches and the resolution of controversy and disagreement by accommodation rather than confrontation. A constitution is a way of governing, not a set of codified specifications for the resolution of disputes among the sovereign branches. There are blank spaces on the constitutional canvas that must be left untouched if the Constitution is to bear the same creative relation to our future that it has to our past.

In our brief, we and the Special Prosecutor have cited *Youngstown Sheet & Tube Co.* v. *Sawyer*, 343 U.S. 579 (1952), to support conflicting arguments. We quote the opening words of Mr. Justice Frankfurter's concurring opinion, confident in the knowledge that they reflect beliefs we and the Special Prosecutor hold in common:

> Before the cares of the White House were his own, President Harding is reported to have said that government after all is a very simple thing. He must have said that, if he said it, as a fleeting inhabitant of fairyland. The opposite is the truth. A constitutional democracy like ours is perhaps the most difficult of man's social arrangements to manage successfully. Our scheme of society is more dependent than any other form of government on knowledge and wisdom and self-discipline for the achievement of its aims.
>
> *　　*　　*　　*　　*
>
> Rigorous adherence to the narrow scope of the judicial function is especially demanded in controversies that arouse appeals to the Constitution. The attitude with which this Court must approach its duty when confronted with such

issues is precisely the opposite of that normally manifested by the general public. So-called constitutional questions seem to exercise a mesmeric influence over the popular mind. This eagerness to settle—preferably forever—a specific problem on the basis of the broadest possible constitutional pronouncements may not unfairly be called one of our minor national traits. An English observer of our scene has acutely described it: 'At the first sound of a new argument over the United States Constitution and its interpretation the hearts of Americans leap with a fearful joy. The blood stirs powerfully in their veins and a new lustre brightens their eyes. Like King Harry's men before Harfleur, they stand like greyhounds in the slips, straining upon the start.' *The Economist*, May 10, 1952, p. 370.

The path of duty for this Court, it bears repetition, lies in the opposite direction. (343 U.S. at 593-594).

Respectfully submitted,

> JAMES D. ST. CLAIR
> MICHAEL A. STERLACCI
> JEROME J. MURPHY
> LOREN A. SMITH
> JAMES R. PROCHNOW
> EUGENE R. SULLIVAN
> JEAN A. STAUDT
> JAMES J. TANSEY
> *Attorneys for the President*

Of Counsel
CHARLES ALAN WRIGHT
LEONARD GARMENT

> The White House
> Washington, D.C. 20500
> Telephone Number: 456-1414

July 1, 1974

X
THE ACLU BRIEF IN UNITED STATES
v.
NIXON

The only amicus brief submitted to the Supreme Court in the case was that of the ACLU. The main emphasis of that brief was on the scope of executive privilege.

SUPREME COURT OF THE UNITED STATES

OCTOBER TERM, 1973

No. 73-1766

UNITED STATES OF AMERICA,
Petitioner,

v.

RICHARD M. NIXON, PRESIDENT
OF THE UNITED STATES, *et al.,*
Respondents.

MOTION FOR LEAVE TO FILE BRIEF AMICUS CURIAE

The attorneys for Richard M. Nixon having refused consent to the filing of this brief by the American Civil Liberties Union,* this Motion is filed pursuant to Rule 42.

The American Civil Liberties Union is a nationwide nonpartisan organization of more than 250,000 members devoted solely to the preservation of the liberties safeguarded by the Bill of Rights. For more than fifty years the ACLU has participated in hundreds of cases in this Court to advance individual liberties and to assure that governmental power is limited as required by the Constitution.

The case at bar involves profound issues concerning the power of the President to resist the processes of law. It is no exaggeration to state that this case presents the question whether the United States is a government of laws in which all citizens, including the President, are subject to the judicial process or whether the President can himself define the reach of the judicial and constitutional rules to which he is subject.

We believe that our brief, which examines the historical and judicial precedents concerning executive privilege, will be of substantial assistance to the court in the resolution of the issues in this case.

NORMAN DORSEN
Attorney for Movant

---

* The letter of consent from the Special Prosecutor has been filed with the Clerk of the Court.

SUPREME COURT OF THE UNITED STATES

OCTOBER TERM, 1973

No. 73-1766

UNITED STATES OF AMERICA,
Petitioner,

v.

RICHARD M. NIXON, PRESIDENT
OF THE UNITED STATES, *et al.,*
Respondents.

BRIEF AMICUS CURIAE OF THE
AMERICAN CIVIL LIBERTIES UNION

INTEREST OF AMICUS

The interest of *Amicus* is set out in the preceding Motion for Leave to File.

QUESTIONS PRESENTED

1.   Whether the President, when he has assumed sole personal and physical control over evidence demonstrably material to the trial of charges of obstruction of justice in a federal court, is subject to a judicial order directing compliance with a subpoena *duces tecum* issued on the application of the Special Prosecutor in the name of the United States.

2.   Whether a federal court is bound by the assertion by the President of an absolute "executive privilege" to withhold demonstrably material evidence from the trial of charges of obstruction of justice by his own White House aides and party leaders, upon the ground that he deems production to be against the public interest.

3.   Whether a claim of executive privilege based on the generalized interest in the confidentiality of government deliberations can block the prosecution's access to evidence material and important to the trial of charges of criminal misconduct by high government officials who participated in those deliberations, particularly where there is a *prima facie* showing that the deliberations occurred in the course of the criminal conspiracy charged in the indictment.

SUMMARY OF ARGUMENT

The President, like other citizens, is not above the law. It is the duty of the courts to determine what the law is and the obligation of every citizen to obey it. The Constitution contains no express privilege or immunity which places the President beyond the reach of compulsory judicial process, nor can one be inferred from the doctrine of separation of powers. For more than a century and a half the courts have reviewed the actions of all three branches of government, including actions by Presidents beyond their statutory or constitutional authority. Indeed, the tradition of holding the Executive accountable for his acts extends deep into our constitutional history, the English Crown having long been held to be subject to the process of the courts.

II

Since the acts of the President are subject to constitutional limitation and judicial review, the President has no authority solely in his discretion to withhold material evidence from a judicial proceeding, particularly a criminal trial. This Court and others have on several occasions reviewed claims of executive privilege to withhold information "in the public interest," while no court has ever recognized an absolute privilege of the kind advanced by the President in this case. Nor does the historical record, despite its ambiguities, support the President's position. Finally, the separation of powers is based not on isolation but on interaction of the three branches of government, each being subject to the checks and balances of the other two.

III

Whatever privilege concerning advisory communications may attach to the office of the presidency, it does not shield the occupant of that office from producing documentary material when there is substantial evidence that it relates to a crime. The unofficial acts of a President, such as conducting a political campaign or otherwise acting outside the scope of his official duties, certainly are not shielded from the scrutiny of a criminal proceeding. This Court has twice held in recent years that an explicit constitutional privilege protecting the speech or debate of Members of Congress may not be used to block criminal investigations, and it must now reject an assertion of presidential privilege with no similar constitutional basis but having the same result. Finally, the public has a right, derived in part from the

First Amendment, to obtain evidence relating to possible crimes committed by high elected officials, whom this Court has held necessarily enjoy fewer privileges than ordinary citizens in a representative democracy.

ARGUMENT

Introduction

There have been few comparable occurrences when this Court has been called upon to reaffirm a bedrock constitutional principle on which our society rests. The closest case is *Youngstown Sheet & Tube Company* v. *Sawyer*, 343 U.S. 579 (1959), where a President beset by heavy responsibility and an ongoing war, sought in manifest good faith to assure needed supplies of steel in order to protect American lives and property and to advance American foreign policy objectives. In a decision that has grown in stature and impact with the years, the Court rejected proffered theories of Executive "inherent power" and reasserted the Rule of Law as it applied to the President even in time of national emergency. See also *United States* v. *United States District Court*, 407 U.S. 297 (1972).

The case at bar presents comparable questions concerning the supremacy of law, although in a different legal and political context. As in the *Youngstown* case, there is no need to consider, much less impugn, the good faith of the President in order to insist with the utmost gravity that attempts to elevate the office of the President above the law as defined by this Court must be decisively rejected. The issue does not depend upon one's view of the current controversy embroiling the nation. It turns on the absolute necessity to preserve the constitutional balance. As Mr. Justice Jackson, concurring in *Youngstown*, observed:

"With all its defects, delays and inconveniences, men have discovered no techniques for long preserving free government except that the Executive be under the law and that the law be made by parliamentary deliberation." 343 U.S. at 655.

I. THE PRESIDENT IS NOT ABOVE THE LAW: HE IS SUBJECT TO JUDICIAL PROCESS

The fundamental issue raised in this case is whether the President, acting in his sole discretion, can disregard an obligation imposed on all other citizens to produce evidence demonstrably material to the trial of criminal charges of obstruction of justice in a federal court. Although the Constitution protects citizens from certain lines of inquiry and methods of gathering evidence in a criminal proceeding, the President does not invoke these protections; rather, he asserts an absolute immunity from any form of legal process.

There is no proposition more dangerous to the health of a constitutional democracy than the notion that an elected head of state is above the law and beyond the reach of judicial review. This proposition, currently advanced by the President, is a frontal attack on the elementary principle set forth by Chief Justice Marshall in *Marbury* v. *Madison*, 5 U.S. (1 Cranch) 137, 177 (1803): "It is emphatically the province and duty of the judicial department to say what the law is."

It is a basic premise of our constitutional government that the judiciary is to determine what the law is and that every citizen is subject to the law. It is inconceivable that a sweeping presidential immunity should arise merely out of implications drawn from custom, untried in the courts; in fact, no such custom exists. Equally basic to the Constitution is the idea that the Executive Branch must be subject to continuing scrutiny, lest, being the most powerful and vigorous, it encroach on the other branches. James Wilson expressed this sentiment to the Pennsylvania Ratification Convention:

> The executive power is better to be trusted when it has no screen. Sir, we have a responsibility in the person of our President; he cannot act improperly, and hide either his negligence or inattention; he cannot roll upon any other person the weight of his criminality . . . Add to all this, that officer is placed high, and is possessed of power far from being contemptible; yet not a *single privilege* is annexed to his character. 2 Elliot 480 (emphasis supplied).

Had the Framers intended to deviate from these principles of constitutional government, or had they wanted to grant novel immunities and privileges, they would have done so plainly and clearly. But nowhere in the Constitution of the United States is the President granted immunity from legal process.

There is ample precedent that the President must submit to compulsory process of the courts. In *United States* v. *Burr* 25 Fed. Cas. 30 (No. 14692d) (C.C.D. Va. 1807), Chief Justice Marshall ruled that a subpoena may be directed to the President. "That the President . . . might be subpoenaed and called upon to produce any paper which is in his possession, is not controverted, indeed that has once been decided." *T. Carpenter, The Trial of Colonel Aaron Burr* 37 (1807), cited in Berger, *The President, Congress, and the Courts*, 83 Yale L.J. 1111, 1117 (1974). Even counsel for President Jefferson in the *Burr* case admitted, "We do not think that the President is above legal process . . . and if the President possesses information of any nature which might tend to serve the cause of Aaron Burr, a subpoena should be issued to him, notwithstanding his elevated position." *Id.* at 75. George Hay, the United States Attorney in the *Burr* case, said:

> I never had the idea of clothing the President . . . with these attributes of divinity . . . That high officer is but a man; he is but a citizen; and, if he knows anything in any case civil or criminal, which might affect the life, liberty, or property of his fellow citizens . . . it is his duty to . . . go before a Court, and declare what he knows. *Id.* at 90-91.

Nor does the tripartite separation of powers imply presidential immunity from judicial process. As Mr. Justice Brandeis observed, dissenting in *Myers* v. *United States*, 272 U.S. 52, 293 (1926):

> The Doctrine of Separation of Powers was adopted by the Convention of 1787 not to promote efficiency but to preclude the exercise of arbitrary power. The purpose was, not to avoid friction, but, by means of the inevitable friction incident to the distribution of the governmental powers among three departments, to save the people from autocracy.

The Constitution provides that: "The judicial power of the United States shall be vested in one Supreme Court, and in such inferior Courts as the Congress may from time to time ordain and establish." U.S. Const. art. III, §1. To hold that the President is immune from judicial scrutiny would deny this express delegation of the judicial power to the courts; to base such a holding on the doctrine of separation of powers would defeat the purpose for which the doctrine was designed.[1]

Furthermore, if the notion of Presidential immunity is to be gleaned from the separation of powers, there are no grounds for distinguishing presidential claims of immunity from the claims of any other officer in the Executive or Legislative Branch. If immunity from judicial process is a necessary element of the doctrine of separation of powers, then a judicial order directed to a lesser executive officer or to an officer of the Congress would prove no less an interference. Yet, for the past century and a half, in the exercise of their duty "to say what the law is," courts

---

[1] As Madison observed: "It may always be expected that the judicial branch . . . will . . . most engage the respect and reliance of the public as the surest expositor of the Constitution, as well as in questions . . . concerning the boundaries between the several departments of the Government as in those between the Union and its members." 4 Letters and Writings of JAMES MADISON 340-50 (1867).

have reviewed the actions of all three branches of government. In a variety of notable cases, courts have invalidated the actions of Presidents (or Cabinet officers acting under presidential orders) as beyond their statutory or constitutional authority, e.g., *Youngstown Sheet & Tube Company* v. *Sawyer*, 343 U.S. 579 (1952); *United States* v. *United States District Court*, 407 U.S. 297 (1972), and having compelled presidents to perform the ministerial obligations of their office, *Marbury* v. *Madison, supra*, as well as their duties as citizens, *United States* v. *Burr, supra*.

Just as no grant of Presidential immunity can be inferred from the separation of powers, no other provision of the Constitution extends immunity from judicial process. While Senators and Representatives enjoy a limited immunity from inquiry concerning "Speech and Debate" on the floors of Congress, U.S. Const., art. I, §6, ¶1, the Constitution is silent as to any such privilege for the President. As Solicitor General Robert H. Bork recently stated: "Since the Framers knew how to, and did, spell out immunity, the natural inference is that no immunity exists where none is mentioned." Memorandum for the United States at 10, *Application of Spiro T. Agnew*, Civil No. 73-965 (D. Md.) cited in Berger, *The President, Congress, and the Courts*, 83 Yale L.J. 1111, 1125 (1974).

The long tradition of holding the President accountable for his acts is not limited to American constitutional history. Lord Coke in 1688 expressed the view, which was to dominate English political thought in the seventeenth century, that the King himself was "under . . . the laws." *Prohibitions del Roy*, 17 Eng. Rep. 1342 (1608). Nearly two centuries later this principle was being applied by the English courts to require the production of Crown documents relevant to civil as well as criminal litigation. For example, in an admiralty case involving a ship seized by British authorities in 1789, the shipowner was permitted to employ judicial process to obtain a secret order of the Privy Council relating to the Crown's seizure policy. In ordering production, the Court pointed out:

> In any cause where the Crown is a party, it is to be observed, that the Crown can no more withhold evidence of documents in its possession than a private person. If the court thinks proper to order the production of the documents, that order must be obeyed. *The Ship Columbus*, 1 Collectanae Juridica 88, 92 (1789), cited in Berger, *Executive Privilege* v. *Congressional Inquiry* (Part II), 12 U.C.L.A. L. Rev. 1287, 1294 (1965).

Summing up the constitutional history establishing judicial

review of executive action, the Supreme Court in *United States* v. *Lee*, 106 U.S. 196, 220 (1882), rejected an argument similar to the President's claim in this case:

No man in this country is so high that he is above the law. No officer of the law may set that law at defiance, with impunity. All the officers of the government, from the highest to the lowest, are the creatures of the law and are bound to obey it. It is the only supreme power in our system of government, and every man who by accepting office, participates in its functions, is only the more strongly bound to submit to that supremacy, and to observe the limitations which it imposes upon the exercise of the authority which it gives.

The Court should apply these settled principles to the case at bar.

II. THE DOCTRINE OF EXECUTIVE PRIVILEGE DOES NOT GIVE THE PRESIDENT UNREVIEWABLE DISCRETION TO WITHHOLD EVIDENCE IN THIS OR ANY OTHER CASE.

The precise issue presented by the President's assertion of executive privilege is whether the President has implied authority to withhold evidence from the Special Prosecutor *solely in his discretion*, or whether his decision to do so is subject to constitutional limitation and judicial review.

A. *Judicial Precedents Do Not Support the President's Claim of Privilege*

At the beginning, Chief Justice Marshall stated that, "[b]y the Constitution of the United States, the President is invested with certain important political powers, in the exercise of which he is to use his own discretion, and is accountable only to his country in his political character, and to his own conscience." *Marbury* v. *Madison*, 5 U.S. (1 Cranch) 135, 165 (1803). The Chief Justice nevertheless recognized the authority of the judiciary to review all acts not explicitly committed by the Constitution to executive discretion and to determine for itself which issues are precluded from judicial review. Such a determination is "peculiarly irksome, as well as delicate," but the task is mandated by the Constitution. 5 U.S. at 168-170.

Most invocations of executive privilege have involved presidential refusal to supply information to Congress. But the issue raised in this case by the President's refusal to submit to the process of the courts with respect to the tapes sought by the Special Prosecutor should be treated in the same way as would a presidential refusal to supply such material to Congress. In both cases the central question is whether the President has an unreviewable power to withhold from another branch of government any information he deems privileged.

There is no need for the Court to address the broad question of whether or not the privilege which the President claims has some basis in law.[2] Rather, "the issue is whether the President has the implied authority under the Constitution to withhold data from Congress [and the courts] *solely in his discretion*, or whether his decision to do so is subject to constitutional limitation and judicial review." Dorsen and Shattuck, *Executive Privilege, the Congress and the Courts*, 35 OHIO ST.L.J. 1, 11 (1974) (emphasis in original.)[3]

The Supreme Court has not yet spoken squarely on the issue. But lower court rulings and statements by this Court reinforce the conclusion that the President cannot be the final arbiter of the so-called "executive privilege."

In *Committee for Nuclear Responsibility, Inc.* v. *Seaborg*, 463 F.2d 788,793 (D.C. Cir. 1971), the Court of Appeals considered and rejected a claim of absolute privilege: "Any claim to executive absolutism cannot override the duty of the court to assure that an official has not exceeded his charter or flouted the legislative will." Following that decision, the Court of Appeals in *Nixon* v. *Sirica*, 487 F.2d 700, 713 (D.C. Cir. 1973) stated:

> [C]ounsel for the President can point to no case in which a court has accepted the Executive's mere assertion of privilege as sufficient to overcome the need of the party subpoenaing the documents. To the contrary, the courts have repeatedly asserted that the applicability of the privilege is in the end for them and not the Executive to decide.

---

[2] Professor Raoul Berger maintains that "executive privilege . . . is a myth . . . , a product of the nineteenth century, fashioned by a succession of presidents who created 'precedents' to suit the occasion." R. BERGER, *Executive Privilege: A Constitutional Myth* 1 (1974). Berger searches the Constitution, history and laws and finds no such justification for executive privilege.

[3] President Nixon, while a Member of Congress, made the following point:
I am now going to address myself to an issue which is very important. The point has been made that the President of the United States has issued an order that none of this information can be released to the Congress and that therefore the Congress has no right to question the judgment of the President in making that decision.
I say that proposition cannot stand from a constitutional standpoint or on the basis of the merits for this very good reason: That would mean that the President could have arbitrarily issued an Executive Order in the Meyers case, the Teapot Dome case, or any other case denying the Congress of the United States information it needed to conduct an investigation of the executive department and the Congress would have no right to question his decision.
Any such order of the President can be questioned by the Congress as to whether or not that order is justified on the merits. Cong. Rec. 4783 (April 22, 1948).

Judicial authority to compel evidence from the President is grounded in its power to issue mandatory orders to officers of the Executive Branch. Issuance of such orders has, on occasion, required a determination of the limits of the President's authority under the Constitution. Mr. Justice Frankfurter, concurring in *Youngstown Sheet and Tube Company* v. *Sawyer*, 343 U.S. at 596, pointed to the necessity of such a determination: "To deny inquiry into the President's power in a case like this, because of the damage to the public interest to be feared from upsetting its exercise by him, would in effect always preclude inquiry into challenged power, which presumably only avowed great public interest brings into action."

While the President himself is a party to this action, in *Youngstown* the Secretary of Commerce was the named defendant. This is obviously but a formal distinction. The decision in *Youngstown* effectively restrained the President; it affirmed a District Court order enjoining an action ordered by President Truman claimed to be authorized by the Constitution. As the Court of Appeals noted in *Nixon* v. *Sirica*, 487 F.2d at 709: "[T]he practice of judicial review would be rendered capricious and very likely impotent—if jurisdiction vanished whener the President personally denoted an executive action or omission as his own."

The extent to which the *Burr* case recognizes a right of "executive privilege" is currently being debated. There is no doubt, however, that the decision rejects the claim of discretionary presidential power of the kind advanced here. In his opinion Chief Justice Marshall stated:

> Whatever difference may exist with respect to the power to compel the same obedience to the process, as if it had been directed to a private citizen, there exists no difference with respect to the right to obtain it. The guard, furnished to this high officer to protect him from being harassed by vexatious and unnecessary subpoenas, is to be looked for in the conduct of a court after these subpoenas have issued, not in any circumstance which is to precede their being issued. *United States* v. *Burr* 25 Fed Cas at 34.

Thus, while the President should be protected from harassment, his protection emanates from the courts: the office of the Presidency—although the highest and most powerful in the land—is not itself a shield from judicial process, nor should it be in any government of laws.

In *United States* v. *Reynolds*, 345 U.S. 1 (1953), where there was a conceded need to protect the Executive from potentially damaging effects flowing from the possible discovery of military secrets, the Court held, "the [trial] court itself must determine whether the circumstances are appropriate for the claim of privilege . . . ," 345 U.S. at 8, because "[j]udicial control over the evidence in a case cannot be abdicated to the caprice of executive officers." *Id.* at 9-10. Even a compelling claim involving secret weapons, therefore, cannot provide immunity from the judicial process where the Constitution is silent.

While a claim of absolute Presidential immunity from judicial process has not been previously raised before this Court, there is a substantial body of law holding that the courts will require the production of departmental records and papers under appropriate circumstances, including copies of documents prepared for the President. One such case is *Environmental Protection Agency* v. *Mink*, 410 U.S. 73, 93 (1973), in which the Court stated that, pursuant to the Freedom of Information Act, the District Court "may order" an *in camera* inspection of unclassified documents to determine whether and to what extent they are subject to the requirements of the Act. Although the Court in *Mink* recognized, as it did in *Reynolds, supra*, that the national interest in safeguarding military secrets may bar certain documents and materials from discovery, whatever privilege exists results from the application of rules that are judicially or legislatively determined. There is, in short, no judicial support for the breathtaking claims of the President in this case.

B. *The Historical Record Does Not Support the President's Position*

While the historical record is at times ambiguous, and therefore open to varying interpretations, compare *Nixon* v. *Sirica*, 487 F.2d 700 (majority opinion), with 487 F.2d at 731-37 (MacKinnon, J., dissenting), it emphatically does not sustain an unreviewable presidential power to withhold information from Congress or the courts.

One of the dissenting opinions in *Nixon* v. *Sirica*, 487 F.2d at 778, correctly points. out that "[t]hroughout this nation's 184-year Constitutional history, Congress and the Executive have succeeded in avoiding any near-fatal confrontation over attempts by Congress to procure documents in the Executive's possession." The absence of such a clash indicates that presidents have refrained from asserting the extraordinary power that is claimed here. The pattern was set by President Washington, who at least once questioned the authority of Congress to demand documents, but eventually complied with congressional requests and never directly confronted Congress with a discretionary refusal to disclose. The one denial by Washington of a request for information—a demand by the House of Representatives for all papers relating to the negotiation of the Jay Treaty—was based on the President's correct conclusion that the House lacked power under the Constitution to demand information relating to the making of treaties. Washington conceded, however, that the Senate could receive the documents.[4]

It is true that during the early presidencies a congressional practice developed of extending to the President an implied "privilege" to withhold certain investigative reports and state secrets from public disclosure. Where the offer extended by Congress was accepted by the President and documents were withheld, however, the arrangement was generally recognized as an accommodation rather than the exercise of an unreviewable presidential power.[5] When Jefferson declined, for example, to produce certain information on the Burr conspiracy in 1807, he was acting upon a House request that expressly excepted "such [information] as he may deem the public welfare to require not to be disclosed."[6] This congressional accommodation, of course, did not exempt Jefferson from compulsory judicial process. See *United States* v. *Burr, supra.*

The historical record, therefore, is at best ambiguous and of no help in supporting the President's claims in this case. As one recent commentator has observed, the post-1787 precedents "bear all of the earmarks of their essential character as political compromises, and thus yield no unitary conception of the Constitutional basis of a privilege."[7]

---

[4] See Berger, *Executive Privilege* v. *Congressional Inquiry,* 12 U.C.L.A. L. Rev. 1043, 1079-80, 1089-93 (1965).

[5] When this "accommodation" broke down, as it did on one occasion during the presidency of Andrew Jackson in 1835, Congress found it appropriate to apply sanctions against the Executive, by, for example, refusing to confirm a presidential nominee. *Id.* at 1095.

[6] Quoted in Mem. of Atty. Gen. William Rogers, submitted to Subcomm. on Constitutional Rights of the Comm. on the Judiciary, United States Senate, 85th Cong., 2nd Sess. (1958), reprinted in 44 A.B.A.J. 941, 944 (1958).

[7] Frohnmayer, "An Essay on Executive Privilege" (ABA Samuel Pool Weaver Constitutional Law Prize Essay for 1974) reprinted in Cong. Rec. 56603 (April 30, 1974) (daily ed.).

C. The Privilege Does Not Inhere
in the Doctrine of the Separation of Powers

In the absence of historical or judicial support for the President's claim of unreviewable power to withhold information from the Congress and the courts, we turn again to the President's argument that such a privilege is necessary to protect the power of the Executive and is therefore required by the doctrine of separation of powers.

Proponents of the President's interpretation of the doctrine of separation of powers argue that if the judicial branch can "coerce" the Chief Executive into surrendering documents and records, "then the Chief Executive is no longer 'master in his own house.' " *Nixon* v. *Sirica*, 487 F.2d at 769 (Wilkey, J., dissenting). This argument is defective on several grounds.

First, it is equally true that if the Special Prosecutor cannot obtain evidence necessary and material to a criminal proceeding because the President asserts an unreviewable executive privilege, the judicial branch is not master in *its* house.

There is a broader perspective on the separation of powers issue. As Hamilton stated, each branch must be given "the necessary constitutional means and personal motives to resist encroachments of the others." Federalist No. 51 at 337. These means and motives preserve a dynamic balance between the three departments. Congress has the power to make appropriations, to vest jurisdiction in the courts and to determine the procedures by which they operate, and to impose legal duties on the Executive. The President has the power to veto congressional action and the power to appoint the officers of the judicial branch. The courts play their constitutional role by checking unconstitutional action on the part of any branch. Thus, *no* branch is entirely "master in its own house." Each branch is subject to checks and balances from the others, and the separation of powers depends on interaction, not isolation. See *Myers* v. *United States*, 272 U.S. at 293 (Brandeis, J., dissenting).

Furthermore, separation of powers was often seen by the Framers as a safeguard against encroachment by the *Executive*. Charles Pinckney, commenting on the express congressional privilege from arrest, said:

. . . They [the Framers] well knew how oppressively the power of undefined privileges had been exercised in Great Britain, and were determined no such authority should be exercised here . . . . Let us inquire why the Constitution should have been so attentive to each branch of Congress . . . . and have shown so little to the President . . .

In this respect no privilege of this kind was intended for our Executive, nor any except that which I have mentioned for your Legislature. 3 Farrand 385.

Having no foundation in law or history, and not being a necessary and explicit element of the doctrine of separation of powers, the President's claim to an unreviewable executive privilege to withhold data from Congress and the courts must be rejected as a dangerous fiction and inconsistent with the rule of law.

III. EXECUTIVE PRIVILEGE CANNOT BE INVOKED TO DEFEAT A SUBPOENA FOR DOCUMENTARY MATERIAL WHEN THERE IS SUBSTANTIAL EVIDENCE THAT IT RELATES TO A CRIME.

If the President is subject to judicial process and "the court itself must determine whether the circumstances are appropriate for the claim of privilege . . . ," *United States* v. *Reynolds*, 345 U.S. at 8, the only remaining question is whether any such claim can withstand judicial scrutiny where the material sought is essential to a criminal prosecution. The only claim of privilege that has any arguable relevance to the subject of this case involves the President's asserted power to withhold materials relating to internal advice within the Executive Branch.[8] We urge that whatever privilege may attach to the office of the Presidency, it does not shield the occupant of that office from producing documentary evidence essential to a criminal trial.[9]

The principle that every citizen has the duty to give evidence is fundamental in Anglo-American law. Mr. Justice White recently asserted " . . . the longstanding principle that the public . . . has a right to every man's evidence except for those persons protected by a constitutional, common law, or statutory privilege. . . . " *Branzburg* v. *Hayes*, 408 U.S. 665, 668 (1972.)[10] The President is not protected in this case by any such

---

[8] See Dorsen and Shattuck, *Executive Privilege, the Congress and the Courts*, 35 Ohio St. L.J. 1, 29-33 (1974).

[9] The Court in this case need not decide what the constitutional privilege should be if (a) the President were subpoenaed personally, or (b) the evidence sought were not material to a fair trial.

[10] A footnote in Mr. Justice White's majority opinion in *Branzburg*, quoting from Jeremy Bentham, vividly illustrates why (408 U.S. at 688):
. . . Were the Prince of Wales, the Archbishop of Canterbury, and the Lord High Chancellor, to be passing by in the same coach while a chimney sweeper and a barrow-woman were in dispute about a halfpenny worth of apples, and the chimney

"constitutional" privilege. There is undoubtedly a principle to be served in protecting the internal decisionmaking process of each branch of government. The justification for this principle is that the development of public policy may be inhibited if individuals in government cannot rely on the confidentiality of their communicated opinions. See, e.g., *Soucie* v. *David*, 448 F.2d 1067, 1080-81 (D.C. Cir. 1971).

The proper scope of an "advice privilege" which may be asserted by the President, subject to judicial review, is as follows:

1. The privilege may be claimed (only by the President personally) with respect to recommendations, advice and suggestions passed on by members of the Executive Branch acting under lawful authority for consideration in formulation of policy. See *Environmental Protection Agency* v. *Mink*, 410 U.S. at 85-89; *Ethyl Corporation* v. *Environmental Protection Agency*, 478 F.2d 47, 51-52 (4th Cir. 1973).

2. The privilege may not be asserted with respect to what has been *done*, as distinct from what has been advised. The President is accountable for his actions and for decisions that he has made leading to action by others. See, e.g., *Grumman Aircraft Engineering Corporation* v. *Renegotiation Board*, 482 F.2d 710, 718-19 (D.C. Cir. 1973).[11]

Whatever the effect of an "advice privilege" in other circumstances, there is no justification for confidentiality when there is substantial evidence that the communications at issue themselves may relate to a crime, such as obstruction of justice. "There is obviously an overriding policy justification for this position, since the opposite view would permit criminal conspiracies at the seat of government to be shrouded by the veil of an advice privilege." Dorsen and Shattuck, *Executive Privilege, the Congress and the Courts*, 35 OHIO ST. L.J. 1, 32 (1974).

This Court has recently underscored its impatience with claims of *explicit constitutional privilege*, based on the separation of powers, when that privilege is used to block investigations concerning "possible third party crimes." In *Gravel* v. *United States*, 408 U.S. 606 (1972), the Court held that Senator Gravel's assistant could be compelled to testify about the publication of

---

sweeper or the barrow-woman were to think proper to call upon them for their evidence, could they refuse it? No, most certainly not. 4 *The Works of Jeremy Bentham* 320-21 (1843).

[11] To the extent there is a privilege protecting certain aspects of the Presidency from public view, ". . . it should extend at most to official acts, not to unofficial acts of a candidate campaigning with the aid of a Reelection Committee that, according to testimony, sought to corrupt the election." R. Berger, *Executive Privilege: A Constitutional Myth* 261 (1974).

the Pentagon papers, which Gravel himself had read on the Senate floor. Mr. Justice White, writing for the majority, stated that even the Senator could be interrogated by a grand jury if his sources of information related to crime, since the Constitution "provides no protection for criminal conduct threatening the security of the person or property of others . . . " 408 U.S. at 622.

A similar result was reached in *United States* v. *Brewster*, 408 U.S. 501 (1972), a case involving a claim of immunity by former Senator Daniel Brewster of Maryland, who was prosecuted for having received a bribe to influence his action on postal legislation. The Court of Appeals had held that the indictment was invalid because it put into question a Senator's constitutionally protected motives for legislative action, but the Supreme Court reversed on the ground that "[t]aking a bribe is, obviously, no part of the legislative process or function." 408 U.S. at 526.

Gravel and *Brewster* appear to foreclose any claim by the President that his taped conversations concerning alleged criminal activities in the White House are covered by a privilege for "advisory communications," because in those cases the Court was dealing with the *explicit* constitutional immunity granted by Article I, Section 6. But there is no such specific immunity based on executive privilege. It is, therefore, all the more plain that the privilege, whatever its reach, does not permit the President to withhold information concerning criminal conduct.

Similarly, it is plain that a common law privilege may be outweighed by the exigencies of a criminal prosecution. In *United States* v. *Clark*, 289 U.S. 1, 16 (1933), the Court held that upon showing of a prima facie case that a jury was tainted, the interest in confidential jury proceedings was outweighed by "the overmastering need, so vital in our polity, of preserving trial by jury in its purity against the inroads of corruption." The privilege fell and "the debates and ballots in the jury room" became admissible in evidence. 289 U.S. at 14. The indictment in the instant case of several parties to alleged conversations recorded on the tapes subpoenaed by the Special Prosecutor easily meets the *Clark* standard of a "prima facie showing."

On May 22, 1973, before the existence of the White House tapes became known, the President issued a statement which accurately and succinctly summarized the law: "Executive privilege will not be invoked as to any testimony concerning possible criminal conduct or discussions of possible criminal

518

conduct, in the matters under investigation."[12] This Court should hold the President to his earlier correct position.

Apart from the President's duty, in common with all citizens, to give evidence in a criminal proceeding, the public has a right to obtain the evidence, particularly when it relates to possible crimes committed by high elected officials. This right derives in part from the First Amendment, the primary purpose of which is to insure that citizens are informed about the activities of their government. It is axiomatic that a free flow of information is essential to democratic self-government.[13]

A corollary of this axiom is the duty of high elected officials, and the President in particular, to account fully to the electorate for their actions. As Mr. Justice Black emphasized, concurring in *New York Times Company* v. *Sullivan*, 376 U.S. 254, 257 (1964), "a representative democracy ceases to exist the minute that the public functionaries are by any means absolved from their responsibility to their constituents" (quoting Blackstone). Indeed, *Sullivan* affirmed the principle that elected officials enjoy fewer privileges than ordinary citizens. It is for this reason that the Court has pointed out that the First Amendment is rooted in the struggle "to establish and preserve the right of the English people to full information in respect to the doings and misdoings of their government." *Grosjean* v. *American Press Company*, 233 U.S. 245, 247 (1936).

While we realize that a criminal proceeding is not primarily a vehicle for informing the public, when the President withholds evidence needed for the prosecution, he frustrates the principle that when criminal charges are made, "society's interest is best served by a thorough and extensive investigation . . . " *Wood* v. *Georgia*, 370 U.S. 375, 392 (1962). As the Court of Appeals for the District of Columbia has stated, if an unqualified executive power to withhold information is sustained by the judicial branch, "the head of an executive department would have the power on his own say so to cover up all evidence of fraud and corruption when a federal court or grand jury was investigating malfeasance in office, and this is not the law." *Committee for Nuclear Responsibility, Inc.* v. *Seaborg, supra,* at 794. See also *Nixon* v. *Sirica,* 487 F.2d at 714.

---

[12] New York Times, May 23, 1973.

[13] Among the many recognitions of this principle throughout our history is the statement by Patrick Henry that, "the liberties of the people never were . . . secure when the transactions of their rulers may be concealed from them." 3 Elliot 170.

CONCLUSION

For the reasons stated above the decision of the District Court should be affirmed.

Respectfully submitted,

NORMAN DORSEN
New York University Law School
40 Washington Square South
New York, New York 10012

MELVIN L. WULF
JOHN H. F. SHATTUCK
American Civil Liberties Union
22 East 40th Street
New York, New York 10016

Attorneys for Amicus Curiae

June 21, 1974

XI
THE ORAL ARGUMENT
IN
UNITED STATES
v.
NIXON

The oral argument before the Supreme Court took place before a packed courtroom. Some spectators had waited for days for the few public seats available. One correspondent wrote that the "echoes of history" were there as the lawyers and Justices argued about the meaning of Marbury v. Madison and "issues of final power in the American system." The oral argument settled a few issues almost immediately. Justice Douglas questioned Mr. Jaworski at once about the relevancy of the fact that the grand jury had named the President as an unindicted co-conspirator. Justice Stewart picked up the point, and it became apparent that the Supreme Court did not have to pass on that issue at all in determining whether the tapes had to be produced. Eventually the Supreme Court refused to consider the question. In addition some of the arguments which seemed reasonable on paper could not withstand the searching questions of the Justices. At one point Mr. St. Clair said that it was important for the President to be able to get candid communications from anyone, particularly when he was considering Presidential appointments, such as judges. Immediately Justice Marshall asked him what would *happen if a lawyer tried to bribe the President to appoint him as a judge. Mr. St. Clair said that he should be impeached. But Justice Marshall continued, "How are you going to impeach him if you don't know about it?" Mr. St. Clair had to admit that nothing could be done if the information was not available. Justice Marshall pointed out: "If you know the President is doing something wrong, you can impeach him; but the only way you can find out [is by a subpoena; therefore] you can't impeach him, so you don't impeach him." His final comment was "You lose me some place along there." The argument that follows shows the Court acting not only as the final court in the criminal justice system but as the ultimate Constitutional arbiter with the final say on how power is distributed between the three separate arms of government.*

IN THE SUPREME COURT OF THE UNITED STATES

OCTOBER TERM, 1973

No. 73—1766

UNITED STATES OF AMERICA, PETITIONER

v.

RICHARD M. NIXON, PRESIDENT OF THE UNITED STATES,
ET AL., RESPONDENTS

No. 73—1834

RICHARD M. NIXON, PRESIDENT OF THE UNITED STATES,

PETITIONER

v.

UNITED STATES OF AMERICA

Washington, D. C.
Monday, July 8, 1974

The above-entitled matters came on for argument at 10:02
o'clock a.m.

BEFORE:

WARREN E. BURGER, Chief Justice of the United States
WILLIAM O. DOUGLAS, Associate Justice
WILLIAM J. BRENNAN, JR., Associate Justice
POTTER STEWART, Associate Justice
BYRON R. WHITE, Associate Justice
THURGOOD MARSHALL, Associate Justice
HARRY A. BLACKMUN, Associate Justice
LEWIS F. POWELL, JR., Associate Justice

APPEARANCES:

LEON JAWORSKI, ESQ., Special Prosecutor, Watergate Special Prosecution Force, Department of Justice, Washington,

D.C. 20005; and

PHILIP A. LACOVARA, ESQ., Counsel to the Special Prosecutor, Watergate Special Prosecution Force, Department of Justice, 1425 K Street, N.W., Washington, D.C. 20005; for the United States.

JAMES D. ST. CLAIR, ESQ., The White House, Washington, D.C., 20500, for the President.

PROCEEDINGS

CHIEF JUSTICE BURGER: We will hear arguments in No. 73—1766, The United States of America against Nixon; and Richard M. Nixon against the United States.

Mr. Jaworski, there has been a request for additional time, and the Court grants that additional time of one-half-hour, I understand. Is that correct?

MR. JAWORSKI: That is correct, sir.

CHIEF JUSTICE BURGER: That will be allowed to each side. And we will not interrupt the argument with any recess. We will go right through until you have finished.

You may proceed whenever you are ready, Mr. Jaworski.

ORAL ARGUMENT ON LEON JAWORSKI, ESQ.,
ON BEHALF OF THE UNITED STATES

MR. JAWORSKI: Mr. Chief Justice, and may it please the Court: On March 1 last, a United States District Court Grand Jury, sitting here, returned an indictment against seven defendants charging various offenses, including among them a conspiracy to defraud the United States, and also to obstruct justice.

John Mitchell, one of the defendants, was a former Attorney General of the United States, and also chairman of the Committee to Re-Elect the President. Another, H. R. Haldeman, was the President's Chief of Staff. Another, John Ehrlichman, was Assistant to the President for Domestic Affairs. The others were either on the President's staff or held responsible positions on the Re-Election Committee.

In the course of its deliberations, the grand jury voted unanimously with nineteen members concurring, that the course of events in the formation and continuation of a conspiracy was such that President Nixon, among a number of others, should be identified as an unindicted co-conspirator in the bill of particulars to be filed in connection with the pre-trial proceedings.

Now, although this particular decision and determination on the part of the grand jury occurred in February, it was a

well-kept secret for two-and-a-half months. The grand jury, of course, knew it; the members of the prosecution staff knew it.

It was done so to avoid affecting the proceedings in the House Judiciary Committee.

And it was so kept during these two-and-a-half months until it became necessary to reveal it as a result of the President's motion to quash the subpoena, as I will indicate subsequently in my argument.

Now, to obtain additional evidence, which the Special Prosecutor has good reason to believe is in the possession of and under the control of the President, and which it is believed by the Special Prosecutor is quite important to the development of the Government's proof in the trial in United States v. Mitchell et al, the Special Prosecutor, on behalf of the United States, moved for a subpoena duces tecum. And it is the subpoena here in question.

The district court ordered the subpoena to issue, returnable on May 2. And the subpoena, of course, called for the production of tape recordings in advance of September 9, 1974, which is the trial date. This was done to allow time for litigation in the event litigation was to ensue over the production of the tapes. And also for transcription and authentication of any tape recordings that were produced in response to the subpoena.

Now, on April 30 the President released to the public and submitted to the House Judiciary Committee 1,216 pages of edited transcripts of 43 conversations dealing with Watergate. Portions of 20 of the subpoenaed conversations were included among the 43. Then on May 1, by his counsel, the President filed a special appearance, a formal claim of privilege and a motion to quash the subpoena.

Now, for the United States to conduct a full and appropriate hearing on the motion to quash the subpoena, it became necessary to reveal the grand jury's finding regarding the President. And this was first done by the Special Prosecutor calling on the Chief of Staff, General Alexander Haig, and the President's counsel, Mr. St. Clair, and advising them of what had occurred two-and-a-half months prior. And then on the following morning advising Judge Sirica of what had occurred, in camera, and pointing out the necessity of this being used in connection with the arguments on a motion to quash because of their relevance and the necessity of these matters being made a part of the proceedings.

Now, the Special Prosecutor joined counsel for the President in urging that the matter be heard in camera, which was done. Three of the defendants had joined the Special Prosecutor in

moving for the subpoena. All of the defendants, at the time of argument in camera to Judge Sirica, opposed the motion to quash.

JUSTICE DOUGLAS: I don't see the relevancy of the fact that the grand jury indicted the President as co-conspirator to the legal issue as to the duty to deliver pursuant to the subpoena that you are asking for.

MR. JAWORSKI: The only relevance, Mr. Justice, lies in it being necessary to show, under Rule 17(c), that there is some relevance to the material that we seek to subpoena.

JUSTICE WHITE: Rule 17(c) presupposes the subpoena running against the party. The President is not a party. He is not a defendant in one of these cases.

MR. JAWORSKI: That is correct, sir. But it was also felt that it would be necessary to show why, in order to prove this conspiracy, and in order to provide all of the links in the conspiracy — it was deemed necessary to show that the President was named as an unindicted co-conspirator and also that this —

QUESTION: I thought that was primarily just for the knowledge, information, of the House Judiciary Committee.

MR. JAWORSKI: No, sir. That is not correct, sir. It became very important, Mr. Justice, for us to have that as a part of the proceedings so that we could use the various links in the testimony so as to show that the conversations were such as to make one admissible as against a co-conspirator.

QUESTION: The grand jury sent it to the House Committee, didn't they?

MR. JAWORSKI: The grand jury sent nothing of an accusatory nature to the House Committee, no, sir. What the grand jury sent to the House Committee was the evidence that had been accumulated, and it very carefully excised from it anything by way of the grand jury's interpretation or anything along that line, Mr. Justice.

Now, in its Opinion and Order of May 20, the district court —

JUSTICE STEWART: You would be here, Mr. Jaworski, whether or not the President had been named as an indicted co-conspirator. That simply gives you another string to your bow —— isn't that about it?

MR. JAWORSKI: It is true that it admits some evidence that would otherwise not be admissible.

JUSTICE STEWART: Right. But even had the President not been named, you would still have subpoenaed at least part of this material.

MR. JAWORSKI: There is no question about that.

JUSTICE STEWART: And you would still be here.

MR. JAWORSKI: That is right, sir. But in order to present the full picture, and in order to present —— that also is a part of it.

The district court denied the motion to quash and a motion to expunge that had also been filed.

QUESTION: No one yet has ever suggested that during a criminal trial, a conspiracy trial, and some evidence is offered of an out-of-court statement, of someone who is alleged to be a co-conspirator, that it is enough for the prosecution to then show that the grand jury had named him a co-conspirator.

MR. JAWORSKI: No.

QUESTION: That will never get you over your ——

MR. JAWORSKI: And we don't so contend.

QUESTION: That was the direction of your —

MR. JAWORSKI: No. This was in connection with the subpoenaing of this evidence, Mr. Justice. In other words this was in connection with showing that we have the right to this evidence.

QUESTION: I understand that.

MR. JAWORSKI: Yes, sir.

QUESTION: But you do not suggest that that is all you need to show, is that it?

MR. JAWORSKI: No, sir. Of course not.

JUSTICE BRENNAN: You don't suggest that the grand jury finding is binding on the Court or not?

MR. JAWORSKI: I do suggest that it makes a prima facie case. And I think under the authorities, it so does.

JUSTICE BRENNAN: Let me understand this, Mr. Jaworski. You don't suggest that your right to this evidence depends upon the President having been named as an unindicted co-conspirator.

MR. JAWORSKI: No, sir.

JUSTICE BRENNAN: And so for the purposes of our decision, we can just lay that fact aside, could we?

MR. JAWORSKI: What I was really doing in pointing to that—

JUSTICE BRENNAN: Well, could we?

MR. JAWORSKI: Yes. Primarily, it was in order to show a reason for the grand jury's action. There is also before this Court a motion to expunge the act of a grand jury in naming the President as an unindicted co-conspirator. And I was trying to lay before the Court the entire situation that warranted that action.

JUSTICE POWELL: Mr. Jaworski, as I understand your brief you go beyond what you have addressed so far. I think you say that the mere fact that the President was named as an unindicted co-conspirator forecloses his claim of privilege.

MR. JAWORSKI: Well, we certainly —

JUSTICE POWELL: That is one of the points in your brief.

MR. JAWORSKI: We certainly make that as one of the points which I intend to discuss at a later point.

JUSTICE POWELL: That reduces him in and of itself to the status of any other person accused of a crime?

MR. JAWORSKI: I don't say that it forecloses. What I think we suggest is that it does present a situation here that should not make the application of executive privilege appropriate. We do say that.

JUSTICE MARSHALL: But only prima facie.

MR. JAWORSKI: Prima facie — that is correct. But when you get to the matter, Mr. Justice Powell, of balancing interests, we do feel that that particular situation is a factor that is important. And this is why we lay stress on it.

The Court's order, of course, was to deliver the originals of all subpoenaed items, as well as an index and an analysis of those items, together with tape copies of those portions of the subpoenaed recordings for which transcripts had been released to the public by the President on April 30.

Now, this case presents for review the action of the lower court.

Now, may I, before I get to the jurisdictional points, briefly state what we consider to be a bird's eye view of this case.

Now enmeshed in almost 500 pages of briefs, when boiled down, this case really presents one fundamental issue. Who is to be the arbiter of what the Constitution says? Basically this is not a novel question — although the factual situation involved is, of course, unprecedented.

There are corollary questions, to be sure. But in the end, after the rounds have been made, we return to face these glaring facts that I want to briefly review for a final answer.

In refusing to produce the evidence sought by a subpoena duces tecum in the criminal trial of the seven defendants — among them former chief aides and devotees — the President invokes the provisions of the Constitution. His counsel's brief is replete with references to the Constitution as justifying his position. And in his public statements, as we all know, the President has embraced the Constitution as offering him support for his refusal to supply the subpoenaed tapes.

Now, the President may be right in how he reads the Constitution. But he may also be wrong. And if he is wrong, who is there to tell him so? And if there is no one, then the President, of course, is free to pursue his course of erroneous interpretations. What then becomes of our constitutional form of government?

So when counsel for the President in his brief states that this case goes to the heart of our basic constitutional system, we agree. Because in our view, this nation's constitutional form of government is in serious jeopardy if the President, any President, is to say that the Constitution means what he says it does, and that there is no one, not even the Supreme Court, to tell him otherwise.

JUSTICE STEWART: Mr. Jaworski, the President went to a court. He went to the district court with his motion to quash. And then he filed a cross-petition here. He is asking the Court to say that his position is correct as a matter of law, is he not?

MR. JAWORSKI: He is saying his position is correct because he interprets the Constitution that way.

JUSTICE STEWART: Right. He is submitting his position to the Court and asking us to agree with it. He went first to the district court, and he has petitioned in this Court. He has himself invoked the judicial process. And he has submitted to it.

MR. JAWORSKI: Well, that is not entirely correct, Mr. Justice.

JUSTICE STEWART: Didn't he file a motion to quash the subpoenas in the district court of the United States?

MR. JAWORSKI: Sir, he has also taken the position that we have no standing in this Court to have this issue heard.

JUSTICE STEWART: As a matter of law —— he is making that argument to a court; that as a matter of constitutional law he is correct.

MR. JAWORSKI: So that of course this Court could then not pass upon the constitutional question of how he interprets the Constitution, if his position were correct. But I ——

JUSTICE STEWART: As a matter of law — his position is that he is the sole judge. And he is asking this Court to agree with that proposition, as a matter of constitutional law.

MR. JAWORSKI: What I am saying is that if he is the sole judge, and if he is to be considered the sole judge, and he is in error in his interpretation, then he goes on being in error in his interpretation.

JUSTICE STEWART: Then this Court will tell him so. That is what this case is about, isn't it?

MR. JAWORSKI: Well, that is what I think the case is about, yes, sir.

CHIEF JUSTICE BURGER: He is submitting himself to the judicial process in the same sense that you are, is that not so, Mr. Jaworski?

MR. JAWORSKI: Well, I can't ——

CHIEF JUSTICE BURGER: You take one position and he takes another.

MR. JAWORSKI: Well, Mr. Chief Justice, in my view, frankly, it is a position where he says the Constitution says this, "and nobody is going to tell me what the Constitution says." Because up to this point he says that he and he alone is the proper one to interpret the Constitution. Now, there is no way to escape that. Because the briefs definitely point that out, time after time.

QUESTION: I think this matter may be one of semantics. Each of you is taking a different position on the basic question, and each of you is submitting for a decision to this Court.

MR. JAWORSKI: That may be, sir.

JUSTICE DOUGLAS: Well, we start with a Constitution that does not contain the words "executive privilege," is that right?

MR. JAWORSKI: That is right, sir.

JUSTICE DOUGLAS: So why don't we go on from there?

MR. JAWORSKI: All right, sir. That is a very good beginning point. But of course there are other things that need to be discussed inasmuch as they have been raised.

CHIEF JUSTICE BURGER: Perhaps we can further narrow the area if, as I take from your briefs, you do emphasize there is no claim here of typical military secrets, or diplomatic secrets, or what in the Burr case were referred to as state secrets. None of those things are in this case, is that right?

MR. JAWORSKI: That is correct, sir. And we do point to the authorities to show that there is a difference in the situation here. I do think that it is proper, as much as I regret to have to do it, to point out that the President's interpretation of what his action should be in this particular set of circumstances is one that really requires judicial intervention perhaps more so than a normal one would. I think that we realize that there is at stake the matter of the supplying of evidence that relates to two former close aides and devotees. I think we are aware of the fact that the President has publicly stated that he believed that these two aides of his, Mr. Haldeman and Mr. Ehrlichman, would come out all right in the end. Added to that the fact that the President has a sensitivity of his own involvement, is also a matter that calls for the exercise of the question to which Mr. Justice Douglas alluded as one that is somewhat unusual.

Turning now to juristiction —— before the Court are the two questions of statutory jurisdiction the Court directed the parties to brief and argue.

JUSTICE BLACKMUN: Mr. Jaworski, at this point, help me over one hurdle. Do you feel that the mandamus case as such is here?

MR. JAWORSKI: Yes, we do, sir.

JUSTICE BLACKMUN: I search your petition for certiorari in vain to find even a mention of it. And I wondered if it is a political question. What is your position —— that the issues in any event are here?

MR. JAWORSKI: Yes, sir.

JUSTICE BLACKMUN: Whether the case is heard or ——

MR. JAWORSKI: Yes, sir, we say it is here, not only because of the appeal itself, but also because of the petition for mandamus.

Now, we did, Mr. Justice, discuss that in one of the briefs. Now, it may be that it wasn't originally when we filed the original brief of jurisdiction. But we certainly ——

JUSTICE BLACKMUN: You mentioned it in your second brief on the merits ——

MR. JAWORSKI: Yes.

JUSTICE BLACKMUN: But not at all in your petition for certiorari.

MR. JAWORSKI: Well, we did in the —— it was in a footnote, on page 2 of the petition for writ of certiorari, Mr. Justice.

JUSTICE BLACKMUN: It usually takes more than a footnote to get a case —

MR. JAWORSKI: Well, I would think so. But there really is no issue here between the parties here on the issue of jurisdiction. I mean there is no argument as between the parties on it. And while the parties cannot agree on it, I must say that on three different bases the jurisdiction does exist as we see it. Now, I am not yet getting to the question of the intra-executive matter that has been raised. But I am discussing now the statutory basis of jurisdiction.

JUSTICE BLACKMUN: Your footnote merely refers to the presence of a mandamus case. It doesn't purport to bring it up here.

But go ahead.

MR. JAWORSKI: But to answer your question directly, sir, this is correct; we are standing upon not only the matter that this is an appeal that properly had been in the Court of Appeals, and for that reason has been moved up here properly under 28 U.S.C. 1254 (1). We also say that the Court has jurisdiction over the petition and cross-petition under 1254(1) because they present for review all questions raised by the petition —— by the President's petition for writ of mandamus. And then we also say that in addition to that the All Writs Act[1] gives this Court the jurisdiction to proceed.

JUSTICE STEWART: Of course, in a mandamus action Judge Sirica would be the party respondent. And he is not a party in this case. And he is not represented by counsel here, is he?

MR. JAWORSKI: As far as I know, he is not, no sir.

JUSTICE STEWART: The mandamus would be *Nixon* v. *Sirica*, would it not?

MR. JAWORSKI: But it was brought up by the President in their petition for mandamus, is that right. That is the way it got into this Court. It raises the same questions actually that were raised on the matter that we brought up on appeal.

QUESTION: What was the chronology, Mr. Jaworski? Notice of appeal from Judge Sirica's order was the first step taken to get to the court of appeals, was it?

MR. JAWORSKI: That is, I believe, right, sir.

QUESTION: And while that was pending, then I gather the President's petition for mandamus was filed.

MR. JAWORSKI: Yes, sir.

QUESTION: And then the last step was that you filed the petition to bypass here.

MR. JAWORSKI: Right.

QUESTION: And that petition to bypass applied I gather to whatever case was pending in the court of appeals?

MR. JAWORSKI: That is correct, sir.

QUESTION: And at that time the case pending was both the appeal from Judge Sirica's order and the President's —

MR. JAWORSKI: Mandamus. Correct, sir.

QUESTION: You feel they are not two cases?

MR. JAWORSKI: No, sir, they raise the same question.

QUESTION: Yet you could bring each up separately if you so chose.

MR. JAWORSKI: Yes, sir, could have.

JUSTICE STEWART: It seems to me they are two cases.

---

[1] Section 1254(1) of Title 28 of the U.S. Code provides that a case in the court of appeals may be reviewed by the Supreme Court "by writ of certiorari granted upon the petition of any party . . . before or after rendition of judgment or decree." The All Writs Act, 28 U.S.C. 1651 provides that the Supreme Court "may issue all writs necessary or appropriate in aid of [its] jurisdiction and agreeable to the usages and principles of law."

(Editor's Note: All the footnotes in this section have been supplied by the editor.)

MR. JAWORSKI: Inasmuch as they present the same questions —— it occurred to us that it was appropriate to rely upon jurisdiction as to both of them.

JUSTICE STEWART: Again, with respect to the mandamus action, one of the parties isn't here in Court represented by counsel. He is the party respondent.

MR. JAWORSKI: Well, I don't have the record before me, but I must say —— and I will not make an outright representation that Judge Sirica is —— and that is why I hesitated a few minutes ago —— was made a party. After all, it was brought up by the President. But I am advised by a note justed passed me that Judge Sirica is a party to that proceeding.

JUSTICE STEWART: Who represents him here?

MR. JAWORSKI: I don't know of anyone representing him here.

JUSTICE STEWART: Has he filed any brief or made any appearance at all in any sense?

MR. JAWORSKI: So far as I know, no.

JUSTICE STEWART: In any event, Judge Sirica's order was an appealable order.

MR. JAWORSKI: Yes, sir, that is correct.

JUSTICE STEWART: If you are correct in that submission —— do we ever have to reach any issues raised by the mandamus?

MR. JAWORSKI: No, you would not. We were pointing out that the jurisdiction rests on a three-pronged basis.

JUSTICE STEWART: But the mandamus is not your act.

MR. JAWORSKI: It is not, no, sir.

JUSTICE STEWART: You are not obliged to defend it.

MR. JAWORSKI: That is correct, sir. We, however, were pointing out that the same issues really were raised by —— if the petition is properly before the Court.

Now, if there are no further questions on the matter of statutory jurisdiction, I would like to pass to the intra-executive dispute.

First, we recognize, of course, that jurisdiction cannot be waived, and nothing that is presented here is with the idea of suggesting even remotely that there is any waiver with respect to the question of jurisdiction. But we do say that the contention that there is an intra-executive dispute and for that reason this Court cannot pass upon these questions is not sound.

Before discussing the cases, however, I think it would be appropriate for us to undertake to place this in the right perspective.

Let me say first that we stand upon two bases: first, that actually the orders that were entered creating the Office of the

Special Prosecutor and delineating his authority, even the original order at the time that my predecessor was acting as Special Prosecutor, had the force and effect of law. We also point to the fact that the arrangement made itself with the Acting Attorney General that I made, if I may point to it — and one reason I have no reticence in discussing the facts is because the facts are undisputed. There has been no dispute raised as to just what actually transpired.

The situation is one of the arrangement itself, which the Acting Attorney General points to, with respect to the matter of independence having been discussed by him with the President — thus meaning that the President himself had approved the setting up of this particular office, and the rights and the responsibilities that it has under the charter.

We set this out in the appendix, of course, pointing precisely to what the authority and the responsibilities and the obligations of the Special Prosecutors are. One of the express duties that is delegated to the Special Prosecutor is that he shall have full authority for investigating and prosecuting — among others — allegations involving the President. And the delegation of authority expressly stated in particular the Special Prosecutor shall have full authority to determine whether or not to contest the assertion of executive privilege, or any other testimony of privilege.

Now, in the instance of my appointment, unlike the appointment that had been made prior thereto, there was an amended order, and it referred to assurances given by the President to the Attorney General that the President will not exercise his constitutional powers to effect the discharge of the Special Prosecutor, or to limit the independence that he is hereby given. And that he will not be removed from his duties except for extraordinary improprieties on his part, and without the President first consulting the majority and minority leaders and the chairman and ranking minority members of the Judiciary Committees of the Senate and House of Representatives, in ascertaining that their consensus is in accord with the proposed action. And then, that the jurisdiction of the Special Prosecutor will not be limited without the President first consulting with such members of Congress and ascertaining that their consensus is in accord with his proposed action.

Now, at the time —

QUESTION: What does "consensus" mean — unanimous?

MR. JAWORSKI: No, sir. It has been interpreted by the Acting Attorney General in conversations as meaning six of eight.

QUESTION: I take it when you make reference to this, you

are in effect suggesting that your position is certainly different than if a United States Attorney were prosecuting this case.

MR. JAWORSKI: That is correct, sir. I think we have what might be termed a quasi-independent status, where there were delegated to this particular office performance of certain functions. And there is no reason why the President could not have delegated those to us.

As a matter of fact ——

QUESTION: Mr. Jaworski —— quasi-independent in the sense of an agency?

MR. JAWORSKI: Yes, sir. For instance, the Comptroller of the Currency —— he has a status somewhat similar to that. And we know that there are suits brought between the Department of Justice and the Comptroller.[2]

QUESTION: I have trouble with your position being similar to a U.S. Attorney, because a U.S. Attorney is absolutely under the thumb of the Attorney General.

MR. JAWORSKI: Well, I didn't say —— what I meant was that we had independent status that was really different from the status of the United States Attorney.

QUESTION: I'm sorry.

MR. JAWORSKI: I thought that was the way I answered the question.

Now, I should say that it is interesting when the case of *Nixon* v. *Sirica* was before the court of appeals, Professor Charles Alan Wright, who was then arguing that case, and who was not on the original brief, but I observe was on the reply brief filed on behalf of the President —— at that time argued with respect to the particular Office of the Special Prosecutor: "Now, in this instance we have a division of function within the Executive in that my friend Mr. Cox" —— referring to Archibald Cox —— "has been given absolute independence. It is for him to decide whom he will seek to indict. It is for him to decide to whom he will give immunity . . . " —— a decision that would ordinarily be made at the level of the Attorney General or in an important enough case at the level of the President.

But the President's present counsel in his motion to quash, as he does here —— except the words here are different, but the effect is the same —— is contending to the Court that the President has the right to determine who, when and with what

[2] In *United States* v. *Marine Bancorporation*, 94 S. Ct. 2856 (1974) the Comptroller of the Currency intervened on behalf of the defendant in an antitrust suit brought by the Justice Department. He argued against the position taken by the Solicitor General in the Supreme Court since he had previously approved the bank mergers challenged by the Justice Department.

information individuals shall be prosecuted.

JUSTICE STEWART: Well, Nixon against Sirica was different in that the parties there were the grand jury on the one hand, represented, to be sure, by the Special Prosecutor —— the grand jury, which is an adjunct of the judicial branch of government on the one hand —— and the Chief Executive, on the other. And here, now that an indictment has been returned, the two parties are both members of the executive branch. Isn't that correct —— that there is that difference?

MR. JAWORSKI: Yes, sir, that is correct. But I don't think it is a disctinction as to the substance.

QUESTION: You are a member —— you are the United States —— the people of the United States, who you represent. You are not a member of the judicial branch, unlike the grand jury in Nixon against Sirica —— you are a member of the executive branch of government, are you not?

MR. JAWORSKI: That is correct, sir, yes.

QUESTION: There is that difference.

MR. JAWORSKI: There is that difference, yes.

QUESTION: And it might be a crucial difference, might it not?

MR. JAWORSKI: But I don't think the description to which I pointed as to the independent status of the independent executor would be any different in the Sirica case than it would be in this case. And I was merely ——

QUESTION: No —— you are if anything more independent than Mr. Cox was under the regulations.

MR. JAWORSKI: That is correct, sir.

JUSTICE STEWART: But that doesn't really go to the question that I am raising.

MR. JAWORSKI: Yes, sir. I realize that.

Now, may I, however, indicate very briefly — and I know this is an important question — but I do feel that the facts ought to be before the Court in detail — indicate just what did transpire with respect to how these particular regulations, this order, was interpreted by the President's Acting Attorney General, and also by the Attorney General Designate, and also by the President himself, and by the President's Chief of Staff General Haig.

Mr. Bork, in hearings at a time when Congress was pressing the bill of an independent Special Prosecutor, testified that "Although it is anticipated that Mr. Jaworski will receive cooperation from the White House in getting any evidence he feels he needs to conduct investigations and prosecutions, it is clear and understood on all sides that he has the power to use judicial processes to pursue evidence if disagreements should develop."

It was further pointed out ——

QUESTION: You are quoting from whom at what time?

MR. JAWORSKI: Acting Attorney General Bork's testimony in the House.

QUESTION: On what occasion?

MR. JAWORSKI: After I had been appointed, and in connection with the hearings on the bill to establish an independent prosecutor by congressional act.

QUESTION: Thank you.

MR. JAWORSKI: Then he further said: "I understand and it is clear to me that Mr. Jaworski can go to court and test out..." and these are the important words —— "and test out any refusal to produce documents on the grounds of confidentiality." And Attorney General Saxbe, then a designate, who was also present at the time that this matter was discussed, and at the time that I accepted the responsibilities, testified that I had the right to contest an assertion of executive privilege and stated that I can go to court at any time to determine that.

Now, the President himself, as we point out in our brief, in announcing the appointment of a new independent prosecutor, stated to the nation that he had no greater interest than to see that the new Special Prosecutor had the cooperation from the executive branch and the independence that he needs to bring about that conclusion of the Watergate investigation.

The President's Chief of Staff at the time that this appointment was accepted, and at the time that the new regulations were then drafted by the Acting Attorney General, had assured me — and this is a part of the record, because a letter was written at the request of Senator Hugh Scott to the White House as a result of discussions that he had with General Haig, in which I sent a copy of the testimony that I had given to the congressional committees to the White House so it would be fully aware of it and the receipt of it was acknowledged without any change in the testimony.

So I had been assured to the right to judicial process by him after he had reviewed the matter with the President and came and told me that I would have the right to take the President to court, and that these were the key words in this arrangement, and that the right would not be questioned.

Of course, this independence that was given to the Special Prosecutor actually was but an echo of public demand. And if I may be permitted to say so, it was the only basis on which, after what had occurred, and a predecessor had been discharged —— it was the only basis on which the Special Prosecutor could have felt that he could have come in and serve and undertake to perform these functions.

It is important, I think, to observe that counsel for the President, in his brief, by accepting the proposition that the President and the Attorney General can delegate certain executive functions to subordinate officers implicitly has conceded we think the validity of the regulations delegating prosecutorial powers to the Special Prosecutor.

The regulations specifically provide, as you will notice from the appendix —— and we have set them out —— the Attorney General will not countermand or interfere with the Special Prosecutor's decisions or actions. This is also a part of the charge.

Thus, to argue, as has been done in these briefs, that the separation of powers preclude the courts from entertaining this action because it is the exclusive prerogative of the executive branch, not the judiciary to determine whom to prosecute, on what charges, and with what evidence, we think misses the point.

What has evolved from the regulations in our view is a prosecutorial force with certain exclusive responsibilities. And this is why I say that to some degree it could be described as a quasi-independent agency.

It is not unlike, our situation is, the case we alluded to a few minutes ago decided by the Court just a week or so ago. It is not unlike the case of the *Secretary of Agriculture* v. the *United States*.[3] This isn't the first time that there has been an action brought by one member of the executive branch against another official in the executive branch. And we refer to these cases in our briefs in detail.

Now, I want to make it clear that the President at no point of course delegated to the Special Prosecutor the exclusive right to pass on the question of executive privilege or any other privilege —— attorney/client privilege, or any other testimonial privilege. What we are merely saying is that we have the clear right to test it in this court. And this is on what we stand.

Well, because of the passage of time, if I may, I think I should get to other discussions—unless there are questions on this particular point.

Passing to the merits, we would say if there is any one principle of law that *Marbury* v. *Madison* decides is that it is up

---

[3] *Secretary of Agriculture* v. *United States,* 350 U.S. 162 (1956). The suit involved the validity of certain tariff regulations promulgated by the Interstate Commerce Commission and challenged by the Secretary of Agriculture.

to the court to say what the law is. And almost to the point of redundancy, but necessary because it was a landmark decision, Chief Justice Marshall reasoned we think with clarity and emphasis that it is emphatically the province and the duty of the judicial department to say what the law is. And this Court, of course, through the years has reaffirmed, consistently applied that rule. It has done it in a number of cases — in *Powell* v. *McCormack*,[4] in the *Youngstown Steel* seizure case,[5] in *Doe* v. *McMillan*,[6] and a footnote, I think a very important one, appears in that opinion, when Mr. Justice White pointed out that "While an inquiry such as involved in the present case, because it involves two coordinate branches of government, must necessarily have separation of power implications, the separation of powers doctrine has not prevented this Court from reviewing acts of Congress, even when, it is pointed out, the executive branch is also involved."

Now, there are a number of cases that speak to that. I think one of the cases that perhaps went into greater detail, and also points out quite a distinguishing feature, is the *Gravel* case;[7] whereas in the Gravel case the Court did hold that it was appropriate to go into certain matters where privilege had been exercised on the part of a Senator on behalf of his aide.

There are two things that I believe clearly help us in that decision, and also other decisions as far as the questions here involved. One is that the speech or debate clause is in the Constitution; it is written in there. And this is what was invoked. I don't find anything written in the Constitution, and nothing has been pointed, that is a writing in the Constitution that relates to the right of the exercise of executive privilege on the part of the President.

[4] In *Powell* v. *McCormack*, 395 U.S. 486 (1969) the Supreme Court held that it could properly examine whether the House of Representatives acted legally in excluding Adam Clayton Powell from his seat in Congress for alleged improprieties. The Court held that Powell was unconstitutionally deprived of his seat.

[5] In *Youngstown Sheet & Tube Co.* v. *Sawyer*, 343 U.S. 579 (1952) the Supreme Court declared illegal President Truman's seizure of certain steel companies during the Korean War.

[6] *Doe* v. *McMillian*, 412 U.S. 306 (1973). The Supreme Court held that it could determine whether the government could publish a Congressional report on the public school system of the District of Columbia which allegedly invaded the right of privacy of certain students. The Court determined the limits of immunity for the Superintendent of Documents.

[7] *Gravel* v. *United States*, 408 U.S. 606 (1973). In that case an aide to Senator Mike Gravel of Alaska was ordered to appear before a federal grand jury to answer certain questions about publication of the Pentagon papers. The Supreme Court rejected the argument that the Speech and Debate Clause of the Constitution barred the grand jury from asking him any questions.

Another very important thing that is pointed out in that case is that it did involve an examination into wrong-doing on the part of those who were seeking to invoke the privilege.

JUSTICE BRENNAN: Is the term "executive privilege" an ancient one?

MR. JAWORSKI: I beg your pardon, sir?

JUSTICE BRENNAN: Is the term "exeuctive privilege" an ancient one?

MR. JAWORSKI: It has been used over a period of time. How ancient, Mr. Justice Brennan, I am not in a position to say. But certainly it has been one that has been used over the years. But it is not one that I find any basis for in the Constitution.

QUESTION: Are you now arguing that there is no such thing as executive privilege?

MR. JAWORSKI: No, sir.

QUESTION: I didn't think so.

MR. JAWORSKI: No, sir. Because I say there is no basis for it in the Constitution.

QUESTION: You think if anything it's a common law privilege? Is that your point?

MR. JAWORSKI: Yes, sir. And it has been traditionally recognized and appropriately so in a number of cases as we see it. We do not think it is an appropriate one in this case. But we certainly do not for a moment feel that it has any constitutional base.

CHIEF JUSTICE BURGER: In *Scheuer* against *Rhodes*[8] I thought we held that there is a common law privilege in the executives dealing at the state level, but that it is a qualified privilege, is that not so?

MR. JAWORSKI: Yes, Mr. Chief Justice, that is exactly the point. This Court has examined a number of situations. And in some situations, as I think was pointed out earlier, where military secrets and such as that were involved, or national secrets of great importance, the Court has taken a good, close look and has upheld privilege. But —

QUESTION: When you say it has taken a good, close look — without looking at the evidence sometimes; taken a good close look at the claim and the basis of the claim, is that what you mean?

MR. JAWORSKI: That is what I mean, yes, sir.

---

[8] *Scheuer* v. *Rhodes*, 413 U.S. 919 (1974) held that certain Ohio State officials could be sued by the survivors of the Kent State students shot by the National Guardsman on the campus. The Court held that state officials had a qualified but not an absolute immunity against suit.

QUESTION: Didn't this Court say that it did have constitutional overtones?

MR. JAWORSKI: It said it had constitutional overtones. And I don't know in what case it may have been used. But —

QUESTION: That was in the Court of Claims, I think.[9]

MR. JAWORSKI: Yes, sir. But it certainly has never placed it in the Constitution so far as I am aware of, and President's counsel who have carefully examined the authorities.

QUESTION: Right.

QUESTION: That was in Kaiser Aluminum and Chemical Corporation case in the Court of Claims that phrase was used.

QUESTION: That is judicially tailored?

MR. JAWORSKI: Yes, sir.

JUSTICE POWELL: Is it your view that there are not influences to be derived from the doctrine of separation of powers? Are you saying this is purely an evidentiary privilege?

MR. JAWORSKI: That the privilege as recognized judically may have been tied into a separation of powers doctrine we don't deny. What we say is that the separation of powers doctrine in the exercise of and calling for executive privilege has not been applied in a number of instances involving both Congress and involving also the Executive — despite the fact that even in the congressional situations the speech and debate clause is there.

What I am saying is that the separation of powers doctrine, as was pointed to in the *Doe* v. *McMillan* case has not been permitted to stand in the way of this Court examining it from a standpoint of whether the executive privilege should be permitted or not.

QUESTION: In *Reynolds*[10] the Court ended up treating the assertion of privilege there as an evidentiary privilege but it did allude to the fact that there was a constitutional question, and it said the Court wasn't reaching it, as I recall.

MR. JAWORSKI: On the issue of executive privilege, I should point out here, it is a very narrow one. And I think it is important that we bear this in mind. It doesn't involve a very large or broad privilege or right. What it really narrows down to is

---

[9] In *Kaiser Aluminum* v. *Chemical Corp.* v. *United States,* 157 F. Supp. 939 (1958) the Court of Claims held that documents involving executive deliberations were "privileged from inspection as against public interest." But the court said that the privilege is not absolute.

[10] In *United States* v. *Reynolds,* 345 U.S. 1 (1953) the Supreme Court upheld a claim of privilege covering an accident report on the crash of a B-29 air force bomber testing secret electronic equipment and said that the government did not have to produce the report to the plaintiffs in a tort action.

somewhat a simple but very important issue in the administration of criminal justice, and that is whether the President, in a pending prosecution, can withhold material evidence from the court, merely on his assertion that the evidence involves confidential communications. And this is what it really gets down to.

We know that there are sovereign prerogatives to protect the confidentiality necessary to carry out responsibilities in the fields of international relations and national defense that are not here involved. And there is no claim of any state secrets or that disclosure will have dire effect on the nation or its people.

Actually, I think when we get to weighing the non-disclosure as against disclosure, and I think when we begin to weigh the balance of interests, it would seem to me that the balance clearly lies in favor of a disclosure in a situation such as the circumstances here.

Of course ——

JUSTICE DOUGLAS: That certainly would not be true if a case of the Fifth Amendment were involved. But that is not present here.

MR. JAWORSKI: Not present, Mr. Justice Douglas. And there is no question but what the Fifth Amendment is very plainly written out in the Constitution and is invoked as a clear constitutional privilege.

I think that it would be of help if I may point out to the Court that there is an excellent article that we have alluded to in our briefs by Professor Berger that appears in the Yale Law Journal, which discusses the Aaron Burr case at length,[11] and also other cases that have been pointed to since the time of that case. And if I may just say, very briefly, that summarizes the situation by saying that the heart of Marshall's opinion was justly summarized by the Court of Appeals in the *Nixon* v. *Sirica* case, in a tapes case, that we have talked about. "The Court was to show respect for the President's reason, but the ultimate decision remained with the Court." And we are not suggesting for a moment here that the matter of executive privilege should not be looked into. It deserves to be tested. It should be tested. And we urge that it be tested. But the ultimate decision is not one of saying that it is absolute, it rests in the Constitution, that it doesn't entitle anyone, it doesn't authorize anyone, it doesn't even authorize this Court to look into it —— because if the courts are the ultimate interpreters of the Constitution and can restrain Congress to

---

[11] Raoul Berger, "The President, Congress and the Courts," 83 *Yale Law Journal* *1111* (1974).

operate within constitutional bounds, they certainly shouldn't be empowered any less to measure Presidential claims of constitutional powers.

I wanted briefly to make mention of the question that had been raised by counsel for the President that involves a motion to expunge the finding of the grand jury's action that the President is to be named as an unindicted co-conspirator along with a number of others when the pre-trial proceedings are gone into and a bill of particulars is being filed.

And I say that the grand jury's finding, painful as it is, I think on the part of the Court, must be considered as being valid and sufficient to show prima facie —— it is suffifient to show prima facie that the President was involved in the proceedings in the course and in the continuation of the particular conspiracy that was charged.

CHIEF JUSTICE BURGER: Well, is that the issue, Mr. Jaworski, or is the issue whether there can be a collateral attack?

MR. JAWORSKI: That is also another issue.

But I merely wanted to point out that I believe that this Court would not go into the grand jury's findings. But it's a prima facie matter. And that this Court would not go into it for the purpose of determining a matter of that kind.

QUESTION: I thought we had put that issue aside. I just don't understand what the relevance of that is to this case.

MR. JAWORSKI: Well, I have to agree with you —— neither do I see what the relevance is of the matter of saying —— there is another argument advanced here, and that is that the President can't be indicted. And I don't know what the relevance of it is in this case, either, very frankly, because it is not before the Court. And yet the argument is made, and many pages of briefs are devoted to it.

QUESTION: I am just wondering, Mr. Jaworski, why you aren't content it is irrelevant without taking on the right ——

MR. JAWORSKI: This is why I skipped the argument with respect to the matter of whether he could be indicted or not —— inasmuch as this question had been raised and briefed and a motion exists before the Court —— I have to agree it is not relevant. But it is a part of the case, and that is the only reason I alluded to it. And I have no interest in spending much time on it.

JUSTICE STEWART: Except part of the grounds on which you rest in subpoenaing this material is the fact that the President has himself been named as a co-conspirator, an unindicted one. That's true, isn't it? That is part of the grounds on which you rest in subpoenaing this material. And the response to that is that the President cannot constitutionally be named as an unindicted co-conspirator. So to that extent it is in this case — the question is in this case.

MR. JAWORSKI: I don't think it is a matter that, very frankly, has any particular basis to it, because I don't see how this Court could be asked to substitute its judgment for that of a grand jury.

JUSTICE STEWART: Well, that is something quite different again — whether or not there was sufficient evidence before the grand jury to justify the grand jury in naming the President. That is quite different, and, as the Chief Justice suggested, a collateral issue.

MR. JAWORSKI: That is right.

JUSTICE STEWART: But the issue of whether or not the President can constitutionally be named by a grand jury as a co-conspirator, even though an unindicted one, is at least tangentially before us. Because it is the fact that he has been named by the grand jury that is part of the grounds and part of the foundation upon which you have based your subpoena duces tecum.

MR. JAWORSKI: Not only that. I think it has been pinpointed in our view in materiality because it does relate to the question of the proof that we are seeking, the relevance of the proof that we are seeking. And this gets into, of course, a discussion of matters that are sealed and which I cannot discuss with the Court.

QUESTION: I understand — right.

QUESTION: Whether or not they had the authority, they did it. It is a fact that the grand jury did it.

MR. JAWORSKI: That is correct, sir.

QUESTION: And so I don't see how we have anything to do with whether they had the authority or not. It is a fact. Is that right?

MR. JAWORSKI: That is, I think, correct.

Now —

JUSTICE DOUGLAS: I thought the heart of this case was the rights of defendants in a criminal trial to that evidence. It may be exculpatory and free them of all liability. I don't know, but I —

MR. JAWORSKI: Well, it certainly is in the case. Now, of course what you have reference to also, I am sure, Mr. Justice Douglas, is *Brady* and the *Jencks—Brady* v. *Maryland,* and the Jencks Act.[12] And this is part of the case. However, it happens

---

[12] In *Brady* v. *Maryland,* 373 U.S. 83 (1973) the Supreme Court held that a prosecutor must give up to a defendant any exculpatory evidence (material helpful to his defense) in the possession of the prosecutor. In *Jencks* v. *United States,* 353 U.S.

not to be a part of the appeal, although it is a part of the case. But as far as our position is concerned, it doesn't relate to that. But certainly it is true that this material, as we have pointed out in our communications to the President, may well involve exculpatory matters. And we time and again pointed out we wanted them not simply because we felt that there were matters that needed to be developed in connection with the prosecution, but that they could well contain exculpatory matter.

CHIEF JUSTICE BURGER: The *Brady* question really lurks just in the background, does it not? That is, if you get information, whatever you get will be available to——you would concede is available to any defendant who can make a showing.

MR. JAWORSKI: Correct, sir.

JUSTICE STEWART: And the question of whether or not the defendants, under the *Brady* doctrine, are entitled to subpoena information and material that is not now in your possession but is in the possession of the President, was an issue that was left undecided by the district court.

MR. JAWORSKI: That is correct, sir.

QUESTION: Am I right about that?

MR. JAWORSKI: Before this Court.

I believe with the permission of the Court, unless there are further questions, I will reserve the rest of the time to close.

CHIEF JUSTICE BURGER: Mr. St. Clair.

ORAL ARGUMENT OF JAMES D. ST. CLAIR, ESQ., ON BEHALF OF THE PRESIDENT

MR. ST. CLAIR: Mr. Chief Justice and Members of the Court, my learned brother has approached this case, I think, from the traditional point of view——namely, this is an attempt by a Special Prosecutor to obtain what he thinks is desirable evidence in a criminal prosecution that he has the responsibility for. Not once, however, have I heard him mention what I think is really involved, at least in significant part, and that is the co-pendency of impeachment proceedings before the House of Representatives, and the realistic fusion that has taken place with respect to these two proceedings, and the promise of continued fusion, as I understand my brother's position.

May I quote from page ——

JUSTICE: Well, those are none of our problems, are they?

MR. ST. CLAIR: I think, sir, they really are. First, by way of factual ——

657 (1957), the Supreme Court held that a federal prosecutor must make available to a defendant any written statements of government witnesses called in his trial. The rule was later codified in the Jencks Act, 18 U.S.C. § 3500.

QUESTION: The sole authority to impeach is in the House.

MR. ST. CLAIR: That is correct.

QUESTION: The sole authority to try is in the Senate.

MR. ST. CLAIR: Right. And the Court shall not be used to implement or aid that process, which is what happening in this case. This case wouldn't be here on July 8 —

QUESTION: Just how is this done? How does this case implement that?

MR. ST. CLAIR: I would like to review some of the facts for you in this regard.

QUESTION: Which are in the record?

MR. ST. CLAIR: Yes. My brother has mentioned them to you.

QUESTION: But are they in the record?

MR. ST. CLAIR: Yes, sir.

JUSTICE DOUGLAS: Well, if we are just an adjunct of the House Judiciary Committee, this case should be dismissed as improvidently granted, shouldn't it?

MR. ST. CLAIR: Exactly right, sir. Not only that, it makes the case unjusticiable, at least.

JUSTICE DOUGLAS: Then the district court's decision stands. Is that what you want?

MR. ST. CLAIR: No. The case should be dismissed, sir.

JUSTICE DOUGLAS: If we dismiss as improvidently granted, I submit that the district court's judgment would stand.

MR. ST. CLAIR: Then I would retract what I said. This case should be dismissed.

QUESTION: The case would be on appeal in the court of appeals.

QUESTION: Are you now talking about the bypassing of the court of appeals?

MR. ST. CLAIR: No, sir. I am talking about the proceeding before the district court, through the court of appeals, to this Court.

QUESTION: If we dismissed this appeal as improvidently granted, it would go back to the court of appeals.

MR. ST. CLAIR: Well, as I say, I think this case should be dismissed—period.

QUESTION: No. Really what you mean is you think that the order of Judge Sirica should be vacated and set aside.

MR. ST. CLAIR: That is right, sir.

QUESTION: That is quite different from dismissing the case.

MR. ST. CLAIR: I agree.

QUESTION: That's deciding it on the merits.

MR. ST. CLAIR: That's right. That is what I am trying to get across to this Court, perhaps unartfully——this case should be disposed of, be it by vacating the order below or not. In any event, it is improper in our view that this case should be heard in the context it is now being heard. We wouldn't be here on July 8, before a crowded courtroom if it was not recognized generally ——

QUESTION: It is a political question here, and it was a political question in the district court.

MR. ST. CLAIR: Exactly. And therefore it is a non-justiciable issue in this and in the district court. What has happened in this case is ——

QUESTION: Did you argue that to the district judge?

MR. ST. CLAIR: I believe we argued the non-justiciability argument, yes, sir. I know we did. But ——

QUESTION: Your position is that the issuance of a subpoena duces tecum is not a justiciable issue.

MR. ST. CLAIR: In this context at this time, sir. What has happened is this.

As you know, on February 24 a grand jury secretly named the President among others as an unindicted co-conspirator. That fact was not made known. On March 1 an indictment was returned against a number of the President's chief aides. Coincident with that, and in an open courtroom, the Assistant Prosecutor——Special Prosecutor, handed up to the judge a bag, together with a sealed letter, requesting that this material be sent over to the House of Representatives. The President took no position regarding that proposal, because he considered it to be probably appropirate, under the belief that there was nothing accusatory in that material. Judge Sirica himself reviewed the material, found nothing accusatory, and said it would therefore be quite appropriate to send this material to the House of Representatives——not realizing and not knowing that the Special Prosecutor had previously obtained a secret charge against the President and others, which was definitely accusatory.

QUESTION: But that, as I understand it, was not among the material that was conveyed to the grand jury. At least that is what I understood Mr. Jaworski to tell us this morning.

MR. ST. CLAIR: The material that was turned over was before the grand jury.

QUESTION: Now, just a moment. I understood Mr. Jaworski to tell us this morning very unambiguously and explicitly, that the fact that the President was named as an unindicted co-conspirator was not conveyed to the grand jury——I mean to the House of Representatives.

MR. ST. CLAIR: No, it was not. The material was sent to the

House of Representatives in the belief that it was non-accusatory in nature——it was simply a recital of facts.

QUESTION: Exactly. And that is what Mr. Jaworski has represented again to us this morning, was the fact of the matter.

MR. ST. CLAIR: Mr. Jaworski had available to him, unknown to the Judge, and unknown to counsel for the President, a secret indictment naming the President as a co-conspirator. The accusatory part followed later.

QUESTION: Followed in what form?

MR. ST. CLAIR: By a newspaper leak.

QUESTION: It wasn't sent from the court over to the House.

MR. ST. CLAIR: It didn't have to be. All they had to do was read the newspaper. There can be no question about it. And therefore I say this case has to be viewed realistically in the context that it is now being heard.

CHIEF JUSTICE BURGER: I am not sure——perhaps you can help me——are you suggesting that there was some duty on the part of the Special Prosecutor to disclose to the district Judge that there was this secret indictment before the Judge passed on whether the material should be sent to the House?

MR. ST. CLAIR: I think it would have been quite appropriate, because the Judge's decision was based on the proposition there was nothing accusatory; that under the circumstances absolute fairness was appropriate and required insofar as the President was concerned. No one could argue that the indictment as a co-conspirator, naming him as a co-conspirator, does anything but impair the President's position before the House of Representatives. That should in my judgment, have been made known to the Judge. I don't know what he would have done under those circumstances. His decision was based solidly on the proposition there was nothing accusatory in the material.

Now, my brother says in his brief that this material he now seeks of course will be available to the House Committee and will be used to determine whether or not the President should be impeached. So this fusion is now going to continue. And under the Constitution, as we view it, only the legislature has the right to conduct impeachment proceedings. The courts have been, from the history involved and from the language of the provisions, excluded from that function. And yet the Special Prosecutor is drawing the Court into those proceedings, inevitably, and inexorably.

No one could stand here and argue with any candor that a decision of this Court would have no impact whatsoever on the pending inquiry before the House of Representatives concerning the impeachment of the President.

JUSTICE STEWART: Well, how far does your point go? Let's assume that a murder took place on the streets of Washington of which the President happened to be one of the very few eye witnesses. And somebody was indicted for that murder. And the President was subpoenaed as a witness. Would you say he cannot be subpoenaed now, because there is an impeachment inquiry going on and the courts absolutely have to stop dead in their tracks from doing their ordinary judicial business?

MR. ST. CLAIR: I would not say that. I don't think he could be necessarily subpoenaed. I don't think the President is subject to the process of the court unless he so determines he would give evidence. But the murder —

JUSTICE STEWART: Putting that to one side. You are saying that the courts, as I understand it, have to stop dead in their tracks from doing their ordinary business in any matter involving even tangentially the President of the United States if, as and when a committee of the House of Representatives is investigating impeachment.

MR. ST. CLAIR: No, Justice Stewart, I am not. The subject matter of these two matters is the same subject matter.

QUESTION: Seven people have been indicted, six of whom remain under indictment. A trial is scheduled for next September 9.

MR. ST. CLAIR: Right.

QUESTION: The prosecutor is preparing for that trial. He is trying under Rule 17 of the Federal Rules of Criminal Procedure to adduce matters to be used in evidence at that trial. You say that cannot go forward because of some tangential effect, or you say a direct effect, upon some other matter going on in another branch of the government.

MR. ST. CLAIR: I say it should not go forward at this time at the very least, because the subject matter being inquired or in large measure before the House Committee is exactly the same subject matter being involved in this argument—namely, should the President produce the tapes.

QUESTION: What in those tapes involves the impeachment proceedings?

MR. ST. CLAIR: Pardon?

QUESTION: What in any of these tapes is involved in the impeachment proceeding?

MR. ST. CLAIR: Well, if Your Honor please, the House of Representatives has subpoenaed —

QUESTION: I don't know what is in the tapes. I assume you do.

MR. ST. CLAIR: No, I don't.

QUESTION: You don't know, either. Well, how do you know that they are subject to executive privilege?

MR. ST. CLAIR: Well, I do know that there is a preliminary showing that they are conversations between the President and his close aides.

QUESTION: Regardless of what it is.

MR. ST. CLAIR: Regardless of what it is. They may involve a number of subjects.

QUESTION: But you don't know.

QUESTION: Does not the Special Prosecutor claim that the subject matter is the same?

MR. ST. CLAIR: He claims that, but he has no way of showing it. In fact, he says it is only probable or likely. He has no way of showing that they in fact involve the subject of Watergate.

QUESTION: If his claim is honored by this Court, all that would happen is the evidence would go to Judge Sirica who would examine it in camera, I assume.

MR. ST. CLAIR: I presume that is so. And it would then be made available to the Special Prosecutor, the Special Prosecutor says this of course would then become part of the impeachment proceedings, and there we are.

CHIEF JUSTICE BURGER: Mr. St. Clair, going back to this murder witness situation, if the President, any President, witnessed an automobile accident, was the sole witness, or a murder, as Mr. Justice Stewart suggested, you are not indicating that his testimony, his evidence would not be available to the Court, but merely that he cannot be subpoenaed, but might give it by deposition, as several Presidents have in the past.

MR. ST. CLAIR: That is quite correct.

CHIEF JUSTICE BURGER: The testimony of Justices of this Court has been given in past times by deposition.

MR. ST. CLAIR: It really is a matter of accommodation, not as a matter of assertion of a right of one branch over another.

But the point I want to make is that the same subject matter is inexorably involved in both proceedings now proceeding at the same time. And, you know, the House of Representatives has not —

QUESTION: And that's final. Nobody can do anything about it.

JUSTICE MARSHALL: Why were you willing to give up twenty-some of them?

MR. ST. CLAIR: That is a very good question, and I would like to answer it. The decisions that are made in the impeachment proceedings, Justice Marshall, are essentially political decisions.

JUSTICE MARSHALL: I'm talking about this case. You say he will give up twenty of them in this case.

MR. ST. CLAIR: Yes, we will——because they have already been made public.

QUESTION: The tapes, or transcriptions?

MR. ST. CLAIR: As soon as the Judge approves some method of validating the accuracy of these tapes, they can have the tapes. But you have to understand, the tape is a part of a reel. A reel may cover a dozen conversations. So there is a mechanical problem of trying to validate or be sure that this is correct. But it is only a mechanical problem. Once that is solved, subject to the approval of the Judge below, they have the availability of that.

QUESTION: Are the tapes that you are willing to release valuable to the Watergate Committee in Congress?

MR. ST. CLAIR: We think so. That is why we made them available.

QUESTION: I thought you said you didn't want them to have any tapes.

MR. ST. CLAIR: No, sir.

QUESTION: That this was merely a way of getting stuff over to them. But you are going to give them some.

MR. ST. CLAIR: I say this. I say the President should decide as a political matter what should be made available to the House.

QUESTION: Oh.

MR. ST. CLAIR: That the Court ought not to be drawn into that decision.

QUESTION: And that's final. Nobody can do anything about it. MR. ST. CLAIR: The House takes a different view. The House has subpoenaed something in the neighborhood of 145 tapes. And that is a political decision.

QUESTION: So that the House can get them, the President can get them, and the only people I know that cannot get them is the courts.

MR. ST. CLAIR: The President has not honored any of the subpoenas other than the first one issued by the House. So that there is a dispute in the House now between the President and the Committee on the Judiciary. It is essentially a political dispute. It is a disupte that this Court ought not be drawn into. And the result of a decision in this case would inexorably result in being brought into it.

JUSTICE BRENNAN: You have not convinced me that we are drawn into it by deciding this case. How are we drawn into the impeachment proceedings by deciding this case?

MR. ST. CLAIR: The impact of a decision in this case undeniably, Mr. Justice Brennan, in my view, cannot have——will not be overlooked.

JUSTICE BRENNAN: Any decision of this Court has ripples.

MR. ST. CLAIR: I think it would be an inappropriate thing to do at this time because there is pending ——

QUESTION: Well, that's a different thing. You've been arguing we have absolutely no authority constitutionally to decide this case.

MR. ST. CLAIR: I will argue that in a moment. But I am arguing now only that you should not. I am arguing now, sir, only that you should not——because it would involve this Court inexorably in a political process which has been determined by the Constitution to be solely the function of the legislative branch. And it cannot be that the impact of this Court's decision in this matter, which is one of the principal matters now pending before the House, would be overlooked. It would certainly as a matter of realistic fact have a significant impact.

JUSTICE DOUGLAS: But as I said before, we have——the beneficiaries here are six defendants being tried for criminal charges. And what the President has may free them completely. Is that true? Theoretically.

MR. ST. CLAIR: Mr. Justice Douglas——it may. The *Brady* issue we don't believe is properly before the Court. It has not been briefed by us nor by my brother.

QUESTION: It was not decided by the district court.

MR. ST. CLAIR: It was not decided by the district court. I would only say this. That in the experience that I have had in connection with cases tried, such as the Stans-Mitchell case in New York, the Chapin case in Washington, the Ehrlichman case now going on, there has never been a claim that the President has not made available appropriate and adequate Brady material. But I do not believe it is before this Court at this time. What is before this Court is a prosecutor's demand for evidence. And I direct my remarks for a moment to that problem. He says that in effect we have no right to be here, that we have delegated the who, the when, and with what issues to him. We have delegated the who and the when, and pursuant to that he has indicted a number of people. And he has indicted them at such time as he thought appropriate. But even he contends that we did not delegate to him what Presidential conversations would be used as evidence. That was reserved. And he concedes that that is the fact. And that is what is at issue here. Not when and who is to be indicted, but what Presidential communications are going to be used as evidence. And that is what the issue is in this case.

CHIEF JUSTICE BURGER: Mr. St. Clair, you left me in a little bit of doubt about this mechanical problem. I think perhaps we diverted you from it. Are you suggesting that on a given tape, which is a reel type of thing, having an hour or more of material, or maybe several hours —

MR. ST. CLAIR: Two or three days.

CHIEF JUSTICE BURGER: Two or three days——I see. That the first three hours might be material which has already been transcribed and released; the next three or four hours might be a conference with the Joint Chiefs of Staff or the Chairman of the Atomic Energy Commission, or a program to give under-developed nations, for example, aid or peaceful uses of atomic energy——matters totally irrelevant but confidential. Is that your argument?

MR. ST. CLAIR: It is my argument, and the fact. For example —

CHIEF JUSTICE BURGER: And you want some mechanism set up so that these things can be screened out.

MR. ST. CLAIR: They have been screened out in the transcripts. Whatever has been published to the public we are quite prepared to verify the accuracy of. Now, in the course of those transcripts there are, of course, portions left out.

CHIEF JUSTICE BURGER: Have you at any time tendered or proferred a statement that a particular tape from eighteen minutes after eleven until three o'clock that afternoon, including the lunch hour, included a conference with the Secretary of State, the Secretary of Defense and someone else having to do with totally unrelated matters. Has that kind of a tender been made?

MR. ST. CLAIR: No. We simply published the portion of that conversation which does not relate to that with the notation that a portion had been left out.

QUESTION: But no explanation of why it is left out.

MR. ST. CLAIR: It was left out because it did not involve Presidential action as it related to Watergate, or something to that effect. We did not disclose the substance of that left-out material.

QUESTION: Is there any particular reason why at least the identity of the conferees could not be made —

MR. ST. CLAIR: There might well be such a reason. My proffer to my brother has been that we will verify the accuracy of the printed transcript, so this 1240-odd pages of Presidential conversations that are available to the public and available to him will be useable in the trial. Now, this may well involve a mechanism approved by the Court involving counsel for the defendant to be satisfied——that they are satisfied that the copy is accurate. But this all has to be expurgated out of a reel of tape that may involve several days of conversation. But it is essentially a mechanical problem.

QUESTION: The tapes that they ask for in this subpoena duces tecum, which is the only thing before us——has any effort been made to say what if any part of that can be released?

MR. ST. CLAIR: Other than the twenty that are already published, no effort has been made as yet, sir.

QUESTION: Why not?

MR. ST. CLAIR: Because, if Your Honor please, we have not felt that it has been necessary to do so, because we firmly feel that the President has every right to refuse to produce them.

QUESTION: You don't think that a subpoena duces tecum is sufficient reason for you to try? You just ignored it, didn't you?

MR. ST. CLAIR: No, sir, we did not. We filed a motion to quash it.

QUESTION: The difference between ignoring and filing a motion to quash is what?

MR. ST. CLAIR: Well, if Your Honor please, we are submitting the matter ——

JUSTICE STEWART: You are submitting the matter to this Court ——

MR. ST. CLAIR: To this Court under a special showing on behalf of the President ——

JUSTICE STEWART: And you are still leaving it up to this Court to decide it.

MR. ST. CLAIR: Yes, in a sense.

JUSTICE STEWART: In what sense?

MR. ST. CLAIR: In the sense that this Court has the obligation to determine the law. The President also has an obligation to carry out his constitutional duties.

JUSTICE STEWART: You are submitting it for us to decide whether or not executive privilege is available in this case.

MR. ST. CLAIR: Well, the problem is the question is even more limited than that. Is the executive privilege, which my brother concedes, absolute or is it only conditional.

JUSTICE STEWART: I said "in this case". Can you make it any narrower than that?

MR. ST. CLAIR: No, sir.

JUSTICE STEWART: Well, do you agree that that is what is before this Court, and you are submitting it to this Court for decision?

MR. ST. CLAIR: This is being submitted to this Court for its guidance and judgment with respect to the law. The President, on the other hand, has his obligations under the Constitution.

JUSTICE STEWART: Are you submitting it to this Court for

this Court's decision?

MR. ST. CLAIR: As to what the law is, yes.

JUSTICE STEWART: If that were not so, you would not be here.

MR. ST. CLAIR: I would not be here. Now, my brother says I have no right to even challenge his right to be here. And I would like to deal with that for a moment.

This is, as we have pointed out in our brief, essentially an executive department matter. Whatever may have been the arrangements between the branches of the executive with respect to evidentiary matter——and in fact there were no arrangements regarding evidentiary matters——it is not the function of the Court to direct or rule what evidence will be presented to it by the executive in the executive's duty of prosecuting.

If this was a United States Attorney, this case would not be here, of course. It is here only because certain things were delegated to the Special Prosecutor. But the Special Prosecutor was not delegated the right to tell the President what of his conversations are going to be made available as evidence. That was specifically reserved. And the only thing that my brother can do is argue about it. And that is what he is doing right here today. Therefore ——

QUESTION: Why wouldn't this case be here if this were a United States Attorney? I think I agree with you. But I would like to ask you to tell me why.

MR. ST. CLAIR: Well, the United States Attorney would be directed ——

QUESTION: By whom?

MR. ST. CLAIR: By the President or the Attorney General at the direction of the President ——

QUESTION: I thought the Attorney General was the one who directed the United States Attorney.

MR. ST. CLAIR: By the Attorney General at the direction of the President.

QUESTION: No, no. In the normal case——the President doesn't know anything about run of the mill federal prosecutions——that's fair to say, isn't it?

MR. ST. CLAIR: I think so, But most cases don't involve ——

QUESTION: And in fact in run of the mill cases, the Attorney General doesn't know much about them.

MR. ST. CLAIR: Yes, sir——with all due respect.

QUESTION: Right. So the United States Attorney brings a prosecution, and in the course of that prosecution he, before trial, subpoenas under Rule 17 of the Federal Rules of Criminal Procedure——he subpoenas material in the custody of the

President. So what happens?

MR. ST. CLAIR: The President says to the Attorney General "I am not going to produce this material."

QUESTION: No. It's the United States Attorney subpoenaing it under your hypothetical case.

MR. ST. CLAIR: That is right.

QUESTION: And so what happens?

MR. ST. CLAIR: In my view the President would instruct the Attorney General to instruct the United States Attorney to withdraw his motion.

QUESTION: And the United States Attorney says "I'm not going to do that because I am sworn to uphold justice."

MR. ST. CLAIR: Then you would have a new United States Attorney.

Well, I'm being a little facetious.

QUESTION: I'm being serious, because I think ——

MR. ST. CLAIR: I think the United States Attorney, with all respect, would and should be removed from that case.

QUESTION: By whom?

MR. ST. CLAIR: The executive power of the government is not vested in the United States Attorney; it is vested in one man and that man is the President of the United States.

QUESTION: By statute it is vested——law enforcement is vested in the Attorney General.

MR. ST. CLAIR: Yes. But that statute which my brother cites in his brief does not deprive, nor could it deprive the President of his constitutional authority to be the chief law enforcement officer. He shall take care to see that the laws are enforced. The executive power is vested in him, in one man. And the Attorney General is nothing but a surrogate for the President of the United States.

JUSTICE STEWART: Your argument is a very good one as a matter of political science, and it would be a very fine one as a matter of constitutional and probably statutory law——except hasn't your client dealt himself out of that argument by what has been done in the creation of the Special Prosecutor? You have just pointed out that the Special Prosecutor is quite different from the United States Attorney.

MR. ST. CLAIR: Right. Perhaps with respect to everything except——the President did not delegate to the Special Prosecutor the right to tell him whether or not his confidential communications should be made available as evidence. So that within the package of executive power normally represented by the executive department as to who shall be prosecuted, that has been delegated to this gentleman and he has exercised that power. When——he has done that. With what evidence——he has done that, as we will deal with in a few moments. But not with that portion of the evidence that is available that constitutes Presidential confidential communications. And the Special Prosecutor cannot, and even if the President did give him that authority, probably could not, as a constitutional matter, delegate that. But in any event —

QUESTION: Delegate what? He probably would not and could not delegate what?

MR. ST. CLAIR: The right to order the President to give up confidential communications. That was not delegated.

QUESTION: Not the unfettered right to get it, but the right to go to court and ask a court to decide whether or not he is entitled to it.

MR. ST. CLAIR: Right. And the President, under no circumstances, gave up any of his defense with respect to that.

QUESTION: And you are making those defenses right here and now.

MR. ST. CLAIR: Making them right now.

QUESTION: No question about that.

MR. ST. CLAIR: And even if we did agree between us that we would vest this Court with jurisdiction, simply because of the politics of the situation, this Court, by all of its decisions, would not accept the vesting of such jurisdiction.

QUESTION: Why not?

MR. ST. CLAIR: Because this Court determines its jurisdiction——the parties can't agree —

QUESTION: We all know that law, yes. And surely you are right, as I say——a lawsuit between the Secretary of Commerce, for example, suing the President over a matter of executive policy, we both agree it would be unthinkable——and since any cabinet officer is the creature of the President who appointed him, the answer would be "You're fired."

MR. ST. CLAIR: If it goes that far.

QUESTION: If it goes that far——that's right.

But aren't we here met both factually and, I suggest, legally, with quite a different situation?

MR. ST. CLAIR: I think not, in terms of separation of powers, if I may. My brother's point of view is he views himself as the United States as distinguished from a member of the executive branch. And in his brief he invokes the United States as really a fourth entity. Constitutionally—, a Special Prosecutor, with the power that my brother suggests he has, is a constitutional anomaly. We have only three branches, not three-and-a-third or three-and-half, or four. There is only one executive branch. And the executive power is vested in a President. Now if for political reasons the President wants to dole out some of those powers, he may so do, and has done in this case. But he cannot vest jurisdiction in a court that otherwise the court would not have. Nor should the court accept jurisdiction.

QUESTION: But hasn't your client also inhibited himself from the ultimate sanction that you suggested he could impose with respect to your hypothetical United States Attorney, i.e., the sanction of dismissing the Special Prosecutor.

MR. ST. CLAIR: That is correct.

QUESTION: And as a matter of law — regulations that the force of law.

MR. ST. CLAIR: That is correct. And he has not been dismissed. Nor is he likely to be.

QUESTION: And until and unless he is, we have a case in controversy of a very real kind.

MR. ST. CLAIR: The point is, if I may make it, the only issue here is whether the President gave up his right to protect the confidentiality of his conversations. No claim is made that he did.

QUESTION: You are living testimony to the fact that he did not give up his right to defend his position in court.

MR. ST. CLAIR: And my brother concedes that.

QUESTION: The fact that the delegation to Mr. Jaworski gave him the right to contest the President's claim of privilege presupposed that the President had a right to assert the privilege——not the right to assert it necessarily with complete finality. That is what we are really arguing about here today, isn't it?

MR. ST. CLAIR: If we get beyond the subject matter situation. Now, if this were the Nixon against Sirica case, where we didn't have what I think is a dispositive problem in this case, namely the lack of jurisdiction of the judicial branch to determine this intra-executive matter——if we had a grand jury subpoena, as was true in the Nixon against Sirica case, then you have intra-branch, and the Court would have a better standing in its responsibility to see the grand jury's return under its jurisdiction to have such evidence as they thought appropriate. But we are well beyond that stage. Rule 17(c) requires much more restrictive form of evidence. It has got to be relevant and admissible. It is nothing like a grand jury.

QUESTION: Mr. St. Clair?

MR. ST. CLAIR: Yes, sir.

QUESTION: In reference to your point of our three branches are three and some fraction, is not the Comptroller General something of an autonomous, factional, more than a third branch figure.

MR. ST. CLAIR: Well, I don't think, if Your Honor please, that the Attorney General represents that the basic constitutional structure has been changed. He may have executive and he may have legislative functions.

QUESTIONS: He may proceed with reference to the Executive Branch and I would assume with reference to expenditures of the Legislative Branch and without consulting either one of them. Is that not so?

MR. ST. CLAIR: I understand. He is created by a legislative——It is very much like a semi-independent agency. In one aspect he's an agent of the legislature and in the other aspect he's an agent of the executive. But we don't have anymore than Legislative, Judicial, and the Executive Branches.

QUESTION: Mr. Jaworski, as I understand it is claiming that he is somewhat like——not necessarily precisely like——but somewhat like the Comptroller General. He may make decisions and Congress cannot recall him short of I believe it is a fifteen year term for the Comptroller General, and the President, no President can fire the Comptroller General and I suppose the Court could not fire him.

MR. ST. CLAIR: Well, I'm sure the Court couldn't. I'm not too clear about the President. In the *Myers* case[13] I really haven't thought that much of it. It could be that he could be fired. But I think that is really somewhat beside the point because this issue really turns on an admission that as to the element of executive power here involved, namely, presidential conversations, they weren't delegated. So whatever else may have been delegated those were not. And this Court has no jurisdiction to resolve a dispute as to whether or not they should be given up. Because that would involve this Court in the prosecution of the case and the judicial ——

QUESTION: Doesn't the Court decide what is necessary for a trial of a criminal case.

MR. ST. CLAIR: It can, sir, with respect to third parties but

---

[13] *Myers v. United States*, 272 U.S. 52 (1926). The Supreme Court held that the President could fire a postmaster at will even if Congress tried to restrict his removal power.

it should not involve itself with the executive function of prosecuting the case.

QUESTION: My only question was that this is a subpoena duces tecum that was issued by a judge. Right?

MR. ST. CLAIR: Yes, sir.

QUESTION: Slightly judicial.

MR. ST. CLAIR: Entirely.

QUESTION: And that's what is before us. And that you move to quash. But that's what is before us.

MR. ST. CLAIR: Our motion to quash is one of the issues before us. That's right.

QUESTION: The only thing before us is as to whether or not the subpoena should issue.

MR. ST. CLAIR: I guess it's about the same thing as whether or not it should be quashed.

QUESTION: That's right.

MR. ST. CLAIR: I think it amounts to the same thing.

QUESTION: So that's not political.

MR. ST. CLAIR: Well, it is not in the context of the proceedings here but in the context of whether or not it is in fact involved in this case it is, I suggest, political in the sense of information being sought. Admittedly it then becomes available to the House.

QUESTION: Well, I don't see where the House has got anything to do with the point that I'm talking about. You say this is political and not judicial and I submit it could be judicial because it involves the issue of subpoena.

MR. ST. CLAIR: Well, the question is is it a proper issue of subpoena.

QUESTION: That's right.

MR. ST. CLAIR: Judges make mistakes and lawyers and even presidents so far as I know. The point I want to make to you, sir, is that this is an executive function and executive decision one not delegated —

QUESTION: The executive function, as I understand your discussion as to whether you should voluntarily turn them over to the special prosecutor. We are passed that stage. We are now at the stage where the prosecutor has asked the Court to assist him and the Court has assisted him. Does that not take it a step beyond pure political or executive?

MR. ST. CLAIR: We submit if the Court had properly assisted him but the Court has no right to determine what the executive will offer in evidence.

QUESTION: I see.

MR. ST. CLAIR: And this is a function of the President. No

one has contended that the President has given up his executive responsibilities under the Constitution and certainly the prosecution of criminal cases is an executive function.

QUESTION: Absolute. Now you're arguing absolute privilege, even though every day you issue other ones.

MR. ST. CLAIR: I beg your pardon.

QUESTION: You turn tapes loose every day or so don't you?

MR. ST. CLAIR: No, we don't turn them loose every day but we have turned a number loose in the President's discretion in which he thought was the right thing to do.

QUESTION: And you're getting ready to turn twenty more tapes loose.

MR. ST. CLAIR: That is repetitious, Your Honor, of what has already been made public.

QUESTION: I thought you said you believed you would turn twenty loose.

MR. ST. CLAIR: Those would be the tapes of the twenty conversations already made public.

QUESTION: And you released those tapes.

MR. ST. CLAIR: We provided a means whereby their accuracy can be verified. We release the whole reel of tape involving a number of conversations —

QUESTION: You are still saying the absolute privilege to decide what shall be released and what shall not be released is vested in one person and nobody can question it.

MR. ST. CLAIR: Insofar as it relates to the presidential conversations, that is correct, sir.

JUSTICE STEWART: Mr. St. Clair, with the jurisdictional question, as I further understand it, that argument of yours—at least I got it from the brief—involves at least two separate concepts, maybe three. One is that this is an intra-branch dispute and that argument would be fully valid under the analogy you use in your brief if this were a dispute between let's say two committees in one of the Houses of the Congress. And one committee sued the other for jurisdiction of a particular matter you suggest, probably quite correctly, that that would not be a matter for the judiciary to determine. That's one argument. But this is purely an intra-executive branch controversy as it would be between two congressional committees. This is intra—Article 2, the hypothetical case would be intra-Article 1 branch. That's one argument.

Then you have quite a separate argument it seems to me, i.e. that the President constitutionally is the chief prosecutor since he is the executive. And that it is not for the courts to decide what a prosecutor shall use in prosecuting a case. Now, aren't those two separate arguments? You bring both of them under this rubric?

MR. ST. CLAIR: That's correct, sir. I don't know how separate they are but it certainly ——

JUSTICE STEWART: It seems to me like they are quite separate.

MR. ST. CLAIR: Well, if they're making both of them separate, fine. Now, as with respect to ——

JUSTICE STEWART: Now, the second argument would have no relevance at all to your analogy of the legislative branch.

MR. ST. CLAIR: Well, I don't want to mislead the Court into thinking that I believe Mr. Jaworski has no right to determine any evidence that he can use.

JUSTICE STEWART: But ultimately you tell us that constitutionally the President as the chief executive and whereas, constitutionally the chief prosecutor——whatever the statutes might provide——has unrestricted discretion in determining whatever he will or will not use in prosecuting the case.

MR. ST. CLAIR: That is correct.

JUSTICE STEWART: Which is quite a different concept from the other concept. You make them both under the same rubric as I say. But it seems to me they are quite separate arguments.

MR. ST. CLAIR: And I think they are well founded.

JUSTICE STEWART: I know you do or you wouldn't make them.

MR. ST. CLAIR: Now, I would like to move if I may to briefly the suggestion that the issue here is non-justiciable on the grounds other than I have already mentioned, namely, the context in which this case unfortunately now finds itself.

It seems to us briefly that the case is non-justiciable for somewhat more technical reasons. First, this is an issue where someone has to exercise some discretion. There are no real bounds or standards by which that discretion should be exercised. And by traditional standards of this Court where that exists then this Court should not take the case. Secondly, it seems to me there is a textual constitutional grant if we assume that the grant of executive power includes the means by which that can be effectively exercised. That's the second ground. The third, of course, there is a political involvement which I have suggested. Therefore, I suggest quite briefly that even if there is subject matter jurisdiction the case is non-justiciable for these additional reasons.

The standards of *Baker* v. *Carr*[14] and *Powell* are not

[14] In *Baker* v. *Carr*, 369 U.S. 186 (1962) the Supreme Court held that federal

applicable here. There is no individual's rights who have been protected against the onslaught of Government. The President is not here as an individual, he is here as the constitutional officer in whom the executive power is vested. There is no philosophy that would support a finding of justiciability on the grounds that we are strengthening the democratic processes as true in *Powell* and also to a greater extent in *Baker* and *Carr.*

If anything, a decision in this case against the President would tend to diminish the democratic process. This President was elected on the theory that he would have all the powers, duties, and responsibilities of any other president. And if it is determined that he doesn't, there is a certain amount of diminution of the political aspect of the case insofar as constituents who voted for him are concerned. This President ought not to have any less powers than any other President ought to have. One of the necessary results as I view them from my brother's argument is that because of the circumstances of this case Richard Nixon is let's say an 85% President, not a 100% President. And that can't be constitutionally. The framers of the Constitution had in mind a strong presidency. As we know they considered a number of alternatives. A presidency consisting of three members all of which suggestions were discarded and a stong presidency was decided upon, may I say, to the distinctive management of this country as history has developed.

Now by reason of the action of a grand jury the special prosecutor suggests that this President has something less than any other president would have. I would only call your attention to the action of the framers of the constitutional convention when the issue was raised as to whether or not a President who was under impeachment should be suspended during the pendency of the impeachment proceeding. And the decision was definitely he should not because the framers envisioned a strong, active President even in the course of impeachment proceedings. They did not want this country to be led by someone who didn't have those full powers even if he was under impeachment. And indeed, this President continues to function as President, as he should, even though there are impeachment inquiries underway.

QUESTION: If I may interrupt you again, is what you're telling us now directed to your point, that this is a non-justiciable political question or is it directed to your point that the executive privilege is absolute and that the determination of it is to be ——

courts could examine the apportionment standards set for legislative districts. It laid down the definition of what constituted a "political question" which could not be reviewed by the courts.

MR. ST. CLAIR: I think that it involves both. It is non-justiciable, if I may, because it does involve the Court in a political matter.

Now, the mere fact that politics is involved is, of course, not preventing the court from taking appropriate action under the cases where individual rights are involved or where the franchise of voters could be strengthened by a decision of the Court. I am suggesting in this case the converse is true. Therefore, the justification between *Baker* and *Carr* and the *Powell* case is not available and not applicable here. Furthermore, however, the argument still in my view has force with respect to the consequences of the grand jury action in naming him as a co-conspirator which we suggest they were not qualified to do. The President is not above the law by any means. But law as to the President has to be applied in a constitutional way which is different than anyone else. Namely, we suggest that he can only be impeached while in office and cannot be indicted until such time as he no longer is in office.

QUESTION: Well, let's assume that we accept that proposition. What follows from it?

MR. ST. CLAIR: Well, then the naming of the President by a grand jury as a co-conspirator. If that has the effect of diminishing the President's rights it is a pro tanto impeachment.

QUESTION: I should think you could run the argument the other way, saying that since the President cannot be indicted then all that can happen to him is that he be, can be named as an unindicted co-conspirator.

MR. ST. CLAIR: That could be said. But by the naming of him as an unindicted co-conspirator we suggest is an intrusion by the grand jury on a function that is solely legislative and not judicial.

JUSTICE DOUGLAS: A president could be sued, couldn't he, for back taxes or penalities or what not?

MR. ST. CLAIR: Well, in questions of immunity I think individually he could be.

JUSTICE DOUGLAS: The Constitution speaks of persons, any person.

MR. ST. CLAIR: That's correct. I think the President could be sued for back taxes in his individual capacity. But in terms of his power to effect the responsibilities of his office, to protect the presidency from unwarranted intrusions into the confidentiality of his communications, that's not a personal matter.

QUESTION: It may be that one of these defendants might be completely exonerated from something in one of those tapes.

MR. ST. CLAIR: As I have suggested, if that defendant will satisfy a Court that there is such a tape and will identify it or will even come close to it and persuade a Court that that would exonerate him or there's reason to believe it might I don't believe we'll have a question. But that's not what my brother here is asking for. He's asking for a set number of tapes, not for that purpose, although he throws that in but he really wants them he says for prosecution. And I would like to review with the Court the question of the necessity shown for this because he went on his theory of a qualified privilege. There has to be a showing of some necessity.

Now we should understand——and I am sure the Court knows——that all of these individuals here involved have testified before the Senate Select Committee, with exception I believe of either Mr. Colson who now has plead quilty under plea bargain where he has agreed to cooperate so that the special prosecutor has the full benefit of his testimony. They have testified on one or more occasions before a grand jury. In addition, the President has furnished to the special prosecutor the transcripts and tapes of the critical conversations involved in this alleged conspiracy and I might review those very briefly with you. Mr. Dean in his Senate Committee testimony suggested that on September 15 the President acknowledged a cover-up. He changed that later to testimony that he believed that was so and it was an inference. In any event the President furnished that portion of that tape of the conversation with Mr. Dean.

Mr. Dean also testified that on March 13, 1973, he discussed the cover-up with the President in efforts to blackmail the President by one of the defendants who broke into the Democratic National Headquarters. Later it developed that that was a mistake in that it was actually on March 21 and the grand jury indictment proceeds on the theory of March 21st. The tape of the conversation of March 13 was furnished, all of the conversations between the principals, being two in number, on March 21st were furnished. The conversations between the individuals and the President on the next day in the afternoon of March 22nd was furnished. And a large number of additional conversations were furnished.

Now if *Reynolds* means anything——and *Reynolds* in addition to the *Kaiser Aluminum* case noted a constitutional question, as I think one of the learned Justices suggested——one of the reasons for not facing that issue in that case was it was not necessary because in the case there was a crash of a bomber that was on a secret mission, and the Court said that the parties had the testimony of the witnesses, the survivors and other testimony that it wasn't necessary to get to the constitutional question. I suggest that's true here. It is difficult for me to conceive a prosecutor who has more evidence than this prosecutor has. He has full benefit of a Senate Select Committee investigation which staff had 50-odd lawyers, existed for a year, he has the benefit of his own investigation of a grand jury that sat for nineteen months with an investigative staff of similar proportions; he simply says I need this because I want to present all of the evidence in the case. He does not say —

QUESTION: I don't understand that. Do you think that a prosecutor could get this from a normal third party witness, he can't get it from the President because of executive privilege; that there must be a further showing beyond the relevance shown in 17(c)?

MR. ST. CLAIR: As we point out in our brief, the tape of the conversation is very —

QUESTION: The answer is "yes" isn't it, that there is a further showing necessary?

MR. ST. CLAIR: That's right. Does he really need it. What does he say he needs it for?

QUESTION: How does a District Court go about deciding a question like that in advance of trial without a prosecutor lays out his entire evidence and says "It is my judgment that this is evidence and without this evidence I might lose the case."

MR. ST. CLAIR: He doesn't say that. He made a showing to the Court below. The showing is available to you here.

QUESTION: But you would suggest that he would have to do that?

MR. ST. CLAIR: He has the burden under *Reynolds*, under *Kaiser Aluminum*, and so forth, to show that he needs it. And what does he say he needs it for? He doesn't say he needs it to obtain conviction.

JUSTICE WHITE: Mr. St. Clair, while I've got you let me interrupt and ask you something else.

MR. ST. CLAIR: Yes, sir.

JUSTICE WHITE: And it is related to this. No matter how absolute the executive privilege is that you claim on behalf of the President I assume you're talking about conversations to which the privilege would apply.

MR. ST. CLAIR: Yes, sir.

JUSTICE WHITE: Now, is it —

MR. ST. CLAIR: We have to make such a showing and I say that is our only burden.

JUSTICE WHITE: You wouldn't suggest that every conversation the President had has, while he's in office would be subject to executive privilege?

MR. ST. CLAIR: No. It would have to be a confidential communication.

JUSTICE WHITE: Well, it has to be in the course of his duties as President.

MR. ST. CLAIR: Yes, but it private —

JUSTICE WHITE: It would be in carrying out his duties as President under the Constitution?

MR. ST. CLAIR: Yes, sir.

JUSTICE WHITE: Now, I don't suppose if he was talking with one of his aides, Mr. Haldeman, Mr. Ehrlichman about an investment of his out in California, you know or some other place —

MR. ST. CLAIR: Or a tennis game or whatever.

JUSTICE WHITE: Yes. You wouldn't suggest that that —

MR. ST. CLAIR: My brother doesn't suggest that that is what he wants either.

JUSTICE WHITE: Well, how about conversations about a campaign, about the Nixon campaign?

MR. ST. CLAIR: That's getting a little closer.

JUSTICE WHITE: It isn't closer to the executing of the laws of the United States, is it, running of a political campaign?

MR. ST. CLAIR: I don't think it is very close, no.

JUSTICE WHITE: Conversations about that subject matter.

MR. ST. CLAIR: My brother isn't seeking any such conversations.

JUSTICE WHITE: I know. But shouldn't the President have to say at least, even if the privilege is as absolute as you say it is, shouldn't he at least have to say I believe or assert that the executive privilege applies to this tape because this conversation is in the course of his performance of his duties as President?

MR. ST. CLAIR: As I read some of —

QUESTION: You haven't done that either, have you?

MR. ST. CLAIR: We have not done that. We have simply responded to an assertion that these all relate to Watergate.

Assuming that to be the facts —

QUESTION: Would you automatically say that every conversation about Watergate is in the course of the performance of the duties of the President of the United States?

MR. ST. CLAIR: I would think it would be, yes, sir.

QUESTION: Why is that, Mr. St. Clair?

MR. ST. CLAIR: Because he has the duty, (a) to enforce the laws; that is, to prosecute these cases; and (b) he has to take care to see that the laws are enforced; that is, to investigate. And much of this material does relate to the investigation as 1,200 and some pages of the public transcript fully discloses. But I would be ready to concede——and I don't think that it is a difficult problem between us——that the President should show that the circumstances are appropriate for the claim of such a privilege and I think such language appears in *Mink*[15] and perhaps even in *Reynolds* and *Kaiser Aluminum*. Simply it has to be a confidential communication first of all and ——

QUESTION: How about——Do you concede or what is your view of the privilege with respect to whether it reaches a factual assertions in a conversation, the difference that was made in the *Mink* case and in others with respect to opinions and judgments as distinguished from facts?

MR. ST. CLAIR: Well, of course, *Mink*, I believe, was a ——

QUESTION: Statutory case.

MR. ST. CLAIR: ——statutory case. But that was one of the exceptions.

QUESTION: Well, what is your view, would you say if conversation is merely a recitation of fact it is still covered by executive privilege?

MR. ST. CLAIR: Yes, it is. If it's confidential and it is between the President and some advisor with respect to ——

QUESTION: Well, that hasn't got much to do with the decision making process, just pure cold facts.

MR. ST. CLAIR: It might well have to do with the decision making process if the facts are such as were developed in the course of an investigation with regard to the existence of an obstruction of justice charge much of which the President was involved in. But the fact-against-opinion decisions really relate to another situation as I suggest in the statute but the conversations that the President has with his advisors which we suggest is absolutely privileged. It is a discretionary matter that he has to exercise in what he is going to release and not release. And since *Marbury* and *Madison*, *Mississippi* and *Johnson*,[16] it has been clear that the Courts will not direct a President to exercise his discretion in any manner. This is not to say the Courts won't strike down as in *Sawyer* excessive action on the part of the President where excessive action on the part of the legislature

[15] In *Environmental Protection Agency* v. *Mink*, 410 U.S. 73 (1973) the Supreme Court held that any documents classified under the provisions of a proper executive order could not be disclosed pursuant to the Freedom of Information Act.

[16] In *Mississippi* v. *Johnson*, 4 Wall. 475 (1867) the Supreme Court refused to entertain a lawsuit against President Andrew Johnson challenging his Reconstruction program in the South after the Civil War.

that has happened a number of times. But it's a far different thing to suggest that the Court undertake to direct the President to exercise his discretion in a certain manner.

It is not a ministerial duty by any means. It is a matter of discretion. There are some things he feels he probably should under the circumstances make available and others he shouldn't.

QUESTION: In that particular instance, the one here involves the relevancy of materials to a criminal trial. And that normally has been a part of the judicial power under Article III and not executive power.

MR. ST. CLAIR: Well, I would like to discuss very briefly *Gregoire*[17] if I may, for example. I think this raises a very important question.

There is, of course, an explicit speech and debate immunity provided in the Constitution. As our brief indicates the reason for this is quite clear. It is to protect the legislature from unwarranted invasion from the executive and perhaps even the judicial. It does not mean the executive is not entitled to substantially the same thing by implication. And at least in the civil field, as we have pointed out, the Courts have worked out by implication as a necessary ingredient to the function of the duties of the executive an absolute immunity from civil liability for actions taken within the sphere of the official. *Spalding* and *Vilas*[18] I guess is the leading case cited in *Barr* and *Matteo*[19] and other cases.

If such a matter can be worked out with respect to the executive on civil matters we suggest there is no reason why in fact the court should spell out a similar exemption in criminal matters especially as they relate to the President himself. Because while I said the President is not above the law, the law can only be made applicable to him in a certain way while he is in office.

Now, if a junior congressman can commit a crime on the floor of the house as apparently is possible under *Gravel* and *Johnson*[20] is it to be said that the President of the United States

---

[17] *Gregoire* v. *Biddle*, 177 F. 2d 579 (2d Cir. 1949) held that the attorney general and other officials of the Justice Department were absolutely immune from suit for activities within the scope of their powers.

[18] *Spalding* v. *Vilas*, 161 U.S. 484 (1896) held that the Postmaster General could not be sued for activities imposed on him by law.

[19] *Barr* v. *Matteo*, 360 U.S. 564 (1959) held that a high executive official could not be sued for libel for releasing a press release relating to his official duties.

[20] *United States* v. *Johnson*, 383 U.S. 169 (1966) held that a Congressman could not be held criminally liable for any speech he made on the floor of Congress even if it was alleged to be an overt act in a criminal conspiracy.

has less immunity than a junior congressman? I think not. So I suggest to you that common sense and the proper construction of the Constitution imply within the plan of executive power all those necessary ingredients to make it work to be effective which would include immunity and criminal immunity. The President we suggest cannot be indicted, cannot be named as a co-conspirator because that is an assumption of a legislative function under the Constitution. And therefore we suggest that even if this is criminal the President is immune from ordinary criminal process. He is not immune from process. But that process that is available to the President is the process of impeachment which does not include the function of the judiciary branch. And therefore we say that if under Gravel the congressman is entitled to immunity even from criminal conduct for actions taken within the legislation sphere of his conduct then it would be very hard to support a proposition that the President as the chief executive of the country is entitled to less.

JUSTICE MARSHALL: Except they didn't put it in the constitution.

MR. ST. CLAIR: Right. And the reason they didn't was it was not found to be necessary. They didn't put civil immunity into the Constitution either for the executive branch and this Court has found ——

JUSTICE MARSHALL: I'm not talking about that. I'm talking about the *Gravel* case. The Gravel case was on the Constitution, wasn't it?

MR. ST. CLAIR: It was a speech and debate case and it even forbade, as I understand the Gravel case, grand jury inquiry into motivations and actions of the senator and his aide.

JUSTICE MARSHALL: Because the Constitution said so.

MR. ST. CLAIR: Right. And I suggest the Constitution by clear implication provides the same not only for the executive but for the judicial as well. And certainly for the executive.

JUSTICE MARSHALL: And if we can't find it in the Constitution what happens to your argument?

MR. ST. CLAIR: Well, I would suggest you should find it in the Constitution. And it need not be explicit. It can well be implied.

JUSTICE MARSHALL: My question is if we can't find it what happens to your argument?

MR. ST. CLAIR: If you cannot find it?

JUSTICE MARSHALL: Yes, sir.

MR. ST. CLAIR: Then, if Your Honor please, that portion of the argument is lost as far as this Court is concerned.

QUESTION: Don't you—You haven't lost your other point

because this Court can set up the same kind of privilege that they've set up in other ones.

MR. ST. CLAIR: That's correct. And we're suggesting that it should in this case. Not necessarily because a great deal is now left to be gained by expunging the grand jury action. My brother is right, the damage has been done and we think quite improperly so. We think the tactics involved with the prosecutor in seeking to enlarge the scope of admissible testimony is hardly worth what has been done here but it has been done.

But it seems to me history would be served by granting of the relief we have prayed for below, namely, to expunge this; secondly, seems to me the American people would feel better about the fairness of the issues now pending before the House if that were expunged.

Insofar as the mechanisms of this case are concerned, it destroys or removes a basis on which they contend they are entitled to these documents. And I would like to address that for a moment.

QUESTION: We have been asked many times to do that in other cases with respect to grand juries, and up to today I don't think we have ever come anywhere near doing it.

MR. ST. CLAIR: And up to today you have never had a President of the United States named as a co-conspirator either, sir.

QUESTION: That is very true.

MR. ST. CLAIR: And the President of the United States——I don't mean to be facetious about it——but the President of the United States, we suggest, can be proceeded against only by impeachment while in office. And his powers are unabated until such time as he leaves that office.

Now with respect to this suggestion that a grand jury finding is prima facie evidence ——

QUESTION: That of course has never been decided either.

MR. ST. CLAIR: No. This case is unusual in many respects.

This suggestion that a grand jury finding is prima facie evidence and therefore the President has lost whatever privilege he otherwise would have had, isn't borne out either by the facts or the legal issues and principles involved. A grand jury finding is not prima facie evidence.

Even if it is mentioned in an opening argument in the criminal trial, there is a grave risk of a mistrial. The cases cited by my brother, particularly the *Clark*[21] case, are clearly cases which require a showing in court, or in *Clark* a showing to the judge that there was prima facie evidence of wrong doing.

You may recall that is a case involving an investigation into a juror as to whether or not the juror had performed properly. And the juror, it had been shown, had testified falsely in the qualifications, that she had never had any business relations with one of the parties when in fact she had. The court said, well, there is a finding of wrong doing, and based on that now I will look into the jury's deliberations to see what she did.

But Justice Cardozo made it very clear that if he hadn't been able to make a prima facie showing of wrong doing by evidence before him, there would have been no cause for letting in the light as he put it.

In the *Carter* case,[22] and other cases, which are relied on by my brothers, are all cases where there was a prima facie showing in a courtroom. Now a grand jury charge is not prima facie. In the first place it is only accusatory. It is not even admissible in, nor can it be referred to in a trial.

Secondly, it can well involve incompetent evidence as this Court has recently decided. And it is totally inappropriate to suggest that a President who otherwise would have a very valuable privilege, and I think I should emphasize the value of this privilege because it is a valuable privilege.

All you have to do is read Justice Reed's decision in *Kaiser Aluminum*, and he spells it out quite clearly, the importance and value of this privilege. To simply say to have a grand jury make a charge, that destroys that privilege, is an argument that I don't think can be sustained.

CHIEF JUSTICE BURGER: Mr. St. Clair, you have not mentioned in your argument, a few moments ago, on the absence of any provision for immunity for judges or presidents—you haven't mentioned the holding of this Court in *Pierson* against *Ray*[23] whereas recall it the Court assumed with a sentence or

---

[21] *Clark v. United States,* 289 U.S. 1 (1933) held that jury deliberations could not be examined in later proceedings unless there was direct and substantial evidence of improprieties such as a juror accepting a bribe.

[22] *United States v. Carter,* 15 F.R.D. 367 (D.D.C. 1954) held that only those documents which would be admissible at trial or which may be used for impeachment purposes can be subpoenaed under Rule 17(c).

[23] *Pierson v. Ray,* 386 U.S. 547 (1967) held that state judges were absolutely immune from suit under the Civil Rights Act and policemen were also immune it they had probable cause for an arrest.

two that there was absolute privilege for the Judiciary but that the privileges of the Executive, in that case a policeman, was qualified. The Court had no difficulty in concluding that it did not require an expressed constitutional provision to spell out an absolute privilege for judges. These were state judges in that case, of course.

MR. ST. CLAIR: That's right. If Your Honor please, I don't believe that simply because the Constitution does not explicitly state ——

QUESTION: Your immunity.

MR. ST. CLAIR: As it does in the Speech and Debate Clause, should this Court hold it does not exist in criminal matters.

I would like to make one point with the Court, however, because I am sure the point will be raised concerning Justice Kerner, for example; there is a distinct difference, as we point out in our reply brief, as we view it, between a President of the United States, a single individual in whom the entire Executive function is vested. A President serves seven days a week, 24 hours a day. And only he, or those under him performing his functions, can exercise the Executive functions of our government.

Now if a congressman or a senator, or even if a judge ——

QUESTION: Who is to determine how much evidence the prosecutor needs? Only the prosecutor.

MR. ST. CLAIR: That's correct.

QUESTION: Don't you agree?

MR. ST. CLAIR: That's correct. Not the Court.

QUESTION: Don't you agree?

MR. ST. CLAIR: And if that evidence constitutes presidential confidential communications, then I suggest, if Your Honor please, the President determines that.

QUESTION: Many a case has been lost because the prosecutor had too much evidence.

MR. ST. CLAIR: Well, I suggest that's probably the fact here.

So when the government says, I don't need this evidence to win these cases, in my opinion, but I need them so I can present all the evidence.

QUESTION: But you're still ——

MR. ST. CLAIR: I've been trying cases long enough to know, and so has he. That's not what he is really after.

QUESTION: Yes, I've tried a few, too.

[Laughter.]

Mr. St. Clair, I was just wondering, where do you see the burden here——is it on the prosecution?

MR. ST. CLAIR: The burden under 17(c) is clearly on the prosecution, and the burden is clearly on the prosecution on every other aspect.

QUESTION: Right. And now, how much is enough for our phrase we've been kicking around, prima facie?

MR. ST. CLAIR: Well, I suggest whatever was considered by this Court in *Reynolds* to be enough, is more than enough in this case. We have the testimony of every individual involved, a number of them have pled guilty. Dean has pled guilty. Colson has pled guilty. Kalmbach has pled guilty, et cetera, et cetera. All under plea bargains, where they are under obligation to fully cooperate.

This Prosecutor is not, nor does he say at any point that he needs this information to prosecute successfully these cases.

QUESTION: Mr. St. Clair, just to pinpoint another issue, let's assume for the moment that we didn't agree with you on your test of privilege, and let's just assume that the only issue that was left in the case was the 17(c) issue.

QUESTION: Or a Vice President?

MR. ST. CLAIR: Or a Vice President, is removed from his duties, matters go on. But a President doesn't have that opportunity to take a vacation. It is vested in one individual and deliberately so.

QUESTION: This is pretty far afield from the basic question here which is the testimonial privilege —

MR. ST. CLAIR: We say it's a constitutional privilege.

QUESTION: Not prosecutorial immunity, but testimonial privilege is what we are dealing with here basically.

MR. ST. CLAIR: That is correct. I think so.

I want to make the point with you that we think that the privilege we are arguing for is both common law and constitutional law.

QUESTION: I understand that.

MR. ST. CLAIR: It is constitutional because it is inherent in the Executive power, and

QUESTION: I understand your argument. But this matter of whether or not a judge can be prosecuted criminally has nothing to do with testimonial privilege, does it?

MR. ST. CLAIR: Well, my brothers seem to think it does, because they say because of the implications of criminality here, the President has lost something he otherwise would not have had.

JUSTICE STEWART: I understand that. Since I have already interrupted you, may I prevail upon your good nature —

MR. ST. CLAIR: Please do.

JUSTICE STEWART: —Mr. St. Clair, to ask you whether it is your claim that any of these materials have to do with what have sometimes been called matters of state, i.e. matters of international relations or national defense? Mr. Jaworski assured us that they did not involve matters of state. Because as you well know, both the commentators and court decisions have made a dichotomy between the privilege that exists with respect to general confidentiality on the one hand of the Executive, and matters of state, on the other, to which a higher privilege is sometimes been thought to have been accorded.

MR. ST. CLAIR: Well, I think if a higher privilege has been accorded, it should not——but in any event the privilege of confidentiality is not unimportant, however ——

JUSTICE STEWART: I know that.

MR. ST. CLAIR: Let me direct myself to your question. The answer to your question is no one knows. You won't know until you listen to these tapes as to what subjects are discussed. My brother can only state that it is probable that they relate at least in part to whatever he says, Watergate, or it's likely that it might. And I have had the experience, for example, where circumstances were such that the House committee felt that it was likely that a conversation took place between the Attorney General, Mr. Mitchell, and the President regarding plans for surveillance of the Democratic party. When you looked at the conversation, it wasn't there at all.

So I have no way of knowing, nor does the Prosecutor know, what additional matters may be interwoven into these conversations. One thing is certain ——

JUSTICE STEWART: Am I mistaken in believing, Mr. St. Clair, in understanding, Mr. St. Clair, that in this case to date no representation has been made by affidavit or professional representation or otherwise that any of these materials have to do with national defense or international relations?

MR. ST. CLAIR: No. And no representation can be made to the contrary either.

QUESTION: And that would be therefore a matter to be, under the existing order now under review of Judge Sirica, that would be submitted to him later in camera.

MR. ST. CLAIR: If this court finds ——

QUESTION: I say under his existing order.

MR. ST. CLAIR: Yes, that is right. And the President presumably if he were to comply with that order, would make such a representation in an appropriate case. But the fundamental point is that we believe for reasons stated that the President's right to confidential advice is important ——

QUESTION: I understand that.

MR. ST. CLAIR: And it is actually fundamental to the proper

functioning of his government. And in many instances I suggest it is even more important in military matters and matters of state, so to speak, because no matter what the conversation is, of course, it is the thought that it might become public that involves then this chilling effect we have made reference to in our brief under the first amendment. But as a practical matter, and I can see it myself, the communications are not free and open because who is to say that you won't be called before a grand jury. Most everyone in the White House has been called before a grand jury sometime several times. The FBI has interviewed every secretary that had any knowledge of any aspect of this case.

This Prosecutor has a plethora of information. He says he wants to try the case with all the evidence. Well, he knows better than that. Nobody tries any case with all the evidence. You would be buried in minutiae. You select the evidence that you think most appropriate to your case. You don't try it with all the evidence.

And this Special Prosecutor has mountains of information.

Now, ——

MR. ST. CLAIR: Then the President wins, in my view.

QUESTION: Well, because?

MR. ST. CLAIR: Because the Prosecutor cannot show that the evidence he seeks is relevant and admissible. Because of the nature of the circumstance, he doesn't know what's in there.

QUESTION: Well, I suppose there are two parts to the question: one, how much of a showing does he have to make as to what might be on the tape; and, secondly, if that matter that he claims is on the tape is on the tape, is that relevant and admissible under 17(c)?

MR. ST. CLAIR: You would have to know what the matter was, what the issues in the case were, but under *Bowman*[24] and *Iozia*,[25] it's not enough to show that it probably is or it might be or is likely to be; it must be shown to be relevant, and must be shown to be admissible.

QUESTION: But, Mr. St. Clair, ——

MR. ST. CLAIR: That's why it's not a third-party ——

QUESTION: Mr. St. Clair, you can't put an impossible task

[24] *Bowman Dairy Co.* v. *United States,* 341 U.S. 214 (1951) held that the government could be ordered to produce, under Rule 17(c), all documents which it had presented to the grand jury or would offer in evidence at trial.

[25] In *United States* v. *Iozia,* 13 F.R.D. 335 (S.D.N.Y. 1952) the court held that a defendant could obtain from the government under Rule 17(c) all relevant material before trial that he needed in good faith to properly prepare for trial.

on someone who wants to subpoena against a third-party witness, or against anybody else, as to showing what is precisely in some documents, I would suppose.

MR. ST. CLAIR: Well, if you want to utilize 17(c), then I suggest that's what you have to do.

QUESTION: He's never listened to the tapes. He doesn't know precisely what's on them. You would say that he could never subpoena a tape unless he had already gotten it.

MR. ST. CLAIR: As a prosecutor, that's right.

QUESTION: Well, that's —

MR. ST. CLAIR: As a grand jury, that's another matter. If he had sought these under a grand jury subpoena, we would then be directly faced with *Nixon* v. *Sirica*, which we happen to think was improperly, incorrectly decided.

But under 17(c) we're dealing with the prosecutor's subpoena. The decided cases make it quite clear there must be a specific showing of relevance and admissibility.

Now, if he can't do it because of the nature of —

QUESTION: Well, that isn't what 17(c) —

MR. ST. CLAIR: That's his problem, not mine.

QUESTION: The cases you're talking about are cases where a defendant sought discovery of evidence from the—or sought material in the prosecutor's files.

MR. ST. CLAIR: Most of those cases are, but there is at least one case, I think it's *Gross*[26]   that says the rules are equally applicable to the prosecution; it's cited in one of the footnotes in our brief.

But a 17(c) subpoena is conceptually a subpoena for known information, conceptually, if the prosecutor is looking for things, he should utilize a grand jury subpoena. In that case, I think in *Bowman* they wanted the prosecutor to produce each document he was going to use in the presentation of his case. That's specific.

It's obviously relevant and admissible.

QUESTION: So once he gets through with the grand jury he can't, he shouldn't be using a subpoena to develop his case?

MR. ST. CLAIR: That's correct.

And certainly not under these circumstances.

QUESTION: Do you think that's the practice in the federal courts —

MR. ST. CLAIR: I think it is the practice. I think that the

[26] *United States* v. *Gross,* 24 F.R.D. 138 (S.D.N.Y. 1959) h ld that Rule 17(c) was applicable to the government as well as a defendant.

grand jury practice is far, far greater perhaps than the Constitution has envisioned. It's really used today, frankly, as an effective discovery tool.

JUSTICE POWELL: Mr. St. Clair, may I get back to what seems rather fundamental to me. Let us assume that it had been established that the conversations we are talking about here today did involve a criminal conspiracy, would you still be asserting an absolute privilege?

MR. ST. CLAIR: Yes, quite clearly. Under the analogy with *Gravel* that I made.

JUSTICE POWELL: Right. And as I understand it, the public interest behind that privilege is the preservation of candor in discussions between the President and his closest aides.

MR. ST. CLAIR: Quite clearly so. The simple reason, sir, ——

JUSTICE POWELL: Right. May I follow that up?

MR. ST. CLAIR: I'm sorry.

JUSTICE POWELL: What public interest is there in preserving secrecy with respect to a criminal conspiracy?

MR. ST. CLAIR: The answer, sir, is that a criminal conspiracy is criminal only after it's proven to be criminal.

JUSTICE POWELL: But my ——

MR. ST. CLAIR: And we're not at that point yet.

JUSTICE POWELL: My question was based on the assumption that it had been established that the conversation did relate to a criminal conspiracy.

MR. ST. CLAIR: That is, the case has been tried and the defendant found guilty.

JUSTICE POWELL: No. Well, it could have been established in various ways, as you just said, a number of people have already confessed, and these people were participants in some of these conversations.

MR. ST. CLAIR: But the fact that one defendant confessed does not make the other defendant quilty.

JUSTICE POWELL: Of course. But, anyway, your answer is that you would still assert absolute privilege.

MR. ST. CLAIR: The answer is yes, even if it is criminal. But, more importantly, it is yes, because criminality is something that is not necessarily determined at the time that you must resolve the issue. And that you should not destroy the privilege in the anticipation of a later finding of criminality which may never come to pass.

It is quite conceivable that a number of these defendants will be found innocent. And, in fact, in theory, they are innocent right now.

QUESTION: What is the public interest in keeping that

secret?

MR. ST. CLAIR: To avail the President, if Your Honor please, of a free and untrammeled source of information, and advice, without the thought or fear that it may be reviewed at some later time, when some grand jury in this case, or some other reason, suggests there is criminality.

For example, ——

QUESTION: But you ——

MR. ST. CLAIR: ——it's very important——I'm sorry.

QUESTION: You did release them for the grand jury in this case.

MR. ST. CLAIR: Yes. In the President's discretion, he did that. And it's a discretionary matter.

But, for example, the simple matter of appointments, if I may, an appointment of a judge, it's very important to the judiciary to have good judges. It's not at all unheard of for lawyers to be asked their opinion about a nominee.

Now, if that lawyer wants to be sure that he's going to be protected in giving candid opinions regarding a nominee for the bench, it's absolutely essential that that be protected. Otherwise, you're not going to get candid advice.

Now, this isn't a State secret, it isn't national defense; I suggest it's more important, because that judge may sit on that bench for thirty years.

QUESTION: Well, don't you think it would be important if the judge and the President were discussing how they were going to make appointments for money?

MR. ST. CLAIR: I'm sorry, sir, I didn't understand your question.

QUESTION: Don't you think it would be important in a hypothetical case if an about-to-be appointed judge was making a deal with the President for money?

MR. ST. CLAIR: Absolutely.

QUESTION: But under yours it couldn't be. In public interest you couldn't release that.

MR. ST. CLAIR: I would think that that could not be released, if it were a confidential communication. If the President did appoint such an individual, the remedy is clear, the remedy is he should be impeached.

Let me give you an example ——

JUSTICE MARSHALL: How are you going to impeach him if you don't know about it?

MR. ST. CLAIR: Well, if you know about it, then you can state the case. If you don't know about it, you don't have it.

JUSTICE MARSHALL: So there you are. You're on the

prongs of a dilemma, huh?

MR. ST. CLAIR: No, I don't think so.

JUSTICE MARSHALL: If you know the President is doing something wrong, you can impeach him, but the only way you can find out is this way; you can't impeach him, so you don't impeach him. You lose me some place along there.

[Laughter.]

MR. ST. CLAIR: Well, this is, I think, what was suggested in the *Seaborg*[27] case, where the Court said, Well, gee, if that is so, then fraud could be all covered over and so forth.

Human experience has not demonstrated that's a fact, very few things forever are hidden.

Secondly, however, this case is not that case. As I pointed out, there is a plethora of information. This is not a case where there is no information. If anything, there is more than enough.

QUESTION: Well, what you're telling us also could be argued the other way, that there's been a waiver and neither you ——

MR. ST. CLAIR: That has been suggested by my brother.

QUESTION: ——nor your brother have talked about waiver. I don't suggest that it's ——

MR. ST. CLAIR: My brother suggests a waiver, but this privilege is not like Fifth Amendment privilege or attorney-client privilege, where if you let out one word you've lost the whole thing. That would defeat the purpose of it.

QUESTION: Yes.

MR. ST. CLAIR: As we've pointed out in our brief, public policy requires as much publicity as the President, in his discretion, determines would be appropriate and the more information the better. And if you require——if you rule that one utterance constitutes a waiver ——

QUESTION: Right.

MR. ST. CLAIR: ——you're not going to get it; you're not going to have that thing. This is a discretionary privilege that the Constitution, by implication of necessity and history, has shown is inherent in the executive function, as indeed it is in other functions.

We've cited in our brief similar examples of the Legislature insisting upon such a privilege, even against subpoenas from courts, Executive, and from the courts themselves.

CHIEF JUSTICE BURGER: Mr. St. Clair, you are cutting into your rebuttal time now.

---

[27] *Committee for Nuclear Responsibility* v. *Seaborg*, 463 F. 2d 788 (D.C. Cir 1971) held that the government could be forced to hand over documents relating to underground nuclear tests if a judge determined they were relevant and contained no military or diplomatic secrets.

MR. ST. CLAIR: I know. I do appreciate being reminded of that, and I think I would preserve it, which I think is ten more minutes of it.

CHIEF JUSTICE BURGER: Mr. Lacovara.

REBUTTAL ARGUMENT OF PHILIP A. LACOVARA, ESQ.,
ON BEHALF OF THE UNITED STATES

MR. LACOVARA: Thank you, Mr. Chief Justice

If I may, I would like to advert first to procedural questions that Mr. Justice Blackmun and Mr. Justice Stewart have raised about whether the mandamus case is properly here.

Mr. Justice, we did, in our certiorari petition, refer to the fact that we were trying to bring before the Court, for review before a judgment in the court of appeals, the order of the district court, which we said the President had tried to obtain review of in two ways in two cases in the district court——in the court of appeals, rather. And we gave the docket numbers of those two cases.

That certiorari petition was filed on the 24th of May, and Judge Sirica, who is the respondent, as Justice Stewart properly notes, in the mandamus case in the court of appeals, was served with a copy of the certiorari petition, as he had been served with the mandamus petition, as, indeed, had all the respondents who were otherwise before the court, the defendants in the *United States* v. *Mitchell.*

On May 28th, in accordance with a motion that was filed in the court of appeals, a copy of which, I believe, is in the files of this Court, the court of appeals transmitted to this Court the records in both of those cases, the appeal and the mandamus cases.

Now, Mr. Justice Stewart, with respect to Judge Sirica's appearance here, he is a party before this Court, and I believe there is a letter on file with the Clerk of this Court from Judge Sirica, in which he states that he will not appear separately, the United States, through the Special Prosecutor, is appearing on behalf of Judge Sirica, as, indeed, we would have in the court of appeals, to uphold his decision enforcing our subpoena.

So the case, procedurally, is properly before the Court, both with respect to the appeal and the mandamus proceeding.

I would like to ——

JUSTICE WHITE: Mr. Lacovara, before you get too far, let's assume you get by the jurisdictional matters and also the standing question, the intra-Executive dispute matter, and we get to the executive privilege or get to the merits, so-called ——

MR. LACOVARA: Yes.

JUSTICE WHITE: —which end of this case should we, would we normally start at, anyway? At the 17(c) end of the executive privilege end?

MR. LACOVARA: Well, I think—normally—I think normally you might start at the 17(c) end, because that would provide for a, conceivably for a disposition on non-constitutional grounds if you found that we had not made a sufficient showing to satisfy the ordinary requirements of that rule.

So, in accordance with the Court's normal jurisprudence —

JUSTICE WHITE: Mr. Lacovara, Judge Sirica found that you had satisfied the requirements.

MR. LACOVARA: Absolutely.

JUSTICE WHITE: Well, then what's the scope of our review?

MR. LACOVARA: We have made the suggestion that any appellate court reviewing this kind of determination applies a standard of whether the district judge, who is intimately familiar with this indictment and with the 49-page appendix, showing that we submitted, in demonstrating why each of these 64 subpoenaed conversations was material, he made the finding that we had clearly demonstrated relevance and an evidentiary nature, and —

JUSTICE WHITE: What's our standard of appellate review?

MR. LACOVARA: And your standard should be whether he has abused his discretion.

JUSTICE WHITE: Clearly erroneous?

MR. LACOVARA: Clearly erroneous standard, yes, sir.

JUSTICE WHITE: What about the standard, though?

MR. LACOVARA: I'm sorry, it's the basis standard, he called it.

JUSTICE WHITE: What about the basic standard of 17(c)?

MR. LACOVARA: I think the parties are in agreement that *Bowman Dairy* and *Iozia*, that district court decision, established the basic criteria.

JUSTICE WHITE: Are you—the government is in agreement that the standards of *Iozia* must be satisfied in this case under 17(c).

MR. LACOVARA: Well, we have suggested that it's possible that a lower standard can be applied.

JUSTICE WHITE: Well, that's what I'm asking you. What is your position?

MR. LACOVARA: Well, my position would be that when you are talking about a subpoena to a third party, as distinguished from an intra-case subpoena between government and defendant, a lower standard of relevancy or materiality should —

QUESTION: So the parties are not in agreement at all?

MR. LACOVARA: Well, we have suggested that even if the proper standard is applied, that we meet that standard because of the showing that we made that each of these items is —

QUESTION: Is it a necessity standard?

MR. LACOVARA: Necessity in the sense of being relevant to the issues to be tried, and being of an evidentiary nature.

Now, the necessity standard comes in more in determining whether the executive privilege claim should be overridden if, apart from the waiver fact and what we call the *Clark* point —

JUSTICE BRENNAN: It was Mr. St. Clair's argument that under 17(c) you can't possibly satisfy its requirements, because you don't know what's in the tapes.

MR. LACOVARA: Oh, well, that obviously we don't think is a proper legal standard, and the courts have said—in fact we go back to Chief Justice Marshall's opinion in the *Burr* case, where exactly the same suggestion was made by the United States Attorney in opposing the subpoena, that Burr hadn't specified which portions of General Wilkinson's letter were really going to be material, and Chief Justice Marshall replied, with his eloquent common sense, "Of course not, because he hasn't seen the letter yet. But he's made a sufficient averment that it does contain something material, that at least it should be brought into court."

Now, we, as I say, have gone much further than Colonel Burr did.

JUSTICE WHITE: You think *Iozia* just means only evidentiary and relevant, is that what you—is that your reading of that case?

MR. LACOVARA: When you're talking about a subpoena between the parties, yes, sir. They talk about other criteria, which I think are really assumed, whether it's a fishing expedition, whether you're going off on a frolic.

But, as the later cases, as, I believe, Judge Sirica indicates, seem to have distilled that —

JUSTICE WHITE: So you don't think *Iozia* and those—and *Bowman* requires any showing that this particular evidence be something more than evidentiary and relevant?

MR. LACOVARA: That it be critical?

JUSTICE WHITE: Yes.

MR. LACOVARA: No, sir, I don't believe so.

JUSTICE WHITE: Yes.

MR. LACOVARA: I think that, as you were suggesting before, and as Judge Sirica held, it's never been the law that once an indictment is returned, the prosecution is not entitled to continue gathering evidence. The burdens of proof before a grand jury and a trial jury are clearly different. It's an abuse of the grand jury process that has been held, to use a grand jury subpoena, as Mr. St. Clair suggested, to continue gathering evidence after an indictment is returned.

JUSTICE BRENNAN: Yes, but you apparently concede that you can't use it just for discovery?

MR. LACOVARA: Yes, sir.

JUSTICE WHITE: And you say that the evidence you're seeking by a subpoena, you must make some kind of a minimal showing of admissibility, you can't, for example, seek something that would admittedly be inadmissible hearsay?

MR. LACOVARA: Well, I hope I'm not conceding more than I should, but the rule does talk about subpoenaing material from a person on a showing that it will be relevant.

It's Rule 17, and I'm taking a position which is narrower than of course you're suggesting, Mr. Justice, that I might take. But, in all candor, the rule talks about subpoenaing documents from a person, not only from a party. Mr. Justice Douglas, I believe you earlier mentioned that the rule applied only to subpoenas to parties. But the rule specifically provides for subpoenas to persons who are not parties to the case.

But it says, and this was the clause that we were relying on here, the Court may direct that the books or papers be produced before the Court at a time prior to the trial or prior to the time when they are to be offered in evidence.

So there does seem to be some natural focus about the evidentiary nature of this case.

JUSTICE WHITE: I just wanted to get the government's position, because it is a rather important part of the case.

MR. LACOVARA: Yes, sir.

We insist, as Judge Sirica found, that the citation of chapter and verse, if I may, in our 49-page showing before the district court, with references to sworn testimony, as well as with representations about what witnesses will testify at trial, we demonstrated why each of these subpoenaed conversations satisfied the *Bowman Dairy*, *Iozia*, Rule 17(c) standard.

Now, that leads me into the related point—what is the relevance of the grand jury's finding that the President was a co-conspirator in this case?

It has been alleged that we did this in order to prejudice the President's rights. I think we have sought to demonstrate in our reply brief that that was —

JUSTICE STEWART: Mr. Lacovara, I don't think it would be very hard to understand the developments of a showing at the trial, for purposes of evidence, that certain people are co-conspirators, for purposes of introduction of evidence. But that's a little different question than the relevance of the grand jury having come to that conclusion.

MR. LACOVARA: Yes. Normally I would concede it is not the practice, as anyone who has been a prosecutor knows, for the grand jury, if it is not identifying the co-conspirators in the body of its indictment, to place them on the record. It is fairly common practice, however, for an indictment to say "In addition to the defendants, the named persons are unindicted co-conspirators." This is not an ordinary case.

JUSTICE WHITE: That may be so. But even if they named them in the indictment, that is not enough on which to base the introduction of out-of-court statements by an unindicted co-conspirator.

MR. LACOVARA: Yes. That was the point that I wanted to get to in discussing what we call our clause argument. We have never argued, and of course there would be no basis for arguing, that the mere grand jury finding, whether on the face of the indictment or in the grand jury's minutes, that the President or any of the other 18 unindicted co-conspirators were members of this conspiracy would itself be enough at trial to warrant the judge's admission of extra-judicial statements given by those co-conspirators. We are not making that contention here. The issue arises because a motion to quash a subpoena was filed prior to trial. And the basis for that motion was a claim of executive privilege, a governmental privilege that exists for the benefit of legitimate governmental processes.

We countered that apart from *Nixon* v. *Sirica* and the balancing process, and apart from the waiver argument that we also developed at some length, this President, as difficult as it was to say this——not because of the evidence but because of the inherent awkwardness of it——this President is not in a position to claim this public privilege, for the reason that a prima facie showing can be made that these conversations were not in pursuance of legitimate governmental processes or the lawful deliberation of the public's business. These conversations, as we showed in our 49-page appendix, and as the grand jury alleged, were in furtherance of a criminal conspiracy to defraud the United States and obstruct justice.

We did not rely, even before Judge Sirica, and we do not rely here, merely on the fact that the grand jury made this determination. We do submit that for purposes of a pre-trial consideration of a subpoena that is challenged on grounds of executive privilege, we are not confronted with the need that we will be confronted with at trial, which we fully intend to discharge, of showing by evidence to the trial judge that the president and the other co-conspirators were members of the co-conspiracy.

JUSTICE STEWART: One of your grounds for the non-applicability of the privilege is that the conversations were in the course of the conspiracy.

MR. LACOVARA: Yes sir.

JUSTICE STEWART: And that you say is satisfied by merely the grand jury?

MR. LACOVARA: No, sir —— absolutely not.

JUSTICE WHITE: Just a moment. It is not satisfied merely by the grand jury finding. So a court must go on and make its own determination——if they were going to agree with you on this ground.

MR. LACOVARA: Let me back up a little. I see the point that you are making. We are taking the position that the grand jury's determination is conclusive on the Court on two issues: (a) that a conspiracy existed, and (b) that President Nixon was a member of the conspiracy. That is not enough, we concede, to override a claim of executive privilege——because, as Mr. St. Clair well says, he is still the President, and he is still in a position to invoke executive privilege. Where we have said we must bear an evidentiary burden to the satisfaction of the Court is on drawing the nexus between the subpoenaed conversations and the conclusively determined prima facie showing that there is a conspiracy of which the President is a member. We made that evidentiary showing to Judge Sirica. That showing is before this Court. Judge Sirica found that that showing was sufficient. And for that reason, as I believe his opinion—although it had to be guarded because these items were placed under seal——reflects that he did make the showing.

JUSTICE WHITE: Well, that showing, or such a showing could arguably have been made whether or not the grand jury had named the President, could it not?

MR. LACOVARA: Yes, sir, it could have been made as evidentiary matter.

JUSTICE WHITE: Exactly.

JUSTICE BRENNAN: Isn't it your position that it was independently of the naming of the President?

MR. LACOVARA: Yes, sir. The evidence that was placed before Judge Sirica we would submit would be sufficient to make that showing. And we have said that that is not legally necessary;

that we didn't have to prove a conspiracy, in effect prove the whole case that may take three months to try in order to defeat a claim of executive privilege before trial.

This Court has frequently said the criminal process would be burdened down unduly if proceedings were preceded by mini-proceedings. That is exactly what we have here. We submit the evidence is sufficient. Judge Sirica —— this is a situation in which the showing that we did submit, intrinsically, we submit, tracks the allegations of the indictment and provides independent evidentiary support for those allegations.

We have said, though, that it is not legally necessary in a proceeding like this for a court independently to decide whether the grand jury had enough evidence before it to say there is a conspiracy, or that a particular individual was a member of the conspiracy. We said all you need to find is that we have shown that these conversations were in furtherance of this conspiracy.

JUSTICE POWELL: Mr. Lacovara, let's back up a minute. Do you concede that an incumbent President of the United States could not be indicted and tried for a crime?

MR. LACOVARA: No, sir.
JUSTICE POWELL: You do not. Do you think he could be?

MR. LACOVARA: We have not expressed a position on that, Mr. Justice Powell.

JUSTICE POWELL: Let's assume for the moment that he could not be. Would you still argue that the grand jury had the power or the right, and if so by virtue of what?

MR. LACOVARA: Yes. We ——
JUSTICE POWELL: To name him as an unindicted co-conspirator.

MR. LACOVARA: We do in fact make that argument at some length. I guess all of our arguments are made with too much length. But we do argue at length, sir, seriously, that the question of Presidential indictability, which we offer some views on, just to show that the question is an open one, because of our obligation we believe to the law and to the courts, is not really determinative of the question that is really in this case, to the extent that the Court reaches the expungement argument advanced by counsel or to the extent that the Court does not reach the so-called Clark argument——that is executive privilege just cannot be invoked here.

The issue of Presidential indictability does not determine the issue which an incumbent President can be named as an unindicted co-conspirator by a grand jury.

We have shown in our brief why even persons who do have some constitutional immunity——and counsel argues that implicitly under the framework of the Constitution, the President should have an implicit immunity from prosecution——even such persons can be and frequently are named by grand juries as unindicted co-conspirators.

The practical arguments that may militate in favor of a judicial recognition of some unique immunity for the President alone——not for circuit judges, not for Supreme Court Justices, not for Members of Congress, but the President alone it may be held at some later date is immune from prosecution——but that by no means suggests the answer to the question here. And the grand jury elected not to test that issue.

JUSTICE POWELL: The thing that I was wondering about is that there is only one President, and executive power is vested in him. And I do wonder whether or not the precedents you set with respect to other people would vest the authority in a grand jury, either on its own motion or because of what some prosecutor suggested, while the President is in office to name him as an unindicted co-conspirator. With grand juries sitting all over the United States, and occasionally you find a politically-motivated prosecutor——that's a rather far-reaching power, if it exists.

MR. LACOVARA: It is, Mr. Justice, and there is no doubt about it. We are conscious of the delicacy of the issue. We have suggested, however, that although there is some conceivable opportunity for abuse, our judicial system, our democratic system is based on several fundamental propositions, one of which is that grand juries usually are not malicious. Even prosecutors cannot be assumed to be malicious. We also assume, as this Court regularly holds in first amendment cases dealing with public officials, that we have a resilient society where people can be trusted to sort out truth from falsehoods. We have a robust debate.

I submit to you, sir, that just as in this case a grand jury would not lightly accuse the President of a crime, so, too, the fear that, perhaps without basis, some grand jury somewhere might maliciously accuse a President of a crime is not necessarily a compelling reason for saying that a grand jury has no power to do that. I think the system may be vibrant enough to deal with that. And I think the inherent dignity of the Presidential office on any incumbent provides him with a notable check against being defeated, or as my colleague says, impeached by the action of a grand jury. This is perhaps the most notorious event, notorious case in recent times. When the grand jury's action was disclosed, I venture to say that although it was a difficult time for all concerned, including the prosecutors as well as other counsel and the country——the President has not been displaced from office, he still is President, he still functions in accordance with his constitutional powers.

CHIEF JUSTICE BURGER: Mr. Lacovara, I wanted to get to this mechanical question that Mr. St. Clair brought up. Assume for the moment that a given tape, one of the 64 tapes is in fact one-eighth of the total time, which might be several hours, apparently, because they are long tapes——but one-eighth of it involves discussions of the people who are under indictment here, but that seven-eights of it in fact now——we have to assume this——includes conferences with the Secretaries of the Cabinet, with the Joint Chiefs of Staff, the Chairman of the Atomic Energy Commission, very high-level people, and perhaps some staff people as well——including in those conversations some highly sensitive material; not sensitive in the sense that it is national military secrets or diplomatic secrets, but sensitive in the sense of confidentiality. Would you not think that some mechanism ought to be available that if the participants are identified, as you have got them all identified by the voluntary submission of the President, as to the 64——that if the participants are identified and the time frame specified that the certificate of the major persons present, that the subject was atomic energy, all sorts of other things, would be sufficient to foreclose a court from examining it in camera?

MR. LACOVARA: Well——

CHIEF JUSTICE BURGER: I am asking would you think so.

MR. LACOVARA: The answer to the question, Mr. Chief Justice, is yes, because these are the procedures that have been set up in the court of appeals decision in *Nixon* v. *Sirica*, which were found to be eminently practical when the tapes subpoenaed by the grand jury were submitted. These are six-hour reels. And under the so-called index and analysis which the court of appeals in that case required to be submitted, and which Judge Sirica here has required to be submitted, counsel for the President says this is a six-hour reel; the Watergate portions are minutes 312——no, that's too many——112 through 146. Prior to that there is a meeting between the President and the Secretary of Health, Education and Welfare on the school bill. After the Watergate-related discussions there is a meeting between the President and representatives of the National Association of Manufacturers.

What has happened is that White House counsel has come to Judge's chambers with the original reels. They have marked the beginning of the Watergate-related portions on those reels for the Court to make an independent determination this is Watergate-related and therefore offset by whatever overcoming of the privilege has been held——and after that is done, a copy of the Watergate-related portions is made. The Judge does not listen to the non-Watergate-related portions which are still covered by a presumptive executive privilege, which we have freely conceded from the time the grand jury began this process in July of 1973 to our brief in this Court.

CHIEF JUSTICE BURGER: Then as to this hypothetical seven-eighths, there is, you suggest, no disagreement between you and Mr. St. Clair and Mr. Jaworski and you, on the one hand?

MR. LACOVARA: That's correct, sir. And I might say that under the procedure that was worked out, this may predate Mr. St. Clair, so you will have to rely solely on my representation, the President indicated a willingness to allow the judge to listen to a few moments of conversation on either end of the portion of the tape that had been listed in this index and analysis as being Watergate-related, just so he would have an assurance that there was a transition from one subject to another subject.

That was agreed to by the President as being, if a minimal intrusion on the confidentiality privilege for an unrelated subject, then certainly by no means an excessive one.

JUSTICE BRENNAN: Mr. Lacovara, you have only a very few minutes. Are you going to address Mr. St. Clair's opening argument that the pendency of the House Judiciary impeachment inquiry either should lead the Court to conclude that this whole business before us in a non-justiciable matter, therefore, necessarily, that Judge Sirica's order should be quashed. Or, in any event, that because of the possible effect of a decision on the issue presented, upon the impeachment inquiry, that the Court should stay its hand.

MR. LACOVARA: That was to be my last point, sir, and I will make it right now.

The notion that because there is concurrently underway an impeachment inquiry before the House of Representatives, that somehow makes this a nonjusticiable political question is, we think, a remarkable notion which is not supported by sound constitutional law or by any of the decisions of this Court, and, indeed, I submit that to the extent that the Court has discretion in the matter, and although this Court has now been given discretionary certiorari power, district courts have no such option, it would not even be a wise exercise of discretion for this Court to stay its hand.

This case before the Court is not a request for an opinion between two congressional committees as to who has jurisdiction over a particular bill. It's not even a request for a dispute between Cabinet officers, or the President and a Cabinet officer, over what proper executive policy ought to be.

This is a criminal proceeding, a federal criminal case against six defendants. A subpoena has been issued to obtain evidence for use at the trial which is scheduled to begin on September 9th.

The Court cannot escape the fact that this is a trial of tremendous national importance, but a trial that was brought to a head without regard to the impeachment inquiry. This is an independent, separate constitutional process that is under way, and a traditional, ordinary, prosaic remedy, a subpoena has been utilized to obtain evidence for that trial.

There is some debate about whether the evidence is critical to our prosectuion. I noted in Justice Rehnquist's opinion a few weeks ago, in *Michigan* v. *Tucker*,[28] that he echoed, or presaged, perhaps, the same point that Judge Sirica made, that it's really the obligation of the prosecution to present all of the material evidence for the jury, for the fact-finder to pass upon.

That's what this case involves.

The same argument would have prevented this Court from deciding *Marbury* v. *Madison.* It's common knowledge that Chief Justice Marshall, himself, was threatened with impeachment if he decided the case against President Jefferson. He went ahead and did his duty on behalf of this Court.

Later, in connection with the Burr trial, ——

CHIEF JUSTICE BURGER: But he really decided it in favor of President Jefferson didn't he?

MR. LACOVARA: No, sir.

CHIEF JUSTICE BURGER: He didn't?

---

[28] *Michigan* v. *Tucker,* 94 S.Ct. 2357 (1974) held that the so-called Miranda rule did not apply to police interrogation that took place before *Miranda* v. *Arizona,* 384 U.S. 436 (1966) was decided.

MR. LACOVARA: No, sir. He said it expressly ——

CHIEF JUSTICE BURGER: He surely decided it, Jefferson won the case——the battle, but lost the war.

MR. LACOVARA: Well, if you ——

CHIEF JUSTICE BURGER: Of judicial supremacy.

MR. LACOVARA: Well, the case is normally thought of as

Now, to say that there will be public consequences, even political consequences to the Court's action does not mean that this is a political question, so that the Court must regard it as non-justiciable.

being solely concerned with original jurisdiction, but if ——

CHIEF JUSTICE BURGER: But in that sense ——

MR. LACOVARA: ——if one reads the case again, sir, I submit, Chief Justice Marshall got to the original jurisdiction point only after he had been very decisive in saying that a lower court could issue and should issue and would be obliged to issue the mandamus to Secretary Madison, because the President had no legal power to order Secretary of State Madison not to issue that commission.

He held that——it might be called dictum, but it certainly at the time was a courageous act.

CHIEF JUSTICE BURGER: But the basic ruling in the case related to the original jurisdiction of the Court under Article III, did it not?

MR. LACOVARA: I concede that, sir.

Later, however, when he did go on, in 1807, to issue the subpoena to President Jefferson, that was an act of profound political consequences, but he stated, again eloquently, that it was the Court's duty to obtain evidence if it were material to the trial.

The notion that political consequences should stay the hand of the Court is a notion that, again speaking through Marshall, the Court rejected in *Cohens* v. *Virginia*,[29] and the *Cherokee Nation* case,[30] where it common knowledge that the States, the Stage Legislatures in Virginia and Georgia would interpose themselves and defy this Court, and Marshall uttered the words, which I think are justly famous, that just as the Court can't reach out for

---

[29] *Cohens* v. *Virginia*, 6 Wheat. 264 (1821) held that the Supreme Court could review a final judgment of the highest state court when a constitutional issue was presented in the case.

[30] In *Worcester* v. *Georgia*, 6 Pet. 515 (1832) the Supreme Court ordered Georgia to surrender a prisoner seized in Cherokee Indian territory. State authorities refused to do so.

jurisdiction it doesn't have, it has an obligation to exercise the jurisdiction it does have, whatever may be the political consequences of that act.

The Court's action in *Ex Parte Milligan*,[31] in telling President Lincoln that he did not have the power to conduct the Civil War the way he wanted to conduct it; again profound political consequences.

We come to the war power cases in World War II, the Japanese Exclusion cases,[32] this Court did not say that because of the consequences for the President, or because of the political reaction to a decision one way or the other the Court should stay its hand.

In *Youngstown*, where our colleague's brief closes by quoting Justice Frankfurter's brilliant concurring opinion, saying how the Court should, as an institution, be reluctant to decide great constitutional questions. But he went on to say: "We have an obligation to look into an assertion of presidential power. And even if the embarrassment to be caused to the President by our disagreeing with him would be profound, it is still the duty of the Court to tell him when he's wrong."

This Court, in *Powell* v. *McCormack*, how could there be a more political case than telling a house of Congress that it had to seat a member that it had excluded? But the Court said the Constitution forbade it, it's up to the Court to decide what the Constitution allows. And even though the Court interprets the Constitution differently from another branch, that's the judicial process.

So, separation of powers here, with the notion of political question, whether something is committed to the final determination of another branch, far from supporting the President's position, demands that the Court affirm the action that Judge Sirica has taken. This is emphatically the province of this Court to decide.

Not to belabor the point, but perhaps the finest chapter in the Court's recent history has come——the finest chapters have come in the fields of reapportionment, civil rights, and the procedural rights of the criminally accused. It would be naive to say that

[31] *Ex parte Milligan*, 4 Wall. 2 (1867) held that a military commission could not try a civilian accused of treasonous activities in the Civil War when the civil courts were open and operating.

[32] In *Hirabayashi* v. *United States*, 320 U.S. 81 (1943) the Supreme Court upheld the validity of the mass relocation of Japanese-Americans from the West Coast shortly after Pearl Harbor. However in *Ex parte Endo*, 323 U.S. 283 (1944) it said that relocation orders could not be applied to concededly loyal Japanese-Americans.

those were not profoundly, politically important decisions. But they were made as decisions of constitutional law, despite the consequences that political branches might face, despite the public reaction, the Court understood its duty to interpret the Constitution.

That's all we ask for today. That's all Judge Sirica has done. We believe he has done it correctly. We believe the case is fully justiciable. We believe the principles that have been briefed by the parties support the correctness of the decision below. And we submit that this Court should fully, explicitly, and decisively, and definitely uphold Judge Sirica's decision.

CHIEF JUSTICE BURGER: Thank you, Mr. Lacovara. Mr. St. Clair, you have fifteen minutes left.

SURREBUTTAL ARGUMENT OF JAMES D. ST. CLAIR, ESQ.,

ON BEHALF OF THE PRESIDENT

MR. ST. CLAIR: Thank you, Mr. Chief Justice. Members of the Court:

In response to my brother's most recent argument: Of course, *Sawyer* was an important case, with political implications. Of course, the other cases were, in and of themselves, important cases, with political implications.

But this case is different, in that the decision in this case will have an undeniable impact on another proceeding. And another proceeding which the Constitution says is essentially a political proceeding, from which the Court is excluded.

And for this Court to be drawn into that thicket, if I may call it that, seems to me highly inappropriate, at least at this time.

As I indicated at the outset, the House Committee has made certain political decisions, the President has made certain political decisions. They will each have to bear the responsibility of those decisions with the American people.

This Court should not impair, interfere with, or otherwise participate directly or indirectly in that proceeding. And it's inevitable that it would happen. This courtroom wouldn't be full today if this were simply a suit on a subpoena brought by the Special Prosecutor against the President, even though that would be an important political matter because the President is involved.

But this is important for other reasons, quite apart from that, other reasons which, I suggest, indicate quite clearly that this Court ought to, in its discretion and in its judgment, stay its hand, at least until such time as those proceedings have run their course.

Because those are political decisions being made, they should not bear the burden either way of a judicial decision.

JUSTICE DOUGLAS: Well, under that theory, all the criminal trials that are going on should stop, then.

MR. ST. CLAIR: That would not be the first time, Mr. Justice Douglas, that a criminal trial was delayed. And in balancing the importance to this nation, I would suggest that this is clearly indicated, and I don't believe the defendants would be crying very bitter tears.

But, in any event, the justiciability of this case seems to me to be the single, important, obvious matter that my brother would prefer not much to talk about, but there can be no doubt about it if you read page 59 in his brief, he says he, the President, is now the subject of an impeachment inquiry by the Committee on the Judiciary of the House of Representatives, and the subpoenaed evidence may have a material bearing on whether he is impeached; and, if impeached, whether he is convicted and removed from office.

And I suggest the Constitution and all of the history of the Framers makes it quite clear that the Framers conceived impeachment as a legislative process, the Court was excluded specifically from that function.

Marbury v. *Madison* itself, I agree with the Chief Justice, that it decided the case in favor of the President. The rule was discharged and the commission was not issued.

But it also held, and it's been the law since that case, that the Courts will not interfere with or direct a discretionary act on the part of the President or any other branch of government. And that's been confirmed in *Mississippi* v. *Johnson* and any case since that time.

And the discretion that the Constitution, by implication and by necessity, that has been vested in the President in determining which of his confidential communications shall be made public or released is a discretionary act that this Court ought not, by its decision, undertake to do for him. Because this Court is not equipped in knowledge, background, and any other way, to exercise that discretion for the President of the United States.

This is not a ministerial act.

Finally, I observe a slight, but significant shift in my brother's position with respect to the prima facie nature of the naming of the President as a co-conspirator. They say it can be made prima facie. I take it that is by examining the evidence before the grand jury in order to determine whether or not that evidence in fact supports that determination.

We have invited this court and Judge Sirica to do just that. The Special Prosecutor has opposed in each instance this or any other court looking behind that to see whether in fact the evidence can be made, as he now states the position, to support a charge of criminality.

Before the argument, the argument was that because it was a finding or a' vote, it was prima facie. Now it is, I take it, somewhat different.

But in any event, the action by a grand jury purporting to assess criminality to a President of the United States is a clear intrusion upon the legislative function and power with respect to impeachment.

As I said earlier, the President is not above the law. Nor does he contend that he is. What he does contend is that as President the law can be applied to him in only one way, and that is by impeachment, not by naming as a co-conspirator in a grand jury indictment, not by indictment or in any other way. And therefore in this case I urge that this court take such action as is appropriate to overrule Judge Sirica's decision in order that this case be dismissed.

MR. CHIEF JUSTICE BURGER: Thank you, Mr. St. Clair. Thank you, Mr. Jaworski and Mr. Lacovara.

The case is submitted.

(Whereupon, at 1:04 o'clock p.m. the case was submitted.)

XII
THE SUPREME COURT DECISION IN UNITED STATES
v.
NIXON

The Supreme Court's decision in United States v. Nixon *was unanimous. Despite press reports that there was considerable internal dispute among the Justices, it appears that they were of one mind from the beginning. The Supreme Court press officer announced that there had been only one conference of the Justices after the argument until the final opinion was issued. This implied that the Chief Justice had assigned himself to write the opinion at the initial conference for a unanimous Court. The opinion carefully examined each of the issues raised by the parties and in logical and inevitable steps declared that the President must deliver the subpoenaed tapes. Mr. St. Clair immediately announced that the President would comply with the ruling.*

No. 73-1766
UNITED STATES, PETITIONER,

v.

RICHARD M. NIXON, PRESIDENT OF THE
UNITED STATES, ET AL.

No. 73-1834
RICHARD M. NIXON, PRESIDENT OF THE
UNITED STATES, PETITIONER,

v.

UNITED STATES

[July 24, 1974]

*ON WRITS OF CERTIORARI TO THE UNITES STATES
COURT OF APPEALS FOR THE DISTRICT OF COLUMBIA
CIRCUIT BEFORE JUDGMENT.*

MR. CHIEF JUSTICE BURGER delivered the opinion of the
Court.

These cases present for review the denial of a motion, filed on
behalf of the President of the United States, in the case of *United
States* v. *Mitchell et al.* (D. C. Crim. No. 74-110), to quash a
third-party supboena *duces tecum* issued by the United States
District Court for the District of Columbia, pursuant to Fed.
Rule Crim. Proc. 17 (c). The subpoena directed the President to
produce certain tape recordings and documents relating to his
conversatĩons with aides and advisers. The court rejected the
President's claims of absolute executive privilege, of lack of
jurisdiction, and of failure to satisfy the requirements of Rule 17
(c). The President appealed to the Court of Appeals. We granted
the United States' petition for certiorari before judgment,[1] and
also the President's responsive cross-petition for certiorari before
judgment,[2] because of the public importance of the issues

---

[1] See 28 U.S.C. § § 1254 (1) and 2101 (e) and our Rule 20. See, *e.g., Youngstown
Sheet & Tube Co.* v. *Sawyer,* 343 U.S. 934, 579, 584 (1952); *United States* v. *United
Mine Workers,* 329 U.S. 708, 709, 710 (1946); 330 U.S. 258, 269 (1947); *Carter* v.
Carter Coal Co., 298 U.S. 238 (1936); *Rickert Rice Mills* v. *Fontenot,* 294 U.S. 110
(1936); *Railroad Retirement Board* v. *Alton R. Co.,* 295 U.S. 330, 344 (1935); *United
States* v. *Bankers Trust Co.,* 294 U.S. 240 243 (1935).

[2] The Cross-petition in No. 73–1834 raised the issue whether the grand jury acted
within its authority in naming the President as a coconspirator. Since we find
resolution of this issue unnessary to resolution of the question whether the claim of
privilege is to prevail, the cross-petition for certiorari is dismissed as improvidently

presented and the need for their prompt resolution. —— U. S. ——, —— (1974).

On March 1, 1974, a grand jury of the United States District Court for the District of Columbia returned an indictment charging seven named individuals[3] with various offenses, including conspiracy to defraud the United States and to an unindicted co-conspirator.[4] On April 18, 1974, upon motion of the Special Prosecutor, see n. 8, *infra*, a subpoena *duces tecum* was issued pursuant to Rule 17 (c) to the President by the United States District Court and made returnable on May 2, 1974. This subpoena required the production, in advance of the September 9 trial date, of certain tapes, memoranda, papers, transcripts, or other writings relating to certain precisely identified meetings between the President and others.[5] The Special Prosecutor was able to fix the time, place and persons present at these discussions because the White House daily logs and appointment records had been delivered to him. On April 30, the President publicly released edited transcripts of 43 conversations; portions of 20 conversations subject to subpoena in the present case were included. On May 1, 1974, the President's counsel, filed a "special appearance" and a motion to quash the subpoena, under Rule 17 (c). This motion was accompanied by a formal claim of privilege. At a subsequent hearing,[6] further motions to expunge

granted and the remainder of this opinion is concerned with the issues raised in No. 73–1766. On June 19,1974, the President's counsel moved for disclosure and transmittal to this Court of all evidence presented to the grand jury relating to its action in naming the President as an unindicted coconspirator. Action on this motion was deferred pending oral argument of the case and is not denied.

[3] The seven defendants were John N. Mitchell, H. R. Haldeman, John D. Ehrlichman, Charles W. Colson, Robert C. Mardian, Kenneth W. Parkinson, and Gordon Strachan. Each had occupied either a position of responsibility on the White House staff or the Committee for the Re-Election of the President. Colson entered a guilty plea on another charge and is no longer a defendant.

[4] The President entered a special appearance in the District Court on June 6 and requested that court to lift its protective order regarding the naming of certain individuals as co-conspirators and to any additional extent deemed appropriate by the Court. This motion of the President was based on the ground that the disclosures to the news media made the reasons for continuance of the protective order no longer meaningful. On June 7, the District Court removed its protective order and, on June 10, counsel for both parties jointly moved this Court to unseal those parts of the record which related to the action of the grand jury regarding the President. After receiving a statement in opposition from the defendants, this Court denied that motion on June 15, 1974, except for the grand jury's immediate finding relating to the status of the President as an unindicted co-conspirator.– U.S. – (1974).

[5] The specific meetings and conversations are enumerated in a schedule attached to the subpoena. 42a–46a of the App.

[6] At the joint suggestion of the Special Prosecutor and counsel for the President, and with the approval of counsel for the defendants, further proceedings in the District Court were held *in camera*.

the grand jury's action naming the President as an unindicted co-conspirator and for protective orders against the disclosure of that information were filed or raised orally by counsel for the President.

On May 20, 1974, the District Court denied the motion to quash and the motions to expunge and for protective orders. —— F. Supp. —— (1974). It further ordered "the President or any subordinate officer, official or employee with custody or control of the documents or objects subpoenaed," *id.*, at ——, to deliver to the District Court, on or before May 31, 1974, the originals of all subpoenaed items, as well as an index and analysis of those items, together with tape copies of those portions of the subpoenaed recordings for which transcripts had been released to the public by the President on April 30, The District Court rejected jurisdictional challenges based on a contention that the dispute was nonjusticiable because it was between the Special Prosecutor and the Chief Executive and hence "intra-executive" in character; it also rejected the contention that the judiciary was without authority to review an assertion of executive privilege by the President. The court's rejection of the first challenge was based on the authority and powers vested in the Special Prosecutor by the regulation promulgated by the Attorney General; the court concluded that a justiciable controversy was presented. The second challenge was held to be foreclosèd by the decision in *Nixon* v. *Sirica*, —— U.S. App. D.C. ——, 487 F. 2d 700 (1973).

The District Court held that the judiciary, not the President, was the final arbiter of a claim of executive privilege. The court concluded that, under the circumstances of this case, the presumptive privilege was overcome by the Special Prosecutor's prima facie "demonstration of need sufficiently compelling to warrant judicial examination in chambers. . . ." ——F. Supp., at ——. The court held, finally, that the Special Prosecutor had satisfied the requirements of Rule 17 (c). The District Court stayed its order pending appellate review on condition that review was sought before 4 p. m., May 24. The court further provided that matters filed under seal remain under seal when transmitted as part of the record.

On May 24, 1974, the President filed a timely notice of appeal from the District Court order, and the certified record from the District Court was docketed in the United States Court of Appeals for the District of Columbia Circuit. On the same day, the President also filed a petition for writ of mandamus in the Court of Appeals seeking review of the District Court order.

Later on May 24, the Special Prosecutor also filed, in this Court, a petition for a writ of certiorari before judgment. On May 31, the petition was granted with an expedited briefing schedule. —— U. S. —— (1974). On June 6, the President filed, under seal, a cross-petition for writ of certiorari before judgment. This cross-petition was granted June 15, 1974, —— U. S. —— (1974), and the case was set for argument on July 8, 1974.

I. JURISDICTION

The threshold question presented is whether the May 20, 1974, order of the District Court was an appealable order and whether this case was properly "in," 28 U.S.C. § 1254, the United States Court of Appeals when the petition for certiorari was filed in this Court. Court of Appeals jurisdiction under 28 U S. C. § 1291 encompasses only "final decisions of the district courts." Since the appeal was timely filed and all other procedural requirements were met, the petition is properly before this Court for consideration if the District Court order was final. 28 U. S. C. § 1254 (1); 28 U. S. C. § 2101 (e).

The finality requirement of 28 U. S. C. § 1291 embodies a strong congressional policy against piecemeal reviews, and against obstructing or impeding an ongoing judicial proceeding by interlocutory appeals. See, *e. g., Cobbledick* v. *United States,* 309 U. S. 323, 324-326 (1940). This requirement ordinarily promotes judicial efficiency and hastens the ultimate termination of litigation. In applying this principle to an order denying a motion to quash and requiring the production of evidence pursuant to a subpoena *duces tecum,* it is has been repeatedly held that the order is not final and hence not appealable. *United States* v. *Ryan,* 402 U.S. 530, 532 (1971); *Cobbledick* v. *United States,* 309 U. S. 322 (1940); *Alexander* v. *United States,* 201 U.S. 117 (1906). This Court has

> "consistently held that the necessity for expedition in the administration of the criminal law justifies putting one who seeks to resist the production of desired information to a choice between compliance with a trial court's order to produce prior to any review of that order, and resistance to that order with the concomitant possibility of an adjudication of contempt if his claims are rejected on appeal." *United States* v. *Ryan,* 402 U.S. 530, 533 (1971).

The requirement of submitting to contempt, however, is not without exception and in some instances the purposes underlying the finality rule require a different result. For example, in *Perlman* v. *United States*, 247 U. S. 7 (1918), a subpoena had been directed to a third party requesting certain exhibits; the appellant, who owned the exhibits, sought to raise a claim of privilege. The Court held an order compelling production was appealable because it was unlikely that the third party would risk a contempt citation in order to allow immediate review of the appellant's claim of privilege. *Id.*, at 12-13. That case fell within the "limited class of cases where denial of immediate review would render impossible any review whatsoever of an individual's claims." *United States* v. *Ryan, supra*, at 533.

Here too the traditional contempt avenue to immediate appeal is peculiarly inappropriate due to the unique setting in which the question arises. To require a President of the United States to place himself in the posture of disobeying an order of a court merely to trigger the procedural mechanism for review of the ruling would be unseemly, and present an unnecessary occasion for constitutional confrontation between two branches of the Government. Similarly, a federal judge should not be placed in the posture of issuing a citation to a President simply in order to invoke review. The issue whether a President can be cited for contempt could itself engender protracted litigation, and would further delay both review on the merits of his claim of privilege and the ultimate termination of the underlying criminal action for which his evidence is sought. These considerations lead us to conclude that the order of the District Court was an appealable order. The appeal from that order was therefore properly "in" the Court of Appeals, and the case is now properly before this Court on the writ of certiorari before judgment. 28 U. S. C. § 1254; 28 U. S. C. § 2101 (e). *Gay* v. *Ruff*, 292 U. S. 25, 30 (1934).[7]

II. JUSTICIABILITY

In the District Court, the President's counsel argued that the court lacked jurisdiction to issue the subpoena because the matter was an intra-branch dispute between a subordinate and superior officer of the Executive Branch and hence not subject to judicial resolution. That argument has been renewed in this Court with emphasis on the contention that the dispute does not

---

[7] The parties have suggested this Court has jurisdiction on other grounds. In view of our conclusion that there is jurisdiction under 28 U.S.C. § 1254 (1) because the District Court's order was appealable, we need not decide whether other jurisdictional vehicles are available.

present a "case" or "controversy" which can be adjudicated in the federal courts. The President's counsel argues that the federal courts should not intrude into areas committed to the other branches of Government. He views the present dispute as essentially a "jurisdictional" dispute within the Executive Branch which he analogizes to a dispute between two congressional committees. Since the Executive Branch has exclusive authority and absolute discretion to decide whether to prosecute a case, *Confiscation Cases*, 7 Wall. 454 (1869), *United States* v. *Cox*, 342 F. 2d 167, 171 (CA5), cert. denied, 381 U. S. 935 (1965), it is contended that a President's decision is final in determining what evidence is to be used in a given criminal case. Although his counsel concedes the President has delegated certain specific powers to the Special Prosecutor, he has not "waived nor delegated to the Special Prosecutor the President's duty to claim privilege as to all materials . . . which fall within the President's inherent authority to refuse to disclose to any executive officer." Brief for the President 47. The Special Prosecutor's demand for the items therefore presents, in the view of the President's counsel, a political question under *Baker* v. *Carr*, 369 U.S. 186 (1962), since it involves a "textually demonstrable" grant of power under Art. II.

The mere assertion of a claim of an "intra-branch dispute," without more, has never operated to defeat federal jurisdiction; justiciability does not depend on such a surface inquiry. In *United States* v. *ICC*, 337 U.S. 426 (1949), the Court observed, "courts must look behind names that symbolize the parties to determine whether a justiciable case or controversy is presented." *Id.*, at 430. See also: *Powell* v. *McCormack*, 395 U.S. 486 (1969); *ICC* v. *Jersey City*, 322 U. S. 503 (1944); *United States ex rel. Chapman* v. *FPC*, 345 U. S. 153 (1953); *Secretary of Agriculture* v. *United States*, 347 U. S. 645 (1954); *FMB* v. *Isbrandsten Co.*, 356 U. S. 481, 482 n. 2 (1958); *United States* v. *Marine Bank Corp.*, — U. S. — (1974), and *United States* v. *Connecticut National Bank*, — U. S. — 1974.

Our starting point is the nature of the proceeding for which the evidence is sought—here a pending criminal prosecution. It is a judicial proceeding in a federal court alleging violation of federal laws and is brought in the name of the United States as sovereign. *Berger* v. *United States*, 295 U. S. 78, 88 (1935). Under the authority of Art. II § 2, Congress has vested in the Attorney General the power to conduct the criminal litigation of the United States Government. 28 U. S. C. § 516. It has also vested in him the power to appoint subordinate officers to assist him in the discharge of his duties. 28 U. S. C. § § 509, 510, 515,

533. Acting pursuant to those statutes, the Attorney General has delegated the authority to represent the United States in these particular matters to a Special Prosecutor with unique authority and tenure.[8] The regulation gives the Special Prosecutor explicit power to contest the invocation of executive privilege in the process of seeking evidence deemed relevant to the performance of these specially delegated duties.[9] 38 Fed. Reg. 30739.

So long as this regulation is extant it has the force of law. In *Accardi* v. *Shaughnessy*, 347 U. S. 260 (1953), regulations of the Attorney General delegated certain of his discretionary powers to the Board of Immigration Appeals and required that Board to exercise its own discretion on appeals in deportation cases. The

---

[8] The regulation issued by the Attorney General pursuant to his statutory authority, vests in the Special Prosecutor plenary authority to control the course of investigations and litigation related to "all offenses arising out of the 1972 Presidential Election for which the Special Prosecutor deems it necessary and appropriate to assume responsibility, allegations involving the President, members of the White House staff, or Presidential appointees, and any other matters which he consents to have assigned to him by the Attorney General." 38 Fed. Reg. 30739, as amended by 38 Fed. Reg. 32805. In particular, the Special Prosecutor was given full authority, *inter alia*, "to contest the assertion of 'Executive Privilege' ... and handl[e] all aspects of any cases within his jurisdiction." *Ibid.* The regulations then go on to provide:

"In exercising this authority, the Special Prosecutor will have the greetest degree of independence that is consistent with the Attorney-General's statutory accountability for all matters falling within the jurisdiction of the Department of Justice. The Attorney General will not countermand or interfere with the Special Prosecutor's decisions or actions. The Special Prosecutor will determine whether and to what extent he will inform or consult with the Attorney General about the conduct of his duties and responsibilities. In accordance with assurances given by the President to the Attorney General that the President will not exercise his Constitutional powers to effect the discharge of the Special Prosecutor or to limit the independence he is hereby given, the Special Prosecutor will not be removed from his duties except for extraordinary improprieties on his part and without the President's first consulting the Majority and Minority Leaders and Chairman and ranking Minority Members of the Judiciary Committees of the Senate and House of Representatives and ascertaining that their consensus is in accord with his proposed action."

[9] That this was the understanding of Acting Attorney General Robert Bork, the author of the regulations establishing the independence of the Special Prosecutor, is shown by his testimony before the Senate Judiciary Committee:

"Although it is anticipated that Mr. Jaworski will receive cooperation from the White House in getting any evidence he feels he needs to conduct investigations and prosecutions, it is clear and understood on all sides that he has the power to use judicial processes to pursue evidence if disagreement should develop." Hearings before the Senate Judiciary Committee on the Special Prosecutor, 93d Cong., 1st Sess., pt. 2, at 470 (1973). Acting Attorney General Bork gave similar assurances to the House Subcommittee on Criminal Justice. Hearings before the House Judiciary Subcommittee on Criminal Justice on H. J. Res. 784 and H. R. 10937, 93d Cong. 1st Sess. 266 (1973). At his confirmation hearings, Attorney General William Saxbe testified that he shared Acting Attorney General Bork's views concerning the Special Prosecutor's authority to test any claim of executive privilege in the courts. Hearings before the Senate Judiciary Committee on the nomination of William B. Saxbe to be Attorney General, 93d Cong., 1st Sess. 9 (1973).

Court held that so long as the Attorney General's regulations remained operative, he denied himself the authority to exercise the discretion delegated to the Board even though the original authority was his and he could reassert it by amending the regulations. *Service* v. *Dulles*, 354 U. S. 363, 388, (1957), and *Vitarelli* v. *Seaton*, 359 U. S. 535 (1959), reaffirmed the basic holding of *Accardi*.

Here, as in *Accardi*, it is theoretically possible for the Attorney General to amend or revoke the regulation defining the Special Prosecutor's authority. But he has not done so.[10] So long as this regulation remains in force the Executive Branch is bound by it, and indeed the United States as the sovereign composed of the three branches is bound to respect and to enforce it. Moreover, the delegation of authority to the Special Prosecutor in this case is not an ordinary delegation by the Attorney General to a subordinate officer: with the authorization of the President, the Acting Attorney General provided in the regulation that the Special Prosecutor was not to be removed without the "consensus" of eight designated leaders of Congress. Note 8, *supra*.

The demands of and the resistance to the subpoena present an obvious controversy in the ordinary sense, but that alone is not sufficient to meet constitutional standards. In the constitutional sense, controversy means more than disagreement and conflict; rather it means the kind of controversy courts traditionally resolve. Here at issue is the production or nonproduction of specified evidence deemed by the Special Prosecutor to be relevant and admissible in a pending criminal case. It is sought by one official of the Government within the scope of his express authority; it is resisted by the Chief Executive on the ground of his duty to preserve the confidentiality of the communications of the President. Whatever the correct answer on the merits, these issues are "of a type which are traditionally justiciable." *United States* v. *ICC*, 337 U. S., at 430. The independent Special Prosecutor with his asserted need for the subpoenaed material in the underlying criminal prosecution is opposed by the President with his steadfast assertion of privilege against disclosure of the material. This setting assures there is "that concrete adverseness which sharpens the presentation of issues upon which the court

---

[10] At his confirmation hearings Attorney General William Saxbe testified that he agreed with the regulations adopted by Acting Attorney General Bork and would not remove the Special Prosecutor except for "gross impropriety." Hearings, Senate Judiciary Committee on the nomination of William B. Saxbe to be Attorney General, 93d Cong., 1st Sess., 5–6, 8–10 (1973). There is no contention here that the Special Prosecutor is guilty of any such impropriety.

so largely depends for illumination of difficult constitutional questions." *Baker* v. *Carr*, 369 U. S., at 204. Moreover, since the matter is one arising in the regular course of a federal criminal prosecution, it is within the traditional scope of Art. III power. *Id.*, at 198.

In light of the uniqueness of the setting in which the conflict arises, the fact that both parties are officers of the Executive Branch cannot be viewed as a barrier to justiciability. It would be inconsistent with the applicable law and regulation, and the unique facts of this case to conclude other than that the Special Prosecutor has standing to bring this action and that a justiciable controversy is presented for decision.

III. RULE 17(c)

The subpoena *duces tecum* is challenged on the ground that the Special Prosecutor failed to satisfy the requirements of Fed. Rule Crim. Proc. 17 (c), which governs the issuance of subpoenas *duces tecum* in federal criminal proceedings. If we sustained this challenge, there would be no occasion to reach the claim of privilege asserted with respect to the subpoenaed material. Thus we turn to the question whether the requirements of Rule 17 (c) have been satisfied. See *Arkansas-Louisiana Gas Co.* v. *Dept. of Public Utilities*, 304 U. S. 61, 64 (1938); *Ashwander* v. *Tennessee Valley Authority*, 297 U. S. 288, 346-347 (1936). (Brandeis, J., concurring.)

Rule 17 (c) provides:

"A subpoena may also command the person to whom it is directed to produce the books, papers, documents or other objects designated therein. The court on motion made promptly may quash or modify the supoena if compliance would be unreasonable or oppressive. The court may direct that books, papers, documents or objects designated in the subpoena be produced before the court at a time prior to the trial or prior to the time when they are to be offered in evidence and may upon their production permit the books, papers, documents or objects or portions thereof to be inspected by the parties and their attorneys."

A subpoena for documents may be quashed if their production would be "unreasonable or oppressive," but not otherwise. The leading case in this Court interpreting this standard is *Bowman Dairy Co.* v. *United States*, 341 U. S. 214 (1950). This case recognized certain fundamental characteristics of the subpoena *duces tecum* in criminal cases: (1) it was not intended to provide a means of discovery for criminal cases. *Id.*, at 220; (2) its chief innovation was to expedite the trial by providing a time and place *before* trial for the inspection of subpoenaed materials.[11] Ibid. As both parties agree, cases decided in the wake of *Bowman* have generally followed Judge Weinfeld's formulation in *United States* v. *Iozia*, 13 F. R. D. 335, 338, (SDNY 1952), as to the required showing. Under this test, in order to require production prior to trial, the moving party must show: (1) that the documents are evidentiary[12] and relevant; (2) that they are not otherwise procurable reasonably in advance of trial by exercise of due diligence; (3) that the party cannot properly prepare for trial without such production and inspection in advance of trial and that the failure to obtain such inspection may tend unreasonably to delay the trial; (4) that the application is made in good faith and is not intended as a general "fishing expedition."

Against this background, the Special Prosecutor, in order to carry his burden, must clear three hurdles: (1) relevancy; (2) admissibility; (3) specificity. Our own review of the record necessarily affords a less comprehensive view of the total situation than was available to the trial judge and we are unwilling to conclude that the District Court erred in the evaluation of the Special Prosecutor's showing under Rule 17 (c) Our conclusion is based on the record before us, much of which is under seal. Of course, the contents of the subpoenaed tapes could not at that stage be described fully by the Special Prosecutor, but there was a sufficient likelihood that each of the

---

[11] The Court quoted a statement of a member of the advisory committee that the purpose of the Rule was to bring documents into court "in advance of the time that they are offered in evidence, so that they may then be inspected in advance, for the purpose ... of enabling the party to see whether he can use [them] or whether he wants to use [them]." 341 U.S., at 220 n. 5. The Manual for Complex and Multi-district Litigation published by the Administrative Office of the United States Courts recommends that Rule 17 (c) be encouraged in complex criminal cases in order that each party may be compelled to produce its documentary evidence well in advance of trial and in advance of the time it is to be offered. P. 142, CCH Ed.

[12] The District Court found here that it was faced with "the more unusual situation ... where the subpoena, rather than being directed to the government by the defendants, issues to what, as a practical matter, is a third party." *United States* v. *Mitchell,*—F. Supp.—(D.C. 1974). The Special Prosecutor suggested that the evidentiary requirement of *Bowman Diary Co.* and *Iozia* does not apply in its full vigor when the subpoena *duces tecum* is issued to third parties rather than to government prosecutors. Brief for the United States 128-129. We need not decide whether a lower standard exists because we are satisfied that the relevance and evidentiary nature of the subpoenaed tapes were sufficiently shown as a preliminary matter to warrant the District Court's refusal to quash the subpoena.

tapes contains conversations relevant to the offenses charged in the indictment. *United States* v. *Gross*, 24 F. R. D. 138 (SDNY 1959). With respect to many of the tapes, the Special Prosecutor offered the sworn testimony or statements of one or more of the participants in the conversations as to what was said at the time. As for the remainder of the tapes, the identity of the participants and the time and place of the conversations, taken in their total context, permit a rational inference that at least part of the conversations relate to the offenses charged in the indictment.

We also conclude there was a sufficient preliminary showing that each of the subpoenaed tapes contains evidence admissible with respect to the offenses charged in the indictment. The most cogent objection to the admissibility of the taped conversations here at issue is that they are a collection of out-of-court statements by declarants who will not be subject to cross-examination and that the statements are therefore inadmissible hearsay. Here, however, most of the tapes apparently contain conversations to which one or more of the defendants named in the indictment were party. The hearsay rule does not automatically bar all out-of-court statements by a defendant in a criminal case.[13] Declarations by one defendant may also be admissible against other defendants upon a sufficient showing by independent evidence,[14] of a conspiracy among one or more other defendants and the declarant and if the declarations at issue were in furtherance of that conspiracy. The same is true of declarations of coconspirators who are not defendants in the case on trial. *Dutton* v. *Evans*, 400 U. S. 74, 81 (1970). Recorded conversations may also be admissible for the limited purpose of impeaching the credibility of any defendant who testifies or any other coconspirator who testifies. Generally, the need for evidence to impeach witnesses is

---

[13] Such statements are declarations by a party defendant that "would surmount all objections based on the hearsay rule ... " and, at least as to the declarant himself "would be admissible for whatever inferences" might be reasonably drawn. *United States* v. *Matlock*, — U.S. — (1974). *On Lee* v. *United States*, 343 U.S. 747, 757 (1953). See also McCormick on Evidence, § 270, at 651-652 (1972 ed).

[14] As a preliminary matter, there must be substantial, independent evidence of the conspiracy, at least enough to take the question to the jury. *United States* v. *Vaught*. 385 F. 2d 320, 323 (CA4 1973); *United States* v. *Hoffa*, 349 F. 2d 20, 41–42 (CA6 1965), aff'd on other grounds, 385 U.S. 293 (1966); *United States* v. *Santos*, 385 F. 2d 43, 45 (CA7 1967), cert. denied, 390 U.S. 954 (1968); *United States* v. *Morton*, 483 F. 2d 573, 576 (CA8 1973); *The United States* v. *Spanos*, 462 F 2d 1012, 1014 (CA9 1972); *Carbo* v. *United States*, 314 F. 2d 718, 737 (Ca9 1963), cert, denied, 377 U.S. 953 (1964). Whether the standard has been satisfied is a question of *admissibility* of evidence to be decided by the trial judge.

insufficient to require its production in advance of trial. See, *e.g., United States v. Carter,* 15 F. R. D. 367, 371 (D. D. C. 1954). Here, however, there are other valid potential evidentiary uses for the same material and the analysis and possible transcription of the tapes may take a significant period of time. Accordingly, we cannot say that the District Court erred in authorizing the issuance of the subpoena *duces tecum.*

Enforcement of a pretrial subpoena *duces tecum* must necessarily be committed to the sound discretion of the trial court since the necessity for the subpoena most often turns upon a determination of factual issues. Without a determination of arbitrariness or that the trial court finding was without record support, an appellate court will not ordinarily disturb a finding that the applicant for a subpoena complied with Rule 17 (c). See, *e.g., Sue v. Chicago Transit Authority,* 279 F. 2d 416, 419 (CA7 1960); *Shotkin v. Nelson,* 146 F. 2d 402 (CA 10 1944).

In a case such as this, however, where a subpoena is directed to a President of the United States, appellate review, in deference to a coordinate branch of government, should be particularly meticulous to ensure that the standards of Rule 17 (c) have been correctly applied. *United States v. Burr,* 25 Fed. Cas. 30, 34 (No. 14,692d) (1807). From our examination of the materials submitted by the Special Prosecutor to the District Court in support of his motion for the subpoena, we are persuaded that the District Court's denial of the President's motion to quash the subpoena was consistent with Rule 17 (c). We also conclude that the Special Prosecutor has made a sufficient showing to justify a subpoena for production *before* trial. The subpoenaed materials are not available from any other source, and their examination and processing should not await trial in the circumstances shown. *Bowman Dairy Co., supra; United States v. Iozia, supra.*

IV. THE CLAIM OF PRIVILEGE

A.

Having determined that the requirements of Rule 17 (c) were satisfied, we turn to the claim that the subpoena should be quashed because it demands "confidential conversations between a President and his close advisors that it would be inconsistent with the public interest to produce." App. 48a. The first contention is a broad claim that the separation of powers doctrine precludes judicial review of a President's claim of privilege. The second contention is that if he does not prevail on the claim of absolute privilege, the court should hold as a matter of constitutional law that the privilege prevails over the subpoena *duces tecum.*

In the performance of assigned constitutional duties each branch of the Government must initially interpret the Constitution, and the interpretation of its powers by any branch is due great respect from the others. The President's counsel, as we have noted, reads the Constitution as providing an absolute privilege of confidentiality for all presidential communications. Many decisions of this Court, however, have unequivocally reaffirmed the holding of *Marbury* v. *Madison,* 1 Cranch 137 (1803), that "it is emphatically the province and duty of the judicial department to say what the law is." *Id.,* at 177.

No holding of the Court has defined the scope of judicial power specifically relating to the enforcement of a subpoena for confidential presidential communications for use in a criminal prosecution, but other exercises of powers by the Executive Branch and the Legislative Branch have been found invalid as in conflict with the Constitution. *Powell* v. *McCormack, supra; Youngstown, supra.* In a series of cases, the Court interpreted the explicit immunity conferred by express provisions of the Constitution on Members of the House and Senate by the Speech or Debate Clause, U. S. Const. Art. I, § 6. *Doe* v. *McMillan,* 412 U. S. 306 (1973); *Gravel* v. *United States,* 408 U. S. 606 (1973); *United States* v. *Brewster,* 408 U. S. 501 (1972); *United States* v. *Johnson,* 383 U.S. 169 (1966). Since this Court has consistently exercised the power to construe and delineate claims arising under express powers, it must follow that the Court has authority to interpret claims with respect to powers alleged to derive from enumerated powers.

Our system of government "requires that federal courts on occasion interpret the Constitution in a manner at variance with the construction given the document by another branch." *Powell* v. *McCormack, supra,* 549. And in *Baker* v. *Carr,* 369 U. S., at 211, the Court stated:

"[d]eciding whether a matter has in any measure been committed by the Constitution to another branch of government, or whether the action of that branch exceeds whatever authority has been committed, is itself a delicate exercise in constitutional interpretation, and is a responsibility of this Court as ultimate interpreter of the Constitution."

Notwithstanding the deference each branch must accord the others, the "judicial power of the United States" vested in the federal courts by Art. III, § 1 of the Constitution can no more be shared with the Executive Branch than the Chief Executive, for example, can share with the Judiciary the veto power, or the Congress share with the Judiciary the power to override a presidential veto. Any other conclusion would be contrary to the basic concept of separation of powers and the checks and balances that flow from the scheme of a tripartite government. The Federalist, No. 47, p. 313 (C. F. Mittel ed. 1938). We therefore reaffirm that it is "emphatically the province and the duty" of this Court "to say what the law is" with respect to the claim of privilege presented in this case. *Marbury* v. *Madison*, *supra*, at 177.

B.

In support of his claim of absolute privilege, the President's counsel urges two grounds one of which is common to all governments and one of which is peculiar to our system of separation of powers. The first ground is the valid need for protection of communications between high government officials and those who advise and assist them in the performance of their manifold duties; the importance of this confidentiality is too plain to require further discussion. Human experience teaches that those who expect public dissemination of their remarks may well temper candor with a concern for appearances and for their own interests to the detriment of the decisionmaking process.[15] Whatever the nature of the privilege of confidentiality of presidential communications in the exercise of Art. II powers the privilege can be said to derive from the supremacy of each branch within its own assigned area of constitutional duties. Certain powers and privileges flow from the nature of enumerated powers;[16] the protection of the confidentiality of presidential communications has similar constitutional underpinnings.

The second ground asserted by the President's counsel in support of the claim of absolute privilege rests on the doctrine of

---

[15]There is nothing novel about government confidentiality. The meetings of the Constitutional Convention in 1787 were conducted in complete privacy. 1 Farrand. The Records of the Federal Convention of 1787, xi-xxv (1911). Moreover, all records of those meetings were sealed for more than 30 years after the Convention. See 3 U.S. Stat. At Large, 15th Cong. 1st Sess., Res. 8 (1818). Most of the Framers acknowledged that without secrecy no constitution of the kind that was developed could have been written. Warren, *The Making of the Constitution*, 134-139 (1937).

[16] The Special Prosecutor argues that there is no provision in the Constitution for a presidential privilege as to his communications corresponding to the privilege of Members oof Congress under the Speech or Debate Clause. But the silence of the Constitution on this score is not dispositive. "The rule of constitutional interpretation announced in *McCulloch* v. *Maryland*. 4 Wheat. 316, that that which was reasonably appropriate and relevant to the exercise of a granted power was considered as accompanying the grant, has been so universally applied it suffices merely to state it." *Marshall* v. *Gordon*, 243 U.S. 521, 537 (1917).

separation of powers. Here it is argued that the independence of the Executive Branch within its own sphere, *Humphrey's Executor* v. *United States,* 295 U. S. 602, 629-630; *Kilbourn* v. *Thompson,* 103 U.S. 168, 190-191 (1880), insulates a president from a judicial subpoena in an ongoing criminal prosecution, and thereby protects confidential presidential communications.

However, neither the doctrine of separation of powers, nor the need for confidentiality of high level communications, without more, can sustain an absolute, unqualified presidential privilege of immunity from judicial process under all circumstances. The President's need for complete candor and objectivity from advisers calls for great deference from the courts. However, when the privilege depends solely on the broad, undifferentiated claim of public interest in the confidentiality of such conversations, a confrontation with other values arises. Absent a claim of need to protect military, diplomatic or sensitive national security secrets, we find it difficult to accept the argument that even the very important interest in confidentiality of presidential communications is significantly diminished by production of such material for *in camera* inspection with all the protection that a district court will be obliged to provide.

The impediment that an absolute, unqualified privilege would place in the way of the primary constitutional duty of the Judicial Branch to do justice in criminal prosecutions would plainly conflict with the function of the courts under Art. III. In designing the structure of our Government and dividing and allocating the sovereign power among three coequal branches, the Framers of the Constitution sought to provide a comprehensive system, but the separate powers were not intended to operate with absolute independence.

> "While the Constitution diffuses power the better to secure liberty, it also contemplates that practice will integrate the dispersed powers into a workable government. It enjoins upon its branches separateness but interdependence, autonomy but reciprocity." *Youngstown Sheet & Tube Co.* v. *Sawyer,* 343 U.S. 579, 635 (1952) (Jackson, J., concurring).

To read the Art. II powers of the President as providing an absolute privilege as against a subpoena essential to enforcement of criminal statutes on no more than a generalized claim of the public interest in confidentiality of nonmilitary and non-diplomatic discussions would upset the constitutional balance of "a workable government" and gravely impair the role of the courts under Art. III.

C.

Since we conclude that the legitimate needs of the judicial process may outweigh presidential privilege, it is necessary to resolve those competing interests in a manner that preserves the essential functions of each branch. The right and indeed the duty to resolve that question does not free the judiciary from according high respect to the representations made on behalf of the President. *United States* v. *Burr*, 25 Fed. Cas. 187, 190, 191-192 (No. 14,694) (1807).

The expectation of a President to the confidentiality of his conversations and correspondence, like the claim of confidentiality of judicial deliberations, for example, has all the values to which we accord deference for the privacy of all citizens and added to those values the necessity for protection of the public interest in candid, objective, and even blunt or harsh opinions in presidential decision making. A President and those who assist him must be free to explore alternatives in the process of shaping policies and making decisions and to do so in a way many would be unwilling to express except privately. These are the considerations justifying a presumptive privilege for presidential communications. The privilege is fundamental to the operation of government and inextricably rooted in the separation of powers under the Constitution.[17] In *Nixon* v. *Sirica*, — U. S. App. D. C. —, 487 F. 2d 700 (1973), the Court of Appeals held that such presidential communications are "presumptively privileged," *id.*, at 717, and this position is accepted by both parties in the present litigation. We agree with Mr. Chief Justice Marshall's observation, therefore, that "in no case of this kind would a court be required to proceed against the President as against an ordinary individual." *United States* v. *Burr*, 25 Fed. Cas. 187, 191 (No. 14,694) (CCD Va. 1807).

But this presumptive privilege must be considered in light of our historic commitment to the rule of law. This is nowhere more profoundly manifest than in our view that "the twofold aim [of criminal justice] is that guilt shall not escape or innocence suffer." *Berger* v. *United States*, 295 U. S. 78, 88 (1935). We have elected to employ an adversary system of

[17] Freedom of communication vital to fulfillment of wholesome relationships is obtained only by removing the specter of compelled disclosure ... [G]overnment ... needs open but protected channels for the kind of plain talk that is essential to the quality of its functioning." *Carl Zeiss Stiftung* v. *V. E. B. Carl Zeiss, Jena*, 40 F.R.D. 318, 325 (D.C. 1966). See *Nixon* v. *Sirica*, — U.S. App. D.C.   487 F. 2d 700, 713 (1973); *Kaiser Aluminun & Chem. Corp.* v. *United States*, 157 F.Supp. 939 (Ct. Cl. 1958) (*per* Recd, J.); The Federalist No. 64 (S.F. Mittel ed. 1938).

criminal justice in which the parties contest all issues before a court of law. The need to develop all relevant facts in the adversary system is both fundamental and comprehensive. The ends of criminal justice would be defeated if judgments were to be founded on a partial or speculative presentation of the facts. The very integrity of the judicial system and public confidence in the system depend on full disclosure of all the facts, within the framework of the rules of evidence. To ensure that justice is done, it is imperative to the function of courts that compulsory process be available for the production of evidence needed either by the prosecution or by the defense.

Only recently the Court restated the ancient proposition of law, albeit in the context of a grand jury inquiry rather than a trial,

> " 'that the public ... has a right to every man's evidence' except for those persons protected by a constitutional, common law, or statutory privilege, *United States* v. *Bryan*, 339 U. S., at 331 (1949); *Blackmer* v. *United States*, 284 U. S. 421, 438; *Branzburg* v. *United States*, 408 U. S. 665, 688 (1973)."

The privileges referred to by the Court are designed to protect weighty and legitimate competing interests. Thus, the Fifth Amendment to the Constitution provides that no man "shall be compelled in any criminal case to be a witness against himself." And, generally, an attorney or a priest may not be required to disclose what has been revealed in professional confidence. These and other interests are recognized in law by privileges against forced disclosure, established in the Constitution, by statute, or at common law. Whatever their origins, these exceptions to the demand for every man's evidence are not lightly created nor expansively construed, for they are in derogation of the search for truth.[18]

In this case the President challenges a subpoena served on him as a third party requiring the production of materials for use in a criminal prosecution on the claim that he has a privilege against disclosure of confidential communications. He does not place his claim of privilege on the ground they are military or diplomatic secrets. As to these areas of Art. II duties the courts have

[18] Because of the key role of the testimony of witnesses in the judicial process, courts have historically been cautious about privileges. Justice Frankfurter, dessenting in *Elkins* v. *United States*, 364 U.S. 206, 234 (1960), said of this: "Limitations are properly placed upon the operation of this general principle only to the very limited extent that permitting a refusal to testify or excluding relevant evidence has a public good transcending the normally predominant principle of utilizing all rational means for ascertaining truth."

traditionally shown the utmost deference to presidential responsibilities. In *C. & S. Air Lines* v. *Waterman Steamship Corp.*, 333 U. S. 103, 111 (1948), dealing with presidential authority involving foreign policy considerations, the Court said: said:

> "The President, both as Commander-in-Chief and as the Nation's organ for foreign affairs, has available intelligence services whose reports are not and ought not to be published to the world. It would be intolerable that courts, without the relevant information, should review and perhaps nullify actions of the Executive taken on information properly held secret." *Id.*, at 111.

In *United States* v. *Reynolds*, 345 U. S. 1 (1952), dealing with a claimant's demand for evidence in a damage case against the Government the Court said:

> "It may be possible to satisfy the court, from all the circumstances of the case, that there is a reasonable danger that compulsion of the evidence will expose military matters which, in the interest of national security, should not be divulged. When this is the case, the occasion for the privilege is
>
> appropriate, and the court should not jeopardize the security which the privilege is meant to protect by insisting upon an examination of the evidence, even by the judge alone, in chambers."

No case of the Court, however, has extended this high degree of deference to a President's generalized interest in confidentiality. Nowhere in the Constitution, as we have noted earlier, is there any explicit reference to a privilege of confidentiality, yet to the extent this interest relates to the effective discharge of a President's powers, it is constitutionally based.

The right to the production of all evidence at a criminal trial similarly has constitutional dimensions. The Sixth Amendment explicitly confers upon every defendant in a criminal trial the right "to be confronted with the witnesses against him" and "to have compulsory process for obtaining witnesses in his favor." Moreover, the Fifth Amendment also guarantees that no person shall be deprived of liberty without due process of law. It is the manifest duty of the courts to vindicate those guarantees and to accomplish that it is essential that all relevant and admissible evidence be produced.

In this case we must weigh the importance of the general privilege of confidentiality of presidential communications in performance of his responsibilities against the inroads of such a privilege on the fair administration of criminal justice.[19] The interest in preserving confidentiality is weighty indeed and entitled to great respect. However we cannot conclude that advisers will be moved to temper the candor of their remarks by the infrequent occasions of disclosure because of the possibility that such conversations will be called for in the context of a criminal prosecution.[20]

On the other hand, the allowance of the privilege to withhold evidence that is demonstrably relevant in a criminal trial would cut deeply into the guarantee of due process of law and gravely impair the basic function of the courts. A President's acknowledged need for confidentiality in the communications of his office is general in nature, whereas the constitutional need for production of relevant evidence in a criminal proceeding is specific and central to the fair adjudication of a particular criminal case in the administration of justice. Without access to specific facts a criminal prosecution may be totally frustrated. The President's broad interest in confidentiality of communications will not be vitiated by disclosure of a limited number of conversations preliminarily shown to have some bearing on the pending criminal cases.

We conclude that when the ground for asserting privilege as to subpoenaed materials sought for use in a criminal trial is based only on the generalized interest in confidentiality, it cannot prevail over the fundamental demands of due process of law in the fair administration of criminal justice. The generalized assertion of privilege must yield to the demonstrated, specific need for evidence in a pending criminal trial.

[19] We are not here concerned with the balance between the President's generalized interest in confidentiality and the need for relevant evidence in civil litigation, nor with that between the confidentiality interest and congressional demands for information, nor with the President's interest in preserving state secrets. We address only the conflict between the President's assertion of a generalized privilege of confidentiality against the constitutional need for relevant evidence to criminal trials.

[20] Mr. Justice Cardozo made this point in an analogous context. Speaking for a unanimous Court in *Clark* v. *United States,* 289 U.S. 1 (1933), he emphasized the importance of maintaining the secrecy of the deliberations of a petit jury in a criminal case. "Freedom of debate might be stifled and independence of thought checked if jurors were made to feel that their arguments and ballots were to be freely published in the world." *Id.*, at 13. Nonetheless, the Court also recognized that isolated inroads on confidentiality designed to serve the paramount need of the criminal law would not vitiate the interests served by secrecy:

"A juror of integrity and reasonably firmness will not fear to speak his mind if the confidences of debate bar barred to the ears of mere impertinence or malice. He will not expect to be shielded against the disclosure of his conduct in the event that there is evidence reflecting upon his honor. The chance that now and then there may be found some timid soul who will take counsel of his fears and give way to their repressive power is too remote and shadowly to shape the course of justice." *Id.*, at 16.

D.

We have earlier determined that the District Court did not err in authorizing the issuance of the subpoena. If a president concludes that compliance with a subpoena would be injurious to the public interest he may properly, as was done here, invoke a claim of privilege on the return of the subpoena. Upon receiving a claim of privilege from the Chief Executive, it became the further duty of the District Court to treat the subpoenaed material as presumptively privileged and to require the Special Prosecutor to demonstrate that the presidential material was "essential to the justice of the [pending criminal] case." *United States* v. *Burr, supra,* at 192. Here the District Court treated the material as presumptively privileged, proceeded to find that the Special Prosecutor had made a sufficient showing to rebut the presumption and ordered an *in camera* examination of the subpoenaed material. On the basis of our examination of the record we are unable to conclude that the District Court erred in ordering the inspection. Accordingly we affirm the order of the District Court that subpoenaed materials be transmitted to that court. We now turn to the important question of the District Court's responsibilities in conducting the *in camera* examination of presidential materials or communications delivered under the compulsion of the subpoena *duces tecum.*

E.

Enforcement of the subpoena *duces tecum* was stayed pending this Court's resolution of the issues raised by the petitions for certiorari. Those issues now having been disposed of, the matter of implementation will rest with the District Court. "[T]he guard, furnished to [President] to protect him from being harassed by vexatious and unnecessary subpoenas, is to be looked for in the conduct of the [district] court after the subpoenas have issued; not in any circumstances which is to precede their being issued." *United States* v. *Burr, supra,* at 34. Statements that meet the test of admissibility and relevance must be isolated; all other material must be excised. At this stage the District Court is not limited to representations of the Special Prosecutor as to the evidence sought by the subpoena; the material will be available to the District Court. It is elementary that *in camera* inspection of evidence is always a procedure calling for scrupulous protection against any release or publication of material not found by the court, at that stage, probably admissible in evidence and relevant to the issues of the trial for which it is sought. That being true of an ordinary situation it 's obvious that the District Court has a very heavy responsibility to see to it that presidential conversations, which are either not relevant or not admissible, are accorded that high degree of respect due the President of the United States. Mr. Chief Justice Marshall sitting as a trial judge in the *Burr* case, *supra*, was extraordinarily careful to point out that:

> "[I]n no case of this kind would a Court be required to proceed against the President as against an ordinary individual." *United States* v. *Burr*, 25 Fed. Cases 187, 191 (No. 14,694).

Marshall's statement cannot be read to mean in any sense that a President is above the law, but relates to the singularly unique role under Art. II of a President's communications and activities, related to the performance of duties under that Article. Moreover, a President's communications and activities encompass a vastly wider range of sensitive material than would be true of any "ordinary individual." It is therefore necessary[21] in the public interest to afford presidential confidentiality the greatest protection consistent with the fair administration of justice. The need for confidentiality even as to idle conversations with associates in which casual reference might be made concerning political leaders within the country or foreign statesmen is too obvious to call for further treatment. We have no doubt that the District Judge will at all times accord to presidential records that high degree of deference suggested in *United States* v. *Burr*, *supra*, and will discharge his responsibility to see to it that until released to the Special Prosecutor no *in camera* material is revealed to anyone. This burden applies with even greater force to excised material; once the decision is made to excise, the material is restored to its privileged status and should be returned under seal to its lawful custodian.

Since this matter came before the Court during the pendency of a criminal prosecution, and on representations that time is of the essence, the mandate shall issue forthwith.

Affirmed.

---

[21] When the subpoenaed material is delivered to the District Judge *in camera* questions may arise as to the excising of parts and it lies within the discretion of that court to seek the aid of the Special Prosecutor and the President's counsel for *in camera* consideration of the validity of particular excisions, whether the basis of excision is relevancy or admissibility or under such cases as *Reynolds, supra*, or *Waterman Steamship, supra*.

MR. JUSTICE REHNQUIST took no part in the consideration or decision of these cases.

LEON JAWORSKI, Special Prosecutor, and PHILIP A. LACOVARA, Counsel to the Special Prosecutor, for petitioner in No. 73-1766 and respondent in No. 73-1834; JAMES D. ST. CLAIR, Attorney for the President (MICHAEL A. STERLACCI, JEROME J. MURPHY, LOREN A. SMITH, JAMES R. PROCHNOW, EUGENE R. SULLIVAN, JEAN A. STAUDT, THEODORE J. GARRISH, JAMES J. TANSEY and LARRY G. GUTTERRIDGE, with him on the brief) for respondent in No. 73-1766 and petitioner in No. 73-1834; NORMAN DORSEN, MELVIN L. WULF and JOHN H. F. SHATTUCK filed brief for American Civil Liberties Union, as amicus curiae, seeking affirmance, in No. 73-1766.

My fellow Americans, our long national nightmare is over. Our Constitution works. Our great republic is a government of laws and not of men. Here, the people rule.

President Gerald R. Ford
Inaugural Address, August 10, 1974